PAGE 50

ON THE ROAD

YOUR COMPLETE DESTINATION GUIDE
In-depth reviews, detailed listings and insider tips

PAGE 329

SURVIVAL GUIDE

HELP YOU HAVE A SMOOTH TRIP

THIS EDITION WRITTEN AND RESEARCHED BY

Brett Atkinson, Sarah Bennett, Peter Dragicevich, Charles Rawlings-Way, Lee Slater

Walk on the Wild Side

With just a million people scattered across 151,215 square kilometres, the South Island has a population density even smaller than Tasmania. Filling in the gaps are the sublime (and very pretty) forests, mountains, lakes, beaches and fiords that have made New Zealand's 'Mainland' one of the best hiking (locals call it 'tramping') destinations on the planet. Tackle one of the South Island's six epic 'Great Walks' – you've probably already heard of the Heaphy, Routeburn or Milford Tracks – or just spend a few dreamy hours wandering through some easily accessible wilderness.

Action Aplenty

The easygoing heritage charms of Arrowtown, Dunedin and Oamaru are undoubted, but the South Island's most iconic experiences are best enjoyed with a healthy sense of adventure. Kayak in the meandering coves of the Marlborough Sounds or amid Fiordland's remote isolation, scare yourself silly with Queenstown's gravity-defying menu of bungy options, or take to two wheels through stunning scenery on the Otago Central Rail Trail. During winter, squeeze in a short ski-field break around Wanaka, Queenstown or Mt Hutt, before adjourning to cosy bars and cafes to watch NZ's rugby legends take on the best of Australia and South Africa.

Welcome to possibly the world's most scenically diverse island; with lakes, mountains and beaches, often incorporating quintessentially Kiwi ways to get active and adventurous.

(left) South Bay from Kaikoura
(below) Franz Josef Glacier

Food, Wine & Beer

After all this honest exercise, visitors can ease further into the local eating and drinking scene. NZ food was once a bland facsimile of a British Sunday dinner, but these days Kiwi chefs dip into new-world culinary oceans for inspiration. Expect a tasty focus on local and seasonal produce, especially around the stone-fruit orchards of Central Otago and the salty marine larder surrounding Kaikoura.

Thirsty? NZ's cool-climate wineries have been collecting wine-award trophies for decades now, and Marlborough, Christchurch and Dunedin are all hoppy hubs for the country's emerging craft-beer movement.

Meet the Locals

Prepare to meet the South Island's idiosyncratic wildlife: whales, fur seals, dolphins and penguins all frequent the coastal waters around Kaikoura, partnered by an armada of pelagic bird species including petrels and albatross. NZ's endangered Hector's dolphins cavort in the waters of Banks Peninsula and the Catlins, and the Otago Peninsula has penguins, royal albatross and sea lions. Further south, often battered by Southern Ocean winds, Stewart Island presents opportunities to spy NZ's iconic but shy kiwi in the wild. More bolshy avian species include the kea, NZ's native alpine parrot. Keep a close eye on your rental car's aerial if they're hanging around.

New Zealand – South Island

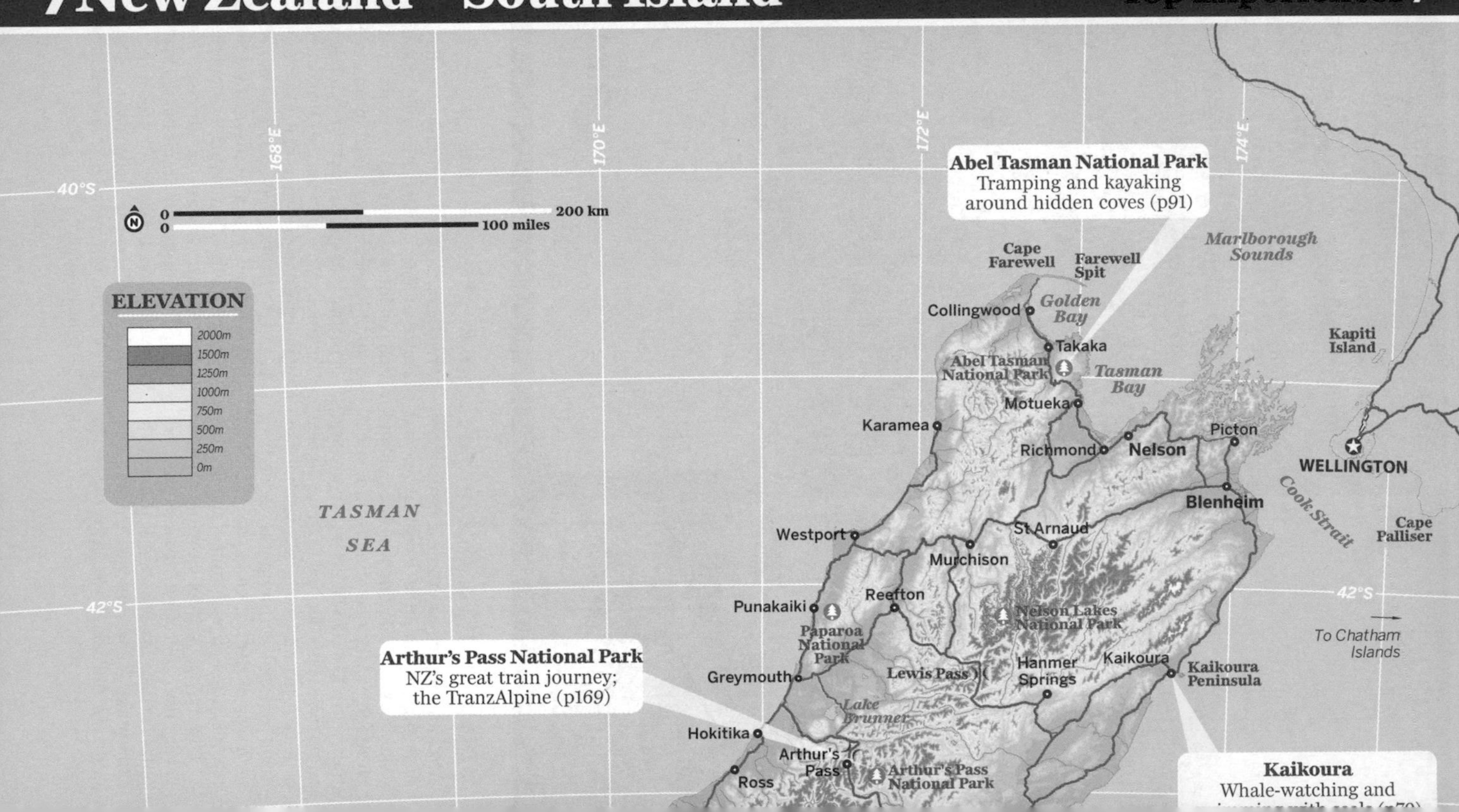

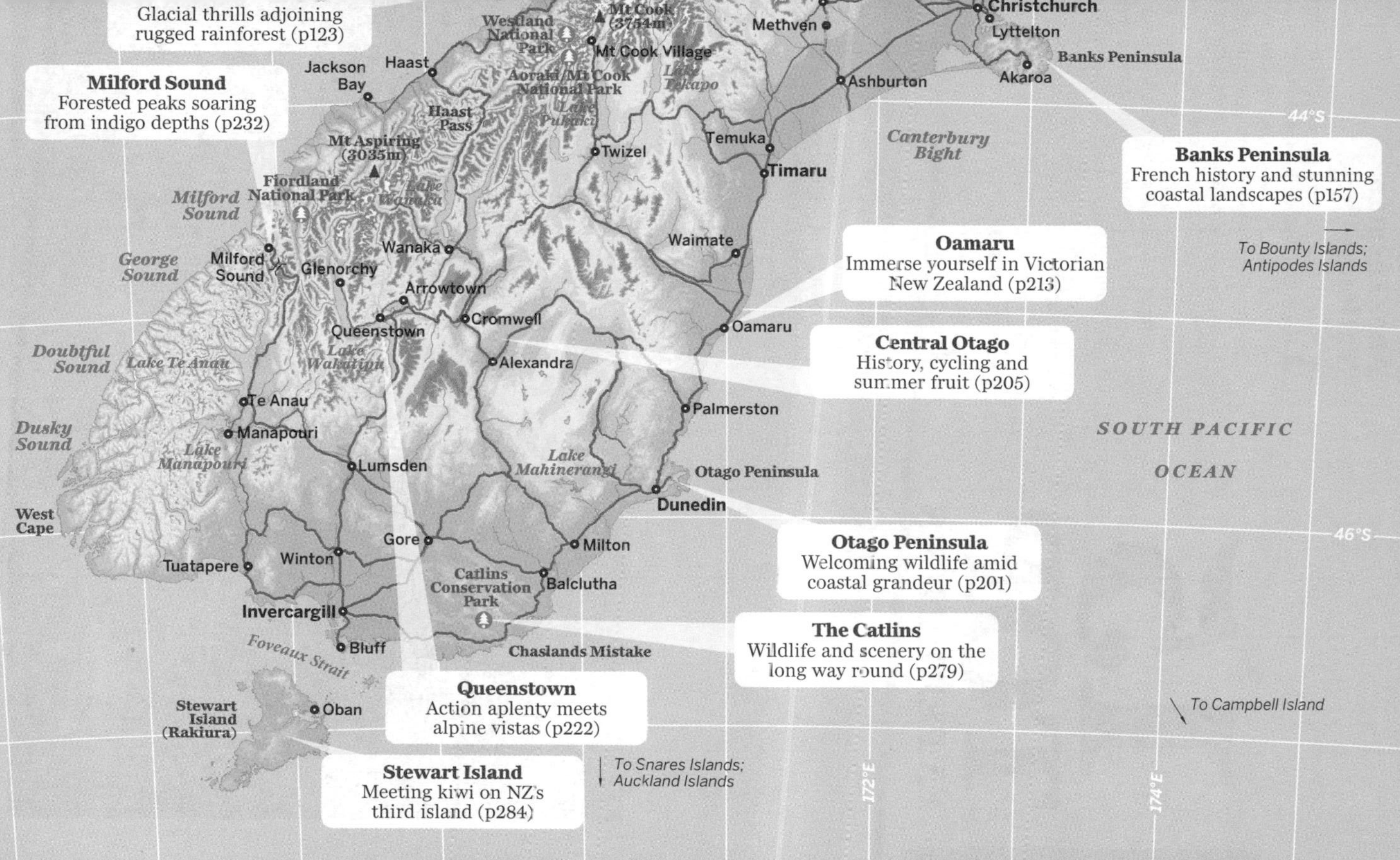
Glacial thrills adjoining rugged rainforest (p123)
Milford Sound
Forested peaks soaring from indigo depths (p232)
Banks Peninsula
French history and stunning coastal landscapes (p157)
Oamaru
Immerse yourself in Victorian New Zealand (p213)
Central Otago
History, cycling and summer fruit (p205)
Otago Peninsula
Welcoming wildlife amid coastal grandeur (p201)
The Catlins
Wildlife and scenery on the long way round (p279)
Queenstown
Action aplenty meets alpine vistas (p222)
Stewart Island
Meeting kiwi on NZ's third island (p284)
Christchurch
Lyttelton
Banks Peninsula
Akaroa
Methven
Ashburton
Canterbury Bight
Temuka
Timaru
Westland National Park
Mt Cook (3754m)
Mt Cook Village
Aoraki/Mt Cook National Park
Lake Tekapo
Lake Pukaki
Twizel
Jackson Bay
Haast
Haast Pass
Mt Aspiring (3035m)
Fiordland National Park
Lake Wanaka
Milford Sound
George Sound
Wanaka
Glenorchy
Arrowtown
Cromwell
Queenstown
Lake Wakatipu
Alexandra
Waimate
Oamaru
Palmerston
Doubtful Sound
Lake Te Anau
Te Anau
Dusky Sound
Manapouri
Lake Manapouri
Lumsden
Lake Mahinerangi
Otago Peninsula
Dunedin
West Cape
Gore
Milton
Winton
Tuatapere
Catlins Conservation Park
Balclutha
Invercargill
Bluff
Foveaux Strait
Chaslands Mistake
Stewart Island (Rakiura)
Oban
To Bounty Islands; Antipodes Islands
SOUTH PACIFIC OCEAN
To Campbell Island
To Snares Islands; Auckland Islands
44°S
46°S
172°E
174°E

15 TOP EXPERIENCES

Abel Tasman National Park

1 Here's New Zealand nature at its most gl ous and seductive: lush green hills fringe with golden sandy coves, slipping gently into warm shallows before meeting a crystal-clea sea of cerulean blue. Abel Tasman National P (p91) is the quintessential postcard paradise where you can put yourself in the picture, assuming an endless number of poses: tramping, kayaking, swimming, sunbathing, or eve makin' whoopee in the woods. This sweet-as corner of NZ's South Island raises the bar ar effortlessly keeps it there.

Kaikoura

2 First settled by Maori with their keen no for seafood, Kaikoura (p70) – meaning 'eat crayfish' – is now NZ's best spot for bot consuming and communing with marine life Whales are definitely off the menu, but you' almost guaranteed a good gander at Moby's mates on a whale-watching tour. There's als swimming with seals and dolphins, or birdsp ting including albatross. When it comes to 'sea food and eat it', crayfish is still king, but on fishing tours you can hook into other edi wonders of the unique Kaikoura deep.

1

2

5

‹karoa & Banks ‹eninsula

3 Infused with a healthy dash of Gallic ambi- ‹nce, French-themed Akaroa ‹ends languidly around one ‹ the prettiest harbours ‹ Banks Peninsula (p157). ‹eek dolphins and plump ‹enguins inhabit clear waters ‹erfect for sailing and explor- ‹g. Elsewhere on the penin- ‹la, the spidery Summit ‹d prescribes the rim of an ‹cient volcano, while wind- ‹g roads descend to hidden ‹ys and coves. Spend your ‹ys tramping and kayak- ‹g amid the improbably ‹autiful land- and seascape, ‹ile relaxing at night in chic ‹stros or cosy bed-and- ‹eakfast accommodation. ‹ctor's dolphin, Akaroa

Franz Josef Glacier

4 The spectacular glaciers of Franz Josef (p123) and Fox (p128) are remarkable for many reasons, including their rates of accumulation and descent, and their proximity to both the loftiest peaks of the Southern Alps and the Tasman Sea around 10km away. Get almost face-to-face with them on a short walk, or take a hike on the ice with Franz Josef or Fox Glacier Guides. The ultimate encounter is on a scenic flight, which often also provides grandstand views of Mt Cook, Westland forest, and a seemingly endless Tasman Sea.

Central Otago

5 Here's your chance to balance virtue and vice, all with a background of some of NZ's most starkly beautiful landscapes. Take to two wheels to negotiate the easygoing Otago Central Rail Trail (p208), cycling into heritage South Island towns such as Clyde (p207) and Naseby (p210). Tuck into well-earned beers in laidback country pubs, or linger for a classy lunch in the vineyard restaurants of Bannockburn. Other foodie diversions include Cromwell's weekly farmers market, and the summer stone-fruit harvest of the country's best orchards. Otago Central Rail Trail

Queenstown

6 Queenstown (p222) may be world-renowned as the birthplace of bungy jumping, but there's more to New Zealand's adventure hub than leaping off a bridge wearing a giant rubber band. Against the ridiculously scenic backdrop of the jagged indigo profile of The Remarkables mountain range, travellers can spend days skiing, hiking or mountain biking, before dining in cosmopolitan restaurants or partying in some of NZ's best bars. Next-day options include hang gliding, kayaking or river rafting, or easing into holiday mode with sleepier detours to Arrowtown or Glenorchy.

Otago Peninsula

7 The Otago Peninsula (p201) is stunning proof there's more to the South Island's outdoor thrills than heart-stopping alpine and lake scenery. Amid a backdrop of coastal vistas combining rugged, hidden beaches with an expansive South Pacific horizon, it's very easy to spot penguins, seals and sea lions. Beyond the rare yellow-eyed penguin, or hoiho, other fascinating avian residents include the royal albatross. Otago Peninsula's Taiaroa Head is the world's only mainland royal albatross colony: visit in January or February to see these magnificent ocean-going birds.

6

DAVID WALL / LONELY PLANET IMAGES ©

DAVID WALL / LONELY PLANET IMAGES ©

CHRISTOPHER GROENHOUT / LONELY PLANET IMAGES ©

ranzAlpine

8 In less then five hours the TranzAlpine (p116) crosses from the Pacific Ocean the Tasman Sea. Leaving Christchurch it eeds across the Canterbury Plains to the othills of the Southern Alps. After negotiat-g tunnels and viaducts, the train enters the oad expanse of the Waimakariri Valley. A op at Arthur's Pass Village is followed by e 8.5km-long Otira tunnel, burrowing right rough the bedrock of New Zealand's alpine ine. Then it's all downhill: through the ramakau River Valley, past Lake Brunner, d finally into sleepy Greymouth.

Milford Sound

9 Fingers crossed you'll be lucky enough to see Milford Sound (p232) on a clear, sunny day. That's definitely when the world-beating collage of waterfalls, verdant cliffs and peaks, and dark cobalt waters is at its best. More likely though is the classic Fiordland combination of mist and drizzle, with the iconic snowcapped profile of Mitre Peak revealed slowly through shimmering sheets of precipitation. Either way, keep your eyes peeled for seals and dolphins, especially if you're exploring New Zealand's most famous fiord by kayak. Fur seals

Skiing & Snowboarding

10 You're guaranteed to find decent South Island snow right through the winter season (June to October). The most famous slopes are around hip Queenstown (p222) and laidback Wanaka (p249), with iconic ski runs such as Coronet Peak, the Remarkables and Treble Cone close at hand. There are also dedicated snowboarding and cross-country (Nordic) snow parks here. Further north the smaller club-operated ski fields of Canterbury offer a more local experience. And when it comes to après-ski time, a cosy bar or restaurant is never far away. Coronet Peak, Queenstown

Stewart Island

11 Stewart Island (p284), the country's rugged southern addendum, is a paradise for trampers, birdwatchers and traveller seeking an authentic NZ travel experience. Test yourself on the challenging North West Circuit Track or spend three days on the easier, but still spectacular, Rakiura Track. Joi the friendly locals at NZ's southernmost pub quiz at the South Sea Hotel in Oban, before making plans to explore the abundant bird lif on nearby Ulva Island, or join a kiwi-spotting tour to see NZ's shy feathered icon mooching around at twilight on isolated beaches. North West Circuit Track

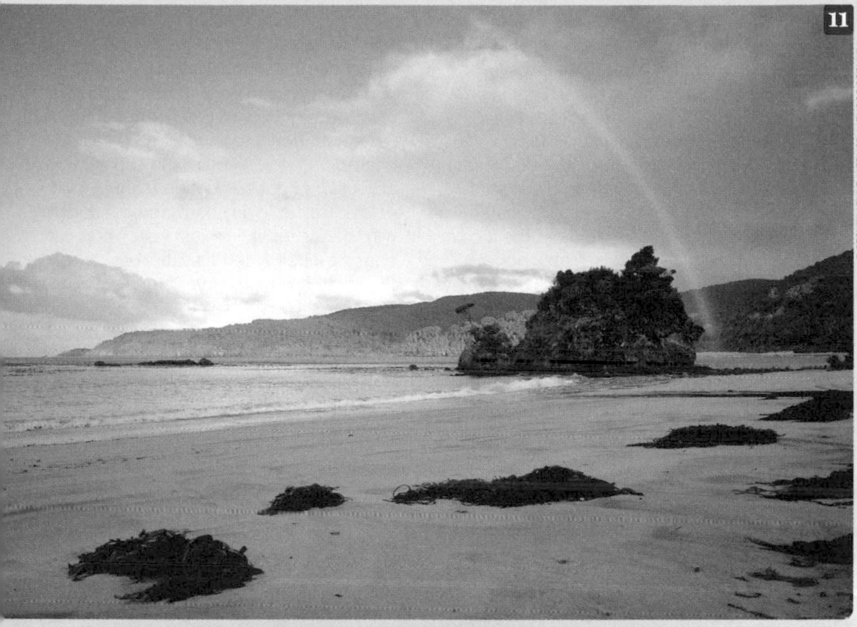

11

12

Oamaru

12 A wonderfully restored Victorian townscape, the quirky celebration of Steampunk culture, or the nightly arrival of hundreds of little blue penguins: surprising Oamaru (p213) has plenty of reasons for a mandatory inclusion on your South Island itinerary. Explore the town's harbourside historic precinct on a penny-farthing bicyle before adjourning for Earl Grey or something stronger in heritage cafes and restaurants. At dusk, grab a grandstand seat to say gidday to penguins returning home after a day's fishing, before toasting their ocean-going bravery with a beer at a corner pub. Bank of NSW building

The Catlins

13 Even for many New Zealanders the rugged Catlins (p279) coast is unknown territory. Avoid the speedy but functional inland route linking Dunedin and Invercargill, and traverse through the Catlins' more diverse and interesting procession of isolated bays and coves, sweeping coastal scenery, and opportunities to meet the locals and the local wildlife. Catlins' highlights include Blair Sommerville's quirky Lost Gypsy Gallery at Papatowai, swimming (or surfing) with dolphins at Curio Bay, and the windswept environs of Slope Point, the southernmost tip of the South Island. Cannibal Bay

Rugby

14 Rugby Union is New Zealand's nationa game and governing preoccupation. If your timing's good you might catch the revered national team (and reigning world champions) the All Blacks in action. The 'ABs' are resident gods: mention Richie McCaw or Dan Carter in any conversation and you'll win friends for life! Or just watch some kids chasing a ball around a suburban field on a Saturday morning, or yell along with the locals in a small-town pub as the big men collide on the big screen.

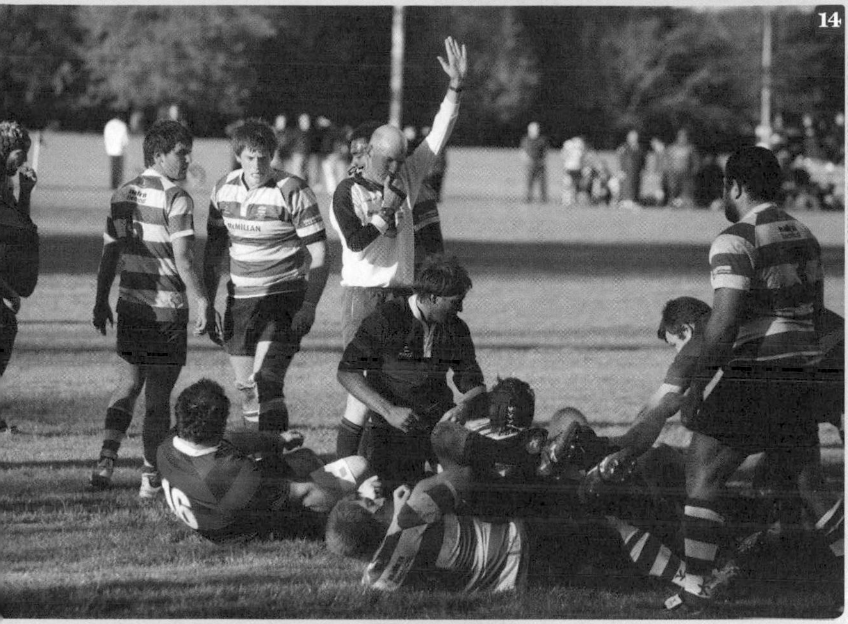

14

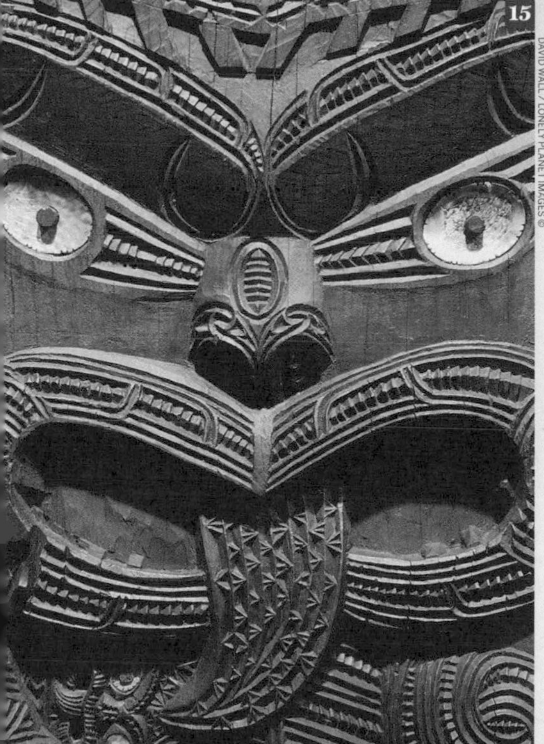

PAUL KENNEDY / LONELY PLANET IMAGES ©

15

DAVID WALL / LONELY PLANET IMAGES ©

Maori Culture

15 New Zealand's indigenous Maori culture is accessible and engaging: join in a *haka* (war dance); chow-down at a traditional *hangi* (Maori feast cooked in the ground); carve a pendant from bone or *pounamu* (jade); learn some Maori language; or check out an authentic cultural performance with song, dance, legends, arts and crafts. Big-city and regional museums around the South Island are crammed with Maori artefacts and historical items, and Timaru's excellent Te Ana Maori Rock Art Centre (p172) showcases the fascinating story of NZ's indigenous rock art. Maori carving, Otago Museum

need to know

Currency
» New Zealand dollars ($)

Language
» English and Maori

When to Go

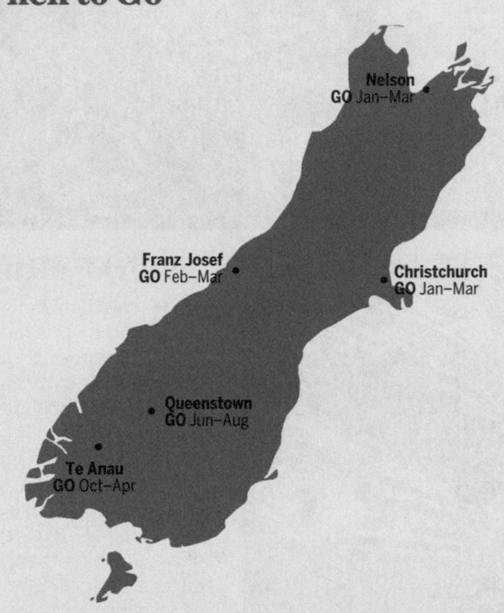

High Season (Dec–Feb)

» Summer: busy beaches, outdoor explorations, festivals and sporting events. City accommodation increases up to 25%.

» High season in the ski towns is during winter (Jun–Aug): chilly days, cold nights and deep powder.

Shoulder Season (Mar–Apr)

» Prime travelling time: fine weather, short queues, kids in school and warm(ish) ocean.

» Long evenings supping Kiwi wines and craft beers.

» Sep–Nov is spring shoulder season too.

Low Season (May–Aug)

» Head for the slopes of the Southern Alps for some brilliant southern hemisphere skiing.

» No crowds, good accommodation deals and a seat in any restaurant.

Your Daily Budget

Budget less than
$130

» Dorm beds or campsites: $25–35 per night

» Big-city food markets for self-catering bargains

» Explore NZ with a money-saving bus pass

Midrange
$130–250

» Double room in a midrange hotel/motel: $100–$180

» Midrange restaurant, a movie or a live band, a few beers at a pub

» Hire a car and explore further

Top end over
$250

» Double room in top-end hotel: from 180

» Three-course meal in a classy restaurant: $70

» Take a guided tour, go shopping or hit some ritzy bars

Money

» ATMs are widely available, especially in larger cities and towns. Credit cards accepted in most hotels and restaurants.

Visas

» Citizens of Australia, the UK and 56 other countries don't need visas for NZ (length of stay allowances vary). Other countries' citizens require visas. See www.immigration.govt.nz.

Mobile Phones

» Australian and European phones will work on NZ's networks, but not most American or Japanese phones. Use global roaming or a local SIM card on prepay.

Driving

» Driving is on the left, with the steering wheel on the right-hand side of the car.

Websites

» **100% Pure New Zealand** (www.newzealand.com) Official tourism site.

» **Department of Conservation** (www.doc.govt.nz) DOC parks and camping info.

» **Destination New Zealand** (www.destination-nz.com) Resourceful tourism site.

» **Lonely Planet** (www.lonelyplanet.com/new-zealand) Advice from travellers who've actually been there.

» **Living Landscapes** (www.livinglandscapes.co.nz) Maori tourism operators.

» **DineOut** (www.dineout.co.nz) Restaurant reviews.

Exchange Rates

Australia	A$1	NZ$1.30
Canada	C$1	NZ$1.23
China	Y10	NZ$1.98
Euro zone	€1	NZ$1.59
Japan	¥100	NZ$1.62
Singapore	S$1	NZ$0.97
UK	UK£1	NZ$1.92
US	US$1	NZ$1.25

For current exchange rates see www.xe.com

Important Numbers

Regular NZ phone numbers have a two-digit area code followed by a seven-digit number. When dialling within a region, the area code is still required. Drop the initial 0 if dialling from abroad.

NZ country code	☎64
International access code from NZ	☎00
Emergency (ambulance, fire, police)	☎111
Directory assistance	☎018
International directory	☎0172

Arriving in the South Island

» **Christchurch Airport**

Bus – City Flyer every 30 minutes, 7.15am to 9.15pm

Shuttle Bus – Pre-booked, 24-hour door-to-door services

Taxi – Around $50; 25 minutes to the city

» **Queenstown Airport**

Bus – Connectabus every 15 minutes from 6.50am to 10.20pm

Shuttle Bus – Pre-booked, 24-hour door-to-door services

Taxi – Around $30; 15 minutes to the city

Driving Around the South Island

There are extensive bus networks and a couple of handy train lines criss-crossing the South Island, but for the best scenery, flexibility and pure freedom it's hard to beat piling into a campervan or rent-a-car and hitting the open road. Scanning the map you might think that driving from A to B won't take long, but remember that many of the roads here are two-lane country byways, traversing hilly landscape in curves, crests and convolutions: allow plenty of time to get wherever you're going. And who's in a hurry anyway? Slow down and see more of the country: explore end-of-the-line towns, stop for a swim/surf/beer, and pack a Swiss Army knife for impromptu picnics at roadside produce stalls.

if you like...

Cities

New Zealand is urbanised: 72% of Kiwis reside in the 16 biggest towns. So it follows that cities here are great fun! Coffee shops, restaurants, bars, boutiques, bookshops, museums, galleries. You're never far from a live gig or an espresso.

Christchurch Re-emerging from recent earthquakes with energy and verve largely due to the determination and resilience of proud locals. Stay longer than you planned to fully experience the city's renaissance, and then explore nearby Banks Peninsula (p136)

Dunedin Exuding history and an artsy, boozy ambience (so many students), and surprisingly close to superb wildlife-viewing opportunities on the Otago Peninsula (p189)

Queenstown Maybe only a town in an international sense, but a global posse of travellers and adventure seekers ensures New Zealand's most scenic alpine resort exudes a cosmopolitan vibe year round (p222)

Beaches

New Zealand has a heck of a lot of coastline: plenty of sun, surf and sand. Top tip: book your trip for summer, or you might find the water a little cooler than you bargained for...especially on the South Island.

Wharariki No car park, no ice-cream van, no swimsuits... This isolated stretch near sweeping Farewell Spit is for wanderers and ponderers (p97)

Kaiteriteri Wildly popular, and for good reason, Kaiteriteri's gorgeous, golden stretch of sand is the gateway to the beautiful Abel Tasman National Park. That's where you can kayak or tramp to more isolated beachy spots like Onetahuti (p89)

Kaka Point Located at the northern point of the rugged Catlins, Kaka Point combines a sweeping surf beach with the occasional seal and sea lion visitor. There's a great pub, and wild and rocky Nugget Point is a short coastal drive away (p283)

History

European NZ history goes back just a couple of hundred years, but Maori have lived here since at least AD 1200.

Dunedin Railway Station One hundred or so years old, trimmed with mosaic tiles and stained-glass windows. One of NZ's most-photographed buildings, and the starting point for the spectacular Taieri Gorge Railway (p190)

Oamaru Historic Precinct Beautifully restored whitestone buildings and warehouses, now housing eclectic galleries, restaurants and artisan workshops. Pack your best sense of balance to ride a penny-farthing bicycle (p213)

Christchurch The earthquakes damaged much of the southern capital's architectural heritage, but some essential historic experiences remain. Punt slowly down the Avon River and explore the excellent Canterbury Museum (p136)

Akaroa Discover the French colonial history of the pretty seaside village of Akaroa. The biannual French Fest in late October is a great time to visit (p157)

» Tramping the Milford Track, Fiordland National Park (p267)

Maori Culture

After you touch down in NZ, it won't take you long to notice how prominent, potent and accessible indigenous Maori culture is in contemporary society, language, music, arts and crafts, performance, tattoos, and of course, rugby.

Shark Nett Gallery Hidden away in Havelock, this is NZ's largest private collection of Maori carvings (p64)

Te Ana Maori Rock Art Centre Learn about traditional Maori rock art in Timaru before exploring remote sites around South Canterbury (p172)

Kokutu Gallery In Whataroa on the West Coast there's greenstone and bone, done the right way, by the right people – this is carving as storytelling (p122)

Maori & Colonial Museum Tucked away in sleepy Okains Bay on the Banks Peninsula, this community-run museum is a surprising storehouse of heritage treasures including a *waka taua* (war canoe) (p158)

Museums & Galleries

Take time out from the wineries, beaches and bars and spend a few hours meandering through a museum or gallery. It's good for the soul.

Otago Museum Harnessing Dunedin's academic firepower, the Otago Museum presents an overview of the region's history, flora and fauna – an excellent primer before wildlife-watching on the Otago Peninsula (p189)

Canterbury Museum One of the few heritage buildings to survive the Christchurch earthquakes unscathed: a fascinating showcase of Maori culture and natural history (p137)

World of WearableArt & Classic Cars Museum Nelson's WOW remains as popular as ever, with the added (and slightly incongruous) bonus of a classic cars display out the back (p81)

Eastern Southland Gallery A real surprise in sleepy Gore – a town more known for moonshine whiskey, country music and trout fishing – this erudite establishment features works by iconic NZ artists Ralph Hotere and Rita Angus (p280)

Tramping

NZ has a worldwide reputation for hiking, with nine epic 'Great Walks' managed by the Department of Conservation. But you needn't be Sir Edmund Hillary: short walks can also deliver a taste of wilderness.

Milford Track Justifiably famous, Milford is our pick of the 'Great Walks': 53.5km of gorgeous fiords, sounds, peaks and raindrops. Good luck dealing with the challenging McKinnon Pass and a few pesky sandflies (p267)

Banks Peninsula Track A four-day meander (or two-day dash) around the perforated Banks Peninsula, southeast of Christchurch (p159)

Robert Ridge & Lake Angelus In Nelson Lakes National Park: an achievable summit and a magical mountain lake (p84)

Tuatapere Hump Ridge Track In the deep southwest of the South Island, the privately run Tuatapere Humpridge Track traverses 53km across rugged subalpine heights from the wonderfully remote Te Waewae Bay (p273)

» Skiing at Coronet Peak, Queenstown (p37)

Pubs, Bars & Beer

Sometimes it's the simple things you encounter on holiday that stay with you: a sunset, a conversation, a splash in the sea, a cold beer at the end of a long day on the road...

Dunedin Bars Eureka, Albar, Tonic and Inch Bar: four great bars in New Zealand's best university town. We'll have an Emerson's pilsner thanks (p197)

Mussel Inn Lose an evening in tiny Takaka with live music and a host of home brews (p98)

Moutere Inn Dating back to 1850, this is reputedly the oldest pub in the land. Surely this alone is excuse enough to visit (p86)

Christchurch Coping with around 10,000 aftershocks is thirsty work, but craft-beer hubs such as Pomeroy's Old Brewery Inn and The Brewery definitely ease the seismic frustration for Christchurch beer fans (p152)

Foodie Experiences

New Zealand is no longer the land of meat-and-three-veg. Eating here these days can be as simple or sophisticated as you like, with the emphasis squarely on fresh regional produce.

Bannockburn Vineyard Restaurants Eye-popping Central Otago scenery combined with the best of NZ food and wine. While you're in the area, don't miss some excellent restaurants in nearby Queenstown and Arrowtown (p206)

Central Otago Drift by the orchards around Alexandra, Cromwell and Roxburgh in February and March for roadside stalls crammed with juicy stone fruit. Apricots, peaches, plums and nectarines – anything goes (p205)

Hokitika Wildfoods Festival You're a big baby, Bear Grylls – eating insects can be lots of fun – especially when they're washed down with Monteith's beers (p119)

Original Kaikoura Seafood BBQ Swing by this fabulous outdoor fish shack for some whitebait, mussels, paua or crayfish, cooked hot and fresh (p74)

Skiing

Snowbunny? Powderhound? Downhill deity? Whatever your snowy persuasion, if you're here to ski you won't be disappointed. The South Island offers hundreds of world-class runs, and interesting diversions like Nordic (cross-country) skiing.

Treble Cone 26km from Wanaka, with everything from challenging downhill terrain to snowboard half-pipes and cross-country skiing at the nearby Cardrona Snow Farm (p38)

Canterbury From Mt Hutt and Methven's après-ski buzz, to smaller fields like Ohau, Round Hill, Porters and Broken River (p168)

Coronet Peak The Queenstown area's oldest ski field, just 18km from town. Night skiing on Friday and Saturday gives you time to hit the slopes before hitting the bars and clubs back in town (p37)

Snow Park NZ This dedicated snowboard park is 36km from Wanaka, with challenging half-pipes and more rails than the Orient Express (p38)

If you like...mountain biking, challenge yourself on the multiple downhill options of the new gondola-assisted Queenstown Bike Park (p229)

If you like...birdwatching, follow your nose to see NZ's iconic kiwi snuffling about in the wild on Stewart Island (p284)

Wine Regions

If you haven't been to your local liquor store in the past decade, you might have missed the phenomenon that is NZ wine. Harnessing a pristine environment, abundant sunshine, and volcanic soils, passionate winemakers have been busy crafting world-beating cool-climate drops.

Marlborough The country's biggest and best wine region keeps on turning out superb sauvignon blanc. Don't be picky – just drink some and see what the fuss is about (p68)

Waitaki Valley In a quiet back road linking Canterbury and North Otago, the South Island's newest wine region produces excellent pinot gris. It's where All Blacks captain Richie McCaw was born, so please pay your respects (p218)

Gibbston Valley Negotiate a tasty pathway through the vineyards of this meandering river valley near Queenstown. You can even visit on a retro bicycle (p239)

Waipara Valley A short hop north of Christchurch are spectacular vineyards producing equally spectacular riesling (p164)

Markets

Weekend markets are big business in NZ, the national appetite for organic, locally grown and artisan produce seemingly bottomless. They're also great places to eat breakfast, drink coffee, watch buskers, meet friends and generally unwind.

Dunedin Farmers Market Organic fruit and veg, Dunedin's own Green Man beer, robust coffee and homemade pies – stock up for life on the road (p197)

Nelson Market A big, busy weekly market featuring everything from Doris's traditional bratwursts to new-age clothing (p77)

Cromwell Central Otago's best farmers' market takes place in Cromwell's small but perfectly formed historic precinct. Come hungry as there are plenty of free samples (p205)

Christchurch Farmers Market The historic surroundings of Riccarton Bush are transformed every Saturday with artisan cheeses, craft beer and international street food. On Sundays an arts and crafts market takes centre stage (p152)

Extreme Activities

We're not sure if it's something that has evolved to lure tourists, or if it's something innate in the Kiwi psyche, but extreme activities (skydiving, bungy jumping, jetboating, zorbing, white-water rafting etc) are part and parcel of today's NZ experience.

Queenstown Bungy Strap yourself into the astonishing Shotover Canyon Swing or Nevis Highwire Bungy and be propelled into the void (p224)

Franz Josef Skydive If you're really up for some super-human thrills, this is the highest skydiving in NZ at 18,000 ft (p126)

U-fly Extreme Yes, YOU fly – a stunt plane, no less – across the clear blue skies above Motueka (p87)

Buller River Look forward to a combo of stunning West Coast scenery and exciting river rafting through tight spots such as 'Earthquake Rapids'. Jetboating the Buller is reputed to be NZ's best – sorry Queenstown (p102)

month by month

Top Events

1 **World Buskers Festival**, January

2 **Marlborough Wine Festival**, February

3 **Queenstown Winter Festival**, July

4 **Oamaru Victorian Heritage Celebrations**, November

January

New Zealand peels its eyes open after New Year's Eve, gathers its wits and gets set for another year. Great weather, the cricket season in full swing and it's happy holidays for the locals.

World Buskers Festival

Christchurch could use a little cheering up: jugglers, musos, tricksters, puppeteers, mime artists, dancers... Shoulder into the crowd, see who's performing in the middle and maybe leave a few dollars. Avoid if you're scared of audience participation.

Nelson Jazz & Blues Festival

Get your groove on at rockin' venues and ad hoc street corner stages. Acts range from international funkateers through to Kiwi hipsters, and Nelson's reputation for great wine and beer makes it very easy to enjoy the diverse beats.

February

The sun is shining, the nights are long, and the sauv blanc and pale ale are chillin' in the fridge: this is prime party time across NZ. Book your festival tickets (and beds) in advance.

Marlborough Wine Festival

NZ's biggest and best wine festival features tastings from around 50 Marlborough wineries (also NZ's biggest and best), plus fine food and entertainment. It's mandatory over-indulgence; remember to keep quiet if you don't like sauvignon blanc.

Rippon Festival

Wanaka's alternative music festival – held in a gently sloping lakeside vineyard – features cool sounds with a dance, reggae, rock and electronica spin. It's an uber-relaxed opportunity to listen to the finely curated best of the NZ music scene.

March

March brings a hint of autumn, and it's harvest time in the vineyards of Marlborough and orchards of Central Otago. Expect long dusky evenings and plenty of festivals plumping out the calendar.

Hokitika Wildfoods Festival

Eat worms, hare testicles or crabs at Hokitika's comfort-zone-challenging food fest. Not for the mild-mannered or weak-stomached... But even if you are, it's still fun to watch! There are plenty of fine quality NZ brews to help subdue any difficult tastes.

Ellerslie Flower Show

Christchurch's glorious Hagley Park is made even more spectacular by the lovingly-crafted introduction of beautiful gardens. Don't come expecting a haven for fuddy-duddy gardeners, as many of the colourful, floral additions are also bold, modern and innovative.

Gibbston Harvest Festival

Make the short trek from Queenstown or Cromwell to the Gibbston Valley. In mid-March, the rugged and meandering river valley showcases award-winning wines from 15 vineyards, local cheese and chocolate, and the recent addition of new riverside walking and mountain-biking trails.

April

April is when canny travellers hit NZ: the ocean is swimmable and the weather still mild, with nary a tourist or queue in sight. Easter equals pricey accommodation everywhere.

Warbirds Over Wanaka

Held every second Easter in even-numbered years, Warbirds Over Wanaka is an internationally renowned airshow set against rugged Central Otago scenery. Heritage and iconic aircraft pull crazy manoeuvres for up to 100,000 spectators. Tally ho chaps, and BYO Biggles goggles.

Clyde Wine & Food Festival

Sleepy Clyde is well-known as the northern terminus of the Otago Central Rail Trail, but the cool-climate pinots and rieslings of local vineyards are also damn fine. Keep an eye out for Two Paddocks, Kiwi actor Sam Neill's vineyard.

May

The nostalgia of autumn runs deep: party nights are long gone and a chilly NZ winter beckons. Thank goodness for the Comedy Festival. It's your last chance to explore Fiordland and Southland in reasonable weather.

New Zealand International Comedy Festival

This three-week laugh-fest in May kicks off in the North Island, but then hits the South Island with the on-the-road Comedy Convoy. International gag-merchants (such as Arj Barker and Danny Bhoy) line up next to home-grown talent.

June

Time to head south: it's ski season. Queenstown and Wanaka hit their strides, and international legions of skiers and snowboarders hit the slopes at Coronet Peak, The Remarkables and Cardrona.

New Zealand Golden Guitar Awards

We like both kinds of music: country and western! With niche-market appeal, these awards in Gore cap off a week of everlovin' country twang and boot-scootin' good times, with plenty of concerts and buskers.

July

Queenstown gets more than a little crazy with the annual winter festival. Expect increases in accommodation prices while it's happening. If you're feeling less active, combine cinema, Cadbury's chocolate and craft beer in Dunedin.

Queenstown Winter Festival

This southern snow-fest has been running since 1975, and now attracts around 45,000 snowbunnies. It's a 10-day party, studded with fireworks, jazz, street parades, comedy, a Mardi Gras, masquerade ball and lots of snow-centric activities on the mountain slopes.

New Zealand International Film Festivals

After separate film festivals in Dunedin (July–August) and Christchurch (August), a selection of flicks hits the road for screenings in regional towns from July to November. Film buffs in Greymouth and Invercargill get very excited at the prospect.

August

Land a good deal on accommodation pretty much anywhere except the ski towns. Winter is almost spent, but there's still not much happening outside: music and art are your saviours...or watch some rugby.

Christchurch Arts Festival

The South Island's biggest arts festival takes place on a biannual basis in odd-numbered years. Celebrate with resilient Cantabrians at an array of new post-earthquake venues, including the innovative Hagley Park Events Village. Music, theatre and dance all feature.

September

Spring has sprung, and baby lambs are running amok on the South Island. There's good accommodation bargains to be had, but definitely

be ready for four seasons in one day. The snow season often lingers.

Snowsports

Forget flying off to Europe or South America. Here's your chance to experience the widest range of snow-sports activities in the southern hemisphere. Focus on your downhill at Coronet Peak, achieve snowboarding nirvana at Cardrona, or go Nordic at Snow Farm New Zealand.

October

Post-rugby and pre-cricket sees sports fans twiddling their thumbs: a trip to Kaikoura perhaps? October is 'shoulder season' with reasonable accommodation rates, minimal crowds and no competition for the good campsites.

Kaikoura Seafest

Kaikoura is a town built on crayfish. Well, not literally, but there sure are plenty of crustaceans in the sea here, many of which find themsleves on plates at Seafest, which is also a great excuse to drink a lot and dance around.

French Fest

Allez très vite to Akaroa's biannual French Fest – held in late October in odd-numbered years and celebrating the harbour town's Gallic heritage. Quirky events include a waiters' race and a French cricket tournament. Sorry Aussies, underarm bowling is not allowed.

(above) Vineyard at Blenheim, Marlborough (p68)
(below) The legacy of 19th-century French settlers lives on in Akaroa (p160)

Wanaka Fest

Wanaka's normally all about exploring the alpine vistas on two legs or two knobbly mountain bike tyres, but the lakeside town's emerging gourmet side is also showcased at the annual Wanaka Fest. Come along and tuck into lots of local produce.

November

Another NZ summer threatens as days get longer following the introduction of daylight saving. Now's a good time to be doing the Milford or Routeburn Tracks, but you'll need to book ahead.

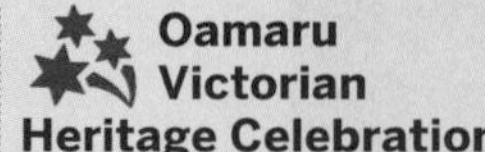

Oamaru Victorian Heritage Celebrations

Ahhh, the good old days: when Queen Vic sat dourly on the throne, the hems were low, collars were high, and civic decency was a matter of course. Old Oamaru thoroughly enjoys this tongue-in-cheek historic homage with dress-ups, penny-farthing races, choirs, guided tours etc.

NZ Cup & Show Week

Christchurch's annual NZ Cup & Show Week is an iconic Canterbury event, and it's a great opportunity for the good people of Christchurch to celebrate with fashion shows, horse racing and the country-comes-to-town appeal of the A&P (agricultural and pastoral) Show.

December

Summertime! The crack of leather on willow resounds across the nation's cricket pitches and office workers surge towards the finish line. Everyone gears up for Christmas: avoid shopping centres like the plague.

Queen Charlotte Track

Beat the summer rush with a December departure on the hugely popular Queen Charlotte Track. Cover the coastal track's spectacular 71km on two legs or two wheels, or even integrate a spot of sea kayaking into your stunning journey.

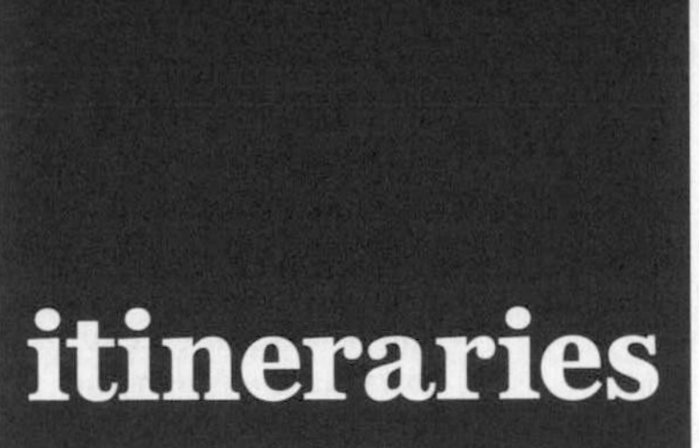

itineraries

Whether you've got one week or two, these itineraries provide a starting point for the trip of a lifetime. Want more inspiration? Head online to lonelyplanet.com/thorntree to chat with other travellers..

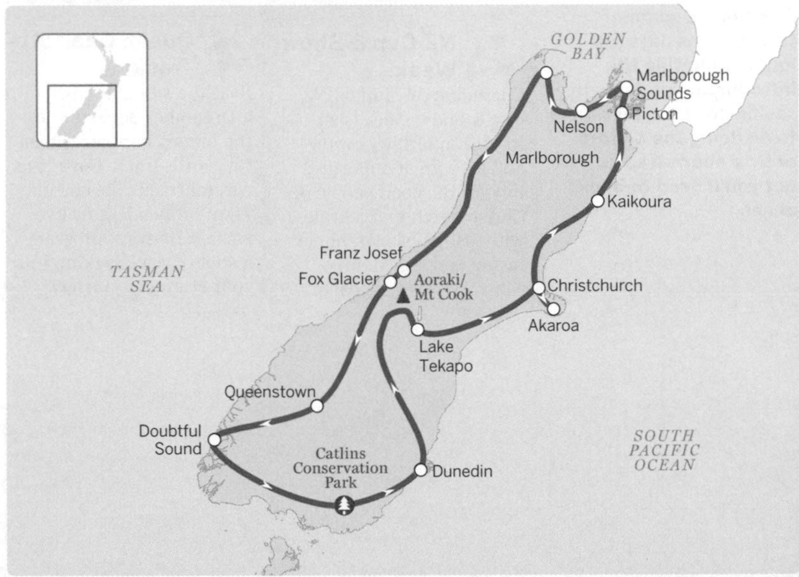

Three Weeks

Southern Circuit

Head to **Christchurch** and see how the city is rebuilding post-earthquakes. Grab a kick-ass coffee, then visit the Canterbury Museum or International Antarctic Centre. The Avon River cuts a lazy ribbon through town, check it out in the Botanic Gardens, or see if the city tramway or Christchurch Art Gallery have reopened yet.

City saturated? Drive out to Banks Peninsula and the French-colonial settlement of **Akaroa**, then head north for whale-watching in **Kaikoura**. Continue to the famous **Marlborough wine region** and pretty harbour town of **Picton** to lose a day in the waterways of the **Marlborough Sounds**.

Detour west past artsy **Nelson** to ecofriendly **Golden Bay**. Heading southbound along the West Coast there's time to check out the town of **Franz Josef** and visit the Franz Josef and **Fox Glaciers** before continuing to ski-central **Queenstown**, the desolate and mesmerising **Doubtful Sound** and the overgrown **Catlins**. Back up the East Coast, drop in to Scottish-flavoured **Dunedin**, then detour through Central Otago to the snowy heights of **Aoraki/Mt Cook** and **Lake Tekapo**, before rolling back into Christchurch.

» (above) Snowcapped Seaward Kaikoura Range (p70)
» (left) Autumn in Otago (p201)

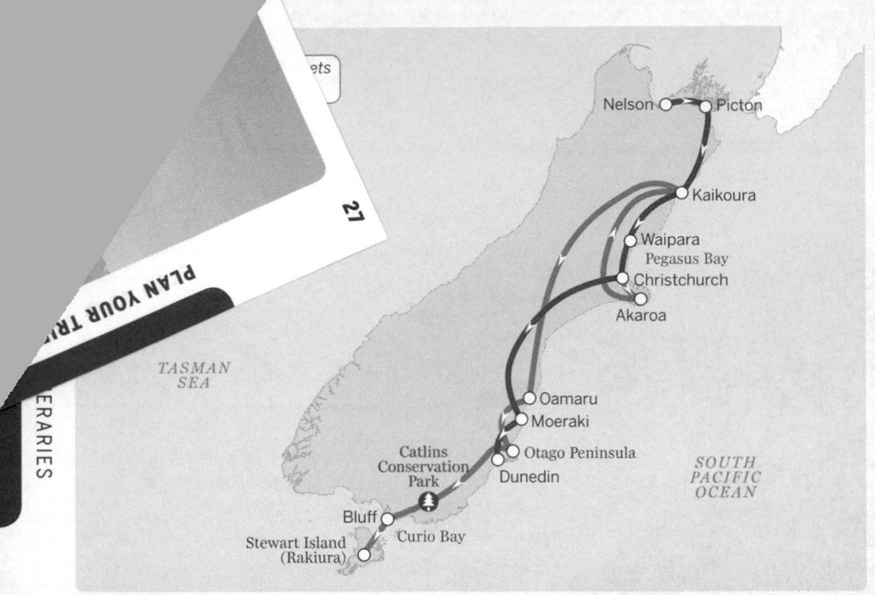

One Week to Ten Days
Food, Beer & Markets

Fire up your tastebuds around **Nelson**, widely regarded as the nation's craft-brewing capital and home to innovative microbreweries such as Renaissance, Moa and 8 Wired. Loop east through **Picton** and down the South Island's rugged East Coast to **Kaikoura** for delicious seafood. Graduate from Kaikoura's rustic seafood eateries to classier dining in the vineyard restaurants of **Waipara**'s wine region, north of Christchurch. Pegasus Bay and Mud House are both great for leisurely lunches.

Journey into **Christchurch** to sample the post-earthquake restaurant scene emerging in Sumner and Addington, and don't miss the excellent Christchurch Farmers Market on a Saturday morning or Wednesday night. More craft-beer heaven awaits beer buffs at Pomeroy's Old Brewery Inn and the Brewery.

From Christchurch continue south to North Otago and award-winning eateries such as Oamaru's Riverstone Kitchen and Fleur's Place in **Moeraki**. Emerson's and Green Man are the microbreweries to check out further south in **Dunedin** – sample a few at Eureka or Tonic – before loading up the car with organic, free-range and locavore goodies at the Dunedin Farmers Market.

One Week to Ten Days
Animal Planet

From **Christchurch** travel to **Akaroa** to swim with Hector's dolphins, NZ's smallest and rarest. Squeeze in a return trip up the coast to **Kaikoura** for whale-watching and swimming with NZ fur seals, before travelling south to **Oamaru**. There's a fascination with Steampunk culture and a wonderful historic precinct, but nature buffs are in town to meet the little blue penguins that swim ashore every night at dusk.

From Oamaru travel to the **Otago Peninsula** for more little blue penguins, and their extremely rare, shuffling cousins, the yellow-eyed penguin, or hoiho. Join a tour with Natures Wonders to get close up and personal with seals and sea lions before admiring the royal albatross colony on nearby Taiaroa Head. A seaborne journey with Elm Wildlife Cruises is another essential Otago Peninsula experience.

Continue south to the rugged and isolated **Catlins**. Little blue penguins, yellow-eyed penguins and Hector's dolphins are all regular visitors to **Curio Bay**. Head further south and leave the South Island at **Bluff** for kiwi-spotting on wild and idiosyncratic **Stewart Island**. Now you can really say you've met a kiwi.

Trekking in the South Island

Top Long Tramps

Heaphy Track, Kahurangi National Park (p98)
Abel Tasman Coast Track, Abel Tasman National Park (p91)
Milford Track, Fiordland (p267)

Top Short Tramps

Parachute Rocks, Nelson Lakes National Park (p84)

Best For Kids or Beginners

Queen Charlotte Track, Marlborough Sounds (p61)
Banks Peninsula Track, Canterbury (p159)

Top Wildlife Encounters

Birdlife, Okarito Three Mile Lagoon Walk, West Coast (p122)
Seals, Cape Foulwind Walkway, West Coast (p104)
Yellow-eyed penguins, Graves Trail, Oamaru (p214)

Trekking (aka bushwalking, hiking, or tramping as Kiwis call it) is the perfect vehicle for a close encounter with the South Island's natural beauty. There are thousands of kilometres of tracks here – some well marked (including six of NZ's celebrated 'Great Walks'), some barely a line on a map – plus an excellent network of huts enabling trampers to avoid lugging tents and (in some cases) cooking gear. Before plodding off into the forest, get up-to-date information from the appropriate authority – usually the Department of Conservation (DOC; see p331), or regional i-SITE visitor information centres.

Planning Your Tramp

When to Go

» **Mid-December–late January** Tramping high season is during the summer school holidays, starting a couple of weeks before Christmas – avoid it if you can.

» **January–March** With summer weather lingering into March, wait until February if you can, when tracks are (marginally) less crowded. Most nonalpine tracks can be walked enjoyably at any time from about October through to April.

» **June–August** Winter is not the time to be out in the wild, especially at altitude – some paths close in winter because of avalanche danger and lower levels of facilities and services.

TRACK SAFETY

Thousands of people tramp across NZ without incident, but every year a few folks meet their maker in the mountains. Some trails are only for the experienced, fit and well-equipped – don't attempt these if you don't fit the bill. Ensure you are healthy and feel comfortable walking for sustained periods.

NZ's climatic changeability subjects high-altitude walks to snow and ice, even in summer: always check weather and track conditions before setting off, and be ready for conditions to change rapidly. Consult a DOC visitor centre and leave your intentions with a responsible person before starting longer walks.

See also www.mountainsafety.org.nz and www.metservice.co.nz for weather updates.

What to Bring

Primary considerations: your feet and your shoulders. Make sure your footwear is tough as old boots, and that your pack isn't too heavy. Wet-weather gear is essential, especially on the South Island's waterlogged West Coast. If you're camping or staying in huts without stoves, bring a camping stove. Also bring insect repellent to keep sandflies away, and don't forget your scroggin – a mixture of dried fruit and nuts (and sometimes chocolate) for munching en route.

Books

DOC publishes detailed books on the flora and fauna, geology and history of NZ's national parks, plus leaflets (50c to $2) detailing hundreds of NZ walking tracks.

Lonely Planet's *Tramping in New Zealand* describes around 50 walks of various lengths and degrees of difficulty. Mark Pickering and Rodney Smith's *101 Great Tramps* has suggestions for two- to six-day tramps around the country. The companion guide, *202 Great Walks: the Best Day Walks in New Zealand* by Mark Pickering, is handy for shorter, family-friendly excursions. *Accessible Walks* by Anna and Andrew Jameson, is an excellent guide for elderly, disabled and family trampers, with detailed access information on 100-plus South Island walks.

New trampers should check out *Don't Forget Your Scroggin* by Sarah Bennett and Lee Slater – all about being safe and happy on the track. The *Birdseye Tramping Guides* from Craig Potton Publishing have fab topographical maps, and there are countless books covering tramps and short urban walks around NZ – scan the bookshops.

Maps

The topographical maps produced by **Land Information New Zealand** (LINZ; www.linz.govt.nz) are a safe bet. Bookshops don't often have a good selection of these, but LINZ has map sales offices in major cities and towns, and DOC offices often sell LINZ maps for local tracks. Outdoor stores also stock them.

The LINZ map series includes park maps (national, state and forest), dedicated walking-track maps, and detailed 'Topo50' maps (you may need two or three of these per track).

Online Resources

» **www.trampingtracks.co.nz** Descriptions, maps and photos of long and short tramps all over NZ.

» **www.tramper.co.nz** Articles, photos, forums and excellent track and hut information.

» **www.trampingnz.com** Region-by-region track info with readable trip reports.

» **www.peakbagging.org.nz** Find a summit and get on top of it.

» **www.topomap.co.nz** Online topographic map of the whole country.

Track Classification

Tracks in NZ are classified according to various features, including level of difficulty. We loosely refer to the level of difficulty as easy, medium, hard or difficult. The widely used track classification system is as follows:

» **Short Walk** Well formed; allows for wheelchair access or constructed to 'shoe' standard (ie walking boots not required). Suitable for people of all ages and fitness levels.

» **Walking Track** Easy and well-formed longer walks; constructed to 'shoe' standard. Suitable for people of most ages and fitness levels.

» **Easy Tramping Track** or **Great Walk** Well formed; major water crossings have bridges and

Great Walks

track junctions have signs. Light walking boots required.

» **Tramping Track** Requires skill and experience; constructed to 'boot' standard. Suitable for people of average physical fitness. Water crossings may not have bridges.

» **Route** Requires a high degree of skill, experience and navigation skills. Well-equipped trampers only.

Great Walks

Six of NZ's nine official 'Great Walks' are on the South Island. Natural beauty abounds, but prepare yourself for crowds, especially during summer.

All six of the South Island's Great Walks are described in Lonely Planet's *Tramping in New Zealand,* and are detailed in pamphlets provided by DOC visitor centres.

To tramp these tracks you'll need to buy **Great Walk Tickets** before setting out. These track-specific tickets cover you for hut accommodation (from $10 to $51.10 per adult per night, depending on the track and season) and/or camping ($5 to $20.40 per adult per night). You can camp only at designated camping

[illegible]AND'S SIX 'GREAT WALKS'

[illegible]	DISTANCE	DURATION	DIFFICULTY	DESCRIPTION
[illegible]	51km	3–5 days	Easy to medium	NZ's most popular walk (or sea kayak); beaches and bays in Abel Tasman National Park
[illegible]eaphy Track	82km	4–6 days	Medium to hard	Forests, beaches and *karst* landscapes in Kahurangi National Park
Kepler Track	60km	3–4 days	Easy to medium	Lakes, rivers, gorges, glacial valleys and beech forest in Fiordland National Park
Milford Track	54km	4 days	Easy	Rainforest, crystal-clear streams and 630m-high Sutherland Falls in Fiordland National Park
Rakiura Track	36km	3 days	Medium	Bird life (kiwi!), beaches and lush bush on remote Stewart Island, off the South Island
Routeburn Track	32km	3 days	Medium	Eye-popping alpine scenery around Mt Aspiring and Fiordland National Parks

grounds; note there's no camping on the Milford Track. In the off-peak season (May to September), you can use **Backcountry Hut Passes** ($92 per adult, valid for six months) or pay-as-you-go **Hut Tickets** (huts $10 to $15, camping $5) instead of Great Walk tickets on Great Walks except for the Heaphy Track, Abel Tasman Coast Track and Rakiura Track. Kids under 18 stay in huts and camp for free on all Great Walks.

There's a booking system in place for Great Walk huts and campsites. Trampers must book their chosen accommodation and specify dates when they purchase their Great Walk tickets:

» The **Abel Tasman Coast Track**, **Heaphy Track** and **Rakiura Track** require bookings year-round.

» The **Kepler Track**, **Milford Track** and **Routeburn Track** require bookings in peak season only (October to April).

Bookings/ticket purchases can be made online (www.doc.govt.nz), by email (greatwalksbooking@doc.govt.nz), or via DOC offices close to the tracks. Bookings open mid-July each year.

Other Tracks

Of course, there are a lot more walks in the South Island than just the Great ones! Try these selections on for size:

» **Banks Peninsula Track** A 35km, two-day (medium) or four-day (easy) walk over the hills and along the coast of Banks Peninsula.

» **Hump Ridge Track** An excellent, three-day, 53km circuit beginning and ending at Bluecliffs Beach on Te Waewae Bay, 20km from Tuatapere.

» **Coast Track** An easy, three-day, 40km walk over private and public land along the spectacular coastline 50km south of Kaikoura.

» **Queen Charlotte Track** A three- to five-day medium walk in the Marlborough Sounds, affording great water views. Top-notch accommodation and water transport available.

» **Rees-Dart Track** A 70km, four- to five-day hard tramping track in Mt Aspiring National Park, through river valleys and traversing an alpine pass.

Backcountry Huts & Conservation Campsites

Huts

DOC maintains more than 950 backcountry huts in NZ's national and forest parks. Hut categories include:

» **Basic huts** Just a shed!

» **Standard huts** No cooking equipment and sometimes no heating, but mattresses, water supply and toilets.

» **Serviced huts** Mattress-equipped bunks or sleeping platforms, water supply, heating, toilets and sometimes cooking facilities.

Details about the hut services can be found on the DOC website. Backcountry hut fees per adult per night range from free to $52, with tickets bought in advance at DOC visi-

» (above) Clinton Valley, Milford Track (p267), Fiordland
» (left) Routeburn Track (p247), Mt Aspiring National Park, Otago

tor centres (some huts can also be booked online: see www.doc.govt.nz). Children under 10 can use huts for free; 11- to 17-year-olds are charged half-price. If you do a lot of tramping, DOC sells a six-month Backcountry Hut Pass (p32), applicable to most huts except Great Walk huts in peak season (October to April, during which time you'll need Great Walk tickets). In the low season (May to September), Backcountry Hut Tickets and Backcountry Hut Passes can also be used to procure a bunk or campsite on some Great Walks.

Depending on the hut category, a night's stay may use one or two tickets. Date your tickets and put them in the boxes provided at huts. Accommodation is on a first-come, first-served basis.

Campsites

DOC also manages 250 'Conservation Campsites' (usually vehicle-accessible) with categories as follows:

» **Basic campsites** Basic toilets and water; free and unbookable.

» **Standard campsites** Toilets and water supply, and perhaps barbecues and picnic tables. $5 to $16; unbookable.

» **Serviced campsites** Full facilities: flush toilets, tap water, showers and picnic tables. They may also have barbecues, a kitchen and laundry. Bookable via DOC visitor centres; $7 to $19.

See the Great Walks section in this chapter for info on Great Walks campsites. Kids aged five to 17 pay half-price for Conservation Campsites; kids four and under stay free.

RESPONSIBLE TRAMPING

If you went straight from the cradle into a pair of hiking boots, some of these tramping tips will seem ridiculously obvious; others you mightn't have considered. Online, the website, Leave No Trace (www.lnt.org), is a great resource for low-impact hiking, and the Department of Conservation (DOC) site (www.camping.org.nz) has plenty more responsible camping tips. When in doubt, ask DOC or i-SITE staff.

The ridiculously obvious:

» Time your tramp to avoid peak season: less people means less stress on the environment and fewer snorers in the huts.

» Carry out *all* your rubbish. Burying rubbish disturbs soil and vegetation, encourages erosion, and animals will probably dig it up anyway.

» Don't use detergents, shampoo or toothpaste in or near watercourses (even if they're biodegradable).

» Use lightweight kerosene, alcohol or Shellite (white gas) stoves for cooking; avoid disposable butane gas canisters.

» Where there's a toilet, use it. Where there isn't one, dig a hole and bury your by-product (at least 15cm deep, 100m from any watercourse).

» If a track passes through a muddy patch, just plough straight on through – skirting around the outside increases the size of the bog.

You mightn't have considered:

» Wash your dishes 50m from watercourses; use a scourer, sand or snow instead of detergent.

» If you *really* need to scrub your bod, use biodegradable soap and a bucket, at least 50m from any watercourse. Spread the waste water around widely to help the soil filter it.

» If open fires are allowed, use only dead, fallen wood in existing fireplaces. Leave any extra wood for the next happy camper.

» Keep food-storage bags out of reach of scavengers by tying them to rafters or trees.

» Feeding wildlife can lead to unbalanced populations, diseases and animals becoming dependent on handouts. Keep your dried apricots to yourself.

TE ARAROA

After a lengthy planning and construction period, **Te Araroa** (The Long Pathway; www.teararoa.org.nz), finally opened in December 2011. A 3000km tramping trail from Cape Reinga in NZ's north to Bluff in the south (or the other way around), the route links existing tracks with new sections. Built over a decade, mostly by volunteers, it's one of the longest hikes in the world. Check the website for maps and track notes, plus blogs and videos from hardy types who have completed the end-to-end epic.

Guided Walks

If you're new to tramping or just want a more comfortable experience than the DIY alternative, several companies can escort you through the wilds, usually staying in comfortable huts (showers!), with meals cooked and equipment carried for you.

On the South Island try Kaikoura, the Milford Track, Heaphy Track or Hollyford Track. Prices for a four-night guided walk start at around $1500, and rise towards $2000 for deluxe guided experiences.

Getting There & Away

Getting to and from trailheads can be problematic, except for popular trails serviced by public and dedicated trampers' transport. Having a vehicle only helps with getting to one end of the track though (you still have to collect your car afterwards). If the track starts or ends down a dead-end road, hitching will be difficult.

Of course, tracks accessible by public transport (eg Abel Tasman) are also the most crowded. An alternative is to arrange private transport, either with a friend or by chartering a vehicle to drop you at one end then pick you up at the other. If you intend to leave a vehicle at a trailhead, don't leave anything valuable inside – theft from cars in isolated areas is a significant problem.

Skiing & Snowboarding in the South Island

Best For Kids or Beginners

Coronet Peak, Queenstown (p37)
Mt Hutt, Central Canterbury (p38)
Mt Dobson, South Canterbury (p38)
Round Hill, South Canterbury (p38)
The Remarkables, Queenstown (p38)

Top Snowboarding

Mt Hutt, Central Canterbury (p38)
Treble Cone, Wanaka (p38)
Snow Park, Wanaka (p38)
Ohau, South Canterbury (p38)

Top Après-Ski Watering Holes

Opium, Wanaka (p256)
Blue Pub, Methven (p171)
Cardrona Hotel, Cardrona (p258)
Atlas Beer Café, Queenstown (p238)
Monty's, Queenstown (p238)

Top Extreme Skiing

Heliskiing is big fun (and big money). Spin your rotor blades up to the high, pristine slopes of **Coronet Peak**, **Cardrona**, **Mt Hutt** and **Treble Cone**.

Global warming is triggering a worldwide melt, but NZ's South Island remains an essential southern hemisphere destination for snow bunnies, with downhill skiing, cross-country (Nordic) skiing and snowboarding all passionately pursued. Heliskiing, where choppers lift skiers to the top of long, isolated stretches of virgin snow, also has its fans. The South Island ski season is generally from June to October, though it varies considerably from one ski area to another, and can run as late as November.

Planning Your Snow Session

Where to Go

The variety of locations and conditions makes it difficult to rate the South Island's ski fields in any particular order. Some people like to be near Queenstown's party scene or Wanaka's snowboarding hub, while others prefer the quality high-altitude runs on Mt Hutt, uncrowded Rainbow, or less-stressed club skiing areas. Club areas are publicly accessible and usually less crowded and cheaper than commercial fields, even though non-members pay a higher fee.

The South Island's commercial ski areas aren't generally set up as 'resorts' with

Skiing & Snowboarding Areas

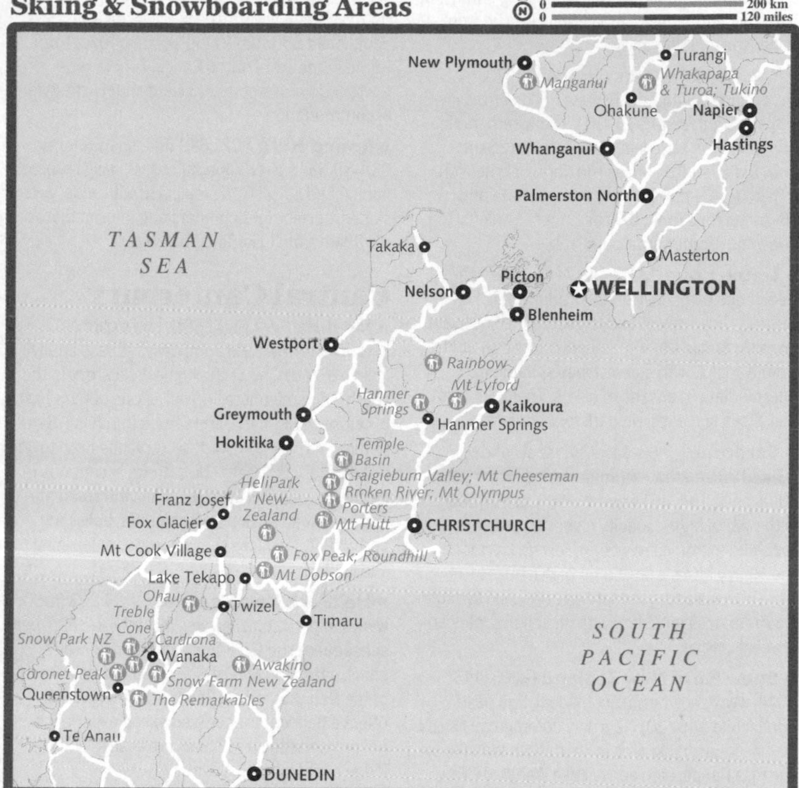

chalets, lodges or hotels. Rather, accommodation and après-ski carousing are often done in surrounding towns, connected to the slopes via daily shuttles. Many club areas have lodges you can stay at, subject to availability.

Visitor information centres in NZ, and Tourism New Zealand (p341) offices internationally, have info on the various ski areas and can make bookings and organise packages. Lift passes cost anywhere from $40 to $95 per adult per day (half-price for kids). Lesson and lift packages are available at most areas. Ski/snowboard equipment rental starts at around $40 a day (cheaper for multiday hire).

Online Resources

» **www.brownbear.co.nz/ski** Brilliant reference detailing all of NZ's ski areas.

» **www.snow.co.nz** Reports, cams and ski info across the country.

» **www.nzski.com** Reports, employment, passes and webcams for Mt Hutt, Coronet Peak and The Remarkables.

» **www.chillout.co.nz** Info on Mt Lyford, Hanmer Springs, Mt Cheeseman, Roundhill, Temple Basin, Fox Peak, Mt Dobson, Mt Olympus, Porters, Craigieburn Valley and Broken River ski areas.

» **www.newzealandsnowtours.com** Snowboarding and skiing tours, north and south.

South Island Ski Regions

Queenstown & Wanaka

» **Coronet Peak** (☎03-450 1970, snow phone 03-442 4620; www.nzski.com; daily lift pass adult/child $95/52) The Queenstown region's oldest ski field. Snow-making systems and treeless slopes provide excellent skiing and snowboarding for all levels. Night skiing Friday and Saturday, July to September. Shuttles run from Queenstown, 18km away.

» **The Remarkables** (☎03-450 1970, snowphone 03-442 4615; www.nzski.com; daily lift pass adult/child $91/49) Visually remarkable, this ski field is also near Queenstown (28km away), with shuttle buses run during ski season. It has a good smattering of intermediate and advanced runs (only 10% beginner). Look for the sweeping 'Homeward Bound' run.

» **Treble Cone** (☎03-443 7443; www.treblecone.com; daily lift pass adult/child $95/48) The highest and largest of the southern lakes ski areas is in a spectacular location 26km from Wanaka, with steep slopes suitable for intermediate to advanced skiers. There are also half-pipes and a terrain park for boarders.

» **Cardrona** (☎03-443 7341, snow phone 03-443 7007; www.cardrona.com; daily lift pass adult/child $94/46) Around 34km from Wanaka, with several high-capacity chairlifts, beginners' tows and extreme snowboard terrain (including the 'Heavy Metal' snowboard park). Buses run from Wanaka and Queenstown during ski season. Good services for skiers with disabilities, plus an on-field crèche.

» **Snow Farm New Zealand** (☎03-443 7542; www.snowfarmnz.com; daily trail pass adult/child $40/20) NZ's only commercial Nordic (cross-country) ski area is 35km from Wanaka on the Pisa Range, high above Lake Wanaka. There is 50km of groomed trails, huts with facilities and thousands of hectares of open snow.

» **Snow Park NZ** (☎03-443 9991; www.snowparknz.com; daily lift pass adult/child $88/41) NZ's only dedicated freestyle ski and snowboard area, with a plethora of pipes, terrain parks, boxes and rails and snow-making facilities. Backpacker-style accommodation, restaurant and bar; 34km from Wanaka, 58km from Queenstown.

South Canterbury

» **Ohau** (☎03-438 9885; www.ohau.co.nz; daily lift pass adult/child $75/30) This commercial ski area is on Mt Sutton, 42km from Twizel. There are plenty of intermediate and advanced runs, excellent snowboarding/cross-country terrain and a ski lodge.

» **Mt Dobson** (☎03-685 8039; www.dobson.co.nz; daily lift pass adult/child $72/28) With a 3km-wide basin and located 26km from Fairlie, Mt Dobson caters for learners and intermediates. It has a terrain park, famously dry powder, and on a clear day you can see Aoraki/Mt Cook and the Pacific Ocean from the summit.

» **Fox Peak** (☎03-685 8539, snow phone 03-688 0044; www.foxpeak.co.nz; daily lift pass adult/child $50/10) A club ski area 40km from Fairlie in the Two Thumb Range. Expect rope tows, good cross-country skiing and dorm-style accommodation.

» **Round Hill** (☎021 680 694, snow phone 03-680 6977; www.roundhill.co.nz; daily lift pass adult/child $72/36) A small field with wide, gentle slopes, perfect for beginners and intermediates. It's 32km from Lake Tekapo village.

Central Canterbury

» **Mt Hutt** (☎03-302 8811, snow phone 03-308 5074; www.nzski.com; daily lift pass adult/child $87/48) One of the highest ski areas in the southern hemisphere, as well as one of NZ's best. It's close to Methven, and Christchurch is 118km to the west, with ski shuttles servicing both towns. Road access is rough – be extremely cautious in lousy weather. Plenty of beginner, intermediate and advanced slopes with chairlifts, heliskiing and wide-open faces that are good for learning to snowboard.

» **HeliPark New Zealand** (☎03-303 9060; www.helipark.co.nz; access incl 1st run $325, per subsequent run $75) One of NZ's snow-white gems, sitting on Mt Potts above the headwaters of the Rangitata River, 75km from Methven. It offers a helicopter-accessed skiing experience. Accommodation and meals are available at a lodge 8km from the ski area.

» **Porters** (☎03-318 4002; www.skiporters.co.nz; daily lift pass adult/child $82/42) The closest commercial ski area to Christchurch (96km away on the Arthur's Pass road). Its 'Big Mama', at 620m, is one of the steepest runs in NZ, but there are wider, gentler slopes too. There's a half-pipe for snowboarders, good cross-country runs along the ridge, and lodge accommodation.

» **Temple Basin** (☎03-377 7788; www.templebasin.co.nz; daily lift pass adult/child $68/37) A club field 4km from the Arthur's Pass township. It's a 50-minute walk uphill from the car park to the ski-area lodges. There's floodlit skiing at night and excellent backcountry runs for snowboarders.

» **Craigieburn Valley** (☎03-318 8711; www.craigieburn.co.nz; daily lift pass adult/child $68/45) Centred on Hamilton Peak, Craigieburn Valley is 40km from Arthur's Pass. It's one of NZ's most challenging club areas, with intermediate and advanced runs (no beginners). Accommmodation is in 'please-do-a-chore' lodges.

» (above) Treble Cone (p38), Wanaka
» (left) Coronet Peak (p37), Wanaka

HELISKIING

NZ's remote heights are tailor-made for heliskiing, with operators covering a wide off-piste area along the Southern Alps. Costs range from around $800 to $1200 for three to eight runs. Heliskiing is also available at Coronet Peak, Treble Cone, Cardrona, Mt Hutt, Mt Lyford, Ohau and Hanmer Springs. Alternatively, independent operators include:

» **Alpine Heli-Ski** (☎03-441 2300; www.alpineheliski.com; Queenstown)

» **Backcountry Helicopters NZ** (☎03-443 9032; www.heliskinz.com; Wanaka)

» **Harris Mountains Heli-ski** (☎03-442 6722; www.heliski.co.nz; Queenstown & Wanaka)

» **Heli Ski Queenstown** (☎03-442 7733, 0800 123 4354; www.flynz.co.nz; Queenstown)

» **Methven Heliski** (☎03-302 8108; www.methvenheli.co.nz; Methven)

» **Southern Lakes Heliski** (☎03-442 6222; www.southernlakesheliski.co.nz; Queenstown)

» **Wilderness Heliski** (☎03-435 1834; www.wildernessheli.co.nz; Aoraki/Mt Cook)

» **Broken River** (☎03-318 8713, snow phone 03-383 8888; www.brokenriver.co.nz; daily lift pass adult/child $65/35) Not far from Craigieburn Valley, this club field is a 15- to 20-minute walk from the car park and has a real sense of isolation. Reliable snow, laid-back vibe. Catered or self-catered lodge accommodation available.

» **Mt Cheeseman** (☎03-344 3247, snow phone 03-318 8794; www.mtcheeseman.co.nz; daily lift pass adult/child $70/35) A cool club area in the Craigieburn Range, this family-friendly operation is 112km from Christchurch (the closest club to the city). Based on Mt Cockayne, it's a wide, sheltered basin with drive-to-the-snow road access. Lodge accommodation is available.

» **Mt Olympus** (☎03-318 5840; www.mtolympus.co.nz; daily lift pass adult/child $70/35) Difficult to find (but worth the search), 2096m Mt Olympus is 58km from Methven and 12km from Lake Ida. This club area has intermediate and advanced runs, and there are solid cross-country trails to other areas. Access is sometimes 4WD-only, depending on conditions. Lodge accommodation available.

Northern South Island

» **Hanmer Springs** (☎027 434 1806; www.skihanmer.co.nz; daily lift pass adult/child $60/30) A commercial field based on Mt St Patrick, 17km from Hanmer Springs township, with mostly intermediate and advanced runs. There are pipe-rides for snowboarders, and a new beginners' tow was installed in 2012.

» **Mt Lyford** (☎03-315 6178, snow phone 03-366 1220; www.mtlyford.co.nz; daily lift pass adult/child $70/35) Around 60km from both Hanmer Springs and Kaikoura, and 4km from Mt Lyford village. It's more of a 'resort' than most NZ ski fields, with accommodation and eating options. There's a good mix of runs and a terrain park.

» **Rainbow** (☎03-521 1861, snow phone 0832 22605; www.skirainbow.co.nz; daily lift pass adult/child $70/35) Bordering Nelson Lakes National Park (100km from Nelson, a similar distance from Blenheim), with varied terrain, minimal crowds and good cross-country skiing. Chains are often required. St Arnaud is the closest town (32km).

Extreme South Island

Top Anti-Gravity Actvities

Queenstown (p222) There are plenty of places on the South Island where you can hurl yourself into oblivion attached to a giant rubber band, but why mess around: head straight to Queenstown for the biggest and the best.

Top White-Water Rafting Trips

Buller Gorge, Murchison (p102)
Kawarau River, Queenstown (p225)
Shotover Canyon, Queenstown (p225)

Top Mountain-Biking Tracks

Queenstown Bike Park, Queenstown (p229)
Otago Central Rail Trail, Otago (p208)

Top Surf Spots

Tauranga Bay, Westport (p46)
St Clair Beach, Dunedin (p191)

The South Island's astounding natural assets encourage even the laziest lounge lizards to drag themselves outside and get active. 'Extreme' sports are abundant and supremely well organised here. Mountaineering is part of the national psyche; skydiving, mountain biking, jetboating and rock climbing are well established; and pant-wetting, illogical activities such as bungy jumping have become everyday pursuits. Adrenaline-pumping activities obviously have an element of risk, but the perception of danger is part of the thrill (just make sure you have travel insurance anyway).

Bungy Jumping

Bungy jumping was made famous by Kiwi AJ Hackett's 1986 plunge from the Eiffel Tower, after which he teamed up with champion NZ skier Henry van Asch to turn the endeavour into a profitable enterprise. And now you can get crazy too!

Queenstown is a spider-web of bungy cords, including a 43m jump off the Kawarau Bridge, a 47m leap from a ledge at the top of a gondola, and the big daddy, the 134m Nevis Highwire. Other South Island bungy jumps are located at Waiau River (near Hanmer Springs) and Mt Hutt Ski Field. Varying the theme, try the 109m-high Shotover Canyon Swing or Nevis Arc in Queenstown, both seriously high rope swings. *Swooosh...*

Caving

Caving (aka spelunking) opportunities abound in NZ's honeycombed *karst* (limestone) regions. In the South Island, you'll find local clubs and organised tours around Westport and Karamea. Golden Bay also has some mammoth caves.

Useful resources:

» **New Zealand Speleological Society** (www.caves.org.nz)

Horse Trekking

Unlike some other parts of the world where beginners get led by the nose around a paddock, horse trekking in NZ lets you really get out into the countryside – on a farm, forest or beach. Rides range from one-hour jaunts (from around $50) to week-long, fully catered treks.

On the South Island, all-day horseback adventures happen around Kaikoura, Nelson, Mt Cook, Lake Tekapo, Hanmer Springs, Queenstown, Glenorchy, Methven, Mt Hutt, Cardrona, Te Anau and Dunedin. Treks are also offered alongside Paparoa National Park on the West Coast.

For info and operator listings:

» **100% Pure New Zealand** (www.newzealand.com)

» **True NZ Horse Trekking** (www.truenz.co.nz/horsetrekking)

Jetboating

Hold onto your breakfast: passenger-drenching, 360-degree spins ahoy! On the South Island, the Shotover and Kawarau Rivers (Queenstown) and the Buller River (Westport) have fab jetboating. The Dart River is less travelled but also good, while the Waiatoto River (Haast) and Wilkin River (Mt Aspiring National Park) are superb wilderness experiences. Try also the Kawarau River (Cromwell), the Waiau River (Te Anau) and the Wairaurahiri River (Tuatapere).

Parasailing & Kiteboarding

Parasailing (dangling from a modified parachute that glides over the water, while being pulled along by a speedboat/jetski) is perhaps the easiest way for humans to achieve assisted flight. After a half-day of instruction you should be able to do limited solo flights. Tandem flights are available in Queenstown and Wanaka. The **New Zealand Hang Gliding and Paragliding Association** (www.nzhgpa/org.nz) rules the roost.

Kiteboarding (aka kitesurfing), where a mini parachute drags you across the ocean on a mini surfboard, can be attempted at Nelson. Lessons are also available if you're a kiteboarding newbie.

Mountain Biking

The South Island is laced with quality mountain-biking opportunities. Bikes can be hired in adventure-sports centres like Queenstown and Wanaka.

Various companies will take you up to the summits of mountains and volcanoes (eg Cardrona and the Remarkables) so you can hurtle down without the grunt-work of getting to the top first.

Key South Island mountain-biking meccas include the Goldfields Heritage Trail in Central Otago, the new Queenstown Bike Park, and Twizel near Mt Cook. Newly opened trails around Queenstown and Wanaka also explore the region's mountain and lake scenery. Other South Island options include Waitati Valley and Hayward Point near Dunedin, Canaan Downs near Abel Tasman National Park, Mt Hutt, Methven and the Banks Peninsula. Increasingly popular are leisurely, multi-day explorations of the Otago Central Rail Trail.

Some traditional tramping tracks are open to mountain bikes, but the Department of Conservation (DOC) has restricted access in many cases due to track damage and the inconvenience to walkers, especially at busy times. Never cycle on walking tracks in national parks unless it's permissible (check with DOC), or risk heavy fines and the unfathomable ire of hikers. The Queen Charlotte Track is a good one to bike, but part of it is closed in summer.

Resources include:

» **Classic New Zealand Mountain Bike Rides** (www.kennett.co.nz) details short and long rides all over NZ.

» **New Zealand Mountain Biker** (www.nzmtbr.com.nz) is a mag which comes out every two months.

Mountaineering

NZ has a proud mountaineering history – this was, after all, the home of Sir Edmund

» (above) Shotover River, Queenstown region (p225)
» (left) Otago Central Rail Trail (p208)

DAVID WALL / LONELY PLANET IMAGES ©

» (above) Bungy jumping, Kawa
Bridge (p225), Queenstown
» (left) Rafting on the Buller Rive
Buller Gorge (p102), West Coa

CYCLE TOURING

OK, so cruising around the country on a bicycle isn't necessarily extreme, but it is super-popular in NZ, especially during summer. Most towns offer bike hire, at either backpacker hostels or specialist bike shops, with bike repair shops in bigger towns.

If you're not after altitude, the Otago Central Rail Trail between Middlemarch and Clyde is a winner. The Little River Rail Trail in Canterbury (en route to Banks Peninsula) is also fabulous. For an off-the-beaten-highway option, try the Southern Scenic Route from Invercargill round Tuatapere to Te Anau. For more detailed touring info, see Lonely Planet's *Cycling New Zealand*.

The $50-million **Nga Haerenga, New Zealand Cycle Trail** (www.nzcycletrail.com) is a national network of bike trails from Kaitaia to Bluff featuring 18 'Great Rides' (a similar concept to tramping's 'Great Walks'). Some sections/trails are still in the developmental stages, but some stages are open: see the website for updates.

Online resources include:

» **Independent Cycle Tours** (www.cyclehire.co.nz)

» **Paradise Press** (www.paradise-press.co.nz) produces *Pedallers' Paradise* booklets by Nigel Rushton.

Hillary (1919–2008), who along with Tenzing Norgay was the first to summit Mt Everest. When he came back down, Sir Ed famously uttered to friend George Lowe, 'Well, George, we knocked the bastard off!'

The Southern Alps are studded with impressive peaks and challenging climbs. The Aoraki/Mt Cook region is outstanding; others extend along the spine of the South Island from Mt Tapuaenuku (in the Kaikoura Ranges) and the Nelson Lakes peaks in the north to the rugged southern mountains of Fiordland. Another area with climbs for all levels is Mt Aspiring National Park. To the south in the Forbes Mountains is Mt Earnslaw, flanked by the Rees and Dart Rivers.

The Christchurch-based **New Zealand Alpine Club** (www.alpineclub.org.nz) proffers professional information, and produces the annual *NZAC Alpine Journal* and the quarterly *The Climber* magazine. Professional outfits for training, guiding and advice can be found at Wanaka, Aoraki/Mt Cook, Lake Tekapo, and the Fox and Franz Josef Glaciers.

Rock Climbing

Time to chalk up your fingers and don some natty little rubber shoes. On the South Island, try the Port Hills area above Christchurch, or Castle Hill on the road to Arthur's Pass. West of Nelson, the marble and limestone mountains of Golden Bay and Takaka Hill provide prime climbing. Other options are Long Beach (north of Dunedin), and Mihiwaka and Lovers Leap on the Otago Peninsula.

Climb New Zealand (www.climb.co.nz) has the low-down on the gnarliest overhangs around NZ, plus access and instruction info.

Sea Kayaking

Sea kayaking is a fantastic way to see the coast, and get close to wildlife you'd otherwise never see.

On the South Island, try the Marlborough Sounds (Picton) and along the coast of the Abel Tasman National Park. Fiordland is also a hot spot with a heap of tour operators in Te Anau, Milford, Doubtful Sound and Manapouri. Also try the Otago Peninsula, Stewart Island and Kaikoura.

Useful resources:

» **Kiwi Association of Sea Kayakers** (www.kask.org.nz)

» **Sea Kayak Operators Association of New Zealand** (www.skoanz.org.nz)

Scuba Diving

Most of NZ's opportunities for diving are off the North Island, but down south, the Marlborough Sounds Maritime Park hosts the *Mikhail Lermontov,* the largest diveable cruise-ship wreck in the world. In Fiordland head for Dusky Sound, Milford Sound and Doubtful Sound, which offer amazingly clear pseudo-deep-water conditions not far below the surface. Invercargill, with its Antarctic waters, also has a diving club.

Expect to pay anywhere from $180 for a short, introductory, pool-based scuba course; and around $600 for a four-day, PADI-approved, ocean-dive course. One-off organised boat- and land-based dives start from around $170.

Resources include:

» **New Zealand Underwater Association** (www.nzunderwater.org.nz)

» **Dive New Zealand** (www.divenewzealand.com)

Skydiving

For most first-time skydivers, a tandem skydive will help you make the leap, even if common sense starts to get the better of you. Tandem jumps involve training with a qualified instructor, then experiencing up to 45 seconds of free fall before your chute opens. The thrill is worth every dollar (around $250/300/350 for a 8000/10,000/12,000ft jump, extra for a DVD/photograph). The **New Zealand Parachute Federation** (www.nzpf.org) is the governing body.

At the time of writing safety concerns had sparked a wholesale review of skydiving in New Zealand, with operators having to comply with stringent new Civil Aviation Authority (CAA) regulations. Ask your operator if it has CAA accreditation before you take the plunge.

White-Water Rafting, Kayaking & Canoeing

There are almost as many white-water rafting and kayaking possibilities as there are rivers in the country, and there's no shortage of companies to get you into the rapids. Rivers are graded from I to VI, with VI meaning 'unraftable'. On the rougher stretches there's usually a minimum age limit of 12 or 13 years.

Popular South Island rafting rivers include the Shotover and Kawarau Rivers (Queenstown), Rangitata River (Christchurch), Buller River (Murchison), Karamea River (Westport) and the Arnold and Waiho Rivers on the West Coast. The grad-

SURFING IN NEW ZEALAND: JOSH KRONFELD

As a surfer I feel particularly guilty letting the reader in on a local secret – NZ has a sensational mix of quality waves perfect for beginners and experienced surfers. As long as you're willing to travel off the beaten track, you can score some great, uncrowded waves. The islands of NZ are hit with swells from all points of the compass throughout the year. So, with a little weather knowledge and a little effort, numerous options present themselves. Point breaks, reefs, rocky shelves and hollow sandy beach breaks can all be found – take your pick!

Surfing has become increasingly popular in NZ and today there are surf schools running at most premier surf beaches. It's worth doing a bit of research before you arrive: **Surfing New Zealand** (www.surfingnz.co.nz) recommends a number of surf schools on its website. If you're on a surf holiday in NZ, consider purchasing a copy of the *New Zealand Surfing Guide* by Mike Bhana.

Surf.co.nz (www.surf.co.nz) provides information on many great surf spots, but most NZ beaches hold good rideable breaks. Some of the ones I particularly enjoy on the South Island are:

» **Marlborough & Nelson** Kaikoura Peninsula, Mangamaunu and Meatworks

» **Canterbury** Taylors Mistake and Sumner Bar

» **Otago** Dunedin is a good base for surfing on the South Island, with access to a number of superb breaks, such as St Clair Beach

» **West Coast** Punakaiki and Tauranga Bay

» **Southland** Porridge and Centre Island

NZ water temperatures and climate vary greatly from north to south. For comfort while surfing, wear a wetsuit. In summer on the North Island you can get away with a spring suit and boardies but on the South Island you'll need a 2–3mm steamer. In winter on the North Island use a 2–3mm steamer, and on the South Island a 3–5mm with all the extras.

Josh Kronfeld, surfer and former All Blacks player

ing of the Shotover Canyon varies from III to V+, depending on the time of year. The Kawarau River is rated IV; the Rangitata River has everything from I to V.

Canoeing is also popular on the South Island's lakes. Many backpacker hostels close to canoe-friendly waters have Canadian canoes and kayaks for hire (or for free).

Resources include:

» **New Zealand Rafting Association** (www.nz-rafting.co.nz)

» **Whitewater NZ** (www.rivers.org.nz)

» **New Zealand Kayak** (www.canoeandkayak.co.nz) NZ's premier kayaking magazine

regions at a glance

Get ready for an oft-changing selection of some of the planet's most surprising scenery. From the marine labyrinth of the Marlborough Sounds to the craggy volcanic legacy of Banks Peninsula, the South Island packs a stunning scenic punch. Along the way, taste test the best of the country's emerging gourmet scene, balancing enjoyment of excellent wine and craft beer with active adventure amid the great outdoors. Kayak through the mist of Doubtful Sound or test yourself on the Milford or Routeburn Tracks – often in the company of NZ's quirky wildlife – before experiencing colonial history around the heritage streets of Dunedin and Oamaru.

Marlborough & Nelson

National Parks
Wineries
Wildlife

National Parks

Not satisfied with just one national park, the Nelson region has three – Nelson Lakes, Kahurangi and the Abel Tasman. You could tramp in all three during a spectacular and active week.

Wineries

Bobbing in Marlborough's sea of sauvignon blanc, riesling, pinot noir and bubbly are barrel loads of quality cellar door experiences and some fine regional food.

Wildlife

The top of the South Island is home to myriad creatures, both in the water and on the wing. Kaikoura is a great one-stop shop for spotting a whale or swimming with dolphins and seals.

p52

The West Coast

Natural Wonders
Tramping
History

Natural Wonders

This area has many natural wonders: around 90% of the land lies within a conservation estate. Don't miss Oparara's famous arch and Punakaiki's pancake rocks.

Tramping

The West Coast offers tracks from an easy hour through to hard-core epics. Old mining and milling routes like Charming Creek Railway and Mahinapua Walkway entice beginners and history buffs.

History

The Coast's pioneering history comes vividly to life at places such as Denniston, Shanty Town, Reefton and Jackson's Bay. Explore old mining communities, replica historic villages, and some of the West Coast's most isolated beaches.

p100

Christchurch & Canterbury

History & Culture
Outdoors
Scenery

History & Culture

Earthquakes have damaged Christ church's architectural heritage, but the Canterbury Museum, Botanic Gardens and Avon River still showcase the city's proud history. Nearby, Akaroa proudly celebrates its French heritage.

Outdoors

Tramp the alpine valleys around Arthur's Pass, kayak with dolphins on Akaroa Harbour, or head inland for tramping and kayaking amid the glacial lakes of the Aoraki/Mt Cook National Park.

Scenery

Descend Banks Peninsula's Summit Rd to explore hidden bays and coves and experience nature's grand scale: river valleys, soaring peaks and glaciers of the Southern Alps.

p134

Dunedin & Otago

Wildlife
Wine Regions
History

Wildlife

Otago Peninsula's wild menagerie – seals, sea lions and penguins – patrol the rugged coastline, while rocky Taiaroa Head is the planet's only mainland breeding location for the magnificent royal albatross.

Wine Regions

Barrel into the craggy valleys of Bannockburn for excellent vineyard restaurants and the world's best pinot noir, or delve into the up-and-coming Waitaki Valley wine scene for riesling and pinot gris.

History

Explore the arty and storied streets of Dunedin, or escape by foot or penny-farthing bicycle into the heritage Victorian ambience of Oamaru's restored Harbour-Tyne Historic Precinct.

p187

Queenstown & Wanaka

Outdoors
Scenery
Wine Regions

Outdoors

Nowhere else on Earth offers so many activities amid such spectacular surroundings, and bungy jumping, river rafting and mountain biking only scratch Queenstown's adrenaline-fuelled surface.

Scenery

Queenstown's combination of Lake Wakatipu and the soaring Remarkables is a real jaw-dropper, or venture into prime New Zealand wilderness near Glenorchy and Mt Aspiring National Park.

Wine Regions

Start with lunch at Amisfield Winery's award-winning restaurant, then explore the Gibbston Valley: stay in cottage accommodation, eat artisan cheeses and drink excellent pinot noir.

p221

Fiordland & Southland

Scenery
National Parks
Outdoors

Scenery

The star of the show is remarkable Milford Sound, but take time to explore the rugged Catlins coast or experience the remote, end-of-the-world appeal of Stewart Island.

National Parks

Fiordland National Park comprises much of New Zealand's precious Southwest NZ (Te Wahipounamu) World Heritage Area. Further south, Rakiura National Park showcases Stewart Island's beauty.

Outdoors

Test yourself by tramping the Milford or Humpridge Tracks, negotiating a sea kayak around gloriously isolated Doubtful Sound, or jetboating on the rugged Wairaurahiri River.

p259

Every listing is recommended by our authors, and their favourite places are listed first

Look out for these icons:

TOP CHOICE Our author's top recommendation  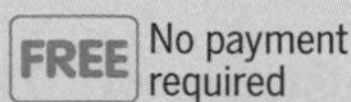

See the Index for a full list of destinations covered in this book.

On the Road

Marlborough & Nelson

Includes »

Best Places to Eat

» Green Dolphin (p76)
» Wither Hills (p69)
» Hopgood's (p82)
» Sans Souci Inn (p96)
» Wakamarinian Cafe (p65)

Best Places to Stay

» Hopewell (p64)
» Ratanui (p96)
» Kerr Bay (p84)
» Dylan's Country Cottages (p76)

Why Go?

For many travellers, Marlborough and Nelson will be their introduction to what South Islanders refer to as the 'Mainland'. Having left windy Wellington, and made a white-knuckled crossing of Cook Strait, folk are often surprised to find the sun shining and the temperature up to 10 degrees warmer.

Good pals, these two neighbouring regions have much in common beyond an amenable climate: both boast renowned coastal holiday spots, particularly the Marlborough Sounds and Abel Tasman National Park. There are two other national parks (Kahurangi and Nelson Lakes) and more mountain ranges than you can poke a stick at.

And so it follows that these two regions have an abundance of luscious produce: summer cherries for a starter, but most famously the grapes that work their way into the wineglasses of the world's finest restaurants. Keep your penknife and picnic set at the ready.

When to Go

The forecast is good: Marlborough and Nelson soak up some of New Zealand's sunniest weather. January and February are the warmest months, with daytime temperatures averaging 22°C; July is the coldest, averaging 12°C. It's wetter and more windswept the closer you get to Farewell Spit and the West Coast.

From around Christmas to mid February, the top of the South teems with Kiwi holidaymakers, so plan ahead during this time and be prepared to jostle for position with a load of jandal-wearing families.

Marlborough & Nelson Highlights

1. Getting up close to wildlife, including whales, seals, dolphins and albatross, in **Kaikoura** (p70)
2. Nosing your way through the **Marlborough Wine Region** (p68)
3. Tramping or biking the **Queen Charlotte Track** (p61) in the Marlborough Sounds
4. Embracing the craft-beer scene around **Nelson** (p77)
5. Sea kayaking in postcard-perfect **Abel Tasman National Park** (p91)
6. Getting blown away at Blenheim's **Omaka Aviation Heritage Centre** (p65), one of New Zealand's best museums
7. Reaching the end of the road around **Farewell Spit** (p98), where there'll be gannets and godwits for company

ESSENTIAL MARLBOROUGH & NELSON

» **Eat** Doris' bratwurst at the weekend markets in Nelson and Motueka

» **Drink** A pint of Captain Cooker at Golden Bay's Mussel Inn (p98)

» **Read** The *Nelson Mail* and the *Marlborough Express*

» **Listen to** the dawn chorus in Nelson Lakes National Park

» **Watch** The tide roll in, and then watch it roll away again...

» **Festival** Marlborough Wine Festival

» **Go Green** on the Heaphy Track, a hotbed of ecological wonderment

» **Online** www.destinationmarlborough.com; www.nelsonnz.com; www.kaikoura.co.nz

» **Area code** ☎03

Getting There & Around

Cook Strait can be crossed slowly and scenically on the ferries between Wellington and Picton, and swiftly on flights servicing key destinations.

InterCity is the major bus operator, but there are also local shuttles. Tranz Scenic's *Coastal Pacific* train takes the scenic route from Picton to Christchurch, via Blenheim and Kaikoura.

Renting a car is easy, with a slew of car-hire offices in Picton and depots throughout the region.

Popular coastal areas such as the Marlborough Sounds and Abel Tasman National Park are best navigated on foot or by kayak, with water-taxi services readily available to join the dots.

MARLBOROUGH REGION

Picton is the gateway to the South Island and the launching point for Marlborough Sounds exploration. A cork's pop south of Picton is agrarian Blenheim and its world-famous wineries, and further south still is Kaikoura, the whale-watching town.

History

Long before Abel Tasman sheltered on the east coast of D'Urville Island in 1642 (more than 100 years before James Cook blew through in 1770), Maori knew the Marlborough area as Te Tau Ihu o Te Waka a Maui ('the prow of Maui's canoe'). When Cook named Queen Charlotte Sound, his detailed reports made the area the best-known sheltered anchorage in the southern hemisphere. In 1827 French navigator Jules Dumont d'Urville discovered the narrow strait now known as French Pass. His officers named the island just to the north in his honour. In the same year a whaling station was established at Te Awaiti in Tory Channel, which brought about the first permanent European settlement in the district.

Picton

POP 4000

Half asleep in winter, but hyperactive in summer (with up to eight fully laden ferry arrivals per day), boaty Picton clusters around a deep gulch at the head of Queen Charlotte Sound. It's the main traveller port for the South Island, and the best place from which to explore the Marlborough Sounds and tackle the Queen Charlotte Track. Over the last few years this little town has really bloomed, and offers visitors plenty of reason to linger even after the obvious attractions are knocked off the list.

Sights & Activities

The majority of activity happens around the Marlborough Sounds (p58), but landlubbers will still find plenty to occupy themselves.

The town has some very pleasant **walks**. A free i-SITE map details many of these, including an easy 1km track to Bob's Bay. The Snout Track (three hours return) continues along the ridge offering superb water views. Climbing a hill behind the town, the Tirohanga Track is a two-hour leg-stretching loop offering the best view in the house.

Edwin Fox Maritime Museum MUSEUM
(www.edwinfoxsociety.co.nz; Dunbar Wharf; adult/child $10/4; ⏲9am-5pm) Purportedly the world's third-oldest wooden ship, the *Edwin Fox* was built of teak in Calcutta and launched in 1853. During its chequered career it carried troops to the Crimean War, convicts to Australia and immigrants to NZ. This museum has maritime exhibits, including the venerable old dear, preserved under cover.

Eco World Aquarium WILDLIFE CENTRE
(www.ecoworldnz.co.nz; Dunbar Wharf; adult/child/family $20/10/55; ⏲10am-8pm Dec-Feb, 10am-5.30pm Mar-Nov) The primary purpose

of this centre is animal rehab, but we're not talking in the Amy Winehouse sense here. All sorts of critters come here for fix-ups and rest-ups, and the odd bit of how's-your-father goes on, too. Very special specimens include NZ's 'living dinosaur' – the tuatara – as well as blue penguins, gecko and giant weta. Fish-feeding time (11am and 2pm) is a splashy spectacle. Sharing the building is the **Picton Cinema** (☎03-573 6030; www.pictoncinemas.co.nz; Dunbar Wharf; adult/child $15/9; ⏰10am-8pm), bringing the likes of Werner Herzog to town. The manager deserves a medal

Picton Museum MUSEUM
(London Quay; adult/child $5/1; ⏰10am-4pm) If you dig local history – whaling, sailing and the 1964 Roller Skating Champs – this will float your boat. The photo displays are well worth a look, especially for five bucks (funds go towards much-needed development).

Sleeping

Villa Backpackers HOSTEL $
(☎03-573 6598; www.thevilla.co.nz; 34 Auckland St; dm $26-30, d with/without bathroom $76/67; @📶) This bright backpackers has a blooming garden and sociable outdoor areas (with spa pool), cheery kitchen and free bikes. In-demand en-suite rooms, switched-on staff, fresh flowers and free apple crumble (fruit supply permitting) make this a real home away from home. Queen Charlotte Track bookings and camping gear for hire.

Tombstone Backpackers HOSTEL $
(☎03-573 7116, 0800 573 7116; www.tombstonebp.co.nz; 16 Gravesend Pl; dm $28, d with/without bathroom $75/81; @📶🏊) Rest in peace in hotel-worthy dorms, double rooms and a self-contained apartment. Also on offer are a spa overlooking the harbour, free breakfast, sunny reading room, pool table, DVD library, free ferry pick-up and drop-off... The list goes on.

Jugglers Rest HOSTEL $
(☎03-573 5570; www.jugglersrest.com; 8 Canterbury St; sites from $19, dm $31, d $66-70; ⏰closed from Jun-Sept; @📶) The jocular host keeps all her balls up in the air at this well-run and homely bunk-free backpackers. Peacefully located 10 minutes' walk from town or even less on a free bike. Cheery, private gardens are a good place to socialise with fellow travellers, especially during the evening fire shows.

Sequoia Lodge Backpackers HOSTEL $
(☎0800 222 257, 03-573 8399; www.sequoialodge.co.nz; 3a Nelson Sq; dm $25-28, d with/without bathroom $78/66; @📶) A well-managed backpackers in a colourful, high-ceilinged Victorian house. It's a little out of the centre, but has bonuses including free internet, DVDs, hammocks, barbecues, spa and nightly chocolate pudding! Free breakfast May to November.

Buccaneer Lodge LODGE $
(☎03-573 5002; www.buccaneerlodge.co.nz; 314 Waikawa Rd; s/d/tr/q $72/80/93/124; @📶) Enthusiastic owners have spruced up this Waikawa Bay lodge to offer good en-suite rooms, many with expansive views from the 1st-floor balcony. Courtesy town transfers, free bike hire and the pretty foreshore just five minutes' walk away.

Parklands Marina Holiday Park HOLIDAY PARK $
(☎0800 111 104, 03-573 6343; www.parktostay.co.nz; 10 Beach Rd, Waikawa; sites from $30, units $50-90; @📶🏊) Large, leafy campground with roomy sites, satisfactory cabins, plus ready access to boat-ilicious Waikawa Bay and Victoria Domain (pleasant 3km walk/cycle from town). Courtesy transfers available.

Picton Top 10 Holiday Park HOLIDAY PARK $
(☎03-573 7212, 0800 277 444; www.pictontop10.co.nz; 70-78 Waikawa Rd; sites from $20, units

MAORI NZ: MARLBOROUGH & NELSON

While Maori culture on the South Island is much less evident than in the north, it can still be found in pockets, and particularly around coastal Marlborough.

Kaikoura is rich in Maori history, into which Maori Tours Kaikoura (p74) can offer an insight. The Marlborough Sounds, too, has some stories to tell. Plug into them on eco-oriented tours and wildlife cruises with Myths & Legends Eco-Tours (p58).

Maori history is no more powerfully relayed than through oral traditions and carving. Encounter both of these *tikanga* (customs) at Shark Nett Gallery (p64) in Havelock, with its impressive collection of contemporary carvings.

Picton

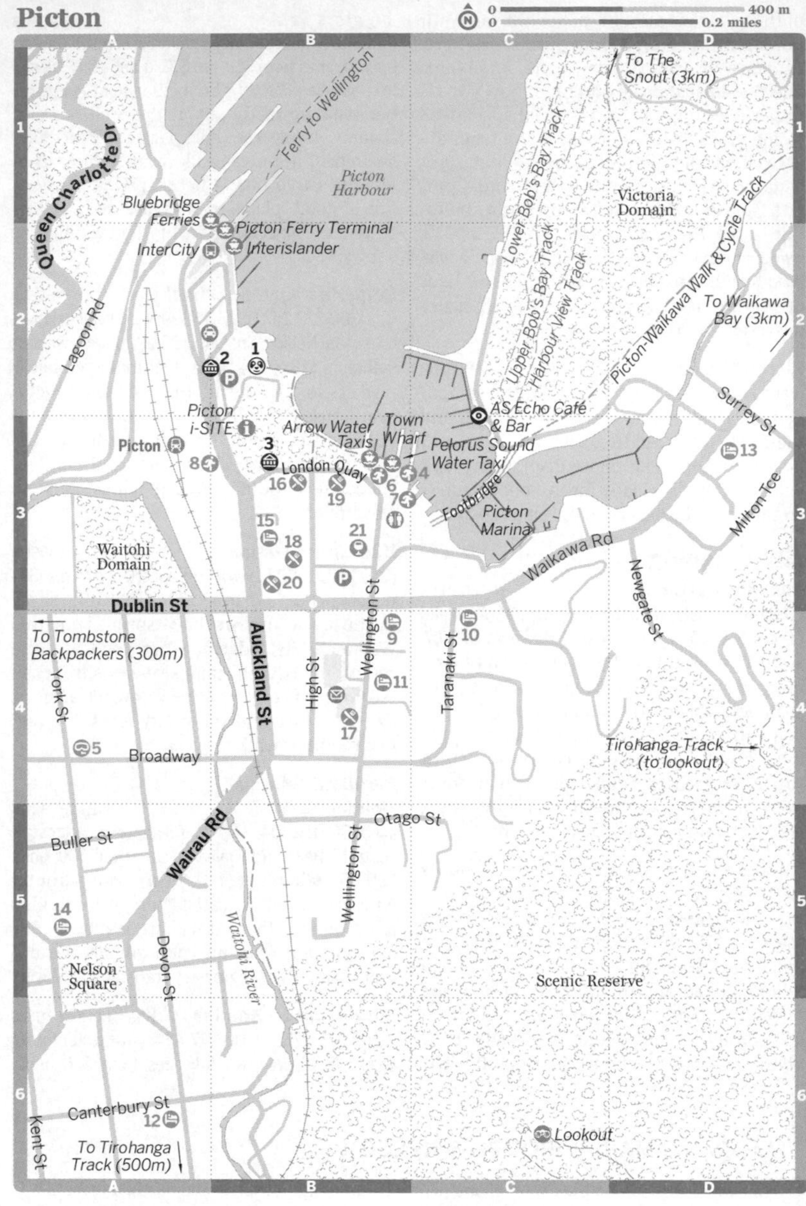

$70–110; @☎≋) About 500m from town, this compact, well-kept place has modern, crowd-pleasing facilities including playground, barbecue area, heated swimming pool and a super recreation room.

Harbour View Motel MOTEL **$$**
(☎03-573 6259, 0800 101 133; www.harbourviewpicton.co.nz; 30 Waikawa Rd; d $125-200; ☎) The elevated position of this motel commands good views of Picton's mast-filled harbour from its tastefully decorated, self-contained studios with timber decks.

Picton

Sights
- 1 Eco World Aquarium B2
- 2 Edwin Fox Maritime Museum B2
- 3 Picton Museum B3

Activities, Courses & Tours
- 4 Beachcomber Fun Cruises B3
- Cougar Line .... (see 4)
- 5 Dive Picton A4
- Dolphin Watch Ecotours .... (see 6)
- 6 Endeavour Express B3
- 7 Marlborough Sounds Adventure Company D3
- 8 Wilderness Guides A3

Sleeping
- 9 Gables B&B B4
- 10 Harbour View Motel C4
- 11 Jasmine Court B4
- 12 Jugglers Rest A6
- 13 Picton Top 10 Holiday Park D3
- 14 Sequoia Lodge Backpackers A5
- 15 Villa Backpackers B3

Eating
- 16 Café Cortado B3
- 17 Fresh Choice Supermarket B4
- 18 Gusto B3
- 19 Le Café B3
- 20 Picton Village Bakkerij B3

Drinking
- 21 Seamus's B3

Entertainment
- Picton Cinema .... (see 1)

Jasmine Court MOTEL $$
(0800 421 999, 03-573 7110; www.jasminecourt.co.nz; 78 Wellington St; d $145-235, f $185-245; @) Top-notch, spacious motel with plush interiors, kitchenette, DVD player, plunger coffee and locally milled soap. Some rooms have a spa, and the odd one has a decent harbour view. Flash new studio units exhibit further excellence.

Bay Vista Waterfront Motel MOTEL
(03-573 6733; www.bayvistapicton.co.nz; 303 Waikawa Rd, Waikawa; d $130-165;) Recently revamped and neat as a new pin, this motel enjoys an enviable position at the water's edge, with lush lawn and views down Queen Charlotte Sound. All units have kitchen facilities. Located 4km from Picton (courtesy transfer available by request).

Gables B&B B&B $$
(03-573 6772; www.thegables.co.nz; 20 Waikawa Rd; s $100, d $140-170, units $155-200, all incl breakfast; @) This historic B&B (once home to Picton's mayor) has three spacious, themed en-suite rooms in the main house and two homely self-contained units out the back. Prices drop if you organise your own breakfast. Lovely hosts show good humour (ask about the Muffin Club).

Whatamonga Home Stay HOMESTAY $$
(03-573 7192; www.whsl.co.nz; 425 Port Underwood Rd; d incl breakfast $140-165; @) Follow Waikawa Rd, which becomes Port Underwood Rd, for 8km and you'll bump into this classy waterside accommodation with two detached, self-contained units with king-sized beds and balconies with magic views. Two other rooms under the main house (also with views) share a bathroom. Free kayaks, dinghies and fishing gear are available.

Eating & Drinking

Picton Village Bakkerij BAKERY $
(cnr Auckland & Dublin Sts; items $2-8; 6am-4pm;) Dutch owners bake trays of European goodies here, including interesting breads, decent pies and filled rolls, cakes and custardy, tarty treats. Be prepared to queue.

Le Café CAFF $$
(London Quay; lunch $10-23, dinner $19-33; 7.30am-10.30pm;) A perennially popular spot both for its quayside location, dependable food and Havana coffee. The likes of salami sandwiches and sweets are in the cabinet, while a good antipasto platter, generous pasta, local mussels, lamb loin and expertly cooked fresh fish feature a la carte. Laid-back atmosphere, craft beer and occasional live gigs make this a good evening hang-out.

Gusto CAFE $
(33 High St; meals $14-20; 7.30am-2.30pm;) This workaday joint, with friendly staff and outdoor tables, does beaut breakfasts including first-class salmon-scrambled egg and a 'Morning Glory' fry-up worth the calories. Lunch options may include local mussels and a steak sandwich.

EXPLORING THE MARLBOROUGH SOUNDS

The Marlborough Sounds are a geographic maze of inlets, headlands, peaks, beaches and watery reaches, formed when the sea flooded into deep valleys after the last ice age. To get an idea of how convoluted the sounds are, Pelorus Sound is 42km long but has 379km of shoreline.

You can reach many spectacular locations by car. The wiggly 35km drive along **Queen Charlotte Drive** from Picton to Havelock is a great Sounds snapshot (even on a rainy day), but if you've got time to burn, take a pilgrimage to **French Pass** (or even **D'Urville Island**) for some big picture framing of the Outer Sounds. Roads are predominantly narrow and occasionally unsealed, so allow plenty of driving time and keep your wits about you.

Sounds travel is invariably quicker by boat (for example, Punga Cove from Picton by car takes two to three hours, but just 45 minutes by boat). Fortunately, a multitude of vessels await to ferry you around, either to schedule or on-demand, with the bulk operating out of Picton for the Queen Charlotte Sound, and some from Havelock for Kenepuru and Pelorus Sounds.

There are loads of walking, kayaking and biking opportunities, but there's **diving** as well – notably the wreck of the *Mikhail Lermontov*, a Russian cruise ship that sank in Port Gore in 1986.

From Picton

Numerous operators ply the Picton waters, most of which can be found at the new Town Wharf. They offer everything from a quick zip across to a lodge and back, to cruises taking in sites such as Ship Cove and Motuara Island bird sanctuary, to round-trip Queen Charlotte Track transport and pack transfers that allow trampers to walk with a small daypack. Bikes and kayaks can also be transported.

Cougar Line (Map p56; ☎0800 504 090, 03-573 7925; www.cougarlinecruises.co.nz; Town Wharf; track round trip $103, full day tour from $75) QC Track transport, plus various half- and full-day cruise/walk trips, including the rather special (and flexible) ecocruise to Motuara Island (p58) and a Ship Cove picnic.

Beachcomber Fun Cruises (Map p56; ☎03-573 6175, 0800 624 526; www.beachcombercruises.co.nz; Town Wharf; mail run $89, cruises $61-99, track round trip $99) Two- to four-hour cruises, some with resort lunches. Cruise/walk, cruise/bike and QC Track options also available.

Endeavour Express (Map p56; ☎03-573 5456; www.boatrides.co.nz; Town Wharf; track round trip $97) Backpacker-friendly company offering QC Track transfers and day adventures. Mountain bikes and camping gear for hire. QCT Pass vendor.

Marlborough Sounds Adventure Company (Map p56; ☎0800 283 283, 03-573 6078; www.marlboroughsounds.co.nz; Town Wharf; half- to 3-day packages $85-545) Bike-walk-kayak trips, with options to suit every inclination. The kayak trip ($105) to Lochmara Lodge includes a fish and chips lunch as reward. Gear rental (bikes, kayaks and camping equipment) also available.

Wilderness Guides (Map p56; ☎0800 266 266, 03-573 5432; www.wildernessguidesnz.com; Picton Railway Station; 1 day trip from $125, kayak or bike hire per day $60) Host of the popular and flexible 'multisport' day trip (kayak/walk/cycle) plus many other guided and independent biking, hiking and kayaking tours around the Queen Charlotte Sound.

Dolphin Watch Ecotours (Map p56; ☎0800 9453 5433, 03-573 8040; www.naturetours.co.nz; Town Wharf; dolphin swimming/viewing $165/100, other tours from $75) Half-day 'swim with dolphins' and wildlife tours including trips to Motuara Island (p58).

Café Cortado CAFE **$$**
(cnr High St & London Quay; mains $17-36; ⌚8am-late) A pleasant corner cafe and bar with sneaky views of the harbour through the foreshore's pohutukawa and palms, this fairly consistent performer turns out fish and chips, meaty mains, good pizza and respectable salads.

Myths & Legends Eco-Tours (☎03-573 6901; www.eco-tours.co.nz; half-/full-day cruises $200/250) A chance to get out on the water with a local Maori family – longtime locals, storytellers and environmentalists. There are six different trips to choose from, including birdwatching and visiting Ship Cove.

GoDive Marlborough (☎03-573 9181, 0800 463 483; www.godive.co.nz; 1-day wreck dive incl lodge accommodation from $255) PADI training and dive trips to the Sounds' most famous wreck, the *Mikhail Lermontov*.

Dive Picton (Map p56; ☎0800 423 483, 03-573 7323; www.divepicton.co.nz; cnr York St & Broadway; half-/full-day $190/290) Dive trips around the Sounds and to the *Mikhail Lermontov*, plus PADi and SSI training.

Active Eco Tours (☎03-573 7199; www.sealswimming.com; half-day dive trip/snorkel/seal swim $185/90/135) See the seals, plus wreck dives and jaunts to other Sounds sights, under and over the water.

Arrow Water Taxis (Map p56; ☎03-573 8229, 027 444 4689; www.arrowwatertaxis.co.nz; Town Wharf) Pretty much anywhere, on demand, for groups of four or more.

Picton Water Taxis (☎027 227 0284, 03-573 7853; www.pictonwatertaxis.co.nz) Water taxi and sightseeing trips around Queen Charlotte, on demand.

Float Plane (☎021-704 248; www.nz-scenic-flights.co.nz; Ferry Terminal; flights from $75) Offers Queen Charlotte Track and Sounds accommodation transfers, scenic flights, and flights and trips to Nelson, the Abel Tasman National Park and across to the lower North Island.

From Anakiwa

Sea Kayak Adventure Tours (Map p60; ☎03-574 2765, 0800 262 5492; www.nzseakayaking.com; cnr Queen Charlotte Dr & Anakiwa Rd; half-/full-day kayak rental $40/60, bike $40/50) Freedom kayak and mountain-bike rental, plus guided and 'guided then go' kayaking trips around Queen Charlotte, Kenepuru and Pelorus Sounds (from $75).

From Havelock

Pelorus Mail Boat (Map p60; ☎03-574 1088; www.mail-boat.co.nz; Jetty 1; adult/child $128/free; ⏱departs 9.30am Tue, Thu & Fri) Popular full-day boat cruise through the far reaches of Pelorus Sound on a genuine NZ Post delivery run. Bookings essential; BYO lunch. Picton and Blenheim pick-up and drop-off available.

Greenshell Mussel Cruise (☎03-577 9997, 0800 990 800; www.greenshellmusselcruise.co.nz; adult/child $115/39; ⏱departs 1.30pm) Three-hour cruise on a catamaran to mussel in on Kenepuru's aquaculture. Includes a tasting of steamed mussels and a glass of wine. Bookings essential.

Waterways Boating Safaris (Map p60; ☎03-574 1372; www.waterways.co.nz; 745 Keneperu Rd; half-day adult/child $110/55, full day $150/75) Be guided around the majestic Marlborough Sounds while piloting your own zippy boat. A unique and fun way to get out on the water, see the scenery and learn about the area's ecology and history. BYO lunch. Local pick-up/drop-offs.

Pelorus Sound Water Taxi (Map p56; ☎027 444 2852, 03-574 2151; www.pelorussoundwatertaxis.co.nz; Jetty 1a) Taxi and sightseeing trips from Havelock, around Pelorus, on demand.

Kenepuru Water Taxi (☎021 455 593, 03-573 4344; www.kenepuru.co.nz; 7170 Kenepuru Rd) Taxi and sightseeing trips around Kenepuru Sound, on demand.

Seamus's PUB
(25 Wellington St; meals $12-27; ⏱noon-1am) Seamus's is a snug little drinking den, pouring a reliable Guinness as well as a good selection of whiskies. Mix it all up with hearty bar food and regular live music, and you've got the recipe for the liveliest joint in town.

Marlborough Sounds

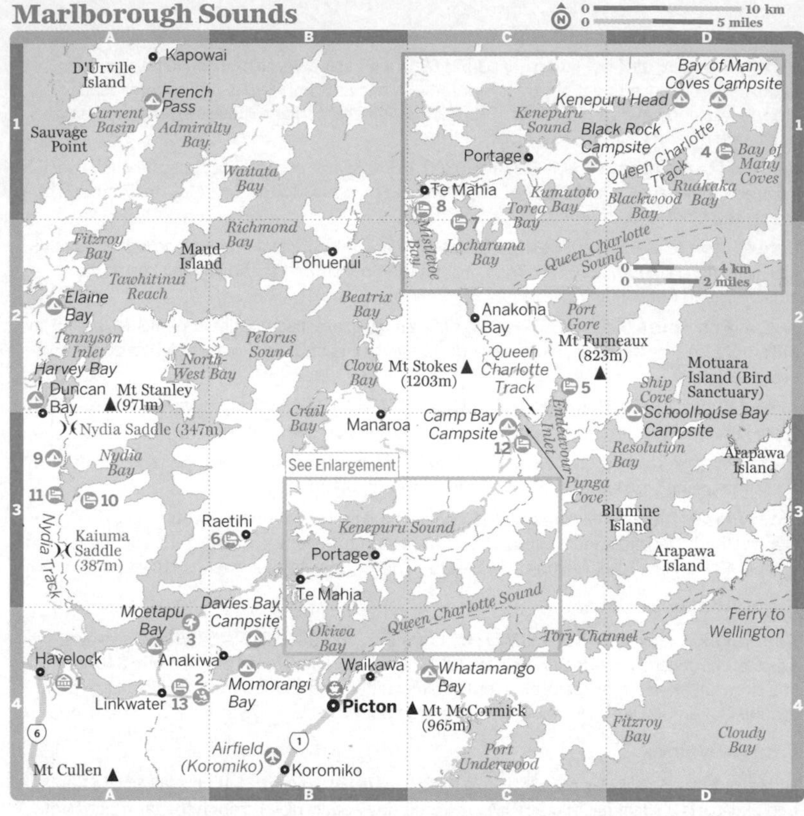

Marlborough Sounds

Sights

1 Shark Nett Gallery A4

Activities, Courses & Tours

Pelorus Mail Boat .... (see 1)
2 Sea Kayak Adventure Tours A4
3 Waterways Boating Safaris A4

Sleeping

4 Bay of Many Coves Resort D1
5 Furneaux Lodge C2
6 Hopewell B3
7 Lochmara Lodge C2
Mahana Lodge .... (see 12)
8 Mistletoe Bay C1
Noeline's Homestay .... (see 12)
9 Nydia Bay DOC Campsite A3
10 Nydia Lodge A3
11 On the Track Lodge A3
12 Punga Cove Resort C3
13 Smiths Farm Holiday Park A4

Fresh Choice Supermarket SUPERMARKET (Mariners Mall, 100 High St; 7am-9pm) Pretty much the only choice, and actually pretty good.

Information

Picton i-SITE (03-520 3113; www.destinationmarlborough.com; Foreshore; 9am-5pm Mon-Fri, to 4pm Sat & Sun) All vital tourist guff including maps, Queen Charlotte Track information, lockers and transport bookings. Department of Conservation (DOC) counter staffed during summer.

Picton Library (03-520 7493; 67 High St; 8am-5pm Mon-Fri, 10am-1pm Sat;) Free wi-fi internet access.

Police Station (03-520 3120; 36 Broadway)

Post Office (03-573 6900; Mariners Mall, 72 High St)

Getting There & Away

Make bookings for ferries, buses and trains at Picton i-SITE.

Air

Soundsair (☎03-520 3080, 0800 505 005; www.soundsair.com) flies daily between Picton and Wellington (adult/child $100/88). There are discounts for online bookings, and a shuttle bus ($7) to/from the airstrip at Koromiko, 8km south.

Boat

There are two operators crossing Cook Strait between Picton and Wellington, and although all ferries leave from more or less the same place, each has its own terminal. The main transport hub (with car-rental depots) is at the Interislander Terminal, which also has public showers, a cafe and internet facilities.

Bluebridge Ferries (☎0800 844 844, in Wellington 04-471 6188; www.bluebridge.co.nz; adult/child from $51/26) crossings takes three hours 20 minutes; there are up to four sailings in each direction daily. Cars and campervans up to 5.5m from $118, motorbikes $51, bicycles $10. Passenger fares are from $51/26 per adult/child.

Interislander (☎0800 802 802, in Wellington 04-498 3302; www.interislander.co.nz; adult/child from $46/23) crossings takes three hours 10 minutes; up to five sailings in each direction daily. Cars are priced from $118, campervans (up to 5.5m) from $133, motorbikes $56, bicycles $15. Passenger fares from adult/child $55/28.

Bus

Buses serving Picton depart from the Interislander terminal or nearby i-SITE.

InterCity (☎03-365 1113; www.intercitycoach.co.nz; Picton Ferry Terminal) runs services south to Christchurch (from $26, 5½ hours) via Kaikoura (from $17, 2½ hours), with connections to Dunedin, Queenstown and Invercargill. Services also run to/from Nelson (from $26, 2¼ hours), with connections to Motueka and the West Coast; and to/from Blenheim (from $10, 30 minutes). At least one bus daily on each of these routes connects with a Wellington ferry service.

Smaller shuttle buses running from Picton to Christchurch include **Atomic Shuttles** (☎03-349 0697; www.atomictravel.co.nz) and **Naked Bus** (☎0900 625 33; www.nakedbus.com).

Ritchies Transport (☎03-578 5467; www.ritchies.co.nz) buses traverse the Picton–Blenheim line daily (from $12), departing from the Interislander ferry terminal.

Train

Tranz Scenic (☎0800 872 467, 04-495 0775; www.tranzscenic.co.nz) runs the *Coastal Pacific* service daily each way between Picton and Christchurch via Blenheim and Kaikoura (and 22 tunnels and 175 bridges!), departing Christchurch at 7am, Picton at 1pm. Adult one-way Picton–Christchurch fares range from $59 to $99. The service connects with the Interislander ferry.

Getting Around

Shuttles (and tours) around Picton and wider Marlborough are offered by **Marlborough Sounds Shuttles** (☎03-573 7122; www.marlboroughsoundsshuttles.co.nz). Between Picton and Havelock (via Anakiwa), you can hitch a van ride with **Coleman Post** (☎027 255 8882; $15). It departs Picton at 8.15am and Havelock at 10.45am, with other services on request.

Renting a car in Picton is easy-peasy – as low as $35 per day if you shop around. Most agencies allow drop-offs in Christchurch; if you're planning to drive to the North Island, most companies suggest you leave your car at Picton and pick up another one in Wellington after crossing Cook Strait. The i-SITE can help you with recommendations and bookings, or try one of the following direct:

Ace (☎03-573 8939; www.acerentalcars.co.nz; Ferry Terminal)

NZ Rent A Car (☎03-573 7282; www.nzrentacar.co.nz; Ferry Terminal)

Omega (☎03-573 5580; www.omegarentalcars.com; 1 Lagoon Rd)

Pegasus (☎03-573 7733; www.carrentalspicton.co.nz; 1 Auckland St)

Queen Charlotte Track

The hugely popular, meandering 71km Queen Charlotte Track offers gorgeous coastal scenery on its way from historic Ship Cove to Anakiwa, passing through a mixture of privately owned land and DOC reserves. Access depends on the cooperation of local landowners; respect their property by utilising designated campsites and toilets, and carrying out your rubbish. Your purchase of the Track Pass ($12), available from operators in town and on the track, provides the co-op the means to maintain and enhance the experience for all.

Queen Charlotte is a well-defined track, suitable for people of average fitness. You can do the walk in sections using local water-taxi transport, walk the whole three- to five-day journey, or embark on a combo of walking, kayaking or biking. We're talking mountain biking here, and a whole lot of fun for fit, competent off-roaders: it's possible to ride the track in two or three days, guided or self-guided. Note that the section between Ship Cove and Camp Bay is off-limits to cyclists from 1 December to the end of February. During these months you can still be dropped by boat at the Saddle and ride to Anakiwa.

Numerous boat and tour operators service the track (p58), allowing you to start and finish where you like, on foot or bike or by kayak.

Sleeping options are no more than a few hours' walk apart; boat operators will transport your pack along the track for you. Ship Cove is the usual (and recommended) starting point – mainly because it's easier to arrange a boat from Picton to Ship Cove than vice versa – but the track can be started from Anakiwa. There's a public phone at Anakiwa but not at Ship Cove.

Estimated walk times:

TRACK SECTION	DISTANCE	DURATION
Ship Cove to Resolution Bay	4.5km	1½-2hr
Resolution Bay to head of Endeavour Inlet	10.5km	2½-3hr
Endeavour Inlet to Camp Bay/Punga Cove	12km	3-4hr
Camp Bay/Punga Cove to Torea Saddle/Portage	24km	6-8hr
Torea Saddle/Portage to Te Mahia Saddle	7.5km	3-4hr
Te Mahia Saddle to Anakiwa	12.5km	3-4hr

Sleeping & Eating

Unless you're camping, it pays to book your Queen Charlotte Track accommodation *waaay* in advance, especially in summer. There are six **DOC campsites** (adult/child $6/3) along the track, each with toilets and a water supply but no cooking facilities. There's also a variety of resorts, lodges, backpackers and guesthouses.

The following select listings are arranged in order heading south from Ship Cove. Your overnight stops will depend on how far you can/want to walk on any given day – do your research and book ahead. Not every accommodation option is covered here; see the map for campsites, and www.qctrack.co.nz for all possibilities.

Furneaux Lodge LODGE **$$**
(03-579 8259; www.furneauxlodge.co.nz; Endeavour Inlet; dm $38, cabins from $45, units $199-269, meals $20-36; @) One of the Sounds' stalwart resorts, Furneaux's highlights are the historic lodge building and a big flat lawn right down to the water's edge. This place welcomes pit-stoppers (coffee, beer, lunch, etc), but there's also adequate accommodation here, the most pleasant of which are the swish but pricey waterfront studios.

Punga Cove Resort RESORT **$$$**
(03-579 8561; www.pungacove.co.nz; Endeavour Inlet; dm $45, lodge $150-180, chalets $180-450, restaurant mains $29-40; @) A rustic but charming resort offering self-contained studios and family and luxury A-frame chalets, most with sweeping sea views. The backpackers is basic but Punga's location easily atones. Ample activities (pool, spa, games, kayak and bike hire), plus a restaurant and boatshed bar/cafe (decent local beers and $25 pizza).

Mahana Lodge LODGE **$$**
(03-579 8373; www.mahanalodge.co.nz; Endeavour Inlet; d $180; closed May-Aug) This beautiful property features a pretty waterside lawn and purpose-built lodge with four en-suite doubles. Eco-friendly initiatives include bush regeneration, pest trapping and organic veggie patch; in fact, feel-good factors abound: free kayaks, robes, home-baking and a blooming conservatory where the evening meal is served (three courses $55).

Noeline's Homestay HOMESTAY **$**
(03-579 8375; Endeavour Inlet; dm without/with linen $30/35) Follow the pink arrows from Camp Bay to this relaxed homestay and be greeted by 70-something Noeline, 'the Universal Grandma', and her home-baked treats. It's a friendly arrangement with beds for five people, cooking facilities and great views.

Bay of Many Coves Resort RESORT **$$$**
(0800 579 9771, 03-579 9771; www.bayofmanycoves.co.nz; Bay of Many Coves; 1-/2-/3-bedroom apt $620/830/995; @) Honeymooning? These plush and secluded apartments are appropriately romantic, with all mod cons and private balconies overlooking the water. The upmarket cafes and restaurant are staffed by a crew of iron chefs. Additional indulgences include room service, massage, spa and a hot tub.

Portage Resort Hotel RESORT $$
(☎03-573 4309; www.portage.co.nz; The Portage; dm $40, d $165-365; @☎≋) This fancy resort is centred upon a smart lodge building housing Te Weka restaurant and Retro Bar (meals $14 to $35), with a sundeck overlooking the pool patio and grounds. The 22-bed backpacker wing has a small lounge and cooking facilities. Moderately stylish rooms climb the price ladder from there. The on-site Kenepuru Store sells limited snacks and groceries, while underneath is an outpost of Marlborough Sounds Adventure Company (p58), offering trips and freedom hire of bikes and boats.

DeBretts & Treetops GUESTHOUSE $
(☎03-573 4522; www.stayportage.co.nz; Portage Bay; s without/with linen $40/45) The family-run enclave of DeBretts and **Treetops** (☎03-573 4404) offers a combined total of six bedrooms in two homely backpackers high on the hill above Portage Resort. Torea Bay bag transfers included.

Lochmara Lodge RESORT $$
(☎0800 562 462, 03-573 4554; www.lochmara lodge.co.nz; Lochmara Bay; units $90-280; @☎) A superb retreat on Lochmara Bay, reached from the Queen Charlotte Track or from Picton aboard the lodge's water taxi ($55 return). Relaxation-inducing facilities include massage and the indulgent bath house overlooking the bay. There are en-suite doubles, units and chalets, all set in lush surroundings, and a fully licensed cafe and restaurant offering fine food and decent coffee.

TOP CHOICE **Mistletoe Bay** HOLIDAY PARK $
(☎03-573 4048; www.mistletoebay.co.nz; unpowered sites adult/child $16/10, dm $20, cabins $140, linen $7.50) Surrounded by bushy hills, sweet Mistletoe Bay offers attractive camping with a brand new communal facilities block, eight irresistible cabins sleeping up to six, and a cottage with bunks for overflow. Environmental sustainability abounds, as does the opportunity to jump off the jetty, kayak in the bay, or walk the Queen Charlotte Track.

Te Mahia Bay Resort RESORT $$
(☎03-573 4089; www.temahia.co.nz; d $140-248; ☎) This lovely low-key resort is within cooee of the Queen Charlotte Track in a picturesque bay on Kenepuru Sound. It has a range of delightful rooms-with-a-view, our pick of which is the great-value heritage units. The on-site store has pre-cooked meals, pizza, coffee and camping supplies (wine!), and there are kayaks for hire and massage.

Anakiwa Backpackers HOSTEL $
(☎03-574 1388; www.anakiwabackpackers.co.nz; 401 Anakiwa Rd, Anakiwa; dm $33, d $85-105, q $155; @☎) This former schoolhouse (1926) greets you at the southern end of the track – a soothing spot to rest and reflect. There are two doubles (one with en-suite), a four-bed dorm and a beachy self-contained unit. Jocular owners will have you jumping off the jetty for joy and imbibing espresso and ice cream (hallelujah) from their little green caravan (open summer afternoons). Provisions available by arrangement and free kayak hire.

ℹ Information

The Picton i-SITE (p60) books and stocks everything Queen Charlotte Track, and loads more besides. Picton's Villa Backpackers (p55) is also a hotbed of info, and handles bookings. Check online details at www.qctrack.co.nz.

Kenepuru & Pelorus Sounds

Kenepuru and Pelorus Sounds, to the west of Queen Charlotte Sound, are less populous and therefore offer fewer traveller services, including transport. There's some cracking scenery, however, and those with time to spare will be well rewarded by their explorations.

Havelock is the hub of this area, the western bookend of the 35km Queen Charlotte Drive (Picton being the eastern) and the self-proclaimed 'Greenshell Mussel Capital of the World'. While hardly the most rock-and-roll of NZ towns, Havelock makes a practical base from which to set off, as you'll readily locate most necessaries, including fuel and food. As you get out into the Sounds be prepared to encounter only the odd service station and the occasional shop, which *may* have frozen bread and and out-of-date Popsicles.

For finer detail, including a complete list of visitor services, visit www.pelorus .co.nz, which covers Havelock, Kenepuru and Pelorus Sounds, and the extreme extremeties of French Pass and D'Urville Island.

DON'T MISS

PELORUS BRIDGE

A pocket of deep, green forest tucked away among paddocks of bog-standard pasture, 18km west of Havelock, this scenic reserve contains one of the last stands of river-flat forest in Marlborough. It survived only because a town planned in 1865 didn't get off the ground by 1912, by which time obliterative logging made this little remnant look precious. The reserve was born, and hats off to that, because now visitors can explore its many tracks, admire the historic bridge, take a dip in the limpid Pelorus River (beautiful enough to star in Peter Jackson's *Hobbit*), and even indulge in some home-baking at the cafe. The fortunate few can stay overnight in the DOC's small but perfectly formed **Pelorus Bridge Campsite** (☎03-571 6019; www.doc.govt.nz; unpowered/powered sites from $10/11), with its snazzy new facilities building.

Sights & Activities

If a stroll through the streets of Havelock leaves you thinking that there *must* be more to this area, you're right – and to get a taste of it you need go no further than the **Cullen Point Lookout**, 10 minutes from Havelock along the Queen Charlotte Drive. A short walk leads up and around a headland overlooking Havelock, the surrounding valleys and Pelorus Sound. The *Havelock Map & Walkway Guide*, available around town, details more walks in the area.

Nydia Track

The Nydia Track (27km, 10 hours) starts at Kaiuma Bay and ends at Duncan Bay (or vice versa). Around halfway is beautiful Nydia Bay, where there's a **DOC campsite** (adult/child $6/3) and **Nydia Lodge** (☎03-520 3002; www.doc.govt.nz; dm $15.30), an unhosted 50-bed lodge (four-person minimum). You'll need water and road transport to complete the journey; Havelock's Blue Moon lodge runs a shuttle to Duncan Bay. **On the Track Lodge** (☎03-579 8411; www.nydiatrack.org.nz; Nydia Bay; dm $40, d/tw $110, d cabins $130) provides alternative accommodation at Nydia Bay in a tranquil, ecofocused lodge offering everything from packed lunches to evening meals and a hot tub.

Shark Nett Gallery GALLERY

(☎03-574 2877; www.sharknett.co.nz; 129 Queen Charlotte Dr, Havelock; adult/child $12/6.50; ⏲10am-4pm) Overlooking the tidal Pelorus estuary, Shark Nett showcases contemporary Maori carving relating to the local Rangitane *iwi* (tribes). Guided tours provide an educational and evocative insight into how carving is used to record tribal *tikanga* (customs) and *whakapapa* (ancestry).

Sleeping & Eating

There's plenty of accommodation along the Kenepuru Road, most of which is readily accessible off the Queen Charlotte Track (p65). Other options in this area include some picturesque DOC campgrounds (most full to bursting in mid-summer), a few remote lodges and a handy holiday park at Linkwater, the cross-roads for Queen Charlotte and Kenepuru, where you'll find a petrol station with snacks. Havelock has a couple of dependable offerings and a smattering that are less so.

Smiths Farm Holiday Park HOLIDAY PARK $

(☎0800 727 578, 03-574 2806; www.smithsfarm.co.nz; 1419 Queen Charlotte Dr, Linkwater; sites from $16, cabins $60-130, units $130; @📶) Located on the apty named Linkwater flat between Queen Charlotte and Pelorus, friendly Smiths makes a handy basecamp. Well-kept cabins and motel units face out onto the bushy hillside, while livestock nibble around the lush camping lawns. Walks extend to a nearby waterfall and glowworm dell.

Hopewell LODGE $

(☎03-573 4341; www.hopewell.co.nz; 7204 Kenepuru Rd, Double Bay; dm from $40, d with/without bathroom from $130/100, 4-person cottage $200; @📶) Beloved of travellers from near and far, remote Hopewell sits waterside surrounded by native bush. Savour the long, winding drive to get there, or take a water taxi from Te Mahia. Stay at least a couple of days, so you can chill out or enjoy the roll-call of activities: mountain biking, kayaking, sailing, fishing, eating gourmet pizza, soaking in the outdoor spa, and more.

Havelock Garden Motel MOTEL $$

(☎03-574 2387; www.gardenmotels.com; 71 Main Rd, Havelock; d 105-160; 📶) Set in a large, graceful garden complete with dear old trees and a duck-filled creek, these 1960s units have been tastefully revamped to offer homely comforts. Local activities are happily booked for you.

Blue Moon GUESTHOUSE $
(☎03-574 2212; www.bluemoonhavelock.co.nz; 48 Main Rd, Havelock; dm $25, d $66-86; @📶) This largely unremarkable lodge has homely rooms in the main house (one with en suite), as well as cabins and a bunkhouse in the yard (along with a spa pool). The lounge and kitchen are pleasant and relaxed, as is the sunny barbecue deck. Hosts run shuttle transport servicing the Nydia Track, Queen Charlotte, and surrounds.

Wakamarinian Café CAFE $
(☎03-574 1180; 70 Main Rd, Havelock; snacks $2-9; ⏲9.30am-5pm) Heavenly home baking in a sweet cottage. Get in early to grab one of the popular pies, or console yourself with proper quiche and a sweet slice – the raspberry and white-chocolate shortcake defies description. Great coffee and excellent value, too, from Beth and Laurie: Havelock's culinary saviours.

Getting There & Away

InterCity (☎03-365 1113; www.intercitycoach.co.nz) runs daily from Picton to Havelock via Blenheim ($22, one hour), and from Havelock to Nelson ($23, 1¼ hours). **Atomic Shuttles** (☎03-349 0697; www.atomictravel.co.nz) plies the same run. You can travel between Havelock and Picton for $15 via the scenic Queen Charlotte Drive with Coleman Post (p61). Buses depart from the high street in the middle of town – look for the restaurant with the mussels on the roof.

Blenheim

POP 26,500

Blenheim (pronounced 'Blenum') is an agricultural town 29km south of Picton on the Wairau Plain between the Wither Hills and the Richmond Ranges. The town has yet to demonstrate any real power as a visitor magnet; it is the neighbours over the back fence that pull in the punters.

Sights & Activities

Omaka Aviation Heritage Centre MUSEUM
(Map p66; www.omaka.org.nz; 79 Aerodrome Rd; adult/child/family $25/10/55; ⏲10am-4pm) Blenheim's 'big attraction' has always been its wineries, but the Omaka Aviation Heritage Centre has blown the wine out of the water. Aided by Peter Jackson and his team of creative types, this captivating collection of original and replica Great War aircraft is brought to life with a series of dioramas depicting dramatic wartime scenes such as the death of Manfred von Richthofen, the Red Baron. Memorabilia and photographic displays deepen the experience. The guided tour is an extra $5 extremely well spent. A cafe and shop are on-site, and next door is **Omaka Classic Cars**, with over 100 vehicles from the '50s to the '80s (adult/child $12.50/5).

Marlborough Museum MUSEUM
(Map p66; www.marlboroughmuseum.org.nz; 26 Arthur Baker Pl off New Renwick Rd; adult/child $10/5; ⏲10am-4pm) Besides a replica township, vintage mechanicals, train rides (every first and third Sunday) and well-presented artefact displays, there's the *Wine Exhibition* for those looking to cap off their vineyard experiences.

Wither Hills Farm Park WALKING
In a town as flat as a pancake, this 1100-hectare park provides welcome relief, offering a range of walks and mountain-bike trails with grand views across the Wairau Valley and out to Cloudy Bay. Pick up a map from the i-SITE or check the information panels at the gates.

High Country Horse Treks HORSE RIDING
(☎03-577 9424; www.high-horse.co.nz; 961 Taylor Pass Rd; 1-3hr treks $70-120) Runs equine exploration from its base 11km southwest of town (call for directions).

Molesworth Tours GUIDED TOUR
(☎03-577 9897; www.molesworthtours.co.nz) New Zealand's largest high-country station – which is complete with cob cottages and vistas galore – can be discovered in depth with Molesworth Tours. It offers one- to four-day all-inclusive heritage and 4WD trips ($190 to $1655), as well as four-day fully supported (and catered) mountain-bike adventures ($1295).

Festivals & Events

Marlborough Wine Festival FOOD & WINE
(www.wine-marlborough-festival.co.nz; tickets $48) Held on the second weekend of February at Montana's Brancott Estate, this is an extravaganza of local wine, fine food and entertainment. Book accommodation well in advance.

Marlborough Wine Region

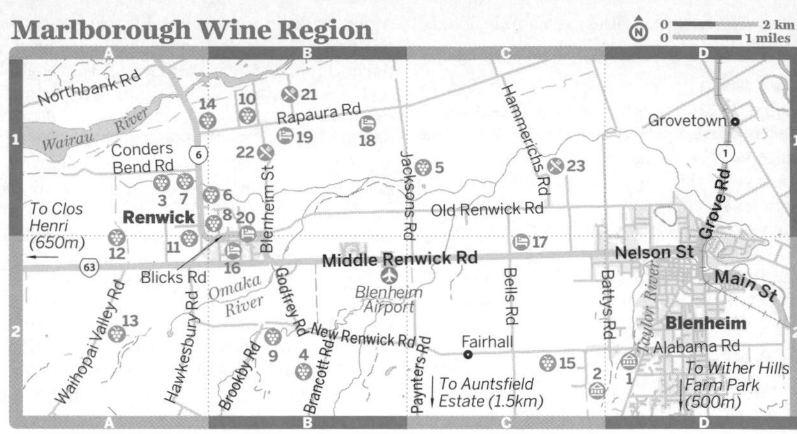

Marlborough Wine Region

Sights
1 Marlborough Museum D2
2 Omaka Aviation Heritage Centre C2

Activities, Courses & Tours
3 Bladen Estate A1
4 Brancott Estate Heritage Centre B2
5 Cloudy Bay C1
6 Forrest B1
7 Framingham A1
8 Gibson Bridge B1
9 Highfield Estate B2
10 Huia B1
11 Mahi Wines A2
12 Seresin Estate A2
13 Spy Valley Wines A2
14 Wairau River A1
15 Wither Hills C2

Sleeping
16 Olde Mill House B2
17 St Leonards C2
18 Stonehaven B1
19 Vintners Hotel B1
20 Watson's Way Lodge B1

Eating
21 Herzog Winery B1
22 La Veranda B1
23 Rock Ferry C1
Wairau River .... (see 14)
Wither Hills .... (see 15)

Sleeping

IN TOWN

Blenheim's budget beds fill with long-stay guests doing seasonal work; hostels will help find work and offer reasonable weekly rates. There are masses of midrange motels, with rich pickings on Middle Renwick Rd west of the town centre, and a handful on SH1 towards Christchurch.

Koanui Lodge & Backpackers HOSTEL $
(☎03-578 7487; www.koanui.co.nz; 33 Main St; dm $25, d with/without bathroom $82/58; @☜) This pink palace on the main street caters to both workers and casual visitors. Both the old villa and newer lodge wing are clean and tidy, but otherwise unremarkable.

Grapevine Backpackers HOSTEL $
(☎03-578 6062; www.thegrapevine.co.nz; 29 Park Tce; tent sites $18, dm $24, d $58-68, tr $81; @☜) Located inside an old maternity home just out of the town centre, Grapevine is a worker-focused hostel with a peaceful sunset deck by Opawa River. There are free canoes, and bike hire is $20 per day. Avoid the three-tier bunks if vertigo is an issue.

Blenheim Top 10 Holiday Park HOLIDAY PARK $
(☎03-578 3667, 0800 268 666; www.blenheimtop10.co.nz; 78 Grove Rd; sites from $35, cabins $78-90, units & motels $110-145; @☜≋) About five minutes north of town, this holiday park has campervan pads and campsites spread out along Opawa River, as well as a spa, a playground and the usual cabin/unit sus-

pects. Bike hire costs $20 per half-day. Park up right at the far end of the camp to mute some of the road and railway noise.

171 on High MOTEL **$$**
(☎0800 587 856, 03-579 5098; www.171onhighmotel.co.nz; 171 High St; d $140-180; @📶) A welcoming option close to town, these tasteful, splash-o-purple studios and apartments are bright and breezy in the daytime, warm and shimmery in the evening. Expect a wide complement of facilities and 'extra mile' service.

WINE REGION ACCOMMODATION

TOP CHOICE **Watson's Way Lodge** LODGE **$**
(Map p66; ☎03-572 8228; www.watsonswaybackpackers.co.nz; 56 High St, Renwick; dm $30, d $70-90; ⏲closed Aug-Sep; @📶) This traveller-focused, purpose-built hostel has spick-and-span rooms, mainly twins and doubles, some with en suite. There are spacious leafy gardens dotted with fruit trees and hammocks, an outdoor claw-foot bath, bikes for hire (guest/public rate $15/25 per day) and local information aplenty.

Olde Mill House B&B **$$**
(Map p66; ☎03-572 8458; www.oldemillhouse.co.nz; 9 Wilson St, Renwick; s/d $120/145; @📶) On an elevated section in otherwise flat Renwick, this charming old house is a treat. Dyed-in-the-wool local hosts run a welcoming B&B, with stately decor and home-grown fruit and homemade goodies for breakfast. Free bikes, outdoor spa and gardens make this a tip-top choice in the heart of the wine country.

St Leonards COTTAGES **$$**
(Map p66; ☎03-577 8328; www.stleonards.co.nz; 18 St Leonards Rd; d $115-310, extra adult $35; 📶) Tucked into the grounds of an 1886 homestead, these four rustic cottages offer privacy and a reason to stay put. (Anyone for tennis?) Each has its own history, layout and individual outlook to the gardens and vines. Our pick is the Stables, with its lemon-grove view.

Stonehaven B&B **$$$**
(Map p66; ☎03-572 9730; www.stonehavenhomestay.co.nz; 414 Rapaura Rd; d incl breakfast $262-288; @📶🏊) A stellar stone-and-timber B&B nestled among the picturesque vines with two ensuite guest rooms. Beds are piled high with pillows, breakfast is served in the summer house, dinner is provided by request with rare wines from the cellar.

Vintners Hotel HOTEL **$$$**
(Map p66; ☎0800 684 190, 03-572 5094; www.mvh.co.nz; 190 Rapaura Rd; d $150-295; 📶) Sixteen architecturally designed suites make the most of wine-valley views, while inside classy suites boast wet-room bathrooms and abstract art. The stylish reception building has a bar and restaurant opening out on to a cherry orchard and organic vegie garden. Staff are keen to connect you with the best experiences the region has to offer.

Eating & Drinking

Hospitality can be pretty hit and miss in Blenny, with some of the best food found yonder at the wineries. While you're at it, keep an eye out for the scrumptious craft beers made by local brewers, **Renaissance** (www.renaissancebrewing.co.nz), and their associate **8-Wired** (www.8wired.co.nz), 2011 Brewer's Guild champion. Josh Scott, a winemaker's son, also brews the good range of bottle-fermented beers and thirst-quenching ciders known as **Moa** (www.moabeer.co.nz).

Café le Cupp CAFE **$**
(30 Market St; snacks $2-5, meals $5-16) The best tearoom in town by a country mile. Ogle your way along the counter (egg sandwiches, mince savouries, luscious lamingtons, carrot cake) or get yourself a brekkie such as the full fry-up, French toast or muesli. Heaven descends on Thursdays in the form of the ginger gem.

Raupo MODERN NZ **$$**
(6 Symons St; breakfast $13-19, lunch & dinner $18-33; ⏲7.30am-late) Blenheim's best restaurant since the day it opened. It boasts stylish timber-and-stone architecture and a pleasant riverside location. This promise is backed up by consistent, modern cafe fare along the lines of macadamia muesli, aged feta and chorizo salad, local mussels and salmon, and super-fine Euro-sweets: truffles, sorbet and pastries.

CPR CAFE
(18 Wynen St) Get a fix of Blenheim's own-roast coffee. There are muffins if you're lucky, but it's really all about the beans.

Information

Blenheim i-SITE (☎0800 777 181, 03-577 8080; www.destinationmarlborough.com; 8 Sinclair St; ⏲8.30am-5.30pm Mon-Fri, 9am-5pm Sat, 9am-4pm Sun) Information on

MARLBOROUGH WINERIES

Marlborough is NZ's vinous colossus, producing around three quarters of the country's wine. At last count, there were 23,900 hectares of vines planted – that's approximately 28,000 rugby pitches! Sunny days and cool nights create the perfect microclimate for cool-climate grapes: world-famous sauvignon blanc, top-notch pinot noir, and notable chardonnay, riesling, gewürztraminer, pinot gris and bubbly. Spending a day or two drifting between tasting rooms and dining among the vines is a quintessential South Island experience.

The majority of Marlborough's nearly 140 wineries lie within the Wairau Valley, mainly around Blenheim and Renwick, with others blanketing the cooler Awatere Valley or creeping up the southern-side valleys of the Wairau. Of the 40 or so that are open to the public, those listed below are well worth a look, and provide a range of quality cellar-door experiences.

A Taste of the Tastings

Most cellar doors are open from around 10.30am till 4.30pm, with some scaling back operations in winter. Wineries may charge a small fee for tasting, normally refunded if you purchase a bottle. Pick up a copy of *The Marlborough Wine Trail* map from Blenheim i-SITE (p67), available online at www.wine-marlborough.co.nz.

Auntsfield Estate (☎03-578 0622; www.auntsfield.co.nz; 270 Paynters Rd) Quality hand-crafted wines from this historic and picturesque vineyard at the foot of the hills. Tours by arrangement ($15).

Bladen Estate (Map p66; www.bladen.co.nz; 83 Conders Bend Rd) Bijou family winery that's big on charm.

Brancott Estate (Map p66; ☎03-520 6975; www.brancottestate.com; 180 Brancott Rd) Ubermodern cellar door and restaurant complex atop a hillock overlooking one of the original sauvignon blanc vineyards.

Clos Henri (www.closhenri.com; 639 SH63) French winemaking meets Marlborough terroir with *très bien* results. Beautifully restored local country church houses the cellar door.

Cloudy Bay (Map p66; www.cloudybay.co.nz; Jacksons Rd) Understated exterior belies the classy interior of this blue-ribbon winery and cellar door. Globally coveted sauvignon blanc, bubbly and pinot noir.

Forrest (Map p66; www.forrest.co.nz; 19 Blicks Rd) Doctor-owners produce and prescribe a range of fine vinous medicines, including some mood-altering riesling.

Framingham (Map p66; www.framingham.co.nz; 19 Conders Bend Rd) Consistent, quality wines including exceptional rieslings and stellar stickies.

Gibson Bridge (Map p66; www.gibsonbridge.co.nz; cnr Gee St & SH6) Peachy pinot gris, and a grandiose cellar door in a miniscule space.

Highfield Estate (Map p66; www.highfield.co.nz; 27 Brookby Rd) Impressive views over the Wairau Valley from the tower atop this rosy Tuscan-style winery. The fizz is the biz.

Huia (Map p66; www.huia.net.nz; 22 Boyces Rd) Sustainable, small-scale winegrowing and the cutest yellow tasting room in town. Delectable dry-style gewürztraminer.

Mahi Wines (Map p66; www.mahiwine.co.nz; 9 Terrace Rd) Knowledgeable and friendly staff who are rightly proud of Mahi's stable of fine wines, with a strong focus on single-vineyard varieties.

Seresin Estate (Map p66; www.seresin.co.nz; 85 Bedford Rd) Organic and biodynamic wines and olive oils from cinematographer Michael Seresin. Shedlike cellar door and groovy sculptures dotted about.

Spy Valley Wines (Map p66; www.spyvalleywine.co.nz; 37 Lake Timara Rd, Waihopai Valley) Stylish, edgy architecture at this espionage-themed winery with great wines across the board. Memorable merchandise.

Wairau River (Map p66; www.wairauriverwines.com; 11 Rapaura Rd) Carbon-neutral family estate with some of Marlborough's oldest vines. Relaxing gardens and a fancy new cellar door.

Wither Hills (Map p66; www.witherhills.co.nz; 211 New Renwick Rd) One of the region's flagship wineries and an architectural gem. Premium wines and enthralling winemaker-for-a-day tours ($35).

Best Wining & Dining

With wine there must be food. This is our pick of the bunch for dining among the vines. Opening hours are for summer, when bookings are recommended.

La Veranda (Map p66; ☎03-572 7230; www.georgesmichel.com; 56 Vintage Ln; platters $19-22; ⊙11am-4pm Tue-Sun) Keenly priced platters of quality charcuterie, fromages and French desserts – the sort of lunch you should be eating at a vineyard. Eat outside or in Domaine George Michel's elegant restaurant.

Wairau River (Map p66; ☎03-572 9800; www.wairauriverwines.com; 11 Rapaura Rd; mains $19-24; ⊙noon-3pm) Modishly modified mudbrick bistro with wide veranda, and beautiful gardens with plenty of shade. Order the mussel chowder or the rare beef salad with noodles. Relaxing and thoroughly enjoyable.

Wither Hills (Map p66; ☎03-520 8284; www.witherhills.co.nz; 211 New Renwick Rd; mains $18-35, platters $25-38; ⊙11am-4pm Tue, 11am-4pm & 6pm-late Wed-Sun) Simple, well executed food in a stylish space. Pull up a beanbag on the Hockneyesque lawns and enjoy a french onion tart, bouillabaisse or platter (after 3pm), before climbing the ziggurat for impressive views across the Wairau.

Rock Ferry (Map p66; ☎03-579 6431; www.rockferry.co.nz; 80 Hammerichs Rd; mains $18-24; ⊙noon-3pm) Pleasant environment inside and out, with a slightly groovy edge. The compact summery menu – think salmon and lime leaves or fish cakes on noodle salad – is accompanied by wines from Marlborough and Otago.

Herzog Winery (Map p66; ☎03-572 8770; www.herzog.co.nz; 81 Jefferies Rd; mains $46-82, 5-course degustation menu with/without wine $197/125; ⊙restaurant 6.30pm-9.30pm, bistro 11am-10pm (closed mid-May to mid-Oct)) Refined dining in Herzog's opulent dining room. Beautifully prepared food and a remarkable wine list. Less extravagant bistro meals (mains $26 to $28) also available.

Wine Tours

Wine tours are generally conducted in a minibus, last between four and seven hours, take in four to seven wineries and range in price from $55 to $90 (with a few grand tours up to around $200 for the day, including a winery lunch). The following are grand crus:

Bubbly Grape (☎0800 228 2253, 027 672 2195; www.bubblygrape.co.nz) Three different tours including a gourmet lunch option.

Highlight Wine Tours (☎03-577-9046, 027 434 6451; www.highlightwinetours.co.nz) Visit a chocolate factory, too. Custom tours available.

Sounds Connection (☎03-573 8843, 0800 742 866; www.soundsconnection.co.nz) This operator partners up with Herzog for a wine and food matched lunch.

Bike2Wine (☎0800 653 262, 03-572 8458; www.bike2wine.co.nz; 9 Wilson St, Renwick; standard/tandem $30/60 per day, delivery/pick-up $5-10 per bike) Your other option is to get around the grapes on two wheels. This operator offers a self-guided, fully geared and supported tours.

Marlborough and beyond. Wine-trail maps and bookings for everything under the sun.

Blenheim Police Station (☎03-578 5279; 8 Main St)

Post Office (cnr Scott & Main Sts)

Wairau Hospital (☎03-520 9999; www.nmdhb.govt.nz; Hospital Rd)

Getting There & Around

Air

Blenheim Airport is 6km west of town on Middle Renwick Rd. **Air New Zealand** (☎03-577 2200, 0800 747 000; www.airnewzealand.co.nz; 29 Queen St; ⊙9am-5pm Mon-Fri) has direct flights to/from Wellington (from $99), Auckland (from $139) and Christchurch (from $99) with onward connections. Soundsair (p61) and **Air2There** (☎0800 777 000; www.air2there.com) connect Blenheim with Wellington and Paraparaumu.

Bicycle

Avantiplus (☎03-578 0433; www.bikemarlborough.co.nz; 61 Queen St; hire per half-/full day touring bike $25/40, mountain bike $40/60) rents bikes; longer hire and delivery by arrangement.

Bus

InterCity (☎03-365 1113; www.intercitycoach.co.nz) buses run daily from the Blenheim i-SITE to Picton (from $11, 30 minutes) continuing through to Nelson (from $18, 1¾ hours). Buses also head down south to Christchurch (from $25, three daily) via Kaikoura (from $16).

Naked Bus (☎0900 625 33; www.nakedbus.com) runs from Blenheim to many South Island destinations, including Kaikoura ($18, two hours), Nelson ($23, 1¾ hours) and Motueka ($36, 3¾ hours). Buses depart the i-SITE. Book online or at the i-SITE; cheaper fares for advance bookings.

Ritchies Transport (p61) buses traverse the Blenheim–Picton line daily (from $12), departing from Blenheim Railway Station.

Shuttles (and tours) around Picton and wider Marlborough are offered by Marlborough Sounds Shuttles (p61).

Taxi

Call for bookings or for a post-wine-tour ride back to your hotel with **Marlborough Taxis** (☎03-577 5511).

Train

Tranz Scenic (☎0800 872 467, 04-495 0775; www.tranzscenic.co.nz) runs the daily *Coastal Pacific* service, stopping at Blenheim en route to Picton (from $29) heading north, and Christchurch (from $59) via Kaikoura (from $59) heading south.

Kaikoura

POP 3850

Take SH1 132km southeast from Blenheim (or 183km north from Christchurch) and you'll wind around the panoramic coast to Kaikoura, a pretty peninsula town backed by the snowcapped peaks of the Seaward Kaikoura Range. There are few places in the world with so much wildlife around: whales, dolphins, NZ fur seals, penguins, shearwaters, petrels and wandering albatross all stop by or make this area home.

Marine animals are abundant here due to ocean-current and continental-shelf conditions: the seabed gradually slopes away from the land before plunging to more than 800m where the southerly current hits the continental shelf. This creates an upwelling, bringing nutrients up from the ocean floor into the feeding zone.

Until the 1980s Kaikoura was a sleepy crayfishing town ('Kai' meaning food, 'koura' meaning crayfish) with grim prospects. These days it's a tourist mecca, with quality accommodation and many other enticements including eye-popping wildlife tours.

History

In Maori legend, Kaikoura Peninsula (Taumanu o Te Waka a Maui) was the seat where the demigod Maui placed his feet when he fished the North Island up from the depths of the sea. The area was heavily settled before Europeans arrived – at least 14 Maori *pa* (fortified village) sites have been identified, and excavations show that the area was a moa-hunter settlement about 800 to 1000 years ago.

James Cook sailed past the peninsula in 1770, but didn't land. His journal states that 57 Maori in four double-hulled canoes came towards the *Endeavour*, but 'would not be prevail'd upon to put along side'.

In 1828 Kaikoura's beachfront was the scene of a tremendous battle. A Ngati Toa war party, led by chief Te Rauparaha, bore down on Kaikoura, killing or capturing several hundred of the Ngai Tahu tribe.

Europeans established a whaling station here in 1842, and the town remained a whaling centre until 1922. Sheep farming and agriculture also flourished. After whaling ended, the sea and fertile farmland continued to sustain the community.

Sights

Point Kean Seal Colony WILDLIFE RESERVE
At the end of the peninsula seals laze around in the grass and on the rocks, lapping up all the attention. Give them a wide berth (10m), and never get between them and the sea – they will attack if they feel cornered and can move surprisingly fast.

Fyffe House HISTORIC BUILDING
(www.fyffehouse.co.nz; 62 Avoca St; adult/child/family $9/2/18; ⌚10am-6pm daily Nov-Apr, to 4pm Thu-Mon May-Oct) Kaikoura's oldest surviving building is Fyffe House, built upon foundations of whale vertabrae. Built by Scotsman George Fyffe, cousin of Kaikoura's first European settler, Robert Fyffe, it started life as a small cottage in 1842. There's plenty to see inside and out, including the original brick oven, historical displays and gardens.

Kaikoura District Museum MUSEUM
(14 Ludstone Rd; adult/child $5/1; ⌚10am-4.30pm Mon-Fri, 2-4pm Sat & Sun) This provincial museum houses the old town jail, historical photos, Maori and colonial artefacts, a huge sperm-whale jaw and the fossilised remains of a plesiosaur.

Point Sheep Shearing Show FARM
(☎03-319 5422; www.pointsheepshearing.co.nz; Fyffe Quay; adult/child $10/5; ⌚shows 1.30pm & 4pm) The 30-minute Point Sheep Shearing Show at the Point B&B is fun and educationally ovine. You can also feed a ram, and lambs between September and February. Classic NZ!

Activities

There's a safe swimming beach in front of the Esplanade, and a pool (adult/child $3/1.50; 10am to 5pm November to March) if you have a salt aversion.

Decent surfing can be found in the area, too, particularly at Mangamaunu Beach (15km north of town), where there's a 500m point break, fun in good conditions. Get the low-down, transport, learn to surf or hire gear from **Board Silly Surf Adventures** (☎0800 787 352, 027 418 8900; 76 West End; 3hr lesson $80, board & suit from $30) based at South Bay. Gear hire and advice is also available from **R&R Sports** (☎03-319 5028; 14 West End; bike hire half-day $20, full day $30-40) and **Surf Kaikoura** (☎03-319 7173; www.surfkaikoura.co.nz; 4 Beach Rd).

Kaikoura Peninsula Walkway WALKING
A foray along this walkway is a must-do if humanly possible. Starting from the town, this three- to four-hour loop heads out to Point Kean, along the cliffs to South Bay, then back to town over the isthmus (or in reverse, of course). En route you'll see fur seals and red-billed seagull and shearwater (aka mutton bird) colonies. Lookouts and interesting interpretive panels abound. Collect a map at the i-SITE or follow your nose.

Dive Kaikoura DIVING
(☎0800 348 352, 03-319 6622; www.divekaikoura.co.nz; Yarmouth St; half-day $250) The whole coastline, with its rocky formations and abundant marine life, offers interesting snorkelling and diving. Dive Kaikoura runs small-group trips and diver training.

Skydive Kaikoura SKYDIVING
(☎0800 843 759; www.skydivekaikoura.co.nz; Kaikoura Airport; 9000-13,000ft $260-380; ⌚closes for winter) Come down to earth with Henk and Sarah, who offer personal service and jumps with stupendous mountain-to-sea views. Handicam and photo packages available. The airport is 7km south of town.

Fyffe View Ranch Adventure Park FARM
(☎03-319 5069; www.kaikourahorsetrekking.co.nz; 82 Chapmans Rd off Postmans Rd; 30min/90min treks $30/120; ⌚10.30am-late) Fun, down-to-earth farmy folk offer horse treks. Hilarious gravity-fuelled mountain kart luge, woolshed archery and farm-animal feeding are also available. The ranch is 9km west of town at the foot of Mt Fyffe.

Clarence River Rafting RAFTING
(☎03-319 6993; www.clarenceriverrafting.co.nz; 3802 SH1, at Clarence Bridge; 5hr trip adult/child $120/80) The bouncy Grade II rapids of the scenic Clarence River can be rafted on a popular half-day trip, or on longer journeys including a five-day journey with wilderness camping ($1300). The operator's base is on SH1, 40 km north of Kaikoura near Clarence Bridge.

Tours

Tours are big business in Kaikoura. It's all about marine mammals: whales (sperm, pilot, killer, humpback and southern right), dolphins (Hector's, bottlenose and dusky) and NZ fur seals up close. During summer, book your tour a few weeks ahead, and give yourself some leeway to allow for lousy weather.

Whale-Watching

Your choices are boat, plane or helicopter. Aerial options are shorter and pricier, but allow you to see the whole whale, as opposed to just a tail, flipper or spout from a boat.

Kaikoura

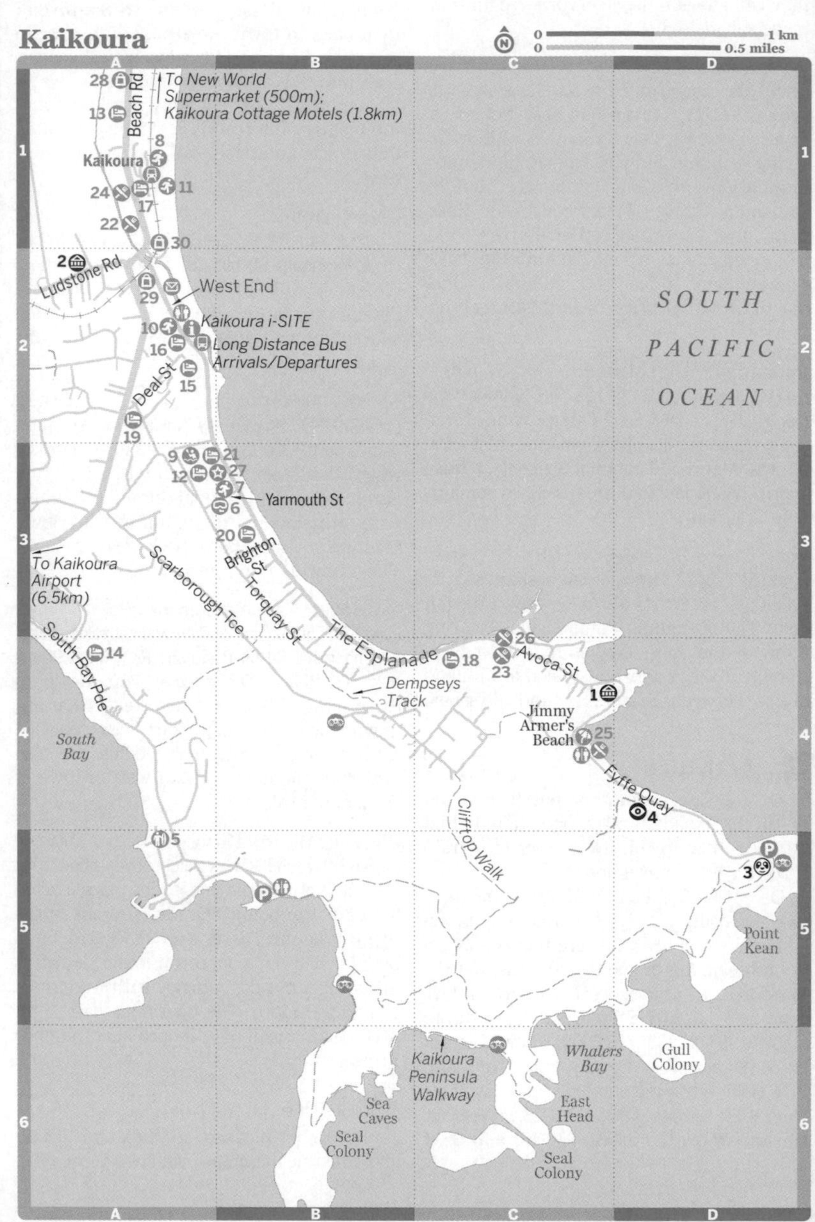

Whale Watch Kaikoura ECOTOUR
(☎03-319 6767, 0800 655 121; www.whalewatch.co.nz; Railway Station; 3hr tour adult/child $145/60) With knowledgeable guides and fascinating 'world of whales' onboard animation, Kaikoura's biggest operator heads out on boat trips (with admirable frequency) to introduce you to some of the big fellers. It'll refund 80% of your fare if no whales are sighted (success rate: 98%). If this trip is a must for you, allow a few days flexibility in case the weather turns to custard.

Kaikoura Helicopters SCENIC FLIGHTS
(☎03-319 6609; www.worldofwhales.co.nz; Railway Station; 15-60min flight from $100-490) Reliable whale-spotting flights (standard tour 30 minutes $220 each for three or more people), plus jaunts around the peninsula, Mt Fyffe and peaks beyond.

Wings Over Whales ECOTOUR
(☎03-319 6580, 0800 226 629; www.whales.co.nz; 30min flight adult/child $165/75) Light-plane flights departing from Kaikoura Airport, 7km south of town. Spotting success rate: 95%.

Dolphin & Seal Spotting

Dolphin Encounter ECOTOUR
(☎03-319 6777, 0800 733 365; www.dolphin.co.nz; 96 Esplanade; swim adult/child $175/160, observation $90/45; ⏲tours 8.30am & 12.30pm year-round, plus 5.30am Nov-Apr) Here's your chance to rub shoulders with pods of dusky dolphins on three-hour tours. Limited numbers, so book in advance.

Seal Swim Kaikoura ECOTOUR
(☎0800 732 579, 03-319 6182; www.sealswimkaikoura.co.nz; 58 West End; tours $70-110; ⏲Oct-May) Two-hour guided snorkelling tours, from shore or boat.

TOP CHOICE **Kaikoura Kayaks** KAYAKING
(☎0800 452 456, 03-319 7118; www.kaikourakayaks.co.nz; 19 Killarney St; seal tours adult/child $95/70; ⏲tours 8.30am, 12.30pm & 4.30pm Nov-Apr, 9am & 1pm May-Oct) Guided sea-kayak tours to view fur seals and explore the peninsula's coastline. Kayaking lessons, freedom hire, family-friendly options and kayak fishing also available.

Birdwatching

Albatross Encounter BIRDWATCHING
(☎03-319 6777, 0800 733 365; www.albatrossencounter.co.nz; 96 Esplanade; adult/child $120/60; ⏲tours 9am & 1pm year-round, plus 6am Nov-Apr) Kaikoura is heaven for bird-nerds, who fly at the opportunity for a close encounter with pelagic species such as shearwaters,

Kaikoura

Sights
1 Fyffe House C4
2 Kaikoura District Museum A2
3 Point Kean Seal Colony D5
4 Point Sheep Shearing Show D4

Activities, Courses & Tours
Albatross Encounter .... (see 7)
5 Board Silly Surf Adventures A5
6 Dive Kaikoura B3
7 Dolphin Encounter B3
8 Kaikoura Helicopters A1
9 Kaikoura Kayaks A3
10 Seal Swim Kaikoura A2
11 Whale Watch Kaikoura A1

Sleeping
12 Albatross Backpacker Inn A3
13 Alpine Pacific Holiday Park A1
14 Bay Cottages A4
15 Dolphin Lodge A2
16 Fish Tank Lodge A2
17 Kaikoura Top 10 Holiday Park A1
18 Maui YHA C4
19 Nikau Lodge A2
20 Sails Motel B3
21 Waves on the Esplanade A3

Eating
Café Encounter .... (see 7)
22 Corianders A1
23 Green Dolphin C4
24 Hislops A1
25 Original Kaikoura Seafood BBQ C4
26 Pier Hotel C4
Reserve Hutt .... (see 10)

Entertainment
27 Mayfair Theatre B3

Shopping
28 Cods & Crayfish A1
29 R&R Sport A2
30 Surf Kaikoura A1

CRAY CRAZY

Among all of Kaikoura's munificent marine life, the one species you just can't avoid is the crayfish, whose delicate flesh dominates local menus. Unfortunately (some say unnecessarily), it's pricey – at a restaurant, you'll shell out (pardon the pun) around $55 for half a cray or over $100 for the whole beast. You can also buy fresh, cooked or uncooked crays from **Cods & Crayfish** (81 Beach Rd; 8am-6pm) and iconic **Nins Bin** (SH1; 8am-6pm), a surf-side caravan 23km north of town. Upwards of $50 should get you a decent specimen.

A good alfresco option is the **Original Kaikoura Seafood BBQ** (Fyffe Quay; 10.30am-early evening), a roadside stall near the peninsula seal colony – the fish or scallop sandwiches (white bread of course) are worthy, affordable substitutes if crayfish doesn't float your boat. Alternatively, take a fishing tour, or buddy-up with a local who might take you crayfishing and share the spoils.

shags, mollymawks, petrels and the inimitable albatross.

Fishing Trips

Fishing is a common obsession in Kaikoura, with local boaties angling for any excuse to go out for a little look-sea. It's a good opportunity to *kai koura* (eat crayfish). Trips start from around $60; the i-SITE has a full list of operators.

Fishing at Kaikoura FISHING
(03-319 3003; gerard.diedrichs@xtra.co.nz) Fishing, crayfishing, scenic tours and waterskiing, on the 6m *Sophie-Rose*.

Kaikoura Fishing Charters FISHING
(03-319 6888, 0800 225 297; www.kaikourafishing.co.nz) Dangle a line from the good ship *Takapu*, then take your filleted, bagged catch home to eat.

Kaikoura Fishing Tours FISHING
(0800 246 6597; www.kaikoura-fishing-tours.co.nz) Serious about scenery and seafood. Your catch is filleted ready for dinner.

Walking Tours

Walks Kaikoura WALKING
(03-319 6617; www.walkskaikoura.com; half-/full day from $95/145) Experienced local guides offering tailored walks around the area, from mountains to coast. Helihikes to mountaintops also possible.

Kaikoura Coast Track WALKING
(03-319 2715; www.kaikouratrack.co.nz; package $215) A three-day, 40km, self-guided walk through private farmland and along the Kaikoura Coast, 43km south of town. The price includes three nights' farm-cottage accommodation and pack transport; BYO sleeping bag and food. A two-day mountain-bike option (BYO bike) costs $85.

Kaikoura Wilderness Walks WALKING
(03-319 6966, 0800 945 337; www.kaikourawilderness.co.nz; 1-/2-night package $1195/1595) Two- or three-day guided walks through the privately owned Puhi Peaks Nature Reserve high in the Seaward Kaikoura range. Package includes accommodation and meals at the luxurious Shearwater Lodge.

Other Tours

Maori Tours Kaikoura CULTURAL TOUR
(0800 866 267, 03-319 5567; www.maoritours.co.nz; 3½hr tour adult/child $125/65; tours 9am & 1.30pm) Fascinating half-day, small-group tours laced with Maori hospitality and local lore. Visit historic sites, hear legends and learn indigenous use of trees and plants. Advance bookings required.

Kaikoura Mountain Safaris DRIVING TOUR
(021 869 643; www.kaikouramountainsafaris.co.nz; half-day tour adult/child $100/55, 1-day tour adult/child $165/100) Journey into the back-country in a 4WD or Unimog – three different tours (departing from the i-SITE) taking in alpine vistas, remote farms and the Clarence River valley.

Festivals & Events

Seafest FOOD & WINE
(www.seafest.co.nz; tickets $35; early Oct) A one-day showcase of piscatorial prowess, plus live bands, family entertainment and a big Friday-night bash to kick things off.

Sleeping

Summer sees accommodation fill up, so book in advance or save your visit for the off-season when reduced rates are in the offing.

Fish Tank Lodge HOSTEL $
(☎03-319 7408; www.fishtanklodge.co.nz; 86 West End; dm/d $25/65; @📶) Nemo meets Michaelangelo at this newly muraled and freshly upgraded hostel in the middle of town. Expect clean, bright and breezy all-round, especially out on the 1st-floor balcony, which enjoys expansive views. Smart management are keen to keep you happy: bike hire and snorkel gear make a good start.

Albatross Backpacker Inn HOSTEL $
(☎0800 222 247, 03-319 6090; www.albatross-kaikoura.co.nz; 1 Torquay St; dm $25-29, s/d $49/69; @📶) This arty backpackers resides in two sweet heritage buildings, one a former post office. It's colourful and close to the beach but sheltered from the breeze. As well as a laid-back lounge, and a separate one for tele-viewers, there are decks and verandas to chill out on.

Dolphin Lodge HOSTEL $
(☎03-319 5842; www.dolphinlodge.co.nz; 15 Deal St; dm $27, d with/without bathroom $67/60; @📶) This small home-away-from-home hostel has onsite managers showing the love and owners visiting often to fuss over their lovely scented garden (hammocks ahoy). Inside is a bit squeezed, but on dry days most of the action will be out on the fantastic deck, or around the barbecue, or in the spa pool...

Maui YHA HOSTEL $
(☎0800 278 299, 03-319 5931; www.yha.co.nz; 270 Esplanade; dm $33, d $89-110, tr $102; @📶) This excellent YHA boasts unimpeded views across the bay to the pine-lined esplanade and mighty peaks beyond. Many rooms enjoy similar views, as does the big-windowed dining room, which you'll find in the same state as the rest of this purpose-built (1962) hostel: tidy, functional and conservatively dressed. Half-/full-day bike hire $20/30.

Alpine Pacific Holiday Park HOLIDAY PARK $
(☎0800 692 322, 03-319 6275; www.alpine-pacific.co.nz; 69 Beach Rd; sites from $40, cabins $75, units & motels $140-180; @📶🏊) This compact and proudly trimmed park copes well with its many visitors, and offers excellent facilities, including a shiny kitchen, resorty pool area and barbecue pavilion. Rows of cabins and units are slightly more stylish than average. Mountain views can be had from many angles.

Kaikoura Top 10 Holiday Park HOLIDAY PARK $
(☎0800 363 638, 03-319 5362; www.kaikoura top10.co.nz; 34 Beach Rd; sites from $44, cabins $80-95, units & motels $150-210; @📶🏊) Hiding from the highway behind a massive hedge, this busy, well-maintained campground offers family-friendly facilities (heated pool, spa, trampoline) and cabins and units to the usual Top 10 standard.

Nikau Lodge B&B
(☎03-319 6973; www.nikaulodge.com; 53 Deal St; d $190-250; @📶) A waggly-tailed welcome awaits at this beautiful B&B high on the hill with grand-scale vistas. Four ensuite rooms are plush and comfy, with additional satisfaction arriving in the form of cafe-quality breakfasts accompanied by fresh local coffee. Good-humour, home-baking, free wi-fi, hot-tub and blooming gardens: you may want to move in.

Bay Cottages MOTEL $$
(☎03-319 5506; www.baycottages.co.nz; 29 South Bay Pde; cottages/motels $100/130) Here's a great value option on South Bay, a few kilometres south of town: five tourist cottages with kitchenette and bathroom sleeping up to four, and two slick motel rooms with stainless-steel benches, low-voltage lighting and flat-screen TVs. The friendly owner may even take you crayfishing in good weather.

Sails Motel MOTEL $$
(☎03-319 6145; www.sailsmotel.co.nz; 134 Esplanade; d $115, q $140; 📶) There are no sea (or sails) views at this motel, so the cherubic owners have to impress with quality. Their four secluded, tastefully appointed self-contained units are down a driveway in a garden setting (private outdoor areas abound).

Kaikoura Cottage Motels MOTEL $$
(☎0800 526 882, 03-319 5599; www.kaikoura cottagemotels.co.nz; cnr Old Beach & Mill Rds; d $120-140; 📶) This enclave of eight modern tourist flats is looking mighty fine, surrounded by attractive native plantings now in full flourish. Oriented for mountain views, the self-contained units sleep four between an open plan studio-style living room and one private bedroom. Soothing sand-and-sky colour scheme and quality chattels.

TOP CHOICE Dylan's Country Cottages COTTAGES $$
(☎03-319 5473; www.lavenderfarm.co.nz; 268 Postmans Rd; d $175; ⊙closed May-Aug;) On the grounds of the delightful Kaikoura Lavender Farm, northwest of town, these two self-contained cottages make for an aromatic escape from the seaside fray. One has a private outdoor bath and a shower emerging from a tree; the other an indoor spa and handkerchief lawn. Homemade scones, preserves and free-range eggs for breakfast. Sweet, stylish and romantic.

Waves on the Esplanade APARTMENT $$$
(☎0800 319 589, 03-319 5890; www.kaikouraapartments.co.nz; 78 Esplanade; apt $240-350;) Can't do without the comforts of home? Here you go: spacious, luxury two-bedroom apartments with Sky TV, DVD player, two bathrooms, laundry facilities and full kitchen. Oh, and superb ocean views from the balcony. Rates are for up to four people.

The Factory B&B $$$
(☎03-319 3034; www.hapukufactory.com; 5 Old Beach Rd, Hapuku; d incl breakfast $480;) About 10 minutes' drive north of Kaikoura in the cute beach settlement of Hapuku is this 100-year-old dairy factory, divinely converted and bejewelled with designer furniture. The guest wing is fully self-contained and sleeps up to six, although it looks like honeymoon heaven. One night will never be enough.

Eating & Drinking

Kaikoura has some very good cafes and restaurants, and some that are well-past their use-by date.

Green Dolphin SEAFOOD $$$
(☎03-319 6666; www.greendolphinkaikoura.com; 12 Avoca St; mains $25-46; ⊙5pm-late) Quality Kaikoura fish multiple ways, and the omnipresent bovine, porcine and lobstery treats, all made with care and a fondness for good local produce. On busy nights, book ahead or nurse a cocktail or aperitif in the pleasant bar or garden. Those with foresight should plump for a table with a view by the floor-to-ceiling windows.

Hislops CAFE $$
(33 Beach Rd; lunch $9-24, dinner $22-37; ⊙9am-late, closed Tue & Wed May-Sep;) This snappy, feel-good cafe maintains its reputation for fresh, wholesome food. Start the morning with a guilt-free fry-up, then come back at night for organic meats plus local seafood, veg and vegan choices. Notable salads, such as goats feta and avocado.

Pier Hotel MODERN NZ $$
(www.thepierhotel.co.nz; 1 Avoca St; snacks $7-18, mains $24-34; ⊙11am-late) Wide views of bay and the mountains beyond make this the grandest dining room in town. A cheerful crew serves up generous portions of honest food, such as fresh local fish, baby back spare ribs and bbq crayfish for those with fat wallets. The enticing public bar has reasonably priced beer and bar snacks, historical photos and a garden bar. Upstairs lodgings are worn and creaky, but good value (double room, including breakfast, from $115).

Café Encounter CAFE $
(96 Esplanade; meals $8-19; ⊙7.30am-5pm;) Housed in the Dolphin Encounter complex, this cafe is more than just somewhere to wait for your trip. Great counter food and coffee, plus cakes, pastries, bagels, toasties and daily specials, such as braised pork belly and fennel slaw. Ocean and esplanade views from the sunny patio.

Reserve Hutt CAFE $
(72 West End; meals $10-18) The best coffee in the town centre, roasted on site and espressed by dedicated baristas in Kaikoura's grooviest cafe. Puttin' out that rootsy retro-Kiwiana vibe we love so much, this is a neat place to linger over a couple of flatties and down a muffin, delicious ham croissant or the full eggy brunch.

Corianders INDIAN $$
(17 Beach Rd; mains $14-20;) Spicing up Kaikoura life, this branch of the Corianders chain keeps the bar raised with dependable Indian food in a pleasant environment. The epic menu has all your favourites and some you've never heard of. Excellent *pakora*, good breads and extensive vegie options.

New World Supermarket SUPERMARKET
(124-128 Beach Rd; ⊙7.30am-9pm) Ten minutes' walk from the town centre.

Entertainment

Mayfair Theatre CINEMA
(☎03-319 5859; 80 Esplanade; adult/child $10/6) Resembling a pink liquorice allsort, this seafront picture house screens almost-recent releases.

Information

Kaikoura i-SITE (☎03-319 5641; www.kaikoura.co.nz; West End; ⌚9am-5pm Mon-Fri, to 4pm Sat & Sun, extended hours Dec-Mar) Helpful staff make tour, accommodation and transport bookings, and help with DOC-related matters.

Coffee Hit (22 Beach Rd; wi-fi) Free wi-fi when you buy a cup or two of top-notch espresso served to you by Mr Good Guy from his coffee caravan right on SH1. Choice.

Paperplus/Post Office (☎03-319 6808; 41 West End) Postal agent.

Getting There & Away

Bus

InterCity (☎03-365 1113; www.intercity.co.nz) buses run between Kaikoura and Nelson (from $49, 3½ hours), Picton (from $17, 2¼ hours) and Christchurch (from $15, 2¾ hours). The bus stop is at the car park next to the i-SITE (tickets and info inside).

Naked Bus (☎0900 625 33; www.nakedbus.com) also runs to/from Kaikoura to most South Island destinations, departing from the i-SITE. Book online or at the i-SITE; cheaper fares for advance bookings.

Train

Tranz Scenic (☎0800 872 467, 04-495 0775; www.tranzscenic.co.nz) runs the *Coastal Pacific* service, stopping at Kaikoura on its daily run between Picton (from $59, 2¼ hours) and Christchurch (from $59, three hours). The northbound train departs Kaikoura at 9.54am; the southbound at 3.28pm.

Getting Around

Hire bicycles from R&R Sport (p71). Surf Kaikoura and Maui YHA also hire bikes.

Kaikoura Shuttles (☎03-319 6166; www.kaikourashuttles.co.nz) will run you around the local sights as well as to and from the airport.

NELSON REGION

The Nelson region, centred upon Tasman Bay but stretching north to Golden Bay and Farewell Spit, and south to Nelson Lakes, is a popular travel destination for both international visitors and locals. It's not hard to see why. Not only does it boast three national parks (Kahurangi, Nelson Lakes and Abel Tasman), but it can also satisfy nearly every other whim, from food, wine and beer to art, craft and festivals, to that most precious of pastimes for which the region is well known: lazing about in the sunshine.

Nelson

POP 60,800

Dishing up a winning combination of great weather and beautiful surroundings, Nelson is hailed as one of New Zealand's most 'liveable' cities. In summer it fills up with local and international visitors, who lap up its offerings, including proximity to diverse natural attractions.

Sights

Nelson has an inordinate number of galleries, most of which are listed in the *Art & Crafts Nelson City* brochure (with walking-trail map) available from the i-SITE. A fruitful wander can be had by starting at the **Fibre Spectrum** (www.fibrespectrum.co.nz; 280 Trafalgar St), where you can pick up hand-woven woollens, before moving on to 'Lord of the Ring' jeweller **Jens Hansen** (www.jenshansen.com; 320 Trafalgar Sq), glassblower **Flamedaisy** (www.flamedaisy.com; 324 Trafalgar Sq), then around the corner to the home of Nelson pottery, **South Street Gallery** (www.nelsonpottery.co.nz; 10 Nile St W). More interesting local creations can be found at the **Nelson Market** (Montgomery Sq; ⌚8am-1pm Sat) on Saturday.

Christ Church Cathedral CHURCH
(www.nelsoncathedral.org; Trafalgar Sq; admission free; ⌚8am-7pm Nov-Mar, to 5pm Apr-Oct) The enduring symbol of Nelson, the art-deco Christ Church Cathedral lords it over the city from the top of Trafalgar St. Work began in 1925, but this architectural hybrid wasn't completed until 1965.

Nelson Provincial Museum MUSEUM
(www.nelsonmuseum.co.nz; cnr Hardy & Trafalgar Sts; admission from adult/child $5/3; ⌚10am-5pm Mon-Fri, 10am-4.30pm Sat & Sun) This modern museum space is filled with cultural heritage and natural history exhibits with a regional bias, as well as regular touring exhibitions (admission price varies). It also features a great rooftop garden.

Suter GALLERY
(www.thesuter.org.nz; 208 Bridge St; adult/child $3/50c, free on Sat; ⌚10.30am-4.30pm) Adjacent to Queen's Gardens, Nelson's public art gallery presents changing exhibitions, floor talks, musical and theatrical performances, and films. It also houses a small but good art store and a popular cafe.

Central Nelson

Founders Heritage Park MUSEUM
(www.founderspark.co.nz; 87 Atawhai Dr; adult/child/family $7/5/15; ⏲10am-4.30pm) Two kilometres from the city centre, this park comprises a replica historic village with a bakery, chocolatier and museums. It makes for a fascinating wander, which you can augment with a visit to the onsite **Founders Brewery & Café** (www.foundersbrewery.co.nz; meals $11-15), NZ's first certified organic brewery, where you can get brunch and wood-fired pizza. Tastings are $10; a 'backpacker special' grants park entry plus a tasting of three beers for $12.

Miyazu Japanese Garden GARDENS
(Atawhai Dr) This serene garden is full of sculptures, lanterns and ducks on placid ponds. Sit for a while and ponder something profound.

Botanical Reserve PARK
(Milton St) Walking tracks ascend Botanical Hill, where a spire proclaims it the 'Centre of New Zealand'. NZ's first-ever rugby match was played at the foot of the hill on 14 May 1870. Nelson Rugby Football Club trounced the lily-livered players from Nelson College 2-0.

Activities

Nelson offers boundless opportunities to embrace the great outdoors.

Walking & Cycling

There's plenty of walking and cycling to be enjoyed in and around the town, for which the i-SITE has maps. The classic walk from town is to the top of the Botanical Reserve, while the new **Dun Mountain Trail** network ranging over the hills to the south of the city centre has lots of interesting options and supberb riding for fit, keen mountain bikers.

Central Nelson

Top Sights

Suter D2

Sights

1 Christ Church Cathedral B4
2 Fibre Spectrum B3
3 Flamedaisy Glass Design B3
4 Jens Hansen B3
5 Nelson Provincial Museum B3
6 South Street Gallery A4

Activities, Courses & Tours

7 Stewarts Avanti Plus Nelson A3
8 UBike C1

Sleeping

9 Accents on the Park B3
10 Almond House D1
11 Lynton Lodge A4
12 Nelson YHA A2
13 Palazzo Motor Lodge A4
14 South Street Cottages A4
15 Trampers Rest D4

Eating

16 DeVille B2
17 Falafel Gourmet B3
18 Ford's B3
19 Hopgood's B3
20 Indian Café C2
21 Organic Greengrocer D1
22 Penguino Ice Cream Café B2
Stefano's .... (see 27)
23 Swedish Bakery & Café B2

Drinking

24 Free House C2
25 Sprig & Fern C3
26 Vic B3

Entertainment

27 State Cinema 6 .... B2
28 Theatre Royal A2

Shopping

29 Nelson Farmers' Market C3
30 Nelson Market A2

UBike CYCLING
(☎0800 282 453; www.ubike.co.nz; Collingwood St Bridge; half-/full day from $40/60) A short walk from the i-SITE, UBike hires city and mountain bikes from its caravan. Trail maps and tips, plus espresso to get you going.

Biking Nelson MOUNTAIN BIKING
(☎0800 224 532, 021 861 725; www.bikingnelson.co.nz; 3hr guided ride $115, bike hire half-/full day $45/65) Hit the hillside mountain-bike trails with Dave and company, who run guided rides (all gear provided) and offer freedom rental and advice.

Paragliding, Hang Gliding & Kiteboarding

Nelson is a great place to get airborne. Most operators are some way out of town, but will pick-up or drop-off in Nelson.

Tandem paragliding costs around $180, while introductory courses are around $250. Tandem hang gliding is around $185, and introductory kiteboarding starts at $150.

Nelson Paragliding PARAGLIDING
(☎03-544 1182, 0508 359 669; www.nelsonparagliding.co.nz)

Adventure Paragliding & Kiteboarding PARAGLIDING, KITEBOARDING
(☎03-540 2183, 0800 212 359; www.skyout.co.nz)

Cumulus Paragliding PARAGLIDING
(☎03-929 5515; www.tandem-paragliding.co.nz)

Kitescool KITEBOARDING
(☎021 354 837; www.kitescool.co.nz)

Kite Surf Nelson KITEBOARDING
(☎0800 548 363; www.kitesurfnelson.co.nz)

Nelson Hang Gliding Adventures HANG GLIDING
(☎03-548 9151; www.flynelson.co.nz)

Hang Gliding New Zealand HANG GLIDING
(☎03-540 2183, 0800 212 359; www.hanggliding.co.nz; flight $180)

Other Activities

TOP CHOICE **Nelson Bonecarving** CARVING
(☎03-546 4275; www.carvingbone.co.nz; 87 Green St, Tahunanui; full-day course $79) Admirers of Maori design will love Stephan's acclaimed bonecarving course. He'll supply all materials, tools, instruction, encouragement and cups of tea (plus free pick-up/drop-off in town if needed); you supply inspiration and talent and you'll emerge with your very own bone carving.

Happy Valley Adventures ADVENTURE SPORTS
(☎03-545 0304, 0800 157 300; www.happyvalleyadventures.co.nz; 194 Cable Bay Rd; Skywire adult/

child $85/55, quad bike tours from $80, horse trek $95) Dangle 150m above the forest in the 'Skywire' (a chairlift/flying-fox hybrid), then soar through the air for its 1.65km length. If that ain't enough, take a quad-bike tour, or if it's too much, try a 2½-hour horse trek. Or just have coffee and cake in the cafe – a 15-minute drive northeast of Nelson along SH6.

Cable Bay Kayaks KAYAKING
(☎0508 222 532, 03-545 0332; www.cablebaykayaks.co.nz; Cable Bay Rd; half-/full day guided trip $85/145) Fifteen minutes' drive from Nelson city, Nick and Jenny offer guided sea-kayaking trips exploring the local coastline where you'll likely meet local marine life (snorkelling gear on board) and may even enter a cave.

Tours

Bay Tours GUIDED TOUR
(☎0800 229 868, 03-548 6486; www.baytoursnelson.co.nz; half-/full-day tours from $89/144) Nelson city, region, wine, beer, food and art tours. The full-day scenic tour includes a visit to Kaiteriteri and a cruise in Abel Tasman National Park.

JJ's Quality Tours GUIDED TOUR
(☎0800 229 868, 03-548 6486; www.jjstours.co.nz; tours from $89) Scenic, wine-focused and craft tours, plus a half-day brewery trail.

Wine, Art & Wilderness GUIDED TOUR
(☎03-539 4477, 0800 326 868; www.wineartandwildernesstours.co.nz; tours from $214) Upmarket wine, scenic and nature tours around Nelson, Marlborough, Golden Bay and the West Coast.

Simply Wild GUIDED TOUR
(☎03-548 8500; www.simplywild.co.nz) A swathe of half- to five-day active wilderness adventures: walking, mountain biking, sailing, caving, rafting and canoeing around Nelson's national parks. Prices on application.

Festivals & Events

For current info on Nelson's active events program, visit www.itson.co.nz.

Nelson Jazz & Blues Festival MUSIC
(www.nelsonjazzfest.co.nz) More than 50 scoobedoobop events over a week in January. Local and international acts in halls and on street corners, regionwide.

Nelson Arts Festival
(www.nelsonfestivals.co.nz) Over two weeks in October; events include a street carnival, exhibitions, cabaret, writers, theatre and music.

Sleeping

Accents on the Park HOSTEL $
(☎03-548 4335, 0800 888 335; www.accentsonthepark.com; 335 Trafalgar Sq; sites $30, dm $20-28, d with/without bathroom from $92/60; @☎) This perfectly positioned hostel has a hotel feel with its professional staff, balconies, groovy cafe-bar (meals around $15), movie nights with free popcorn, free daily bread and wi-fi, soundproofed rooms, quality linen, fresh bathrooms and bikes for hire. Bravo! (Book early.)

Bug Backpackers HOSTEL $
(☎03-539 4227; www.thebug.co.nz; 226 Vanguard St; dm $25-28, d $66-80; @☎) A fresh, excellent hostel about 15 minutes' walk from town, occupying a converted villa and a modern building next door. The Bug emits joie de vivre, with an unashamedly bold colour scheme and a swarm of cutesy VW Beetle paraphernalia. Quality beds, nice kitchens, girls' dorm and a homely backyard. Free bikes and pick-up/drop-offs.

Tasman Bay Backpackers HOSTEL $
(☎03-548 7950, 0800 222 572; www.tasmanbaybackpackers.co.nz; 10 Weka St; sites from $18, dm $25-27, d $66-85; @☎) Typical of Nelson's breed of quality backpackers, this well-designed hostel has airy communal spaces, hyper-coloured rooms, a sunny outdoor deck and a well-used hammock. Good freebies: bikes, breakfast during winter, and chocolate pudding and ice cream year-round.

Trampers Rest HOSTEL $
(☎03-545 7477; 31 Alton St; dm/s/d $29/46/66; @☎) With just a few beds (no bunks), the tiny but much-loved Trampers is hard to beat for a homely environment. The enthusiastic owner is a keen tramper and cyclist, and provides comprehensive local information and free bikes. It has a small kitchen, a book exchange, and a piano for evening singalongs.

Almond House HOSTEL $
(☎03-545 6455; www.almondbackpackers.co.nz; 63 Grove St; dm/s/d $29/46/68; @☎) Stylish and homely addition to Nelson's collection of quality backpackers. Four-bed dorms and

THE WONDROUS WORLD OF WEARABLE ART

Nelson exudes creativity, so it's hardly surprising that NZ's most inspiring fashion show was born here. It began humbly in 1987 when creator Suzie Moncrieff held a local off-beat fashion show. The concept was to create a piece of art that could be worn and modelled. The idea caught on, and the World of WearableArt Awards Show became an annual event. Wood, papier mâché, paua shell, earplugs, soft-drink cans, ping-pong balls and more have been used to create garments; 'Bizarre Bra' entries are showstoppers.

The awards show has been transplanted to Wellington, but you can ogle entries at Nelson's **World of WearableArt & Classic Cars Museum** (WOW; ☎03-547 4573; www.wowcars.co.nz; 1 Cadillac Way; adult/child $22/8; ⏲10am-5pm). High-tech galleries include a carousel mimicking a catwalk, and a glow-in-the-dark room.

More car than bra? Under the same roof are 50 mint-condition classic cars and motorbikes. Exhibits change, but may include a 1959 pink Cadillac, a yellow 1950 Bullet Nose Studebaker convertible and a BMW bubble car. You can view another 70 vehicles in *The Classic Collection* next door ($8 extra). Cafe and art gallery on-site.

double rooms are decked out with colourful local art and quality linen, while the friendly vibe makes you feel like part of the family. Free internet and bikes.

Shortbread Cottage HOSTEL **$**
(☎03-546 6681; www.shortbreadcottage.co.nz; 33 Trafalgar St; dm/s/d $26/60/60; @📶) This renovated 100-year-old villa has room for only a dozen or so beds but it's packed with charm and hospitality. It offers free internet, fresh-baked bread, and shortbread on arrival. It's also only a stone's throw from the town centre.

Nelson YHA HOSTEL **$**
(☎03-545 9988; www.yha.co.nz; 59 Rutherford St; dm/s/d from $28/60/86, d with bathroom $100; @📶) A tidy, purpose-built, central hostel with high-quality facilities including a soundproof TV room (free DVDs), two well-organised kitchens and a sunny outdoor terrace. Solid service on tour and activity bookings.

Paradiso Backpackers HOSTEL **$**
(☎0800 269 667, 03-546 6703; www.backpackernelson.co.nz; 42 Weka St; sites from $18, dm $25-29, d $66; @📶🏊) Club Med for the impoverished, Paradiso is a sprawling place that lures a backpacker-body-beautiful crowd to its poolside terrace. There are two kitchens, hammocks, volleyball court, spa and sauna. Bikes for hire ($15 per day).

Tahuna Beach Accommodation Park HOLIDAY PARK **$**
(☎03-548 5159, 0800 500 501; www.tahunabeach.co.nz; 70 Beach Rd; sites/cabins/units from $17/50/110; @📶) A few minutes' walk from the beach, 5km from the city, this huge park is home to thousands in high summer, which you'll find hellish or bloody brilliant, depending on your mood. During the shoulder season, you'll have the minigolf mostly to yourself.

Palazzo Motor Lodge MOTELS **$$**
(☎03-545 8171, 0800 472 5293; www.palazzomotorlodge.co.nz; 159 Rutherford St; studios $130-225, apt $225-390; @📶) Hosts with the most offer a cheerful welcome at this popular, modern, Italian-tinged motor lodge. The stylish studios and one- and two-room apartments feature enviable kitchens with decent cooking equipment, classy wineglasses and a dishwasher. The odd bit of dubious art is easily forgiven, particularly as Doris' sausage is available for breakfast.

Te Maunga House B&B **$$**
(☎03-548 8605; www.nelsoncityaccommodation.co.nz; 15 Dorothy Annie Way; s $90, d $100-135; @📶) Aptly named ('the mountain'), this is a grand old family home on a knoll with exceptional views. Two doubles and a single, with their own bathrooms, are filled with characterful furniture and made up with good linens. Your hearty breakfast can be walked off up and down *that* hill. It's only a 10-minute climb (15 minutes in all, from town), but only the leggy ones will revel in it. Closed from May to September.

Nelson City Holiday Park HOLIDAY PARK **$**
(☎03-548 1445, 0800 778 898; www.nelsonholidaypark.co.nz; 230 Vanguard St; sites $40, cabins & units $60-120; @📶) The closest option to town: convenient, well-maintained, clean, but cramped

(although the motel units are pretty good). Limited campsites by the creek out back.

Lynton Lodge LODGE $$
(☎03-548 7112; www.lyntonlodge.co.nz; 25 Examiner St; apt $95-130; 📶) On the hill near the cathedral and with city views, unashamedly dated Lynton Lodge offers self-contained apartments and a guesthouse vibe – try for one of the balcony units. Affable hosts, grassy garden and super-close to town.

South Street Cottages RENTAL HOUSE $$$
(☎03-540 2769; www.cottageaccommodation.co.nz; South St; d from $225) Stay on NZ's oldest preserved street in one of several endearing, two-bedroom self-contained cottages built in the 1860s. Each has all the comforts of home, including kitchen, laundry and courtyard garden; breakfast provisions supplied. There is a two-night minimum stay.

Eating

Nelson has a lively cafe scene as well as a varied array of restaurants. Self-caterers should steer resolutely towards the fruitful Nelson Market (p77) on Saturday and the **Farmers Market** (Fashion Island, cnr Morrison & Hardy Sts ; ⏰12pm–4.30pm Wed) on Wednesday.

DeVille CAFE $$
(22 New St; meals $13-20; ⏰9am-4pm Mon-Sat; 🥕) Most of DeVille's tables lie in its sweet walled courtyard, a hidden boho oasis in the inner city and the perfect place for a meal or morning tea. The food's good – from fresh baked goods to the eggy brunch, caesar salad and sticky pork sandwich. Open late for live music Friday and Saturday in summer.

Stefano's PIZZERIA $
(☎03-546 7530; 91 Trafalgar St; pizzas $6-29; ⏰lunch & dinner; 🥕) Located upstairs in the State Cinema complex, this Italian-run joint turns out some of NZ's best pizza. Thin, crispy and delicious, and some variations really very cheap. Wash it down with a beer or wine in the ambience-free interior or out on the tiny balcony.

Swedish Bakery & Café BAKERY $
(54 Bridge St; snacks $2-7; ⏰8.30am-3.30pm Mon-Fri, 9am-1.30pm Sat) Delicious breads, pastries, cakes and small chocolate treats from the resident Scandinavian baker. Lovely fresh filled rolls such as meatball and beetroot salad. Take your goodies away or eat in the bijou cafe.

Indian Café INDIAN $$
(94 Collingwood St; mains $16-21; ⏰lunch Mon-Fri, dinner daily; 🥕) This saffron-coloured Edwardian villa houses an Indian restaurant that keeps the *bhaji* raised with impressive interpretations of Anglo-Indian standards, such as chicken tandoori, rogan josh and beef madras. Share the mixed platter to start, then mop up your mains with one of 10 different breads.

Hopgood's MODERN NZ $$$
(☎03-545 7191; 284 Trafalgar St; mains $34-37; ⏰5.30pm-late Mon-Sat) Tongue-and-groove-lined Hopgood's is perfect for a romantic dinner or holiday treat. The food is decadent and skilfully prepared but unfussy, allowing quality local ingredients to shine. The Asian crispy duck followed by twice-cooked pork belly with butter beans, spinach and bacon are knockouts. Desirable, predominantly Kiwi wine list. Bookings advisable.

Penguino Ice Cream Café ICE CREAM $
(Montgomery Sq; ice creams $4-7; ⏰noon-5pm) Indulge yourself with superb gelato and sorbet, from traditional vanilla and boysenberry to apple pie and beyond. Next day, visit for a shake, fruit smoothie, sundae, mango lassi...

Ford's MODERN NZ $$
(www.fordsnelson.co.nz; 276 Trafalgar St; lunch $16-22; ⏰from 8am) Sunny pavement tables at the top of Trafalgar Street make this a popular lunchtime spot, as does the chef-owner's menu of modern classics such as the excellent seafood chowder, steak sandwich on sourdough, and tuna niçoise. Make a short stop for coffee and a scone, or linger over dinner which leaps up a tenner.

Falafel Gourmet MIDDLE EASTERN $
(195 Hardy St; meals $9-23; 🥕) A cranking joint dishing out the best kebabs in town, full of salad.

Haven Fish & Chips FISH & CHIPS $
(268 Wakefield Quay; fish & chips $8-10; ⏰11.30am-1.30pm & 4.30-8pm) Pick your own fillet, then eat your meal by the waterfront. What could be better?

Organic Greengrocer FOOD, DRINK $
(cnr Tasman & Grove Sts; ⏰9am-6pm Mon-Fri, to 3pm Sat; 🥕) Stocks foods for the sensitive, plus produce, organic tipples and natural bodycare. Food to go and coffee also on offer.

IN PURSUIT OF HOPPINESS

The Nelson region lays claim to the title of craft-brewing capital of New Zealand. With world-class hops grown here since the 1840s, and a dozen breweries spread between Nelson and Golden Bay, it's got a pretty good case.

Pick up a copy of the *Nelson Craft Beer Trail* map (available from the i-SITE and other outlets, and online at www.craftbrewingcapital.co.nz) and wind your way between brewers and pubs. Top picks for a tipple include the Free House (p429), the Moutere Inn (p432), Golden Bear (p432), and the Mussel Inn (p444).

Drinking

Nelson's got a bad (read: good) case of craft-beer fever, so if your budget allows it, hoppiness awaits. Cheaper thrills can be found at numerous establishments clustered on Bridge St towards the intersection with Collingwood. If you're out late, walk home with a friend.

Free House CRAFT BEER
(www.freehouse.co.nz; 95 Collingwood St) Come rejoice at this church of ales. Tastefully converted from its original, more reverent purpose, it's now home to an excellent, oft-changing selection of NZ craft beers. You can imbibe inside or out. Hallelujah.

Sprig & Fern CRAFT BEER
(www.sprigandfern.co.nz; 280 Hardy St) The Sprig & Fern brewery in Richmond supplies an extensive range of beers to S&F pubs springing up around the region. Around 20 brews on tap, from lager through to doppelbock and berry cider. No pokies, no TV, just decent beer, occasional live music and a pleasant outdoor area. Pizzas can be ordered in.

Vic PUB
(www.vicbrewbar.co.nz; 281 Trafalgar St) A commendable example of a Mac's Brewbar, with trademark, quirky Kiwiana fit-out, including a striped, knitted stag's head. Quaff a few handles of ale, maybe grab a bite to eat (mains $10 to $30) and tap a toe to regular live music, including Tuesday night jazz. Good afternoon sun and people-watching from streetside seating.

☆ Entertainment

Theatre Royal THEATRE
(☎03-548 3840; www.theatreroyalnelson.co.nz; 78 Rutherford St) Joan Rivers, eat your heart out, because the 'grand old lady of Nelson' (aged 134) has just had the face lift to end all face lifts. If you love heritage buildings and the performing arts, visit **Everyman Records** (249 Hardy St), find out what she's showing and book a ticket.

State Cinema 6 CINEMA
(☎03-548 3885; www.statecinema6.co.nz; 91 Trafalgar St) This is the place to see mainstream, new-release flicks.

Information

Banks and ATMs pepper Trafalgar St.

After Hours & Duty Doctors (☎03-546 8881; 96 Waimea Rd; ⊙8am-10pm)

Nelson i-SITE (☎03-548 2304; www.nelsonnz.com; cnr Trafalgar & Halifax Sts; ⊙8.30am-5pm Mon-Fri, 9am-5pm Sat & Sun; @) A slick centre complete with DOC information desk for the low-down on national parks and walks (including Abel Tasman and Heaphy tracks). Pick up a copy of the *Nelson Tasman Visitor Guide*.

Police Station (☎03-546 3840; cnr St John & Harley Sts)

Post Office (www.nzpost.co.nz; 209 Hardy St)

Nelson Hospital (☎03-546 1800; www.nmdhb.govt.nz; Waimea Rd)

Getting There & Away

Air

Air New Zealand (☎03-546 3100, 0800 737 000; www.airnewzealand.co.nz; cnr Trafalgar & Bridge Sts; ⊙9am-5pm Mon-Fri) has direct flights to/from Wellington (from $79), Auckland (from $99) and Christchurch (from $79).

Soundsair (☎03-520 3080, 0800 505 005; www.soundsair.com) flies daily between Nelson and Wellington (from $107).

Air2there (p70) flies between Nelson and Paraparaumu on the Kapiti Coast ($135).

Bus

Book Abel Tasman Coachlines, InterCity, Tranz Scenic and Interisland ferries at the **Nelson SBL Travel Centre** (☎03-548 1539; www.nelsoncoaches.co.nz; 27 Bridge St).

Also based here are **Abel Tasman Coachlines** (☎03-548 0285; www.abeltasmantravel.co.nz; 27

Bridge St, departs SLB Travel Centre), operating services to Motueka ($12, one hour), Takaka ($35, two hours), Kaiteriteri and Marahau (both $20, two hours). These services also connect with Golden Bay Coachlines (p96) services for Takaka and around. Transport to/from the three national parks is provided by **Trek Express** (☎0800 128 735; www.trekexpress.co.nz).

Atomic Shuttles (☎03-349 0697; www.atomictravel.co.nz) runs from Nelson to Picton ($25, 2¼ hours), and daily to West Coast centres like Greymouth ($54, 5¾ hours) and Fox Glacier ($78, 9½ hours). Services can be booked at (and depart from) Nelson i-SITE.

InterCity (☎03-548 1538; www.intercity.co.nz; Bridge St, departs SLB Travel Centre) runs from Nelson to most key South Island destinations including Picton (from $18, two hours), Kaikoura (from $49, 3½ hours), Christchurch (from $54, seven hours) and Greymouth (from $40, six hours).

Getting Around

To/From the Airport

Nelson Airport is 6km southwest of town, near Tahunanui Beach. A taxi from there to town will cost around about $25, or **Super Shuttle** (☎03-522 5100, 0800 748 885; www.supershuttle.co.nz) offers door-to-door service for $21 (additional passengers $17).

Bicycle

Hire a bike from **Stewarts Avanti Plus Nelson** (☎03-548 1666; www.avantiplusnelson.co.nz; 114 Hardy St; hire per day $30-95, per week from $140) or UBike (p79).

Bus

Nelson Suburban Bus Lines (SBL; ☎03-548 3290; www.nelsoncoaches.co.nz; 27 Bridge St, departs SLB Travel Centre, Bridge St) operates NBUS, the local service between Nelson, Richmond via Tahunanui and Stoke until about 7pm weekdays, 4.30pm on weekends. It also runs the **Late Late Bus** (hourly 10pm-3am Fri & Sat) from Nelson to Richmond via Tahunanui, departing from the Westpac Bank on Trafalgar St. Maximum fare for these services is $4.

Taxi

Nelson City Taxis (☎03-548 8225, 0800 108 855)

Sun City Taxis (☎03-548 2666, 0800 422 666)

Nelson Lakes National Park

Pristine Nelson Lakes National Park surrounds two lakes – Rotoiti and Rotoroa – fringed by sweet-smelling beech forest with a backdrop of greywacke mountains. Located at the northern end of the Southern Alps, and with a dramatic glacier-carved landscape, it's an awe-inspiring place to get up on high.

Part of the park, east of Lake Rotoiti, is classed as a 'mainland island' where a conservation scheme aims to eradicate introduced pests (possums, stoats), and regenerate native flora and fauna. It offers excellent tramping, including short walks, lake scenery and one or two sandflies... The park is flush with bird life, and is famous for brown-trout fishing.

Activities

Many spectacular walks allow you to appreciate this rugged landscape, but before you tackle them, stop by the DOC Visitor Centre for maps and track/weather updates, to leave intentions and to pay your hut or camping fees.

The five-hour **Mt Robert Circuit Track** starts south of St Arnaud and circumnavigates the mountain, with options for a side trip along Robert Ridge. Alternatively, the **St Arnaud Range Track** (five hours return), on the east side of the lake, climbs steadily to the ridgeline via Parachute Rocks. Both tracks are strenuous, but reward with jaw-dropping views of glaciated valleys, arête peaks and Lake Rotoiti. Only attempt these walks in fine weather. At other times they are both pointless (no views) and dangerous.

There are also plenty of shorter (and flatter) walks starting from Lake Rotoiti's Kerr Bay and the road end at Lake Rotoroa. These and the longer day tramps in the park are described in DOC's *Walks in Nelson Lakes National Park* pamphlet ($2).

The fit and well-equipped can enjoy the **Lake Angelus Routes**, including a magnificent overnight (or three-day) tramp along Robert Ridge to Lake Angelus. Stay at the fine Angelus Hut (adult/child $20/10) before returning to St Arnaud via one of three routes. Pick up or download DOC's *Angelus Hut Tracks & Routes* pamphlet ($2) for more details.

Sleeping & Eating

DOC Campsites CAMPSITE **$**
(☎03-521 1806; www.doc.govt.nz; Kerr Bay sites from $10, West Bay $6) Located on the shores of Lake Rotoiti at Kerr Bay, this inviting and hugely popular site has toilets, hot showers, a laundry and a kitchen. Three kilometres from St Arnaud, West Bay campsite has the bare necessities and is open in summer only.

Bookings are essential over the Christmas and Easter holidays.

Travers-Sabine Lodge LODGE $
(☎03-521 1887; www.nelsonlakes.co.nz; Main Rd; dm/d $26/62; @📶) This modern lodge is a great base for outdoor adventure, being a short walk to Lake Rotoiti, inexpensive, clean and comfortable. It also has particularly cheerful technicolour linen in the dorms, doubles and a family room. The owners are experienced adventurers themselves, so tips come as standard; tramping equipment and snowshoes available for hire.

Nelson Lakes Motels MOTEL $$
(☎03-521 1887; www.nelsonlakes.co.nz; Main Rd; d $115-135; @📶) These log cabins and newer board-and-batten units offer all the creature comforts, including kitchenettes and Sky TV. Bigger units sleep up to six.

Alpine Lodge LODGE $$
(☎03-521 1869; www.alpinelodge.co.nz; Main Rd; d $150-205; @📶) Trying its darnedest to create an alpine mood, this lodge has a a range of accommodation, the pick of which are the split-level doubles with mezzanine bedroom, spa and pine timberwork aplenty. The adjacent backpacker lodge (dorm/double $27/69) is spartan but clean and warm. The in-house restaurant is snug, with mountain views, and serves very good food (meals $10 to $29). Long may the Sunday night barbecue continue.

Tophouse Historic Hotel HISTORIC HOTEL $$
(☎0800 544 545, 03-521 1848; www.tophouse.co.nz; Tophouse Rd; s/d $110/135, lunch $10-18) Nine kilometres from St Arnaud, this 1887 hotel retells fireside tales, tall and true. A good stop for refreshments (cake and coffee, wild game pies, and a $49 four-course dinner, for which bookings are essential), Tophouse also boasts New Zealand's smallest bar and a garden with mountain views. There are old-fashioned rooms within the hotel, and four chalets sleeping up to five.

St Arnaud Alpine Village Store SUPERMARKET $
(Main Rd; ⏲8am-6pm, takeaways 4.30-8pm Fri & Sat, daily Dec-Feb) The settlement's only general store sells groceries, petrol, beer and possum-wool socks. Mountain-bike hire per half-/full day is $20/40. It has tramping food, sandwiches, pies and milkshakes, with the fish and chips cranking up on weekends and daily in peak season ($6 to $10).

ℹ Information

The **DOC Visitor Centre** (☎03-521 1806; www.doc.govt.nz; View Rd; ⏲8am-4.30pm) proffers park information (weather, activities), hut passes, plus displays on park ecology and history. See also www.starnaud.co.nz.

ℹ Getting There & Around

Nelson Lakes Shuttles (☎021 490 095, 03-521 1900; www.nelsonlakesshuttles.co.nz) provides on-demand transport from St Arnaud to (all prices per person) Mt Robert car park ($15), Lake Rotoroa ($30), Nelson ($35), Picton ($45) and tramping trailheads as far away as Canterbury. Minimum numbers apply; check the website for budget fares and up-to-the minute movements.

Rotoiti Water Taxis (☎021 702 278; www.rotoitiwatertaxis.co.nz) runs to/from Kerr Bay and West Bay to Lakehead Jetty ($90, up to four people) and Coldwater Jetty ($105, up to four people). Kayaks, canoes and rowboats can also be hired from $40 per half-day; fishing trips and scenic lake cruises by arrangement.

Nelson to Motueka

From Richmond, south of Nelson, there are two routes to Motueka: the busier, more populated coastal highway (SH60) and the inland Moutere Hwy, a pleasant alternative, particularly if you want to make a loop. Either way, this area is densely packed with attractions, so you should allow enough time to pull off the road.

There are numerous wineries in this area; the *Nelson Wine Guide* pamphlet (www.wineart.co.nz) will help you find them.

Art and craft galleries are also in the vicinity. Find these in the *Nelson Art Guide* or *Nelson's Creative Pathways* pamphlets, both available from local i-SITEs, where you can also get information on accommodation around these parts.

SH60 via Mapua

Skirting around Waimea Inlet and along the Ruby Coast, this is the quickest route from Nelson to Motueka (around 45 minutes), although there are various distractions to slow you down. Here are just a few highlights.

Just 10 from Richmond you'll hit **Waimea** (www.waimeaestates.co.nz; SH60; ⏲11am-5pm) winery with its jazzy cafe and tables by the vines. Located a little further away, masterpiece glass is blown at **Höglund Glass Art** (www.hoglundartglass.com; 52 Lansdowne Rd, Appleby; ⏲10am-5pm), where you can watch Ola and his trainees working the furnace.

Just up the road is the turn-off to **Rabbit Island**, a recreation reserve offering estuary views from many angles, sandy beaches and plenty of quiet pine forest. The bridge to the island closes at sunset; overnight stays are not allowed.

Seifried (www.seifried.co.nz; cnr SH60 & Redwood Rd; ⏲10am-5pm) winery sits at the Rabbit Island turn off. It's one of the region's biggest, and is home to a pleasant garden restaurant and the delicious Sweet Agnes riesling.

As you reach the end of the inlet, you can either continue along SH60, or detour along the original coast road, now named the Ruby Bay Scenic Route. Along it lies the settlement of Mapua at the mouth of the Waimea River. It features numerous pleasant establishments including the **Smokehouse** (www.smokehouse.co.nz; Mapua Wharf; fish & chips $7-12; ⏲11am-8pm). Order up fish and chips, and eat them on the wharf while the gulls eye up your crispy bits. Delicious wood-smoked fish and pâté to go.

In the same wharfside cluster you will undoubtedly sniff out the **Golden Bear Brewing Company** (www.goldenbearbrewing.com; Mapua Wharf; meals $8-19), a micro-brewery with tons of stainless steel out back and a dozen or so brews out front. Authentic Mexican food (burritos, quesadillas and *huevos rancheros*) will stop you from getting a sore head. Occasional live music, takeaway beers and tours.

Art browers will enjoy Mapua's **Cool Store Gallery** (www.coolstoregallery.co.nz; 7 Aranui Rd; ⏲11am-4.30pm), packed with high-quality work.

A few kilometres before the scenic route rejoins SH60 is **Jester House** (320 Aporo Rd, Tasman; meals $13-23; ⏲9am-5pm). It alone is a good reason to take this detour, as much for its tame eels as for the peaceful sculpture gardens that encourage you to linger over lunch. A short, simple menu puts a few twists into the staples (wild pork burger, lavender shortbread), and there are local beer and wines. It's 8km to Mapua or Motueka.

Moutere Hwy

This drive traverses gently rolling countryside, dotted with farms, orchards and lifestyle blocks. Visitor attractions are fewer and farther between along here, but it's a nice drive nonetheless, and will prove particularly fruitful in high summer when the berry farms are on song.

The turn-off to the Moutere is sign-posted at Appleby on SH60. Not far along is the turn off to Old Coach Rd, from where you can follow the signposts to **Woollaston** (www.woollaston.co.nz; School Rd; ⏲11am-5pm), a flash hilltop winery complete with tasting room and contemporary art gallery. The patio is a spectacular place to enjoy a platter for lunch.

Upper Moutere is the main settlement along this route. First settled by German immigrants and originally named Sarau, today it's a sleepy hamlet with a shop, a cafe and allegedly New Zealand's oldest pub, the **Moutere Inn** (www.moutereinn.co.nz; 1046 Moutere Hwy; meals $5-27). This welcoming establishment serves honest meals (toasties, pizza, mussels and hot-pot) and very good beer, including its own house brews. Pull up a pew with a beer-tasting platter, play pool, sit outside on the sunny patio, or come along at night to hear regular live music.

Continuing along the Moutere Highway, Neudorf Rd is well signposted, leading as it does to berries and other delectables. Call into **Neudorf Dairy** (www.neudorfdairy.co.nz; 226 Neudorf Rd) for award-winning hand-crafted sheeps'-milk cheeses, or **Neudorf** (www.neudorf.co.nz; 138 Neudorf Rd) winery for gorgeous pinot noir and some of the country's finest chardonnay.

Motueka

POP 6900

Motueka (pronounced Mott-oo-ecka, meaning 'Island of Wekas') is a bustling town, one which visitors will find handy for stocking up en route to Golden Bay and the Abel Tasman and Kahurangi National Parks. It has all the vital amenities, ample accommodation, cafes, roadside fruit stalls, and a clean and beautiful river offering swimming and fishing.

Sights & Activities

While most of Mot's drawcards are out of town, there are a few attractions worth checking out, the best of which is the active aerodrome, home to several air-raising activities. With a coffee cart on site, it's a good place to soak up some sun and views, and watch a few folks drop in.

To get a handle on the town, visit the i-SITE and collect the *Motueka Art Walk* pamphlet, detailing sculpture, murals and occasional peculiarities around town.

Motueka District Museum MUSEUM
(140 High St; admission by donation; ⏲10am-4pm Mon-Fri Dec-Mar, 10am-3pm Tue-Fri Apr-Nov) An interesting collection of regional artefacts, housed in a dear old school building; cafe on site.

Skydive Abel Tasman EXTREME SPORTS
(☎0800 422 899, 03-528 4091; www.skydive.co.nz; Motueka Aerodrome, College St; jumps 13,000ft/16,500ft $299/399) Move over Taupo tandems: we've jumped both and think Mot takes the cake (presumably so do the many sports jumpers who favour this drop zone, some of whom you may see rocketing in). DVDs and photos cost extra, but pick-up/drop-off from Motueka and Nelson are free.

Tasman Sky Adventures SCENIC FLIGHTS
(☎027 229 9693, 0800 114 386; www.skyadventures.co.nz; Motueka Aerodrome, College St; 30min flight $185) A rare opportunity to fly in a microlight. Keep your eyes open and blow your mind on a scenic flight above Abel Tasman National Park. Wow. And there's tandem hang gliding for the eager (15/30 minutes, 2500ft/5280ft $185/275).

U-fly Extreme SCENIC FLIGHTS
(☎0800 360 180, 03-528 8290; www.uflyextreme.co.nz; Motueka Aerodrome, College St; 15min $299) Here's one for the courageous: you handle the controls doing aerobatics in an open cockpit Pitts Special plane. No experience necessary, just a stomach for stunts.

Sleeping

Numerous midrange B&Bs and holiday homes are secreted in the surrounds – ask the i-SITE for suggestions.

TOP CHOICE **Motueka TOP 10 Holiday Park** HOLIDAY PARK $
(☎03-528 7189, 0800 668 835; www.motuekatop10.co.nz; 10 Fearon St; sites from $40, cabins $50-125, units/motels $95-140; @📶🏊) Busy it may

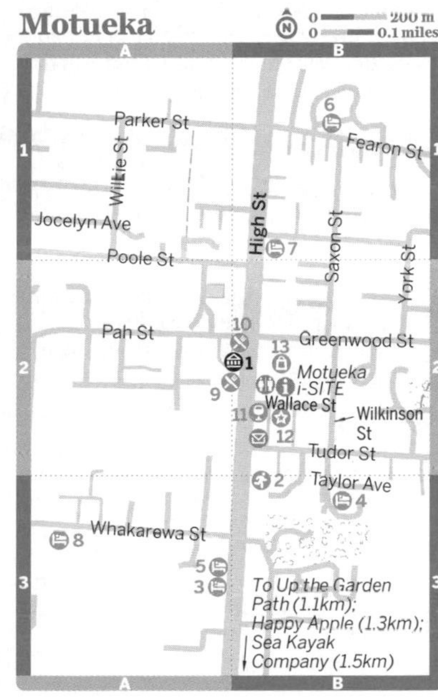

Motueka

Sights
1 Motueka District Museum B2

Activities, Courses & Tours
2 Wilsons Abel Tasman B3

Sleeping
3 Avalon Manor Motel A3
4 Equestrian Lodge Motel B3
5 Laughing Kiwi A3
6 Motueka TOP 10 Holiday Park B1
7 Nautilus Lodge B1
8 White Elephant A3

Eating
9 Patisserie Royale A2
10 Simply Indian B2

Drinking
11 Sprig and Fern B2

Entertainment
12 Gecko Theatre B2

Shopping
13 Motueka Sunday Market B2

be, but this park retains plenty of grassy, green charm. Love those lofty kahikatea trees! All the bells and whistles are in evidence, including several amenities blocks and family-friendly facilities such as swimming pool and jumping pillow. Local wine tours by arrangement.

Eden's Edge Backpacker Lodge HOSTEL $
(☎03-528 4242; www.edensedge.co.nz; 137 Lodder Ln, Riwaka; sites from $17, dm $28, d with/without bathroom $80/70; @ 🛜 ≋) Surrounded by orchards, 4km from Motueka, this purpose-built lodge comes pretty close to backpacker heaven. Well-designed facilities include a gleaming kitchen and inviting communal areas. It even has a a rainwater pool and a star-gazing jetty, and it's all within walking distance of beer, ice cream and coffee.

Equestrian Lodge Motel MOTEL $$
(☎03-528 9369, 0800 668 782; www.equestrianlodge.co.nz; Avalon Ct; d $115-145, q $165-195; @ 🛜 ≋) No horses, no lodge, but no matter. This is a lovely option: quiet and close to town (off Tudor St), with expansive lawns, rose gardens and shady corners. Family-friendly amenities include trampolines and a heated pool and spa. Rooms are plainly dressed; many have ovens.

Happy Apple HOSTEL $
(☎0800 427 792, 03-528 8652; www.happyapplebackpackers.co.nz; 500 High St; sites from $15, dm/s/d $26/41/60; @ 🛜) There's nothing rotten about this apple. Tidy rooms are divided between the house (nice doubles) and dorm wing, but the action is all in the yard out back, where there's an expansive lawn (camping allowed), gardens, fireplace, lounging areas and spa pool.

Nautilus Lodge MOTELS $$
(☎0800 628 845, 03-528 4658; www.nautiluslodge.co.nz; 67 High St; d $160-220; @ 🛜) A top-notch motel complex with 12 units decorated in neutral tones with low-profile furniture including European slatted beds. There are kitchenettes in larger units, spa baths in some, full Sky TV and classy bathrooms in all, and balconies and patios collecting afternoon sun.

Avalon Manor Motel MOTEL $$
(☎0800 282 566, 03-528 8320; www.avalonmotels.co.nz; 314 High St; d $150-215; 🛜) Prominent L-shaped motel five minutes' walk from the centre of town. Spacious four-star rooms have a contemporary vibe, with cooking facilities, Sky TV and free DVDs. Sumptuous studios have king-size beds and large flat-screen TVs. It also has a guest barbecue, a laundry and views of Mt Arthur.

Resurgence LODGE, CHALETS $$$
(☎03-528 4664; www.resurgence.co.nz; Riwaka Valley Rd; lodge from $625, chalets from $525; @ 🛜 ≋) Choose a luxurious en-suite lodge room or self-contained chalet at this magical 50-acre bushland retreat 15 minutes' drive north of Motueka, and half an hour's walk from the picturesque source of the Riwaka River. Lodge rates include cocktails and a four-course dinner as well as breakfast, or you can fire up the barbecue if you're staying in one of the chalets. Chalet rates are for B&B; lodge dinner extra ($90).

Laughing Kiwi HOSTEL $
(☎03-528 9229; www.laughingkiwi.co.nz; 310 High St; dm $27, d with/without bathroom $68/62; @ 🛜) Constant upgrades and improvements at this smart hostel keep the punters smiling. Rooms are spread between an old villa and a purpose-built backpacker lodge with an excellent kitchen/lounge, while the self-contained bach is ideal for groups (double $120).

White Elephant HOSTEL $
(☎03-528 6208; www.whiteelephant.co.nz; 55 Whakarewa St; dm $27, d with/without bathroom $76/72; @ 🛜) Dorms in a high-ceilinged colonial villa have a creaky charm, but your best bets are the en-suite cabins in the garden. Free wi-fi.

Eating & Drinking

TOP CHOICE **Patisserie Royale** BAKERY $
(152 High St; baked goods $2-8; ⏲6am-4pm Mon-Sat, 6am-2pm Sat & Sun) The best of several Mot bakeries and worth every delectable calorie. Lots of French fancies and a darn good pie.

Up the Garden Path CAFE $$
(473 High St; meals $15-27; ⏲9am-5pm Mon-Sun; 🖉) Perfect for lunch or a peppy coffee, this licensed cafe-gallery kicks back in an 1890s house amid idyllic gardens. Unleash the kids in the playroom and linger over your panini, cheese platter, mushroom burger, seafood chowder, pasta or lemon tart. Vegetarian, gluten- and dairy-free options, too.

Simply Indian INDIAN $$
(130 High St; mains $16-23; ⏲lunch & dinner Mon-Sat, dinner Sun; 🖉) As the name suggests:

no-nonsense curry in a no-frills setting. The food, however, is consistently good and relatively cheap. Expect the usual suspects such as tikka, tandoori, madras and vindaloo, and the ubiquitous naan prepared eight different ways. Takeaways are available.

Sprig and Fern PUB
(www.sprigandfern.co.nz; Wallace St; meals $14-19; ⏲2pm-late) Recently born of the expanding Sprig and Fern family, this branch has upped the ante among Motueka's drinking holes. Small but pleasant, with two courtyards, it offers 20 hand-pulled beers, simple food (burgers, pizza, platters) and occasional live music.

☆ Entertainment

Gecko Theatre CINEMA
(☎03-528 9996; www.geckotheatre.co.nz; 23b Wallace St; Tue & Wed $9, Thu-Sun $13; ⏲5pm-midnight) When the weather closes in, pull up an easy chair at this wee, independent theatre for interesting art-house flicks.

Shopping

Motueka Sunday Market MARKET
(Wallace St; ⏲8am-1pm) On Sunday the car park behind the i-SITE fills up with trestle tables for the Motueka Sunday Market: produce, jewellery, buskers, arts, crafts and Doris's divine bratwurst.

Information

Motueka i-SITE (☎03-528 6543; www.abeltasmanisite.co.nz; 20 Wallace St; ⏲8.30am-5pm Mon-Fri, 9am-4pm Sat & Sun) An excellent centre with helpful staff who will make bookings from Kaitaia to Bluff and provide local national-park expertise and necessaries.

Motueka Police Station (☎03-528 1220; 68 High St)

Take Note/Post Office (207 High St) Bookshop moonlighting as a post office.

Getting There & Away

All services depart from Motueka i-SITE.

Abel Tasman Coachlines (☎03-528 8850; www.abeltasmantravel.co.nz) runs two to four times daily from Motueka to Nelson ($12, one hour), Marahau ($10, 30 minutes), Kaiteriteri ($10, 25 minutes) and Takaka ($26, one hour). In summer these services connect with Golden Bay Coachline services to the Heaphy Track, Abel Tasman National Park and other Golden Bay destinations; from May to September all buses run less frequently.

Golden Bay Coachlines (☎03-525 8352; www.goldenbaycoachlines.co.nz) runs from Motueka to Takaka ($26, one hour) and Collingwood ($39, 1½ hours), as well as other Golden Bay destinations in summer, including the Heaphy Track and Totaranui.

Naked Bus (☎0900 625 33; www.nakedbus.com) runs from Motueka to Nelson ($11, one hour). Book online or at the i-SITE; cheaper fares for advance bookings.

Motueka to Abel Tasman

KAITERITERI

Known simply as 'Kaiteri', this seaside hamlet 13km from Motueka is the most popular resort town in the area. On a sunny summer's day, its gorgeous, golden, safe-swimming beach feels more like Noumea than NZ, with more towels than sand. Compounding this is the fact that it's a major gateway to Abel Tasman National Park (various trips depart Kaiteriteri beach, though Marahau is the main base). Kaiteri now also boasts an all-comers mountain-bike park; see www.kaiteriterimtbpark.org.nz for more info.

Sleeping & Eating

Kaiteri Lodge LODGE $
(☎03-527 8281; www.kaiterilodge.co.nz; Inlet Rd; dm $20-35, d $80-160; @ 📶) Modern, purpose-built lodge with small, simple rooms – dorms and en-suite doubles. A nautical navy-and-white colour scheme has been splashed throughout, and there are tidy communal facilities including a barbecue area, as well as bike hire. The on-site **Beached Whale** (dinner $13-28; ⏲4pm-late) bar is a sociable affair serving wood-fired pizza, burgers, fish dinners and the like. Drink and dine while the host busts out a few tunes on his guitar. The Whale will be open when the big bus pulls in.

Kaiteriteri Beach Motor Camp HOLIDAY PARK $
(☎03-527 8010; www.kaiteriteribeach.co.nz; Sandy Bay Rd; sites from $18, cabins $43-75; @ 📶) A gargantuan park in pole position across from the beach. It's hugely popular, so book in advance. The on-site general store is very well stocked, as is the ice-cream hatch were a queue often forms.

Bellbird Lodge B&B $$$
(☎03-527 8555; www.bellbirdlodge.co.nz; Sandy Bay Rd; d $275-325; @ 📶) An upmarket B&B located 1.5km up the hill from Kaiteri Beach, offering two ensuite rooms, bush and sea views, extensive gardens, spectacular breakfasts (featuring homemade muesli and fruit compote), and gracious hosts. Dinner

by arrangement in winter, when local restaurant hours are irregular.

Torlesse Coastal Motels MOTELS $$
(☎03-527 8063; www.torlessemotels.co.nz; Kotare Pl, Little Kaiteriteri Beach; d $120-170, q & f $180-280; 📶) Just 200m from Little Kaiteriteri Beach (around the corner from the main beach) is this congregation of roomy hillside units with pitched ceilings, full kitchens and laundries. Most have water views.

Shoreline RESTAURANT $$
(cnr Inlet & Sandy Bay Rds; meals $15-28; ⏰8am-9pm, reduced hours Apr-Nov) A modern, beige cafe-bar-restaurant right on the beach. Punters chill out on the sunny deck, lingering over sandwiches, pizzas, burgers and other predictable fare, or pop in for coffee and cake. Erratic winter hours; takeaway booth out the back.

Getting There & Away

Kaiteriteri is serviced by **Abel Tasman Coachlines** (☎03-528 8850; www.abeltasmantravel.co.nz).

MARAHAU

POP 200

Further along the coast from Kaiteriteri and 18km north of Motueka, Marahau is the main gateway to the Abel Tasman National Park. It's less of a town, more like a procession of holiday homes and tourist businesses.

If you're in an equine state of mind, **Pegasus Park** (☎0800 200 888; www.pegasuspark.co.nz) and **Marahau Horse Treks** (☎03 527-8425), both along Sandy Bay Rd, offer the chance to belt along the beach on a horse, your hair streaming out behind you (children's pony rides $35, two-hour rides $85 to $90).

Sleeping & Eating

Kanuka Ridge HOSTEL $
(☎03-527 8435; www.abeltasmanbackpackers.co.nz; Moss Rd, off Marahau-Sandy Bay Rd; dm $28, d & tw with/without bathroom $82/62) Five minutes' drive from Marahau and the start of the Abel Tasman track, this purpose-built cottage arrangement is ringed by forest, offering birdy, bushy surroundings for a bit of peace and quiet. Hosts are willing and able to hook you up to the nature buzz, with mountain bikes, activity bookings and car storage.

Ocean View Chalets CHALET $$
(☎03-527 8232; www.accommodationabeltasman.co.nz; 305 Sandy Bay-Marahau Rd; d $118-180, q $235-280; 📶) Positioned on a leafy hillside for maximum privacy, these well-priced cypress-lined chalets are 300m from the Abel Tasman Track and have views across Tasman Bay to Fisherman Island. All are self-contained; breakfast and packed lunches available.

Barn HOSTEL $
(☎03-527 8043; www.barn.co.nz; 14 Harvey Rd; sites from $12, dm $26-30, d $64-76; @📶) Architecturally chaotic, this rustic place surrounded by eucalypts offers no-frills micro-cabins, and bunks and attic doubles in the main house. The centrepiece of the outfit is a deck with shade sails, bean bags and a fireplace, but there are also the necessaries, including tour bookings, secure parking and a separate kitchen for the cabins and campers.

Abel Tasman Marahau Lodge MOTELS $$
(☎03-527 8250; www.abeltasmanmarahaulodge.co.nz; Marahau Beach Rd; d $130-255; @📶) Enjoy halcyon days in this arc of 12 lovely studios and self-contained units with cathedral ceilings, fan, TV, phone and microwave. There's also a fully equipped communal kitchen for self-caterers, plus spa and sauna. Cuckoos, tui and bellbirds squawk and warble in the bushy surrounds.

Fat Tui BURGERS $
(Franklin St, next to Kahu Kayaks; burgers $11-14; ⏰noon-8.30pm Wed-Sun; ✎) Everyone's heard about this bird, based in a caravan that ain't rollin' anywhere fast. Thank goodness. Superlative burgers, such as the Cowpat (beef), the Ewe Beaut (lamb) and the Sparrow's Fart breakfast burger. Fish and chips, and coffee, too.

Hooked on Marahau CAFE $$
(☎03-527 8576; Marahau-Sandy Bay Rd; lunch $10-28, dinner $26-34; ⏰8am-late Dec-Apr, 6pm-late Oct-May) This place has the natives hooked – dinner reservations are prudent. The art-bedecked interior opens onto an outdoor terrace with distracting views. Lunch centres on sandwiches and salads, while the dinner menu boasts fresh fish of the day, green-lipped mussels and NZ lamb.

Park Café CAFE $
(Harvey Rd; lunch $7-18, dinner $15-28; ⏰8am-late mid-Sep–May; ✎) Sitting at the start (or the end) of the Abel Tasman Track, this breezy, licensed cafe is perfectly placed for fuelling up or restoring the waistline. High-calorie options include the big breakfast, burgers, seafood pasta and homemade cakes. Enjoy

Abel Tasman National Park

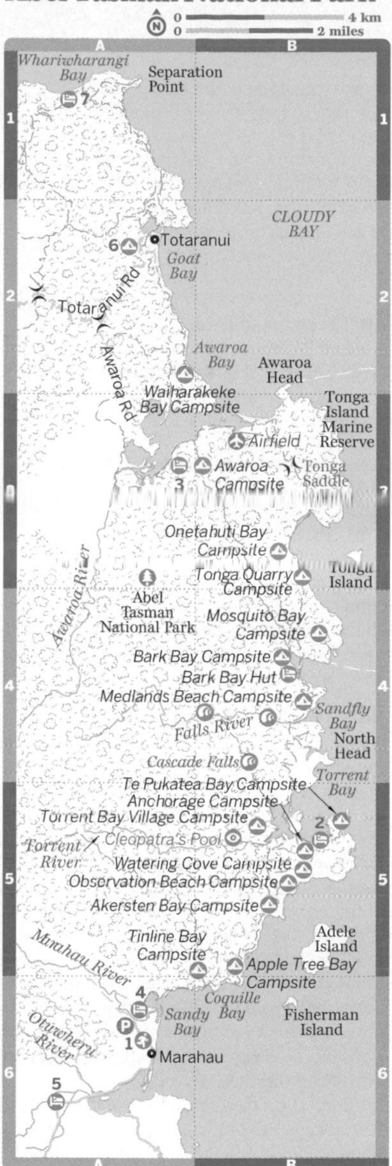

in the the room with a view or in the sunny courtyard garden.

Getting There & Away

Marahau is serviced by **Abel Tasman Coachlines** (☎03-528 8850; www.abeltasmantravel.co.nz).

Abel Tasman National Park

Activities, Courses & Tours

1 Abel Tasman Seal Swim A6

Sleeping

2 Anchorage Hut B5
Aquapackers .... (see 2)
3 Awaroa Hut A3
4 Barn A6
5 Kanuka Ridge A6
Ocean View Chalets .... (see 1)
6 Totaranui DOC Campsite A2
7 Whariwharangi Hut A1

Eating

Park Café .... (see 4)

ABEL TASMAN NATIONAL PARK

The accessible, coastal Abel Tasman National Park blankets the northern end of a range of marble and limestone hills extending from Kahurangi National Park. Various tracks in the park include an inland route, although the coast track is what everyone is here for – it sees more foot traffic than any other Great Walk in New Zealand.

ABEL TASMAN COAST TRACK

This 51km, three- to five-day track is one of the most scenic in the country, passing through native bush overlooking golden beaches lapped by gleaming azure water. Numerous bays, small and large, are like a travel brochure come to life. Visitors can walk into the park, catch water taxis to beaches and resorts along the track, or kayak along the coast.

In summer hundreds of trampers tackle the track at the same time. Track accommodation works on a booking system: huts and campsites must be prebooked year-round. There's no charge for day walks – if you're after a taster, the two- to three-hour stretch from Tonga Bay to Bark Bay is as photogenic as any, or get dropped at a beach and just hang out.

Between Bark Bay and Awaroa Head is an area classified as the **Tonga Island Marine Reserve** – home to a seal colony and visiting dolphins. Tonga Island itself is a small island offshore from Onetahuti Beach.

For a full description of the route, see DOC's *Abel Tasman Coast Track* brochure.

WALKING THE TRACK

The Abel Tasman area has crazy tides (up to a 6m difference between low and high tide),

LOCAL KNOWLEDGE

HAYLEY WESTENRA, SINGER & SONGWRITER

The Abel Tasman National Park, situated at the very top of the South Island, is a place of breathtaking beauty. Whether you opt for the three- to five-day tramp along the coastal track, some sea-kayaking around the bays or just a short half-day walk, you will be left spellbound by the native flora and fauna you encounter and mesmerised by the spectacular ocean views, not to mention the region's famous golden beaches. If you're feeling a little lazy, you could perhaps take a water taxi from Kaiteriteri to Awaroa, passing by Split Apple Rock and a seal colony on the way. However you go about your trip, though, the Abel Tasman National Park will surely leave you enchanted.

which has an impact on walking. Two sections of the main track are tidal, with no high-tide track around them: Awaroa Estuary and the narrow channel at Onetahuti Beach. Tide tables are posted along the track and on the DOC website; regional i-SITES also have them.

Take additional food so that you can stay longer should you have the inclination. Bays around all the huts are beautiful, but definitely bring plenty of sandfly repellent and sunscreen.

Estimated walking times from south to north:

ROUTE	TIME
Marahau to Anchorage Hut	4hr
Anchorage Hut to Bark Bay Hut	4hr
Bark Bay Hut to Awaroa Hut	4hr
Awaroa Hut to Totaranui	1½hr

Many walkers finish at Totaranui, the final stop for the boat services and bus pick-up point, but it is possible to keep walking around the headland to Whariwharangi Hut (p92) (three hours) and then on to Wainui (1½ hours), where buses service the car park.

Tours

Tour companies usually offer free Motueka pick-up/drop-off, with Nelson pick-up available at extra cost.

Abel Tasman Sailing Adventures SAILING
(☎03-527 8375, 0800 467 245; www.sailingadventures.co.nz; Kaiteriteri; half-/full day $85/169) A catamaran that offers the only scheduled sailing trips into the park. Sail/walk/kayak combos available; day-trip includes lunch.

Abel Tasman Seal Swim WILDLIFE TOUR
(☎0800 252 925, 03-527 8383; www.sealswim.com; Aqua Taxi Base, Sandy Bay-Marahau Rd, Marahau; 5hr seal swim adult/child $179/130, seal watch $90/70) Tide-scheduled trips to the seal colony.

Abel Tasman Tours & Guided Walks WALKING
(☎03-528 9602; www.abeltasmantours.co.nz; $220) Small-group, day-long walking tours (minimum of two people) that include packed lunch and water taxis.

Wilsons Abel Tasman WALKING, KAYAKING
(☎0800 221 888, 03-528 2027; www.abeltasman.co.nz; 265 High St, Motueka; half-day cruise $70, cruise & walk $55-70, kayak & walk $89-195) Impressive array of cruises, walking, kayaking and combo tours, including $32 backpacker special and the barbecue cruise (great winter option). Luxurious beachfront lodges at Awaroa and Torrent Bay for guided-tour guests.

Sleeping & Eating

At the southern edge of the park, Marahau is the main jumping-off point for the Abel Tasman National Park. From the northern end of the park, the nearest towns with accommodation are Pohara and Takaka. The whopping **Totaranui DOC Campsite** (☎03-528 8083; www.doc.govt.nz; summer/winter $15/10) is also in the north, 32km from Takaka on a narrow, winding road (12km unsealed – check with DOC or the Golden Bay i-SITE for latest conditions). It's serviced by Abel Tasman Coachlines (p90) from October to April. Sites at Totaranui from December to mid-February are now allocated via ballot; download a booking form from the DOC website.

Along the Coast Track there are four huts: **Anchorage** (24 bunks), **Bark Bay** (34 bunks), **Awaroa** (26 bunks) and **Whariwharangi** (20 bunks), plus 19 designated campsites. None have cooking facilities – BYO stove. Some of the campsites have fireplaces but, again, you must carry cooking equipment. Hut and camp passes should be purchased before you enter the park. From Christmas Day to February, huts and campsites fill to the rafters (book with DOC).

Moored permanently in Anchorage Bay, the **Aquapackers** (☎0800 430 744; www.aquapackers.co.nz; Anchorage; dm/d incl breakfast $70/195) is a rockin' option. This specially converted 13m *Catarac* catamaran provides unusual but buoyant backpacker accommodation for 22. Facilities are basic but decent; prices include bedding, dinner and breakfast. Bookings essential.

Further sleeping options in the park (accessible on foot, by kayak or water taxi, but not by road) are largely confined to holiday homes. Ask about these at the Nelson (p83) or Motueka (p89) i-SITEs or browse online.

ℹ Information

The track operates on DOC's **Great Walks Pass** (sites/huts per person $12.20/35.70). Children are free but booking is still required. Book online (www.doc.govt.nz), contact the **Nelson Marlborough Bookings Helpdesk** (☎03-546 8210; nmbookings@doc.govt.nz), or book in person at the Nelson (p83), Motueka (p89) and Takaka i-SITES or DOC offices, where staff can offer suggestions to tailor the track to your needs and organise transport at each end. Book your trip well ahead of time, especially the huts between December and March.

ℹ Getting Around

Common setting-out points for the Abel Tasman are Kaiteriteri and Marahau in the south, and Takaka in the north. All are serviced by Abel Tasman Coachlines (p90), with connections to Nelson and Motueka. Totaranui is serviced by **Golden Bay Coachlines** (☎03-525 8352; www.gbcoachlines.co.nz) from November to April ($22 from Takaka).

Once you hit the park, it is easy to get to/from any point on the track by water taxi, either from

PADDLING THE ABEL TASMAN

The Abel Tasman Coast Track has long been trampers' territory, but its coastal beauty makes it an equally seductive spot for sea kayaking, which can be combined with walking and camping. A variety of professional outfits are able to float you out on the water, and the possibilities and permutations for guided or freedom trips are vast. You can kayak from half a day up to three days, camping ($14 per night) or staying in DOC huts ($32 per night), baches, even a floating backpackers, either fully catered for or self-catering. You can kayak one day, camp overnight then walk back, or walk further into the park and catch a water taxi back.

Most operators offer similar trips at similar prices. Marahau is the main base, but trips also depart from Kaiteriteri. A popular choice if time is tight is to spend a few hours kayaking in the Tonga Island Marine Reserve, followed by a walk from Tonga Quarry to Bark Bay. This will cost around $160 including water taxis. Three-day trips usually drop you at the northern end of the park, then you paddle back (or vice versa) and cost around $600 including food. One-day guided trips are around $200.

Freedom rentals (double-kayak and equipment hire) are around $100 per person for two days; none allow solo hires, and all depart from Marahau with the exception of Golden Bay Kayaks (p96), which is based at Tata Beach in Golden Bay.

Instruction is given to everyone, and most tour companies have a minimum age of either eight or 14, depending on the trip. Camping gear is usually provided on overnight trips; if you're disappearing into the park for a few days, most operators provide free car parking.

November to Easter is the busiest time, with December to February the absolute peak. You can, however, paddle all year round, with winter offering its own rewards. The weather is surprisingly amenable, the seals are more playful, there's more bird life and less haze.

The following are the main players in this competitive market; shop around.

Abel Tasman Kayaks (☎03-527 8022, 0800 732 529; www.abeltasmankayaks.co.nz; Main Rd, Marahau)

Kahu Kayaks (☎03-527 8300, 0800 300 101; www.kahukayaks.co.nz; cnr Marahau Valley Rd)

Kaiteriteri Kayaks (☎03-527 8383, 0800 252 925; www.seakayak.co.nz; Kaiteriteri Beach)

Marahau Sea Kayaks (☎03-527 8176, 0800 529 257; www.msk.co.nz; Abel Tasman Centre, Franklin St, Marahau)

Sea Kayak Company (☎03-528 7251, 0508 252 925; www.seakayaknz.co.nz; 506 High St, Motueka)

Wilsons Abel Tasman (☎0800 221 888, 03-528 2027; www.abeltasman.co.nz; 265 High St, Motueka)

Kaiteriteri or Marahau. Typical one-way prices from either Marahau or Kaiteriteri: Anchorage and Torrent Bay ($33), Bark Bay ($38), Tonga ($40), Awaroa ($43) and Totaranui ($45). The following are key operators:

Abel Tasman Aqua Taxi (☎03-527 8083, 0800 278 282; www.aquataxi.co.nz; Kaiteriteri & Marahau) Scheduled and on-demand services as well as boat/walk options.

Abel Tasman Sea Shuttle (☎03-527 8688, 0800 732 748; www.abeltasmanseashuttles.co.nz; Kaiteriteri) Scheduled services plus cruise/walk options. Also runs between Nelson and Kaiteriteri during peak season (adult/child $30/15).

Wilsons Abel Tasman (☎03-528 2027, 0800 223 582; www.abeltasman.co.nz; 265 High St, Motueka; pass adult/child $145/72.50) Offers an explorer pass for unlimited taxi travel on three days over a five-day period, plus backpacker specials and an array of tours.

Marahau Water Taxis (☎03-527 8176, 0800 808 018; www.abeltasmancentre.co.nz; Abel Tasman Centre, Franklin St, Marahau) Scheduled services plus boat/walk options.

Golden Bay

MOTUEKA TO TAKAKA

From Motueka, SH60 takes a stomach-churning meander over Takaka Hill. On the way it passes dramatic lookouts over Tasman Bay and Abel Tasman National Park before swooping down towards Takaka and Collingwood. The best way to tackle this region is with your own wheels.

Takaka Hill (791m) butts-in between Tasman Bay and Golden Bay. Just below the summit (literally) are the **Ngarua Caves** (SH60; adult/child $15/7; ⏱45min tours hourly 10am-4pm Sep-May, open Sat & Sun only Jun-Aug), a rock-solid attraction karst in stone, where you can see myriad subterranean delights including moa bones. Access is restricted to tours – you can't go solo spelunking.

Also just before the summit is the turn-off to **Canaan Downs Scenic Reserve**, reached at the end of an 11km gravel road. This area stars in both the *Lord of the Rings* and *Hobbit* movies, but **Harwood's Hole** is the most famous feature here. It's one of the largest *tomo* (caves) in the country at 357m deep and 70m wide, with a 176m vertical drop. It's a 30-minute walk from the car park, and allow us to state the obvious: the cave is off-limits to all but the most experienced cavers.

Canaan is mountain-bikers' heaven. Riders with reasonable off-road skills can venture along a couple of new loop tracks, while those of intermediate skill can head off on the famous **Rameka Track** (bikes and drop-offs can be negotiated from Takaka). There's a basic **DOC Campsite** (per person $6) here, too.

Close to the zenith also lies the **Takaka Hill Walkway**, a three-hour loop walk through marble karst rock formations, native forest and private farmland (owned by the Harwoods, of Hole fame), and **Harwood Lookout**, affording fine views down the Takaka River Valley to Takaka and Golden Bay.

TAKAKA

POP 1230

Boasting NZ's highest concentration of yoga pants, dreadlocks and various types of drop-outs, Takaka is nevertheless a largely a down-to-earth town and the last 'big' centre before the road west ends at Farewell Spit. You'll find most things you need here, and a few things you don't, but we all have an unworn tie-dye tanktop in our wardrobe, don't we?

Sights & Activities

Te Waikoropupu Springs SPRING

'Pupu Springs' are the largest freshwater springs in Australasia and reputedly the clearest in the world. About 14,000 litres of water per second surges from underground vents dotted around the reserve, including one with 'dancing sands' propelled upwards by gushing water. The water looks enticing, but swimming or even touching the water is a no-no. From Takaka, head 4km northwest on SH60, turn inland at Waitapu Bridge and keep going for 3km.

Grove Scenic Reserve LOOKOUT

(signposted down Clifton Rd) Around 10 minutes' drive from Takaka, a signpost at Clifton Rd points you to this worthwhile stop, where a 10-minute walk leads through a crazy limestone maze punctuated by gnarled old Rata trees. The lookout point is quite something. If you dig this, look out for the signpost to **Labyrinth Rocks Park** (Scotts Rd; admission free) closer to Takaka.

Rawhiti Cave CAVE

(www.doc.govt.nz) The ultimate in geological eye-candy around these parts are the phytokarst features of Rawhiti Cave. Get there from Motupipi, by driving along Packard Rd for 2.5km. Walk from the farm gates, then clamber along the river bed and up a zigzag track to the right. The rugged two-hour-return walk (steep in places; dangerous in the wet) may well leave you speechless (although we managed 'monster', 'fangs', and even 'Sarlacc').

Golden Bay Museum & Gallery MUSEUM
(Commercial St; admission by donation; ⏲10am-4pm) This small museum's stand-out exhibits include a diorama depicting Abel Tasman's 1642 landing and some dubious human taxidermy. Ask about the albatross. The adjoining gallery offers satisfying browsing of local and national knickknackery and quite possibly the purchase of a quality souvenir. For additional arty ambling, look for the free *Artists in Golden Bay* pamphlet.

Pupu Hydro Walkway WALKING
Not far from Pupu Springs, this enjoyable two-hour circuit passes through beech forest, past engineering and gold-mining relics to the restored (and operational) Pupu Hydro Powerhouse, built in 1929. To get here, take the 4km gravel road (signed 'Pupu Walkway') off Pupu Springs Rd.

Escape Adventures CYCLING
(☎03-525 8783; www.escapeadventures.co.nz; behind the Post Shop; bike hire per day $75, 1-day guided ride from $150) The Bay offers a range of fantastic cycling opportunities, on- and off-road, for riders of every ability. The flinty folk at Escape can get you out there (including Canaan and Rameka tracks) with guided trips, bike hire and transport.

Remote Adventures SCENIC FLIGHTS
(☎0800 150 338, 03-525 6167; www.remoteadventures.co.nz; Takaka Airfield) Scenic flights around Golden Bay and over Kahurangi National Park for as little as $40.

Golden Bay Air SCENIC FLIGHTS
(☎0800 588 885; www.goldenbayair.co.nz) Scenic and charter flights around the Golden Bay, and Farewell Spit, Abel Tasman and Kahurangi; from $49.

Sleeping & Eating

Kiwiana HOSTEL $
(☎03-525 7676, 0800 805 494; www.kiwianabackpackers.co.nz; 73 Motupipi St; tent sites per person $18, dm/s/d $28/44/68; @wifi) Beyond the welcoming garden is a cute cottage where rooms are named after classic Kiwiana (the jandal, Buzzy Bee...). The garage has been converted into a fun games room, with wood-fired stove, pool table, CD player, books and games, and free bikes for guest use.

Annie's Nirvana Lodge HOSTEL $
(☎03-525 8766; www.nirvanalodge.co.nz; 25 Motupipi St; dm/d $28/66; @wifi) It's clean, it's tidy, and it smells good: dorms in the main house, four doubles at the bottom of the secluded courtyard garden. This YHA hostel is lovely and has friendly owners. Fluffy the cat seals the deal – what a charmer. Free bikes for guests.

Golden Bay Motel MOTEL $$
(☎0800 401 212, 03-525 9428; www.goldenbaymotel.co.nz; 132 Commercial St; d $95-140, extra person $20; wifi) It's golden, all right: check out the paint job. Clean, spacious, self-contained units with decent older-style fixtures and decent older-style hosts. The rear patios overlook a lush green lawn with a playground.

Dangerous Kitchen CAFE $
(46a Commercial St; meals $12-28; ⏲10am-10pm Mon-Sat) Dedicated to Frank Zappa ('In the kitchen of danger, you can feel like a stranger'), DK serves largely healthy, good-value fare such as falafel, pizza, burritos, mega-cake and fresh juice. Mellow and laid-back, with a sun-trap courtyard out back and a people-watching patio on the main drag.

Top Shop DAIRY
(9 Willow St; items $2-9) One of your best bets for a quick eat. A dairy, tearoom and takeaway at the entrance to town; high-rating pies.

Fresh Choice SUPERMARKET
(☎03-525 9383; 13 Willow St; ⏲8am-7pm) Stock up while you can.

Drinking

Brigand CAFE, BAR
(www.brigand.co.nz; 90 Commercial St; meals $16-35; ⏲11am-late Mon-Sat) Beyond the gates you'll find good food such as sandwiches, chowder and meaty mains served in a relaxed atmosphere. A garden bar and great baking feature, too. Equally important, the Brigand is the mainstay of the local entertainment scene; go for Thursday open mic and look out for other gigs.

Roots Bar BAR
(www.rootsbar.co.nz; 1 Commercial St) Popular with the young 'uns and those who can still tap a toe, this music-focused joint has decent beer on tap, a garden bar, lively evenings and the odd tree root lending a little rusticity.

Paul's Coffee Caravan CAFE
The dude with the tunes does the best brew in town from his van tucked into the Library carpark.

☆ Entertainment

Village Theatre CINEMA
(☎03-525 8453; www.villagetheatre.org.nz; 32 Commercial St; adult/child $12.50/7) Demonstrating, yet again, provincial New Zealand's appetite for quality movies.

ℹ Information

DOC Office (☎03-525 8026; www.doc.govt.nz; 62 Commercial St; ⊙8.30am-4pm Mon-Fri) Information on Abel Tasman and Kahurangi National Parks, the Heaphy Track, Farewell Spit and Cobb Valley. Sells hut passes.

Golden Bay i-SITE (☎03-525 9136; www.goldenbaynz.co.nz; Willow St; ⊙9am-5pm Nov-Apr, 10am-4.30pm Mon-Fri, to 4pm Sat & Sun May-Oct; @) A friendly little information centre with all the necessary information, including the indispensible yellow map. Bookings and DOC passes.

ℹ Getting There & Around

Abel Tasman Coachlines (☎03-528 8850; www.abeltasmantravel.co.nz) runs between Takaka and Nelson ($35, 2½ hours).

Golden Bay Air (☎03-525 8725, 0800 588 885; www.goldenbayair.co.nz) flies daily between Wellington and Takaka ($139 to $189) and between Takaka and Karamea for Heaphy Track trampers (minimum two people, per person $175).

Golden Bay Coachlines (☎03-525 8352; www.gbcoachlines.co.nz) works in conjunction with Abel Tasman Coachlines. Connects Takaka with Collingwood ($19, 25 minutes), the Heaphy Track ($33, one hour), Totaranui ($22, one hour) and other stops en route.

Remote Adventures (☎03-525 6167, 0800 150 338; www.remoteadventures.co.nz) offers daily flights between Takaka and Nelson (from $150).

A sustainable, butt-enhancing method of transport is available from the **Quiet Revolution Cycle Shop** (☎03-525 9555; www.quietrevolution.co.nz; 11 Commercial St; bike hire per day $25-45). Local ride maps and a car-relocation service for the Heaphy Track in winter, too.

POHARA

POP 350

About 10km northeast of Takaka is pint-sized Pohara, a beachside resort with a population that quadruples over summer. It's more 'yuppified' than other parts of Golden Bay, with large modern houses cashing in on sea views, but an agreeable air persists and there's some good accommodation.

The beach is on the way to the northern end of the Abel Tasman Coastal Track; the largely unsealed road into the park passes Tarakohe Harbour (Pohara's working port) where **Golden Bay Kayaks** (☎03-525 9095; www.goldenbaykayaks.co.nz; Tata Beach; half-day guided tours adult $75-80, child $35, freedom hire half-/full day $90/110) rents kayaks for hour-long paddles, or can launch you on a three-day exploration of Abel Tasman National Park.

Further along, **Ligar Bay** has a lookout and a memorial to Abel Tasman, who anchored here in December 1642.

Signposted from the Totaranui Rd at Wainui Bay is a leafy walk to the best cascade in the bay: **Wainui Falls**. It's a 1½-hour return trip, but you could easily take longer by dipping a toe or two in the river.

Sleeping & Eating

Pohara Beach Top 10 Holiday Park HOLIDAY PARK $
(☎0800 764 272, 03-525 9500; www.poharabeach.com; 809 Abel Tasman Dr; sites from $20, cabins & units $72-164; @📶) Wow, what a big 'un! On a long grassy strip between the dunes and the main road, this place has a primo location – love that beach! – but in summer it can feel more like a suburb than the seaside. General store and takeaway on site.

Nook GUESTHOUSE $
(☎03-525 8501, 0800 806 665; www.thenookguesthouse.co.nz; 678 Abel Tasman Dr; sites from $15, dm/tw/d $32/65/75, cottage $180-200; 📶) Low-key, nook-sized guesthouse with timber floors, and rooms opening out onto gardens. A self-contained straw-bale cottage sleeps six, while the back paddock has space for tents. Bikes available.

Sans Souci Inn LODGE $$
(☎03-525 8663; www.sanssouciinn.co.nz; 11 Richmond Rd; s/d/f $90/115/135, self-contained unit from $180, dinner mains $32 to $35; ⊙closed Jul-mid-Sep; 📶) Sans Souci means 'no worries' in French, and this will be your mantra too after staying in one of the seven mudbrick, Mediterranean-flavoured rooms. Guests share a plant-filled, mosaic bathroom that has composting toilets, and an airy lounge and kitchen opening out onto the semi-tropical courtyard. Dinner in the on-site restaurant (bookings essential) is highly recommended; breakfast is by request.

Ratanui LODGE $$
(☎03-525 7998; www.ratanuilodge.com; 818 Abel Tasman Dr; d $155-269; @📶🏊) This beautiful new boutique lodge is a contender for NZ's most romantic, with plush and elegant rooms, and sensual stimulators such as swimming pool, massage room, mean mar-

LOCAL KNOWLEDGE

RHYS DARBY, ACTOR & STAND-UP COMIC

Golden Bay has all the elements of wonder for me: beautiful, rugged terrain, an amazing array of artists and world-class food. It's my annual trip there, however, that really gets the wildlife excited. You haven't lived until you've been chased by a wild seal. That's what happened to me the last time I visited Wharariki Beach with its wild windswept dunes and giant rock formations. It really is the land of the lost. You must traverse farmland, hills and bush to get there, but it's well worth it for the stunning ocean views. Then, to complete the day, you should aim for the Mussel Inn (p98) for its wonderful Captain Cooker Manuka Honey Beer, but be sure to stop on the way for a cold dip in any one of the refreshing rivers.

garitas and a candleabra-lit restaurant (open to the public; bookings required). Victorian grandeur inside; colourful cottage garden out the front. Affordable luxury that delivers.

Penguin Café & Bar PUB **$$**
(818 Abel Tasman Dr; lunch $13-22, dinner $20-33; ⌚10am-late Nov-Apr; 4pm-late Mon-Wed & 11am-late Thu-Sun May-Oct) A buzzy spot with a large outdoor area suited to sundowners and thirst-quenchers on sunny days. There's an open fire inside for the odd inclement day. Brunch treats include chowder, mussels and steak sandwiches. Come dinner time, keep an eye out for the local seafood specials.

Getting There & Away

Golden Bay Coachlines (☎03-525 8352; www.gbcoachlines.co.nz) runs daily from Takaka to Pohara ($15, 15 minutes) on the way to Totaranui.

COLLINGWOOD & AROUND

Far-flung Collingwood (population 250) is the last town in this part of the country, and has a real end-of-the-line vibe. It's busy in summer, though for most people it's simply a launch pad for the Heaphy Track or trips to Farewell Spit.

The **Collingwood Museum** (Tasman St; admission by donation; ⌚10am-4pm) fills a tiny, unstaffed corridor with a quirky collection of saddlery, Maori artefacts, moa bones, shells and old typewriters, while the **Aorere Centre** next-door houses multimedia presentations, including the works of the wonderful pioneer photographer, Fred Tyree.

No Collingwood visit would be complete without visiting **Rosy Glow** (54 Beach Rd; chocolates $3-5; ⌚10am-5pm Sat-Thu). Chocoholics: this is your cue. Don't miss it!

A foray to Farewell Spit is essential. From there, follow the sign to **Wharariki Beach** (☎03-524 8507; www.whararikibeachholidaypark.co.nz; sitres from $16, dm $25) (6km unsealed road, then a 20-minute walk through Puponga Farm Park). It's a wild introduction to the West Coast, with mighty dune formations, looming rock islets just offshore and a seal colony at its eastern end (keep an eye out for seals in the stream on the walk here). As inviting as a swim here may seem, there are strong undertows – what the sea wants, the sea shall have...

Befitting a frontier, this is the place to saddle up: **Cape Farewell Horse Treks** (☎03-524 8031; www.horsetreksnz.com; McGowan St, Puponga; ⌚treks from $75). Treks in this wind-blown country range from 1½ hours (to Pillar Point) to three hours (to Wharariki Beach), with longer (including overnight) trips by arrangement.

On the road to Wharariki Beach you'll pass **Wharariki Beach Holiday Park** (☎03-524 8507; www.whararikibeachholidaypark.co.nz; sitres from $16, dm $25), a pretty, young campground with a pleasant communal building.

Sleeping & Eating

There's little in the way of refreshment round these parts, so keep some cheese and crackers up your sleeve.

Innlet Backpackers & Cottages HOSTEL **$**
(☎03-524 8040; www.goldenbayindex.co.nz; Main Rd; sites from $24, dm/d $31/73, cabins from $83; @) A great option 10km from Collingwood on the way to Farewell Spit. The main house has elegant backpacker rooms, and there are various campsites and self-contained options, including a cottage sleeping six. Bush walks and bike hire raise the environmental-consciousness quotient.

Somerset House HOSTEL **$**
(☎03-524 8624; www.backpackerscollingwood.co.nz; 10 Gibbs Rd, Collingwood; dm/s/d incl breakfast $30/46/72; @) A small, low-key hostel

DON'T MISS

FAREWELL SPIT

Bleak, exposed and slighly sci-fi, **Farewell Spit** is a wetland of international importance and a renowned bird sanctuary – the summer home of thousands of migratory waders, notably the godwit (which flies all the way from the Arctic tundra), Caspian terns and Australasian gannets. The 35km beach features colossal, crescent-shaped dunes, from where panoramic views extend across Golden Bay and a vast low-tide salt marsh. Walkers can explore the first 4km of the spit via a network of tracks, but beyond that point access is via tour only.

At the time of writing, the visitor centre and cafe at the spit was between managers; this we take as a positive because the only way is up.

Farewell Spit Eco Tours (☎0800 808 257, 03-524 8257; www.farewellspit.com; Tasman St, Collingwood; tours $120-145) Operating for more than 65 years, this outfit runs tours that range from three to 6½ hours, taking in the spit, lighthouse, gannets and godwits. Tours depart from Collingwood.

Farewell Spit Nature Experience (☎0800 250 500, 03-524 8992; www.farewellspittours.com; tours $120-135) Four-hour spit tours depart Farewell Spit Visitor Centre; six-hour tours depart the Old School Café, Pakawau.

in a bright, historic building on a hill with views from the deck. Get tramping advice from the knowledgeable owners, who offer track transport, free bikes and kayaks, and freshly baked bread for breakfast.

Collingwood Park Motel MOTEL $$
(☎03-524 8499, 0800 270 520; www.collingwoodpark.co.nz; 1 Tasman St; d $100-140; @📶) Clean, spacious self-contained units in excellent nick, wedged between the road and Aorere estuary. Good-value family-sized units have nifty mezzanine floors, plus compact campervan sites ($35) and a backpacker double ($85 to $95).

TOP CHOICE **Mussel Inn** PUB $$
(www.mussellinn.co.nz; 1259 SH60, Onekaka; all-day menu $5-18, dinner $23-29; ⏰11am-late, closed Jul-Aug) Halfway between Takaka and Collingwood, this earthy tavern-cafe-brewery is a Golden Bay institution. A totem pole with crucified mobile phones heralds the mood: this is no place for urban trappings, just excellent beer, wholesome food (mussels, seasonal scallops, fresh fish and steak), open fires and live music. Try a handle (beer glass) or two of 'Captain Cooker', a brown beer brewed naturally with manuka, or the delicious 'Bitter Ass'.

Old School Cafe CAFE $$
(1115 Collingwood Puponga Rd; mains $14-30; ⏰4pm-late Thu-Fri, 11am-late Sat & Sun) These folks get an A for effort by providing honest food to an unpredictable flow of passing trade. What it lacks in imagination (steak, pizza and even a shrimp cocktail), it more than makes up for with arty ambience, a garden bar and a welcoming disposition.

ℹ Getting There & Away

Golden Bay Coachlines (☎03-525 8352; www.goldenbaycoachlines.co.nz) runs from Takaka to Collingwood ($19, 25 minutes, two daily).

Kahurangi National Park

Kahurangi, meaning 'Treasured Possession', is the second largest of NZ's national parks and undoubtedly one of the greatest. Its 452,000 hectares are a hotbed of ecological wonderment: 18 native bird species, over 50% of all NZ's plant species, including over 80% of its alpine plant species, a karst landscape and the largest known cave system in the southern hemisphere (explored by local caving groups, but only for the experienced).

HEAPHY TRACK

One of the best-known tracks in NZ, the four- to six-day 78.5km Heaphy Track doesn't have the spectacular scenery of the Routeburn or Milford Tracks, but revels in its own distinct beauty. The track is almost entirely within Kahurangi National Park, and its highlights include the mystical Gouland Downs, and the nikau-palm-dotted coast, especially around Heaphy Hut, where you could easily spend spend a day or two.

There are seven huts en route, the smallest accommodating only eight people, the largest 28; all have gas stoves, except Brown and Gouland Downs, which need wood. There are nine campsites along the route, with limited capacity (eight campers maximum at James Mackay Hut, as many as 40 at Heaphy Hut). Huts/campsites cost $32/14; all must be prebooked through DOC and the Nelson and Golden Bay i-SITEs.

WALKING THE TRACK

Most people tramp southwest from the Collingwood end to Karamea. From Brown Hut the track passes through beech forest to Perry Saddle. The country opens up to the swampy Gouland Downs, then closes in with sparse bush all the way to Mackay Hut. The bush becomes more dense towards Heaphy Hut, with beautiful nikau palms growing at lower levels.

The final section is along the coast through nikau forest and partly along the beach. Unfortunately, sandflies love this beautiful stretch too. The climate here is surprisingly mild, but don't swim in the sea, as the undertows and currents are vicious. The lagoon at Heaphy Hut is good for swimming, and the Heaphy River is full of fish.

Kilometre markers crop up along the track – the zero marker is at the track's southern end at Kohaihai River near Karamea. Estimated walking times:

ROUTE	TIME
Brown Hut to Perry Saddle Hut	5hr
Perry Saddle Hut to Gouland Downs Hut	2hr
Gouland Downs Hut to Saxon Hut	1½hr
Saxon Hut to James Mackay Hut	3hr
James Mackay Hut to Lewis Hut	3½hr
Lewis Hut to Heaphy Hut	2½hr
Heaphy Hut to Kohaihai River	5hr

CYCLING THE TRACK

For a trial period ending in September 2013, the Heaphy Track can be cycled by experienced mountain bikers from May to September each year. The ride takes two to three days. Two local companies can help you with gear and advice: Escape Adventures (p95) and Quiet Revolution Cycle Shop (p96).

Information

The best spot for detailed Heaphy Track information and bookings is the DOC counter at the Nelson i-SITE (p83). You can also book at the Golden Bay i-SITE (p96) or DOC (p96) in Takaka, online at www.doc.got.nz, by email (nmbookings@doc.govt.nz) or phone (03-546 8210). See also www.heaphytrack.com. For a detailed track description, see DOC's *Heaphy Track* brochure.

OTHER KAHURANGI TRACKS

After tackling the Heaphy north to south, you can return to Golden Bay via the more scenic (though harder) **Wangapeka Track**. It's not as well known as the Heaphy, but many consider the Wangapeka a more enjoyable walk. Taking about five days, the track starts 25km south of Karamea at Little Wanganui, running 52km east to Rolling River near Tapawera. There's a chain of huts along the track.

See www.doc.govt.nz for detailed information on both tracks, and for some excellent full-day and overnight walks around the Cobb Valley, Mt Arthur and the Tableland.

Tours

Bush & Beyond TRAMPING
(☎03-528 9054; www.bushandbeyond.co.nz) Offers various tramping trips, ranging from Mt Arthur or Cobb Valley day walks ($220) through to a guided six-day Heaphy Track package ($1795).

Southern Wilderness TRAMPING
(☎03-545 7544, 0800 666 044; www.southernwilderness.com) Guided four- to five-day tramps on the Heaphy Track ($1495 to $1595) and day walks in Nelson Lakes National Park ($220).

Kahurangi Guided Walks TRAMPING
(☎03-525 7177; www.kahurangiwalks.co.nz) Small-group adventures such as five-day Heaphy tramps ($1500) and various one-day trips, including Abel Tasman and the Cobb (from $170).

Getting There & Away

Golden Bay Coachlines (☎03-525 8352; www.gbcoachlines.co.nz) will get you to the Heaphy Track from Takaka via Collingwood ($33, one hour).

Heaphy Bus (☎0800 128 735, 03-540 2042; www.theheaphybus.co.nz) offers a round-trip shuttle service: drop off and pick up from Kohaihai ($110), and other on-demand local track transport.

Heaphy Track Help (☎03-525 9576; www.heaphytrackhelp.co.nz) offers car relocations ($200 to $300, depending on the direction and time), food drops, shuttles and advice.

Remote Adventures (p95) flies Takaka to Karamea from $170 per person (up to four people and bicycles). Golden Bay Air (p95) flies the same route from $155 per person, as does Helicopter Charter Karamea (p109), who will take up to three people for $675 ($750 with three mountain bikes).

The West Coast

Includes »

Best Outdoors

- Heaphy Track (p107)
- Hokitika Gorge (p119)
- Charming Creek Walkway (p107)
- Denniston Plateau (p106)

Best Places to Stay

- Fox Glacier Holiday Park (p130)
- Lantern Court Motels (p112)
- Okarito Campground (p123)
- Beaconstone Eco Lodge (p109)

Why Go?

What a difference a mountain range makes. Hemmed in by the wild Tasman Sea and the Southern Alps, the West Coast (aka Westland) is like nowhere else in New Zealand.

Both ends of the coast have a remote end-of-the-road feel. In the north the surf-battered highway leads to sleepy Karamea, surrounded by farms and home to alternative lifestylers drawn by its isolation and surprisingly mild climate. The southern end of spectacular State Hwy 6 continues to Haast, gateway to a magnificent pass and Central Otago beyond.

Built on the wavering fortunes of gold, coal and timber, the stories of Coast settlers are hair-raising. Today just 32,000 reside here, typically a hardy and individual breed: they make up less than 1% of NZ's population, scattered amid almost 9% of the country's area.

During summer a phalanx of campervans and tourist buses tick off the 'must see' Punakaiki Rocks and Franz Josef and Fox Glaciers. Deviate from the trail even a short way, however, and be awed by the spectacles that await you alone.

When to Go

During summer the coast road gets relatively busy. May to September can be warm and clear, with fewer crowds and cheaper accommodation. The West Coast has serious rainfall (around 5m annually) but Westland sees as much sunshine as Christchurch. When it's pouring in the east it's just as likely to be fine here.

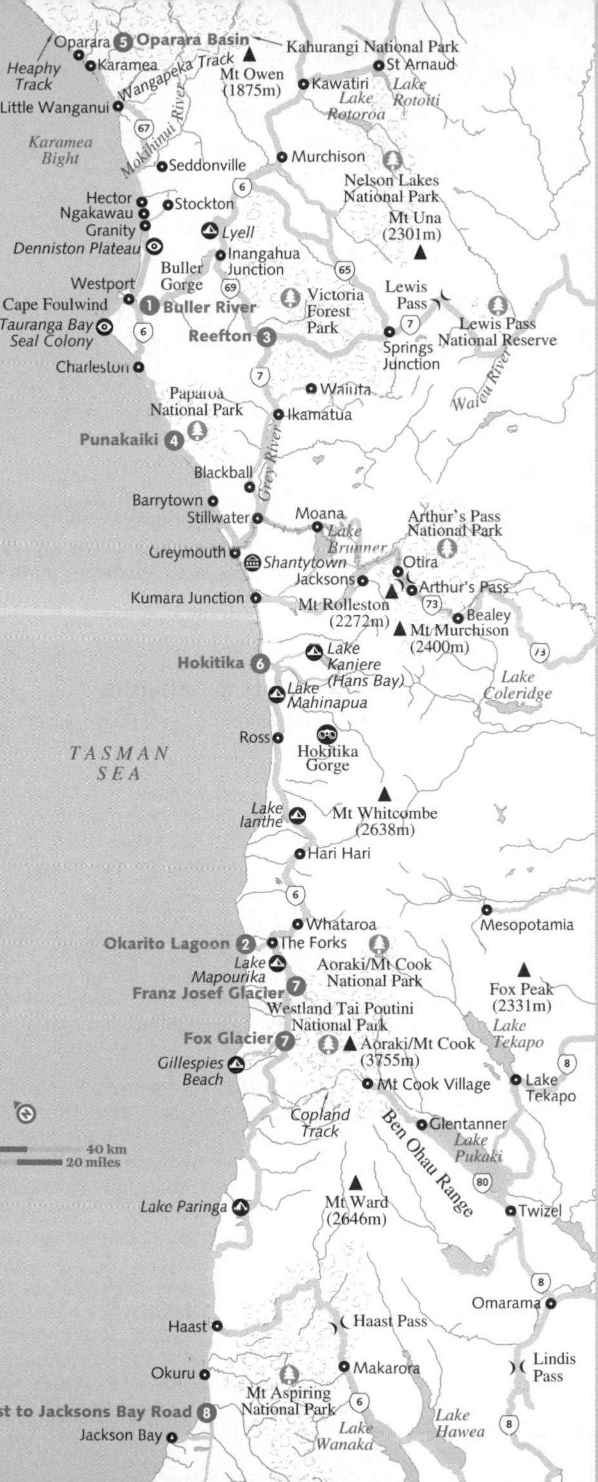

The West Coast Highlights

1. Getting wet 'n' wild on the mighty **Buller River** (p102)
2. Kayaking through the bird-filled channels of **Okarito Lagoon** (p122)
3. Delving into the golden past around **Reefton** (p111)
4. Marvelling at nature's beautiful fury at the Pancake Rocks at **Punakaiki** (p109)
5. Exploring the limestone landscape of the **Oparara Basin** (p107)
6. Hunting out authentic local greenstone in the galleries of **Hokitika** (p117)
7. Flying high into the Southern Alps via **Franz Josef** (p123) and **Fox Glaciers** (p128)
8. Reaching the end of the line on the scenic and historical highway from **Haast** to **Jackson Bay** (p132)

ESSENTIAL WEST COAST

» **Eat** Whitebait, bought from an old-timer's back door at an honest price

» **Drink** The only roast on the coast, Kawatiri Coffee

» **Read** Jenny Pattrick's *The Denniston Rose*, a colourful history of black gold

» **Listen to** Karamea's laid-back community radio station on 107.5FM; you can even choose your own tracks

» **Watch** *Denniston Incline* on YouTube, then imagine sitting in the wagon on the way down

» **Festival** Go bush-food crazy at Hokitika's Wildfoods Festival (p119)

» **Go Green** At West Coast Wildlife Centre (p123) – baby kiwis! Too cute!

» **Online** www.westcoastnz.com

» **Area code** ☎03

Getting There & Around

Air New Zealand (☎0800 737 000, 09-357 3000; www.airnz.co.nz) flies between Westport and Wellington, and Hokitika and Christchurch.

Coaches and shuttles connect centres like Christchurch, Dunedin, Queenstown and Nelson; major players are **Atomic Shuttles** (☎03-349 0697; www.atomictravel.co.nz), InterCity (p348), **Naked Bus** (www.nakedbus.com) and **West Coast Shuttle** (☎03-768 0028; www.westcoastshuttle.co.nz).

The TranzAlpine (p116), one of the world's great train journeys, links Greymouth and Christchurch.

MURCHISON & BULLER GORGE

POP 800

Murchison, 125km southwest of Nelson and 95km east of Westport, is the northern gateway to the West Coast. It sits alongside the Buller River, just one of scores of rivers around this area. Kayaking, rafting and trout-fishing are popular here, but those who want to keep their feet dry might *just* manage it on a number of good walks.

From Murchison, State Hwy 6 snakes through Buller Gorge, a journey that could easily take a day or two by the time you've taken a rafting or jetboating trip and stopped at other interesting points along the way.

Your big decision on the gorge road is which way to head when you reach the forks at Inangahua Junction. Either continue along SH6 through the Lower Buller Gorge to Westport, or head south to Greymouth via Reefton on SH69.

The longer, more scenic SH6 leads to the many attractions up north. It also passes the Lyell, an interesting historic reserve and end of the Old Ghost Road trail which will soon reach right through to Mokihinui north of Westport (part of the New Zealand Cycle Trail). That said, Reefton certainly has its own merits.

Sights & Activities

Ask at the Murchison i-SITE for a copy of the *Murchison District Map*, which lists numerous short walks and the local mountain-bike loop. Bicycles can be hired from Murchison Motels (p103). The i-SITE can also hook you up with guided trout-fishing trips, which will cost around $350 for two people per half-day.

Murchison Museum MUSEUM
(60 Fairfax St; admission by donation; ⏲10am-4pm) This museum showcases all sorts of local memorabilia, the most interesting of which relates to the 1929 and 1968 earthquakes.

Ultimate Descents RAFTING
(☎0800 748 377, 03-523 9899; www.rivers.co.nz; 51 Fairfax St; half-/full day rafting $130/220, half-day kayaking $125) Offers white-water rafting and kayaking trips on the Buller, including half-day, gentler family excursions (adult/child $105/85). Heli-rafting trips by arrangement.

TOP CHOICE **Wild Rivers Rafting** RAFTING
(☎0508 467 238; www.wildriversrafting.co.nz; 3hr trip adult/child $110/85) White-water rafting with Bruce and Marty on the particularly exciting Earthquake Rapids section of the beautiful Buller River (good luck with 'gunslinger' and the 'pop-up toaster'!).

Buller Gorge Swingbridge BRIDGE
(www.bullergorge.co.nz; SH6; bridge crossing adult/child $5/2; ⌚8am-7pm Oct-Apr, 9am-5pm May-Sep) About 14km west of Murchison is NZ's longest swingbridge (110m). Across it are some short walks, one to the White Creek Faultline, epicentre of the 1929 earthquake. Coming back, ride the 160m Cometline Flying Fox, either seated (adult/child $30/15) or 'Supaman' ($45, or tandem adult/child $30/15).

Buller Canyon Jet JETBOATING
(☎03 523 9883; www.bullercanyonjet.co.nz; SH6; adult/child $95/50; ⌚Sept-Apr) Claiming 'NZ's best jet boating', and it might just be right: 40 minutes of ripping through the Buller. Whoo hoo! It's located at the Buller Gorge Swingbridge.

Festivals & Events

Buller Festival SPORTS
(www.bullerfestival.co.nz) A kayaking and rafting extravaganza held over the first weekend in March.

Sleeping & Eating

Murchison is decent place for stocking up on supplies, with a dairy, mini-supermarket and a butchery curing notable bacon.

Lazy Cow HOSTEL $
(☎03-523 9451; www.lazycow.co.nz; 37 Waller St; dm $28, d $74-84; @📶) It's easy to be a lazy cow here, with all the comforts of home including free muffins or cake and freshly cooked evening meals ($12). The great hosts take pride in their pad, and it shows throughout the house and gardens.

Commercial Hotel HOTEL $
(☎03-523 9696; www.commercialhotel.co.nz; cnr Waller & Fairfax Sts; s/d/tr $40/75/100; ⌚8am-8.30pm; @📶) Super street-appeal and brightly coloured bar walls are just the starters. The guest wing offers the best possible shock with its checkerboard and crimson hallway clashing with the heritage-charm bedrooms. Great value; all share bathrooms and a cupboard-sized kitchen. The popular pub offers bar snacks and meals ($13 to $29).

Murchison Motorhome Park HOLIDAY PARK $
(☎03-523 9666; www.murchisonmotorhomepark.co.nz; SH6; sites from $26; ⌚closed Jul & Aug; 📶) The landscaping at this new park has yet to reach maturity, but warm and well-designed facilities more than make up for it, as does the lovely stretch of Buller River (with swimming holes) that runs alongside. It's 8km north of Murchison.

Murchison Lodge B&B $$
(☎03-523 9196; www.murchisonlodge.co.nz; 15 Grey St; s incl breakfast $130-190, d incl breakfast $155-215; ⌚closed May-Aug; @📶) Surrounded by native trees, this B&B has access to the Buller River and some decent swimming holes. Nice interior design touches and friendly hosts add to the comfortable feel. Evening meals by arrangement, if you can't be bothered with the short walk to town.

Murchison Motels MOTEL $$
(☎0800 166 500, 03-523 9026; www.murchisonmotels.co.nz; 53 Fairfax St; d $140-180; 📶🏊) Tucked behind Rivers Cafe, with snazzy one- and two-bedroom units complete with kitchenettes. There's also a swimming pool, and mountain bikes for hire (half-day $15).

Hu-Ha Bikepackers FARMSTAY $
(☎03-548 2707; huhabikepackers@farmside.co.nz; 2937 Kohatu-Kawatiri Hwy, Glenhope; unpowered sites from $14, dm $28, d with/without bathroom $72/62; 📶) Friendly hosts give their ground floor over to guests who can enjoy a charming open-plan communal area with wooden floors, log-burner, and a dining table with a rural view. There's a piano, an enviable collection of vinyl records, and farm animals including a very fat pig. It's 45km to Murchison from here. Cash only.

Rivers Cafe CAFE $$
(51 Fairfax St; meals $12-30; ⌚8.30am-9pm Oct-Mar, 9am-3pm Apr-Sep) The town's old garage is now home to a questionable craft gallery,

MAORI NZ: THE WEST COAST

For Maori, the river valleys and mountains of the West Coast were the traditional source of highly prized *pounamu* (greenstone), carved into tools, weapons and adornments. View the Pounamu exhibit at Holitika Museum (p117) to polish your knowledge of the precious rock before admiring the classy carving done by the town's artists. Kotuku Gallery (p122), further south in Whataroa, is also a good spot for the genuine article.

but myriad quality pastries. Sample the delicious lamb shank pie with decent coffee or a pint of craft beer.

Information

There is no ATM in town; the postal agency is on Fairfax St.

The **Murchison i-SITE** (☎03-523 9350; www.nelsonnz.com; 47 Waller St; ⊙10am-6pm Oct-May, reduced hours Apr-Sept) has info on local activities and transport.

Getting There & Away

Buses passing through Murchison between the West Coast and Picton are **InterCity** (☎03-365 1113; www.intercity.co.nz) and **Naked Bus** (www.nakedbus.com), both of which stop at Beechwoods Café on Waller St.

WESTPORT & AROUND

POP 4850

The port of Westport made its fortune in coal mining, though today the main mine is at Stockton, 38km north. The proposed expansion of West Coast coal mining is the subject of heated debates which pit traditional adversaries – the greens versus the go-aheads – against each other. There's no doubt that this industry keeps the town stoked up: it's looking purposeful, pretty, and even slighly 'go ahead'. Beyond some respectable hospitality, the town contains little of prolonged interest, but makes a good base for exploring the fascinating coast north to Karamea, Oparara and the Heaphy Track.

Sights & Activities

Westport is good for a stroll – the i-SITE can direct you to the **Millenium Walkway** and the freshly revamped **Kawatiri Beach Reserve**. The most thrilling adventure in the area is cave rafting with Norwest Adventures (p104).

Tauranga Bay Seal Colony WILDLIFE

Depending on the season, anything from 20 to 200 NZ fur seals dot the rocks at this seal colony, 16km from Westport. Pups are born from late November to early December.

The Cape Foulwind Walkway (1½ hours return) extends from the seal colony near its southern end, 4km along the coast to Cape Foulwind, passing a replica of Abel Tasman's astrolabe (a navigational aid) and a lighthouse. The walk's northern end is car-accessible from Lighthouse Rd.

The Maori called the cape Tauranga, meaning 'Sheltered Anchorage'. The first European here was Abel Tasman in December 1642; he named it Clyppygen Hoek (Rocky Point). When James Cook moored the *Endeavour* here in March 1770, a furious storm made it anything but a 'sheltered anchorage', hence Cape Foulwind's modern name.

West Coast Brewing Co BREWERY

(www.westcoastbrewing.com; 10 Lyndhurst St; tastings $10; ⊙8.30am-5pm Mon-Fri, 10am-4pm Sat & Sun) Taste up to a dozen craft beers, including the organic Green Fern lager and a notable India pale ale. Pop in for a tasting, or get a rigger to go (or, quite possibly, pull up a stool and struggle to leave).

Coaltown Museum MUSEUM

(165 Queen St; adult/child $12.50/5; ⊙9am-4.30pm) This earnest but decidedly old-fashioned museum will appeal to those with an interest in local history. Expect plenty of musty mining artefacts, maritime displays, and a huge engine from a steam dredge. The Denniston film is worth watching.

Norwest Adventures CAVING, RAILWAY

(☎0800 116 686, 03-788 8168; www.caverafting.com; SH6, Charleston) At Charleston, 26km south of Westport, this friendly bunch run 'Underworld' cave-rafting trips ($165, four hours) into the glowworm-filled Nile River Caves. If you want the glow without the flow (no rafting), it's $105 per person. Both options start with a fun rainforest railway ride, available separately (adult/child $20/15, 1½ hours). The Adventure Caving trip ($330, five hours) includes a 40m abseil into Te Tahi *tomo* (hole) with rock squeezes, waterfalls, prehistoric fossils and trippy cave formations.

Sleeping

Archer House B&B **$$**

(☎03-789 8778, 0800 789 877; www.archerhouse.co.nz; 75 Queen St; d incl breakfast $185; @ᯤ) This big and beautiful 1890 heritage home sleeps up to eight in three rooms with their own bathrooms, all sharing no less than three lounges and peaceful gardens. Lovely hosts, complimentary sherry, generous continental breakfast and free wi-fi make this Westport's most refined accommodation option.

Buller Court Motel MOTEL **$$**

(☎03-789 7979; www.bullercourtmotel.co.nz; 253 Palmerston St; d $120-170, q $195-215; ᯤ) One of many main road options, this older-style complex has had a tasteful make-over and impresses with an away-from-the-road aspect and small but private grassy gardens.

Trip Inn HOSTEL $
(☎0800 737 773, 03-789 7367; www.tripinn.co.nz; 72 Queen Street; dm/s/d $27/55/66; @📶) Feel like lord of the manor at this grand 150-year old villa with beautiful gardens. There's a variety of tidy rooms in and out of the house to choose from, and voluminous communal areas.

Seal Colony TOP 10 Holiday Park HOLIDAY PARK $
(☎0508 937 876, 03-789 8002; www.top10westport.co.nz; 57 Marine Pde, Carters Beach; sites from $36, units $70-140; @📶) Right on Carters Beach and conveniently located between Westport (4km) and the Tauranga Bay seal colony (12km), this no-frills outfit offers a full range of facilities of a more than acceptable standard. A good option for tourers seeking a clean and peaceful stop-off, and perhaps even a swim.

Omau Settlers Lodge LODGE $
(☎03-789 5200; www.omausettlerslodge.co.nz; 1054 Cape Rd; r incl breakfast $135-155; 📶) Close to Cape Foulwind and across the road from the excellent Star Tavern, these contemporary and stylish units offer rest, relaxation and huge buffet breakfasts. Rooms have kitchenette, but you can also share a kitchen and dining room. A hot tub surrounded by bush maximises the take-it-easy quotient.

Westport Holiday Park HOLIDAY PARK $
(☎03-789 7043; www.westportholidaypark.co.nz; 31 Domett St; sites from $32, d $95-145; @📶) A-frame 'chalets' stud this back-street park with adequate amenities and a mini-golf course.

Eating & Drinking

A small town it may be, but Westport has more than its fair share of pubs, along with plenty of places to eat and a couple of supermarkets for stocking up.

TOP CHOICE **Town House** MODERN NZ $$
(☎03-789 7133; www.thetownhouse.co.nz; cnr Cobden & Palmerston Sts; mains $15-32; ⏲10am-4pm Sun & Mon, 10am-late Tue-Sat) The most upmarket option in town, fit for the finest of cities. Shift between the sunny terrace, groovy bar and dining room with art deco styling while you enjoy excellent contemporary fare from morning til night. Too many highlights to mention, but the home-cured confit duck leg and gingernut ice-cream did it for us.

Jay's Cafe CAFE $
(260 Palmerston St; mains $9-17; ⏲8am-5pm Mon-Sat) Mimicking the cafe's native bird theme, locals flock here for the best coffee in town and consistent cafe food, ranging from eggy brekkies through to grilled turbot and steak sammies.

Porto Bello BAR $$
(www.westportrestaurant.co.nz; 62 Palmerston St; meals $12-29; ⏲4pm-late Mon-Thur, 11am-late Fri-Sun) Roman columns and renaissance artwork give this place a Coliseum feel, but the food has its roots firmly in the US of A. Six local craft beers on tap, $15 steak specials and occasional live music keep the locals happy.

Information

The major banks are along Palmerston St. There's free wi-fi at the **Westport Library** (87 Palmerston St).

Buller Hospital (☎03-788 9030; Cobden St)

Department of Conservation Office (DOC; ☎03-788 8008; www.doc.govt.nz; 72 Russell St; ⏲8am-noon & 1-4.30pm Mon-Fri) Tickets for the Heaphy and Wangapeka Tracks plus general tramping info.

Police Station (☎03-788 8310; 13 Wakefield St)

Post Office (cnr Brougham & Palmerston Sts)

Westport i-SITE (☎03-789 6658; www.westport.org.nz; 1 Brougham St; ⏲9am-5pm Nov-Mar, to 4.30pm Apr-Oct) Information on local tracks, walkways, tours, accommodation and transport.

Getting There & Around

Air

Air New Zealand (☎0800 737 000; www.airnewzealand.co.nz) has one or two flights per day to/from Wellington (from $89).

Bus

InterCity (☎03-365 1113; www.intercity.co.nz) buses depart daily from outside the i-SITE and **Caltex Petrol Station** (197 Palmerston St) to Nelson (from $30, 3½ hours), Greymouth (from $17, 2¼ hours) and Franz Josef (from $38, six hours).

Naked Bus (www.nakedbus.com) goes three times a week to Nelson (from $10, four hours), Greymouth (from $10, two hours) and Franz Josef (from $10, 5¼ hours), departing from the i-SITE.

East West Coach (p112) operates a Christchurch service ($63, Sunday to Friday, 4¾ hours) departing from the Caltex Petrol Station.

Karamea Express (☎03-782 6757; info@karamea-express.co.nz) links Westport and Karamea ($30, two hours, 11.30am Monday to Friday May to September, plus Saturday from October to April), departing from the i-SITE.

Car

Hire some wheels at **Wesport Hire** (☎0508 974 473, 03-789 5038; wesporthire@xtra.co.nz; 294 Palmerston St).

Taxi

Buller Taxis (☎03-789 6900) can take you to/from the airport (around $20).

WESTPORT TO KARAMEA

North along SH67, the road is pressed against the rocky shoreline by verdant hills. If you're heading all the way up to Karamea, fill your tank in Westport as it's 98km to the next petrol station.

The first town beyond Westport is **Waimangaroa**, with a shop worth a stop for a home-made pie and ice cream. Here you'll also find the turn-off to the **Denniston Plateau**, 9km inland and 600m above sea level.

Denniston was once NZ's largest coal producer, with 1500 residents in 1911. By 1981 there were eight. Its claim to fame was the fantastically steep **Denniston Incline**, an engineering spectacular. Empty coal trucks were hauled back up the 45-degree slope by the weight of descending loaded trucks.

Today this historic site is a fascinating place to visit, recently improved and enhanced with information panels. The *Denniston Rose Walking Tour* brochure ($2 from DOC and Westport Llibrary) may lead keen readers to the local bookshop to buy Jenny Pattrick's evocative novels set in the area. The **Denniston Mine Experience** (☎0800 881 880; www.dennistonminexperience.co.nz; Denniston; 2hr tour adult/child $85/55) guided tours ride the 'gorge express' train into the historic Banbury mine for what is a slightly spooky but fascinating exploration of the tunnels. Other features of the plateau include the **Denniston Bridle Track**, which follows sections of the Incline, excellent mountain biking (maps and bikes from Habitat Sports (p108)) and some picnic sports with awesome views.

At sleepy **Granity**, 30km north of Westport, head 5km uphill to the semi-ghost town of **Millerton**, and a further 3km to **Stockton**, home of NZ's largest operational coal mine. (Orange fluro vests ahoy!) The **Millerton Incline Walk** (20 minutes return) takes in parts of the old Incline, a bridge and dam. Just north at **Hector** you can see a monument to Hector's dolphins, NZ's smallest, although you'll be lucky to see them unless your timing is impeccable.

In these parts you'll find the Charming Creek Walkway (p107). Further north, the Seddonville road leads to the **Rough and Tumble Bush Lodge** (☎03-782 1337; www.roughandtumble.co.nz; Mokihinui Rd; r $200; 📶). In a gentle bend of the Mohikinui River, this upmarket self-catering option is surrounded by forest and walking trails. The rooms and shared main lodge house exude rustic chic, while the kitchen is equipped to feed a small army. Advance bookings are essential.

At the Mohikinui River mouth, 3km off the highway, is the not-so-gentle **Gentle Annie Beach** and the **Gentle Annie Coastal Enclave** (☎03-782 1826, 0274 188 587; www.gentleannie.co.nz; De Malmanche Rd, Mohikinui; sites from $12, s/d $25/50, cabins $120-200), perfect for quiet contemplation. There are campsites, a lodge, a range of self-contained accommodation and a seasonal cafe. There's also a maze on top of a lookout point, and glow worms if you know who to ask.

Between Mohikinui and Little Wanganui the road meanders over **Karamea Bluff**, with rata and matai forests, and expansive views of the Tasman Sea below. It's worth stopping to do the **Lake Hanlon** walk (30 minutes return) on the Karamea side of the hill.

KARAMEA & AROUND

The relaxed town of Karamea (population 650) considers itself the West Coast's 'best kept secret', but those who've visited tend to boast about its merits far and wide. An end-of-the-road town it may well be, but it still has a bit of the 'hub' about it, servicing the end (or start) of the Heaphy and Wangapeka Tracks, and the unmissable Oparara Basin. With a friendly climate, and a take-it-easy mix of locals and chilled-out imports, the Karamea area is a great place to jump off the well-trodden tourist trail for a few lazy days.

Sights & Activities

Hats off to the Karamea community who have established the very pleasant **Karamea Estuary Walkway**, a short stroll (one

DON'T MISS

A CHARMING CREEK INDEED

One of the best day-walks on the Coast, the **Charming Creek Walkway** (six hours return) is an all-weather trail following an old coal line through the Ngakawau River Gorge. Along its length are rusty relics galore, tunnels, a suspension bridge and waterfall, and lots of interesting plants and geological formations.

You can start the track at **Ngakawau**, where you'll find the **Charming Creek B&B** (☎0800 867 3529, 03-782 8007; www.bullerbeachstay.co.nz; Ngakawau; d incl breakfast $139-169; 📶) – a good base for the track. The rooms are clean and, well, charming, and there's a driftwood-fired hot tub right by the sea. A two-night walking package ($420) includes dinners and a picnic lunch while on the track.

You can also start the track at the northern trailhead 10km beyond **Seddonville**, a small bush town on the Mohikinui River where **Seddonville Holiday Park** (☎03-782 1314) offers respectable camping in the grounds of the old school. A local may fix you up with transport if you don't want to walk it both ways.

Experienced mountain bikers can make a loop of it: park your car at the Seddonville pub and ride in a clockwise direction. The coastal highway is a fab way to finish, as is a pint at the pub when you're done.

hour) bordering the estuary and Karemea River. You can ask a local where it is, follow your nose, or pick up a leaflet from the Karamea Information & Resource Centre. While you're there, pick up the free *Karamea* brochure, which details other walks, including **Big Rimu** (45 minutes return), **Flagstaff** (one hour return) and the **Zig Zag** (one hour return).

Longer walks around Karamea include the **Fenian Track** (four hours return) leading to **Cavern Creek Caves** and **Adams Flat**, where there's a replica gold-miner's hut; and the first leg of the **Wangapeka Track** to Belltown Hut. The Wangapeka Track is a day traverse of Kahurangi National Park, generally started at Tapawera in the Motueka Valley.

Other activities include swimming, fishing, whitebaiting, kayaking and mountain biking. Your best bet for advice on these is to ask a local and always use common sense – especially when it comes to the watery stuff. **Karamea Outdoor Adventures** (☎03-782 6181, 03-782 6646; www.karameaadventures.co.nz; Bridge St; guided kayak trips from $45, kayak hire 2hrs $25, bike hire 2hrs $25) offers guided kayaking trips on the Oparara and Karamea Rivers, plus kayak and mountain-bike hire, and advice on local excursions.

OPARARA VALLEY

North of Karamea, the **Oparara Basin** contains justifiably famous natural wonders. Spectacular limestone arches and unique caves are surrounded by a karst landscape blanketed by primitive rainforest. To get here from Karamea, drive 10km along the main north road north and turn off at McCallum's Mill Rd. Continue 15km past the sawmill along a winding gravel (sometimes rough) road.

It's an easy walk (45 minutes return) through old-growth forest to the 200m-long, 37m-high **Oparara Arch**, spanning its namesake river. Its rival is the **Moria Gate Arch** (43m long, 19m high), accessed via a similar track (one hour return). Other highlights are **Mirror Tarn** (an easy 20 minutes return), and the **Crazy Paving & Box Canyon Caves** (10 minutes return, BYO torch).

Beyond these, in a protected area of Kahurangi National Park, are the superb **Honeycomb Hill Caves & Arch**, accessible only by prebooked guided tours (five hours, $150) run by the people at the Karamea Information and Resource Centre (p108). Ask about their other guided tours of the area.

For a full-day freedom walk, the rewarding **Oparara Valley Track** takes you through ancient forest, along the river, and will take five hours and pop you out at the **Fenian Walk** carpark. Ask at the Information & Resource Centre about track transport, and also about gentle river kayaking trips on offer from mid-December to April (two hours, $95).

HEAPHY TRACK

The West Coast road runs out at **Kohaihai**, the western trailhead (and most commonly, the finish point) of the Heaphy Track, where there's also a **DOC campsite** (per person $6). A day walk or overnight stay can readily be had from here. Walk to **Scotts Beach** (1½ hours return), or go as far as **Heaphy Hut** (huts/campsites $32/14) (five hours) and stay a night or two before returning.

This section can also be mountain-biked, as can the whole track (two to three days) from May to September under a trial period ending in September 2013; ask at Westport's **Habitat Sports** (☎03-788 8002; www.habitatsports.co.nz; 204 Palmerston St) for bike hire and details.

Helicopter Charter Karamea (p109) will fly up to three people through to the northern trailhead in Golden Bay for $675 ($750 with three bikes); ask about other possible drop-off/pick-up points.

For detailed information on negotiating the Heaphy Track, see www.heaphytrack.com.

Sleeping & Eating

Cafes and restaurants are thin on the ground around these parts, so stock up at Karamea's 4 Square and keep an eye out for 'open' signs.

Last Resort RESORT $
(☎0800 505 042, 03-782 6617; www.lastresort.co.nz; 71 Waverley St, Karamea; dm $37, d $78-155; @☜) When we visited, renovations were well underway at this iconic, rambling and rustic resort. Rooms and facilities are simple but hallmarked by the extensive use of local timbers and artwork. The communal areas are warm and welcoming, including the cafe (lunch $9 to $15, dinner $18 to $29) serving simple all-day food like burgers, fish and chips and Caesar salad.

Rongo Backpackers HOSTEL $
(☎03-782 6667; www.rongobackpackers.com; 130 Waverley St, Karamea; sites from $20, dm $30-32, d & tw $75; @☜) Part neo-hippie artists' haven and part organic vegie garden, this uber-relaxed hostel even has its own community radio station (107.5 FM, www.karamearadio.com). Popular with long-term guests who often end up working within – either tending the garden or as de facto DJs. Every fourth night free.

Karamea Farm Baches CABINS $
(☎03-782 6838; www.karameamotels.com; 17 Wharf Rd, Karamea; d/tr/q $90/115/140; @☜) Pushing reuse/recycle to the limit, these 1960s fully self-contained baches are the real McCoy, right down to cobwebby corners and frayed bedspreads. If you dig organic gardening, friendly dogs and colourful hosts, this will win you over.

Karamea River Motels MOTEL $$
(☎03-782 6955; www.karameamotels.co.nz; 31 Bridge St, Karamea; r $125-165; ☜) The smart rooms at this modern, rural motel range from studios to two-bedroom units. Features include long-range views, barbecues and lush gardens complete with lily pond.

Karamea Holiday Park HOLIDAY PARK $
(☎03-782 6758; www.karamea.com; Maori Point Rd, Karamea; sites from $28, cabins $40-50, d $86; @☜) A simple, old-fashioned camp alongside the estuary in bush surrounds, 3km south of Market Cross. The classic weatherboard cabins are clean and well maintained.

Wangapeka Backpackers Retreat & Farmstay HOSTEL $
(☎03-782 6663; www.wangapeka.co.nz; Atawhai Farm, Wangapeka Valley; campsites from $10, dm $20, s/d $45/75; ☜) This laid-back and friendly farmstay close to the Wangapeka Track has crusty dorms with clean linen, and meals by arrangement. Turn down Wangapeka Rd just north of Little Wanganui and follow the signs. It's a 20km drive south of Karamea.

Karamea Village Hotel PUB $$
(karameahotel@xtra.co.nz; cnr Waverley St & Wharf Rd, Karamea; mains $18-29; ⊙11am-11pm) Treat yourself to life's simple pleasures: a game of pool with the locals, a pint of Monteith's Original Ale, and a whitebait-fritter sandwich. Sorted.

Information

Karamea Information & Resource Centre (☎03-782 6652; www.karameainfo.co.nz; Market Cross; ⊙9am-5pm daily Jan-May, 9am-1pm Sat & Sun only Jun-Dec; @) This excellent, community-owned centre has the local low-down, internet access, maps and DOC hut tickets. It also doubles as the petrol station.

Getting There & Away

Karamea Express (p106) links Karamea and Westport ($30, two hours, 7.50am Monday to Friday May to September, plus Saturday from October to April). It also services Kohaihai twice daily during peak summer, and other times on demand. Wangapeka transport is also available.

Heaphy Bus (☎0800 128 735, 03-540 2042; www.theheaphybus.co.nz), based in Nelson, also runs between both ends of the Heaphy, as well as the Wangapeka.

Fly from Karamea to Takaka with **Helicopter Charter Karamea** (☎03-782 6111; www.adventuresnz.co.nz; 79 Waverley St, Karamea) or Golden Bay Air (p96), for around $175 per person, then walk back on the Heaphy Track; contact the Information & Resource Centre for details.

Rongo Backpackers run on-demand track and town transport around the place including to Heaphy, Wangapeka, Oparara Basin and Westport.

WESTPORT TO GREYMOUTH

SH6 along the surf-pounded coastline here proffers fine ocean views. Fill up in Westport if you're low on petrol and cash – there's no fuel until Runanga, 92km away, and the next ATM is in Greymouth. The main attractions along this stretch are the geologically fascinating Pancake Rocks at Punakaiki. To break the journey, consider the following.

Set on 52 serene hectares 17km south of Westport, solar-powered, energy-efficient **Beaconstone Eco Lodge** (☎027 431 0491; www.beaconstoneecolodge.co.nz; Birds Ferry Rd; dm $28-31, d $66-74; ⏲Oct-Jun) is both earth- and guest-friendly. The style is a little bit Americana cool, while the comforts are many, including cosy beds and a laid-back communal area. Bush walks on the doorstep. There's only room for 12, so booking is recommended.

Jack's Gasthof (☎03-789 6501; www.jacksgasthof.co.nz; SH6; sites from $5, d $50; ⏲Oct-May) is 21km south of Westport on the Little Totara River. Laconic Jack swapped Berlin for this gentle spot more than 22 years ago, and he and Petra still run this eternally popular pizzeria (mains $10 to $25; open from 11am) with adjacent bar improbably bejewelled with a disco ball. Rooms and camping for horizonal dancing.

For a true taste of the region's gold mining past, swing into **Mitchell's Gully Gold Mine** (☎03-789 6553; www.mitchellsgullygoldmine.co.nz; SH6; adult/child $10/free; ⏲9am-5pm), 22km south of Westport, where you'll meet a pioneer's descendants and explore the family mine. There are interesting tales, relics, tunnels and railtracks, plus a giant waterwheel and the odd trap-door spider.

The next stop is **Charleston**, 26km south of Westport. It's hard to believe it now, but this place boomed during the 1860s gold rush, with 80 hotels, three breweries and hundreds of thirsty g… the Nile Riv… cept a motel … houses and t… (p104) with v… terly amazing…

From here … mixture of lo… green forest a… matically scul… Drive as slowl… allow.

Punakaiki & Paparoa National Park

Located midway between Westport and Greymouth is Punakaiki, a small settlement beside the rugged 38,000-hectare Paparoa National Park. For most travellers, it's a quick stop for an ice cream and a squiz at the Pancake Rocks; a shame because there's excellent tramping on offer and some tragically underused accommodation.

Sights

Paparoa National Park is blessed with sea cliffs, a dramatic mountain range, gorgeous limestone river valleys, diverse flora and a Westland petrel colony, the world's only nesting site of this rare sea bird.

Pancake Rocks NATURAL FEATURE

Punakaiki is famous for its fantastic Pancake Rocks and blowholes. Through a layering-weathering process called stylobedding, the Dolomite Point limestone has formed into what looks like piles of thick pancakes. When the tide is high (tide times are posted at the visitor information centre), the sea surges into caverns and booms menacingly through blowholes. See it on a wild day and be reminded that Mother Nature really is the boss. An easy 15-minute walk loops from the highway out to the rocks and blowholes.

Activities

Tramps around Punakaiki include the **Truman Track** (30 minutes return) and the **Porari River Track** (3½ hours), which goes up the spectacular limestone Pororari River gorge before popping over a hill to come down the bouldery Punakaiki River to rejoin the highway.

Surefooted types can visit the **Fox River Tourist Cave** (three hours return), 12km

pen to amateur ex- sturdy shoes.

he national park are de- C *Paparoa National Park* , and include the **Inland Pack** o to three days), a route estab- y miners in 1867 to dodge difficult al terrain.

Many of Paparoa's inland walks are susceptible to river flooding; check in with the DOC Visitor Centre in Punakaiki before you depart. Better still, go with a guide.

Nature's Tours ECOTOUR
(☎03-731 1442; www.naturestours.co.nz; 4hr tour $125) Fresh-faced Zane of Nature's Tours brims with passion for the wilderness and successfully translates this into insightful hiking tours packed with stories with a dash of fun. Four-hour trips take in the Pancake Rocks, the Truman Track and Pororari River, with customised trips (two hours to two days) by arrangement.

Punakaiki Canoes KAYAKING
(☎03-731 1870; www.riverkayaking.co.nz; SH6; canoe hire 2hr/full day $35/55, family rates avail) The Pororari River offers gentle, family-friendly paddling. This outfit rents canoes near the Pororari River bridge.

Punakaiki Horse Treks HORSE RIDING
(☎03-731 1839; www.pancake-rocks.co.nz; SH6; 2½hr ride $145; ⏲Oct-June) Punakaiki Horse Treks, based at Hydrangea Cottages, conducts four-legged outings in the Punakaiki Valley, with river crossings, finishing at the beach.

Sleeping & Eating

There's good news and bad news. The good news is that there's heaps of good accommodation in Punakaiki. The bad news is that there's no grocery shop or petrol, and that the two cafes next to the main visitor car park may well fail to please. The tavern down the road, however, has proven a consistently good performer. Keep it up, Team Pub!

TOP CHOICE **Punakaiki Beach Hostel** HOSTEL $
(☎03-731 1852; www.punakaikibeachhostel.co.nz; 4 Webb St; sites per person $20, dm/s/d $27/53/71; @📶) A canary-yellow, beach-bumming hostel with a sea-view verandah, just a short way from Pancake Rocks. Co-operative owners have been-there-done-that and know exactly what you want: a clean hostel with good beds, great communal facilities, and staff who smile because they mean it.

Punakaiki Beach Camp HOLIDAY PARK $
(☎03-731 1894; beachcamp@xtra.co.nz; 5 Owen St; sites $31, d $46) With a back-drop of sheer cliffs, this salty park with good grass is studded with clean, old-style cabins and shipshape amenities.

Te Nikau Retreat LODGE $
(☎03-731 1111; www.tenikauretreat.co.nz; Hartmount Pl; sites from $18, dm $27, d $71-86, cabins from $96; @📶) This unconventional property consists of numerous buildings nestled into their own rainforest nooks, just a short walk to the beach. There are dorms in the main building, several cute cabins, and the larger Nikau Lodge sleeping up to 10. The clear-roofed stargazer hut is tiny, but fun for those who want to sleep under the night sky.

Hydrangea Cottages COTTAGES $$
(☎03-731 1839; www.pancake-rocks.co.nz; SH6; d $140-220; 📶) On a hillside overlooking the Tasman, these five stand-alone and mostly self-contained cottages (largest sleeping up to seven) are built from salvaged river timber and river stones. It's a classy but relaxed enclave, with splashes of colourful mosaic and pretty cottage gardens. The owners also run the horse-trekking stables.

Punakaiki Tavern PUB $$
(www.punakaikitavern.co.nz; SH6; mains $19-32; ⏲8am-late) Whether it's breakfast, lunch or dinner, this pub does decent portions of honest food served in comfortable surrounds. Most nights the punters are a mix of local and international, so there's ample opportunity for conversation and friendly debate over the rules of pool.

Information

The **Paparoa National Park visitor information centre and i-SITE** (☎03-731 1895; www.doc.govt.nz; SH6; ⏲9am-5pm Oct-Nov, to 6pm Dec-Mar, to 4.30pm Apr-Sep) has information on the park and track conditions, and handles bookings for local attractions and accommodation, including hut tickets.

See also www.punakaiki.co.nz.

Getting There & Away

InterCity (☎03-365 1113; www.intercity.co.nz) links to Westport daily (from $13, three hours), Greymouth (from $10, 45 minutes) and Franz Josef (from $33, four hours). **Naked Bus** (www.nakedbus.com) has a similar service along SH6 operating three days a week. Both companies allow enough time to check out Pancake Rocks.

The Coast Road

The highway from Punakaiki to Greymouth is flanked by white-capped waves and rocky bays on one side, and the steep, bushy Paparoa Ranges on the other.

At **Barrytown**, 16km south of Punakaiki, Steve and Robyn run **Barrytown Knifemaking** (☎0800 256 433, 03-731 1053; www.barrytownknifemaking.com; 2662 SH6, Barrytown; classes $130; ⏰closed Mon), where you can make your own knife – from hand-forging the blade to crafting a handle from native rimu timber. The day-long course features lunch, archery, axe-throwing and a stream of entertainingly bad jokes from Steve. Bookings essential, and transport from Punakaiki can be arranged.

With a backdrop of subtropical rainforest, **Ti Kouka House** (☎03-731 1460; www.tikoukahouse.co.nz; 2522 SH6, Barrytown; d incl breakfast $295; 📶) is all rugged sea views, global antiques and lots of recycled wood including history-laden doors and windows. It's an excellent B&B, with three luxury rooms.

Breakers (☎03-762 7743; www.breakers.co.nz; 1367 SH6, Nine Mile Creek; d incl breakfast $215-355; @📶), 14km north of Greymouth, is one of the best-kept secrets on the coast. Beautifully appointed en suite rooms overlook the sea, with fine surfing opportunities at hand for the intrepid. The hosts are both friendly and mountain-biking mad.

REEFTON & GREY VALLEY

From Murchison, an alternative to the SH6 coast route is to turn off at Inangahua Junction and travel inland across winding valley roads via Reefton, and over the mountains into the Grey Valley.

Amid the regenerating forests, small towns are reminders of futile farming attempts, and of the gold rush of the 1860s.

Reefton

POP 1000

For generations, Reefton's claims to fame have been mining and its early adoption of the electricity grid and street lighting. Hence the tagline, 'the city of light'. Today, however, it's a different story, one that starts – improbably – with the building of the world-class Roller Park, which attracts stunt-lovers from all corners of NZ. To quote a local, 'It's more than we deserve.' We disagree. If so many volunteers and sponsors are prepared to build such an edgy civic amenity in a town that still looks like the set of *Bonanza*, we suggest there's something a little bit special about this crazy little town.

Sights & Activities

With loads of crusty old buildings within a 200m radius, Reefton is a fascinating town for a stroll. To find out who lived where and why, undertake the short **Heritage Tour** outlined in the woefully photocopied Historic Reefton leaflet ($1), available from the i-SITE.

The i-SITE also stocks the free Reefton leaftlet, detailing historic sites and more short walks including the **Reefton Walkway** (40 minutes), and **Powerhouse Walk** (40 minutes). Rewarding walks can be had at the old goldfields around Blacks Point and Murray Creek, with the enjoyable **Murray Creek loop** taking five hours (round trip). It's mountain-biking heaven around here, with bikes available to hire from the **Picture Framers** (☎03-732 8293; 45 Broadway; bikes from $10).

Reefton lies on the edge of the 206,000-hectare **Victoria Forest Park** (NZ's largest forest park), sporting five different species of beech tree. Tramps here include the three-day **Kirwans**, **Lake Christabel** and **Robinson River Tracks**, and the two-day **Big River Track**, which is fast becoming a must-do for mountain bikers. It ends at historic Waiuta, 21km south of Reefton, once a burgeoning gold town but abandoned in 1951 after the mine collapsed. Ask at the i-SITE for information and maps.

Blacks Point Museum MUSEUM
(Blacks Point, SH7; adult/child/family $5/3/15; ⏰9am-noon & 1-4pm Wed-Fri & Sun year-round, plus 1-4pm Sat Oct-Apr) This community-run museum, 2km east of Reefton on the Christchurch road, is inside an old church and crammed with prospecting paraphernalia. Just up the driveway is the still functional **Golden Fleece Battery** (adult/child $1/free; ⏰1-4pm Wed & Sun Oct-Apr), used for crushing gold-flecked quartz. The Blacks Point walks also start from here.

Bearded Mining Company ODDBALL ENCLAVE
(Broadway; admission by donation; ⏰9am-2pm) Looking like a ZZ Top tribute band, the fellers hangin' at this high-street mining hut

are champing at the bit to rollick your socks off with tales tall and true. If you're lucky you'll get a cuppa from the billy.

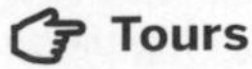

Tours

Globe Gold Mine Tours CULTURAL TOUR
(027 442 4777; www.reeftongold.co.nz) If you want to dig deeper into Reefton, book into Paul and Ronnie's tours at the i-SITE or pop into their Broadway Tearooms. The Heritage Tour (two hours, $25) takes in town highlights. The Gold Mine Tour (adult/child/family $55/30/120) visits the local mine. You'll get views over the pit-edge and see plenty of huge machiney in action. Tours run at noon and 2pm, with evening tours in summer.

Festivals & Events

Reefton Summer Festival CULTURAL
(www.reefton.co.nz) Go-ahead Reefton has cobbled together a month of fun from mid-December onwards, kicking off with carols and a visit from Santa, and pressing on with quiz nights, go-kart races and the Reefton Gallops.

Sleeping & Eating

Lantern Court Motels MOTEL **$$**
(03-732 8574, 0800 526 837; www.lanterncourtmotel.co.nz; 63 Broadway; old units d $95-120, new units d $140-165;) The original accommodation in this heritage hotel has had a right old spruce-up, and offers great-value self-catering for everyone from singles to family groups. The verandah is the best chilling-out spot in town. Meanwhile, the well-assimilated motel block next door offers all mod cons with a nod to classical styling.

Reefton Motor Camp HOLIDAY PARK **$**
(03-732 8477; roa.reuben@xtra.co.nz; 1 Ross St; sites from $25, d $45) On the Inangahua River and a minute's walk to Broadway, this older style camp ticks the right boxes and offers the bonuses of a big green sportsfield and shady fir trees.

Old Nurses Home GUESTHOUSE **$**
(03-732 8881; reeftonretreat@hotmail.com; 104 Shiel St; s/d $40/80; @) Your best bet for a cheap sleep, this stately old building is warm and comfortable, with noteworthy communal areas including pretty gardens and patios. Bedrooms are clean and airy with comfy beds.

Broadway Tearooms BAKERY **$**
(31 Broadway; snacks $3-8, meals $10-20; 5am-3pm) This rustic old joint gets by far the most day-time traffic, and for good reason. The bakers out back turn out everything from cream-filled donuts to decent meat pies to meticulous golden shortbread. Hot meals range from the egg breakfast to a whitebait lunch. Good alfresco, or eat in and survey the cute cruet set collection.

Wilson's PUB
(32 Broadway; mains $15-29; 11am-11pm) A solid town pub pleasing all, from smokin' youth through to soup-slurping pensioners. Meat and two veg dominate the menu, but it's all hearty and homemade. Occasional bands and DJs raise the excitement level to somewhere under fever pitch.

Information

The **Reefton i-Site** (03-732 8391; www.reefton.co.nz; 67 Broadway; 9am-5pm Nov-Mar, to 4.30pm Apr-Oct; @) has helpful staff, and a compact re-creation of the Quartzopolis Mine (gold coin entry). There's internet at the library, which doubles as the postal agency.

Getting There & Away

East West Coach (03-789 6251, 0800 142 622; eastwestco@xtra.co.nz) runs daily to Westport ($29, 1¼ hours) and Christchurch ($54, 3¾ hours).

Blackball

In the Grey Valley northeast of the river, about 25km north of Greymouth, is Blackball – established in 1866 to service gold diggers; coal mining kicked in between 1890 and 1964. The National Federation of Labour (a trade union) was conceived here, born from influential strikes in 1908 and 1931.

The hub of Blackball is **Formerly the Blackball Hilton** (03-732 4705, 0800 425 225; www.blackballhilton.co.nz; 26 Hart St; s without/with breakfast $40/55), famous because a certain global hotel chain got antsy when it was renamed a few years back. Hence the 'formerly'. This official Historic Place has memorabilia galore, hot meals, cold beer, heaps of afternoon sun, and a host of clean rooms oozing the charm of yesteryear.

Competing with the Hilton in the fame stakes are smallgoods made by the **Blackball Salami Co** (www.blackballsalami.co.nz; 11 Hilton St; 8am-4pm Mon-Fri, 9am-2pm Sat). The venison and beef salami are super tasty, as are the snarlers (as they say in Kiwi-speak) – that's sausages for the uninitiated.

Lake Brunner

Lying inland from Greymouth, Lake Brunner can be reached via the SH7 turn-off at Stillwater (or from the south via Kumara Junction). Locals reckon Lake Brunner and the Arnold River have the world's best trout fishing – not an uncommon boast in NZ. The Greymouth i-SITE can hook you up with a guide.

Moana is the main settlement, and where several short walks start including the **Velenski Walk** (20 minutes one way) and the **Rakaitane** (45 minutes return), between them taking in lake, river and forest views.

The **Station House Cafe** (40 Koe St; lunch $12-19, dinner $28-30; ⏲9.30am-10pm Dec-Feb, 10.30am-10pm Mar-Nov) is a reliable stop for refreshment, sitting on a hillside opposite the station where the *TranzAlpine* train pulls in. With a view that grand a glass of wine might be in order.

Lake Brunner Country Motel (☎03-738 0144; www.lakebrunnermotel.co.nz; 2014 Arnold Valley Rd; sites from $30, cabins $54-145) is a wonderful place for a night or two, even if the lake wasn't on your itinerary. Cabins, cottages and campervan sites are tucked into native plantings, while tenters can enjoy the lush grassy camping field down the back. This is proper peace and quiet, unless you count birdsong and the bubbling of the spa pool. It's 37km from Greymouth, 2km north of Moana.

GREYMOUTH

POP 10,000

Welcome to the 'Big Smoke' of Westland. Crouched at the mouth of the imaginatively named Grey River, the West Coast's largest town has a proud gold-mining history, and a legacy of occasional river floods, now somewhat alleviated by a flood wall.

On the main road and rail route through Arthur's Pass and across the Southern Alps from Christchurch, Greymouth sees its fair share of travellers. The town is well geared to looking after them, with all the necessary services and the odd tourist attraction, the most famous of which is Shantytown.

Sights & Activities

Shantytown MUSEUM
(www.shantytown.co.nz; Rutherglen Rd, Paroa; adult/child/family $31.50/15.50/74; ⏲8.30am-5pm) Eight kilometres south of Greymouth and 2km inland from SH6, Shantytown recreates an 1860s gold-mining town, complete with steam-train rides, post office, pub and Rosie's House of Ill Repute. There's also gold panning, a flying fox, sawmill, a gory hospital and 10-minute holographic movies in the new Princess Theatre.

TOP CHOICE **Left Bank Art Gallery** GALLERY
(www.leftbankarts.org.nz; 1 Tainui St; admission by donation; ⏲10am-4pm daily) This 90-year-old former bank houses contemporary NZ jade carvings, prints, paintings, photographs and ceramics. The gallery also fosters and supports a wide society of West Coast artists.

History House Museum MUSEUM
(www.history-house.co.nz; 27-29 Gresson St; adult/child $6/2; ⏲10am-4pm Mon-Fri) This museum documents Greymouth's pre-1920 history with an impressive collection of photographs.

Floodwall Walk WALKING
Take a 10-minute stroll along Mawhera Quay from Cobden Bridge, or keep going for an hour or so taking in the fishing harbour, breakwater and Blaketown Beach.

Point Elizabeth Walkway WALKING
Starting 6km north of Greymouth at Dommett Esplanade, this impressive walkway (three hours return) heads up the coast to the Rapahoe Range Scenic Reserve and a fine tract of mixed podocarp forest with flashes of bright-red rata blooming in the summer.

Tours

Kea Heritage Tours GUIDED TOURS
(☎0800 532 868; www.keatours.co.nz) Top-quality tours with well-informed guides, visiting coast sites and those beyond. Short tours include the half-day Punakaiki Tour ($105), and the day-long Twin Glaciers ($287). Myriad other options include a multi-day exploration of the Maori greenstone trails.

Monteith's Brewing Co GUIDED TOUR
(www.monteiths.co.nz; cnr Turumaha & Herbert Sts) When we visited, Monteith's brand-new brewery was getting ready to open: testatment to the power of a loyal public. Tours and tastings are available: ask for details at the i-SITE or just turn up at the front door.

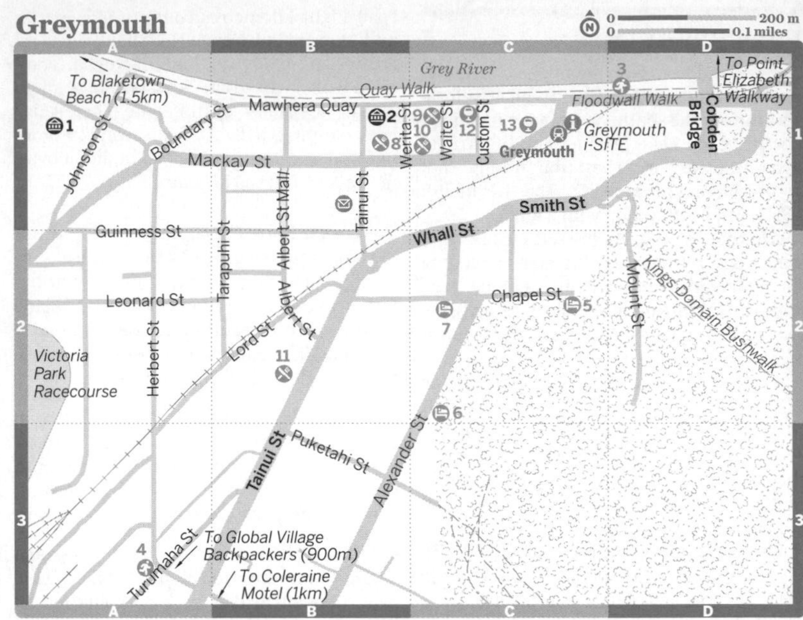

Greymouth

Sights

1 History House Museum A1
2 Left Bank Art Gallery B1

Activities, Courses & Tours

3 Floodwall Walk D1
4 Monteith's Brewing Co. A3

Sleeping

5 Ardwyn House C2
6 Kaianga-ra YHA C2
7 Noah's Ark Backpackers C2

Eating

8 Ali's Eating & Drinking B1
9 DP:One Cafe C1
10 Frank's Late Night Lounge C1
11 Priya B2

Drinking

12 Royal Hotel C1
13 Speight's Ale House C1

Sleeping

Global Village Backpackers HOSTEL $
(☎03-768 7272; www.globalvillagebackpackers.co.nz; 42 Cowper St; sites from $17, dm/d/tr/q $28/68/96/120; @📶) A collage of African and Asian art is infused with a passionate travellers' vibe here. Free kayaks – the Lake Karoro wetlands reserve is just metres away – and mountain bikes are on tap, and relaxation comes easy with a spa, sauna, barbecue and fire pit.

Noah's Ark Backpackers HOSTEL $
(☎0800 662 472, 03-768 4868; www.noahsarkbackpackers.co.nz; 16 Chapel St; sites $32, dm/s/d $27/52/66; @📶) Originally a monastery, Noah's now has eccentric animal-themed rooms and a sunset-worthy balcony. In true Ark style, the camping price is for two people. Mountain bikes and fishing rods are provided free of charge.

Kaianga-ra YHA HOSTEL $
(☎03-768 4951; www.yha.co.nz; 15 Alexander St; dm $31, s/d $68/80; @📶) Built in 1937 as a Marist Brothers' residence, this hostel is big, clean, functional and well behaved – everything you'd expect from YHA. A good night's sleep in the chapel dorm is sacrosanct.

Ardwyn House B&B $
(☎03-768 6107; ardwynhouse@hotmail.com; 48 Chapel St; s/d incl breakfast from $55/85; 📶)

This old-fashioned B&B nestles amid steep gardens on a quiet dead-end street. Mary, the well-travelled host, cooks a splendid breakfast.

Greymouth Seaside Top 10 Holiday Park HOLIDAY PARK $
(☎03-768 6618, 0800 867 104; www.top10greymouth.co.nz; 2 Chesterfield St; sites $44, d $64-193; @📶) This well-appointed beachside park is 2.5km south of town. The facilities are a little worn, but there are plenty of accommodation options, and a jumping pillow and go-karts to keep the kids amused.

Coleraine Motel MOTEL $$
(☎03-768 077, 0800 270 0027; www.colerainemotel.co.nz; 61 High St; d $152-225; @📶) Rattan furniture, spa baths and king-sized beds add up to the smartest luxury rooms in town. Cheaper one- and two-bedroom studios are not far behind. Extra-mile courtesy is shown in the provision of a communal guest lounge.

South Beach Motel & Motorpark MOTEL, HOLIDAY PARK $
(☎0800 101 222, 03-762 6768; www.southbeach.co.nz; 318 Main South Rd; sites $30, d $50-110, tr $125; @📶) Run by good-humoured hosts, this low-rise accommodation complex offers a range of simple but cosy accommodation, unless you count the campsites on a rainy day. Decent communal facilities will help on that score, and as it's only 6km to town this is a pleasant alternative to the big town camp.

Paroa Hotel HOTEL $$
(☎03-762 6860, 0800 762 6860; www.paroa.co.nz; 508 Main South Rd, Paroa; d $125-140; 📶) This family-owned hotel (60 years and counting) is located opposite the Shantytown turn-off and has spacious, garden-fronted units. The onsite restaurant plates up notable schnitzel and huge roasts ($17 to $31) amid a display of rugby jerseys.

New River Bluegums B&B $$
(☎03-762 6678; www.bluegumsnz.com; 985 Main South Rd, Camerons; d incl breakfast $180; @📶) Stay in the cosy upstairs room in the rustic family home, or settle into one of two self-contained units with a rural outlook. Take a bush bath or a farm walk, or work off that extra rasher of bacon or Sharon's gooey brownies on the tennis court. Look for the signpost, 11km south of Greymouth.

Jacksons Retreat HOLIDAY PARK $
(☎03-738 0474; www.jacksonscampervanretreat.co.nz; Jacksons, SH73; sites from $35; @📶) Heading east across Arthur's Pass on SH73, 63km from Greymouth, the tiny settlement of Jackons can be found nestled beside the Taramakau River. Campervan travellers and tenters can stay at Jacksons Retreat, a superb holiday park set upon 15 sloping acres with exceptional views and stacks of excellent amenities. Up the road, the historic Jackson's Tavern can fix you up with a pie and a pint.

Eating & Drinking

Just in case you've missed the gist, big supermarkets are few and far between on the Coast. In Greymouth there are several, so stock up while the going is good.

DP:One Cafe CAFE $
(104 Mawhera Quay; meals $6-15; ⏲9am-9pm; @📶) A stalwart of the Greymouth cafe scene, this hip cafe cups up the best espresso in town, along with good-value grub. Groovy NZ tunes, wi-fi, a relaxed vibe and quayside tables make this a great place for a meet-up to while away a grey day.

THE COAST TO COAST

Kiwis really are a mad bunch. Take, for instance, the annual **Coast to Coast** (www.coasttocoast.co.nz), the most coveted one-day multisport race in the country. Held in mid-February, the race starts in Kumara on the West Coast. Intrepid racers start in the wee hours of the morning with a gentle 3km run, followed by a 55km cycle. Next it's a 33km mountain run over Goat Pass – you know any pass named after a goat isn't going to be flat. From there all there is to do is ride your bike another 15km, paddle your kayak 67km and get back on the bike for the final 70km to Christchurch.

The strong, the brave and the totally knackered will cross the finish line to much fanfare. The course is 243km long and the top competitors will dust it off in just under 11 hours – with slowpokes taking almost twice that.

THE TRANZALPINE

The **TranzAlpine** (☎0800 872 467, 03-768 7080; www.tranzscenic.co.nz; adult/child one way from $89/62), one of the world's great train journeys, traverses the Southern Alps between Christchurch and Greymouth, from the Pacific Ocean to the Tasman Sea – a sequence of unbelievable landscapes. Leaving Christchurch at 8.15am, it speeds across the flat, alluvial Canterbury Plains to the Alps' foothills. Here it enters a labyrinth of gorges and hills called the Staircase, a climb made possible by three large viaducts and a plethora of tunnels.

The train emerges into the broad Waimakariri and Bealey Valleys and (on a good day) the vistas from the new carriages with their panoramic windows are stupendous. The beech-forested river valley gives way to the snowcapped peaks of Arthur's Pass National Park. At Arthur's Pass itself (a small alpine village), the train enters the longest tunnel, the 8.5km 'Otira', burrowing under the mountains to the West Coast.

The western side is just as stunning, with the Otira, Taramakau and Grey River valleys, patches of podocarp forest, and the trout-filled Lake Brunner, fringed with cabbage trees. The train rolls into Greymouth at 12.45pm, heading back to Christchurch an hour later, arriving at 6.05pm.

This awesome journey is diminished only when the weather's bad, but if it's raining on one coast, it's probably fine on the other.

Ali's Eating & Drinking CAFE **$$**
(9 Tainui St; mains $15-27; ⏲10am-late Mon-Sat, to 3pm Sun) Offering little in the way of ambience other than a splash of deep purple, Ali's atones with all-day food made from scratch. Salads, soup and homemade cheesecake make an appearance, although our pick is the chicken parmigiana and the $15 pasta, which filled us to the brim.

Frank's Late Night Lounge INTERNATIONAL **$$**
(☎03-768 9075; 115 Mackay St; mains $19-28; ⏲5pm-late Thu-Sat; 🖉) This effortlessly cool, retro late-night lounge-bar-cafe is your best bet for getting a groove on. Art deco architecture, eclectic decoration and excellent fresh food (including stellar fish dishes and salads) are just a few reasons for visit. Regular gigs, and it's family friendly. Nice one, Frank.

Priya INDIAN **$$**
(☎03-768 7377; 84 Tainui St; mains $16-22; ⏲lunch & dinner) With an explosion of subcontinental Indian spices on temperate West Coast taste buds, this seasoned performer is heavily patronised.

Speight's Ale House PUB
(130 Mawhera Quay; lunch $12-29, dinner $19-35; ⏲11am-late) Housed in the imposing 1909 'Brick House' building, one of the big brands of NZ beer stands its ground with a well-stocked bar, manly meals and several epic dining and drinking rooms of such warmth and style that you could probably bring your granny here.

Royal Hotel PUB
(128 Mawhera Quay; ⏲11am-late) The old-fashioned Royal welcomes all comers with gusto, and flies a little flag for independent NZ brewing while it's at it. Get yourself a pint of something fine, get chatting or watch the soccer on Sky TV.

ℹ Information

Free town and regional maps are available at the i-SITE. Major banks huddle around Mackay and Tainui Sts. There's internet access at the i-SITE and at the **library** (18 Albert St; @📶).

Greymouth i-SITE (☎03-768 5101; www.greydistrict.co.nz; Railway Station, 164 Mackay St; ⏲8.30am-7pm Mon-Fri, 9am-6pm Sat, 10am-5pm Sun Nov-Apr, reduced hours May-Oct; @📶) Inside the railway station you'll find a very helpful crew, and an abundance of local and DOC information.

Grey Base Hospital (☎03-769 7400; High St)

Police Station (☎03-768 1600; 45-47 Guinness St)

Post Office (36 Tainui St)

ℹ Getting There & Around

Sharing the old railway station with the i-SITE, the **West Coast Travel Centre** (☎03-768 7080; www.westcoasttravel.co.nz; Railway Station, 164 Mackay St; ⏲9am-5pm Mon-Fri, 10am-4pm Sat & Sun; @📶) books all forms of transport, including buses, trains and inter-island ferries, and has luggage-storage facilities. It also serves as the bus depot.

Bus

All buses stop at the railway station.

InterCity (☎03-365 1113; www.intercity.co.nz) has daily buses north to Westport (from $17, two hours) and Nelson (from $40, six hours), and south to Franz Josef Glacier (from $29, 3½ hours) and Fox Glacier (from $31, 4¼ hours).

Naked Bus (p102) runs north to Nelson and south to Queenstown stopping at Hokitika, Franz Josef and Fox Glaciers, Haast and Wanaka.

Atomic Shuttles (p102) runs daily to Queenstown ($70, 10½ hours) stopping at Hokitika (from $13, one hour), Franz Josef (from $30, 3½ hours) and Fox Glaciers (from $35, 4¼ hours), Haast ($65, 5¾ hours) and Wanaka ($65, nine hours). It also heads north daily to Nelson ($54, 6¼ hours) on the InterCity service, via Westport ($24, 2¾ hours).

Car

The West Coast Travel Centre will hook you up with hire cars.

Local companies include **Alpine West** (☎0800 257 736, 03-736 4002; www.alpinerentals.co.nz; 11 Shelley St) and **NZ Rent-a-Car** (☎0800 800 956, 03-768 0379; www.nzrentacar.co.nz; 170 Tainui St).

Taxi

Try **Greymouth Taxis** (☎03-768 7078).

HOKITIKA

POP 3100

Visit Hokitika's wide and quiet streets in the off-season, and you might be excused for thinking you've stumbled into a true Wild West town. Throughout summer, though, there's no room for rogue tumbleweeds in the expansive thoroughfares, and 'Hoki' gets as busy with visitors as when the town was a thriving port during the 1860s gold rush, only now, green (stone), and not gold, is the colour of choice.

Sights & Activities

An extensive network of moutain-biking trails lurks near Hokitika. Hire bikes and get maps and advice from **Sports World & Hokitika Cycles** (☎03-755 8662; 33 Tancred St; per day $30-65).

Sunset Point LOOKOUT

(Gibson Quay) A spectacular vantage point at any time of day, this is – as the name suggests – the primo place to watch the light fade away. Surfers, seagulls, and fish and chips: *this* is New Zealand.

Hokitika Museum MUSEUM

(☎03-755 6898; www.hokitikamuseum.co.nz; 17 Hamilton St; adult/child $5/2.50; ⊙9.30am-5pm) Housed in the imposing Carnegie Building (1908), this is an exemplary provincial museum, with intelligently curated exhibitions presented in a clear, modern style. Highlights include the fascinating *Whitebait!* exhibition, and the *Pounamu* room – the ideal primer before you hit the galleries looking for greenstone treasures.

Glowworm Dell NATURAL FEATURE

Just north of town, a short stroll from SH6 leads to a Glowworm Dell, an easy opportunity to enter the other-wordly home of NZ's native fungus gnat lavae (so not even a worm at all). An information panel at the entrance will further illuminate your way.

Hokitika Heritage Walk WALK

Pick up the free leaflet from the i-SITE and wander the waterfront, imagining when the wharves were choked with old-time sailing ships.

Galleries

Art and craft galleries are a strong spoke in Hoki's wheel, and you could easily spend a day spinning around the lot. There are plenty of opportunities to meet the artists, and in some studios you can watch them at work. Be aware that some galleries sell jade imported from Europe and Asia, as precious local *pounamu* (greenstone) is not given up lightly by the wilds.

Hokitika Craft Gallery GALLERY

(www.hokitikacraftgallery.co.nz; 25 Tancred St) The town's best one-stop shop, this co-op showcases a wide range of stunning local work including greenstone, jewellery, textiles, ceramics and some feel-good woodwork.

Tectonic Jade GALLERY

(www.tectonicjade.com; 67 Revell St) The work by local carver Rex Scott is arguably the best in town.

Te Waipounamu Maori Heritage Centre GALLERY

(www.maoriheritage.co.nz; 39 Weld St) Scrupulously authentic, selling only NZ *pounamu* handcrafted into both traditional and contemporary designs.

Jagosi Jade GALLERY

(246 Sewell St) Carver Aden Hoglund produces traditional and modern Maori designs

Hokitika

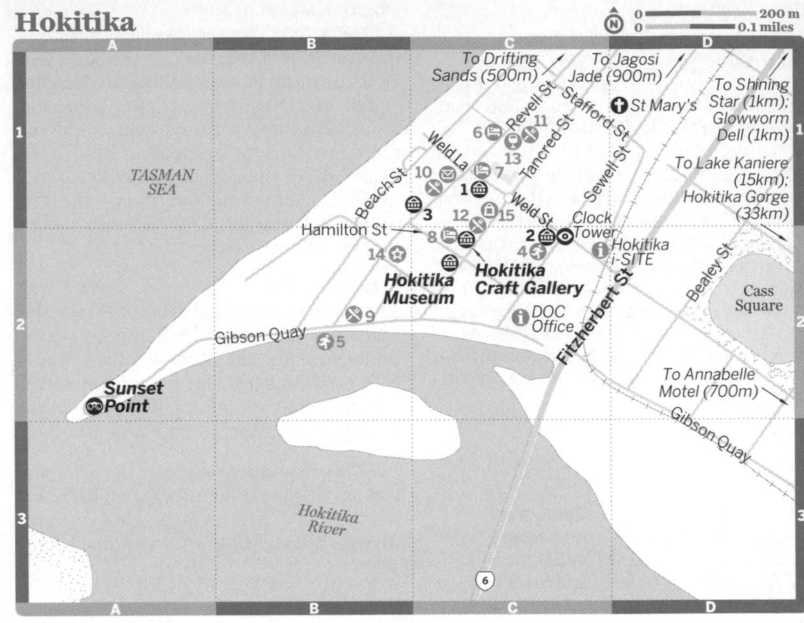

Hokitika

from jade sourced from around the South Island.

Hokitika Glass Studio GALLERY
(www.hokitikaglass.co.nz; 9 Weld St) Glass art and covering a continuum from garish to glorious; watch the blowers at the furnace on weekdays.

Bonz 'N' Stonz CARVING
(www.bonz-n-stonz.co.nz; 27 Sewell St; full-day workshop $75-150) Design, carve and polish your own jade, bone or paua masterpiece, with tutelage from Steve. Prices vary with materials and design complexity. Bookings are recommended.

Tours

Wilderness Wings SCENIC FLIGHTS

(☎0800 755 8118; www.wildernesswings.co.nz; Hokitika Airport; flights $375) Offers 75-minute flights over Hokitika, Aoraki (Mt Cook) and the glaciers.

Festivals & Events

Wildfoods Festival FOOD

(www.wildfoods.co.nz) Held in early March, this festival attracts 20,000 curious and brave gourmands. It's your chance to eat a whole lot of things you would usually either run away from or flick out of your hair. Legendary fun; book early.

Sleeping

Shining Star Beachfront Accommodation HOLIDAY PARK $

(☎0800 744 646, 03-755 8921; www.shiningstar.co.nz; 11 Richards Dr; sites from $30, d $90-169; @) Attractive and versatile beachside spot with everything from camping to classy self-contained seafront units. Kids will love the menagerie, including ducks and alpacas straight from Dr Doolittle's appointment book. Mum and dad might prefer the spa and sauna ($15 for two).

Drifting Sands HOSTEL $

(☎03-755 7654; www.driftingsands.co.nz; 197 Revell St; sites from $15, dm/s/d $29/58/74; @) Access to the beach from the back garden and this hostel's family-home feel make it our pick of Hoki's budget accommodation. The cheery manager and crisp new linen don't hurt either.

Birdsong HOSTEL $

(☎03-755 7179; www.birdsong.co.nz; SH6; dm/s $29/58, d $74-89; @) Located 2.5km north of town, this bird-themed hostel has sea views and a homely atmosphere. Free bikes, handy beach access and hidden extras will entice you into extending your stay.

Stumpers HOTEL $

(☎03-755 6154, 0800 788 673; www.stumpers.co.nz; 2 Weld St; d $70-120; @) Stumpers has a range of rooms above its bustling cafe-bar, including freshly renovated en-suite doubles and simple doubles with shared facilities. Winner of the award for continuous improvement.

Teichelmann's B&B B&B $$$

(☎03-755 8232; www.teichelmanns.co.nz; 20 Hamilton St; d $195-240;) Once home to surgeon, mountaineer and professional beard cultivator Ebenezer Teichelmann, now a charming B&B with amicable hosts. All rooms have en suites, including the more private Teichy's Cottage, situated in the garden oasis out back.

Beachfront Hotel HOTEL $$

(☎0800 400 344, 03-755 8344; www.beachfronthotel.co.nz; 111 Revell St; d $125-330;) This split-personality hotel offers budget rooms in the original wing (where noise from the adjacent pub can be an issue at times), and fancy rooms in the modern Ocean View building with fabulous views from the balconies. The in-house bar is a good spot for a sundowner.

WORTH A TRIP

THE GORGEOUS HOKITIKA GORGE

A picturesque 33km drive leads to **Hokitika Gorge**, a ravishing ravine with turquoise waters. Glacial flour (suspended rock particles) imbues the milky hues. Cross the swing bridge for a couple of short forest walks. To get here, head up Stafford St past the dairy factory and follow the signs.

Kowhitirangi, en route to the gorge, was the scene of a massive 12-day manhunt involving the NZ army in 1941. Unhinged farmer Stanley Graham shot dead four Hokitika policemen, disappeared into the bush then returned to murder three others, before eventually being killed. A grim roadside monument lines up the farmstead site through a stone gun shaft. The 1982 film *Bad Blood* re-enacts the awful incident.

To loop back to Hokitika, take the narrow and winding 10km gravel forest road that skirts **Lake Kaniere**, passing **Dorothy Falls**, **Kahikatea Forest** and **Canoe Cove**. The Hokitika i-SITE has details on these and other local walks, including the **Lake Kaniere Walkway** (3½ hours one way), along the lake's western shore, the historic **Kaniere Water Race Walkway** (3½ hours one way),

Annabelle Motel MOTEL $$
(☎0508 549 494, 03-755 8160; www.annabellemotel.co.nz; 214 Weld St; s $130, d $140-180; 📶) Less than 1km from the Hoki clock tower, pretty Annabelle is away from beach and town action but well located for peace and convenience. Tip-top units, decorated in green garden hues with plush furnishings, meet middle-of-the-road modern standards.

Stations Inn MOTEL $$
(☎0508 782 846, 03-755 5499; www.stations.co.nz; Blue Spur Rd; d $170-250) King-sized beds and spa baths feature in these new units amid rolling hills and rocking alpacas. Next door an ambient restaurant shows off its award-winning relationship with venison, beef and lamb. Follow Hampden St and Hau Hau Rd to Blue Spur Rd.

Awatuna Homestead B&B $$$
(☎0800 006 888, 03-755 6834; www.awatunahomestead.co.nz; 9 Stafford Rd; d incl breakfast $290-370; 📶) Set down on a quiet road 11km north of Hokitika, Awatuna Homestead has three lovely guest rooms and a self-contained apartment. Dinner is available by prior arrangement, and in the evening owners Hemi and Pauline may share fascinating stories of Maori culture and Pacific exploration.

Eating & Drinking

TOP CHOICE **Fat Pipi Pizza** PIZZERIA $$
(89 Revell St; pizzas $19-24; ⏲noon-9pm; 🌿) Vegetarians, carnivores and everyone in between will be salivating for the pizza (including a whitebait version) made with love right before your eyes. Lovely cakes, honey buns and Bengers juices. The beachfront garden bar is shaping up to be the best dining spot in town.

Dulcie's on the Quay FISH & CHIPS $
(cnr Gibson Quay & Revell St; fish & chips $5-10; ⏲lunch & dinner) Net yourself some excellent fush 'n' chups (try the turbot or blue cod), then scoff them straight from the paper at Sunset Point – a Hokitika highlight.

Sweet Alice's Fudge Kitchen SWEETS $
(27 Tancred St) Treat yourself with a slice of Alice's handmade all-natural fudge ($6), or a real fruit ice cream, or a bag of boiled lollies, or maybe all three.

Stumpers Cafe & Bar CAFE, BAR $$
(2 Weld St; lunch $11-21, dinner $18-34; ⏲7am-late) There's something for everyone here, at any time of the day. In the evening you'll find meaty mains, along with a whole host of locals meeting up for a pint and a powwow.

West Coast Wine Bar WINE BAR
(108 Revell St; ⏲11am-4pm Tue-Thu & Sat, 11am-late Fri) Upping Hoki's sophistication factor, this weeny joint with a cute garden bar pours all sorts of deliciousness, and plates up some cheese. Cigars for puffers; fine wines to go.

New World SUPERMARKET
(116 Revell St; ⏲8am-8pm Mon-Fri, 8am-7pm Sat, 9am-7pm Sun) If you're heading south, this is your last proper supermarket before Wanaka, 426 km away!

Entertainment

Crooked Mile Talking Movies CINEMA
(www.crookedmile.co.nz; 36 Revell St; tickets adult/child $12/10) Vintage building, plus old couches, plus organic chocolate and house bar, plus art-house films, equals a perfect night out.

Information

Banks can be found on Weld and Revell Sts.

DOC Office (☎03-756 9100; 10 Sewell St; ⏲8am-4.45pm Mon-Fri) Get basic information from the i-SITE; intrepid adventurers should come to the source.

Hokitika i-SITE (☎03-755 6166; www.hokitika.org; Weld St; ⏲8.30am-6pm Mon-Fri, 9am-5pm Sat & Sun) Extensive bookings including all bus services, car rental agent, DOC information and passes, plus local maps and guides.

Police Station (☎03-756 8310; 50 Sewell St)

Post Office (Revell St)

Westland Medical Centre (☎03-755 8180; 54a Sewell St; ⏲8.30am-10pm)

Getting There & Around

Air

Hokitika Airport (Airport Dr, off Tudor St) is 1.5km east of the centre of town. Air New Zealand (p102) has four flights daily (from $65 one way) to/from Christchurch.

Bus

InterCity (☎03-365 1113; www.intercity.co.nz) buses depart from Tancred St daily for Greymouth (from $14, 45 minutes), Nelson (from $44, seven hours) and Franz Josef Glacier (from $30, two hours).

Atomic Shuttles (☎03-349 0697; www.atomictravel.co.nz) departs i-SITE to Fox Glacier ($36, 3½ hours), Greymouth ($15, one hour) and Queenstown ($70, 10 hours).

WHITEBAIT FEVER

On even the swiftest of visits to the Coast, you are sure to come across a little whitebait or two, whether being sold from the back door of Womble's house, in sandwiches, in museums or in tales tall and true.

These tiny, transparent fish are the young of some of NZ's precious native fish, including inanga, kokopu, smelt and and even eels. Strangely enough, they all look and taste the same, especially once transformed into a fritter.

Commanding up to $80 a kilo round these parts (and much elsewhere), competition is tough to net the elusive fish. The season runs from August to November, when riverbanks and fishing stands are busy from Karamea to Haast.

The classic fritter recipe involves little more than an egg, and is accompanied by a wedge of lemon, although some would say that mint sauce is the best embellishment. The *Whitebait!* exhibition at Hokitika Museum (p117) will give you some idea as to what all the fuss is about.

Naked Bus (www.nakedbus.com) heads north to Greymouth, and south to Queenstown stopping at Franz Josef and Fox Glaciers, Haast and Wanaka.

Car

There are several car-hire branches at Hokitika Airport. **Hokitika Airport Car Rental** (☎0800 556 606; www.hokitikaairportcarhire.co.nz) offers on-line price comparisons, or you could enquire and book at the i-SITE.

Taxi

Try **Hokitika Taxis** (☎03-755 5075).

HOKITIKA TO WESTLAND TAI POUTINI NATIONAL PARK

From Hokitika it's 140km south to Franz Josef Glacier. Most travellers fast forward without stopping, but there are some satisfying stopping points for the inclined. Intercity and Atomic Shuttles stop along this stretch of SH6.

Lake Mahinapua to Okarito

LAKE MAHINAPUA

Eight kilometres south of Hokitika there's a signpost and car park for the **Mahinapua Walkway** (two hours one way), a wonderful walk along an old logging tramway with relics and a diverse range of forest. It's an even better bike ride. Two kilometres further on is the entrance to **Lake Mahinapua Scenic Reserve**, with a picnic area, DOC campsite and several short walks.

ROSS

Ross, 30km south of Hokitika, is where the unearthing of NZ's largest gold nugget, the 2.772kg 'Honourable Roddy', caused a kerfuffle in 1907. The **Ross Goldfields Information Centre** (☎03-755 4077; www.ross.org.nz; 4 Aylmer St; ⏲9am-4pm Dec-Mar, to 3pm Apr-Nov) displays a replica Roddy, along with a scale model ($2) of the town in its shiny years.

The **Water Race Walk** (one hour return) starts near the museum, passing old gold-diggings, caves, tunnels and a cemetery. Try **gold panning** by hiring a pan from the information centre ($10) and head to Jones Creek to look for Roddy's great, great grandnuggets.

The bar at the **Empire Hotel** (19 Aylmer St; meals $15-20) is one of the West Coast's hidden gems – imported directly from a bygone era. It reeks of authenticity, especially when propped up by a few locals. Look out for jam night.

HARI HARI

About 22km south of Lake Ianthe, Hari Hari made headlines in 1931 when swashbuckling Australian aviator Guy Menzies completed the first solo trans-Tasman flight from Sydney. Menzies crash-landed his plane into La Fontaine swamp. Menzies' flight took 11¾ hours, 2½ hours faster than fellow Australian Charles Kingsford Smith's flight in 1928. At the southern end of town is a replica of Menzies' trusty biplane, and there are good photo displays at the Motor Inn.

The **Hari Hari Coastal Walk** (2¾ hours return) is a well-trodden low-tide loop passing the Poerua and Wanganui Rivers. The walk starts 20km from SH6, the last 8km unsealed; follow the signs from Wanganui

Flats Rd. Tide times are posted at the Pukeko Tearooms, which also has decent food and coffee.

Flaxbush Motels (☎03-753 3116; www.flaxbushmotel.co.nz; SH6; d $65-120; wi-fi) has characterful cabins and units covering a wide range of budgets. The owners are certainly animal lovers, with peacocks wandering the grounds and a pet possum that has its own room – in the house. Prices negotiable for extra nights.

The **Hari Hari Motor Inn** (☎0800 833 026, 03-753 3026; hhmi@xtra.co.nz; 42 Main Road; unpowered/powered sites from $12.50/17.50, dm $22.50, d $65-110) has serviceable doubles but doesn't have a shared kitchen for campers or backpackers. The bistro (mains $12 to $28; open noon till late) is Hari Hari's only evening eatery, with pizzas, whitebait sammies, steak, roasts and cold pints of beer.

WHATAROA

Near Whataroa, 35km south of Hari Hari, is the **Kotuku Sanctuary**, NZ's only nesting site for the kotuku (white heron), which roost here between November and February. The herons then fly off individually to reconsider the single life over winter.

White Heron Sanctuary Tours (☎03-753 4120, 0800 523 456; www.whiteherontours.co.nz; SH6; adult/child $120/55; ⏱4 tours daily late Oct-Mar) has the only DOC concession to see the herons. An enjoyable 2½-hour tour involves a gentle jetboat ride and short boardwalk to a viewing hide. Seeing the scores of birds perched in the bushes is a magical experience. A scenic rainforest tour without the herons is available year-round for the same price.

The tour people also run the **Sanctuary Tours Motel** (☎0800 523 456, 03-753 4120; www.whiteherontours.co.nz; SH6; cabins $55-65, d $95-125), with basic cabins with shared facilities ($8 extra for bedlinen), and enthusiastically painted motel units.

Kotuku Gallery (☎03-753 4249; SH6, Whataroa) is chock-full of beautiful Maori bone and pounamu carving. This is a great place to pick up an authentic memento of your visit to Aotearoa.

Glacier Country Scenic Flights (☎0800 423 463, 03-753 4096; www.glacieradventures.co.nz; SH6, Whataroa; flights $175-415) offers a range of scenic flights and heli-hikes, lifting off from Whataroa Valley. These guys give you more mountain-gawping for your buck than many of the operators flying from the glacier townships.

OKARITO

Fifteen kilometres south of Whataroa is the Forks, the turn-off to the tiny seaside hamlet of Okarito, 13km further away on the coast. It sits alongside **Okarito Lagoon**, the largest unmodified wetland in NZ. Okarito has no shops and limited visitor facilities, so stock up and book up before you arrive.

Sights & Activities

From a carpark on the Strand you can begin the easy **Wetland Walk** (25 minutes), or two spectacular longer walks to **Three Mile Lagoon** (three hours return; beach section passable low tide only) and to **Okarito Trig** (1½ hours return). Expect Southern Alps and Okarito Lagoon views.

Andris Apse Wilderness Gallery GALLERY
(☎03-753 4241; www.andrisapse.com; 109 The Strand) Okarito is home to world-class landscape photographer Andris Apse. His precisely composed gallery showcases his beautiful works, printed on site and available to purchase, as are infinitely more affordable books. Ring ahead to check it's open, or look for the sandwich board at the end of the driveway.

Okarito Nature Tours TOURS
(☎0508 652 748, 03-753 4014; www.okarito.co.nz; kayak half-/full day $55/65; wi-fi) Hires out kayaks for paddles into the lagoon and up into the stunning rainforest channels where all sorts of birds hang out. Guided tours are available (from $75), while overnight rentals ($80) allow experienced paddlers to check out deserted North Beach or Lake Windemere. There's excellent espresso and wi-fi in the welcoming office and lounge.

Okarito Boat Tours TOURS
(☎03-753 4223; www.okaritoboattours.co.nz) The lagoon can be explored with Okarito Boat Tours, on morning and afternoon sightseeing tours starting at $45. Bookings are recommended for the nature tour, which departs in the mornings for better wildlife-viewing potential (two hours, $85). Paula and Swade can also fix you up with accommodation in the town

Okarito Kiwi Tours TOURS
(☎03-753 4330; www.okaritokiwitours.co.nz; 2-3hr tours $75) Runs nightly expeditions to spot the rare bird (95% success rate) with a interesting education along the way. Numbers are limited to eight, so booking is recommended

Sleeping

Okarito Campground CAMPSITE

(off Russell St; sites adult/child $10/free) Okarito Campground is a breezy patch of community-managed greenery complete with kitchen and hot showers ($1). Drop your cash in the honesty box and you're sweet as. Gather driftwood from the beach for the fire-pit, or build your bonfire on the beach while the sun goes down.

Old School House GUESTHOUSE

(03-752 0796; www.doc.govt.nz; The Strand; house $100) An old 1892 school building is now the DOC-run Old School House, a charming heritage building available for rent (sleeps up to 12).

Okarito Beach House HOSTEL

(03-753 4080; www.okaritohostel.com; The Strand; dm $25, d $60-100;) The Okarito Beach House has a variety of accommodation. The weathered, self-contained 'Hutel' ($100) is worth every cent. The Summit Lodge has commanding views and the best dining-room table you've ever seen.

WESTLAND TAI POUTINI NATIONAL PARK

Literally the biggest highlights of the Westland Tai Poutini National Park are the Franz Josef and Fox Glaciers. Nowhere else at this latitude do glaciers come so close to the ocean. The glaciers' staggering development is largely due to the West Coast's ample rain. Snow falling in the glaciers' broad accumulation zones fuses into clear ice at 20m depth then surges down the steep valleys.

The rate of descent is mind-blowing: wreckage of a plane that crashed into Franz Josef in 1943, 3.5km from the terminal face, made it down to the bottom 6½ years later – a rate of 1.5m per day. Franz usually advances about 1m per day, but sometimes ramps it up to 5m per day, over 10 times faster than the Swiss Alps' glaciers.

Some say Franz Josef is the superior ice experience, and while it's visually more impressive, the walk to Fox is shorter, more interesting and often gets you closer to the ice. Both glacier faces are roped off to prevent people being caught in icefalls and river surges. The danger is very real – in 2009 two tourists were killed after being hit by falling ice when they ventured too close. Take a guided tour to get close without being too close.

Beyond the glaciers, the park's lower reaches harbour deserted Tasman Sea beaches, rising up through colour-splashed podocarp forests to NZ's highest peaks. Diverse and often unique ecosystems huddle next to each other in interdependent ecological sequence. Seals frolic in the surf as deer sneak through the forests. The resident endangered bird species include kowhiowhio, kakariki (a parrot), kaka and rowi (Okarito brown kiwi), as well as kea, the South Island's native parrot. Kea are inquisitive and endearing, but feeding them threatens their health.

Heavy tourist traffic often swamps the twin towns of Franz and Fox, 23km apart. Franz is the more action-packed of the two, while Fox has a more subdued alpine charm. From December to February, visitor numbers can get a little crazy in both, so consider travelling in the off-season (May to September) for cheaper accommodation.

Franz Josef Glacier

The early Maori knew Franz Josef as Ka Roimata o Hine Hukatere (Tears of the Avalanche Girl). Legend tells of a girl losing her lover who fell from the local peaks, and her flood of tears freezing into the glacier. The glacier was first explored by Europeans in 1865, with Austrian Julius Haast naming it after the Austrian emperor. The glacier is 5km from Franz Josef village; the terminal face is a 40-minute walk from the car park.

Sights & Activities

West Coast Wildlife Centre WILDLIFE

(www.wildkiwi.co.nz; cnr Cron & Cowan Sts; day pass adult/child/family $25/15/75, backstage pass $20/15/60;) This feel-good attraction ticks all the right boxes (exhibition, cafe and retail, wi-fi), then goes a whole lot further by actually breeding the rowi – the rarest kiwi in the world. The day-pass is well worthwhile by the time you've viewed the conservation, glacier and heritage displays, and hung out with real, live kiwi in their ferny enclosure. The additional backstage pass into the incubating and chick-rearing area is a rare opportunity to learn how a species can be brought back from the brink of extinction, and a chance to go ga-ga over what may be the cutest babies on the planet.

Franz Josef Glacier & Village

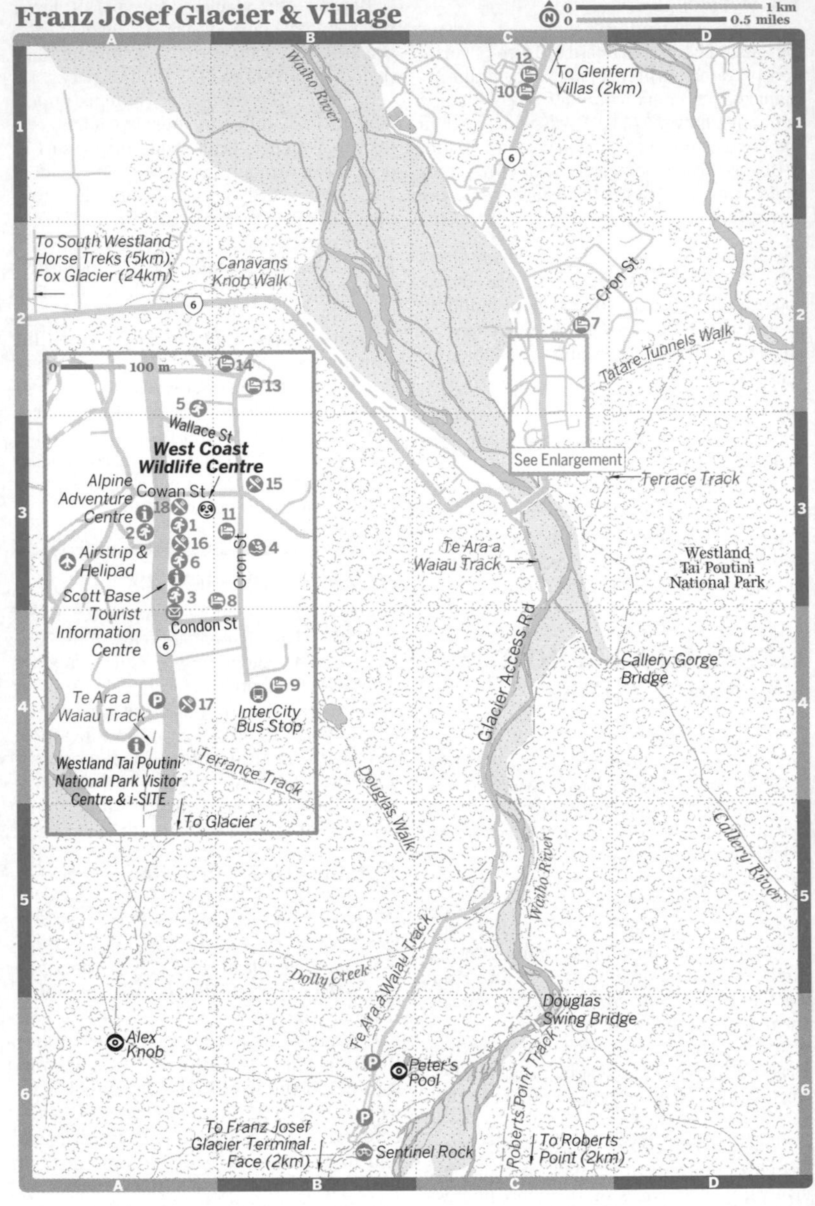

Independent Walks

Courtesy of DOC, the new **Te Ara a Waiau Walkway/Cycleway** provides pleasant rainforest trail access to the glacier car park. Pick up the track at the DOC Visitor Centre. It's an hour each way to walk, 30 minutes maximum to cycle (leave your bikes at the car park – you can't cycle on the glacier walkways). Hire bikes from Across Country Quad Bikes (p126).

Several glacier viewpoints are accessed from the car park, including **Sentinel Rock**

Franz Josef Glacier & Village

Top Sights

West Coast Wildlife Centre.................A3

Activities, Courses & Tours

Across Country Quad Bikes.........(see 1)
1 Air Safaris.................A3
2 Fox & Franz Josef Heliservices...........A3
3 Franz Josef Glacier Guides.................A3
4 Glacier Country Tours & Kayaks.................B3
5 Glacier Hot Pools.................A2
Mountain Helicopters...................(see 1)
6 Skydive Franz.................A3

Sleeping

7 58 on Cron.................C2
8 Alpine Glacier Motel.................B3
9 Franz Josef Glacier YHA.................B4
10 Franz Josef Top 10 Holiday Park.................C1
11 Glow Worm Cottages.................B3
12 Holly Homestead.................C1
13 Rainforest Retreat.................B2
14 Te Waonui Forest Retreat.................B2

Eating

15 Alice May.................B3
16 Four Square Supermarket.................A3
17 Picnics.................A4
18 Speights Landing Bar & Restaurant.................A3

(20 minutes return) and the **Ka Roimata o Hine Hukatere Walk** (1½ hours return), leading you to the terminal face (read the signs; respect the barriers).

Other longer walks include the **Douglas Walk** (one hour return), off the Glacier Access Rd, which passes moraine from the 1750 advance and Peter's Pool, a small kettle lake. The **Terrace Track** (30 minutes return) is an easy amble over bushy terraces behind the village, with Waiho River views. Two good rainforest walks, **Tatare Tunnels** and **Callery Gorge Walk** (both around 1½ hours return), start from Cowan St.

The rougher **Roberts Point Track** (approximately five hours return) heads off from the Douglas swing bridge (access via the Douglas Walk). The **Alex Knob Track** (eight hours return) runs from the Glacier Access Rd to the 1303m peak of Alex Knob. Look forward to three glacier lookouts and views to the coast (cloud cover permitting). Both **Roberts Point** and Alex Knob are suitable only for well-equipped and experienced trampers.

Check out the glacier in the morning or evening, before the cloud cover sets in or after it lifts. Expect fewer tour buses as well.

Guided Walks & Helihikes

Small group walks with experienced guides (boots, jackets and equipment supplied) are offered by **Franz Josef Glacier Guides** (☎0800 484 337, 03-752 0763; www.franzjosefglacier.com). Half-/full-day walks are $123/180 per adult (slightly cheaper for children). Full-day trips have around six hours on the ice, half-day trips up to two hours. Full-day ice climbing trips ($256 including training), and three-hour helihikes ($399), which take you further up the glaciers to see more interesting formations and include two hours on the ice, are also available.

Aerial Sightseeing

Forget sandflies and mozzies. The buzzing you're hearing is more likely to be helicopters and planes cruising past the glaciers and Aoraki/Mt Cook. Many flights also include a snow landing. A 20-minute flight to the head of Franz Josef (or Fox Glacier) costs around $200. Flights past both of the glaciers and to Aoraki/Mt Cook cost from $300 to $380. These are adult prices; fares for children under 15 are between 60% and 70% of the adult price. Shop around: most operators are situated on the main road in Franz Josef.

Air Safaris SCENIC FLIGHTS
(☎03-752 0716, 0800 723 274; www.airsafaris.co.nz) Fixed wing.

Fox & Franz Josef Heliservices SCENIC FLIGHTS
(☎03-752 0793, 0800 800 793; www.scenic-flights.co.nz)

Helicopter Line SCENIC FLIGHTS
(☎0800 807 767, 03-752 0767; www.helicopter.co.nz)

Mountain Helicopters SCENIC FLIGHTS
(☎0800 369 432, 03-752 0046; www.mountainhelicopters.co.nz)

Other Activities

TOP CHOICE **Glacier Hot Pools** BATHHOUSE
(www.glacierhotpools.co.nz; 63 Cron St; adult/child $23/16.50; ⏲noon-10pm) Setting a new standard for outdoor hot pools, this complex has been skillfully built within dense rainforest.

GLACIERS FOR DUMMIES

During the last ice age (15,000 to 20,000 years ago) the Franz Josef and Fox Glaciers reached the sea; in the ensuing thaw they may have crawled back further than their current positions. In the 14th century a mini ice age descended and for centuries the glaciers advanced, reaching their greatest extent around 1750. The terminal moraines from this time are still visible. Since then the West Coast's twin glaciers have both ebbed and advanced on a cyclic basis.

If you get rained in during your time in glacier country, here are a few glacier-geek conversation starters for the pub.

Ablation zone – where the glacier melts.

Accumulation zone – where the snow collects.

Bergschrund – a large *crevasse* in the ice near the glacier's starting point.

Blue ice – as the accumulation zone *(névé)* snow is compressed by subsequent snowfalls, it becomes *firn* and then *blue ice.*

Crevasse – a crack in the glacial ice formed as it crosses obstacles while descending.

Dead ice – isolated chunks of ice left behind when a glacier retreats.

Firn – partly compressed snow en route to becoming *blue ice.*

Glacial flour – finely ground rock particles in the milky rivers flowing off glaciers.

Icefall – when a glacier descends so steeply that the upper ice breaks into ice blocks.

Kettle lake – a lake formed by the melt of an area of isolated *dead ice.*

Moraine – walls of debris formed at the glacier's sides (lateral moraine) or end (terminal moraine).

Névé – snowfield area where *firn* is formed.

Seracs – ice pinnacles formed, like *crevasses,* by the glacier rolling over obstacles.

Terminal – the final ice face at the bottom of the glacier.

Perfect après-hike or on a rainy day. Enjoy the communal pools, or private ones ($42 per 45 minutes) and massages ($85 per half-hour) if you want to really indulge.

Skydive Franz SKYDIVING
(☎0800 458 677, 03-752 0714; www.skydivefranz.co.nz; Main Rd) Claiming NZ's highest jump (18,000ft, 75 seconds freefall, $549), this company also offers 15,000 for $399, and 12,000 for $299. With Aoraki/Mt Cook in your sights, this could be the most scenic jump you ever do.

Glacier Country Tours & Kayaks KAYAKING
(☎03-752 0230, 0800 423 262; www.glacierkayaks.com; 20 Cron St; 3hr tours $95) Take a guided kayak trip on Lake Mapourika (7km north of Franz), and get ecological commentary, mountain views and a serene channel detour. The family deal (from $210) is suitable for the whole crew, with mornings generally offering better conditions. You can also hire kayaks ($60 for 2½ hours).

Eco-Rafting RAFTING
(☎0508 669 675, 03-755 4254; www.ecorafting.co.nz; 6hr trip $450) Rafting adventures throughout the coast, including the six-hour 'Grand Canyon' trip on the Whataroa River with its towering granite walls. Includes a 15-minute helicopter ride.

South Westland Horse Treks HORSE RIDING
(☎0800 187 357, 03-752 0223; www.horsetreknz.com; Waiho Flats Rd; 2h trek $99) Located 5km south of town, this trekking company runs one- to six-hour equine excursions across farmland and remote beaches.

Glacier Valley Eco Tours GUIDED TOUR
(☎0800 999 739; www.glaciervalley.co.nz) Offers leisurely three- to eight-hour walks around local sights ($70 to $160), packed with local knowledge.

Across Country Quad Bikes QUAD BIKING
(☎0800 234 288, 03-752 0123; www.acrosscountryquadbikes.co.nz; Air Safaris Bldg, SH6) Four-wheeled outings, rockin' and rollin' through

the rainforest (two hours, rider/passenger $160/70). A heliquad option ($435, 2½ hours) traverses the mountains and coastline by air before taking on a remote West Coast beach. Mountain bike hire available (half-/full day $25/40).

Sleeping

Franz Josef Top 10 Holiday Park HOLIDAY PARK $
(☎03-752 0735, 0800 467 897; www.franzjoseftop10.co.nz; 2902 Franz Josef Hwy; sites from $40, d $65-165; @📶) This spacious holiday park, 1.5km from the township, has tip-top facilities and more sleeping options than you can shake a stick at. Tenters are well catered for with their own attractive, free-draining grassy area at the back of the park.

Glow Worm Cottages HOSTEL $
(☎03-752 0172, 0800 151 027; www.glowwormcottages.co.nz; 27 Cron St; dm $24-26, d $65-100; @📶) Relax at this quiet haven with homely communal areas and a nice nod to local history in the bedrooms. If you are back by 6pm, there's free vegie soup on offer. If the rain settles in, chill out in the spa or with a good DVD.

Te Waonui Forest Retreat HOTEL $$$
(☎0800 696 963, 03-752 0555; www.tewaonui.co.nz; 3 Wallace St; s/d $620/795; @📶) The damp, earthy surrounds and unflashy exterior of Franz's fancy new hotel hide the fact that inside is porter service, degustation dinners (included, along with breakfast, in the price) and a snazzy bar. The interior is dark – there's definitely a rainforest feel to the place – but you'll sleep like a log in the luxurious beds, and appreciate the modern styled rooms, all natural tones textured in wood and stone.

58 on Cron MOTEL $$
(☎0800 662 766, 03-752 0627; www.58oncron.co.nz; 58 Cron St; d $175-245; 📶) No prizes for the name, but these newish units impress with refreshed furnishings and all mod cons. A smart, clean, consistent performer.

Rainforest Retreat LODGE $
(☎0800 873 346, 03-752 0220; www.rainforestretreat.co.nz; 46 Cron St; sites from $19.50, dm $27-29, d $85-215; @📶) This large complex has something for everyone, from slightly unruly dorms to quieter double units, a handful of cottages and tree houses sleeping up to seven. Campervans can park up in leafy nooks. The on-site Monsoon Bar (motto: 'It rains, we pour') may be enjoyed by the young 'uns.

Franz Josef Glacier YHA HOSTEL $
(☎03-752 0754; www.yha.co.nz; 2-4 Cron St; dm $27-32, s $57, d $83-120; @📶) A large, tidy and colourful place with over 100 beds, and warm, spacious communal areas. There are family rooms available, a free sauna (keep your bathers on, please) and the rainforest at the back door.

Alpine Glacier Motel MOTEL $$
(☎03-752 0226, 0800 757 111; www.alpineglaciermotel.com; 14 Cron St; d $135-230; 📶) Standard motel offerings in the middle of the township. Two units have spas, and most have cooking facilities. Opt for the newer, more stylish units.

Glenfern Villas APARTMENT $$$
(☎03-752 0054, 0800 453 633; www.glenfern.co.nz; SH6; d $210-266; 📶) A handy 3km out of the tourist hubbub, these delightful one- and two-bedroom villas sit amid nikau palms and have top-notch beds, full kitchens, and private decks with views. This is the sort of place that says 'holiday', not 'stop-off'.

Holly Homestead B&B $$$
(☎03-752 0299; www.hollyhomestead.co.nz; SH6; d $265-430; @📶) Guests are welcomed with fresh home baking at this wisteria-draped 1926 B&B. Choose from three character en-suite rooms and a suite, all of which share a deck perfect for that sun-downer. Children over 12 welcome.

Eating & Drinking

Alice May MODERN NZ $$
(cnr Cowan & Cron Sts; mains $18-33; ⌚4pm-late) Resembling an old staging post, this sweet dining room serves up meaty, home-style meals like pork ribs and venison casserole. Park yourself outside and enjoy mountain views and bar snacks during happy hour (4pm to 7pm).

Picnics BAKERY $
(SH6; snacks $2-10; ⌚7am-5pm) Follow your nose (and the stream of foot traffic) to this fantastic little bakery. Heaps of good-value ready-to-scoff baked goods, including epic pasties suitable for bagging for a picnic lunch, or heating up later at dinner time.

Speights Landing Bar & Restaurant PUB $$
(SH6; mains $19-39; ⏲7.30am-late) A slighty frenzied but well-run pub serving up mega-portions of crowd-pleasing food; think big burgers, steaks and pizzas. The patio – complete with heaters and umbrellas – is a good place to unwind after a day on the ice.

Four Square Supermarket SUPERMARKET $
(SH6; ⏲7.45am-9.30pm) Mr Four Square comes to the party, big time.

Information

There's internet at Glacier Country Tours & Kayaks (p126) and Scott Base Tourist Information Centre (p128), and an ATM on the main street – if travelling south this is the last one you will see until Wanaka. The postal agency is located at the Mobil service station.

Alpine Adventure Centre (☎03-752 0793, 0800 800 793; www.scenic-flights.co.nz; SH6) Books activities and screens the 20-minute *Flowing West* movie (adult/child $12/6) on a giant screen. Shame about the '80s soundtrack.

Franz Josef Health Centre (☎03-752 0700, after hours 027 464 1192; 97 Cron St; ⏲8.30am-4pm Mon-Fri) South Westland's main medical centre.

Scott Base Tourist Information Centre (☎03-752 0288; SH6; 9am-9pm; @📶) Internet, Atomic agent, and bookings.

Westland Tai Poutini National Park Visitor Centre & i-SITE (☎03-752 0796; www.glaciercountry.co.nz; SH6; ⏲8.30am-6pm Oct-Apr, to 5pm May-Sept) Regional DOC office with good exhibits, weather information and track updates.

Getting There & Around

Buses leave from outside the Four Square supermarket.

InterCity (☎03-365 1113; www.intercity.co.nz) has daily buses south to Fox Glacier (from $10, 35 minutes) and Queenstown (from $62, eight hours); and north to Nelson (from $56, 10 hours). Book at the DOC Visitor Centre or YHA.

Atomic Shuttles (☎03-349 0697; www.atomictravel.co.nz) has services Sunday to Thursday south to Queenstown ($50, 6½ hours) via Fox Glacier ($15, 35 minutes), and north to Greymouth ($30, four hours). Book at the Scott Base Tourist Information Centre.

Glacier Valley Eco Tours (☎03-752 0699, 0800 999 739; www.glaciervalley.co.nz) runs scheduled shuttle services to the glacier car park (return trip $12.50).

Naked Bus (www.nakedbus.com) runs north to Hokitika, Greymouth and Nelson, and south to Fox Glacier.

Fox Glacier

Fox is smaller and quieter than Franz Josef, with a farmy feel and more open aspect. Lake Matheson is a highlight, as is the beach and historic walk down at Gillespies Beach.

Sights & Activities

Glacier Valley Walks

It's 1.5km from Fox Village to the glacier turn-off, and a further 2km to the car park. Thanks to DOC you can now reach the car park under your own steam via the new **Te Weheka Walkway/Cycleway**, a pleasant rainforest trail starting just south of the Bella Vista motel. It's just over an hour each way to walk, or 30 minutes to cycle (leave your bikes at the car park – you can't cycle on the glacier walkways). Hire bikes from Westhaven (p130).

From the car park, the terminal face is 30 to 40 minutes' walk. How close you can get to it depends on conditions. Obey all signs: this place is dangerously dynamic.

Short walks near the glacier include the **Moraine Walk** (over a major 18th-century advance) and **Minnehaha Walk**. The **River Walk** extends to the **Chalet Lookout Track** (1½ hours return) leading to a glacier lookout. The fully accessible **River Walk Lookout Track** (20 minutes return) starts from the Glacier View Road car park and allows people of all abilities the chance to view the glacier.

Fox Glacier Guiding WALKS
(☎03-751 0825, 0800 111 600; www.foxguides.co.nz; 44 Main Rd) Guided walks (equipment provided) are organised by Fox Glacier Guiding. Half-day walks cost $115/95 per adult/child; full-day walks are $165 (over-13s only). Helihikes cost $399 per person, while a day-long introductory ice-climbing course costs $275 per adult. There are also easy-going two-hour interpretive walks to the glacier (adult/child $49/35). Longer guided heli-hike adventures are also available.

Skydiving & Aerial Sightseeing

With Fox Glacier's backdrop of Southern Alps, rainforest and ocean, it's hard to imagine a better place to jump out of a plane. Aerial sightseeing costs at Fox

Fox Glacier & Village

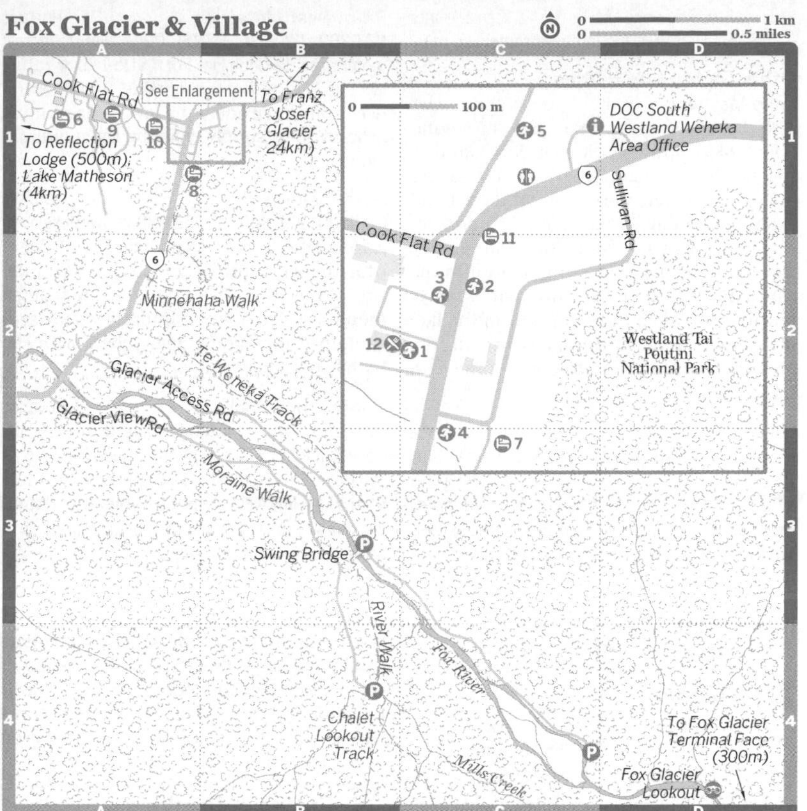

parallel those at Franz Josef. All four operators can be found on SH6 in Fox Glacier Village.

Skydive Glacier Country SKYDIVING
(☎03-751 0080, 0800 751 0080; www.skydivingnz.co.nz; Fox Glacier Airfield, SH6) This professional outfit challenges Isaac Newton, with thrilling leaps from 16,000ft ($399) or 12,000ft ($299).

Fox & Franz Josef Heliservices SCENIC FLIGHTS
(☎03-751 0866, 0800 800 793; www.scenic-flights.co.nz)

Glacier Helicopters SCENIC FLIGHTS
(☎0800 800 732, 03-751 0803; www.glacierhelicopters.co.nz)
See p125.

Helicopter Line SCENIC FLIGHTS
(☎0800 807 767, 03-752 0767; www.helicopter.co.nz)

Fox Glacier & Village

Mountain Helicopters SCENIC FLIGHTS
(☎03-751 0045; www.mountainhelicopters.co.nz)

Other Sights & Activities

Lake Matheson LAKE
The famous 'mirror lake' can be found about 6km down Cook Flat Rd. Wandering slowly (as you should), it will take 1½ hours to complete the circuit. At the far end – on a clear day – you may, just *may*, get the money shot, but failing that you can buy a postcard at the excellent gift store in the car park. The best time to visit is early morning, or when the sun is low in the late afternoon, although the presence of the Matheson Café means that any time is a good time.

Gillespies Beach BEACH
From the highway, turn down Cook Flat Rd for its full 21km (unsealed for the final 12km) to the remote black-sand Gillespies Beach, site of an old mining settlement. Various interesting walks can be had from here, from a five-minute zip to the old miners' cemetery, to the 3½ hour return walk to Galway Beach where seals are wont to haul out. Don't disturb their lazing about.

Sleeping

Fox Glacier Holiday Park HOLIDAY PARK $
(☎03-751 0821, 0800 154 366; www.fghp.co.nz; Kerrs Rd; sites from $38, cabins $58-60, d $94-199; @☎) This park has a range of different sleeping options to suit all budgets. Renovations, including a swanky facilities block, playground and barbecues, have improved what was already a good choice.

Fox Glacier Inn HOSTEL $
(☎03-751 0022; www.foxglacierinn.co.nz; 39 Sullivan Rd; dm $23-27, d $60-90; @☎) Hardworking managers have transformed this backpackers from hellhole to haven. Improvements include female-only 'sanctuary rooms' and bright new linen. Bar/restaurant and information centre on-site.

Lake Matheson Motels MOTEL $$
(☎0800 452 2437, 03-751 0830; www.lakematheson.co.nz; cnr Cook Flat Rd & Pekanga Dr; d $135-145, q $190; ☎) From the outside this place looks pretty ordinary, but inside the rooms come into their own. The owners have continued to pour profits back into the property, where you'll find ultra-tidy rooms with up-market amenities that contradict the mid-range price.

Rainforest Motel MOTEL $$
(☎0800 724 636, 03-751 0140; www.rainforestmotel.co.nz; 15 Cook Flat Rd; d $115-145; ☎) Rustic log cabins on the outside with neutral decor on the inside. Epic lawns for running around on or simply enjoying the mountain views.

Fox Glacier Lodge B&B $$$
(☎0800 369 800, 03-751 0888; www.foxglacierlodge.com; 41 Sullivan Rd; d $195-225; ☎) Beautiful timber adorns the exterior and interior of this attractive property, imparting a mountain chalet vibe. Similarly woody self-contained mezzanine apartments with spa baths are also available.

Reflection Lodge B&B $$$
(☎03-751 0707; www.reflectionlodge.co.nz; 137 Cook Flat Rd; d $210; ☎) The gregarious hosts of this ski-lodge style B&B go the extra mile to make your stay a memorable one. Grand gardens complete with Monet-like pond and alpine views seal the deal.

Westhaven MOTEL $$
(☎0800 369 452, 03-751 0084; www.thewesthaven.co.nz; SH6; d $125-185; ☎) These architecturally precise suites are a classy combo of corrugated steel and local stone amid burnt red and ivory walls. The deluxe king rooms have spas, and there are bikes to hire for the energetic (half-/full day $20/40).

Eating & Drinking

TOP CHOICE **Matheson Café** MODERN NZ $$
(www.lakematheson.com; Lake Matheson Rd; breakfast & lunch $9-19, dinner $24-36; ⊙7.30am-late Nov-Mar, 8am-4pm Apr-Oct) Near the shores of Lake Matheson, this cafe does everything right: slick interior design, inspiring mountain views, strong coffee and upmarket Kiwi fare. Get your sketchpad out and while away the afternoon. Next door is the ReflectioNZ Gallery stocking quality, primarily NZ-made art and souvenirs.

Plateau Café & Bar CAFE $$
(cnr Sullivan Rd & SH6; lunch $10-23, dinner $22-33; ⊙noon-late) Buzzy and sophisticated (for the West Coast anyway), Plateau combines snappy service with rustic faves like lamb burgers, Akaroa salmon and decent veggie creations. If the sun is shining, you can chill out on the wisteria-covered deck with a Kiwi craft beer or glass of wine.

Hobnail Café CAFE $
(44 Main Rd; meals $11-19; ⌚7.30am-3pm) Cabinets full of high-quality stodge including mightily stuffed jacket potatoes, pastries, panini, biscuits and cake. Hearty breakfasts such as bubble and squeak fuel folk headed for the ice. Located in the same building as Fox Glacier Guiding.

Information

At the time of research there were plans afoot to build a Four Square supermarket on the corner of SH6 and Frames Road; here you should find an ATM. The BP petrol station is the last fuel stop until Haast, 120km south. Get online at the Internet Outpost, beside the Helicopter Line office.

DOC South Westland Weheka Area Office (☎03-751 0807; SH6; ⌚9am-noon & 1-4.30pm Mon-Fri) This is no longer a general visitor information centre, but has the usual DOC information, hut tickets and weather and track updates.

Fox Glacier Guiding (☎0800 111 600, 03-751 0825; www.foxguides.co.nz; 44 Main Rd) Books Atomic Shuttles, and provides postal and currency exchange services.

Fox Glacier Health Centre (☎03-751 0836, after hours 027 464 1193; SH6) Staffed most mornings from 9am to noon; doctor available on Tuesdays. Call the clinic for the latest hours.

Getting There & Around

Most buses stop outside the Fox Glacier Guiding building.

InterCity (☎03-365 1113; www.intercity.co.nz) runs two buses a day north to Franz Josef (from $10, 40 minutes), the morning bus continuing to Nelson (from $57, 11 hours). Daily southbound services run to Queenstown (from $58, 7½ hours).

Atomic Shuttles (☎03-349 0697; www.atomictravel.co.nz) runs daily to Franz Josef ($15, 30 minutes), continuing to Greymouth (from $35, 3¼ hours). Southbound buses run daily to Queenstown ($45, 6½ hours).

Fox Glacier Shuttles & Tours (☎0800 369 287) will drive you around the immediate surrounds such as Lake Matheson, Gillespies Beach, the glaciers or beyond (from $10 return).

Naked Bus (www.nakedbus.com) runs north to Franz Josef Glacier, Hokitika, Greymouth, Westport and Nelson, and south to Queenstown, stopping at Haast and Wanaka.

SOUTH TO HAAST

About 26km south of Fox Glacier, along SH6, is the **Copland Valley** trailhead, the western end of the **Copland Track**. Earn one of the best pay-offs of any walk in Aotearoa by tramping six to seven hours to the **Welcome Flat DOC Hut** (adult/child $15/7.50) where thermal springs bubble just metres from the hut door. Backcountry Hut Passes don't apply here, but you can buy tickets online or at any West Coast DOC office or visitor information centres.

Popular with Haast–Fox cyclists and Copland Track trampers, the **Pine Grove Motel** (☎03-751 0898; SH6; sites $25, d $50-90) is 8km south of the trailhead. Units are affordable and in reasonable shape, and the owners offer secure parking.

Lake Moeraki, 31km north of Haast, is a rippling fishing lake. An easy 40-minute walk from here brings you to **Monro Beach**, a gravel beach copping the full Tasman Sea force. There's a breeding colony of Fiordland crested penguins here (July to December) and fur seals. **Wilderness Lodge Lake Moeraki** (☎03-750 0881; www.wildernesslodge.co.nz; SH6; d incl breakfast & dinner $640-1000) is ecofriendly accommodation in a vibrant wilderness setting. The comfortable rooms and four-course dinners are lovely, but the real treats here are the outdoor activities, including nature tours guided by people with conservation in their blood.

About 5km south of Lake Moeraki is the much-photographed **Knights Point** (named after a surveyor's dog) where the Haast road was eventually opened in 1965. Stop here if humanly possible.

Ship Creek, 15km north of Haast, has a lookout platform and two interesting interpretive walks: the **Dune Lake Walk** (30 minutes return) and the **Kahikatea Swamp Forest Walk** (20 minutes return).

If you haven't had your fill of whitebait yet, call into the **Curly Tree Whitebait Company** (☎03-750 0097), 5km north of Haast at the Waita River bridge. Exemplary whitebait patties for $7, plus bait to go at the market price.

HAAST REGION

The Haast region is a major wilderness area. The area's kahikatea and rata forests, wetlands, sand dunes, seal and penguin

WORTH A TRIP

JACKSON BAY ROAD

From Haast Junction, the road most travelled is SH6, upwards or across. But there is another option, and that is south… to the end of the line.

The road to Jackson Bay is quiet and intensely scenic. Towered over by Southern Alps, the farms on the flat and the settlements dotted between them stand testament to some of the hardiest souls who ever attempted settlement in NZ. Until the 1950s, the only way to reach Haast overland was via bush tracks from Hokitika and Wanaka. Supplies came in by a coastal shipping service that called in every couple of months or so.

Besides the ghosts and former glories, which make an appearance here and there, there's plenty to warrant a foray down to Jackson Bay.

Near Okuru is the **Hapuka Estuary Walk** (20 minutes return), a winding boardwalk that loops through a sleepy wildlife sanctuary with good interpretation panels en route.

The road continues west to **Arawhata Bridge**, where a turn-off leads to the **Ellery Creek Walkway**, 3.5km away. This pleasant amble through mossy beech forest (1½ hours return) leads to **Ellery Lake**, where a picnic bench encourages lunch with perhaps a skinny dip for afters.

It's less than an hour's drive from Haast town to the fishing hamlet of **Jackson Bay**, the only natural harbour on the West Coast. Migrants arrived here in 1875 under a doomed settlement scheme, their farming and timber-milling aspirations mercilessly shattered by never-ending rain and the lack of a wharf, not built until 1938. Those families who stayed turned their hands to largely subsistence living.

With good timing you will arrive when the **Cray Pot** (☎03-750 0035; fish & chips $17-29; ⏰11am-8pm Nov-Mar) is open. This place is just as much about the dining room (a caravan) and location (looking out over the bay) as it is about the honest seafood, including a good feed of fish and chips, crayfish, chowder and whitebait.

Walk off your fries on the **Wharekai Te Kou Walk** (40 minutes return) to Ocean Beach, a tiny bay that hosts pounding waves and some interesting rock formations.

colonies, bird life and sweeping beaches ensued its inclusion in the Southwest New Zealand (Te Wahipounamu) World Heritage Area.

Haast & Jackson Bay

Some 120km south of Fox Glacier, Haast crouches around the mouth of the wide Haast River in three distinct pockets: Haast Junction, Haast Village and Haast Beach. While certainly a handy stop for filling the tank and tummy, it's also the gateway to some spectacular scenery, and the end of the line at Jackson Bay.

Activities

Haast River Safari JETBOATING

(☎0800 865 382, 03-750 0101; www.haastriver.co.nz; Haast Village; adult/child $132/55; ⏰trips 9am, 11am & 2pm) Based in the Red Barn between Haast Village and the visitor information centre, these folks runs leisurely 90-minute covered-jetboat cruises on the Haast River.

Waiatoto River Safaris JETBOATING

(☎03-750 0780; www.riversafaris.co.nz; Jackson Bay Rd; adult/child $139/59; ⏰trips 10am, 1pm & 4pm) Take a hair-tousling 2½-hour 'sea to mountain' jetboat trip on the wild Waiatoto River, 30km south of Haast.

Sleeping

Haast Beach Holiday Park HOLIDAY PARK $

(☎03-750 0860, 0800 843 226; www.haastbeachholidaypark.co.nz; 1348 Jackson Bay Rd, Haast Beach; sites from $28, dm $25, d $45-110) New managers are working hard to improve this old but pleasant holiday park with a variety of accommodation options. It's a 20-minute walk from an epic West Coast beach and about 14km south of the Haast Junction. The Hapuka Estuary Walk is across the road.

Haast River Top 10 HOLIDAY PARK $

(☎0800 624 847, 03-750 0020; www.haasttop10.co.nz; SH6, Haast Village; sites from $25, dm $30, s $60, d $90-130, q $130-170; @📶) New holiday park with top-notch amenities including a bright-red, open-plan shed housing facilities for campers and great communal areas in the converted lodge. Motel units are light, spacious and enjoy great views when the weather's kind.

Haast Lodge LODGE **$**
(☎0800 500 703, 03-750 0703; www.haastlodge.com; Marks Rd, Haast Village; sites from $16, dm/d $25/65, units d $95-120; @📶) Covering all bases, Haast Lodge offers well-maintained, clean lodgings from dorms and doubles complete with an excellent communal area, to motel units at the Aspring Court next door. Powered bays for campervans.

Collyer House B&B **$$$**
(☎03-750 0022; www.collyerhouse.co.nz; Cuttance Rd, Haast Village; r from $220; @📶) This gem of a B&B has thick bathrobes, quality linen, beach views and a sparkling host who cooks a terrific breakfast. This all adds up to make Collyer House an indulgent and comfortable choice. Follow the signs off SH6 for 12km down Jackson Bay Rd.

Eating & Drinking

Hard Antler PUB **$$**
(Marks Rd, Haast Village; dinner $20-30; ⏲dining 11am-9pm) This expanding array of deer antlers is enough to give you the horn. So is the fine home cooking (meat all ways) and welcoming attitude of this big, bold pub.

Okoto Espresso CAFE **$**
(Haast Village; snacks $2-10) Look out for the rusty hut being towed by the orange Landrover. Where you find it you'll encounter Robyn and her excellent coffee, whitebait fritters, smoothies, biscotti and pancakes.

Information

The **DOC Haast Visitor Information Centre** (☎03-750 0809; www.haastnz.com; cnr SH6 & Jackson Bay Rd; ⏲9am-6pm Nov-Mar, to 4.30pm Apr-Oct) has wall-to-wall regional information and screens the all-too-brief Haast landscape film *Edge of Wilderness* (adult/child $3/free).

Getting There & Away

InterCity (☎03-365 1113; www.intercity.co.nz) and **Atomic Shuttles** (☎03-349 0697; www.atomictravel.co.nz) buses stop at the visitor information centre on their Fox to Wanaka runs.

Naked Bus (www.nakedbus.com) runs north to the glaciers, Hokitika, Greymouth and Nelson, and south to Queenstown, stopping at Wanaka.

Haast Pass Highway

Turning inland from Haast towards Wanaka (145km, 2½ hours), SH6 snakes alongside the Haast River, climbing up to Haast Pass and Mt Aspiring National Park. As you move inland the vegetation thins away until you reach the 563m pass – snow country covered in tussock and scrub. There are some stunning waterfalls en route (especially if it's been raining), tumbling down just minutes from the highway: **Fantail** and **Thunder Creek** falls are worth a look. There's also the **Bridle Track** (1½ hours one-way) between the pass and Davis Flat. See the DOC booklet *Walks along the Haast Highway* ($2).

The Haast Pass road (Tioripatea, meaning 'Clear Path' in Maori) opened in 1965; before then Maori walked this route bringing West Coast greenstone to the Makarora River in Otago. The pass (and river and township) take their European name from geologist Julius Haast, who passed through in 1863.

There are food and fuel stops at Makarora and Lake Hawea. If you're driving north, check your fuel gauge: Haast petrol station is the last one before Fox Glacier, 120km north.

Christchurch & Canterbury

Includes »

Best Places to Eat

» Bodhi Tree (p149)

» Simo's Deli (p151)

» Christchurch Farmers Market (p152)

» Almeidas Tapas Bar (p150)

» The Little Bistro (p163)

Best Places to Stay

» Orari B&B (p146)

» Le Petit Hotel (p150)

» Coombe Farm (p162)

» Okuti Garden (p162)

Why Go?

Nowhere in New Zealand is changing and developing as fast as post-earthquake Christchurch, and visiting the country's second largest city as it's being rebuilt and reborn is both interesting and inspiring.

A short drive from Christchurch's dynamic re-emergence, Banks Peninsula conceals hidden bays and beaches – a backdrop for kayaking and wildlife cruises with a sunset return to the attractions of Akaroa. To the north are the vineyards of the Waipara Valley and the family-holiday ambience of Hanmer Springs. Westwards, the well-ordered farms of the Canterbury Plains morph quickly into the rough-and-tumble wilderness of the Southern Alps.

Canterbury summertime attractions include tramping along the braided rivers and alpine valleys around Arthur's Pass and mountain biking around the turquoise lakes of the Mackenzie Country. During winter, the attention switches to the mountains, with skiing at Mt Hutt. Throughout the seasons, Aoraki/Mt Cook, the country's tallest peak, stands sentinel over this diverse region.

When to Go

Overall Canterbury is one of NZ's driest regions because moisture-laden westerlies from the Tasman Sea dump their rainfall on the West Coast before hitting the eastern South Island. Head to Christchurch and Canterbury from January to March for settled summer weather and plenty of opportunities to get active amid the region's spectacular landscapes. It's also festival time in Christchurch with January's World Buskers Festival and the Ellerslie International Flower Show in March. Hit the winter slopes from July to October at Mt Hutt or on Canterbury's smaller club ski fields.

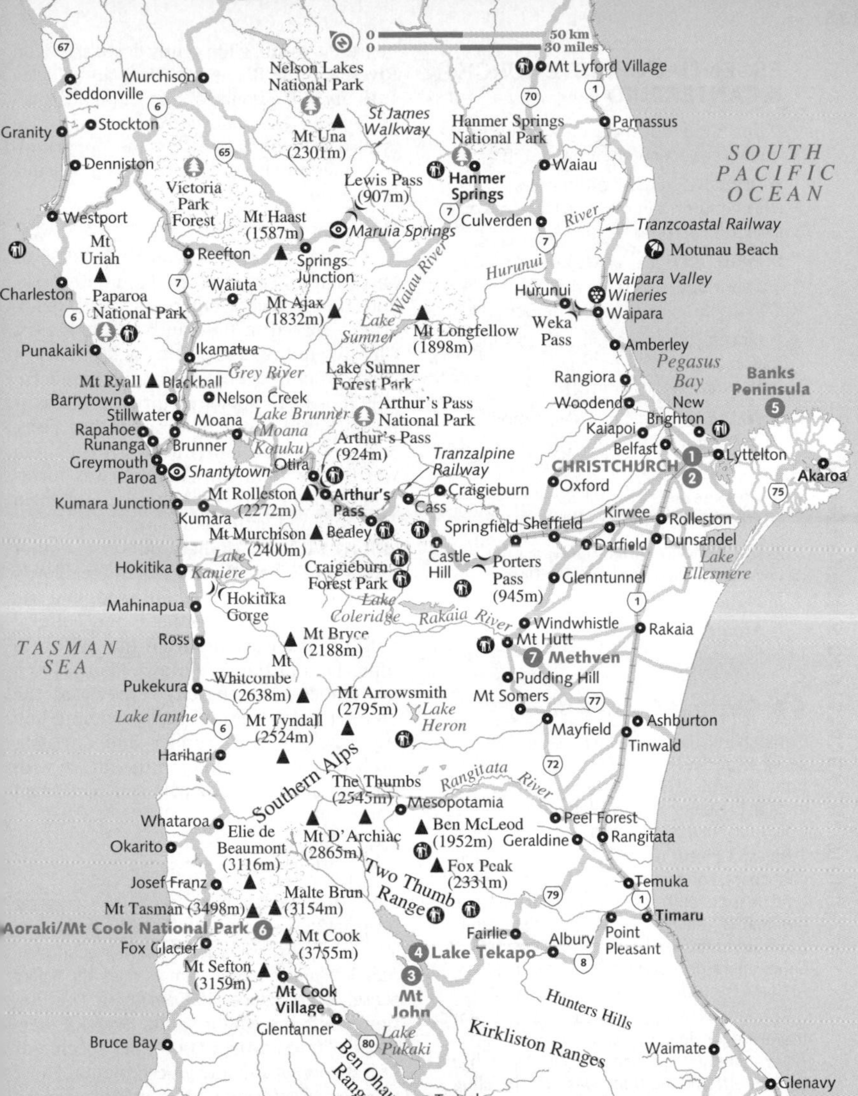

Christchurch & Canterbury Highlights

1. Supporting the exciting rebuilding and re-emergence of **Christchurch** (p136)
2. Meandering along Christchurch's **Avon River** (p141) by punt or bicycle
3. Marvelling at the views of the Mackenzie Country from atop **Mt John** (p178)
4. Taking a soothing soak at Lake Tekapo's **Alpine Springs & Spa** (p178)
5. Negotiating the outer reaches of **Banks Peninsula** (p157) by bike, kayak or boat
6. Tramping in the shadow of NZ's highest peak in **Aoraki/ Mt Cook National Park** (p182)
7. Being surprised by the size of the Canterbury Plains on a balloon flight from **Methven** (p170)

ESSENTIAL CHRISTCHURCH & CANTERBURY

» **Eat** Amid the emerging Addington restaurant scene in Christchurch

» **Drink** NZ's best craft beer at Christchurch's Pomeroy's Old Brewery Inn (p152)

» **Read** *Old Bucky & Me*, a poignant account of the 2011 earthquake by Christchurch journalist Jane Bowron

» **Listen** To the best up-and-coming bands at Christchurch's Dux Live (p153) and darkroom (p153)

» **Watch** *When a City Falls*, a moving documentary about the 2010 and 2011 earthquakes

» **Go green** At the ecofriendly Okuti Garden (p162) on Banks Peninsula

» **Online** www.christchurchnz.com, www.mtcooknz.com; www.lonelyplanet.com/new-zealand/christchurch

» **Area code** ☎03

ℹ Getting There & Away

Christchurch has an international airport serviced by domestic airlines flying to key destinations around NZ. International connections include Brisbane, Sydney, Melbourne and the Gold Coast in Australia, and Singapore in Asia.

Bus and shuttle operators scurry along the east coast, connecting Canterbury's coastal (and near-coastal) settlements with northern destinations such as Picton and Nelson, and southern towns like Dunedin and Queenstown. Other operators connect Christchurch to Arthur's Pass, the West Coast and Mt Cook.

Rail options for east-coast and coast-to-coast travel are provided by KiwiRail Scenic. The *TranzAlpine* service connects Christchurch and Greymouth, and the *TranzCoastal* trains chug north to Picton, with ferry connections across Cook Strait to the North Island.

CHRISTCHURCH

POP 380,900

Welcome to a vibrant city in transition, coping resiliently and creatively with the aftermath of NZ's second-biggest natural disaster (especially as tremors can still be felt regularly). Traditionally the most English of NZ cities, Christchurch is now adding a modern and innovative layer to its damaged heritage heart. Punts still glide gently down the Avon River, and the Botanic Gardens and Hagley Park are still among NZ's finest public spaces, but an energetic entrepreneurial edge is also evident, harnessing the opportunities emerging from the city's recent seismic heartache.

History

The settlement of Christchurch in 1850 was an ordered Church of England enterprise, and the fertile farming land was deliberately placed in the hands of the gentry. Christchurch was meant to be a model of class-structured England in the South Pacific, not just another scruffy colonial outpost. Churches were built rather than pubs, and wool made the elite of Christchurch wealthy. In 1862, Christchurch was incorporated as a very English city, and town planning and architecture assumed a close affinity with the 'Mother Country'. As other migrants arrived, the city's character slowly evolved. New industries followed, and the city forged its own aesthetic and cultural notions, often derived from the rich rural hinterland of the Canterbury Plains. From September 2010, the city's reverie as the South Island's cultural and economic hub was savagely torn asunder, and Christchurch was forced to look to the future with both significant challenges and significant opportunities.

◉ Sights

Botanic Gardens GARDENS

(Map p142; www.ccc.govt.nz; Rolleston Ave; admission free, guided walks $10, train tour adult/child $18/9; ⌚grounds open 7am & close 1hr before sunset, conservatories 10.15am-4pm) The Botanic Gardens comprise 30 riverside hectares planted with 10,000-plus specimens of indigenous and introduced plants. There are conservatories and thematic gardens to explore, lawns to sprawl on, and a cafe at the **Botanic Gardens visitors centre** (Map p142; ⌚pam-4pm Mon-Fri, 10.15-4pm Sat & Sun). Get the kids active in the playground adjacent to the cafe. Guided walks ($10) depart daily at 1.30pm (September to April) from the Canterbury Museum, or you can ride around the gardens in the electric **Caterpillar train** (www.gardentour.co.nz; hop on/hop-off tickets adult/child $18/9; ⌚10am-4pm). Tickets are valid for two days and include a commentary.

Canterbury Museum MUSEUM

(Map p142; ☎03-366 5000; www.canterburymuseum.com; Rolleston Ave; admission by donation; ⏲9am-5pm Apr-Sep, to 5.30pm Oct-Mar) The absorbing Canterbury Museum has a wonderful collection of items of significance to NZ. Highlights include the Maori gallery, with some stunning *pounamu* (greenstone) pieces on display; the coracle in the Antarctic Hall that was used by a group shipwrecked on Disappointment Island in 1907; and a wide array of stuffed birds from the Pacific and beyond: don't miss the statuesque Emperor penguin. Guided tours (donations appreciated) run from 3.30pm to 4.30pm on Tuesday and Thursday. Kids will enjoy the interactive displays in the Discovery Centre (admission $2). Don't miss the gloriously kitsch Kiwiana of Fred & Myrtle's Paua Shell House.

Arts Centre HISTORIC SITE

(Map p142; www.artscentre.org.nz; 2 Worcester St; admission free) This precinct is currently closed, pending strengthening and repairs estimated to cost $240 million. An enclave of Gothic Revival buildings (built from 1877), it was the original site of Canterbury College, which later became Canterbury University. One graduate of the college was Sir Ernest Rutherford, the NZ-born physicist who first split the atom in 1917. Before the earthquakes, the Arts Centre was a popular cultural precinct comprising artists' studios and galleries, weekend craft markets, restaurants and cinemas. One business still operating from a modern building within the Arts Centre is the excellent Canterbury Cheesemongers (p152).

Cathedral Square SQUARE

(Map p142; ☎03-366 0046; www.christchurchcathedral.co.nz; admission free; ⏲8.30am-7pm Oct-Mar, 9am-5pm Apr-Sep) Christchurch's historic hub is Cathedral Square. At the time of research the square was in the heart of the city's cordoned-off CBD (Central Business District), but was planned to be reopened sometime from mid-2012. See the CBD Red Zone Cordon Map (www.cera.govt.nz) for the latest information.

At the centre of the square is (or was) ChristChurch Cathedral, originally constructed in 1881, and a much-loved icon of the city. The February 2011 earthquake caused devastating damage, bringing down the Gothic church's 63m-high spire and leaving only the bottom half of the tower remaining. It was feared up to 20 people had been in the spire when it collapsed, but it was later found that no one had died at the site. Subsequent earthquakes in June 2011 and December 2011 destroyed the cathedral's prized stained-glass rose window, and the cathedral was deconsecrated in October 2011.

The deconstruction and demolition of the cathedral was announced in March 2012 by the Anglican Diocese of Christchurch,

MAORI NZ: CHRISTCHURCH & CANTERBURY

Only 5% of NZ's Maori live on the South Island. The south was settled a few hundred years later than the north, with significant numbers coming south only after land became scarcer on the North Island. Before that, Maori mostly travelled to the south in search of moa, fish and West Coast *pounamu* (greenstone).

The major *iwi* (tribe) of the South Island is **Ngai Tahu** (www.ngaitahu.iwi.nz), ironically now one of the country's wealthiest as it's much richer in land and natural resources (per person) than the North Island tribes. In Christchurch, as in other cities, there are urban Maori of many other *iwi* as well.

Ko Tane at the Willowbank Wildlife Reserve (p140) features traditional dancing, including the *haka* and the *poi* dance. Future plans at Willowbank include the establishment of a replica Maori village.

If you're feeling creative, the Bone Dude (p144), John Fraser, teaches visitors to do their own bone carving at his studio in Christchurch.

You'll unearth Maori artefacts at Christchurch's Canterbury Museum (p137), and at Akaroa Museum (p158) and Maori & Colonial Museum (p158) in Okains Bay on the Banks Peninsula.

Further south in Timaru, the Te Ana Maori Rock Art Centre (p172) presents the fascinating story of NZ's indigenous rock art, and also arranges tours to see the centuries-old work in situ.

Greater Christchurch

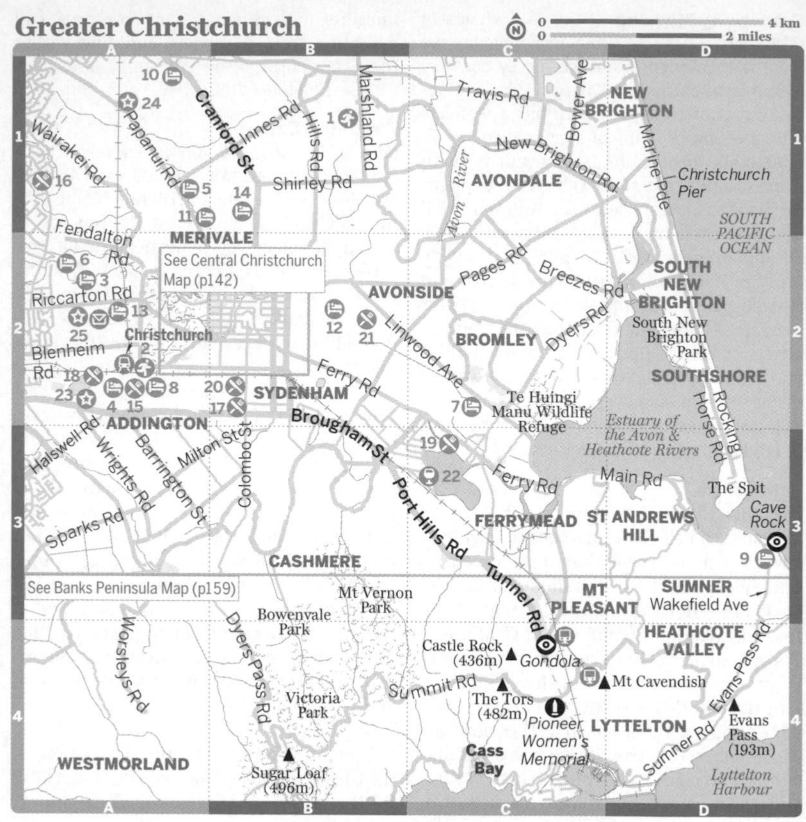

but at the time of research there remained significant public opposition to this decision. See www.christchurchcathedral.co.nz for the latest information. The draft plan to rebuild Christchurch recommends that Cathedral Square be transformed into a park. In April 2012, plans were announced to build a 'cardboard cathedral' designed by Japanese architect Shigeru Ban. Located on the corner of Madras and Hereford Sts near Latimer Square, the $5 million construction would seat 700 worshippers and is planned to open in December 2012. The cathedral will become the temporary centre for Christchurch's Anglican St John's parish, and will also be used for concerts and art exhibitions.

Other heritage buildings around Cathedral Square were also badly damaged, but one modern landmark left unscathed is the 18m-high metal sculpture *Chalice*, designed by Neil Dawson. It was erected in 2001 to commemorate the new millennium.

International Antarctic Centre WILDLIFE
(☎03-353 7798, 0508 736 4846; www.iceberg.co.nz; 38 Orchard Rd, Christchurch Airport; adult/child/family from $35/20/95; ⏰9am-5.30pm) The International Antarctic Centre is part of a huge complex built for the administration of the NZ, US and Italian Antarctic programs. See penguins and learn about the icy continent via historical, geological and zoological exhibits. There's also an aquarium of creatures gathered under the ice in McMurdo Sound. Other attractions include a '4D' theatrette – a 3D film plus moving seats and a watery spray – and the Antarctic Storm chamber, where you can get a first-hand taste of -18°C wind chill. An Extreme Pass (adult/child/family $65/35/165) includes unlimited rides on the Hägglund outdoor adventure course. An optional extra is the Penguin Backstage Pass (adult/child/family $25/15/80), which takes visitors behind the scenes of the Penguin Encounter. Transport

Greater Christchurch

Activities, Courses & Tours
1 Bone Dude B1
2 Turners Auctions A2

Sleeping
3 Anslem House A2
4 Arena Motel A2
5 Elm Tree House A1
6 Fendalton House A2
7 Haka Lodge C2
8 Jailhouse A2
9 Le Petit Hotel D3
10 Meadow Park Top 10 Holiday Park A1
11 Merivale Manor A1
12 Old Countryhouse B2
13 Roma on Riccarton A2
Sumner Bay Motel and Apartments .... (see 9)
14 Wish B1

Eating
15 Addington Coffee Co-op A2
Almeidas Tapas Bar .... (see 9)
Bamboozle .... (see 9)
16 Bodhi Tree A1
17 Burgers & Beers Inc B2
Christchurch Farmers Market .... (see 3)
Cornershop Bistro .... (see 9)
18 Edesia A2
19 Holy Smoke C3
20 Honey Pot Cafe B2
Serious Sandwich .... (see 17)
Simo's Deli .... (see 15)
21 Under the Red Verandah B2

Drinking
22 The Brewery C3
Volstead Trading Company .... (see 13)
Wood's Mill .... (see 15)

Entertainment
23 Christchurch Stadium A2
24 Club 22 .... A1
Court Theatre .... (see 15)
Hollywood 3 .... (see 9)
25 Hoyts Riccarton A2

Shopping
Backpackers Car Market .... (see 20)
Sunday Artisan Market .... (see 3)
Westfield Riccarton Mall .... (see 25)

options include the City Flyer (p156) airport bus (it's just a short walk from the main terminal) or the free Penguin Express shuttle that departs from outside the Canterbury Museum.

FREE Christchurch Art Gallery GALLERY
(Map p142; www.christchurchartgallery.org.nz; cnr Worcester & Montreal Sts; ⌚10am-5pm Thu-Tue, to 9pm Wed) Set in an eye-catching metal-and-glass construction built in 2003, the city's art gallery – closed at the time of writing, with a definite reopening being planned – has an engrossing permanent collection divided into historical, 20th-century and contemporary galleries, plus temporary exhibitions featuring NZ artists. Before the gallery closed following the earthquakes, free guided tours were offered at 11am Monday to Sunday, plus 2pm Saturday and Sunday and 7.15pm Wednesday. Check the website for the latest information about gallery reopenings. The gallery's shop is currently open.

Tramway TRAM
(☎03-366 7830; www.tram.co.nz) Prior to the February 2011 earthquake, historic trams operated on a 2.5km inner-city loop, taking in local attractions and shopping areas. At the time of writing the tramway was not operating because the city's CBD was closed. Check the website for an update.

Orana Wildlife Park WILDLIFE RESERVE
(www.oranawildlifepark.co.nz; McLeans Island Rd, Papanui; adult/child $25/8; ⌚10am-5pm) Orana has an excellent, walk-through native-bird aviary, a nocturnal kiwi house and a reptile exhibit featuring the wrinkly tuatara. Most of the grounds are devoted to Africana, including lions, rhinos, giraffes, zebras, lemurs, oryx and cheetahs. Guided walks start at 10.40am daily, taking in feeding time for the Sumatra tigers; the 2.30pm departure visits the lion enclosure. Check the website for feeding times and other optional Orana experiences for more personal interactions with some of the animals. Phone ☎03-379 1699 for shuttle transport to Orana.

THE CHRISTCHURCH EARTHQUAKES

Christchurch's seismic nightmare began at 4.35am on 4 September 2010. Centered 40km west of the city, a 40-second, 7.1-magnitude earthquake jolted Cantabrians from their sleep, and caused widespread damage to older buildings in the central city. Close to the quake's epicentre in rural Darfield, huge gashes erupted amid grassy pastures, and the South Island's main railway line was bent and buckled. Because the tremor struck in the early hours of the morning, when most people were home in bed, there were no fatalities, and many Christchurch residents felt the city had dodged a bullet.

Fast forward to 12.51pm on 22 February 2011, when central Christchurch was busy with shoppers and office and retail workers enjoying their lunch break. This time the 6.3-magnitude quake was much closer, centred just 10km southeast of the city and only 5km deep. The tremor was significantly more extreme, and many locals report being flung violently and almost vertically into the air. The peak ground acceleration (PGA) exceeded 1.8, almost twice the acceleration of gravity.

When the dust settled after 24 traumatic seconds, NZ's second-largest city had changed forever. The towering spire of the iconic ChristChurch Cathedral lay in ruins; walls and verandahs had cascaded down on the city's central retail hub; and two multistorey buildings had pancaked, causing scores of deaths. Around half of the 185 deaths (including 20 nationalities) occurred in the Canterbury TV building, where many international students at a language school were killed. Elsewhere in the city, the historic port town of Lyttelton was badly damaged; roads and bridges were crumpled; and residential suburbs in the east were inundated as a process of rapid liquefaction saw tonnes of oozy silt rise from the ground

After 22 February, the resilience and bravery of Cantabrians quickly became evident. From the region's rural heartland, the 'Farmy Army' descended on the city, armed with shovels and food hampers. Social media mobilised 10,000 students, and the Student Volunteer Army became a vital force for residential clean-ups in the city's beleaguered eastern suburbs. Heartfelt aid and support arrived from among NZ's close-knit population of just 4.4 million, and seven other nations sent specialised urban-search-and-rescue teams.

At the time of writing, the city's population was still bravely getting on with their lives, besieged by thousands of aftershocks, including significant jolts in June 2011 and December 2011. Most tremors, however, have been small and there have been no fatalities or injuries since February 2011. The earthquake activity is reported to be moving further east into the Pacific Ocean, and peak ground acceleration is decreasing.

The impact of a warm summer's day in early 2011 will take longer than a generation to resolve. Around a quarter of the buildings within the city's famed four avenues need to be demolished. Entire streets and family neighbourhoods in the eastern suburbs will be abandoned, and Christchurch's heritage architecture is irrevocably damaged. The cost to repair and rebuild the city could exceed NZ$30 billion, making it history's third most costly natural disaster.

In December 2011, the influential United States magazine *Foreign Policy* nominated Christchurch one of the urban centres of the 21st century, opining that the 'massive rebuilding effort is a unique opportunity to rethink urban form'. Draft plans for the city's rebuilding over 20 years include a compact, low-rise city centre, neighbourhood green spaces, and parks and cycleways along the Avon River. Coupled with the endurance and energy of the people of Christchurch, the city's future promises to be both interesting and innovative.

Willowbank Wildlife Reserve WILDLIFE RESERVE
(www.willowbank.co.nz; 60 Hussey Rd, Northwood; adult/child/family $25/10/65; ⌚9.30am-dusk) About 6km north of the city, Willowbank focuses on native NZ animals and hands-on enclosures with alpacas, wallabies and deer. Tours are held several times a day, and the after-dark tours are a good opportunity to see a kiwi. Phone ☎03-359 6226 or ask at the Christchurch i-SITE about free shuttle transport to Willowbank.

Gondola CABLE CAR
(www.gondola.co.nz; 10 Bridle Path Rd; return adult/child/family $24/10/59; ⌚10am-9pm) At the time

of writing, this attraction was closed but was planned to reopen by September 2012. Check the website for the latest information.

Activities

Christchurch's most popular activities are gentler than the adrenaline-fuelled pursuits of Queenstown and Wanaka: the city is better suited to punting down the Avon River, cycling through the easy terrain of Hagley Park or negotiating the walking trails at Lyttelton Harbour. The closest **beaches** to the city are Waimairi, North Beach, New Brighton and South Brighton; buses 5, 49 and 60 head here. Sumner, to the city's southeast, is another popular beach, with good restaurants (take bus 3), while further east at Taylors Mistake are some good **surfing** breaks. Several **skiing** areas lie within a two-hour drive of Christchurch. Other active options accessible from Christchurch include cruising on Akaroa Harbour, rafting on the Rangitata River, tandem skydiving, hot-air ballooning, jetboating the Waimakariri River and horse trekking. Inquire at the Christchuch i-SITE (p155).

Walking

The i-SITE has information on walks around Christchurch and in the Port Hills. Some popular walks were closed at the time of writing due to rock falls and instability following the earthquakes, so it's vital to check the current situation at the i-SITE before setting off. Also search www.ccc.govt.nz with the keywords 'Port Hills' for the current status of the following tracks.

For great views of the city, take the walkway from the Sign of the Takahe on Dyers Pass Rd. The various 'Sign of the...' places in this area were originally roadhouses built during the Depression as rest stops. This walk leads up to the Sign of the Kiwi through Victoria Park and then along Summit Rd to Scotts Reserve, with several lookout points along the way.

You can walk to Lyttelton on the Bridle Path (1½ hours), which starts at Heathcote Valley (take bus 28). The Godley Head Walkway (two hours return) begins at Taylors Mistake, crossing and recrossing Summit Rd, and offers beautiful views on a clear day.

The Crater Rim Walkway (nine hours) around Lyttelton Harbour goes some 20km from Evans Pass to the Ahuriri Scenic Reserve. From the gondola terminal on Mt Cavendish, walk to Cavendish Bluff Lookout (30 minutes return) or the Pioneer Women's Memorial (one hour return).

Cycling

City Cycle Hire BICYCLE RENTAL
(☎0800 424 534; www.cyclehire-tours.co.nz; bike half/full day $25/35, mountain bike half/full day $30/45) Mountain bikes will get you nicely off-road: before the earthquakes, a mountain-bike ride from the top of the gondola was on offer (check the website for the latest updates). Bikes can be delivered to where you're staying.

Natural High BICYCLE RENTAL
(☎03-982 2966, 0800 444 144; www.naturalhigh.co.nz; 690a Harewood Rd, Harewood; per day/week from $40/154) Rents touring and mountain bikes, and can advise on guided and

CHRISTCHURCH IN...

Two Days

After breakfast at the Addington Coffee Co-op (p150), amble back to the city through leafy South Hagley Park. Stop at the Antigua Boatsheds (p144) for punting on the Avon, and put together your own informal lunch at Canterbury Cheesemongers (p152) in the Arts Centre. After lunch, explore the excellent Canterbury Museum (p137) before heading to meet the locals over NZ craft beers and great pub food at Pomeroy's Old Brewery Inn (p152).

On day two, explore Hagley Park on a vintage bike courtesy of Vintage Peddler Bike Hire Co (p144), or walk through the lovely Botanic Gardens (p136), perhaps picking up some goodies from Vic's Cafe & Bakery (p151) or Simo's Deli (p151) for a riverside picnic. In the evening, jump on a bus to hit the excellent restaurants at Lyttelton or Sumner.

Four Days

Follow the two-day itinerary, then head to Akaroa to explore its wildlife-rich harbour and the peninsula's beautiful outer bays. On day four it's time for shopping in the funky Re:START (p154) precinct before chilling at the International Antarctic Centre (p138) or enjoying a traditional Maori feast at Willowbank Wildlife Reserve (p140).

Central Christchurch

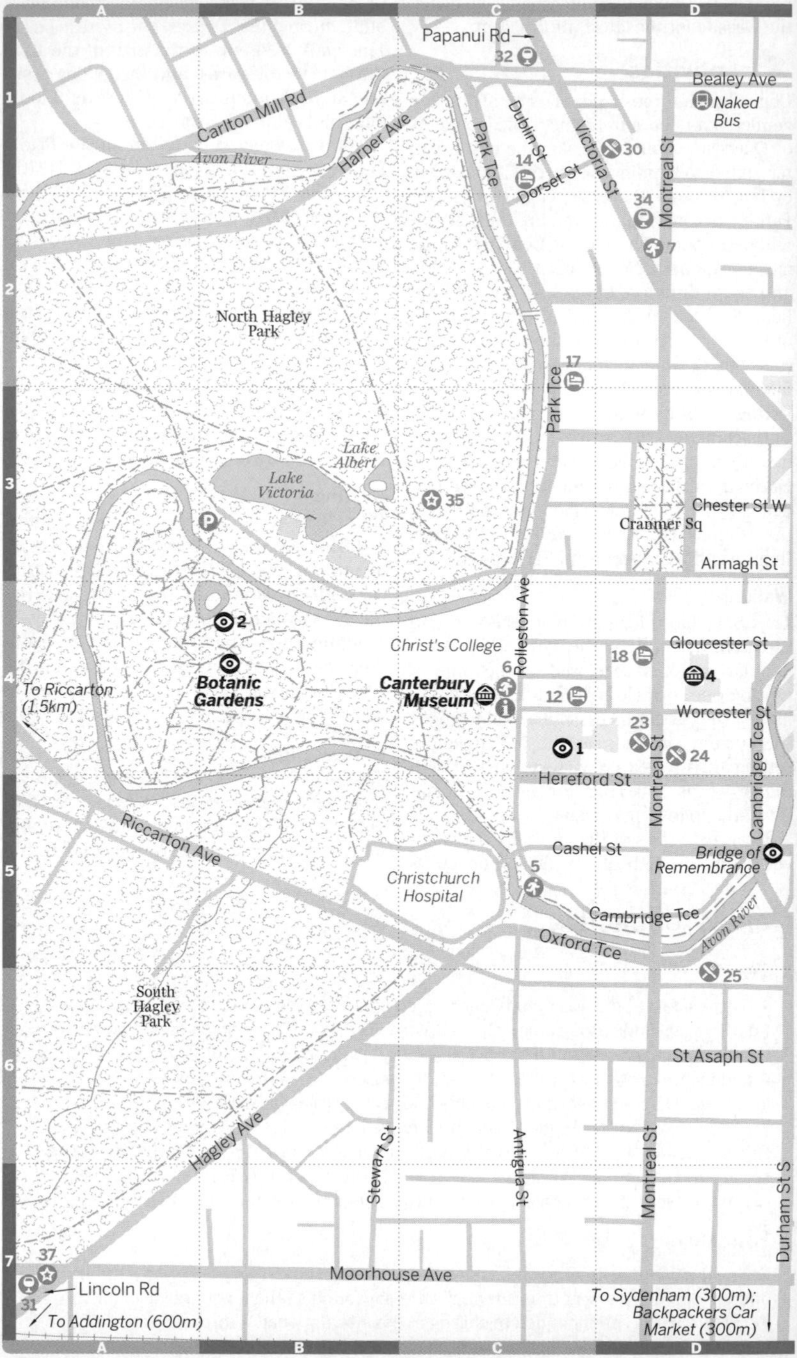

A B C D

1 2 3 4 5 6 7

Papanui Rd
32
Bealey Ave
Naked Bus
Carlton Mill Rd
Avon River
Harper Ave
Park Tce
Dublin St
14
Dorset St
Victoria St
30
Montreal St
34
7
North Hagley Park
17
Park Tce
Lake Albert
Lake Victoria
35
Chester St W
Cranmer Sq
Armagh St
Rolleston Ave
2
Christ's College
Gloucester St
18
4
Botanic Gardens
Canterbury Museum
6
12
Worcester St
To Riccarton (1.5km)
23
1
24
Hereford St
Montreal St
Cambridge Tce
Riccarton Ave
Cashel St
Bridge of Remembrance
5
Christchurch Hospital
Cambridge Tce
Avon River
Oxford Tce
25
South Hagley Park
St Asaph St
Hagley Ave
Stewart St
Antigua St
Montreal St
Durham St S
37
Moorhouse Ave
Lincoln Rd
31
To Addington (600m)
To Sydenham (300m); Backpackers Car Market (300m)

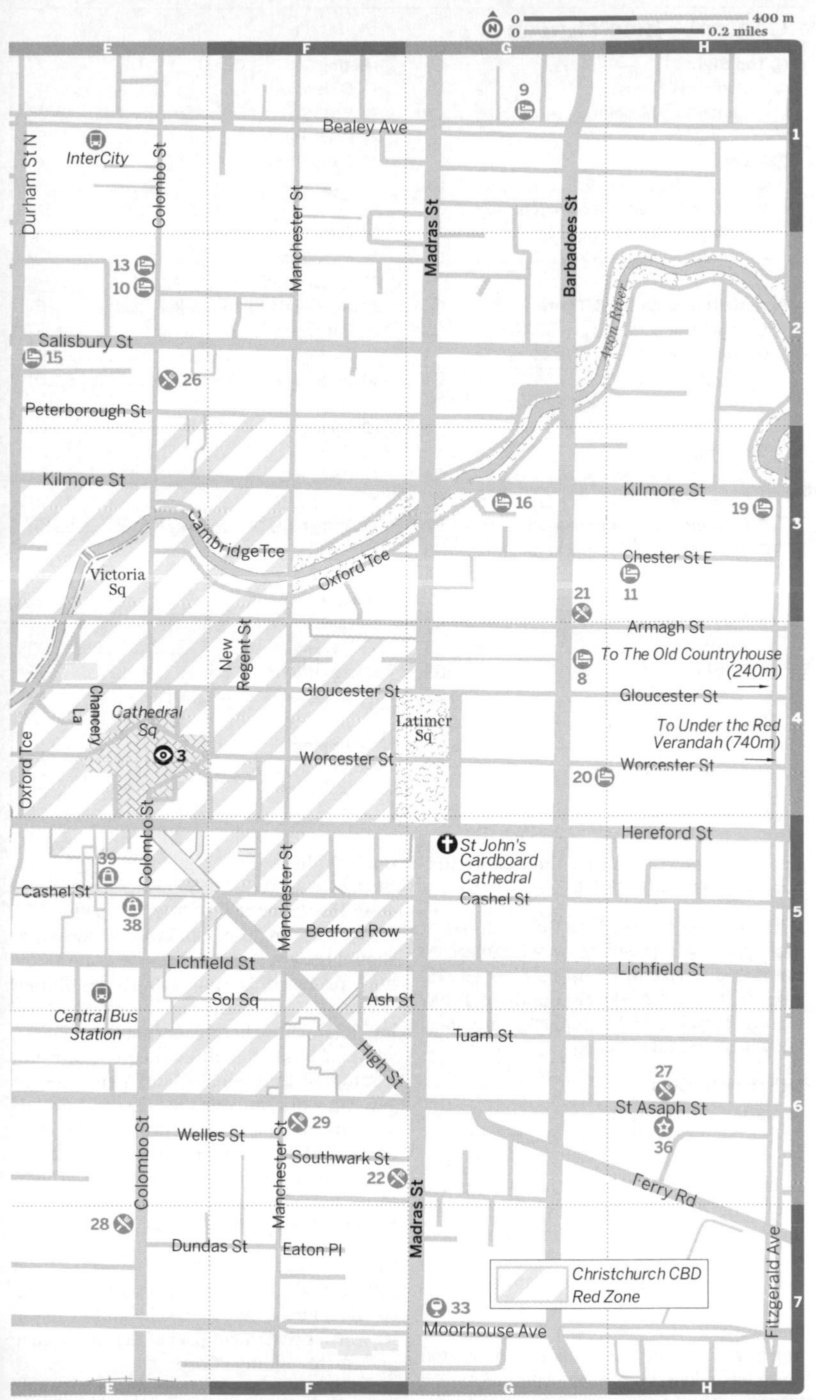
0 400 m
0 0.2 miles
E
F
G
H
1
2
3
4
5
6
7
9
Bealey Ave
InterCity
Durham St N
Colombo St
Manchester St
Madras St
Barbadoes St
13
10
Avon River
Salisbury St
15
26
Peterborough St
Kilmore St
Kilmore St
16
19
Cambridge Tce
Victoria Sq
Oxford Tce
Chester St E
11
21
Armagh St
New Regent St
8
To The Old Countryhouse (240m)
Gloucester St
Gloucester St
Chancery La
Cathedral Sq
Latimer Sq
To Under the Red Verandah (740m)
3
Oxford Tce
Worcester St
Worcester St
20
Hereford St
St John's Cardboard Cathedral
39
Cashel St
Cashel St
38
Bedford Row
Lichfield St
Lichfield St
Sol Sq
Ash St
Central Bus Station
Tuam St
High St
27
St Asaph St
36
29
Welles St
Southwark St
22
Ferry Rd
28
Dundas St
Eaton Pl
Christchurch CBD Red Zone
33
Moorhouse Ave
Fitzgerald Ave

Central Christchurch

Top Sights
Botanic Gardens B4
Canterbury Museum C4

Sights
1 Arts Centre C4
2 Botanic Gardens Visitors Centre B4
3 Cathedral Square E4
4 Christchurch Art Gallery D4

Activities, Courses & Tours
5 Antigua Boatsheds C5
6 Christchurch Personal Guiding Service C4
7 Vintage Peddler Bike Hire Co D2

Sleeping
8 Around the World Backpackers G4
9 Canterbury House G1
10 CentrePoint on Colombo E2
11 Chester Street Backpackers H3
12 Classic Villa C4
13 Colombo in the City E2
14 Dorset House C1
15 Focus Motel E2
16 Foley Towers G3
17 George C2
18 Orari B&B D4
19 Pomeroy's on Kilmore H3
20 Vagabond Backpackers G4

Eating
50 Bistro .... (see 17)
21 Beat St G3
22 Black Betty F6
23 Canterbury Cheesemongers D4
24 Coffee House D4
25 Dose D6
26 Himalayas E2
27 Lotus Heart H6
28 New World Supermarket E7
Pescatore .... (see 17)
29 Topkapi F6
30 Vic's Cafe & Bakery D1

Drinking
31 Cargo A7
32 Carlton Country Club C1
33 Monday Room G7
Pomeroy's Old Brewery Inn .... (see 19)
34 Revival D2

Entertainment
35 Christchurch Events Village C3
36 darkroom H6
37 Dux Live A7

Shopping
38 Ballantynes E5
39 Re:START Mall E5

self-guided bicycle touring through Canterbury and the South Island.

Vintage Peddler Bike Hire Co BICYCLE RENTAL
(Map p142; ☎03-365-6530; www.thevintagepeddler.co.nz; 399 Montreal St; per hour/day $10/25) Take to two retro wheels on these funky vintage bicycles. Helmets, locks and local knowledge are all supplied.

Other Activities

Antigua Boatsheds BOATING
(Map p142; www.punting.co.nz; 2 Cambridge Tce; punting adult/child/family $25/12/65; ⏲9am-6pm) Dating from 1882, the photogenic green-and-white Antigua Boatsheds are the starting point for **Punting on the Avon**, where someone else does all the work during a half-hour return trip in a flat-bottomed boat. There's also an excellent cafe (open 7am to 5pm), which is a great spot for brunch or lunch. Kayaks and rowboats can be rented for independent Avon River exploration.

Bone Dude ART
(Map p138; ☎03-385 4509; www.thebonedude.co.nz; 153 Marshland Rd, Shirley; per person $60; ⏲1-4pm Mon-Fri, 10am-1pm Sat) Creative types should book a session with the Bone Dude, now relocated to the suburb of Shirley, where you can craft your own bone carving (allow three hours). Owner John Fraser, who's of Ngati Rangitihi ancestry, provides a range of traditional Maori templates, or you can work on your own design. Sessions are limited to eight participants, so booking ahead is highly recommended. John can also run evening sessions for a group of at least three participants. Catch bus number 60 from the Central Bus Station.

Garden City Heliflights SCENIC FLIGHT
(☎03-358 4360; www.helicopters.net.nz; per person $145) Flights above the city and Lyttelton let you observe the impact of the earthquake and the rebuilding efforts.

Tours

Ask at the i-SITE about city tours and excursions to Lyttelton, Akaroa, Arthur's Pass, Hanmer Springs and the Waipara Valley.

Canterbury Leisure Tours GUIDED TOUR
(☎03-384 0999, 0800 484 485; www.leisuretours.co.nz; tours from $60) Touring options in and around Christchurch, with everything from three-hour city tours to full-day outings to Akaroa, Mt Cook, Arthur's Pass and Kaikoura.

Canterbury Wine Tours WINE TASTING
(☎0800 081 155; www.waiparavalley.co.nz; tours from $90) Experience three Waipara vineyards on the half-day trip, or make a day of it and sample four different wineries with lunch ($125).

Christchurch Bike Tours GUIDED TOUR
(☎0800 733 257; www.chchbiketours.co.nz; tours from $40; ⏲departs 2pm) Informative, two-hour tours loop around the city along quiet cycleways and leafy park tracks. Also available is a gourmet food tour and a Saturday morning foodie spin that takes in the Christchurch Farmers Market. Prior booking is essential. Tours leave from the Antigua Boatsheds (p144).

Christchurch Personal Guiding Service WALKING TOUR
(Map p142; ☎03-379 9629; tours $15; ⏲11am & 1pm Oct-Apr, 1pm May-Sep) Nonprofit organisation offering informative two-hour city walks. Buy tickets and join tours at the i-SITE departure point.

Christchurch Sightseeing Tours GUIDED TOUR
(☎03-366 9660, 0508 669 660; www.christchurchtours.co.nz; tours from $75) City tours, plus further-afield detours to Akaroa, Hanmer Springs and the Waipara wine region.

Discovery Tours GUIDED TOUR
(☎0800 372 879; www.discoverytravel.co.nz; tours from $130) Excursions to Akaroa, Hanmer Springs, Kakoura and the Waipara Valley wine region. The Alpine Safari option (adult/child $375/276) packs the *TranzAlpine*, jetboating and a spin in a 4WD into one action-packed day.

Hassle Free Tours GUIDED TOUR
(☎0800 141 146; www.hasslefree.co.nz; tours from $29) Explore Christchurch on an open-top, bright-red double-decker bus. Regional options include a 4WD alpine safari, jetboating on the Waimakariri River, and visiting the location of Edoras from the *Lord of the Rings* trilogy. Combo deals with the International Antarctic Centre (p138) are also available.

Hiking Guys TRAMPING
(☎09-281 4481; www.hikingguys.co.nz; adult/child $395/198) Day trips incorporating the *Tranz Alpine* train and tramping around Arthur's Pass.

Welcome Aboard GUIDED TOUR
(☎0800 242 486; www.welcomeaboard.co.nz; adult/child $79/49) The operators of the gondola and tramway operate this comprehensive tour taking in punting on the Avon River, the Botanic Gardens, Sumner and the Re:START container mall.

Festivals & Events

Check www.bethere.co.nz for a comprehensive listing of festivals and events.

CHRISTCHURCH FOR CHILDREN

There's no shortage of kid-friendly sights and activities in Christchurch. If family fun is a priority, consider planning your travels around NZ's biggest children's festival, **KidsFest** (www.kidsfest.org.nz). It's held every July and is chock-full of shows, workshops and parties. The annual World Buskers Festival (p146) is also bound to be a hit.

For picnics and open-air frolicking, visit the Botanic Gardens (p136); there's a playground beside the cafe, and the kids will love riding on the Caterpillar train. Extend your nature-based experience with a wildlife encounter at the Orana Wildlife Park (p139) or the Willowbank Wildlife Reserve (p140), or get them burning off excess energy in a rowboat or paddleboat from the Antigua Boatsheds (p144). At the engrossing International Antarctic Centre (p138), kids will love the Antarctic Storm chamber, the Hägglund Ride and (of course) the penguins. Educational and attention-getting factors also run high at the Discovery Centre at Canterbury Museum (p137).

If the weather's good, hit the beaches at Sumner or New Brighton.

WORTH A TRIP

THE SLOW ROAD TO LITTLE RIVER

The **Little River Rail Trail** (www.littleriverrailtrail.co.nz) will eventually traverse 45km, from the Christchurch suburb of Hornby to the Banks Peninsula hamlet of Little River. At the time of writing, all sections excluding a 14km stretch were open: see the website for the latest information. Join the trail 20km from Little River at Motukarara for the best of the ride. Ask at the Christchurch i-SITE about bike rental and public transport options. Rail trail day trips including transport can be booked with Natural High (p141). Natural High also rents out bikes and offers advice for multiday, self-guided cycling trips incorporating the Little River Rail Trail. Two funky accommodation options at Little River are Okuti Garden (p162) and the Little River Campground (p163); both are also well placed for exploring Akaroa and Banks Peninsula.

World Buskers Festival ARTS
(www.worldbuskersfestival.com) National and international talent entertain passers-by for 10 days in mid- to late January. Check the website for locations – and don't forget to put money in the hat.

Garden City SummerTimes MUSIC
(www.summertimes.co.nz) Say g'day to summer at a huge array of outdoor events between December and March. Sweet as.

Festival of Flowers CULTURAL
(www.festivalofflowers.co.nz) A blooming spectacle around Christchurch's heritage gardens in February and March.

Ellerslie Flower Show CULTURAL
(www.ellersliefiowershow.co.nz) Hagley Park comes alive in early March with NZ's biggest flower show.

Christchurch Arts Festival ARTS
(www.artsfestival.co.nz) Midwinter arts extravaganza in August and September celebrating music, theatre and dance.

NZ Cup and Show Week CULTURAL
(www.nzcupandshow.co.nz) Includes the NZ Cup horse race, fashion shows, fireworks and the centrepiece A&P Show, where the country comes to town. Held in November.

Sleeping

At the time of writing, Christchurch's CBD was closed following earthquake damage, and accommodation was focused in and around the city's inner suburbs. Several international hotels within the CBD were demolished after the earthquake, but the Novotel (www.novotel.com), Ibis (www.ibishotel.com) and Rendezvous (www.rendezvoushotels.com) hotels were preparing to reopen once the CBD cordon was lifted. Check the hotel websites and www.cera.govt.nz for the status of Christchurch's CBD.

Motels are clustered around Bealey Ave and Papanui Rd, north of the centre, and Riccarton Rd, west of town beyond Hagley Park. Many inner-city hostels closed after the earthquake. Most of the hostels still operating are located to the east of the CBD or in Addington.

Booking ahead for accommodation is recommended as motels and hostels in the city are in high demand for tradespeople working on the city's rebuilding.

Orari B&B B&B $$$
(Map p142; ☎03-365 6569; www.orari.net.nz; 42 Gloucester St; d $195-255; P 📶) Orari is a late-19th-century home that has been stylishly updated with light-filled, pastel-toned rooms and inviting guest areas, as well as a lovely front garden. Art connoisseurs take note: it's right across the road from Christchurch Art Gallery. Wine connoisseurs can look forward to complimentary wine after a busy day.

Pomeroy's on Kilmore B&B $$
(Map p142; ☎03-365 1523; www.pomeroysonkilmore.co.nz; 292 Kilmore St; d $145-245; P) What could be better than staying in an elegantly furnished five-room boutique guesthouse? How about knowing it's just a short, thirsty stroll to Pomeroy's Old Brewery Inn (p152), Christchurch's best craft beer pub? Rates include breakfast, and you're also welcome to have a private beer tasting with the friendly owners. Several of the rooms open onto a sunny garden.

Wish B&B $$
(Map p138; ☎03-356 2455; www.wishnz.com; 38 Edgeware Rd, St Albans; s/d incl breakfast from $125/150; P @ 📶) The rooms and beds at the

stylish Wish are supercomfy, but it could be the locally sourced, sustainable and organic breakfasts that you recommend to other travellers. Contemporary NZ art dots the walls, and the huge native-timber kitchen table is just made for catching up with other guests over an end-of-day glass of wine. Wish is very popular and booking ahead is necessary. It's located slightly north of the CBD, in St Albans.

Jailhouse HOSTEL **$**
(Map p138; ☎03-982 7777, 0800 524 546; www.jail.co.nz; 338 Lincoln Rd, Addington; dm/s/d $30/79/85; P@📶) Housed in an old prison that was built in 1874 (and only decommissioned in 1999), the Jailhouse is one of NZ's most unique hostels. Twins and doubles are a bit on the small side – remember, it *was* a prison – but it's still an exceptionally well run and friendly spot. The surrounding Addington area has good cafes, restaurants and entertainment venues.

CentrePoint on Colombo MOTEL **$$**
(Map p142; ☎0800 859 000, 03-377 0859; www.centrepointoncolombo.co.nz; 859 Colombo St; d $155-165, apt $180-260; P@📶) CentrePoint on Colombo has super-comfortable facilities and the bonus of a friendly Kiwi-Japanese management. The owners are a mine of information on how Christchurch is bouncing back after the earthquakes, and happily provide guests with up-to-date information on the best places to eat around town.

George BOUTIQUE HOTEL **$$$**
(Map p142; ☎0800 100 220, 03-379 4560; www.thegeorge.com; 50 Park Tce; d $506-886; P@📶) The George has 53 handsomely decorated rooms and suites on the fringe of Christchurch's sweeping Hagley Park. Discreet staff attend to every whim; there are two excellent restaurants; and ritzy features include huge TVs, luxury toiletries and glossy magazines. Check online for good-value packages and discounts.

Classic Villa B&B **$$$**
(Map p142; ☎03-377 7905; www.theclassicvilla.co.nz; 17 Worcester Ave; d incl breakfast $269-489; P📶) Ideally located near the Botanic Gardens and Canterbury Museum, the Classic Villa is one of Christchurch's most elegant accommodation options. Rooms are trimmed with antiques and Turkish rugs for a classy ambience, and the expansive, Mediterranean-style breakfast is a shared social occasion around the dining room's big wooden table. No children under 12 years old allowed.

Elm Tree House B&B **$$$**
(Map p138; ☎03-355 9731; www.elmtreehouse.co.nz; 236 Papanui Rd, Merivale; d $365-445; P@📶) Originally built in the 1920s, the elegant Elm Tree House has six stylish rooms, a dining area leading to sunny rose gardens, and a spacious, wood-lined guests' lounge. Top-end shopping and Merivale's good restaurants are a short walk away, and yes, the classic Wurlitzer jukebox downstairs is still in working order.

Anslem House B&B **$$$**
(Map p138; ☎03-343 4260; www.anselmhouse.co.nz; 34 Kahu Rd, Fendalton; s/d $190/230; P📶) Designed by renowned NZ architect Heathcote Helmore and constructed partially of unique Oamaru pink marble, Anselm House in Fendalton is one of the city's iconic heritage residences. The decor is elegant and restrained, and the property features a beautiful riverside garden, just perfect for an end-of-the-day glass of wine and conversation with the friendly, well-travelled owners.

Merivale Manor MOTEL **$$**
(Map p138; ☎03-355 7731; www.merivalemanor.com; 122 Papanui Rd, Merivale; d $145-185; P📶) A gracious 19th-century Victorian residence is now the hub of an elegant motel. Accommodation ranges from studios (some with spa baths) to one- and two-bedroom apartments. In keeping with the property's history, decor is understated, and the classy shopping and good bars and restaurants of Merivale are just a few hundred metres away.

Roma on Riccarton MOTEL **$$**
(Map p138; ☎03-341 2100; www.romaonriccarton.com; 38 Riccarton Rd, Riccarton; d $150-205; P📶) Handily located near Hagley Park and the city end of Riccarton Rd, the Mediterranean-style Roma on Riccarton is also a short stroll from cinemas, bars and restaurants, and Christchurch's best shopping mall. Studio units – some with spa baths – and larger, two-bedroom apartments are all spotless and thoroughly modern.

Chester Street Backpackers HOSTEL **$**
(Map p142; ☎03-377 1897; www.chesterst.co.nz; 148 Chester St E; dm/tw/d $30/64/66; P@) This relaxed wooden villa is painted in bright colours and has a huge library in the sunny front room. The friendly house cat is a regular guest at hostel barbecues. It's popular,

so try to book ahead. The equally charming Entwhistle Cottage across the road is often used as an overflow facility, offering twin and double rooms.

Fendalton House B&B $$
(Map p138; ☎03-343 1661, 0800 374 298; www.fendaltonhouse.co.nz; 28a Kotare St, Fenadlton; d $145; P) A friendly, homestay-style B&B amid the pleasant streets of leafy Fendalton. Rates include a cooked breakfast, and on Wednesday nights and Saturday mornings, the foodie attractions of the Christchurch Farmers Market (p152) are just around the corner.

Foley Towers HOSTEL $
(Map p142; ☎03-366 9720; www.backpack.co.nz/foley.html; 208 Kilmore St; dm $24-26, d with/without bathroom $68/62; P@) Sheltered by well-established trees, Foley Towers provides well-maintained rooms encircling quiet inner courtyards and a friendly welcome in dorms warmed by underfloor heating. Check-in after 9pm is available only by arrangement.

Dorset House HOSTEL $
(Map p142; ☎03-366 8268; www.dorsethouse.co.nz; 1 Dorset St; dm/s/d $32/69/84; P@) This 145-year-old wooden villa has a large regal lounge with log fire, pool table, DVDs and beds instead of bunks. It's a short stroll to Hagley Park and the bars and restaurants of Victoria St and Papanui Rd.

Old Countryhouse HOSTEL $
(Map p138; ☎03-381 5504; www.oldcountryhousenz.com; 437 Gloucester St; dm $31-35, d $90-110; P@) The Old Countryhouse features two separate villas with handmade wooden furniture, a reading lounge and a lovely garden filled with native ferns. It's slightly further out than other hostels, but still only 1km east of Latimer Sq. Bus 21 stops opposite.

Around the World Backpackers HOSTEL $
(Map p142; ☎03-365 4363; www.aroundtheworld.co.nz; 314 Barbadoes St; dm/d/tw $30/68/68; P@) Around the World gets rave recommendations for its 'Kiwiana' decor and sunny back garden (complete with a private outdoor bath). Ask about the hostel's 'Love Shack' if you're visiting with the closest of travelling companions.

Haka Lodge HOSTEL $
(Map p138; ☎03-980 4252; www.hakalodge.com; 518 Linwood Ave, Woolston ; dm $28, d&tw $70, self-contained apt $160; P) Sprawled across three floors of a modern suburban house, Haka Lodge is one of Christchurch's newest hostels. Shared dorms and rooms are spotless and colourful, and end-of-day treats include a comfy lounge with big-screen TV and a bird-friendly garden. The lodge is around 10 minutes' drive from the city, and there's a bus stop nearby.

Arena Motel MOTEL $$
(Map p138; ☎03-338 4579, 0800 232 565; www.arenamotel.co.nz; 30 Whiteleigh Ave, Addington; d $130-180;) Handily located in up-and-coming Addington, the Arena Motel is also the closest accommodation to the Christchurch Railway Station – convenient if you're planning a morning departure on the *Tranz Alpine* (p116) through the Southern Alps.

Colombo in the City MOTEL $$
(Map p142; ☎0800 265 662, 03-366 8775; www.motelcolombo.co.nz; 863 Colombo St; d $160-185, apt $185-270; P@) Colombo in the City has attractive units that are luxuriously equipped with Sky TV, CD players, double-glazed windows and spa baths.

Focus Motel MOTEL $$
(Map p142; ☎03-943 0800, 0800 943 0800; www.focusmotel.com; 344 Durham St N; d $150-200; P@) Sleek and centrally located, with big-screen TVs, self-contained studios and super-modern decor.

Airport Gateway Motor Lodge MOTEL $$
(☎0800 242 8392, 03-358 7093; www.airportgateway.co.nz; 45 Roydvale Ave, Burnside; d $155-195; P@) Handy for those early flights, this motel has a variety of rooms with good facilities. A 24-hour airport pick-up is available at no extra charge. The newly opened Premier Suites are very comfortable and good value.

Vagabond Backpackers HOSTEL $
(Map p142; ☎03-379 9677; vagabondbackpackers@hotmail.com; 232 Worcester St; dm/s/d $26/42/60; P@) This small, friendly place is reminiscent of a big shared house. There's an appealing garden, rustic but comfy facilities, and frisbees and barbecues that remind you that you're definitely in NZ. Take the airport shuttle to Cathedral Sq.

Canterbury House HOSTEL $
(Map p142; ☎03-377 8108; http://canterburyhousebp.web.fc2.com; 257 Bealey Ave; dm/s $30/45, d&tw $70; P) More of a homestay than a hostel, Canterbury House is run by a friendly Kiwi-Japanese couple, and enjoys a quiet right-of-

way location off busy Bealey Ave. The decor is slightly chintzy and old-fashioned, but the spacious and well-kept garden is a real asset during summer.

Meadow Park Top 10 Holiday Park HOLIDAY PARK $

(Map p138; ☎0800 396 323, 03-352 9176; www.christchurchtop10.co.nz; 39 Meadow St, Papanui; sites from $40, units $75-169; P@) Wall-to-wall campervans here, while other accommodation ranges from cabins to motel units. It's also well equipped for leisure activities, with an indoor pool, games rooms and a playground for the kids.

North South Holiday Park HOLIDAY PARK $

(☎03-359 5993, 0800 567 765; www.northsouth.co.nz; cnr John's & Sawyers Arms Rds, SH1, Harewood; sites from $35, units $58-125; P@) This place is just five minutes from the airport, and a good place to spend the night after you've picked up your campervan. Facilities include a pool, sauna, playground and newer motel units. Airport transfers are available.

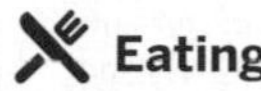

Eating

Following the February 2011 earthquake, many cafes and restaurants were damaged, or left shuttered behind the cordon around the city's CBD. The CBD was scheduled to reopen sometime from mid-2012, and the area will again become a focus for dining out. However, for this edition we have only included restaurants and cafes that were open at the time of research; check www.christchurchnz.com for the latest updates. Bookings are recommended for dinner.

Key dining precincts are along Victoria St to the immediate northwest of the CBD. South of Moorhouse Ave, Addington and Sydenham have become hubs for new post-earthquake eateries.

To the west and north respectively of the CBD, Riccarton and Merivale are dotted with cafes and restaurants, and the beachside suburb of Sumner also features great eating. To the southeast, Lyttelton is again emerging as one Christchurch's best areas for eating and drinking.

Restaurants

Bodhi Tree BURMESE $$

(Map p138; ☎03-377 6808; www.bodhitree.co.nz; 39 Ilam Rd, Bryndwr; dishes $13-24; ⊙6-10pm Tue-Sun;) Christchurch's only Burmese restaurant is also one of the city's best eateries. Don't come expecting spicy flavours from neighbouring Thailand, but look forward to subtle food crafted from exceptionally fresh ingredients. Standout dishes include the *le pet thoke* (pickled tea-leaf salad) and the *ciandi thoke* (grilled eggplant). Meat and seafood also feature. Dishes are starter-sized, so drum up a group and sample lots of different flavours. Bookings are essential.

50 Bistro RESTAURANT $$

(Map p142; ☎03-371 0250; www.thegeorge.com; 50 Park Tce, The George; dinner from $35; ⊙6.30am-late) The more casual restaurant at the George is a bustling affair, doing savvy local twists on classic bistro flavours. Try the Nifty 50 lunch menu – $29 for soup and a main dish – or sample more robust evening meals like lamb shoulder ragu with kumara (sweet potato) gnocchi.

Pescatore RESTAURANT $$$

(Map p142; ☎03-371 0250; www.thegeorge.com; 50 Park Tce; mains $42-50; ⊙6pm-late Tue-Sat) Travelling gourmands should book for Pescatore, the George's more formal restaurant. Dishes like citrus-cured salmon or Canterbury lamb help make Pescatore a regular finalist in *Cuisine* magazine's NZ Restaurant of the Year awards.

Edesia MODERN NZ $$

(Map p138; ☎03-943 2144; www.edesia.co.nz; 12 Show Pl, Addington ; lunch $21-29, dinner $28-39; ⊙11.30am-3pm Mon-Fri & 5.30pm-late Mon-Sat) Ignore the office-park location; Edesia's version of fine dining is worth seeking out. The dinner menu includes innovative spins on local venison, salmon and quail, while lunch is a more informal affair, with prime Canterbury steaks and gossamer-light pasta. The wine list is one of Christchurch's best, and after work Edesia morphs into a cosy bar for local desk jockeys.

Himalayas INDIAN $$

(Map p142; ☎03-377 8935; www.himalayas.co.nz; 830a Colombo St; mains $18-22; ⊙11.30am-2pm Tue-Fri & 5pm-late Tue-Sun;) Every city needs a great Indian eatery, and Himalayas ticks the box in Christchurch. A stylish dining room showcases lots of subcontinental favourites, including vegetarian options like the creamy *dal makhani* (black lentils cooked with aromatic spices). The *kadhai* chicken is studded with chilli, ginger and coriander – perfect with a cold beer. Takeaways are also available.

WORTH A TRIP

SEASIDE AT SUMNER

Just 12km southeast of Christchurch by bus 3, the beachy suburb of Sumner is a relaxing place to stay. Commute to central Christchurch for sightseeing and return to Sumner for good restaurants and an arthouse cinema at night.

Le Petit Hotel (Map p138; ☎03-326 6675; www.lepetithotel.co.nz; 16 Marriner St; d $135; P@🛜) Relaxed coffee, croissant breakfasts and Kara the friendly Scottish terrier are among the highlights at this intimate, French-themed boutique hotel. Factor in the friendly owners, the close proximity to Sumner beach and some of Christchurch's best restaurants, and it's a definite *oui* from us.

Sumner Bay Motel and Apartments (Map p138; ☎0800 496 949, 03-326 5969; www.sumnermotel.co.nz; 26 Marriner St; d $159-185) Studios and one- and two-bedroom units all have a balcony and courtyard, quality furniture, and Sky TV and DVD players. Bikes and surfboards can be rented.

Almeidas Tapas Bar (Map p138; ☎03-326 5220; 41a Nayland St; tapas $8-12; ⏲5pm-late Wed-Sat) Beachy Sumner meets the back streets of Barcelona at this rustic, Spanish-themed tapas bar. More than 20 different small-plate offerings include haloumi and roasted garlic in prosciutto, artichoke hearts wrapped in lemon and mint, and prawns sautéed in garlic, lime and coriander. Try and resist the urge for 'just one more plate' before settling on *churros* (Spanish donuts) for dessert.

Bamboozle (Map p138; ☎03-326 7878; 6 Wakefield St; mains $25-30) Asian fusion is the name of the game at the stylish Bamboozle, where talented chefs conjure up innovative spins on traditional flavours. Dishes include Burmese-style fish with chilli, and wasabi, salmon and cream-cheese dumplings. Leave room for dessert with one of Christchurch's best crème brûlées, or ginger steamed-pudding topped with a lime sauce and coffee ice cream.

Cornershop Bistro (Map p138; ☎03-326 6720; www.cornershopbistro.co.nz; 32 Nayland St; brunch & lunch $12-17, dinner $23-34; ⏲5pm-late Wed-Fri & 10am-late Sat-Sun) This is a superior, French-style bistro that never forgets it's in a relaxed beachside suburb. Spend longer than you planned to lingering over brunch.

Holy Smoke STEAKHOUSE **$$**
(Map p138; www.holysmoke.co.nz; 650 Ferry Rd, Woolston; brunch & lunch $18-25, dinner $26-36; ⏲9am-late Mon-Sat, to 4pm Sun) Here's your chance to get acquainted with the unique smoky character of *manuka* (NZ tea tree). At Holy Smoke, the native wood is used to smoke everything from pork ribs and chicken wings to bacon and salmon. Other menu items include robust slabs of venison, lamb and beef, all teamed with Kiwi craft beers and Central Otago wines.

Lotus Heart VEGETARIAN **$$**
(Map p142; www.thelotusheart.co.nz; 363 St Asaph St; mains $14-25; ⏲8am-4pm daily & 6-10pm Thu-Sat; ✎) Relocated to the edge of the CBD, this organic and vegetarian eatery does curries, freshly squeezed organic juices and filled pita pockets. Try the chilli, coriander and garlic-studded eggs Akoori for breakfast, or drop by for a healthy pizza, wrap or shared platter for lunch or dinner. Organic, vegan and gluten-free options abound, and there's an interesting gift shop onsite.

Topkapi TURKISH **$$**
(Map p142; www.topkapi.co.nz; 64 Manchester St; mains $14-22; ⏲closed Mon) Grab yourself a cushioned, low-slung bench in the tapestry-draped interior and enjoy some great Turkish food, including a wide range of meat or veg kebabs and the all-important baklava finisher. The takeaway counter also does brisk business.

Cafes

TOP CHOICE **Addington Coffee Co-op** CAFE **$**
(Map p138; www.addingtoncoffee.org.nz; 297 Lincoln Rd, Addington; snacks & mains $6-20; 🛜✎) One of Christchurch's biggest and most bustling cafes is also one of its best. Fair-trade coffee and a compact stall selling organic cotton T-shirts jostle for attention with delicious cakes and slices, while a cross-section of the city comes for the free wi-fi, gourmet pies and wraps, and the legendary big breakfasts. An onsite laundromat completes the deal for busy travellers.

Black Betty CAFE $
(Map p142; www.blackbetty.co.nz; 163a Madras St; mains $10-20;) Infused with glorious caffeine-enriched aromas from Switch Espresso's roasting operation, Black Betty's chic industrial warehouse is a popular destination for students from nearby CPIT. Essential culinary attractions include all-day breakfasts – try the ciabatta toast with creamy mushrooms – and excellent counter food including wraps and bagels, as well as the best of NZ wine and craft beers.

Under the Red Verandah CAFE $$
(Map p138; www.utrv.co.nz; cnr Tancred & Worcester Sts, Linwood; mains $15-25;) After losing their original premises in the 2011 earthquake, Under the Red Verandah reopened in a spacious villa at the same location. Christchurch foodie types quickly returned, and now fill the shady garden for leisurely combinations of coffee, oaty pancakes and the city's best corn fritters. Look forward also to lots of organic and gluten-free baking.

Beat St CAFE $
(Map p142; 324 Barbadoes St; snacks & mains $8-16;) Welcome to the grungy hub of Christchurch cafe-cool. Free range this and organic that combine with terrific eggy breakfasts, gourmet pies (try the feta and vegie one) and robust Havana coffee. Beat Street hosts a bohemian open mic night featuring music and poetry on the third Thursday of every month from 6pm.

Honey Pot Cafe CAFE $$
(Map p138; www.honeypotcafe.co.nz; 458 Colombo St, Sydenham ; mains $20-30) One of the first CBD cafes to relocate after the earthquakes, the Honey Pot Cafe set the scene for the emergence of Sydenham as a dining destination. Great eggs Benedict for breakfast give way to spiced lamb and feta salad for lunch, and sirloin steak and chunky, hand-cut chips for dinner. Christchurch's very own 3 Boys beer is on tap.

Coffee House CAFE $$
(Map p142; 290 Montreal St; breakfast & lunch $11-22 & dinner $27-32) Housed in a heritage villa complete with sunny patio, the Coffee House has a great location near the Arts Centre and the Botanic Gardens. Highlights include feta-studded Mediterranean scrambled eggs for breakfast and herb-marinated lamb for dinner. Emerson's beer on tap and a concise wine list will probably see you lingering over something stronger than coffee.

Dose CAFE $
(Map p142; 77 Tuam St; snacks & mains $8-18; closed Sun) Excellent coffee from the Lyttelton Coffee Company and superior counter food combine here with toasted bagels and what may just be Christchurch's best eggs Benedict. Downstairs is almost unbearably cosy, so head upstairs for bigger tables and a quirky ambience with graffiti-style art. From Wednesday to Saturday from 4pm, Dose morphs into a *yakitori* bar with tasty grilled skewers and ice-cold Japanese beer.

Vic's Cafe & Bakery CAFE $
(Map p142; www.vics.co.nz; 132 Victoria St; snacks & mains $8-20) Always busy, Vic's attracts a wide cross-section of Christchurch folk – we even saw the city's mayor there on our Sunday-morning visit. Pop in for a robust breakfast on the big shared tables, or grab baked goodies and still-warm artisan bread for an affordable DIY riverside picnic. Get there early (before 10am) for Vic's world-famous-in-Christchurch nutty porridge ($10.50).

Quick Eats

TOP CHOICE **Simo's Deli** MOROCCAN $
(Map p138; www.simos.co.nz; 3/300 Lincoln Rd, Addington; wraps $6.50-$9.50, tapas & mains $7-17) Part cafe and part deli, Simo's in Addington is popular for its takeaway *bocadillos* (grilled wraps filled with a huge selection of Middle Eastern and African-inspired fillings, sauces and toppings). Other tasty offerings include small plates of grilled calamari or spicy *merguez* sausages, or more robust *tagines* (Moroccan casseroles) and beef kofta with pomegranate sauce.

Serious Sandwich SANDWICHES $
(Map p138; www.theserioussandwich.com; 363 Colombo St, Sydenham; sandwiches $7-10) Serious in name and serious in flavour. Concealed in Sydenham's new Colombo shopping mall, this compact kitchen dishes up tasty gourmet sammies, including the breakfast BLAT (available from 9am) and a meatballs-on-toasted-ciabatta variant (available from around 11am). Look forward to a serious attitude to good coffee, too.

Burgers & Beers Inc BURGERS $
(Map p138; www.burgersandbeersinc.co.nz; 355 Colombo St, Sydenham; burgers $12-16) Quirkily named gourmet burgers – try the Moroccan-spiced Woolly Sahara Sand Hopper (lamb with lemon yoghurt) or the Shagged Stag (venison with tamarillo and plum

chutney) – give this place a funky, laid-back air. An ever-changing selection of Kiwi craft beers give you further reasons to tarry longer. Definitely worth the short hop south to Sydenham.

Self-Catering

Canterbury Cheesemongers SANDWICHES $
(Map p142; www.cheesemongers.co.nz; Arts Centre Old Registry Building, 301 Montreal St; sandwiches from $7; ⏲Tue-Sat) Pop in to buy artisan cheeses, or craft your own sandwich by combining freshly baked *ficelles* and ciabatta with a whole cheese shop of dairy goodies. Coffee and juices are also available to complete a good-value lunch. No Monty Python jokes, please.

TOP CHOICE **Christchurch Farmers Market** FARMERS MARKET $
(Map p138; www.christchurchfarmersmarket.co.nz; Riccarton House, 16 Kahu Rd, Riccarton ; ⏲9am-noon Sat year-round & 4-7pm Wed Nov-Sat) Welcome to one of New Zealand's best farmers markets, a tasty labyrinth of organic fruit and vegies, South Island cheeses and salmon, local craft beer and ethnic treats including Colombian *empanadas* and Moroccan *briouats* (filo parcels). Other tasty stalls to track down are Posh Porridge and She Chocolat. Check out the website before you go to create your own foodie hit list.

New World Supermarket SUPERMARKET
(Map p142; South City Centre, Colombo St) Centrally located.

Drinking

Before the earthquakes, Christchurch's after-dark scene was focused around Oxford Tce ('the Strip') and the inner-city laneways around SOL ('South of Lichfield') Sq and Poplar St. Both precincts were closed at the time of research, and areas like Riccarton, Addington, Victoria St and Merivale were becoming popular.

TOP CHOICE **Pomeroy's Old Brewery Inn** CRAFT BEER
(Map p142; www.pomeroysonkilmore.co.nz; 292 Kilmore St) The welcoming Pomeroy's is the city's hoppy hub for fans of NZ's rapidly expanding craft beer scene. A wide range of guest taps showcase brews from around the country, often including seasonal beers and limited releases. Check the website for what's coming up. There's occasional live music, and the attached Victoria's Kitchen does great pub food (mains $20 to $30).

Volstead Trading Company BAR
(Map p138; www.volstead.co.nz; 55 Riccarton Rd, Riccarton) Volstead is a great example of what Christchurch has always done better than the rest of NZ: shabbily chic bars with a real sense of individuality. Comfy old sofas from your last student flat combine with quirky artwork, interesting beers from the Moa Brewery, and funky cocktails. If you're peckish, dig into unpretentious popcorn, nachos and toasted sandwiches.

The Brewery CRAFT BEER
(Map p138; www.casselsbrewery.co.nz; 3 Garlands Rd, Woolston) Out in Woolston, it's a fair schlep from the city, but the Brewery is an essential destination for beer-loving travellers. Cassels & Sons craft all their beer using a wood-fired brew kettle, resulting in big, bold beers like their 1PA and Best Bitter. Tasting trays are available for the curious and the indecisive, and the food – including wood-fired pizzas – is top-notch, too.

Monday Room WINE BAR
(Map p142; www.themondayroom.co.nz; 367 Moorhouse Ave; ⏲8am-late) Part cafe, part restaurant and part wine bar, the versatile Monday Room is the kind of place to hang out at any time of any day of the week. Occupying a restored heritage building, the funky interior is a background for interesting brunch and lunch options; later in the day, tapas, craft beers and cocktails take centre stage.

Cargo BAR
(Map p142; 379 Lincoln Rd, Addington) Welcome to the city of shipping containers, a popular option for business owners re-establishing after the earthquake. In the case of Addington's Cargo, there's even an astroturf putting green in the corner. The utilitarian decor won't score points for a romantic night out, but on Friday and Saturday nights it's crammed with locals celebrating the end of the working week.

Carlton Country Club PUB
(Map p142; 1 Papanui Rd) Only in innovative, post-earthquake Christchurch would a bunch of shipping containers and a truck-and-trailer come together as one of the city's most popular pubs. Perched on a busy urban corner, the Carlton is a thoroughly unpretentious spot, with lots of thirsty locals tucked away in its nooks and crannies. Don't miss the rooftop deck on a sunny afternoon.

Revival BAR
(Map p142; www.revivalbar.co.nz; 94 Victoria St) More shipping-container bar tomfoolery, this time with the added attraction of its own onsite Lebanese food caravan, Revival is the hippest of Christchurch's container bars, with regular DJs and a funky lounge area dotted with a quirky collection of automotive rear ends and vintage steamer trunks. Yet another classic example of post-earthquake Christchurch drinking chic.

Wood's Mill BAR, CAFE
(Map p138; Addington) Before the earthquakes, Christchurch had a thriving eating and drinking scene in the bricklined thoroughfares around SOL Sq and Lichfield Lane. At the time of research these areas were still cordoned off, but the Wood's Mill precinct in Addington was being repurposed as a similar precinct. The area is scheduled to open in mid-2012.

☆ Entertainment

Like the city's pub and bar scene, many of Christchurch's traditional entertainment venues were damaged by the earthquakes, and newer, more suburban areas have emerged. For live music and club listings, see www.christchurchmusic.org.nz or www.mukuna.co.nz. Also look out for the *Groove Guide* magazine in cafes.

Pomery's Old Brewery Inn (p152) and the Brewery (p152) are good live-music venues. Check their websites for listings.

Christchurch Events Village CONCERT VENUE
(Map p142; www.eventsvillage.co.nz; Hagley Park) This Hagley Park collection of temporary venues is being used for everything from concerts to live theatre.

Dux Live LIVE MUSIC
(Map p142; www.duxlive.co.nz; 363 Lincoln Rd; ⌚hours vary) Dux de Lux was an excellent restaurant, microbrewery and live-music venue in Christchurch's Arts Centre, but it was forced to close after the February 2011 earthquake. The beer is still being brewed (try it here and at Dux de Lux in Queenstown) and in late 2011 this Addington venue opened for live music.

Darkroom LIVE MUSIC
(Map p142; www.facebook.com/darkroom.nz; At the Archive, 336 St Asaphs St; ⌚5pm-late Thu-Sun) A hip combination of live-music venue and bar, darkroom has lots of Kiwi beers, great cocktails and the moreish delights of mini-pizzas and the 'Pie of the Week'. There's lots of live gigs, often free – it's a cool introduction to the renaissance of Christchurch's music scene. Check its Facebook page for gig info.

Court Theatre THEATRE
(Map p138; www.courttheatre.org.nz; off Bernard St, Addington) Christchurch's original Court Theatre was an iconic part of the city's Arts Centre, but it was forced to relocate after the earthquakes. Its new premises in up-and-coming Addington are more modern and spacious, and it's a great venue to see popular international plays and works by NZ playwrights. Check the website for what's playing.

Club 22 CLUB
(Map p138; 22 Harewood Rd, Papanui; ⌚8pm-2am Thu-Sat) Energetic DJ-driven dance club for the younger traveller – some nights the good people of suburban Papanui don't know what's hit them. Search Facebook for Club 22 to see what's planned and who's playing.

The Venue CLUB
(6 Tower St, Hornby; ⌚Wed-Sat 4pm-2am) Another suburban nightclub worth the trek to Hornby for occasional hip hop, dubstep and gloriously noisy rock and roll from Kiwi acts. Check www.christchurchmusic.org.nz for what's on or search Facebook for the Venue.

Christchurch Stadium STADIUM
(Map p138; www.crfu.co.nz; 95 Jack Hinton Drive, Addington) Along with much of Christchurch's sporting infrastructure, the earthquakes forced the closure of AMI Stadium, the traditional home of rugby and cricket in the city. After a 2011 season playing all their games away from home – and still coming in as runners-up – the Canterbury Crusaders Super 15 rugby team moved to a new ground in Addington for the 2012 season. Super-15 games are played from late February to July; from July to September, Canterbury plays in NZ's domestic championship.

Hoyts Riccarton CINEMA
(Map p138; www.hoyts.co.nz; Riccarton Rd, Westfield Riccarton; adult/child $16.50/11.50) Hollywood blockbusters and the occasional arthouse gem feature at Christchurch's most central multiplex. Catch a bus to Riccarton Mall from platform C at the Central Bus Station. Check listings in the *Press* newspaper or at www.flicks.co.nz.

Hollywood 3 CINEMA
(Map p138; www.hollywoodcinema.co.nz; 28 Marriner St; adult/child $16/10) Mainly arthouse and foreign language flicks in the seaside suburb of Sumner. Catch bus 3 from platform A at the Central Bus Station.

Shopping

Since the earthquakes, shopping in Christchurch has largely been focused on the city's suburban malls. The most convenient for visitors is the Westfield Riccarton Mall. At the time of writing, the CBD was closed, but green shoots of retail commerce were evident nearby in the new RE:Start shopping precinct. The gift shops at the Canterbury Museum (p137) and the Christchurch Art Gallery (p139) are also worth browsing.

Re:START Mall MALL
(Map p142; www.restart.org.nz; Cashel Mall) Opened in late October 2011, this colourful labyrinth of shops based in shipping containers was the first retail activity in the Christchurch CBD after the February 2011 earthquake. With a couple of decent cafes, and including two iconic Christchurch stores – Scorpio Books and Johnson's Grocers – it's a pleasant place to stroll. Visit Hapa for a good selection of design and crafts from local artists.

Ballantynes DEPARTMENT STORE
(Map p142; cnr Colombo & Cashel Sts) A venerable Christchurch department store selling men's and women's fashions, cosmetics, travel goods and speciality NZ gifts. Ballantynes was one of the first stores to reopen in the CBD following the earthquakes.

Sunday Artisan Market MARKET
(Map p138; www.sundayartisanmarket.co.nz; Riccarton House, 16 Kahu Rd, Riccarton; 11am-3pm Sun) This Sunday morning market in the leafy grounds of Riccarton House combines local arts and crafts vendors with gourmet food stalls and live music and entertainment.

Westfield Riccarton Mall MALL
(Map p138; www.westfield.co.nz; Riccarton Rd, Riccarton) To the west of central Christchurch, this mega mall has a huge selection of fashion, homeware and entertainment outlets. There's a cinema multiplex and the surrounding area around Riccarton Rd also has many shops. Catch a bus from platform C at Christchurch's Central Bus Station

Information

Emergency

Ambulance, fire service & police (111)

Police station (03-348 6640; www.police.govt.nz; Church Corner, Riccarton Rd, Riccarton) The police kiosk in Cathedral Sq was inaccessible at the time of research, so the station in Riccarton is the most central police station.

Internet Resources

Christchurch & Canterbury (www.christchurchnz.com) Official tourism website for the city and region. Also see www.popupcity.co.nz for its blog of new eating and drinking opportunities around town.

Christchurch.org.nz (www.christchurch.org.nz) The Christchurch City Council's website.

CERA (www.cera.govt.nz) Check the website of the Canterbury Earthquake Recovery Authority for up-to-date maps of the cordon around the city's CBD. Also available is a download of the draft plan to rebuild the city.

Neat Places (www.neatplaces.co.nz) A local blogger's authoritative view of the best of Christchurch's shopping, eating and drinking.

Media

Cityscape (www.cityscape-christchurch.co.nz) Entertainment and events magazine available in inner-city cafes and retailers. Check its website for updates on new openings around town.

Press (www.stuff.co.nz) Christchurch's newspaper, published Monday to Saturday. Check out Friday's edition for the best entertainment listings.

Medical Services

24-Hour Surgery (03-365 7777; www.pegasus.org.nz; Bealey Ave Medical Centre, cnr Bealey Ave & Colombo St; 24hr) Located north of town, with no appointment necessary.

After-Hours Pharmacy (03-366 4439; 931 Colombo St; 6-11pm Mon-Fri, 9am-11pm Sat & Sun, plus public holidays) Located beside the 24-Hour Surgery.

Christchurch Hospital (03-364 0640, emergency dept 03-364 0270; www.cdhb.govt.nz; 2 Riccarton Ave) Centrally located.

Post

Post Office (103 Riccarton Rd) At the time of research, Christchurch's main post office was closed. The most central location is in Riccarton.

Tourist Information

Airport Information Desks (03-353 7774; www.christchurchairport.co.nz; 7.30am-8pm) Transport and accommodation bookings, and a handy post office (open 8am to 4.30pm)

Christchurch i-SITE (☎03-379 9629; www.christchurchnz.com; Rolleston Ave, beside the Canterbury Museum; ⏰8.30am-5pm, later in summer) Transport, activities and accommodation. Note that this location may change during the life of this book. Check online for the current location when you visit.

Department of Conservation (DOC; ☎03-371 3700; www.doc.govt.nz; 38 Orchard Rd, International Antarctic Centre; ⏰8.30am-5pm Mon-Fri) Has information on South Island national parks and walkways. At the time of writing DOC had relocated to the International Antarctic Centre near the airport, but check online for the current location.

 Getting There & Away

Air

Christchurch Airport (CHC; ☎03-358 5029; www.christchurchairport.co.nz) is the South Island's main international gateway. The newly modernised and expanded airport has excellent facilities, including baggage storage and visitor information desks in both the domestic and international terminals.

INTERNATIONAL

Air New Zealand (☎0800 737 000; www.airnewzealand.co.nz) Direct flights (one-way prices) to/from Melbourne (from $139), Sydney ($159) and Brisbane ($159).

Jetstar (☎800 800 995; www.jetstar.com) Direct flights (one-way prices) to/from Melbourne (from $139), Sydney (from $139), Brisbane (from ($169) and the Gold Coast (from $139). Corporate cousin Qantas also flies the same routes at higher fares.

Singapore Airlines (www.singaporeair.com) Direct flights to/from Singapore from around $1100 one way.

Virgin Australia (www.virginaustralia.com) Direct flights (prices one-way) to/from Sydney (from $149), Melbourne (from $149) and Brisbane (from $149).

DOMESTIC

Air New Zealand (☎0800 737 000; www.airnewzealand.co.nz) Direct flights (prices one-way) to/from Auckland (from $79), Blenheim (from $99), Dunedin (from $79), Hamilton (from $109), Hokitika (from $109), Invercargill (from $109), Napier (from $109), Nelson (from $79), New Plymouth (from $109), Palmerston North (from $119), Queenstown (from $59), Rotorua (from $119), Tauranga (from $109), Wanaka (from $99) and Wellington (from $59).

Jetstar (☎0800 800 995; www.jetstar.com) Direct flights (prices one-way) to/from Auckland ($79),Queenstown ($59) and Wellington ($59).

Bus

Shuttles run to Akaroa, Arthur's Pass, Dunedin, Greymouth, Hanmer Springs, Picton, Queenstown, Twizel, Wanaka, Westport and points in between; see the Christchurch i-SITE. Departure points vary, so check when you book.

InterCity (☎03-365 1113; www.intercity.co.nz; 118 Bealey Ave) Buses depart from 118 Bealey Ave, but that may change during the life of this book – check the website. North bound buses go to Kaikoura (2¾ hours), Blenheim (five hours) and Picton (5½ hours), with connections to Nelson (eight hours). One daily bus also goes southwest to Queenstown direct (eight hours). There are services to Wanaka (seven hours) involving a change in Tarras. Heading south, two buses run daily along the coast via the towns along SH1 to Dunedin (six hours), with connections via Gore to Invercargill (9¾ hours) and Te Anau (10½ hours). Book online or at the i-SITE.

Naked Bus (www.nakedbus.com; 70 Bealey Ave, cnr Montreal & Bealey Ave) Heads north to Picton and Nelson, south to Dunedin and southwest to Queenstown. Most buses depart from 70 Bealey Ave, but buses to Kaikoura, Picton and Nelson depart from outside the Canterbury Museum (p137). Check the website or when you book.

Train

Christchurch railway station (☎0800 872 467, 03-341 2588; www.tranzscenic.co.nz; Troup Dr; ⏰ticket office 6.30am-3.30pm Mon-Fri, to 3pm Sat & Sun) is serviced by a free shuttle that picks up from various accommodation; ring the i-SITE to request pick-up. An alternative is Steve's Airport Shuttle (p155) for $5.

The *Coastal Pacific* runs daily each way between Christchurch and Picton via Kaikoura and Blenheim, departing from Christchurch at 7am and arriving at Picton at 12.13pm. The standard adult one-way fare to Picton is $99, but fares can be discounted to $59.

The *TranzAlpine* has a daily route between Christchurch and Greymouth via Arthur's Pass. The standard adult one-way fare is $129, but fares can be discounted to $89.

Contact **Kiwi Rail Scenic** (☎0800 872 467; www.tranzscenic.co.nz) for timetables and tickets.

Getting Around

To/From the Airport

The airport is 12km from the city centre.

Super Shuttle (☎0800 748 885; www.supershuttle.co.nz) operates 24 hours and charges $24 for one person between the city and the airport, plus $5 for each additional person. A cheaper alternative is **Steve's Airport Shuttle**

(☎0800 101 021; 1 person $15, 2&3 people $20) offering a door-to-door service from 3am.

The airport is serviced by the **City Flyer bus** (☎0800 733 287; www.redbus.co.nz; adult/child $7.50/4.50), which runs to/from the Central Bus Station between 7.15am and 10.15pm Monday to Friday and 7.15am to 9.15pm Saturday and Sunday. Pick up the red City Flyer timetable at the i-SITE.

A taxi between the city centre and airport costs around $45 to $55.

Car & Motorcycle

HIRE Most major car- and campervan-rental companies have offices in Christchurch, as do numerous smaller local companies. Operators with national networks often want cars to be returned from Christchurch to Auckland because most renters travel in the opposite direction, so special rates may apply on this northbound route.

Ace Rental Cars (☎03-360 3270, 0800 202 029; www.acerentalcars.co.nz; 20 Abros Pl) Located near the airport.

First Choice (☎03-357 3243, 0800 736 822; www.firstchoice.co.nz; 577 Wairekei Rd) Located near the airport.

Omega Rental Cars (☎03-377 4558, 0800 112 121; www.omegarentalcars.com; 20 Lichfield St) Centrally located.

Pegasus Rental Cars (☎0800 354 504; www.rentalcars.co.nz; 578 Wairakei Rd) Located near the airport.

New Zealand Motorcycle Rentals & Tours (☎03-348 1106; www.nzbike.com; 22 Lowther St) Also does guided motorbike tours.

PURCHASE Many vehicles are offered for sale on noticeboards at hostels, cafes and internet places. Check out **Backpackers Car Market** (Map p138; ☎03-377 3177; www.backpackerscarmarket.co.nz; 33 Battersea St; ⌚9.30am-5pm), or the weekly **Canterbury Car Fair** (☎03-338 5525; Wrights Rd entrance; ⌚9am-noon Sun) held at Addington Raceway. Turners Auctions (p697) buys and sells used cars by auction; vehicles priced under $7000 are auctioned at 6pm on Tuesday and Thursday.

Online see www.trademe.co.nz and www.autotrader.co.nz.

Public Transport

The Christchurch **bus network** (Metro; ☎03-366 8855; www.metroinfo.org.nz; ⌚7am-9pm Mon-Sat, 9am-7pm Sun) is inexpensive and efficient. Most buses run from the **Central Bus Station** (46-50 Lichfield St) between Tuam and Lichfield Sts. Get timetables from the i-SITE or the station's information kiosk. Tickets (adult/child $3.20/1.60) include one free transfer within two hours. Metrocards allow unlimited two-hour/full-day travel for $2.30/4.60, but the cards must be loaded up with a minimum of $10.

Taxi

Blue Star
(☎0800 379 979; www.bluestartaxis)

First Direct
(☎0800 505 555; www.firstdirect.nz.nz)

Gold Band
(☎0800 379 5795; www.goldbandtaxis.co.nz)

AROUND CHRISTCHURCH

Lyttelton

POP 3100

Southeast of Christchurch are the prominent Port Hills, which slope down to the city's port at Lyttelton Harbour. Christchurch's first European settlers landed here in 1850 to embark on their historic trek over the hills.

Lyttelton was badly damaged during the 2010 and 2011 earthquakes, and many of the town's heritage buildings along London St were subsequently demolished. Also fatally damaged was the neogothic **Timeball Station** (www.timeball.co.nz), built in 1876, and where for 58 years a huge time-ball was hoisted on a mast and then dropped at exactly 1pm Greenwich Mean Time. This allowed ships in Lyttelton Harbour to set their clocks and thereby accurately calculate longitude.

Following the earthquakes, Lyttelton has re-emerged as one of Christchurch's most interesting and resilient communities. The town's artsy, independent and bohemian vibe is stronger than ever, and it's again becoming a hub for good bars, cafes and restaurants. It's well worth catching the bus from Christchurch and getting immersed in the local scene.

From Lyttelton, ferries and boat cruises provide access to sheltered Quail Island, as well as to sleepy Diamond Harbour. See www.blackcat.co.nz for details.

If you've got your own transport, the harbour road wends a scenic 15-minute route to pretty Governors Bay, with a couple of good spots for lunch.

The **Lyttelton visitor information centre** (☎03-328 9093; www.lytteltonharbour.info; London St; ⌚9am-5pm Sep-May, to 4pm Jun-Aug) has accommodation and transport information.

Sights

Lyttelton is linked to Christchurch via a road tunnel, but there's a more scenic (and 10km longer) route along the narrow Summit Rd, which has breathtaking city, hill and harbour views, as well as vistas of the Southern Alps.

Eating & Drinking

Freeman's Dining Room RESTAURANT **$$**
(www.freemansdiningroom.co.nz; 47 London St; pizza $20, mains $25-35; ⏲3pm-late Mon-Thu, from 11.30am Fri, from 9am Sat & Sun) Freeman's does fresh pasta, top-notch pizzas and regular wine and beer specials featuring brews from Christchurch's Cassels & Son Brewery. Grab a spot on the deck for great town and harbour views, and take in Sunday afternoon jazz concerts from 3pm. Definitely the kind of neighbourhood local you'd like in your town.

Lyttelton Coffee Company CAFE **$**
(www.lytteltoncoffee.co.nz; 29 London St; mains $10-20) This iconic Lyttelton cafe was destroyed in the February 2011 earthquake, but at the time of writing was planning to reopen in late 2012. Check the website: hopefully you can drop by to sample some of Canterbury's best coffee and tasty and robust brunches. Live music on Saturday afternoons was also a pre-earthquake staple.

Fisherman's Wharf SEAFOOD **$$**
(www.lytteltonwharf.co.nz; 39 Norwich Quay; snacks $7-12, mains $26-34; ⏲11am-8pm) Part alfresco bar and part gourmet fish-and-chippie, Fisherman's Wharf is a top spot for a cold beer and tasty seafood bar snacks and mains. Try the fish of the day – prepared any of three ways – or smaller plates like salmon with lemongrass, chilli and lime, and look forward to views of the harbour and the rugged working port.

Porthole BAR
(cnr Canterbury & London Sts) On the former site of the much-loved Volcano Cafe and Lava Bar, Porthole is another funky reinvention of the humble shipping container. Local wines and Kiwi craft beers are served in the buzzy interior, while laid-back Lyttelton folk chill on the alfresco deck. The Volcano Cafe is still involved too, serving up tasty bar snacks.

Wunderbar BAR
(www.wunderbar.co.nz; 19 London St; ⏲5pm-late Mon-Fri, 1pm-late Sat & Sun) Wunderbar is a top spot to see NZ's more interesting acts, from raucous rock to late-night/early-morning dub. The funky decor alone is worth a trip to Lyttelton. Following the earthquakes, Wunderbar reopened in March 2012. Check the website or www.christchurchmusic.org.nz for what's on.

Governor's Bay Hotel PUB **$$**
(☎03-329 9433; www.governorsbayhotel.co.nz; Main Rd; mains $14-33) Serves tasty burgers, steaks and fish and chips, and more international meals like slow-cooked lamb shanks with Moroccan cous cous. Enjoy a beer on the cool verandah that's dotted with mementos of the hotel's 145 years of history. Upstairs is accommodation in chic and recently refurbished rooms with shared bathrooms (doubles $100 to $150).

She Chocolat CAFE **$$**
(☎03-329 9825; www.shechocolat.com; 79 Main Rd; mains $15-34) She Chocolat serves excellent brunches and lunches with an organic and New Age tinge. After ricotta-and-raisin crepes, make room for locally made Belgian chocolates and take in the harbour views. The cafe is also open for dinner on Friday and Saturday nights; the menu includes a unique chocolate-imbued degustation menu with Pegasus Bay wine matches (per person $125). Bookings recommended.

Farmers Market
(www.lyttelton.net.nz; ⏲10am-1pm Sat) Lyttelton's foodie credentials are enhanced by the farmers market held in the local primary school on Saturdays.

Getting There & Away

Buses 28 and 35 run from Christchurch to Lyttelton (25 minutes). From Lyttelton by car, you can continue around Lyttelton Harbour on to Akaroa. This winding route is longer and more scenic than the route via SH75 between Christchurch and Akaroa.

Akaroa & Banks Peninsula

Banks Peninsula and its hills were formed by two giant volcanic eruptions about 8 million years ago. Small harbours such as Le Bons, Pigeon and Little Akaloa Bays radiate out from the peninsula's centre, giving it a cogwheel shape. The historic town of Akaroa, 83km from Christchurch, is a highlight, as is the absurdly beautiful drive along Summit Rd around the edge of the original crater.

Akaroa ('Long Harbour' in Maori) was the site of the country's first French settlement; descendants of the original French settlers still reside here. It's a charming town that strives to re-create the feel of a French provincial village, down to the names of its streets (Rues Lavaud, Balguerie and Jolie) and houses (Langlois-Eteveneaux). There are also a few choice eateries.

If you're not in a hurry, it's definitely worth spending a few leisurely days in the excellent budget accommodations that dot the outer bays of Banks Peninsula. Most accommodation will arrange pick-up in Akaroa.

History

James Cook sighted the peninsula in 1770. Thinking it was an island, he named it after the naturalist Sir Joseph Banks. The Ngai Tahu tribe, who occupied the peninsula at the time, was attacked at the fortified Onawe *pa* (Maori village) by the Ngati Toa chief Te Rauparaha in 1831 and its population was dramatically reduced.

In 1838, whaling captain Jean Langlois negotiated the purchase of Banks Peninsula from local Maori and returned to France to form a trading company. With French government backing, 63 settlers headed for the peninsula in 1840, but only days before they arrived, panicked British officials sent their own warship to raise the flag at Akaroa, claiming British sovereignty under the Treaty of Waitangi. Had the settlers arrived two years earlier, the entire South Island could have become a French colony, and NZ's future might have been quite different.

The French did settle at Akaroa, but in 1849 their land claim was sold to the New Zealand Company, and in 1850 a large group of British settlers arrived. The heavily forested land was cleared and soon farming became the peninsula's main industry.

Sights

The Giant's House GARDEN

(Map p161; www.thegiantshouse.co.nz; 68 Rue Balguerie; adult/child/family $20/10/45; ⌚noon-5pm Dec 26-April 22, 2-4pm in May-late Dec) An ongoing labour of love from local artist Josie Martin, this playful and whimsical combination of sculpture and mosaics cascades down a hillside garden above Akaroa. Echoes of Gaudí and Miró can be found in the intricate collages of mirrors, tiles and broken china, and there are many surprising nooks and crannies to discover and explore. Martin also exhibits her paintings and sculpture in the lovely 1880 house, the former residence of Akaroa's first bank manager.

Akaroa Museum MUSEUM

(Map p161; cnr Rues Lavaud & Balguerie; adult/child/family $4/1/8; ⌚10.30am-4.30pm Oct-Apr, to 4pm May-Sep) This interesting museum is spread over several historic buildings, including the old courthouse; the tiny Custom House by Daly's Wharf; and one of NZ's oldest houses, Langlois-Eteveneaux. It has modest displays on the peninsula's once-significant Maori population, a courtroom diorama, a 20-minute audiovisual on peninsular history, and Akaroa community archives.

Tree Crop Farm WALKING

(☎03-304 7158; www.treecropfarm.com; admission $10; ⌚10am-5pm in good weather only; 📶) The quirky Tree Crop Farm is 1.8km off the main road through Akaroa (take Rue Grehan). This private wilderness garden has rambling, overgrown tracks, sheepskin-covered couches on a ramshackle verandah, and a cafe and travel library with loads of old *National Geographic* magazines. Rustic, romantic accommodation ($200 to $250) is also available.

Maori & Colonial Museum MUSEUM

(Map p159; www.okainsbaymuseum.co.nz; adult/child $10/2; ⌚10am-5pm) At Okains Bay, northeast of Akaroa, this collection of indigenous and pioneer artefacts includes a reproduction Maori meeting house, a sacred 15th-century god stick and a war canoe.

Barrys Bay Cheese

(Map p159; ☎03-304 5809; www.barrysbaycheese.co.nz; ⌚9am-5pm) At Barrys Bay, on the western side of Akaroa Harbour (12km from Akaroa), is the enticing Barrys Bay Cheese, where you can taste and purchase fine cheddar, havarti and gouda. Crackers and chutney are available for a spontaneous seaside snack.

Activities

See the visitor information centre if you like the sound of jetboating, kayaking or sailing on Akaroa Harbour, touring a working sheep farm or visiting a seal colony.

The *Akaroa – An Historic Walk* booklet ($9.50) details a walking tour starting at the 1876 **Waeckerle Cottage** (Map p161; Rue Lavaud) and finishing at the old Taylor's Emporium premises near the main wharf. The route takes in the old wooden buildings

Banks Peninsula

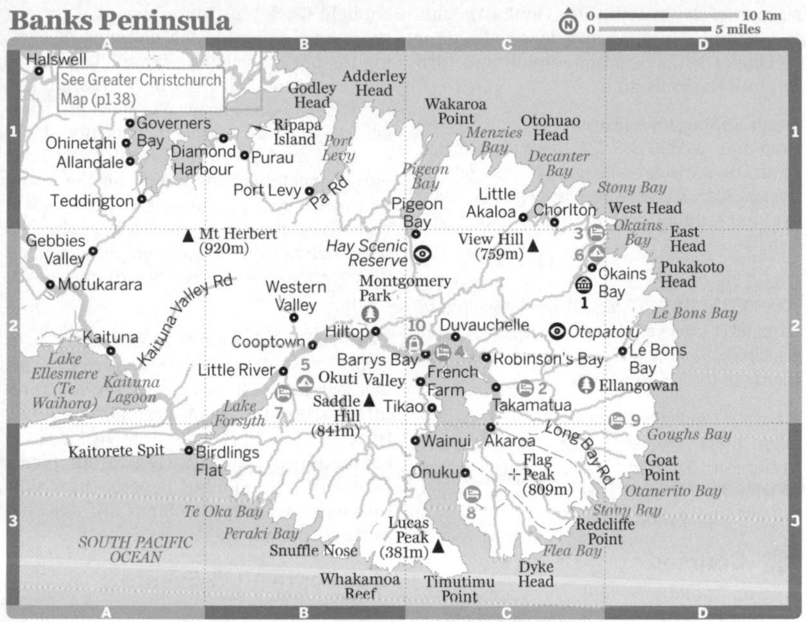

Banks Peninsula

Sights

1 Maori & Colonial Museum C2

Sleeping

2 Coombe Farm C2
3 Double Dutch C2
4 Halfmoon Cottage C2
5 Little River Campground B2
6 Okains Bay Camping Ground C2
7 Okuti Garden B2
8 Onuku Farm Hostel C3
9 Purple Peak Backpackers D2

Shopping

10 Barrys Bay Cheese C2

and churches that give Akaroa its character. Audio guides for self-guided walking tours ($10 per 90 minutes) are also available at the visitor information centre.

Banks Peninsula Track WALKING
(☎03-304 7612; www.bankstrack.co.nz; per person $220) This 35km four-day walk traverses private farmland around the dramatic coastline of Banks Peninsula. Costs includes transport from Akaroa and hut accommodation. A two-day option ($145) covers the same ground at twice the speed.

Akaroa Walk WALKING
(☎0800 377 378, 03-962 3280; www.tuataratours.co.nz; per person $1575; ⊙Nov-Apr) A leisurely upmarket 46km stroll, across three days, from Christchurch to Akaroa. Includes good accommodation and lots of gourmet food. You'll only need to carry your daypack.

Akaroa Adventure Centre ADVENTURE SPORTS
(Map p161; ☎03-304 8709; Rue Lavaud; ⊙8.30am-5.30pm) The Akaroa Adventure Centre rents out sea kayaks, bikes, golf clubs, fishing rods and windsurfing gear. Ask here about staying at Purple Peak Backpackers (p163).

Pohatu Plunge WILDLIFE
(☎03-304 8552; www.pohatu.co.nz) Runs evening penguin-viewing tours (adult/child $70/55); spying the white-flippered penguin is best between August and January. Sea kayaking (adult/child $80/60) and 4WD nature tours (adult/child $90/50) are also available, with the option of staying overnight in a secluded cottage (additional $20 per person) in the Pohatu Nature Reserve.

Onuku Heights Horse Treks HORSE RIDING
(☎03-304 7112; www.onuku-heights.co.nz; 166 Haylocks Rd; from $110; ⊙Nov-May) Surround yourself with the best of the spectacular

scenery of Banks Peninsula. Onuku Heights is 15 minutes from Akaroa: follow the signs to Onuku Marae, continue uphill and turn left into Haylocks Rd.

Fox II Sailing Adventures SAILING
(Map p161; ☎0800 369 7245; www.akaroafoxsail.co.nz; Daly's Wharf; adult/child $70/30; ⊙departures 10.30am & 1.30pm Dec-May) History, scenery and wildlife on NZ's oldest gaff-rigged ketch.

Coast Up Close BOAT TOUR
(☎0800 126 278, 021 228 8091; www.coastupclose.co.nz; adult/child from $65/25; ⊙departs 10.15am & 1.45pm) Fishing and scenic boat trips with plenty of birds and wildlife.

Captain Hector's Sea Kayaks KAYAKING
(Map p161; ☎03-304 7866; www.akaroaseakayaks.co.nz; Beach Rd; kayak hire per half-/full day $35/60) Rental kayaks, canoes and rowboats for self-exploration.

Courses

Akaroa Cooking School COOKING COURSE
(Map p161; ☎021 166 3737; www.akaroacooking.co.nz; 81 Beach Rd; per person $195) Options include popular 'Gourmet in a Day' sessions (10am to 4pm) on Saturdays, and occasional specialised seafood and barbecue classes. All sessions end with tucking into your self-prepared feast, all accompanied by local wines. Check the website for the school's occasional forays into specific ethnic cuisines, including Thai and Italian. Booking ahead is highly recommended.

Tours

Akaroa Dolphins WILDLIFE
(Map p161; ☎0800 990 102, 03-304 7866; www.akaroadolphins.co.nz; 65 Beach Rd; adult/child $70/35; ⊙departures 10.15am, 12.45pm & 3.15pm Oct-Apr, 10.15am only May-Sep) Two-hour wildlife cruises, plus evening cruises and birdwatching trips by arrangement. Say hi to Murphy – wildlife-spotting dog extraordinaire – for us. He even stars in his own children's picture book, available at the Akaroa Dolphins office.

Black Cat Cruises WILDLIFE
(Map p161; ☎03-304 7641; www.blackcat.co.nz; Main Wharf; cruise & swim adult/child $139/115, cruise only $72/35; ⊙5 tours daily 6am-3.30pm Oct-April, 1 tour daily 11.30am May-Sep) The waters around Akaroa are home to the world's smallest and rarest dolphin, the Hector's dolphin, found only in NZ waters. If viewing the dolphins on a harbour cruise isn't enough, Black Cat Cruises can also get you swimming alongside the dolphins (assuming it's not the calving season). Trips operate year-round and carry only 10 swimmers per trip, so book ahead. Wet suits and snorkelling gear are provided, plus hot showers back on dry land. Count on a 2½-hour outing including time in and on the water, and a $59 refund if you don't get to swim with the dolphins. Cruises have around a 98% success rate in seeing dolphins, and an 81% success rate in actually swimming with them.

Eastern Bays Scenic Mail Run TOUR
(☎03-304 8600; tour $60; ⊙9am Mon-Fri) This is a 120km, 4½-hour delivery service to remote parts of the peninsula, and visitors can travel along with the posties to visit isolated communities and bays (beachfront picnic included). The minibus departs the visitor information centre; bookings are essential as there are only eight seats available.

Festivals & Events

French Fest Akaroa FOOD & WINE
(www.frenchfest.co.nz) French Fest Akaroa is a Gallic-inspired get-together, with an emphasis on food, wine, music and art. Don't miss (or stand on) *Le Race D'Escargots*, where sleek, highly trained snails negotiate a compact course. There's also a French Waiter's Race. It's held in late October on a biannual basis in odd-numbered years.

Sleeping

Most Banks Peninsula accommodation is around Akaroa, but the outer bays are also blessed with excellent and interesting budget lodgings. Akaroa has some splurge-worthy, romantic B&B accommodation.

AKAROA

Garthowen B&B $$$
(Map p161; ☎03-304 7419; www.garthowen.co.nz; 7 Beach Rd; s & d incl breakfast $280-345; @☜) With two vintage Citroën cars, two friendly Jack Russell terriers and four super-comfy en suite rooms, (almost) everything comes in twos at this upscale B&B rebuilt in heritage style using recycled cedar. Breakfast on the deck comes with a side order of the best view in town.

Oinako Lodge B&B $$$
(☎03-304 8787; www.oinako.co.nz; 99 Beach Rd; d incl breakfast $245-285; @☜) This glorious timber mansion was built in 1865 for the

Akaroa

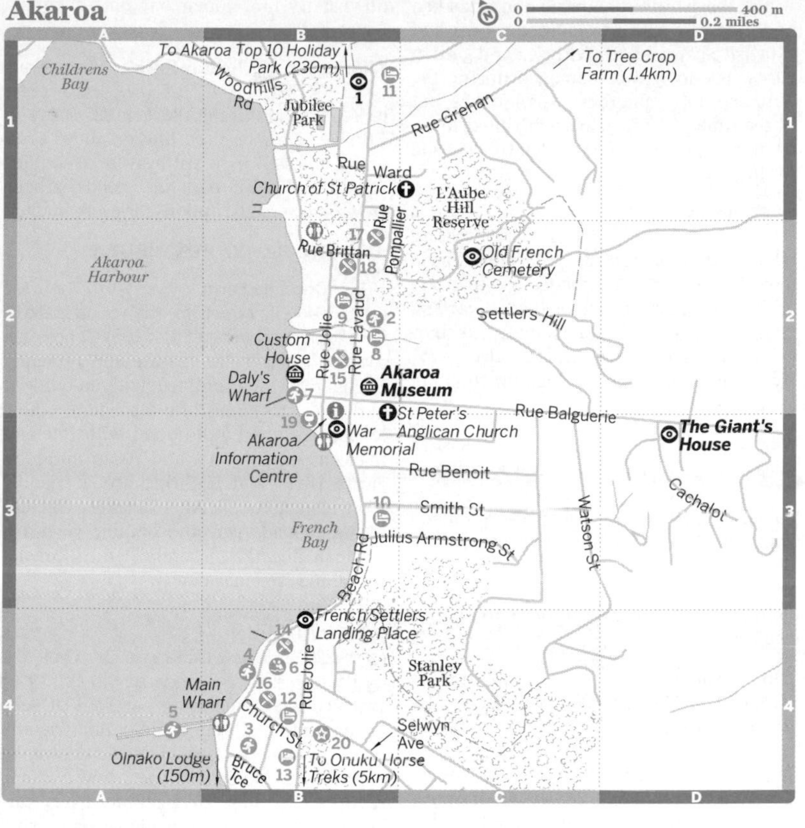

Akaroa

Top Sights

Akaroa Museum ... B2
The Giant's House ... D3

Sights

1 Waeckerle Cottage ... B1

Activities, Courses & Tours

2 Akaroa Adventure Centre ... B2
3 Akaroa Cooking School ... B4
4 Akaroa Dolphins ... B4
5 Black Cat Cruises ... A4
6 Captain Hector's Sea Kayaks ... B4
7 Fox II Sailing Adventures ... B2

Sleeping

8 Bon Accord ... B2
9 Chez la Mer ... B2
10 Garthowen ... B3
11 La Rive Motel ... B1
12 Old Shipping Office ... B4
13 Tresori Motor Lodge ... B4

Eating

14 Akaroa Fish & Chips ... B4
Bully Hayes ... (see 14)
15 Four Square Supermarket ... B2
16 L'Escargot Rouge ... B4
17 The Little Bistro ... B2
18 Vangionis ... B2

Drinking

19 Truby's Bar on the Beach ... B3

Entertainment

20 Cine Café ... B4

British magistrate. It's now an upmarket bed and breakfast with five themed rooms and expansive bay windows with sea and garden views. The lodge was damaged during the 2010 and 2011 Canterbury earthquakes, but at the time of writing was scheduled to reopen in September 2012. Check the website for the latest news.

Chez la Mer HOSTEL **$**
(Map p161; ☎03-304 7024; www.chezlamer.co.nz; 50 Rue Lavaud; dm $25-28, d with/without bathroom $80/70; @📶) A friendly backpackers with well-kept rooms and a shaded garden, complete with fish ponds, hammocks, barbecue and outdoor seating; it's also a TV-free zone. Free bikes and fishing rods are available.

Bon Accord HOSTEL **$**
(Map p161; ☎03-304 7782; www.bon-accord.co.nz; 57 Rue Lavaud; dm $27-30, d $59-89; @📶) This colourful and quirky backpackers fills a compact 155-year-old house. Relax on the deck or in the two cosy lounges, or dive into the herb-filled garden to release your inner French chef. There are free bikes to get you exploring.

Old Shipping Office APARTMENT **$$$**
(Map p161; ☎0800 695 2000; www.akaroavillageinn.co.nz; Church St; d $230) A self-contained apartment in a restored heritage building with an interesting past. (No prizes for guessing the building's former incarnation.) Two bedrooms, a spacious shared lounge and an outdoor spa pool make the Old Shipping Office a good option for families or for two couples. Check-in is at the adjacent Akaroa Village Inn.

Tresori Motor Lodge MOTEL **$$**
(Map p161; ☎03-304 7500, 0800 273 747; www.tresori.co.nz; cnr Rue Jolie & Church St; d $155-205; @📶) For designer-conscious lodgings treat yourself to the Tresori; its rich, colourful decor is anything but bland. It's a short walk to Akaroa's waterfront cafe and restaurant strip.

La Rive Motel MOTEL **$$**
(Map p161; ☎03-304 7651, 0800 247 651; www.larive.co.nz; 1 Rue Lavaud; d $125-135; 📶) Old-style motel with big rooms and good facilities; well priced considering each unit (studio, two- and three-bedroom options) is fully self-contained. The decor is slightly dated compared to other, more modern motels, but La Rive represents good value in a sometimes pricey destination. Most downstairs units open out onto compact courtyards.

Akaroa Top 10 Holiday Park HOLIDAY PARK **$**
(☎03-304 7471, 0800 727 525; www.akaroa-holidaypark.co.nz; 96 Morgans Rd; sites from $35, units $70-118; @📶) On a terraced hillside above town and connected by a pathway to Woodhills Rd, this pleasant park has good harbour views and versatile options for every budget.

AROUND BANKS PENINSULA

TOP CHOICE **Coombe Farm** B&B
(☎03-304 7239; www.coombefarm.co.nz; 18 Old Le Bons Track; d incl breakfast $145-165) Choose between staying in the private and romantic Shepherd's Hut – complete with an outdoor bath – or in the historic farm house, now lovingly restored and dotted with interesting contemporary art and Asian antiques. Hosts Hugh and Kathrine are a friendly Kiwi-English couple. After breakfast (including homemade jam and organic yoghurt), you can negotiate Coombe Farm's private forest and stream walkway.

Okuti Garden ECO-STAY **$**
(☎03-325 1913; www.okuti.co.nz; 216 Okuti Valley Rd; per person $40; ⊙closed May-Oct; @📶) Part eco-aware homestay, part WWOOFer's haven and an all-round funky and friendly place to stay. Options include sleeping in a teepee, a Mongolian yurt, house truck, earth-brick cottage or farmhouse. Vegetarian breakfasts ($15) are available, with many ingredients sourced from Okuti's own gardens. There are plenty of natural nooks and crannies for reading or relaxing, and there's a generous supply of fresh herbs to kickstart your creativity in the shared kitchen.

Halfmoon Cottage HOSTEL **$**
(Map p159; ☎03-304 5050; www.halfmoon.co.nz; dm/s/d $30/52/75; ⊙often closed Jun-Sep; 📶) This marvellous cottage at Barrys Bay (12km from Akaroa) is a blissful place to spend a few days lazing on the big verandahs or in the hammocks dotting the lush gardens. The rooms – mostly doubles – are warmly decorated, and the local landscapes and seascapes can be explored by bicycle or kayak.

Double Dutch HOSTEL **$**
(Map p159; ☎03-304 7229; www.doubledutch.co.nz; 32 Chorlton Rd; dm/s $30/55, d with/without bathroom $76/70; @) Posh enough to be a B&B but budget-friendly, this relaxed hostel is perched on a secluded river estuary

in farmland. There's a general store (and a beach) just a short walk away, but it's best to bring your own ingredients for the flash kitchen.

Onuku Farm Hostel HOSTEL $
(Map p159; ☎03-304 7066; www.onuku.co.nz; Onuku Rd; sites per person from $12.50, dm/d from $28/66; ⊙closed Jun-Aug; @📶) An eco-minded backpackers with basic huts, tent sites and a comfy house on a sheep farm near Onuku, 6km south of Akaroa. From November to March the owners organise swimming-with-dolphins tours ($100) and kayaking trips ($50) for both guests and non-guests, and will pick up from Akaroa. The same family has owned the farm since the 1860s, so you should trust them when they say there's some great walks on the 340-hectare spread. A newly-developed campsite area makes it a great option for travellers with tents or campervans.

Purple Peak Backpackers HOSTEL $
(Map p159; ☎03-420 0199; www.purplepeak.co.nz; camping by donation, dm/d $25/60; @) This rustic surf lodge and backpackers has glorious sea views and a rugged, out-of-the-way location. Accommodation is simple but clean, and during summer there's the occasional tasty seafood barbecue, and pizzas served up from the outdoor wood-fired pizza oven. Surfboards and gear are available for hire. Free shuttles are provided from Akaroa. See Darin at the Akaroa Adventure Centre (p159) for accommodation.

Little River Campground HOLIDAY PARK $
(☎03-325 1014; www.littlerivercampground.co.nz; 287 Okuti Valley Rd; sites from $25, cabins $40-110) This sprawling campground near the hamlet of Little River is arrayed around a forest and riverside setting. Accommodation ranges from grassy tent sites through to rustic Kiwiana cabins. There's a really cruisy family atmosphere: added benefits for the kids include campfires, trampolines and a natural swimming hole in the river.

Okains Bay Camping Ground CAMPSITE $
(Map p159; ☎03-304 8789; www.okainsbaycamp.co.nz; 1162 Okains Bay Rd; sites adult/child $12/6) On pine tree–peppered ground right by a beach, with spick-and-span kitchen facilities and coin-operated hot showers. Pay your fees at the house at the camping ground's entrance. There's a small general store around 1km down the road, and a terrific adventure playground for the kids.

Eating & Drinking

TOP CHOICE **The Little Bistro** FRENCH $$
(Map p161; ☎03-304 7314; 33 Rue Lavaud; mains $27-35; ⊙6pm-late Tue-Sun; 🍷) *Très petite, très chic* and very tasty. Look forward to classic bistro style given a proud Kiwi spin with local seafood, South Island wines and Canterbury craft beers. The menu changes seasonally, but usually includes favourites like pistachio-encrusted lamb or Akaroa salmon terrine; vegetarians are not ignored. Booking ahead is definitely necessary. Sometimes open for lunch in summer – check the blackboard out the front.

Vangionis ITALIAN
(Map p161; www.vangionis.co.nz; Rue Brittan; tapas $8-18, pizza $18-28) Thin-crust pizzas, tapas, pasta and Canterbury beers and wines all feature at this Tuscan-style trattoria. Secure an outside table and while away lunchtime, afternoon or evening. Takeaway pizzas are also available.

L'Escargot Rouge CAFE $
(Map p161; www.lescargotrouge.co.nz; 67 Beach Rd; meals $8-14) Tasty gourmet pies ($7), picnic fixings and French-accented breakfasts are the main attractions at the 'Red Snail'. Try the homemade toasted muesli with fruit, yoghurt and honey ($12) before exploring Akaroa harbour by kayak.

Bully Hayes RESTAURANT $$
(Map p161; www.bullyhayes.co.nz; 57 Beach Rd; lunch $15-25, dinner mains $22-35) Named after a well-travelled American buccaneer, the menu at this sunny spot kicks off with Akaroa salmon before touching down for gourmet burgers, pasta and tapas. Try the seafood platter ($31) for lots of briny bounty from local waters. Monteith's beers and a good local wine list make it a worthwhile place to linger. It's a good spot for breakfast, too.

Akaroa Fish & Chips FISH & CHIPS $
(Map p161; 59 Beach Rd; snacks & meals $6-15) Order takeaways and sit beside the ocean, or grab a table and tuck into blue cod, scallops, oysters and other assorted deep-fried goodness. Either way, keep a close eye on the local posse of eager cats and seagulls.

Truby's Bar on the Beach BAR
(Map p161; Rue Jolie) A perfect waterfront location combines with rustic outdoor seating to produce Akaroa's best place for a sundowner

drink. Truby's blue cod and chips for dinner are world-famous in Akaroa, and baked cheesecake and good coffee are other distractions earlier in the day.

Four Square Supermarket SUPERMARKET $ (Map p161; Rue Lavaud; ⏲8am-8pm) Good deli and wine selection.

☆ Entertainment

Cine Café CINEMA (Map p161; ☎03-304 7678; www.cinecafe.co.nz; cnr Rue Jolie & Selwyn Ave; adult/child $15/13; ⏲2-10pm; 📶) Part cafe with excellent pastries, soups and wi-fi, and part cinema showing art-house flicks.

ℹ Information

Akaroa Information Centre (☎03-304 8600; www.akaroa.com; 80 Rue Lavaud; ⏲9am-5pm) Tours, activities and accommodation.

ℹ Getting There & Away

From November to April the **Akaroa Shuttle** (☎0800 500 929; www.akaroashuttle.co.nz; return $45) departs Christchurch daily at 8.30am and 2pm, returning from Akaroa at 10.30am, 3.35pm and 4.30pm. Bookings are recommended. From May to September, there's only a 10am departure from Christchurch. Check the website for Christchurch pick-up options. Scenic tours from Christchurch exploring Banks Peninsula are also available.

French Connection (☎0800 800 575; www.akaroabus.co.nz; return $45) has a year-round daily departure from Christchurch at 9.15am, returning from Akaroa at 4pm.

NORTH CANTERBURY

From Christchurch, SH1 heads north for 57km through Woodend and Amberley to Waipara. From here it continues northeast to Kaikoura, while SH7 branches due north to Hurunui, through flat farming country, to reach Culverden. About 27km from Culverden is the turn-off from SH7 to Hanmer Springs, a thermal resort. The *Alpine Pacific Triangle Touring Guide* (available from Hanmer Springs and Christchurch i-SITES) outlines things to see and do in this region. See also www.visithurunui.co.nz.

If you're a wine buff or foodie, look for the *North Canterbury Food & Wine Trail* touring map at the i-SITE in Christchurch. Online, see www.foodandwinetrail.co.nz.

The **Brew Moon Garden Café & Brewery** (www.brewmooncafe.co.nz; 150 Ashworths Rd; mains $15-26; @👪) on SH75 in Amberley crafts four different beers; sample them all for $12. Our favourite is the gloriously hoppy Hophead IPA. Gourmet pizzas ($20 to $25) and meals including Akaroa salmon and steak sandwiches are also available. Coffee and New York–style baked cheesecake ($10) are other tasty options.

A few kilometres up SH1, the scenic **Waipara Valley** is home to around 20 wineries; see www.waiparawines.co.nz. Sample a pinot noir or riesling and stop for lunch at one of the spectacular vineyard restaurants. **Waipara Springs** (www.waiparasprings.co.nz; SH1, north of Waipara), **Pegasus Bay** (www.pegasusbay.com; Stockgrove Rd, south of Waipara; mains $27-39; ⏲noon-4pm) and the **Mud House** (www.themudhousewinery.co.nz; SH1, south of Waipara) are open daily for wine tasting and sales, and all have restaurant-cafes for a leisurely lunch. During summer, the Mud House also hosts occasional local and international concerts; see www.adayonthegreen.com.au. The annual **Waipara Wine and Food Festival** (www.waiparawineandfood.co.nz) is held in early March. Wine tours are available from several Christchurch-based companies.

The **Pegasus Bay Restaurant** (☎03-314 6869; www.pegasusbay.com; Stockgrove Rd, south of Waipara; mains $27-39; ⏲noon-4pm) has an old-world ambience set amid a lovely European-style garden. The menu takes advantage of superb local produce and recommends appropriate wine matches – Pegasus Bay is a regular contender for NZ's Best Winery Restaurant award. Booking ahead is recommended.

Near the intersection with SH7 is **Waipara Sleepers** (☎03-314 6003; www.waiparasleepers.co.nz; 12 Glenmark Dr; sites from $20, dm $25, s $35-45, d $55-65; @📶), where you can camp, bunk down in converted train carriages and cook your own meals in the 'station house'. The local pub and general store are located close by.

Hanmer Springs

POP 750

Hanmer Springs, the main thermal resort on the South Island, is 10km off SH7. It's a pleasantly low-key spot to indulge in bathing in hot pools and being pampered in the spa complex. There are good restaurants and lots of family-friendly activities.

Hanmer Springs

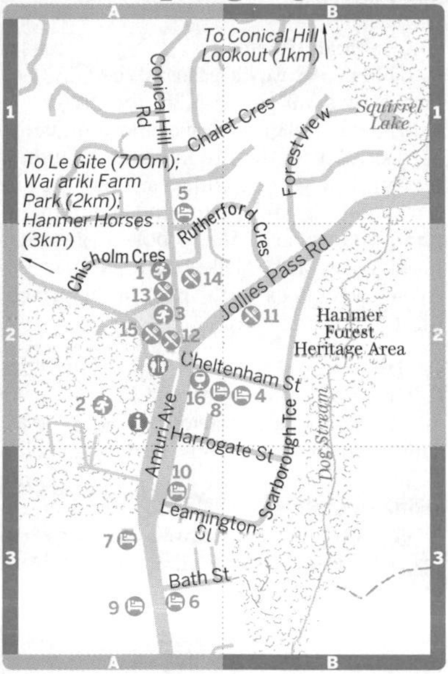

Hanmer Springs

Activities, Courses & Tours

1 Hanmer Springs Adventure Centre A2
2 Hanmer Springs Thermal Pools A2
3 Thrillseekers Canyon Booking Office A2

Sleeping

4 Cheltenham House B2
5 Hanmer Backpackers A1
6 Hanmer Springs Top 10 Holiday Park A3
7 Kakapo Lodge A3
8 Rosie's A2
9 Scenic View Motels A3
10 Tussock Peak Motor Lodge A3

Eating

11 Chantellini's B2
12 Four Square Supermarket A2
13 Hanmer Springs Bakery A2
14 Malabar Restaurant & Bar A2
15 Powerhouse Café A2
Thai Chilli .... (see 15)

Drinking

16 Monteith's Brewery Bar A2

Sights & Activities

Hanmer Springs Thermal Pools BATHHOUSE
(03-315 0000; www.hanmersprings.co.nz; entry on Amuri Ave; adult/child $18/9; 10am-9pm) Visitors have been soaking in the waters of Hanmer Springs Thermal Pools for over 100 years. Local legend has it that the thermal springs are the fires of Tamatea, which fell from the sky after an eruption of Mt Ngauruhoe on the North Island; Maori call the springs Waitapu (Sacred Waters).

The hot-spring water mixes with freshwater to produce pools of varying temperatures. In addition to mineral pools, there are landscaped rock pools, a freshwater 25m lap pool, private thermal pools ($25 per 30 minutes) and a restaurant. There are loads of fun for kids of all ages, including a waterslide and the exciting Superbowl ($10). The adjacent **Hanmer Springs Spa** (03-315 0029, 0800 873 529; www.hanmerspa.co.nz; 10am-7pm) has massage and beauty treatments from $70. A recent refurbishment has lifted the spa to international standards, and entry to the pools is discounted to $12 if you also partake of the spa's facilities.

Molesworth Station WORKING FARM
At 180,500 hectares, Molesworth Station, northeast of Hanmer Springs, is NZ's largest farm, with the country's largest cattle herd (up to 10,000). Inquire at the i-SITE about independent visits to Molesworth, which is under DOC control. Visits are usually possible only when the Acheron Rd through the station is open from late December to early April (weather permitting). The drive from Hanmer Springs north to Blenheim on this narrow, unsealed backcountry road takes around six hours; note that the gates are open only from 7am to 7pm, and overnight camping (adult/child $6/1.50) is permitted in certain areas (no open fires allowed). Pick up the Department of Conservation's *Molesworth Station* brochure from the Hanmer Springs i-SITE or download it from www.doc.govt.nz. **Molesworth Heritage Tours** (03-315 7401; www.molesworth.co.nz; tours $198-695; Oct-May) offer 4WD tours of the station and the remote private land stretching north to St Arnaud. Day tours include a picnic lunch, but there's also a five-hour 'no frills' option.

Other Activities

Other Hanmer Springs activities include kayaking, scenic flights, fishing trips and claybird shooting. Family-friendly activities include mini-golf and tandem bicycles.

There are two skiing areas nearby. **Hanmer Springs Ski Field** is the closest, 17km (unsealed road) from town, and **Mt Lyford Ski Field** is 60km away. They're cheaper than larger resorts. The Hanmer Springs Adventure Centre operates transport.

Thrillseekers Adventures ADVENTURE SPORTS
(☎03-315 7046; www.thrillseekers.co.nz; SH7) Bungy off a 35m-high bridge ($169), jetboat the Waiau Gorge (adult/child $115/60) or go white-water rafting (Grade II to III) down the Waiau River (adult/child $149/79). Other activities include quad-biking (adult/child $129/99). Book at the Thrillseekers Adventure centre, next to the bridge where the Hanmer Springs turn-off meets SH7. There's another **booking office** (☎03-315 7346; www.thrillseekerscanyon.co.nz; Conical Hill Rd; ⏲10am-6pm) in town.

Hanmer Springs Adventure Centre ADVENTURE SPORTS
(☎03-315 7233, 0800 368 7386; www.hanmeradventure.co.nz; 20 Conical Hill Rd; ⏲9am-5pm) Books activities, and rents quad bikes (from $129), mountain bikes (per hour/day from $19/45), fishing rods (per day $25) and ski and snowboard gear. Mountain biking maps are available at the i-SITE.

Wai Ariki Farm Park FARM
(☎03-315 7772; www.waiariki-farmpark.co.nz; 108 Rippingale Rd; adult/child/family $12/6/35; ⏲10am-4pm Tue-Sat, open daily during school holidays) With more animals than Dr Dolittle's Facebook page, Wai Ariki is a great spot for kids. Llamas, Tibetan yaks, rabbits, guinea pigs and goats all feature, and many of the critters can be hand-fed; horse treks for the young ones are also available. For mum and dad there's a cafe and craft gallery.

Hanmer Horses HORSE RIDING
(☎0800 873 546; www.hanmerhorses.co.nz; 1hr rides adult/child $59/49, 2½hr treks $99) Rides depart from a forested setting 10 minutes from town on Rogerson Rd. Younger children can be led on a pony for 30 minutes ($25).

Sleeping

Woodbank Park Cottages COTTAGES $$
(☎03-315 5075; www.woodbankcottages.co.nz; 381 Woodbank Rd; d $180-200) These two matching cottages in a woodland setting are around 10 minutes' drive from Hanmer, but feel a million miles away. Decor is crisp and modern, bathrooms and kitchens are well appointed and expansive wooden decks come equipped with gas barbecues and rural views.

Cheltenham House B&B $$$
(☎03-315 7545; www.cheltenham.co.nz; 13 Cheltenham St; s $195-235, d $235-265; @📶) Centrally located B&B with six snooze-inducing suites, all with bathroom, and including two in cosy garden cottages; there's a billiard table, grand piano and complimentary pre-dinner wine. Cooked gourmet breakfasts can be delivered to your room. Avoid the crowds up the road in the private hot tub.

Le Gîte HOSTEL $$
(☎03-315 5111; www.legite.co.nz; 3 Devon St; dm $28, d with/without bathroom $76/64; @📶) This charming old converted home is a 10-minute walk from the centre. Large rooms (no bunks), relaxing gardens and a lovely lounge area are drawcards. For extra privacy, book a garden 'chalet' with private bathroom.

Tussock Peak Motor Lodge MOTEL $$
(☎0800 8877 625, 03-315 5191; www.tussockpeak.co.nz; cnr Amuri Ave & Leamington St; d $145-225; 📶) Modern, spotless and central, Tussock Peak has colourful decor and friendly service that's an eclectic cut above other motels on Hanmer's main drag. The hardest part is choosing what kind of room to get: studio, one- or two-bedroom unit, spa, courtyard or balcony.

Scenic View Motels MOTEL $$
(☎03-315 7419; www.hanmerscenicviews.co.nz; 10 Amuri Ave; d $135-200; @📶) An attractive timber-and-stone complex with modern, colourful studios and two- and three-bedroom apartments. Mountain views come as standard.

Hanmer Backpackers HOSTEL $
(☎03-315 7196; www.hanmerbackpackers.co.nz; 41 Conical Hill Rd; dm $27, s $55, d $58-70; @📶) Centrally located, the township's original backpackers is a cosy, woodlined haven with a friendly and well-travelled host. Well-maintained shared social areas, cheap wi-fi access and free fruit and coffee all add further big ticks. There's even another edible surprise that we can't talk about.

Rosie's B&B $
(☎03-315 7095; roxyrosie@clearnet.nz; 9 Cheltenham St; s incl breakfast $55-90, d incl breakfast $85-130) Rosie is originally from Australia, but she's now offering great Kiwi hospitality at

this welcoming and reader-recommended spot. Rooms offer either en suite or shared facilities. Look forward to recently decorated bathrooms and a friendly cat called Kiri. The garden cottage ($130) is a nicely private option. Rates include breakfast.

Hanmer Springs Top 10 Holiday Park HOLIDAY PARK $
(03-315 7113, 0800 904 545; www.mountainviewtop10.co.nz; Bath St; sites from $32, units $80-160;) Family-friendly park a few minutes' walk from the Hanmer thermal reserve. Kids will love the playground and the trampoline. Take your pick from basic cabins (BYO everything) to two-bedroom motel units with everything supplied. There are two more camping grounds in town if it's full.

Kakapo Lodge HOSTEL $
(03-315 7472; www.kakapolodge.co.nz; 14 Amuri Ave; dm $28, d $66-90;) The spartan, YHA-affiliated Kakapo has a roomy kitchen and lounge, chill-busting underfloor heating and an outdoor deck. Bunk-free dorms (some with bathroom) are joined by a motel-style unit ($100) with TV and cooking facilities.

Eating & Drinking

Chantellini's FRENCH $$
(03-315 7667; www.chantellinis.com; 11 Jollies Pass Rd; mains $30-36; 10am-10:30ampm) Tucked away behind the main street, this quiet oasis is a relaxed cafe with outdoor garden seating by day, and an intimate French bar and restaurant by night. Chandeliers and black drapes create an elegant ambience. Portions are generous, and the daily two/three-course lunch for $25/30 is great value – try the leek tart or onion soup. Bookings are recommended for dinner.

Powerhouse Café CAFE $$
(03-315 5252; www.powerhousecafe.co.nz; 6 Jacks Pass Rd; mains $12-20;) Recharge your batteries with a huge High Country breakfast, or linger for a more sophisticated lunch of a creamy goats-cheese salad. During summer, return for dinner of Akaroa salmon in the Powerhouse's spacious courtyard. An organic fair-trade coffee is a good trade for wi-fi access, and there are plenty of gluten-free and vegetarian options.

Thai Chilli THAI $$
(The Mall; mains $14-20) Run by a friendly Thai family, the cosy Thai Chilli respects requests for 'spicy, please', and also offers good-value lunch specials ($14). Service – usually by the family's kids – can be hit and miss, but that's part of the low-key charm. Takeaways are also available.

Malabar Restaurant & Bar ASIAN $$
(03-315 7745; www.malabar.co.nz; 5 Conical Hill Rd; lunch & breakfast $10-22 dinner $28-36) This elegant eatery presents Asian cuisine from Beijing to Bangalore. Try the Malabar *thali* showcasing four different curries, or the moreish five-spice crackling pork belly. Breakfast and lunch options are less Asian influenced – think bagels, omelettes or burgers – but equally tasty. A limited takeaway menu of Indian, Chinese and Thai favourites is also available (around $13).

Monteith's Brewery Bar PUB
(wwww.mbbh.co.nz; 47 Amuri Ave) The best pub in town features lots of different Monteiths beers and tasty tucker from bar snacks ($10 to $17) to full meals ($17 to $32). Platters ($27 to $54) are good value if you've just met some new friends in the hot pools across the road.

Hanmer Springs Bakery BAKERY $
(16 Conical Hill Rd; pies $5; 6am-4pm) Grab a takeaway coffee or gourmet pie.

Four Square Supermarket SUPERMARKET $
(Conical Hill Rd) In Hanmer's shopping mall.

Information

Hanmer Springs i-SITE (0800 733 426, 03-315 7128; www.visithanmersprings.co.nz; 42 Amuri Ave; 10am-5pm) Books transport, accommodation and activities.

Getting There & Away

Hanmer Backpackers run daily shuttles between Hanmer and Christchurch (90 minutes) and also operates a convenient service to and from Kaikoura (two hours; Monday, Wednesday and Friday). **Hanmer Connection** (0800 242 663; www.atsnz.com) also links Hanmer Springs to Christchurch. Shuttles depart from the Hanmer i-SITE.

Check the websites of both companies for current departure points from Christchurch.

Lewis Pass Hwy

At the northern end of the Southern Alps, the beautiful Lewis Pass Hwy (SH7) wiggles west from the Hanmer Springs turn-off to Lewis Pass, Maruia Springs and Springs Junction. The 907m-high **Lewis Pass** is not as steep or the forest as dense as Arthur's and Haast Passes, with mainly red and silver beech and kowhai trees growing along river terraces.

The area has some interesting tramps; see the DOC pamphlet *Lake Sumner & Lewis Pass* ($2). Most tracks pass through beech forest with a backdrop of snow-capped mountains, lakes, and alpine tarns and rivers. The most popular tramps are around Lake Sumner in the Lake Sumner Forest Park and the **St James Walkway** (66km; three to five days) in the Lewis Pass National Reserve. Subalpine conditions apply, so make sure you sign the intentions books at the huts.

Maruia Springs (03-523 8840; www.maruiasprings.co.nz; SH7; d $179-199, f $259; @) is a small, Japanese-style hot-spring resort on the banks of the Maruia River, 69km from the Hanmer turn-off, with fairly spartan accommodation, a cafe-bar and a Japanese restaurant (breakfast & dinner only). Despite the name, the cheaper Garden View rooms actually offer the best mountain views. In the **thermal pools** (adult/child $19/9, free for guests), water with black mineral flakes of 'hot spring flowers' is pumped into a gender-segregated traditional Japanese bathhouse and outdoor rock pools. It's a magical setting during a winter snowfall, but mind the sandflies in summer. Massages (30/50 minutes $45/65) and private spa houses (per person 45 minutes for $25) are available.

SH7 continues to **Springs Junction**, where the Shenandoah Hwy (SH65) branches north to meet SH6 near Murchison, while SH7 continues west to Reefton and down to Greymouth. Springs Junction has a petrol station and cafe.

CENTRAL CANTERBURY

Two hours west from Christchurch on SH73 is Arthur's Pass National Park. The trans-island crossing from Christchurch to Greymouth over Arthur's Pass is covered by buses and the *TranzAlpine* train.

From Christchurch the road traverses the Canterbury Plains and then escalates rapidly into the Porters and Craigieburn skiing areas before following the Waimakariri and Bealey Rivers and Lakes Pearson and Grasmere to Arthur's Pass. Southwest of Christchurch (reached by SH73 and SH77) is the Mt Hutt ski resort and Methven.

Craigieburn Forest Park

Accessed from SH73, this forest park is 110km northwest of Christchurch and 42km south of Arthur's Pass. The park has many walking tracks, with longer tramps possible in the valleys west of the Craigieburn Range; see the DOC pamphlet *Craigieburn Forest Park: Day Walks* ($1). The surrounding country is also suitable for skiing and rock climbing. Dominating the vegetation is beech, tussock and turpentine scrub, and even a few patches of South Island edelweiss *(Leucogenes grandiceps)*.

Craigieburn has a rise of 503m so is one of NZ's best skiing areas, with wild-country slopes that suit advanced skiers.

Near Broken River Bridge is the **Cave Stream Scenic Reserve**, with a 594m-long cave with a small waterfall at one end. Take all the necessary precautions (two light sources per person etc) if you're doing the one-hour walk in waist-deep cold water through the pitch-black cave. For details, get the DOC brochure *Cave Stream Scenic Reserve* (50c). The reserve is in the **Castle Hill** area, with prominent limestone outcrops loved by rock climbers and boulderers. Scenes from *The Chronicles of Narnia: The Lion, the Witch and the Wardrobe* were filmed in the area.

Sleeping & Eating

Smylie's Accommodation HOSTEL $
(03-318 4740; www.smylies.co.nz; Main Rd; dm/s/d $28/45/60; @) This welcoming YHA-associated hostel and ski lodge is in the town of Springfield, around 30km southeast of Craigieburn. A handful of self-contained motel units ($85 to $120) and a three-bedroom cottage ($180) are also available. In winter, packages including ski-equipment rental and ski-field transport are on offer. Nearby year-round activities include jetboating, rock climbing, mountain biking and horse trekking.

Flock Hill Lodge LODGE $$
(03-318 8196; www.flockhill.co.nz; SH73; sites from $30, dm/d $31/155; @) This is a high-country sheep station 44km east of Arthur's Pass, adjacent to Lake Pearson and the Craigieburn Forest Park. Backpackers can stay in rustic shearers' quarters, while large groups can opt for two-bedroom motel units or large cottages with kitchenettes. After fishing, exploring, horse riding or mountain

biking, recharge in the cosy bar-restaurant. Unpowered camping sites are also available.

Wilderness Lodge LODGE $$$
(☎03-318 9246; www.wildernesslodge.co.nz; SH73; s incl breakfast $499-649 d incl breakfast $798-998; @) Luxurious lodge on a mountain-beech-speckled sheep station (2400 hectares in size), 16km east of Arthur's Pass. Alpine views and the world's longest driveway produce an absolute middle-of-nowhere atmosphere, and standalone studios with private spa baths feel even more remote. Walking, birdwatching and canoeing are all on tap.

Bealey Hotel HOTEL $$
(☎03-318 9277; www.bealeyhotel.co.nz; s/d without bathroom $60/80, units $150-180; @) Just 12km east of Arthur's Pass, tiny Bealey is famous for a hoax by the local pub owner in 1993. He reckoned he'd seen a real live moa, hence the bogus Big Bird statue standing on a rocky outcrop. There are self-contained motel units and the budget and basic Moa Lodge. Enjoy expansive alpine views from the Mad Moa restaurant.

Famous Sheffield Pie Shop BAKERY $
(Main Rd; pies $4-6) This roadside bakery in the quiet Canterbury Plains hamlet of Sheffield turns out some of NZ's best pies. There are more than 20 different varieties on offer.

Arthur's Pass

POP 62

Arthur's Pass village is 4km from the pass of the same name and is NZ's highest-altitude settlement. The 924m pass was used by Maori to reach Westland, but its European discovery was made by Arthur Dobson in 1864, when the Westland gold rush created the need for a crossing over the Southern Alps from Christchurch. A coach road was completed within a year, but later on the coal and timber trade demanded a railway, duly completed in 1923.

The town is a handy base for tramps, climbs, views and wintertime skiing in Arthur's Pass National Park. Online see www.arthurspass.com. For specific information on weather conditions see www.softrock.co.nz.

Sights & Activities

Near DOC is a small interfaith chapel, with wonderful views.

Day tramps offer 360-degree views of snowcapped peaks, many of them over 2000m; the highest is Mt Murchison (2400m). There are huts on the tramping tracks and several areas suitable for camping. Tramping is best in the drier months (January to April). The leaflet *Walks in Arthur's Pass National Park* ($2) details walks to scenic places including **Devils Punchbowl Waterfall** (one hour return), **Temple Basin** (three hours return) and the **Bealey Spur** track (four to six hours return) with expansive views of the Waimakariri River valley and surrounding mountains. The pleasant **Dobson Nature Walk** (30 minutes return) is best from November to February when the alpine flowers are blooming. Recommended for fit trampers is the **Avalanche Peak** track (six to eight hours return). Longer tramps with superb alpine backdrops include the **Goat Pass Track** (two days) and the longer and more difficult **Harman Pass** and **Harpers Pass Tracks**. These tracks require previous tramping experience as flooding can make the rivers dangerous and the weather is extremely changeable; ask DOC first.

Sleeping & Eating

Camp within Arthur's Pass township at the basic **public shelter** (adult/child $6/3), opposite DOC, where there's running water, a sink, tables and toilets. At the time of research, camping was free at **Klondyke Corner**, 8km south of Arthur's Pass, where there is a toilet. Note that the water here must be boiled before drinking.

Arthurs Pass Village B&B B&B $$
(☎021 394 776; www.arthurspass.org.nz; d $100;) This former railway cottage is now a cosy B&B, complete with open fire, free-range bacon and eggs and homebaked bread for breakfast, and the company and conversation of the interesting owners. Ask Geoff about his time working for Greenpeace, and tuck into tasty, home-cooked dinners like organic roast chicken ($35). The two guest bedrooms share one bathroom.

Mountain House YHA Backpackers & Cottages HOSTEL $
(☎03-318 9258, 027 419 2354; www.trampers.co.nz; SH73; dm $27-29, s/d/tr/q $79/82/99/124, cottage d $140 plus $15 per person; @) Excellent dorms and private rooms on one side of the highway, and older, but still comfortable, rooms across the road. The owners also provide transport to trailheads. Self-

contained cottages with cosy open fires are also available. Bookings are recommended from November to April. You can sometimes camp ($20 per person) near the cottages. Phone ahead to check availability first.

Arthur's Pass Alpine Motel MOTEL **$$**
(☎03-318 9233; www.apam.co.nz; SH73; d $115-135; @☜) In the southern part of town, with comfortable motel units (some recently refurbished) and with new beds. If you're snowed in there's a good DVD library and Freeview satellite TV.

Arthur's Pass Village Motel MOTEL **$$**
(☎021 131 0616, 03-318 9233; www.apmotel.co.nz; SH73; d $145) Centrally located, with two luxury units with cosy leather furniture and warm, natural colours. Booking ahead from November to April is highly recommended.

Wobbly Kea CAFÉ **$$**
(www.wobblykea.co.nz; SH73; meals $15-32) This friendly cafe-bar serves steaks, pasta and pizza. Takeaway pizza ($28) is also available. Breakfast at the Wobbly Kea ($10 to $18) is a local tradition designed to set you up for the most active of days.

Arthur's Pass Store CAFE **$**
(SH73; @☜) Sells sandwiches, burgers, pies and good breakfasts.

Information

There is no ATM in Arthur's Pass. Limited groceries and petrol are very expensive, so fill up in Christchurch or Greymouth.

DOC Arthur's Pass Visitor Centre (☎03-318 9211; www.doc.govt.nz; SH73; ⊗8am-5pm) Information on all park tramps, including route guides for longer hut-lined tramps. It doesn't make onward bookings or reservations, but can help with local accommodation and transport information. The centre screens a 17-minute video on the history of Arthur's Pass. Purchase detailed topographical maps ($9) and hire locator beacons ($30, highly recommended). DOC also advises on the park's often savagely changeable weather. Check conditions here and fill out an intentions card before venturing out. Sign in again after returning to avoid a search party being organised.

Getting There & Around

Arthur's Pass sees buses travelling between Christchurch (two hours) and Greymouth (2½ hours). **Atomic Shuttles** (www.atomictravel.co.nz) and **West Coast Shuttle** (☎027 492 7488, 03-768 0028; www.westcoastshuttle.co.nz) stop here; check their websites for current departure ponts in Christchurch. Bus tickets are sold at the Arthur's Pass Store.

The *TranzAlpine* train runs between Christchurch and Greymouth via Arthur's Pass.

The road over the pass was once winding and very steep, but the spectacular Otira viaduct has removed many of the treacherous hairpin bends.

Mountain House Shuttle (☎03-318 9258, 027 419 2354), based at Mountain House YHA Backpackers, provides transport to various trailheads. See the Trampers Shuttle tab on www.trampers.co.nz for costs.

Methven

POP 1140

Methven is busiest in winter, when it fills up with snow-sports fans heading to nearby Mt Hutt. In summer, Methven town is a laid-back option with quieter (and usually cheaper) accommodation than elsewhere in the country, and a 'what shall I do today?' range of warm-weather activities.

Activities

Ask at the i-SITE about walking trails, horse riding, mountain biking, fishing, scenic helicopter flights and jetboating through the nearby Rakaia Gorge.

Aoraki Balloon Safaris BALLOONING
(☎0800 256 837, 03-302 8172; www.nzballooning.co.nz; flights $385) Early-morning combos of snowcapped peaks and a champagne breakfast.

Methven Heliskiing SKIING
(☎03-302 8108; www.methvenheli.co.nz; Main St; 5-run day trips $950; ⊗May-Oct) Trips include guide service, safety equipment and lunch.

Black Diamond Safaris SKIING
(☎03-302 1884; www.blackdiamondsafaris.co.nz; ⊗May-Oct) Provides access to uncrowded club ski fields by 4WD. Prices start at $150 for 4WD transport only, while $270 gets you transport, a lift pass, guiding and lunch.

Skydiving NZ SKYDIVING
(☎03-302 9143; www.skydivingnz.com; Pudding Hill Airfield) Offers tandem jumps from 3600m ($440).

Sleeping

Some accommodation is closed in summer, but the following are open year-round, with lower prices often available outside the ski season. During the ski season, it pays to book well ahead, especially for budget accommodation.

Alpernhorn Chalet HOSTEL **$**
(☎03-302 8779; www.alpenhorn.co.nz; 44 Allen St; dm $28, d $60-85; @📶) This small, inviting home has a conservatory housing an indoor garden and a spa pool; a log fire, free internet and complimentary espresso coffee seal the deal. Bedrooms are spacious and brightly coloured, there's lots of warm, natural wood, and an in-house reflexologist and massage therapist are on hand if you've come a-cropper on the slopes.

Beluga Lodge B&B **$$**
(☎03-302 8290; www.beluga.co.nz; 40 Allen St; d incl breakfast $165-260; @) Highly relaxing B&B with king-sized beds, fluffy bathrobes, luscious bathrooms and private decks. Extreme privacy-seekers should consider the garden suite, with its own patio and barbecue. A four-bedroom cottage is also available ($275 to $375 per night; minimum three-night stay from June to October).

Glenthorne Station LODGE **$$**
(☎0800 926 868, 03-318 5818; www.glenthorne.co.nz; lodges per person $25-35, holiday house per person $50) This beautifully isolated 25,800-hectare sheep station is 60km northwest of Methven, on the northern shore of Lake Coleridge. The high-country accommodation ranges from budget lodges to a self-contained holiday house. Activities include 4WD tours, fishing, horse riding and walking.

Redwood Lodge LODGE **$**
(☎03-302 8964; www.snowboardnz.com; 3 Wayne Pl; r $58-130; @📶) Turkish rugs and a bright decor give this family-friendly spot with single, double, triple and quad rooms plenty of charm. En suite rooms with TV provide privacy and there's a huge shared TV lounge and kitchen. Larger rooms can be reconfigured to accommodate families.

Big Tree Lodge LODGE **$**
(☎03-302 9575; www.bigtreelodge.co.nz; 25 South Belt; dm $30-32, d/tw/tr $69/69/95; @📶) Transformed from a one-time vicarage, this relaxed lodge has lovely, wood-trimmed bathrooms and a comfy, heritage ambience. Long-term discounts are available. Tucked just behind is Little Tree Studio, a self-contained unit sleeping up to four people ($90/110 summer/winter).

Flashpackers Methven YHA HOSTEL **$**
(☎03-302 8999; www.methvenaccommodation.co.nz; cnr McMillan & Bank Sts; dm/d $25/70, d with bathroom $80; @📶) This YHA-associated lodge has appealing dining and living areas, a large kitchen and indoor and outdoor spa pools. Prices include breakfast and equipment hire (bikes, golf clubs, fishing gear etc).

Eating & Drinking

Café Primo CAFE **$$**
(38 McMillan St; meals $10-18) A treasure trove of retro Kiwiana, and the coolest part is that everything is for sale. Sandwiched in and around the souvenir teaspoons and Buzzy Bee bookends are tasty cakes, panini and legendary bacon and egg sandwiches. You'll also unearth Methven's best coffee. Grab a sunny table in the recently added courtyard and kick-start your day with super-healthy granola.

Cafe 131 CAFE **$**
(Main St; meals $10-20; 📶) A warm space with polished timber and leadlight windows. Serves up all-day breakfasts, good-value platters and soup, pasta, and sandwiches. Beer and wine takes over later in the day. There's also paid wi-fi.

Blue Pub PUB **$$**
(www.thebluepub.co.nz; Main St; mains $15-30) Drink at the bar crafted from a huge slab of native timber, or tuck into robust meals like sausage and mash or blue cod in the quieter restaurant. Challenge the locals to a game of pool or watch rugby on the big screen (most Friday and Saturday nights from March to June). Across the road, the Brown Pub is the rowdier choice of locals.

Supervalue Supermarket SUPERMARKET **$**
(cnr The Mall & MacMillan St; ⏰7am-9pm) Good wine and beer selection.

Entertainment

Cinema Paradiso CINEMA
(☎03-302 1957; www.cinemaparadiso.co.nz; Main St; adult/child $14/10) Quirky cinema with an arthouse skew.

Information

Methven i-SITE (☎03-302 8955; www.methveninfo.co.nz; 160 Main St; ⏰9am-5pm; @) Books accommodation, skiing packages, transport and activities.

Medical Centre (☎03-302 8105; Main St)

Getting There & Around

Methven Travel (☎03-302 8106, 0800 684 888; www.methventravel.co.nz; 93 Main St) picks up from Christchurch (one hour; once daily Monday, Wednesday, Friday and Saturday Nov-Apr; up to three times daily May-Oct). Christchurch airport departures are also available.

Shuttles operate from Methven to Mt Hutt ski field in winter ($38).

Mt Somers

Mt Somers is a small settlement just off SH72, the main road between Geraldine and Mt Hutt. The **Mt Somers Subalpine Walkway** (17km, 10 hours) traverses the northern face of Mt Somers, linking the popular picnic spots of Sharplin Falls and Woolshed Creek. Trail highlights include volcanic formations, Maori rock drawings, deep river canyons and botanical diversity. There are two huts on the tramp: Pinnacles Hut and Woolshed Creek Hut ($10 each). This route is subject to sudden changes in weather and precautions should be taken. Download the Mt Somers track guide from www.doc.govt.nz. Hut tickets and information are available at the **Mt Somers General Store** (Pattons Rd). There are other shorter walks in the area.

The **Mt Somers Holiday Park** (☎03-303 9719; www.mountsomers.co.nz; Hoods Rd; sites from $22, cabins $54-79) is small and well maintained.

At the highway turn-off to Mt Somers is **Stronechrubie** (☎03-303 9814; www.stronechrubie.co.nz; SH72; d $120-160), with studios and luxury chalets. The intimate restaurant (mains $33 to $38, open 6.30pm to late Wednesday to Saturday, noon to 2pm Sunday) features excellent Canterbury lamb and local venison and duck. Consider a DB&B package (per two people $230 to $280).

SOUTH CANTERBURY

SH1 heading south from Christchurch along the coast passes through the port city of Timaru on its way to Dunedin, and carries a lot of traffic. The inland route along SH8 is also busy, but showcases the stunning landscapes of the Mackenzie Country. Studded with the intense blue lakes of Tekapo and Ohau, SH80 veers off at Twizel in the Mackenzie Country to hug Lake Pukaki all the way to the magnificent heights of Aoraki/Mt Cook National Park.

Timaru

POP 26,750

The port city of Timaru is a handy stopping-off point halfway between Christchurch and Dunedin. Many travellers prefer to kick on 85km further south to the smaller, more charming Oamaru, but a few good restaurants and good-value motels means Timaru is worthy of a spot of travellers' R&R. The recently opened Te Ana Maori Rock Art Centre is also of interest for travellers seeking to understand NZ's indigenous Maori heritage.

The town's name comes from the Maori name Te Maru, meaning the 'Place of Shelter'. No permanent settlement existed here until 1839, when the Weller brothers from Sydney set up a whaling station. The *Caroline,* a sailing ship that picked up whale oil, gave the picturesque bay its name.

Sights

Te Ana Maori Rock Art Centre MUSEUM
(☎0800 468 3262; www.teana.co.nz; 2 George St; adult/child/family $20/10/50; ⏲10am-3pm) Interesting showcase of the significance of Maori rock art to the Ngai Tahu tribe. Passionate Maori guides really bring the innovative exhibition to life. You can also take a three-hour excursion (departing 3pm, adult/child/family $125/50/250) around the surrounding region to see isolated rock art in situ. Prior booking is essential for the tours. Entrance is via the i-SITE.

South Canterbury Museum MUSEUM
(www.timaru.govt.nz; Perth St; admission by donation; ⏲10am-4.30pm Tue-Fri, 1.30-4.30pm Sat & Sun) Historical and natural artefacts of the region, including a replica of the aeroplane designed and flown by local pioneer aviator and inventor Richard Pearse. Many believe his mildly successful attempts at manned flight came before the Wright brothers first flew in 1903.

FREE **Aigantighe Art Gallery** GALLERY
(www.aigantighe.org; 49 Wai-iti Rd; ⏲10am-4pm Tue-Fri, noon-4pm Sat & Sun) One of the South Island's largest public galleries, with a 900-piece collection of NZ and European art from the past four centuries set up in a 1908 mansion, and adorned externally by a sculpture garden (always open). The gallery's Gaelic name means 'at home' and is pronounced 'egg-and-tie'.

Timaru

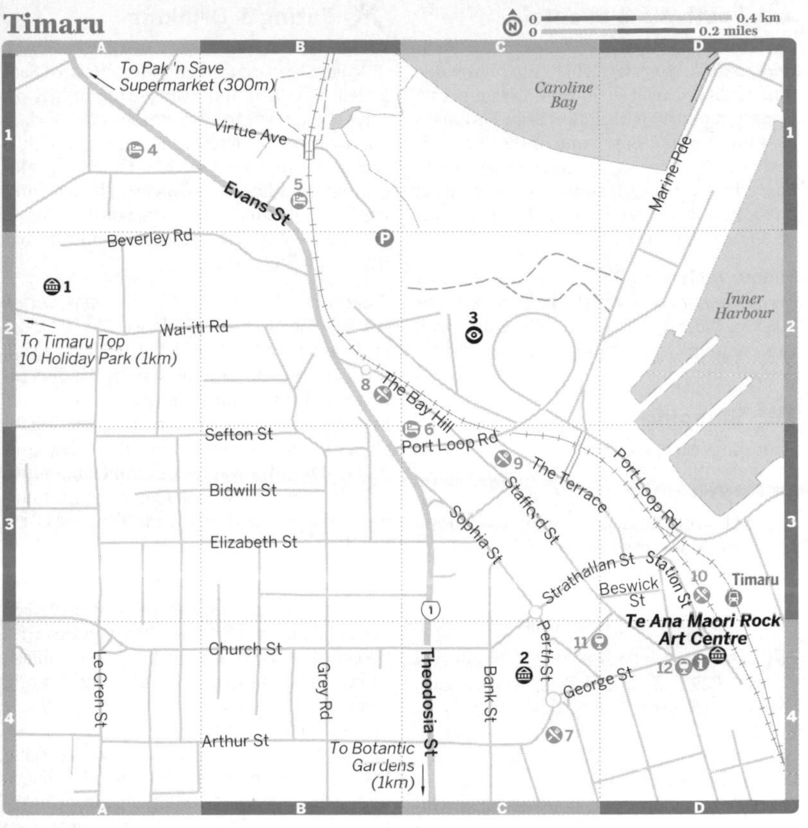

Timaru

Top Sights
Te Ana Maori Rock Art Centre D4

Sights
1 Aigantighe Art Gallery A2
2 South Canterbury Museum C4
3 Trevor Griffiths Rose Garden C2

Sleeping
4 Anchor Motel and Timaru Backpackers A1
5 Baywatch Motor Lodge B1
6 Panorama Motor Lodge C3

Eating
7 Arthur St Café C4
8 Fusion B2
9 Ginger & Garlic C3
10 Off the Rail Café D3

Drinking
11 Petite Wine & Dine C4
12 Speight's Ale House D4

FREE **Botanic Gardens** GARDENS
(cnr King & Queen Sts; 8am-dusk) Established in 1864, Timaru's Botanic Gardens feature ponds, a conservatory and a notable collection of roses and native tree ferns. The gardens are south of town; enter from Queen St.

FREE **Trevor Griffiths Rose Garden** GARDENS
(Caroline Bay; open daylight hours) Rose fans should visit the Trevor Griffiths Rose Garden, with more than 1000 romantic blooms set around arbours and water features. The finest display is from December to February.

Festivals & Events

Christmas Carnival MUSIC
(www.carolinebay.org.nz) This fun, crowded Christmas Carnival (held from December 26 to early January) with concerts and events is held on Caroline Bay – one of the few safe, sheltered beaches on the east coast. South Canterbury's biggest annual summer bash celebrated its centenary in 2012, so it must be doing something right.

Timaru Festival of Roses CULTURAL
(www.festivalofroses.co.nz) The Festival of Roses fills two blooming weeks in November with garden tours, exhibitions and floral workshops.

Sleeping

Panorama Motor Lodge MOTEL $$
(03-688 0097, 0800 103 310; www.panorama.net.nz; 52 The Bay Hill; d from $135; @) Modern, well-appointed units with spa, sauna and gym. More greenery to soften the concrete would be nice, but Caroline Bay Park and Bay Hill's cafes are a short walk away. Family units are particularly spacious.

Baywatch Motor Lodge MOTEL $$
(0800 929 828, 03-688 1886; www.baywatchtimaru.co.nz; 7 Evans St; d $130-145; @) Busy Evans St is wall-to-wall motels, but one of the best options along Timaru's main drag is the Baywatch Motor Lodge. Units here offer fantastic bay views, and double-glazed windows mask the worst of the road noise from SH1, though it's worth asking for a room at the back if you're a light sleeper.

Anchor Motel and Timaru Backpackers MOTEL $
(03-684 5067; www.anchormotel.co.nz; 42 Evans St; backpackers dm/d $25/60, motels s/d $49/99; @) Following a recent refurbishment and with energetic new management, the sprawling Anchor complex is a good-value spot a shortish walk from Caroline Bay. Rooms and dorms are simple, but kept spotless, and just fine if you're transiting north or south.

Timaru Top 10 Holiday Park HOLIDAY PARK $
(03-684 7690, 0800 242 121; www.timaruholidaypark.co.nz; 154a Selwyn St; sites from $34, units $65-120; @) Parkland site with excellent amenities and a golf course next door that's included in your park tariff.

Eating & Drinking

Arthur St Café CAFE $
(8 Arthur St; snacks & meals $15-18; closed Sun) Excellent coffee and cruisy Kiwi dub is always a good way to ease into the day. Decked out with retro furniture and tinged with a green and sustainable ethic, Timaru's funkiest eatery offers sandwiches, bagels and world-famous-in-Timaru breakfasts. There's also occasional live music with an alternative and folkie spin.

Fusion RESTAURANT $$
(64 Bay Hill; lunch $17-20, dinner $26-30) Cool and cosmopolitan in red and black, Fusion's modern cuisine channels both Mediterranean and Asian flavours. Pair a Kiwi craft beer with shared plates of kofta or felafel ($12.50), or partner confit duck leg and Asian slaw with a spicy Central Otago pinot gris. Between meals it's a good spot for coffee and cake, complete with views of Caroline Bay.

Ginger & Garlic MODERN NZ $$
(03-688 3981; www.gingerandgarlic.co.nz; 335 Stafford St; mains $25-34; noon-2pm Mon-Fri & 5-10pm Mon-Sat) Timaru's take on sophisticated food is showcased at this long-running local favourite. Asian-influenced standouts include roasted prawn and sesame toast, and tandoori-style marinated chicken with a laksa cream. The menu also includes dishes with a European and Middle Eastern influence. Try the garlic-crusted Canterbury lamb with a walnut and pumpkin salad. Desserts include a mighty mandarin-infused crème brûlée.

Petite Wine & Dine BAR
(18 Royal Arcade; 4pm-late Tue-Sat) The coolest spot in town is concealed in an arcade showcasing Timaru's most funky and interesting shopping. Look forward to cannily mixed cocktails and a stellar array of local and international beers. Tuck into shared antipasto platters ($29) and gourmet pizzas ($12 to 25). A guaranteed bogan-free zone.

Speight's Ale House PUB
(www.timarualehouse.co.nz; 2 George St) Hands down the best of Timaru's pubs, and also worth a visit to see the 19th-century Landing Building. Hearty pub meals – burgers, steak and seafood – and the full range of Speight's beers on tap definitely make a trek downtown worthwhile.

Off the Rail Café CAFE $

(Station St; meals $10-20; @ 📶) This funky licensed cafe is at the train station. Fire up the jukebox crammed with '70s tunes, and sample Kiwi baked goodies and more contemporary globally influenced dishes. It's open late for drinks and occasional live music on Saturday night.

Pak'n Save Supermarket SUPERMARKET $

(cnr Ranui & Evans Sts; ⏲8am-9pm Mon-Fri, to 7pm Sat & Sun) On the main road north.

Information

Timaru i-SITE (☎03-687 9997; www.southisland.org.nz; 2 George St; ⏲8.30am-5pm Mon-Fri, 10am-3pm Sat & Sun; @) Activities, information, and transport and accommodation bookings. Inside is the Te Ana Maori Rock Art Centre.

Getting There & Away

InterCity (www.intercity.co.nz) stops outside the train station, with buses to Christchurch (2½ hours), Oamaru (one hour) and Dunedin (three hours).

Atomic Shuttles (www.atomictravel.co.nz) stop in Timaru en route to Christchurch and Dunedin. Departs Timaru from the i-SITE.

There are no direct buses from Timaru to Lake Tekapo and Mt Cook – you'll need to first get to Geraldine or Fairlie to catch buses to the Mackenzie Country. Ask at the i-SITE.

Inland & Mackenzie Country

Heading to Queenstown and the southern lakes from Christchurch means a turn off SH1 onto SH79, a scenic route towards the high country and the Aoraki/Mt Cook National Park's eastern foothills. The road passes through Geraldine and Fairlie before joining SH8, which heads over Burkes Pass to the blue intensity of Lake Tekapo.

The expansive high ground from which the scenic peaks of Aoraki/Mt Cook National Park escalate is known as Mackenzie Country, after the legendary James 'Jock' Mackenzie, who ran his stolen flocks in this then-uninhabited region in the 1840s. When he was finally caught, other settlers realised the potential of the land and followed in his footsteps. The first people to traverse the Mackenzie were the Maori, trekking from Banks Peninsula to Otago hundreds of years ago.

See www.mtcooknz.com and www.mackenziewinter.co.nz for more information.

GERALDINE

POP 2210

Geraldine has a country-village atmosphere with pretty private gardens and an active arts scene.

The **Geraldine i-SITE** (☎03-693 1006; www.gogeraldine.co.nz; cnr Talbot & Cox Sts; ⏲8.30am-5pm Mon-Fri, 10am-4pm Sat & Sun) has brochures detailing the gardens and galleries in town, and can book rural B&Bs and farmstays.

Sights

Vintage Car & Machinery Museum MUSEUM

(178 Talbot St; adult/child $8/free; ⏲10am-4pm mid-Sep–early Jun) The Vintage Car & Machinery Museum has more than 30 vintage and veteran cars from as far back as 1907. There's also a rare 1929 Spartan biplane.

FREE **Medieval Mosaic** MUSEUM

(www.1066.co.nz; 10 Wilson St; ⏲9am-5pm Mon-Fri, 10am-4pm Sat-Sun, closed Aug) The mind-bending Medieval Mosaic is ideal for fans of medieval history, word games and clever-clogs mathematics. If you're feeling chilly, the world's biggest woollen jersey is also on display.

Sleeping

Scenic Route Motor Lodge MOTEL $$

(☎0800 723 643; www.motelscenicroute.co.nz; 28 Waihi Terrace; d $125-160; @ 📶) This spacious motel is built in early-settler style, but the modern studios include double-glazing, flat-screen TVs and broadband internet. Larger studios have spa baths. You'll find Scenic Route at the northern end of town.

Rawhiti House HOSTEL $

(☎03-693 8252; www.rawhitihouse.co.nz; 27 Hewlings St; dm/s/d/tr $32/50/72/96; @ 📶) This former maternity hospital is now a sunny and spacious budget accommodation with solar electricity and colourfully furnished rooms. Mountain bikes are available, and guests rave about the comfy beds. It's above town off Peel St. If you ask when you book, they'll usually pick you up from the bus stop.

Geraldine Holiday Park HOLIDAY PARK $

(☎03-693 8147; www.geraldineholidaypark.co.nz; 39 Hislop St; sites from $24, cabins & units $45-105; @) This holiday park is set amid well-established trees across the road from a grassy oval. Besides budget cabins and self-contained units, there's a TV room and playground.

WORTH A TRIP

MT COOK SALMON FARM

Some 15km west of Lake Tekapo along SH8 is the signposted turn-off to the **Mt Cook Salmon Farm** (www.mtcookaplinesalmon.com; Canal Rd; adult/child $2/free), the highest salmon farm on the planet. The farm, 12km from the turn-off, operates in a hydroelectric canal system; a scenic drive along the canal has popular fishing spots and enjoys great views of Mt Cook. Stop at the farm to feed the fish, or pick up something smoked or fresh for dinner. The sashimi ($15) is the freshest you'll ever have, guaranteed.

Eating

Four Peaks Plaza (cnr Talbot & Cox Sts; ⏲9am-5pm) has a bakery, cafes and the Talbot Forest cheese shop. Also here is **Barker's** (www.barkers.co.nz), a fruit-products emporium selling (and sampling) kiwifruit wines, juices, sauces, smoothies and jams. Look out also for **Prenzel** (www.prenzelofgeraldine.co.nz), offering regular tastings of luscious fruit schnapps. Every Saturday during summer the town kicks into organic action with a **farmers market** (⏲9.30am-12.30pm).

Cafe Verde CAFE $

(45 Talbot St; mains $10-18; ⏲9am-4pm) Down the lane beside the old post office is this delightful garden cafe. Grown-ups will appreciate the tasty lunch options such as salmon in filo pastry, while the kids can go crazy – with a small, well-behaved 'c', please – in the sweet, postage stamp–sized playground.

Taste RESTAURANT $$

(www.tasterestaurant.co.nz; 7 Talbot St; mains $28-34; ⏲5pm-9pm Tue-Sat) The ritziest place in town features robust meals with a cosmopolitan spin. Try the Canterbury lamb rump dusted with *horopito* (a native NZ pepper). Gourmet pizzas or shared platters and a few local beers are more informal alternatives.

Village Inn PUB $$

(41 Talbot St; mains $15-24) Geraldine's best pub meals are available for alfresco dining in the garden bar at the Village Inn. Indecisive travellers may struggle with the 13 different beers on tap.

Coco SWEETS $

(10 Talbot St) For a quality sugar rush, visit Coco for handmade choccies, plus designer teas, coffee, hot chocolate and cake.

Entertainment

Geraldine Cinema CINEMA

(www.facebook.com/GeraldineCinema; Talbot St; adult/child $12/8) This quirky local cinema has old sofas and features a mix of Hollywood favourites and arthouse surprises. There's also occasional live music, usually with a folk, blues or country spin. Check Facebook for what's on.

PEEL FOREST

Peel Forest, 22km north of Geraldine (signposted off SH72), is among NZ's most important indigenous podocarp (conifer) forests. A road from nearby Mt Peel station leads to **Mesopotamia**, the run of English writer Samuel Butler (author of the satire *Erewhon*) in the 1860s.

Sights & Activities

The magnificent podocarp forest consists of totara, kahikatea and matai. One fine example of totara on the **Big Tree Walk** (30 minutes return) has a circumference of 9m and is over 1000 years old. Local bird life includes the rifleman, kereru (NZ pigeon), bellbird, fantail and grey warbler. There are also trails to **Emily Falls** (1½ hours return), **Rata Falls** (two hours return) and **Acland Falls** (one hour return).

Get the *Peel Forest Park: Track Information* brochure ($1) from Peel Forest Store.

Rangitata Rafts WHITEWATER RAFTING

(☎03-696 3534, 0800 251 251; www.rafts.co.nz; ⏲Oct-Apr) Rangitata goes white-water rafting on the Rangitata River, which contains exhilarating Grade V rapids. The company's base is at Mt Peel, 13km past the camping ground, and includes budget accommodation (sites/dm/d $20/25/48). Rafting trips can be joined from either the Rangitata lodge ($185) or from Christchurch ($195 including return transport), and include hot showers and a barbecue. Count on three hours on the river. A less frantic option for families is a Family Fun trip (adult/child $165/120) on the Grade II Lower Rangitata River. Inflatable kayaks are used, and you'll have around two hours on the river followed by a meal at the lodge.

Hidden Valleys WHITEWATER RAFTING
(☎03-696 3560; www.hiddenvalleys.co.nz; from $200; ⏲Sep-May) If you can't get enough of NZ's rivers, consider a longer three-day rafting expedition with Hidden Valleys. See its website for other rafting journeys exploring the most exciting and remote of the South Island's rivers. One-day rafting trips on the Rangitata River are also available.

Peel Forest Horse Trekking HORSE RIDING
(☎03-696 3703, 027 246 4423; www.peelforesthorsetrekking.co.nz; 1hr/2hr/half-day/full day $55/110/220/380) Horse trekking in the lush forest is on offer at Peel Forest Lodge, even if you're not staying there. Longer multiday treks ($982 to $1623), and accommodation and horse-trekking packages ($550) are available in conjunction with the lodge.

Sleeping & Eating

Peel Forest Lodge LODGE
(☎03-696 3703; www.peelforestlodge.co.nz; d $350) This self-contained log cabin–style lodge is deep in the forest. Bring your own food along for leisurely barbecues; meals are also available (breakfast/dinner per person $25/50) if you don't want cook. The owners don't live on-site so you'll need to book ahead.

DOC Camping Ground CAMPSITE
(☎03-696 3567; www.peelforest.co.nz; sites from $17 per person, cabins per person $22) The pleasant DOC camping ground beside the Rangitata River, about 3km beyond the Peel Forest Store, is equipped with basic two- to four-berth cabins, showers, a kitchen, laundry and card phone. Check in at the Peel Forest Store and ask about renting a mountain bike ($12/35 per hour/day).

Peel Forest Store
(☎03-696 3567; www.peelforest.co.nz; ⏲9am-6pm Mon-Thu, to 7pm Fri & Sat, 10am-5.30pm Sun) Stocks petrol, groceries and takeaway food, and has internet access. The attached Little Mt Peel Cafe & Bar is a cosy spot for steaks, burgers and beers. Also manages the DOC camping ground.

FAIRLIE

POP 725

Fairlie is often described as 'the gateway to the Mackenzie'. To the west the landscape changes as the road ascends Burkes Pass to the open spaces of Mackenzie Country. It's a great place to stop for lunch. Make time to stroll around the **Fairlie Heritage Museum** (www.fairlieheritagemuseum.co.nz; Mt Cook Rd; ⏲9am-5pm), packed full of fascinating mementos of NZ rural life.

The **Fairlie visitor information centre** (☎03-685 8496; www.fairlie.co.nz; Allandale St; ⏲10am-4pm) can provide information on nearby **mountain biking** tracks. There's **skiing** 29km northwest at Fox Peak in the Two Thumb Range. Mt Dobson, 26km northwest of Fairlie, is in a 3km-wide basin.

Sleeping & Eating

Fairlie Gateway Top 10 Holiday Park HOLIDAY PARK $
(☎0800 324 754, 03-685 8375; www.fairlietop10.co.nz; 10 Allandale Rd; sites from $40, units $60-129; @📶) Tranquil, creek-side park that's perfect for families, with mini-golf and a large playground for the kids. Fishing gear is available for hire. Options range from campsites to motel units.

Pinewood Motels MOTEL $$
(☎03-685 8599, 0800 858 599; www.pinewoodmotels.co.nz; 25-27 Mt Cook Rd; d $99-115; 📶) Comfortable, good-value and self-contained units, recently redecorated, and with Sky TV and new flat-screen TVs.

Eat Deli & Bar CAFE $$
(www.eatdeliandbar.co.nz; 76 Main St; mains $10-20; ⏲8am-5pm Tue-Sun; @) Family-friendly, with a kids' play area, Eat also drags in grown-ups with its excellent coffee and counter food, often with a subtle Asian spin. More robust appetites should go for a steak sandwich ($19). There's also beer, wine and complimentary internet access.

Old Library Café CAFE $$
(6 Allandale Rd; dinner $18-35; @) Damaged in a fire in 2011, this cafe-restaurant in a former Andrew Carnegie library opened better than ever in 2012. Look forward to fresh, award-winning local food such as roasted Mackenzie rack of lamb or blue cod with a citrus butter. There's also a more casual all-day menu featuring pasta, salads and soups.

Whisk & Page CAFE $
(49 Mt Cook Rd; coffee & cake $5-7; ⏲closed Sat) Scones, chocolate brownies and damn fine coffee partner with a retro bookshop. You'll probably recognise a few of the iconic tomes from your childhood, and there's also a good selection of NZ-themed books.

LAKE TEKAPO

POP 315

At the southern end of its namesake lake, this town has unobstructed views across turquoise water and a backdrop of rolling hills and mountains.

Lake Tekapo is a popular stop on tours of the Southern Alps, with buses bound for Mt Cook and Queenstown allowing passengers to pop in for a quick ice cream or coffee. Rather than rushing on, it's actually worth staying to experience the region's glorious night sky from atop nearby Mt John.

Sights & Activities

Popular walks include the track to the summit of **Mt John** (three hours return), accessible from just beyond the camping ground. From there, continue on to Alexandrina and McGregor Lakes, making it an all-day walk. Other walks are detailed in the brochure *Lake Tekapo Walkway* ($1). Mountain bikes can be hired (per hour/half day $10/25) from Lakefront Backpackers Lodge and the Lake Tekapo YHA.

In winter, Lake Tekapo is a base for **downhill skiing** at Mt Dobson or Round Hill, and **cross-country skiing** on the Two Thumb Range.

Church of the Good Shepherd CHURCH
(⌚9am-5pm) The lakeside Church of the Good Shepherd was built of stone and oak in 1935, and is a firm favourite for weddings. Nearby is a statue of a collie dog, a tribute to the sheepdogs that helped develop the Mackenzie Country. It's at its scenic best before and after the tour buses, so come early morning or late afternoon.

Earth & Sky ASTRONOMY TOURS
(☎03-680 6960; www.earthandskynz.com; SH1; stargazing adult/child $105/60) Thanks to clear skies and its distance from any main towns, Lake Tekapo has top-notch stargazing, and the area is known as one of the finest spots on the planet to explore the heavens. Departure times vary, so check when you book. On some night tours visitors can use their own cameras to delve into astrophotography with local photographer Fraser Gunn (www.laketekapo.cc). Forty-minute daytime tours (adult/child $50/25) of the University of Canterbury observatory also operate on demand from 10am to 4pm.

Alpine Springs & Spa DAY SPA
(☎0800 353 8283; www.alpinesprings.co.nz; 6 Lakeside Dr; hot pools adult/child $18/10; ⌚10am-9pm) Open all year round, with hot pools scattered amid quickly growing native trees. Private pools and saunas ($26 per hour) are also available, and spa packages start at $120. 'Skate and Soak' combo deals are available at the adjacent Winter Park. There's a good cafe (snacks $5 to $10, open 10am to 7pm) for coffee and cake, or a snack and something stronger.

Lake Tekapo Winter Park SNOW SPORTS
(☎0800 353 8283; www.alpinesprings.co.nz; 6 Lakeside Dr; skating adult/child $16/12, snow tubing adult/child $19/15; ⌚10am-9pm) At the western edge of the lake, the Lake Tekapo Winter Park at the Alpine Springs complex features a year-round skating rink and a winter mini-snow slope for gentle snow-tubing action. Loads-of-fun tubing is even available in summer on a specially constructed artificial slope.

Cruise Tekapo BOAT TOUR
(☎027 479 7675; www.cruisetekapo.co.nz; cruises per person $40-125, fishing per hour $60-80) Fishing and lake cruises from 25 minutes to two hours.

Mackenzie Alpine Horse Trekking HORSE RIDING
(☎0800 628 269; www.maht.co.nz; 1/2hr ride $50/90, half-/full day $140/260) Organises high-country equine explorations. Overnight camping trips ($350) are also available.

Tours

Air Safaris SCENIC FLIGHTS
(☎03-680 6880; www.airsafaris.co.nz; SH8) Does 50-minute 'Grand Traverse' flights over Mt Cook and its glaciers (adult/child $325/215), taking you up the Tasman Glacier, over the upper part of the Fox and Franz Josef Glaciers, and by Mts Cook, Tasman and Elie de Beaumont. A similar flight goes from Glentanner Park, but with higher prices (adult/child $375/265).

Tekapo Helicopters SCENIC FLIGHTS
(☎03-680 6229, 0800 359 835; www.tekapohelicopters.co.nz; SH8) Has five options, from a 25-minute flight ($195) to a 70-minute trip taking in Mt Cook and Fox and Franz Josef Glaciers ($500). All flights include icefield landings and views of Mt Cook.

Sleeping

Hamilton Drive and the surrounding streets in the eastern part of town have other good B&Bs.

Glacier Rock Bed and Breakfast B&B $$
(☎03-680 6669; www.glacierrock.co.nz; 35 Lochinver Ave; d incl breakfast $195-250; @📶) This architecturally designed home doubles as an art gallery. An artist's – or maybe an architect's – eye is evident in the spacious and airy rooms. Breakfast is served in sunny rooms with huge picture windows.

Tailor-Made-Tekapo Backpackers HOSTEL $
(☎03-680 6700; www.tailor-made-backpackers.co.nz; 9-11 Aorangi Cres; dm $29-33, s $60, d with/without bathroom $80/70; @) This hostel favours beds rather than bunks and is spread over a pair of well-tended houses on a peaceful street away from the main road. The interior is spick and span and there's a barbecue-equipped garden complete with well-established trees, lovely birdsong and a children's playground.

Lakefront Backpackers Lodge HOSTEL $
(☎03-680 6227; www.laketekapo-accommodation.co.nz; Lakeside Dr; dm/d $28/80; @📶) An impressive lakeside place owned by the nearby holiday park (about 1km from the township). Relax by the open fire in the comfy lounge area or take in the sensational views from the front deck. Rooms are modern and bathrooms are top-notch. Backpacker buses stop by so it can get a tad social.

Lake Tekapo Motels & Holiday Park HOLIDAY PARK $$
(☎0800 853 853, 03-680 6825; www.laketekapo-accommodation.co.nz; Lakeside Dr; sites from $30, units $60-150; @📶) Has a pretty and peaceful lakeside locale, plus accommocation options from basic cabins to motel units with full kitchens and Sky TV. Newer chalets come with shared picnic tables, barbecues and spectacular lake vistas.

Peppers Bluewater Resort MOTEL $$
(☎0800 275 373; www.peppers.co.nz; SH8; d from $140; 📶) A sprawling resort arrayed around rocky pools and tussocky gardens. Rooms are chic and modern – if sometimes on the small side – but last-minute online discounts make this a place worth considering.

Lake Tekapo YHA HOSTEL $
(☎03-680 6857; www.yha.co.nz; 3 Simpson Lane; dm $37-78, d&tw $96; @📶) Friendly, well-equipped little place with a living room adorned with open fireplaces, a piano and outstanding views across the lake to the mountains beyond.

Eating

The dining scene at Lake Tekapo has traditionally been lacklustre, but a few recent openings have improved culinary choices.

TOP CHOICE **Astro Café** CAFE $
(Mt John Observatory; coffee & cake $4-8, snacks $7-12) This glass-walled pavilion atop Mt John has spectacular 360-degree views across the entire Mackenzie Basin – quite possibly one of the planet's best locations for a cafe. Tuck into bagels with local Aoraki salmon, or fresh ham-off-the-bone sandwiches; the coffee and cake is pretty good, too. After dark, Astro becomes the location for astrophotography with local photographer Fraser Gunn.

Kohan JAPANESE $$
(SH8; lunch $10-16, dinner $22-35) The Japanese food at Kohan is among the South Island's best, and with a salmon farm just up the road, you know the sashimi is ultrafresh. Lunch specials are good value, and you should definitely leave room for their handmade green-tea ice-cream.

Pepe's ITALIAN $$
(SH8; mains $15-30; ⏲6pm-late) With large booths and walls decorated with skiing paraphernalia, the rustic Pepe's is a cosy little place, with good pizza and pasta. Some of the names are a bit naff (Vinnie's Venison or Spag Bol Bada Bing, anyone?), but the dishes are tasty, and later at night it becomes a good spot for a few quiet drinks.

Mackenzie's Bar & Grill PUB $$
(SH8; mains $22-34) Serving up interesting spins on steak, chicken and seafood, everything at Mackenzie's comes with a side order of stellar lake and mountain views. Robust dishes like lamb shanks and beef Wellington are the perfect response to an active day's adventuring. Even if you're dining somewhere else, pop in for a Monteiths Summer Ale or glass of sauvignon blanc.

Run 77 CAFE $
(SH8; mains $10-24) Relax on chunky wooden furniture and enjoy Tekapo's good coffee, or sandwiches, burgers and pies made from local salmon and organic, free-range beef and venison from the owner's high-country spread (the *real* Run 77). Soups, salads and anitipasto platters tick both the healthy and tasty boxes.

Four Square Supermarket SUPERMARKET
(SH8) Located beside a handy bakery.

Information

There are no ATMs at Lake Tekapo (p180).

Lake Tekapo i-SITE (☎03-680 6579; www.laketekapountouched.co.nz; Godley Hotel, SH8; ⌚9am-6pm) Accommodation, activities and transport information.

Getting There & Away

Southbound services to Queenstown (four hours) and Wanaka (three hours via Tarras), and northbound services to Christchurch (four hours), are offered by **Atomic Shuttles** (www.atomictravel.co.nz), **InterCity** (www.intercity.co.nz) and **Southern Link Coaches** (☎0508 458 835; www.southernlinkcoaches.co.nz).

Cook Connection (☎0800 266 526; www.cookconnect.co.nz) operates to Mt Cook (two hours) and Twizel (one hour). Travel can be over more than one day.

LAKE PUKAKI

On the southern shore of Lake Pukaki, 45km southwest of Lake Tekapo and 2km northeast of the turn-off to Mt Cook, is the **Lake Pukaki visitor information centre** (☎03-435 3280; www.mtcooknz.com; SH8; ⌚9am-6pm Oct-Apr, 10am-4pm May-Sep). The real highlight here is the sterling **lookout**, which on a clear day gives a picture-perfect view of Mt Cook and its surrounding peaks, with the ultrablue lake in the foreground.

TWIZEL

POP 1015

It wasn't long ago that New Zealanders maligned the town of Twizel, just south of Lake Pukaki. The town was built in 1968 to service construction of the nearby hydroelectric power station, and was due to be abandoned in 1984 when the construction project was completed. Now the town's residents are having the last laugh as new lakeside subdivisions have been built to take advantage of the area's relaxed lakes-and-mountains lifestyle. Accommodation and eating options are better value in Twizel than in Mt Cook, but you will be forgoing waking up right in the mountains.

The **Twizel i-SITE** (☎03-435 0066; www.twizel.info; Twizel Events Centre; ⌚9am-6pm Mon-Fri, noon-3pm Sat-Sun; @) is right in town, and there's an ATM in the main shopping area. Note there's no ATM at Mt Cook or Lake Tekapo. Self-drive travellers should also fill up with petrol in Twizel before heading to Mt Cook.

Sights & Activities

Nearby Lake Ruataniwha is popular for rowing, boating and windsurfing. Fishing in local rivers, canals and lakes is also big business and there are a number of guides in the region. Ask at the i-SITE.

Kaki Visitor Hide WILDLIFE RESERVE

(☎03-435 3124; adult/child $15/7; ⌚9.30am & 4.30pm late Oct-Apr) The rare *kaki* (black stilt bird) is found only in NZ, and a breeding program is aiming to increase the population at the Ahuriri Conservation Park. Just south of Twizel, the Kaki Visitor Hide gives you a close-up look at these elusive birds. Bookings are essential for the one-hour tour. Book at the Twizel i-SITE (you'll need your own transport).

Tours

Discovery Tours GUIDED TOUR

(☎03-435 0114, 0800 213 868; www.discoverytours.co.nz) Guided, small-group tours around the Mackenzie Country, including hiking and helibiking, plus a popular two-hour tour (adult/child $75/40) to the site of the Pelennor battlefield in the *Lord of the Rings* movies. You can even charge around like a mad thing wearing *LOTR* replica gear. A shorter one-hour *LOTR* tour (adult/child $55/30) is also available.

Helicopter Line SCENIC FLIGHTS

(☎03-435 0370, 0800 650 652; www.helicopter.co.nz; SH8, Pukaki Airport) Helicopter Line fly over the Mt Cook region, departing from the Lake Pukaki aiport. Sightseeing flights last from 25 minutes ($230) to 60 minutes ($535) and include a snow landing.

BLUE CRUSH

The blazing turquoise colour of Lake Pukaki, a characteristic it shares with other regional bodies of water such as Lake Tekapo, is due to 'rock flour' (sediment) in the water. This so-called flour was created when the lake's basin was gouged out by a stony-bottomed glacier moving across the land's surface, with the rock-on-rock action grinding out fine particles that ended up being suspended in the glacial melt water. This sediment gives the water a milky quality and refracts the sunlight beaming down, hence the brilliant colour.

Sleeping

Matuka Lodge B&B $$$
(☎03-435 0144; www.matukalodge.co.nz; Old Station Rd; d $465-535; @☎) Surrounded by farmland and mountain scenery, this luxury B&B blends modern design with antiques and Oriental rugs sourced on the owners' travels. A library of well-thumbed Lonely Planet guides is testament to their wanderlust, so look forward to interesting chats over pre-dinner drinks. Breakfast often includes salmon smoked just up the road at the Twizel Aoraki Smokehouse.

Omahau Downs B&B $$
(☎03-435 0199; www.omahau.co.nz; SH8; cottages d $135, B&B d $165; closed Jun-Aug) This rural homestead 2km north of Twizel has two cosy, self-contained cottages sleeping up to four, and a B&B lodge with sparkling, modern rooms and a deck looking out on the Ben Ohau Range. An essential experience is a moonlit, wood-fired outdoor bath ($20). Don't make the mistake of booking for only one night.

Mountain Chalet Motels MOTEL $$
(☎03-435 0785, 0800 629 999; www.mountain chalets.co.nz; Wairepo Rd; dm $25, d $95-135; ☎) A reader-recommended place with friendly owners and cosy, well-equipped, self-contained A-frame chalets. The cheapest units are studios, but there are a number of two-bedroom set-ups for larger groups or families. There's also a small, laid-back lodge that's perfect for backpackers.

Parklands Alpine Tourist Park HOLIDAY PARK $
(☎03-435 0507; www.parklandstwizel.co.nz; 122 Mackenzie Dr; sites from $36, dm $30, units $90-150; @☎) Offers green, flower-filled grounds and accommodation in a colourfully refurbished maternity hospital. There are a few basic cabins, and room for tents and campervans. The modern, self-contained cottages are particularly good value.

High Country Lodge & Backpackers HOSTEL $
(☎03-435 0671; www.highcountrylodge.co.nz; Mackenzie Dr; dm $29-35, d $50-90, units $125-155; @☎) This sprawling place used to be a basic hostel for construction workers, and is now trimmed with colourful curtains and bright bed linen. Beyond the dorms and the double rooms, a few standalone motel units also see your Kiwi pesos going a long way.

Eating & Drinking

Poppies Cafe CAFE $$
(www.poppiescafe.com; 1 Benmore Pl; breakfast & lunch $9-18, dinner $24-32) Lunch showcases lighter meals like salmon filo parcels, while dinner is a more formal experience with lamb rump or an Asian-style trio of duck; excellent pizzas ($18 to 26) occupy a tasty middle ground. Where possible, organic and locally sourced produce is used. Poppies is on the outskirts of town near the Mackenzie Country Inn.

Shawty's Café CAFE $$
(4 Market Pl; breakfast & lunch $9-19, dinner mains $21-31; ☎) Cool beats and craft beers create a mood that's surprisingly sophisticated for Twizel. Big breakfasts and gourmet pizzas ($12 to $25) are a good way to start and end an active day amid the surrounding alpine vistas. The adjacent Grappa Lounge has occasional DJs and live music from Wednesday to Saturday across summer.

Jasmine Thai Café THAI $$
(1 Market Pl; lunch $12, dinner $17-22; noon-2pm Tue-Sun & 5-9pm daily) Thailand comes to Twizel, and the zesty and zingy flavours of your favourite Southeast Asian beach holiday have travelled well to get this far inland. Alcohol is BYO, so grab a few cold beers from the Four Square supermarket to ease Jasmine's authentic Thai heat.

Getting There & Away

Onward services to Mt Cook (one hour) and Queenstown (three hours), and northbound services to Christchurch (five hours) are offered by **Atomic Shuttles** (www.atomictravel.co.nz) and **InterCity** (☎03-365 1113; www.intercity.co.nz).

Cook Connection (☎0800 266 526; www.cookconnect.co.nz) operates to Mt Cook (one hour) and Lake Tekapo (one hour). Travel can be over more than one day.

Naked Bus (www.nakedbus.com) travel to Christchurch and Queenstown/Wanaka.

LAKE OHAU & OHAU FORESTS

Six forests in the Lake Ohau area (Dobson, Hopkins, Huxley, Temple, Ohau and Ahuriri) are administered by DOC. The numerous walks in this vast recreation grove are detailed in the DOC pamphlet *Ohau Conservation Area* ($1); huts and camping areas are also scattered throughout for adventurous trampers.

Lake Ohau Lodge LODGE $$
(☎03-438 9885; www.ohau.co.nz; Lake Ohau Rd; s $99-175, d $105-200) Lake Ohau Lodge is idyllically sited on the western shore of rower-friendly Lake Ohau, 42km west of Twizel. Prices listed are for accommodation only (everything from backpacker-style to upmarket rooms with deck and mountain views). DB&B packages are good value. The lodge is the wintertime service centre for the Ohau Ski Field. In the summer it's a quieter retreat.

Aoraki/Mt Cook National Park

The spectacular 700-sq-km Aoraki/Mt Cook National Park, along with Fiordland, Aspiring and Westland National Parks, incorporates the Southwest New Zealand (Te Wahipounamu) World Heritage Area, which extends from Westland's Cook River down to Fiordland. Fenced in by the Southern Alps and the Two Thumb, Liebig and Ben Ohau Ranges, more than a third of the park has a blanket of permanent snow and glacial ice.

Of the 27 NZ mountains over 3050m, 22 are in this park. The highest is the mighty Mt Cook – at 3755m it's the tallest peak in Australasia. Known to Maori as Aoraki (Cloud Piercer), after an ancestral deity in Maori mythology, the mountain was named after James Cook by Captain Stokes of the survey ship HMS *Acheron*.

The Mt Cook region has always been the focus of climbing in NZ. On 2 March 1882, William Spotswood Green and two Swiss alpinists failed to reach the summit of Cook after an epic 62-hour ascent. But two years later a trio of local climbers – Tom Fyfe, George Graham and Jack Clarke – were spurred into action by the news that two well-known European alpinists were coming to attempt Cook, and set off to climb it before the visitors. On Christmas Day 1884 they ascended the Hooker Glacier and north ridge, a brilliant climb in those days, and stood on the summit.

In 1913, Australian climber Freda du Faur became the first woman to reach the summit. In 1948, Edmund Hillary's party, along with Tenzing Norgay, climbed the south ridge; Hillary went on to become the first to reach the summit of Mt Everest. Since then, most of the daunting face routes have been climbed. Among the region's many great peaks are Sefton, Tasman, Silberhorn, Malte Brun, La Perouse, Hicks, De la Beche, Douglas and the Minarets. Many can be ascended from Westland National Park, and there are climbers' huts on both sides of the divide.

Mt Cook is a wonderful sight, assuming there's no cloud in the way. Most visitors arrive on tour buses, stop at the Hermitage hotel for photos, and then zoom off back down SH80. Hang around to soak up this awesome peak and the surrounding landscape and to try the excellent short walks. On the trails, look for the thar, a goatlike creature and excellent climber; the chamois, smaller and of lighter build than the thar; and red deer. Summertime brings the large mountain buttercup (the Mt Cook lily), and mountain daisies, gentians and edelweiss.

Sights

TASMAN GLACIER
The Tasman Glacier is a predictably spectacular sweep of ice, but further down it's downright ugly. Normally as a glacier retreats it melts back up the mountain, but the Tasman is unusual because its last few kilometres are almost horizontal. In recent decades it has melted from the top down, exposing a jumble of stones, rocks and boulders and forming a lake. In other words, in its 'ablation zone' (where it melts), the Tasman is covered in a solid mass of debris, which slows down its melting rate and makes it unsightly.

Despite this considerable melt, the ice by the site of the old Ball Hut is still estimated to be over 600m thick. In its last major advance (17,000 years ago), the glacier crept south far enough to carve out Lake Pukaki. A later advance did not reach out to the valley sides, so the Old Ball Hut Rd runs between the outer valley walls and the lateral moraines of this later advance.

Like the Fox and Franz Josef Glaciers on the other side of the divide, the Mt Cook glaciers move fast. The **Alpine Memorial**, near the old Hermitage site on the Hooker Valley Track, commemorating one of the mountain's first climbing disasters. Three climbers were killed by an avalanche in 1914; only one of the bodies was recovered at the time, but 12 years later a second one melted out of the bottom of the Hochstetter Icefall, 2000m below where the party was buried, illustrating the glaciers' speed.

HERMITAGE
With fantastic views of Mt Cook, this is arguably the most famous hotel in NZ. Originally constructed in 1884, when the trip from

Aoraki/Mt Cook National Park

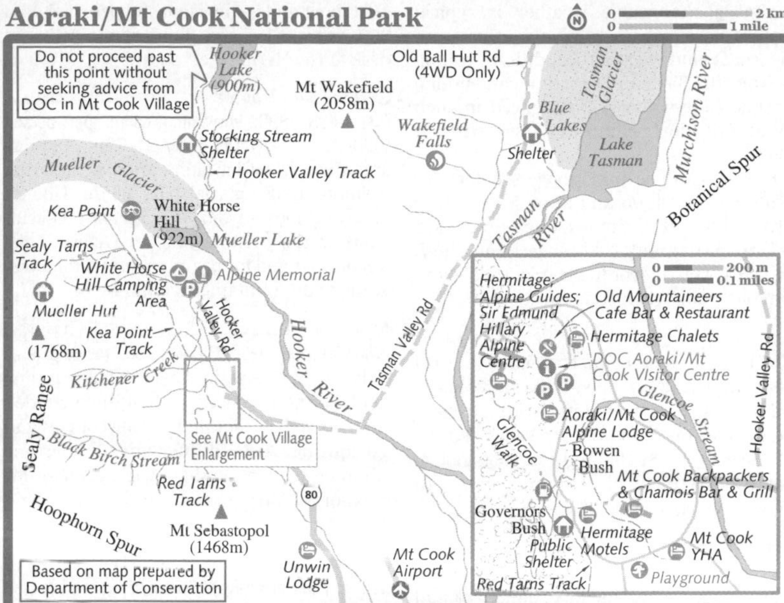

Christchurch took several days, the first hotel was destroyed in a flash flood in 1913. You can still see the foundations in Hooker Valley, 2km from the current Hermitage. Rebuilt, it survived until 1957, when it burnt down. The present Hermitage was built on the same site and a new wing was added for the new millennium.

Sir Edmund Hillary Alpine Centre MUSEUM, PLANETARIUM

(www.hermitage.co.nz; The Hermitage; 1 movie adult/child $18/8, 6 movies adult/child/family $27/14/54; ⌚7.30am-8.30pm) The Sir Edmund Hillary Alpine Centre opened in late 2007 – just three weeks before the January 2008 death of the man often regarded as the greatest New Zealander of all time. His commentary tracks were recorded only a few months before he died. The centre includes a full-dome digital planetarium showing four different digital presentations, and a cinema screen showing the *Mt Cook Magic* 3D movie and a fascinating 75-minute documentary about Sir Ed's conquest of Mt Everest. Another documentary, screened in the museum on a continual basis, reflects the charity and development work that Sir Edmund Hillary achieved in the decades after his conquest of Mt Everest in 1953. Admission to the museum itself is free.

Big Sky ASTRONOMY

(www.hermitage.co.nz; adult/child $50/25; ⌚nightly, weather permitting) NZ's southern sky is introduced by a 30-minute presentation in the Alpine Centre's digital planetarium, before participants venture outside to study the celestial real deal with telescopes, binoculars and an astronomy guide.

Activities

Various easy walks from the Hermitage area are outlined in the brochures available from DOC. Always be prepared for sudden weather changes. Longer walks are recommended only for those with mountaineering experience, as conditions at higher altitudes are severe and the tracks dangerous. Many people have died here, and most walkers shouldn't consider tackling these trails. If you intend on staying at any of the park's huts, it's essential to register your intentions at the DOC visitor centre and pay the hut fee.

For the experienced, there's unlimited scope for climbing, but regardless of your skills, take every precaution – more than 200 people have died in climbing accidents in the park. The bleak In Memoriam book in the visitor information centre begins with the first death on Mt Cook in 1907, and since then more than 70 climbers have died on the peak.

Highly changeable weather is typical around here; Mt Cook is only 44km from the coast and weather conditions rolling in from the Tasman Sea can mean sudden storms. Unless you're experienced in such conditions, don't climb anywhere without a guide.

Check with the park rangers before attempting any climb and always heed their advice. Fill out a climbers-intentions card before starting out – so rangers can check on you if you're overdue coming out – and sign out again when you return.

Kea Point TRAMPING
The trail to Kea Point (two-hours return from the village) is lined with native plant life and ends at a platform with excellent views of Mt Cook, the Hooker Valley and the ice faces of Mt Sefton and the Footstool. If you're lucky, you might share your walk with a few inquisitive kea.

Sealy Tarns TRAMPING
The walk to Sealy Tarns (three to four hours return) branches off the Kea Point Track and continues up the ridge to Mueller Hut (dorm $36), a comfortable 30-bunk hut with gas and cooking facilities.

Hooker Valley TRAMPING
The walk up the Hooker Valley (three hours return) crosses a couple of swing bridges to Stocking Stream and the terminus of the Hooker Glacier. After the second swing bridge, Mt Cook totally dominates the valley.

Tasman Glacier View Track TRAMPING
The Tasman Valley walks are popular for their views of the Tasman Glacier. Walks start at the end of the unsealed Tasman Valley Rd, 8km from the village. The Tasman Glacier View Track (50 minutes return) leads to a viewpoint on the moraine wall, passing the Blue Lakes (more green than blue these days) on the way.

Ultimate Hikes TRAMPING
(☎03-435 1899, 0800 686 800; www.ultimatehikes.co.nz; adult/child $108/67; ⏲Nov-Apr) Offers a day-long 8km walk from the Hermitage through the Hooker Valley to the terminal lake of the Hooker Glacier.

Glacier Explorers BOAT TOUR
(☎0800 686 800, 03-435 1809; www.glacierexplorers.com; per person $145) Heads out on the terminal lake of the Tasman Glacier. It starts with a 20-minute walk to the shore of Lake Tasman, where you board a custom-built MAC boat and get up close and personal with 300-year-old icebergs. Book at the activities desk at the Hermitage.

Glacier Sea-Kayaking KAYAKING
(☎03-435 1890; www.mtcook.com; per person $130-145; ⏲early Oct–mid-Apr) Has half-day and three-hour kayaking trips negotiating icebergs across glacial bays in the Hooker Valley. Choose from the Tasman Glacier Lake or the pristine Mueller Glacier Lake (recommended for beginner kayakers). Book at the Old Mountaineers Cafe.

Alpine Recreation TRAMPING
(☎0800 006 096, 03-680 6736; www.alpinerecreation.com) Based in Lake Tekapo, Alpine Recreation organises high-altitude guided treks, as well as mountaineering courses and ski touring. Also on offer are summertime climbing courses, and guided ascents of Mt Cook or Mt Tasman.

Alpine Guides SNOW SPORTS
(☎03-435 1834; www.alpineguides.co.nz; Retail Centre, The Hermitage) Ski-touring, heliskiing, and guided climbs and mountaineering courses.

Southern Alps Guiding SNOW SPORTS
(☎03-435 1890, 027 342 277; www.mtcook.com) Heliskiing and boarding options including the Tasman Glacier. Ask at the Old Mountaineers Cafe

Glentanner Horse Trekking HORSE RIDING
(☎03-435 1855; www.glentanner.co.nz; 1/2/3hr ride $60/80/150; ⏲Nov-Apr) Leads guided treks on a high-country sheep station. All levels of experience are welcome.

☞ Tours

Mount Cook Ski Planes SCENIC FLIGHTS
(☎0800 800 702, 03-430 8034; www.mtcookskiplanes.com) Based at Mt Cook Airport, offering 40-minute (adult/child $405/295) and 55-minute (adult/child $530/405) flights, both with snow landings. Flightseeing without a landing is a cheaper option; try the 25-minute Mini Tasman trip (adult/child $275/255).

Helicopter Line SCENIC FLIGHTS
(☎03-435 1801, 0800 650 651; www.helicopter.co.nz) From Glentanner Park, the Helicopter Line does 20-minute Alpine Vista flights ($215), an exhilarating 30-minute flight over the Ben Ohau Range ($295) and a 45-minute Mountains High flight over the Tasman Glacier and by Mt Cook ($399). All feature snow landings.

Tasman Valley 4WD Argo Tours 4WD TOUR
(☎0800 686 800, 03-435 1601; www.mountcooktours.co.nz; adult/child $75/38; ⊙year round) Offers a 90-minute Argo (actually an *8WD* all-terrain vehicle) tour checking out the Tasman Glacier and its terminal lake. Expect plenty of alpine flora and an interesting commentary along the way. Pre-book online (recommended) or book at the Hermitage hotel activities desk.

Sleeping

Accommodation is more expensive in Mt Cook Village than in Twizel, but the thrill of waking up so close to the mountains is definitely worth the additional expense.

Campers and walkers can use the **public shelter** (⊙8am-7pm Oct-Apr, to 5pm May-Sep) in the village, which has running water, toilets and coin-operated showers. Note that this shelter cannot be used for overnight stays.

Aoraki/Mt Cook Alpine Lodge LODGE $$
(☎03-435 1860; www.aorakialpinelodge.co.nz; Bowen Dr; d $159-189, tr/q $164/164, f $220-240; @☰) This modern lodge – with twin, double and family rooms – is the best place to stay in the village. With Turkish rugs and underfloor heating, you're guarenteed a warm welcome. Shared facilities include a huge lounge and kitchen area, and the alfresco barbecue with superb mountain views will have you arguing over who's going to grill the steak for dinner.

Mt Cook Backpackers HOSTEL $
(☎03-436 1653, 0800 100 512; www.mountcookbackpackers.co.nz; Bowen Dr; dm $35, d/tw $120, unit $170; @☰) Recently redecorated and refurbished, Mt Cook Backpackers is a sprawling, double-storey spot with four-bed dorms, twins and doubles, and self-contained flats with kitchens. All rooms have en suite facilities and feature private balconies, perfect for taking in the superb alpine views. Attached is the Chamois Bar & Grill.

Hermitage HOTEL $$$
(☎0800 686 800, 03-435 1809; www.hermitage.co.nz; Terrace Rd; r $209-575; @☰) This sprawling complex has long monopolised Mt Cook accommodation in the village. Rooms in well-equipped A-frame chalets (double $269) sleep up to four and include a kitchen. Also available are motel units ($239) and refurbished rooms in various wings of the hotel proper. The higher-end hotel rooms are very smart indeed, and include cinematic views of Mt Cook through huge picture windows.

Mt Cook YHA HOSTEL $
(☎03-435 1820; www.yha.co.nz; cnr Bowen & Kitchener Dr; dm $37, d&tw $118; @☰) This excellent hostel has a free sauna, drying room, warming log fires and DVDs. Rooms are clean and spacious, and family rooms and facilities for travellers with disabilities are also available. Try to book a few days in advance. If you're mountain-bound you can store luggage here.

Glentanner Park Centre HOLIDAY PARK $
(☎0800 453 682, 03-435 1855; www.glentanner.co.nz; SH80; sites from $34, dm $28, units $80-155) On the northern shore of Lake Pukaki, this is the nearest facility-laden camping ground to the national park and has great views of Mt Cook, 25km to the north. It's well set up with various cabins and motel units, a dormitory (open October to April) and a restaurant. Tours and activities can also be booked.

Unwin Lodge HOSTEL $
(☎03-435 1100, 027 817 6860; www.alpineclub.org.nz; SH80; dm $30) About 3.5km before the village, this lodge belongs to the New Zealand Alpine Club (NZAC). Members get preference, but beds are usually available for climbing groupies. There are basic bunks in a recently renovated bunkroom, and a big common room with a fireplace and kitchen.

White Horse Hill Camping Area CAMPSITE $
(☎03-435 1186; Hooker Valley; adult/child $10/5) A basic DOC-run, self-registration camping ground at the starting point for the Hooker Valley Track, 2km from Aoraki/Mt Cook village. There's running water (boil before drinking) and toilets, but no electricity or cooking facilities.

Eating & Drinking

Old Mountaineers Café, Bar & Restaurant CAFE $$
(www.mtcook.com; Bowen Dr; lunch $17-24, dinner $22-35; @☰) This place is cosy in winter, and offers mountain views from outside tables in summer. It delivers top-notch burgers, pizza, pasta and salad, and is a good-value alternative to the eateries at the Hermitage. Linger to study the old black-and-white pics and mountaineering memorabilia. The menu features lots of organic, free-range and GM-free options as well.

TITANIC SCENE ON LAKE TASMAN

When you're only a few kilometres from NZ's highest mountain, the last thing you expect to see is a maze of huge icebergs straight from the planet's polar regions. It's a surreal feeling cruising in an inflatable boat amid 500-year-old islands of ice on Lake Tasman in the Aoraki/Mt Cook National Park. An icing-sugar-like dusting of snow may have fallen overnight, and even that could be enough to rebalance an iceberg and send it spinning and rotating in the frigid water. With a decent wind the location of the floating islands can change by the hour.

The ice may be centuries old, but the lake has been around only a few decades. Lake Tasman was first formed around 30 years ago, when huge swathes of ice sheared off the Tasman Glacier's terminal face. The ice-strewn lake continues to be a dynamic environment and there's always the danger of one of the icebergs breaking up. On 22 February 2011, the Christchurch earthquake caused a 30-million-tonne chunk of ice to shear away from the Tasman Glacier. The huge piece of ice was 1.3km long and 300m high, causing substantial waves to roll into tourist boats on the lake at the time. (Fortunately, no one was injured by the waves.)

The ongoing impact of climate change continues to increase the size of one of NZ's newest and coldest lakes, and it's estimated it will eventually grow to a maximum length of 16km.

Glentanner Restaurant CAFE $
(SH80, Glentanner; meals $10-20) The decor might resemble a school cafeteria, but there's plenty of robust Kiwi tucker on offer. Steak sandwiches and fish and chips will get you through the longest of exploring days.

Hermitage RESTAURANT $$
(☎0800 686 800, 03-435 1809; www.hermitage.co.nz; Terrace Rd) Dining options at the Hermitage include a cafe with light meals and pizzas; fine dining in the Panorama Room (mains $35 to $42); and breakfast, lunch and dinner buffets in the Alpine Room.

Chamois Bar & Grill PUB
(www.mountcookbackpackers.co.nz; Bowen Dr) Chamois Bar & Grill is upstairs in Mt Cook Backpackers, 500m from the YHA, where it entertains with a pool table, big-screen TV and the occasional live gig.

Shopping

Alpine Guides OUTDOOR EQUIPMENT
(www.alpineguides.co.nz; Retail Centre, The Hermitage; ⌚8am-5pm) Sells travel clothing, outdoor and mountaineering gear, and rents ice axes, crampons, daypacks and sleeping bags.

Information

Stock up on groceries and petrol at Twizel or Lake Tekapo. The nearest ATM is in Twizel.

DOC Aoraki/Mt Cook Visitor Centre (☎03-435 1186; www.doc.govt.nz; 1 Larch Grove; ⌚8.30am-5pm Oct-Apr, to 4.30pm May-Sep) Advises on weather conditions, guided tours and tramping routes, and hires out beacons for trampers ($35). The centre includes excellent displays on the flora, fauna and history of the Mt Cook region. Most activities can be booked here. Trampers must complete intentions cards when leaving for walks.

Getting There & Away

The village's small airport only serves aerial sightseeing companies. Some of these may be willing to combine transport to the West Coast (ie Franz Josef) with a scenic flight, but flights are heavily dependent on weather.

InterCity (www.intercity.co.nz) links Mt Cook to Christchurch (five hours), Queenstown (four hours) and Wanaka (with a change in Tarras; 4¼ hours). Buses stop at the YHA and the Hermitage, both of which handle bookings.

The **Cook Connection** (☎0800 266 526; www.cookconnect.co.nz) has services to Twizel (one hour) and Lake Tekapo (two hours). Bus services in these towns link to Christchurch, Queenstown, Wanaka and Dunedin.

If you're driving, fill up at Lake Tekapo or Twizel. There is petrol at Mt Cook, but it's expensive and involves summoning an attendant from the Hermitage (for a fee).

Dunedin & Otago

Includes »

Best Places to Eat

» Dunedin Farmers Market (p197)

» Plato (p195)

» Riverstone Kitchen (p216)

» Fleur's Place (p220)

» Mt Difficulty Wines (p206)

Best Places to Stay

» Arden Street House (p194)

» Kaimata Retreat (p204)

» Sublime Bed & Breakfast (p219)

» The Church Mouse (p210)

Why Go?

Coastal Otago has attractions both urban and rural, offering a chance to escape Queenstown's crowds, party in the South Island's coolest city, and come face to face with the island's most accessible wildlife.

Otago's historic heart is Dunedin. With excellent bars, restaurants and cafes, it also hosts a vibrant student culture and arts scene. From Dunedin's stately Victorian train station, catch the famous Taieri Gorge Railway inland, and continue further on the craggily scenic Otago Central Rail Trail.

Those seeking backcountry NZ can soak up historic Clyde, atmospheric St Bathans and scenic, rustic Naseby. For wildlife, head to the Otago Peninsula, where penguins, albatross, sea lions and seals are easily sighted. Seaside Oamaru has a wonderful historic precinct, resident penguin colonies and a quirky devotion to Steampunk culture.

Unhurried, and overflowing with picturesque scenery, Otago is undeniably generous to explorers after something a little less intense.

When to Go

February and March have settled, sunny weather (usually...), and the juicy appeal of fresh apricots, peaches and cherries. Take to two wheels on the Otago Central Rail Trail during the quieter months of May and December, or ride graciously into the past on a penny farthing bicycle at Oamaru's Victorian Heritage Celebrations in November.

Dunedin & Otago Highlights

1. Sampling local beers and gastronomic excellence in the cafes and restaurants of **Dunedin** (p189)

2. Discovering laid-back charm along the quiet northern shore of **Otago Harbour** (p199)

3. Peering at penguins, admiring albatross and staring at sea lions and fur seals on **Otago Peninsula** (p201)

4. Cycling through lonely vistas of brown and gold along the **Otago Central Rail Trail** (p208)

5. Tasting some of the planet's best pinot noir amid the vineyards of **Bannockburn** (p206)

6. Winding through gorges, alongside canyons and across tall viaducts on the snaking **Taieri Gorge Railway** (p200)

7. Exploring NZ's southern heritage in villages like **Clyde** (p207) and **Naseby** (p210)

8. Experiencing a heritage past and a Steampunk future in historic **Oamaru** (p213)

Getting There & Around

Air New Zealand (☎0800 737 000; www.airnewzealand.co.nz) flies from Dunedin to Christchurch, Wellington and Auckland. Australian destinations are Brisbane, Sydney and Melbourne. **Virgin Australia** (www.virginaustralia.com) links Dunedin to Brisbane, and **Jetstar** (☎0800 800 995; www.jetstar.com) flies to Auckland.

Major bus and shuttle operators include InterCity (p200), Atomic Shuttles (p200), Bottom Bus (p200), **Catch-A-Bus** (☎03-449 2024; www.catchabus.co.nz), Naked Bus (p200) and Wanaka Connexions (p200).

DUNEDIN & THE OTAGO PENINSULA

Nestled at the end of Otago Harbour, Dunedin is a surprisingly artsy town with lots of bars and eateries. If you can unglue yourself from the city's live music and cafe scene, the rugged Otago Peninsula and northern harbour provide easy day trips (or longer), rich with wildlife and outdoor activities.

Dunedin

POP 123,000

Dunedin's compact town centre blends the historic and the contemporary, reflected in its alluring museums and tempting bars, cafes and restaurants. Weatherboard houses ranging from stately to ramshackle pepper its hilly suburbs, and bluestone Victorian buildings punctuate the centre. The country's oldest university provides loads of student energy to sustain thriving theatre, live-music and after-dark scenes.

MAORI NZ: DUNEDIN & OTAGO

In pre-European times, the Otago region was known as Otakou, a name still referenced at the Otakou *marae* (Maori meeting place) on the far reaches of the Otago Peninsula.

Dunedin's Otago Museum (p189) has the finest Maori exhibition in the South Island, including an ornately carved *waka* (war canoe) and finely crafted *pounamu* (green stone). Explore the Maori rock art locations of the Waitaki Valley.

Dunedin is an easy city in which to while away a few days, and many travellers find themselves staying here longer than expected as they recover from the buzz of Queenstown. The wildlife-viewing opportunities of the Otago Peninsula are also nearby.

History

The Otakou area's early history was particularly bloody, involving a three-way feud between peninsular tribes that escalated in the early 19th century. This brutal warfare was followed by devastating diseases and interracial conflict ushered in via coastal sealing and whaling. The first permanent European settlers, two shiploads of pious, hard-working Scots, arrived at Port Chalmers in 1848, and included the nephew of the patron saint of Scottish poetry, Robbie Burns. That the city's founders were Scottish is a source of fierce pride today. A statue of Robbie still frowns down upon the city centre, there are a handful of civic haggis 'n' bagpipe occasions every year, and the city even has its own tartan.

Sights

Some popular things to do in Dunedin involve leaving town, including visiting the Otago Peninsula, the Otago Central Rail Trail and the Taieri Gorge Railway.

Otago Museum MUSEUM

(www.otagomuseum.govt.nz; 419 Great King St; admission by donation; ⏲10am-5pm) Explores Otago's cultural and physical past and present, from geology and dinosaurs to the modern day. The Tangata Whenua Maori gallery houses an impressive *waka taua* (war canoe), wonderfully worn old carvings and some lovely *pounamu* (greenstone) works. If you've already been out on the peninsula admiring penguins and albatrosses, the museum's wildlife collection will also fascinate. Join themed guided tours ($12, see website for times and themes). Children can explore at the hands-on Discovery World (adult/child/family $10/5/25). Check the website for always-excellent temporary exhibitions and special gallery talks.

FREE **Otago Settlers Museum** MUSEUM

(www.otago.settlers.museum; 31 Queens Gardens; ⏲10am-5pm) This eclectic collection gives insights into past residents, whether Maori or Scots, whalers or farmers. Petrol heads and trainspotters will love the old Buick straight eight and 1872-built steam engine, now showcased in the museum's stunning entrance area. A $38 million upgrade in 2012 introduced many new interactive displays.

Railway Station HISTORIC BUILDING
(Anzac Ave) Featuring mosaic-tile floors and glorious stained-glass windows, Dunedin's striking Edwardian Railway Station claims to be NZ's most-photographed building. The station houses the NZ Sports Hall of Fame (p190), hosts the Dunedin Farmers Market (p197), and is the departing point for the Taieri Gorge Railway (p200). If you get in early enough, grab a tasty haggis pie ($5) at the cafe.

Orokonui Ecosanctuary WILDLIFE RESERVE
(www.orokonui.org.nz; adult/child/family $15.90/7.90/39.90; ⌚9.30am-4.30pm) This ecosanctuary occupies a 300-hectare nature reserve on Otago Harbour's north shore. Its mission is to provide a predator-free refuge to repopulate species previously exiled to smaller offshore islands. Around 20 different species of birds now make the sanctuary their forest home. Options to visit include self-guided tours, or to join a one-guided tour (adult/child/family $29.90/14.90/74.90; departs daily at 11am) or a two-hour guided tour (adult/child/family $44.90/22.50/112.50; departs daily at 1.30pm). Two-hour twilight tours (adult/child/family $69.90/39.90/186) depart one hour before sunset on Tuesday and Sunday afternoons. Check the website for current times. The sanctuary can also visited on the Orokonui Express, a combination rail and road excursion on the Seasider train (p200) departing from the Dunedin Railway Station. Check the website or ask at the i-SITE.

FREE **Public Art Gallery** GALLERY
(www.dunedin.art.museum; 30 The Octagon; ⌚10am-5pm) Explore NZ's art scene at Dunedin's expansive and airy Public Art Gallery. Works on permanent show are mainly contemporary, including a big NZ collection featuring local kids Ralph Hotere and Frances Hodgkins, Cantabrian Colin McCahon and some old CF Goldie oils. Climb the iron staircase for great city views.

New Zealand Sports Hall of Fame MUSEUM
(www.nzhalloffame.co.nz; Dunedin Railway Station; adult/child $5/2; ⌚10am-4pm) At the New Zealand Sports Hall of Fame you can try and match bike-champ Karen Holliday's average speed of 45.629km/h, or check out the high-stepping style of iconic All Black fullback George Nepia.

ESSENTIAL DUNEDIN & OTAGO

» **Eat** Alfresco from the diverse stalls at the Dunedin Farmers Market

» **Drink** The fine brews from Dunedin's Emerson's and Green Man breweries

» **Read** *Owls Do Cry* by Oamaru's Janet Frame

» **Listen to** *Tally Ho! Flying Nun's Greatest Bits, a* 2011 compilation marking the 30th anniversary of the iconic record label

» **Watch** *Scarfies* (1999), about murderous Dunedin university students

» **Festival** Oamaru's Victorian Heritage Celebrations in late November

» **Go green** Tiptoe down to Otago Peninsula beaches in search of yellow-eyed penguins

» **Online** www.dunedinnz.com, www.centralotagonz.com

» **Area code** ☎03

FREE **Temple Gallery** GALLERY
(29 Moray Pl; ⌚10am-6pm Mon-Fri, 10am-2pm Sat) Up the staircase, the Temple Gallery was Dunedin's first synagogue (1864), and then for 30 years a Masonic temple. The building retains marks of both, and is a fabulous art space. Artists represented are predominantly Otago locals and exhibitions change regularly.

FREE **Dunedin Botanic Gardens** GARDENS
(cnr Great King St & Opoho Rd; ⌚dawn-dusk) The Dunedin Botanic Gardens date from the 1860s and spread across 22 peaceful, grassy and shady hectares. There's also a playground and a cafe.

Baldwin St STREET
The world's steepest residential street (or so says the *Guinness Book of World Records*), Baldwin St has a gradient of 1 in 1.286 (19°). From the city centre, head 2km north up Great King St to where the road branches sharp left to Timaru. Get in the right-hand lane and continue straight ahead. This becomes North Rd, and Baldwin St is on the right after 1km. Alternatively, grab a Normanby bus at the Octagon and ask the driver. The annual 'Gutbuster' race in Febru-

ary sees up to 1000 athletes run to the top of Baldwin St and back. The record is just under two minutes.

Activities

There's excellent walking and kayaking out on the Otago Peninsula.

Swimming, Surfing & Diving

St Clair and St Kilda are both popular swimming beaches (though you need to watch for rips at St Clair). Both have consistently good left-hand breaks, and you'll also find good surfing at Blackhead further south, and at Aramoana on Otago Harbour's North Shore.

For St Clair, catch bus 8, 9, 28 or 29 from the Octagon. For St Kilda, catch bus 27, also from the Octagon

St Clair Pool SWIMMING
(Esplanade, St Clair Beach; adult/child $5.70/2.60; 6am-7pm Mon-Fri, 7am-7pm Sat & Sun Nov-Mar) A heated, outdoor saltwater pool.

Esplanade Surf School SURFING
(455 8655; www.espsurfschool.co.nz; lessons from $60) Based at St Clair Beach and provides equipment and lessons.

Moana Pool SWIMMING
(60 Littlebourne Rd; adult/child $5.70/2.60; 6am-10pm Mon-Fri, 7am-7pm Sat & Sun) Waterslides, wave machines and a spa.

Tramping & Walking

The **Otago Tramping and Mountaineering Club** (www.otmc.co.nz) organises weekend day and overnight tramps, often to the Silver Peaks Reserve north of Dunedin. Nonmembers are welcome, but must contact trip leaders beforehand.

TUNNEL BEACH WALKWAY

The Tunnel Beach Walkway (45 minutes return; closed August 20 to October 31 for lambing) crosses farmland before descending the sea cliffs to Tunnel Beach. Sea stacks, arches and unusual rock shapes have been carved out by the wild Pacific, and a few fossils stud the sandstone cliffs. It impressed civic father John Cargill so much that he had a hand-hewn stone tunnel built to give his family access to secluded beachside picnics. The walk is southwest of central Dunedin. Catch a Corstorphine bus from the Octagon to Stenhope Cres and walk 1.4km along Blackhead Rd to Tunnel Beach Rd, then 400m to the start of the walkway. Strong currents make swimming here dangerous.

MT CARGILL-BETHUNES GULLY WALKWAY

Catch a Normanby bus to the start of Norwood St, which leads to Cluny St and the Mt Cargill-Bethunes Gully walkway (3½ hours return). The highlight is the view from Mt Cargill (also accessible by car). From Mt Cargill, a trail continues to the 10-million-year-old, lava-formed Organ Pipes and, after another half-hour, to Mt Cargill Rd on the other side of the mountain.

Climbing

Traditional rock climbing (nonbolted) is popular at Long Beach and the cliffs at Mihiwaka, both accessed via Blueskin Rd north of Port Chalmers, and Lovers Leap (bolted and natural) on the peninsula.

Other Activities

Cycle Surgery BICYCLE RENTAL
(www.cyclesurgery.co.nz; 67 Lower Stuart St; per day $40) Rents out bikes and has mountain-biking information.

Hare Hill HORSE RIDING
(0800 437 837, 03-472 8496; www.horseriding-dunedin.co.nz; 207 Aramoana Rd) Horse treks ($75 to $210) including thrilling beach rides and farm treks.

Tours

See the Dunedin i-SITE for more specialised city tours.

Cadbury World FACTORY TOUR
(www.cadburyworld.co.nz; 280 Cumberland St; from adult/child/family $14/7/37; full tour 9am-3.30pm Mon-Fri, reduced tour 9am-3.30pm Sat & Sun) The full 75-minute tour of the factory includes a spiel on history and production, a liquid-chocolate waterfall, and a taste of the end product. The shorter 45-minute weekend tour omits the factory tour and concentrates the yummy parts. Combination tickets (adult/child $39/20) also visiting Speight's Brewery are available.

Speight's Brewery BREWERY
(www.speights.co.nz; 200 Rattray St; adult/child/family $23/10/48) Speight's has been churning out beer on this site since the late 1800s. The 90-minute tour (noon, 2pm, 4pm, 6pm, plus 10am and 7pm in summer) offers samples of Speight's six different beers.

First City Tours BUS TOUR
(adult/child $20/10; buses depart the Octagon 9am, 10.15am, 1pm, 2.15pm & 3.30pm) Hop-on/hop-off double-decker bus tour that loops around the city. Stops include the Otago

Dunedin

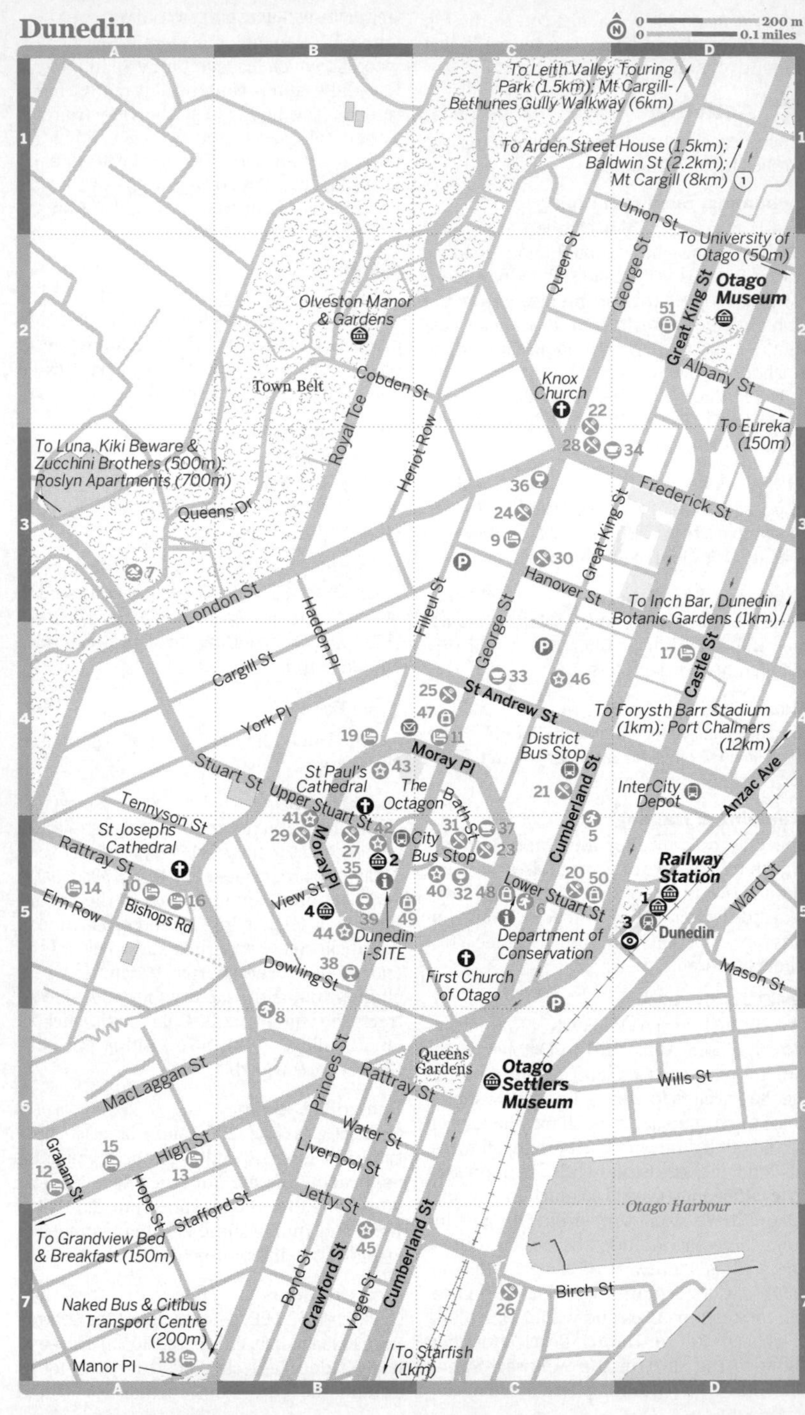

To Leith Valley Touring Park (1.5km); Mt Cargill-Bethunes Gully Walkway (6km)
To Arden Street House (1.5km); Baldwin St (2.2km); Mt Cargill (8km)
Union St
To University of Otago (50m)
Otago Museum
Queen St
George St
Great King St
Olveston Manor & Gardens
Albany St
Town Belt
Cobden St
Knox Church
Royal Tce
Heriot Row
To Eureka (150m)
To Luna, Kiki Beware & Zucchini Brothers (500m); Roslyn Apartments (700m)
Frederick St
Queens Dr
Hanover St
London St
Haddon Pl
Filleul St
To Inch Bar, Dunedin Botanic Gardens (1km)
Cargill St
Castle St
St Andrew St
York Pl
To Forysth Barr Stadium (1km); Port Chalmers (12km)
District Bus Stop
Moray Pl
Stuart St
St Paul's Cathedral
The Octagon
Bath St
Cumberland St
InterCity Depot
Anzac Ave
Tennyson St
Upper Stuart St
St Josephs Cathedral
City Bus Stop
Railway Station
Rattray St
Ward St
Lower Stuart St
Elm Row
Bishops Rd
View St
Dunedin i-SITE
Department of Conservation
Dunedin
Dowling St
First Church of Otago
Mason St
Queens Gardens
Otago Settlers Museum
Wills St
MacLaggan St
Princes St
Rattray St
Water St
High St
Liverpool St
Graham St
Hope St
Jetty St
Stafford St
Otago Harbour
To Grandview Bed & Breakfast (150m)
Bond St
Crawford St
Vogel St
Cumberland St
Birch St
Naked Bus & Citibus Transport Centre (200m)
To Starfish (1km)
Manor Pl

Dunedin

Museum, Speight's, Botanic Gardens and Baldwin St.

Tasty Tours FOOD & WINE
(☎03-453 1455, 021 070 1658; www.tastytours.co.nz; adult/child from $89/59) Tuck into local seafood, cheese, chocolate and beer on specialised foodie tours.

Walk Dunedin WALKING TOUR
(☎03-477 5052; 2hr walk $20; ⏲10am) History-themed strolls around the city, organised by the Otago Settlers Museum. Book at the i-SITE, or pick up a self-guided tour brochure ($4).

Walk This Way WALKING
(☎03-473 8338; www.walkthisway.co.nz; per person $65-75) Bush and coastal walks.

Wine Tours Otago WINE TASTING
(☎021 070 1658, 03-453 1455; www.winetoursotago.co.nz; per person $159) Wine-tasting excursions exploring Central Otago or the Waitaki Valley.

Sleeping

Most accommodation is within easy walking distance of the city centre, though some spots offer a challenging uphill stroll back from town. Most motels are at the northern end of George St.

TOP CHOICE Arden Street House B&B $
(☎03-473 8860; www.ardenstreethouse.co.nz; 36 Arden St; s/d/tw/tr $50/60/60/90, s/d incl breakfast from $75/85; P@☎) North of the city up Northeast Valley, this pair of homes atop a (steep) hill share an organic garden and a very welcoming host. With crazy artworks and a porthole in the bathroom, the main B&B is an amazing space. Readers rave about the shared dinners ($15 to $25) with neighbours, artists, wwoofers and assorted guests. Next door is a comfortable backpacker villa ($30). Head up North Rd from the city, turn right into Glendining St and then left into Arden St.

Grandview Bed & Breakfast B&B $$
(☎03-474 9472, 0800 749 472; www.grandview.co.nz; 360 High St; d incl breakfast $125-200; P@☎) Bold colours, exposed brick walls and snazzy art deco bathrooms are the highlights at this family-owned B&B. The building dates back to 1861, there are superb harbour views from the barbecue and deck area, and lots of sunny shared spaces. The larger rooms have private spa baths, and there's even a compact gym and sauna.

Roslyn Apartments APARTMENT $$
(☎03-477 6777; www.roslynapartments.co.nz; 23 City Rd; d $150-300; P☎) Modern decor and brilliant city and harbour views are on tap at these chic apartments just a short walk from the restaurants and cafes of Roslyn Village. Leather furniture and designer kitchens add a touch of class, and it's a quick 10-minute downhill walk to the Octagon. You may need to consider a taxi on the way back up, though.

315 Euro MOTEL $$
(☎0800 387 638, 03-477 9929; www.eurodunedin.co.nz; 315 George St; d $150-250; P☎) This sleek complex is in the absolute heart of George St's daytime retail strip and after-dark eating and drinking hub. Choose from modern studio apartments or larger one-bedroom apartments with full kitchens. Access via an alleyway is a bit odd, but soundproofing and double-glazed windows keeps George St's irresistible buzz at bay.

Brothers Boutique Hotel BOUTIQUE HOTEL $$$
(☎0800 477 004, 03-477 0043; www.brothershotel.co.nz; 295 Rattray St; d incl breakfast $170-320; P@☎) Rooms in this distinctive old 1920s Christian Brothers residence have been refurbished beyond any monk's dreams, while still retaining many unique features. The chapel room ($320) includes the original arched stained-glass windows of its past life. There are great views from the rooftop units.

Dunedin Palms Motel MOTEL $$
(☎0800 782 938, 03-477 8293; www.dunedinpalmsmotel.co.nz; 185-195 High St; d $170-210; P@☎) A short stroll from the Speight's Ale House, the art deco Palms has smartly decorated studios and one- and two-bedroom units arrayed around a central courtyard. You're handily just out of the CBD, but don't have to endure a long walk uphill.

Fletcher Lodge B&B $$$
(☎03-477 5552; www.fletcherlodge.co.nz; 276 High St; d $325-595, apt $650-750; P@☎) Originally home to one of NZ's wealthy industrialist families, this gorgeous redbrick manor is just minutes from the city, but the secluded gardens feel wonderfully remote. Rooms are elegantly trimmed with antique furniture and ornate plaster ceilings.

Hotel St Clair HOTEL $$
(☎03-456 0555; www.hotelstclair.com; 24 Esplanade; d $175-235; ☎) Southern ocean views and chic and modern rooms provide a surfside haven in beachy St Clair. Downstairs it's just metres to top cafes and restaurants.

Hogwartz HOSTEL $
(☎03-474 1487; www.hogwartz.co.nz; 277 Rattray St; dm $25-28, s $60, d $62-76; @☎) The Catholic bishop's residence since the 1870s, this beautiful building is now a fascinating warren of comfortable and sunny rooms, many with harbour views. The five-bed dorm is actually the bishop's old formal dining room. In a renovated heritage building nearby, the recently opened Coach House has a modern kitchen and features cosy ensuite rooms (per person $45).

Chalet Backpackers HOSTEL $
(☎0800 242 538, 03-479 2075; www.chaletbackpackers.co.nz; 296 High St; dm/s/d $26/40/60; @☎) This rambling old building quickly makes guests feel at home. The kitchen is big, sunny and festooned with flowers, and the dining room has one long table to help you meet your neighbours. There's also a compact garden, pool table, piano and rumours of a ghost.

Elm Lodge HOSTEL $
(☎03-474 1872; www.elmlodge.co.nz; 74 Elm Row; dm/s/d from $26/47/62; @☎) Elm Lodge is a

popular, laidback choice for travellers looking to relax a while. Rooms are quaint but comfortable, and the back garden – including a spa pool – is just made for barbecues and a few cold beers. Elm Lodge is a fairly steep walk into (or particularly *out from*) town.

Living Space HOTEL **$$**
(☎03-951 5000; www.livingspace.net; 192 Castle St; d $89-119; P@📶) Living Space combines kitchenettes in funky colours, whip-smart ergonomic design and a central location. There's an on-site laundry and huge shared kitchen, conversation-friendly lounges and a private DVD cinema. Some rooms are pretty compact, but they're good value and all you need.

On Top Backpackers HOSTEL **$**
(☎03-477 6121, 0800 668 672; www.ontopbackpackers.co.nz; cnr Filleul St & Moray Pl; dm $26-$27, s $54, d with/without bathroom $88/64; @📶) A modern, well-located hostel sitting atop a pool hall and bar, with a large sundeck, shared barbecue area and free basic breakfast. The three new ensuite doubles are hotel quality.

Central Backpackers HOSTEL **$**
(☎0800 423 6872; www.centralbackpackers.co.nz; 243 Moray Pl; dm/tw/d $27/66/70; @📶) Located in the heart of town, this hostel has inviting common TV lounge and kitchen areas, and a welcoming host in Gizmo the cat. Dorm rooms sleep four to 10 on bunks, and private rooms are spacious.

Manor House Backpackers HOSTEL **$**
(☎03-477 0484, 0800 477 0484; www.manorhousebackpackers.co.nz; 28 Manor Pl; dm $22-26, s $53, d $64-74; @) Two stately old villas surrounded by gardens and trees.

Leith Valley Touring Park HOLIDAY PARK **$**
(☎0800 555 331, 03-467 9936; www.leithvalleytouringpark.co.nz; 103 Malvern St; sites $36, units $56-106; P@📶) This holiday park is surrounded by native bush studded with walks, glowworm caves and a wee creek. Self-contained modern motel units are spacious, and tourist flats are smaller but have a more earthy feel (linen required).

Eating

Inexpensive Asian restaurants are clustered along George St around the intersection with St Andrew St. Most also do takeaways.

Uphill from the Octagon, Roslyn has good restaurants and cafes, and the beachy ambience of St Clair is great for a lazy brunch.

TOP CHOICE **Plato** MODERN NZ **$$**
(☎03-477 4235; www.platocafe.co.nz; 2 Birch St; brunch $15-23, dinner $27-33; ⏰6pm-late Mon-Sat, 11am-late Sun) A regular contender in *Cuisine* magazine's Best of NZ gongs, Plato has a retro-themed location near the harbour and a strong beer and wine list. Try standouts like the Indian seafood curry or grilled salmon on potato gnocchi. Sunday brunch is worth the shortish trek from the CBD. Bookings are recommended.

Scotia RESTAURANT **$$**
(☎03-477 7704; www.scotiadunedin.co.nz; 199 Upper Stuart St; mains $18-32; ⏰lunch Mon-Fri, dinner Mon-Sat) Occupying a cosy heritage townhouse, Scotia toasts all things Scottish with a wall full of single malt whisky, and hearty fare such as smoked salmon and Otago rabbit. The two Scottish Robbies – Burns and Coltrane – look down approvingly on a menu that also includes haggis, and duck and whisky pâté.

Best Cafe FISH & CHIPS **$$**
(30 Stuart St, from $8; ⏰lunch & dinner, takeaway until late) Serving up fish and chips since 1932, this local icon has its winning formula down pat, complete with vinyl tablecloths, hand-cut chips and curls of butter on white bread. If there's two or more of you, try the 'Old School' platter with juicy oysters, whitebait, scallops, squid rings and fish of your choice ($29.50, or $35 with Bluff oysters).

Luna MODERN NZ **$$**
(☎03-477 2227; www.lunaroslyn.co.nz; 314 Highgate; lunch $13-22, dinner $27-36; ⏰11am-late) Make the trek to Roslyn for outstanding harbour views from this hilltop glass-encased pavilion. Ask for a window seat when you book, and tuck in dishes like nori-encased salmon with wasabi mash, or gnocchi with pumpkin, sage and walnuts. A more relaxed option is a drink in the classy bar and shared plates including scallops with chilli, lime and ginger.

Zucchini Bros PIZZA **$$**
(www.zucchinibros.co.nz; 292 Highgate; pizza & pasta $15-21; ⏰from 5pm) Unpretentious, colourful and bustling, Zucchini Bros is the go-to spot for Dunedin folk for great pizza and pasta. Work from local photographers fills the walls, and Central Otago wines and Dunedin's own Emerson's beers are the perfect adjunct to all the wood-fired and hand-rolled goodness. Takeaways are also available.

Paasha TURKISH **$$**
(www.paasha.co.nz; 32 St Andrew St; kebabs & mains $12-25;) Authentic Turkish kebabs, dips and salads are faithfully created at this long-running Dunedin icon. It's a top place for takeaways, and most nights the spacious and warm interior is filled with groups drinking Efes Turkish beer and sharing heaving platters of tasty Ottoman goodness.

Izakaya Yuki JAPANESE **$$**
(29 Bath St; dishes $5-12; lunch Mon-Sat, dinner Mon-Sun;) Cute and cosy, with a huge array of small dishes on which to graze, Yuki is a lovely spot for supper or a relaxed, drawn-out Japanese meal. Make a night of it with sake or draught Asahi beer, sushi and sashimi, and multiple plates of *kushiyaki* (grilled skewers) such as asparagus with bacon.

Saigon Van VIETNAMESE **$**
(66 St Andrew St; mains $10-15; lunch & dinner Tue-Sun;) The elegant decor looks high-end Asian, but the Vietnamese food is definitely budget-friendly. Try the combination spring rolls ($8 for six) and a bottle of Vietnamese beer to recreate lazy nights in Saigon. The bean-sprout-laden *pho* (noodle soup) and salads are also good.

Seoul KOREAN **$**
(11 Frederick St; lunch $8, mains $15-17; 11am-9pm Mon-Sat) Behind the unprepossessing exterior lurks a warm orange space filled with students merrily tucking into cast-iron pots of authentic Korean fare. Warm up with *dolsot bibimbap* ($15), a sizzling-hot stone bowl of rice and myriad toppings, and cool down with a chunky red-bean ice cream ($3).

The Perc CAFE **$**
(142 Lower Stuart St; mains $10-18) Always busy, and for good reason – the Perc is a grand place to kick-start your day. The decor's kinda retro and kinda art deco, and there's hearty cafe fare ranging from salmon bagels and panini to warming porridge.

Kiki Beware CAFE **$**
(302 Highgate; snacks & light meals $8-15; Mon-Fri) This friendly neighbourhood cafe sees a loyal band of Roslyn locals popping in for excellent coffee, lots of design and travel magazines, and classy counter food including top-notch salmon bagels and classy cupcakes.

Governors CAFE **$**
(438 George St; mains $9-16) Popular with students, Governors does a nice line in early morning pancakes and other light meals. If you're feeling a little off the pace after the previous night, a strong coffee and an eggy omelette are just what the doctor ordered.

The Good Oil CAFE **$**
(314 George St; mains $10-18) This sleek little cafe is Dunedin's top spot for coffee and cake. Try the lemon and sour cream cake ($4). If you're still waking up, maybe resurrect the day with innovative brunches such as kumara hash with hot smoked salmon ($16).

Nova Cafe CAFE **$$**
(29 The Octagon; mains $15-30;) Not surprisingly, this extension of the Public Art Gallery has a stylish look about it. Cakes and snacks are famously creative, and Nova is also licensed for beer and wine. Escape into Dunedin's best choice of interesting food, travel and arts magazines.

Tangenté CAFE **$**
(111 Moray Pl; meals $7.50-17; 8am-3pm Tue-Sat, 9am-3pm Sun, 4.30-9pm Fri;) A cheerful, welcoming space with mismatched tables, toys for the kids, a funky soundtrack and the glorious aroma of freshly baked bread. Tangente's food is generally organic, free-range and locally sourced.

Modaks CAFE **$**
(337-339 George St; snacks & meals from $9;) This funky little cafe and bar, with brick walls, mismatched Formica tables and couches for slouching, is popular with students and those who appreciate chilled-out reggae while they nurse a pot of tea. Sundaes, smoothies and beer make it a great escape from summer's heat, while plump toasted bagels warm the insides in winter.

Circadian Rhythm Café CAFE
(72 St Andrew St; curry buffet $10; 9am-8pm Mon-Sat) Specialising in organic Indian curries, this all-vegan cafe is also known for its cookies and cakes. Circadian Rhythm is also a music venue, with a variety of interesting acts on Friday nights from 5.30pm. Dunedin's Emerson's and Green Man beers are both available, so you don't have to be *too* healthy.

Starfish CAFE
(www.starfishcafe.co.nz; 7/240 Forbury Rd; mains $18-30) Starfish is part of the growing restaurant scene at St Clair Beach. Pop out on a

weekday to score an outside table to enjoy a gourmet pizza ($19.50) and wine. Dinner is more sophisticated with aged beef fillet on smoky bacon and onion mash. Catch bus 8, 9, 28 or 29 from the Octagon.

Dunedin Farmers Market FARMERS MARKET **$**
(www.otagofarmersmarket.org.nz; Dunedin Railway Station; ⏲8am-12.30pm Sat) The thriving Dunedin Farmers Market is all local, all eatable (or drinkable) and mostly organic. Grab felafels or espresso to sustain you while you browse, and stock up on fresh meats, seafood, vegies and cheese for your journey. Also pick up some locally brewed Green Man organic beer. Sorted.

Velvet Burger BURGERS **$**
(150 Lower Stuart St; mains $10-18; ⏲11.30am-late;) Best consumed after a few beers, but Velvet Burger is also licensed if the night is young. There's another VB at 375 George St (same hours).

Guilty by Confection SWEETS **$**
(www.guiltybyconfection.co.nz; 44-46 Lower Stuart St; ⏲10am-4pm Mon, Wed, Sat, noon-5pm Thu-Fri) Handmade chocolates, fudges and sweets.

Countdown Supermarket SUPERMARKET **$**
(309 Cumberland St; ⏲6am-midnight) Self-catering central.

Drinking

Mou Very BAR
(www.mouvery.co.nz; 357 George St) Welcome to one of the world's smallest bars – it's only 1.8m wide, but is still big enough to host regular funk and soul DJ sessions most Fridays from 5pm. There are just six bar stools, so Mou Very's boho regulars usually spill out into an adjacent laneway. By day, it's a handy refuelling spot for your morning or afternoon espresso.

Eureka BAR
(www.eurekadunedin.co.nz; 116 Albany St) Despite its proximity to occasional student sofa burnings around the corner on Hyde St, Eureka attracts a diverse crowd from first-year university newbies to their more grizzled tutors and other academics. The food's hearty and good value, and it's yet another Dunedin bar showcasing Kiwi microbreweries.

Inch Bar BAR
(8 Bank St) Bigger than Mou Very, but not by much. Make the short trek from town for lots of Kiwi craft beers, tasty tapas including prawns and calamari, and the company of a bohemian team of regulars.

Pequeno BAR
(www.pequeno.co.nz; behind 12 Moray Pl; ⏲Mon-Sat) Down the alleyway opposite the Rialto cinema, Pequeno attracts a more sophisticated crowd with leather couches, a cosy

LOCAL KNOWLEDGE

RICHARD EMERSON, BREWER

Richard Emerson is the head brewer at Dunedin's iconic Emerson's Brewery.

Which of the Emerson's beers is the quintessential Dunedin brew? Our Pilsner is a twist on the classic German Pilsner, and features that distinctive NZ 'sauvignon blanc' hop flavour,

Where are Dunedin's best places to drink Emerson's? The funky Inch Bar (p197) near the Botanic Gardens, Albar (p198) in Stuart St, and Eureka (p197), which is always a favourite with lunching academics. Tonic (p198) is a great craft beer bar, and down Dunedin's laneways is Pequeno (p197), just off Moray Pl. Another must-visit spot is Mou Very (p197), the tiny 'hole in the wall' bar on George St.

What's your favourite Dunedin food and beer match? The Carey's Bay Hotel (p199) near Port Chalmers serves excellent Queen scallops harvested by the local fishermen. They're really good served with Emerson's Pilsner.

Enough about beer – where do you recommend for a coffee? Nova Café (p196).

What are your favourite Dunedin and Otago experiences? The Farmer's Market (p197) held at Dunedin Railway Station on a Saturday morning is hard to beat. Also take the Taieri Gorge Railway (p200) from Dunedin to Middlemarch to start the Otago Central Rail Trail, a brilliant bike ride through to Clyde. Definitely stop at the Waipiata Country Hotel (p211) for a cold beer.

JUST GIVE ME THE COFFEE & NO ONE WILL GET HURT

Dunedin has some excellent coffee bars where you can refuel and recharge.

Fix (15 Frederick St; ⏲Mon-Sat) Wage slaves queue at the pavement window every morning, while students and others with time on their hands relax in the courtyard. Fix doesn't serve food, but you can bring along your own food or takeaways.

Mazagran Espresso Bar (36 Moray Pl; ⏲Mon-Sat) The godfather of Dunedin's coffee scene, this compact wood-and-brick coffee house is the source of the magic bean for many of the city's restaurants and cafes.

Strictly Coffee (23 Bath St; ⏲8am-4pm Mon-Fri) Stylish retro coffee bar hidden down grungy Bath St. Different rooms provide varying views and artworks to enjoy while you sip and sup.

fireplace and an excellent wine and tapas menu. Music is generally laid-back and never too loud to intrude on conversation.

Albar BAR
(135 Lower Stuart St) This former butchers is now a bohemian little bar attracting just maybe the widest age range in Dunedin. Most punters are drawn by the 50 single-malt whiskies, interesting tap beers and cheap-as-chips bar snacks ($4 to $8).

Tonic BAR
(www.tonicbar.co.nz; 138 Princes St; ⏲4pm-late Tue-Fri, 6pm-late Sat) Limited-release Kiwi craft beers, single-malt whiskies and good cocktails appeal to an older crowd than Dunedin's student pubs. Antipasto plates and cheese boards are good reasons to stay for another drink.

Speight's Ale House PUB
(200 Rattray St) Busy even in non-university months, the Ale House is a favourite of strapping young lads in their cleanest dirty shirts. A good spot to watch the rugby on TV, and to try the full range of Speight's beers.

XIIB BAR
(www.bennu.co.nz/xiib.html; alleyway behind 12 Moray Pl; ⏲Tue-Sat) XIIB (aka 12 Below) is an intimate underground bar with comfy seats and couches, and cosy nooks aplenty. There's also floor space for live-music acts (look forward to lots of funk and reggae), or to wriggle along to hip-hop and drum 'n' bass.

☆ Entertainment

di lusso BAR
(www.dilusso.co.nz; 12 The Octagon; ⏲Wed-Sat) Cool with crimson walls and a backlit drinks display, di lusso serves seriously good cocktails.

Urban Factory CLUB
(www.urbanfactory.co.nz; 101 Great King St) The hippest of NZ's touring bands, regular DJ sessions and carefully crafted cocktails.

Pop BAR
(downstairs, 14 The Octagon; ⏲9pm-late Wed-Sat) Pop serves Dunedin's best martinis and prides itself on seriously good DJs playing funk and house.

Hoyts Cinema CINEMA
(☎03-477 3250, info line 03-477 7019; www.hoyts.co.nz; 33 The Octagon; adult/child $16/10) Blockbuster heaven. Rates are often cheaper on Tuesdays.

Metro Cinema CINEMA
(☎03-471 9635; www.metrocinema.co.nz; Moray Pl; adult/student $13/12) Behind the town hall, Metro shows art-house and foreign flicks.

Rialto Cinemas CINEMA
(☎03-474 2200; www.rialto.co.nz; 11 Moray Pl; adult/child $15.50/9.50) Blockbusters and art-house flicks. Rates often cheaper on Tuesdays.

Fortune Theatre THEATRE
(☎03-477 8323; www.fortunetheatre.co.nz; 231 Upper Stuart St; adult/student/child $40/20/15) The world's southernmost professional theatre company has been running dramas, comedies, pantomimes, classics and contemporary NZ productions for almost 40 years. Shows are performed – watched over by the obligatory theatre ghost – in a Gothic-style old Wesleyan church.

Sammy's LIVE MUSIC
(65 Crawford St) Dunedin's premier live-music venue draws an eclectic mix of genres from noisy-as-hell punk to chilled reggae and gritty dubstep. It's also usually venue of choice for visiting Kiwi bands and up-and-coming international acts.

Chicks Hotel LIVE MUSIC
(2 Mount St) Across in Port Chalmers, Chicks is the archetypal rock-and-roll pub, hosting everything from US alt-country bands to local metal noise merchants. Search Facebook for 'Friends of Chicks'. Catch bus 13 or 14 from Cumberland St in Dunedin.

Forsyth Barr Stadium STADIUM
(www.forsythbarrstadium.co.nz; Awatea St) Constructed for the 2011 Rugby World Cup, Dunedin's best sports venue is 1.5km from the centre of town. It's the only major stadium in NZ with a fully covered roof and hosts the Highlanders Super 15 rugby team (www.highlanders-rugby.co.nz) and the Otago NPC rugby team (www.orfu.co.nz).

Shopping

George St is Dunedin's main shopping strip. Moray Pl is also a funky area. Note the following harder-to-find and more interesting spots.

De Novo Art Prints and Posters ARTS & CRAFTS
(www.gallerydenovo.co.nz; 91 Lower Stuart St) Everything from vintage NZ tourism posters and Kiwiana to fine art prints by modern Kiwi artists such as Colin McCahon and Ralph Hotere.

Stuart St Potters Cooperative ARTS & CRAFTS
(14 Lower Stuart St; ⏲Mon-Sat) Locally designed and made pottery and ceramic art from 12 Dunedin and Otago region craftspeople.

Fern JEWELLERY
(67 Princes St; ⏲Mon-Sat) Unique clothing, design and jewellery, often from up-and-coming Dunedin artists and designers.

Bivouac Outdoor OUTDOOR EQUIPMENT
(www.bivouac.co.nz; 171 George St) Clothing, footwear and rugged gear.

University Book Shop BOOKS
(www.unibooks.co.nz; 378 Great King St) Fiction, poetry, Maori, Pacific and NZ titles.

Information

Call ☎111 for ambulance, fire service and police. Internet access is available at most hostels and accommodation. Wi-fi can be found at the airport and the Otago Museum.

Urgent Doctors & Accident Centre (☎03-479 2900; 95 Hanover St; ⏲8am-11.30pm) Also a pharmacy open outside normal business hours.

Dunedin Hospital (☎03-474 0999, Emergency Department 0800 611 116; www.southerndhb.govt.nz; 201 Great King St)

Post Office (233 Moray Pl)

Department of Conservation (DOC; ☎03-477 0677; www.doc.govt.nz; 1st fl, 77 Lower Stuart St; ⏲8.30am-5pm Mon-Fri) Information and maps on regional walking tracks and Great Walks bookings.

Dunedin i-SITE (☎03-474 3300; www.dunedinnz.com; 26 Princes St; ⏲8.30am-5pm Mon-Fri, 8.45am-5pm Sat & Sun) Accommodation, activities, transport and walking tours.

WORTH A TRIP

OTAGO HARBOUR'S NORTH SHORE

The north shore of Otago Harbour provides a worthy detour from the main tourist track.

Little **Port Chalmers** (population 3000) is only 15km out of the city (15 minutes' drive, or bus 13 or 14 from Dunedin's Cumberland St), but it feels a world away. Somewhere between working class and bohemian, Port Chalmers has a history as a port town but has increasingly attracted Dunedin's arty types. Dunedin's best rock-and-roll pub, **Chicks Hotel** is an essential after-dark destination, and daytime attractions include a few raffish cafes, design stores and galleries.

The 150-year-old bluestone **Carey's Bay Hotel** (www.careysbayhotel.co.nz; 17 MacAndrew Rd, Carey's Bay; mains $15-30), 1km past the docks, has a bar with views of fishing boats and the harbour. There is a great collection of art from local painter Ralph Hotere, plus other Otago artworks. Meals tend to be focused on seafood. The salmon fish cakes ($18.50) are good.

On a sheep-and-deer farm 5km down the road from Port Chalmers, **Billy Brown Backpackers** (☎03-472 8323; www.billybrowns.co.nz; 423 Aramoana Rd, Hamilton Bay; dm/d $28/70) has magnificent views across the harbour to the peninsula. There's a lovely rustic shared lounge with a cosy wood-burner, and plenty of retro vinyl to spin.

WORTH A TRIP

TAIERI GORGE RAILWAY

With narrow tunnels, deep gorges, winding tracks, rugged canyons and more than a dozen stone and wrought-iron viaduct crossings (up to 50m high), the scenic **Taieri Gorge Railway** (☎03-477 4449; www.taieri.co.nz; Dunedin Railway Station, Anzac Ave; ⏰office 8am-5pm Mon-Fri, 8.30am-3pm Sat-Sun) consistently rates highly with visitors.

The four-hour return trip aboard 1920s heritage coaches travels to Pukerangi (one-way/return $56/84), 58km away. Some trips carry on to Middlemarch (one-way/return $65/97) or you can opt for a train–coach trip to Queenstown (one-way $138). From Middlemarch, you can also bring your bike along and hit the Rail Trail. In summer (October to April), trains depart 2.30pm daily for Pukerangi, plus trips to Middlemarch or Pukerangi some mornings. In winter (May to September) trains depart for Pukerangi at 12.30pm daily.

ℹ Getting There & Away

Air

Air New Zealand (p189) flies from Dunedin to Christchurch, Wellington and Auckland. Australian destinations are Brisbane, Sydney and Melbourne. Virgin Australia (p189) links Dunedin to Brisbane, and Jetstar (p189) flies to Auckland.

Bus

Buses and shuttles leave from the Dunedin Railway Station, excluding InterCity and Naked Bus. Check when you make your booking.

InterCity (☎03-471 7143; www.intercity.co.nz; 205 St Andrew St; ⏰ticket office 7.30am-5pm Mon-Fri, 11am-3pm Sat, 11am-5.15pm Sun, tickets by phone 7am-9pm daily) has services to Oamaru (one hour 40 minutes), Christchurch (six hours), Queenstown (4½ hours), Te Anau (4½ hours) and Invercargill – via Gore (4 hours). Buses leave from St Andrew St.

Naked Bus (www.nakedbus.com) connects Dunedin with Christchurch (six hours) and Invercargill (four hours). Buses leave from the **Citibus Transport Centre** (630 Princes St).

Southern Link (☎0508 458 835; www.southernlinkcoaches.co.nz) connects Dunedin to Christchurch (six hours), Oamaru (one hour 50 minutes) and Invercargill (three hours 40 minutes). **Coastline Tours** (☎03-434 7744; www.coastline-tours.co.nz) runs between Dunedin and Oamaru (two hours), and will detour to Moeraki or the airport if needed. Coastline departures leave Dunedin from The Octagon.

A couple of services connect Dunedin to the Catlins and Southland. The **Bottom Bus** (☎03-477 9083; www.bottombus.co.nz) does a circuit from Dunedin through the Catlins to Invercargill, Te Anau, Queenstown and back to Dunedin. **Catlins Coaster** (☎03-477 9083; www.catlinscoaster.co.nz) connects Dunedin with Invercargill, returning via the scenic Catlins.

Other services:

Atomic Shuttles (☎03-349 0697; www.atomictravel.co.nz) To/from Christchurch (six hours), Oamaru (two hours), Invercargill (four hours), and Queenstown and Wanaka (both four hours).

Trail Journeys (☎03-449-2024; www.trailjourneys.co.nz) Door-to-door daily between Dunedin and Wanaka stopping at Otago Central Rail Trail towns along the way. Bikes can be transported.

Knightrider (☎03-342 8055; www.knightrider.co.nz) Night-time service to Christchurch (six hours), Oamaru (two hours) and Invercargill (four hours). A handy service if you've got an early morning departure from Christchurch airport.

Wanaka Connexions (☎03-443 9120; www.alpinecoachlines.co.nz) Shuttles between Dunedin and Wanaka (four hours) and Queenstown (four hours). Alternate seven-hour services also include key stops for participants on the Otago Central Rail Trail. See the website for details.

Train

Two interesting train journeys start at Dunedin's railway station (p190): the Taieri Gorge Railway journey, and the **Seasider** (www.seasider.co.nz; one-way/return $54/81; ⏰departs 9.30am, returns 1.30pm), which journeys along the coast to Palmerston and back. Book via the Taieri Gorge Railway (p200).

ℹ Getting Around

To & From the Airport

Dunedin Airport (DUD; ☎03-486 2879; www.dnairport.co.nz) is 27km southwest of the city. A door-to-door shuttle is around $15 per person. Try **Kiwi Shuttles** (☎03-487 9790; www.kiwishuttles.co.nz), **Super Shuttle** (☎0800 748 885; www.supershuttle.co.nz) or **Southern Taxis** (☎03-476 6300; www.southerntaxis.co.nz). There is no public bus service.

A standard taxi ride between the city and the airport costs around $80.

Bus

City buses (☎03-474 0287; www.orc.govt.nz) leave from stops in the Octagon, while buses to districts around Dunedin depart a block away from stands along Cumberland St near the Countdown supermarket. Buses run regularly during the week, but services are greatly reduced (or nonexistent) on weekends and holidays. View the Dunedin bus timetable at the Dunedin i-SITE (p199), or see www.orc.govt.nz.

Car

The big rental companies all have offices in Dunedin, and inexpensive local outfits include **Getaway** (☎0800 489 761, 03-489 7614; www.getawaycarhire.co.nz) and **Driven Rentals** (☎03-456 3600; www.drivenrentals.co.nz).

Taxi

Dunedin Taxis (☎03-477 7777, 0800 50 50 10; www.dunedintaxis.co.nz) and **Otago Taxis** (☎03-477 3333).

Otago Peninsula

Otago Peninsula has the South Island's most accessible diversity of wildlife. Albatross, penguins, fur seals and sea lions are some of the highlights of the region, as well as rugged countryside, wild walks and beaches, and interesting historical sites. Despite a host of tours exploring the peninsula, the area maintains its quiet rural air. Get the *Otago Peninsula* brochure and map from the Dunedin i-SITE and visit www.otago-peninsula.co.nz.

Sights

FREE Royal Albatross Centre WILDLIFE RESERVE

(☎03-478 0499; www.albatross.org.nz; Taiaroa Head; ⏲9am-dusk summer, 10am-4pm winter) Taiaroa Head, at the peninsula's eastern tip, has the world's only mainland royal albatross colony. The best time to visit is from December to February, when one parent is constantly guarding the young while the other delivers food throughout the day. Sightings are most common in the afternoon when the winds pick up, and calm days don't see much bird action. The only public access is through the Royal Albatross Centre where 45-minute tours (adult/child/family $40/20/100) include viewing from a glassed-in hut overlooking the nesting sites. There's no viewing from mid-September to late November. From late November to December the birds are nestbound so it's difficult to see their magnificent wingspan. The first tour of each day runs at 10.30am; bookings can be made online. Ask the staff whether the birds are flying before you pay.

Discounted combo deals are available with Nature's Wonders (p202) and Monarch Wildlife Cruises & Tours (p203). Visit www.albatross.org.nz for details.

Fort Taiaroa HISTORIC SITE

(www.albatross.org.nz) Nearby are the remains of Fort Taiaroa and its 1886 Armstrong Disappearing Gun, built when NZ was certain a Russian invasion was imminent. The gun was loaded and aimed underground, then popped up like the world's slowest jack-in-the-box to be fired. The Fort Taiaroa tour (adult/child/family $20/10/50) or the Unique Taiaroa Experience (adult/child/family $50/25/125) include the guns and the birds.

Yellow-Eyed Penguin Conservation Reserve WILDLIFE RESERVE

(☎03-478 0286; www.penguinplace.co.nz; McGrouther's Farm, Harington Point Rd; tours adult/child $49/12) Activities include building nesting sites, caring for sick and injured birds, and trapping predators. Ninety-minute tours focus on penguin conservation and close-up viewing from a system of hides. Between October and March, tours run regularly from 10.15am to 90 minutes before sunset. Between April and September they run from 3.15pm to 4.45pm. Booking ahead is recommended.

Larnach Castle CASTLE

(www.larnachcastle.co.nz; Camp Rd; castle & grounds adult/child $27/10, grounds only $12.50/4; ⏲9am-7pm Oct-Mar, 9am-5pm Apr-Sep) Standing proudly on the peninsula's highest point, Larnach Castle was an extravagance of the Dunedin banker, merchant and politician, William Larnach. Built in 1871 to impress his French-nobility-descended wife, the Gothic mansion is filled with exquisite antique furnishings. The gardens offer fantastic views of the peninsula and harbour. Without your own transport, a tour is the only way to visit.

Glenfalloch Woodland Garden GARDENS

(www.glenfalloch.co.nz; 430 Portobello Rd; admission by donation; ⏲gardens 9.30am-dusk, cafe-wine bar 11am-3.30pm Mon-Fri, 11am-4.30pm Sat & Sun Sep-Apr) Glenfalloch Woodland Garden covers 12 hectares with flowers, walking tracks and swaying, mature trees including a 1000-year-old matai. Expect spectacular

Otago Peninsula

harbour views. The Portobello bus stops out the front.

Marine Studies Centre AQUARIUM
(www.marine.ac.nz; Hatchery Rd; adult/child/family $12.50/6/25; ⏲10am-4.30pm) View octopuses, seahorses, crayfish and sharks, help with fish-feeding (Wednesday and Saturday 2pm to 3pm), or join a guided tour at 10.30am (adult/child/family $21.50/11/49 including entry). The centre showcases the work of the adjacent university-run marine laboratory.

Activities

The peninsula's coastal and farmland walkways offer stunning views and the chance to see wildlife on your own. Pick up a free copy of the detailed *Otago Peninsula Tracks* from the Dunedin i-SITE. A popular walking destination is the beautiful **Sandfly Bay**, reached from Seal Point Rd (moderate; 40 minutes) or Ridge Rd (difficult; 40 minutes). From the end of Sandymount Rd, you can follow a trail to the impressive **chasm** (20 minutes). Note that the Lovers Leap track and the Chasm track at Sandymount are closed from 20 August to 31 October for lambing.

Wild Earth Adventures KAYAKING
(☎03-489 1951; www.wildearth.co.nz; trips from $115) Offers trips in double sea kayaks, with wildlife often being sighted en route. Trips run between four hours and a full day. Some trips start in Dunedin and some on the peninsula.

Tours

Nature's Wonders WILDLIFE
(☎0800 246 446, 03-478 1150; www.natureswonders naturally.com; Taiaroa Head; tours adult/child/family $55/45/170; ⏲tours from 10.15am) Situated 1km past the albatross colony, and based on a sprawling coastal sheep farm, Nature's Won-

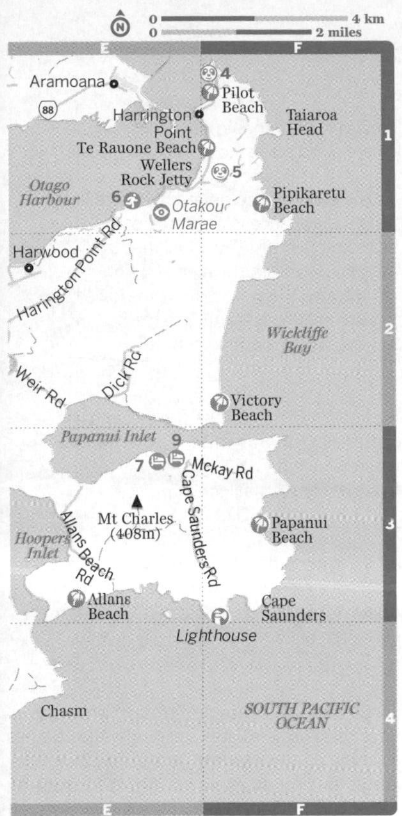

Otago Peninsula

Sights

- Fort Taiaroa ....(see 4)
- 1 Glenfalloch Woodland Garden C3
- 2 Larnach Castle D3
- 3 Marine Studies Centre D2
- 4 Royal Albatross Centre F1
- 5 Yellow-Eyed Penguin Conservation Reserve F1

Activities, Courses & Tours

- 6 Monarch Wildlife Cruises & Tours E1
- Nature's Wonders ....(see 4)

Sleeping

- 7 Betty's Bach E3
- 8 Hotel St Clair A4
- 9 Kaimata Retreat E3
- Larnach Lodge ....(see 2)
- 10 McFarmers Backpackers D3
- Penguin Place Lodge ....(see 5)
- 11 Portobello Motels D2
- 12 Portobello Village Tourist Park D3

Eating

- 1908 Café ....(see 13)
- 13 Portobello Coffee Shop & Café D2
- 14 Portobello Hotel D2
- Starfish ....(see 8)

Drinking

- 15 Carey's Bay Hotel D1
- 16 Chick's Hotel D2

ders runs one-hour tours taking in Stewart Island shags, NZ fur seals and yellow-eyed penguins. The tour is conducted in 'go-anywhere' Argos vehicles and is an exciting combo of improbable scenery and wildlife adventure.

Back to Nature Tours WILDLIFE
(☎03-478 0499, 0800 528 767; www.backtonaturetours.co.nz; adult/child $95/55) Good value peninsula tours getting you up close and personal with yellow-eyed penguins, NZ fur seals and sea lions. From November to March they also offer a tour including a spectacular coastal hike (adult/child $85/45).

Citibus WILDLIFE
(☎03-477 5577; www.citibus.co.nz; adult/child from $95/47.50) Tours combining albatross and penguin viewing.

Elm Wildlife Tours WILDLIFE
(☎03-454 4121, 0800 356 563; www.elmwildlifetours.co.nz; standard tour $99) Small-group tours of up to six hours. Pick-up and drop-off from Dunedin is included.

Monarch Wildlife Cruises & Tours WILDLIFE
(☎03-477 4276; www.wildlife.co.nz) One-hour boat trips from Wellers Rock (adult/child $49/22), and half- ($89/32) and full-day ($235/118) tours from Dunedin. Tours include breeding grounds for sea lions, penguins, albatross and seals often inaccessible by land.

Otago Explorer CULTURAL TOUR, WILDLIFE
(☎03-474 9083; www.otagoexplorer.com) Runs 2½-hour tours of Larnach Castle (adult/child $65/32.50) and summertime wildlife tours.

BEST PLACES TO SPOT...

Yellow-Eyed Penguins

One of the world's rarest penguins, the hoiho (yellow-eyed penguin) is found along the Otago coast, and several peninsula beaches are good places to watch them come ashore (any time after 4pm).

There are two private operators leading tours to yellow-eye colonies on private land, and other tours also visit habitats on private farmland not accessible to the public. The birds also nest at a couple of public beaches, including Sandfly Bay, which has a DOC hide. If you go alone, stay on the trails, view penguins only from the hide and don't approach these shy creatures; even loud voices can disturb them. The penguins have been badly distressed by tourists using flash photography or traipsing through the nesting grounds. Don't loiter on the beach, as this deters them from coming ashore.

Blue Penguins

Blue penguins can be viewed at Pilots Beach, just below the albatross centre car park. The penguins come ashore just before dusk. Walk down the gravel road to the viewing area near the beach, and remain there until the birds have returned to their burrows. There may be as many as 80 or more in summer, but sometimes none in winter.

Sea Lions

Sea lions are most easily seen on a tour, but are regularly present at Sandfly Bay, Allans and Victory Beaches. They are predominantly bachelor males vacationing from Campbell Island or the Auckland Islands. Give them plenty of space, as they can really motor over the first 20 metres.

Sleeping

TOP CHOICE Kaimata Retreat LODGE **$$$**
(☎03-456 3443; www.kaimatanz.com; 297 Cape Saunders Rd; s/d incl breakfast $390/460) This luxury ecolodge has three rooms overlooking a gloriously isolated inlet on the eastern edge of Otago Peninsula. Watch sea lions and bird life from the spacious decks, or get even closer with an eco-expedition with local farmer Dave. Be sure to include a private three-course dinner ($99 per person), and don't make the mistake of staying just one night.

Betty's Bach RENTAL HOUSE **$$**
(☎03-456 3443; www.bettysbach.co.nz; 267 Cape Saunders Rd; d $160) This cute retro bach enjoys superb, ever-changing views of Otago Peninsula's isolated Papanui Inlet. Get busy in the funky kitchen, fire up the wood-burning heater and have an old-school Kiwi holiday. Kaimata Retreat (p204) is nearby, and guests at Betty's Bach can join their eco-expeditions exploring the surrounding area.

McFarmers Backpackers LODGE **$**
(☎03-478 0389; www.otago-peninsula.co.nz; 774 Portobello Rd; s $50, d/tw $60-90) On a working farm with harbour views, this rustic timber lodge and self-contained cottage are steeped in character and feel instantly like home. Lounge on the window seat or sundeck, barbecue out the back or get warm in front of the wood-burning stove. The cottage is great for families, and the Portobello bus goes past the gate.

Larnach Lodge LODGE **$$**
(☎03-476 1616; www.larnachcastle.co.nz; Camp Rd; incl breakfast stable d $155, lodge d $260-280; @☎) Larnach Castle's back-garden lodge has 12 individually decorated rooms. The Queen Victoria Room has a giant four-poster bed, while in the Goldrush Room guests sleep in an old horse-drawn carriage. Less frivolous are the atmospheric rooms in the 125-year-old Coach House with sloping Tudor ceilings. Dinner is available by arrangement. A few hundred metres from Larnach Castle, the newly opened Camp Estate country house has luxury suites (doubles $380) worthy of a romantic splurge.

Portobello Village Tourist Park HOLIDAY PARK **$**
(☎03-478 0359; www.portobellopark.co.nz; 27 Hereweka St; sites from $31, units $55-130; ☎) With lots of trees and grass, this is a pleasant place to stake your tent. There's a kids' play

area, a modern kitchen and wheelchair-accessible facilities. Backpacker rooms are BYO everything – bed linen can be hired – and self-contained units are smartly decorated.

Portobello Motels MOTEL **$$**
(☎03-478 0155; www.portobellomotels.com; 10 Harington Point Rd; d $135-145; 📶) Sunny, modern, self-contained units just off the main road in Portobello. Studio units have small decks overlooking the bay. One- and two-bedroom units are also available, but lack the stunning views.

Penguin Place Lodge LODGE **$**
(☎03-478 0286; McGrouther's Farm, Harington Point Rd; adult/child $25/10) Atop the hill and surrounded by farmland, this lodge has a good shared kitchen, a bright lounge, and basic double and twin rooms. There are views across the farm and harbour, you're close to seals and albatross, and you're next-door neighbours with the penguins. Linen costs $5 extra.

Eating

Other Otago Peninsula dining options include the **Portobello Hotel**, and the **Portobello Coffee Shop & Café** for excellent burgers ($15). There's takeaways at the Portobello Store, and cafes attached to Larnach Castle, Nature's Wonders, Glenfalloch Woodland Garden and the Royal Albatross Centre.

There are also plenty of 'hey-let's-stop-here' places for picnics, so stock up before you leave Dunedin.

1908 Café RESTAURANT **$$**
(www.1908cafe.co.nz; 7 Harington Point Rd; mains $20-34; ⏲11.30am-2pm Wed-Sat, 6-10pm daily) Salmon, venison and steak are joined by fresh fish and blackboard specials, and there's a box of toys for the kids. It's a beautiful old building, cheerfully embellished with local art.

Getting There & Around

Up to 10 buses travel each weekday between Dunedin's Cumberland St and Portobello Village, with one or two a day continuing on to Harington Point. Weekend services are more limited. Once on the peninsula, it's tough to get around without your own transport. Most tours will pick you up from your Dunedin accommodation.

There's a petrol station in Portobello, but opening hours are unpredictable. Fill up in Dunedin before driving out.

CENTRAL OTAGO

Rolling hills, grassy paddocks and a succession of tiny, charming gold-rush towns make this region worth exploring. Naseby and Clyde compete for the title of NZ's cutest towns, and rugged, laconic 'Southern Man' types can be seen propping up the bar in backcountry hotels. There are also fantastic opportunities for those on two wheels, whether mountain biking along old gold-mining trails, or taking it easy on the Otago Rail Trail.

Visit www.centralotagonz.com.

Cromwell

POP 2610

Cromwell has a charming lakeside historic precinct, a great weekly farmers market and, courtesy of local farms and orchards, a few good eateries. If you're travelling east to Dunedin or west to Queenstown, it's a good spot to stop for lunch. The nearby Bannockburn region has fine vineyards crafting excellent pinot noir and also some lovely vineyard restaurants. The **Cromwell i-SITE** (☎03-445 0212; www.centralotagonz.com; ⏲9am-6pm; @) is in the central shopping mall. Its *Walk Cromwell* brochure covers local mountain-bike and walking trails, including the nearby gold-rush ghost-town of Bendigo.

Sights & Activities

Old Cromwell Town HISTORIC BUILDINGS
(www.oldcromwell.co.nz) When the Clyde Dam was completed in 1992, it flooded the original Cromwell village including the town centre, 280 homes, six farms and 17 orchards. Many historic buildings were disassembled before the flooding and have since been restored as Old Cromwell Town. This pedestrianised zone sits beside Lake Dunstan and now showcases good eating and interesting galleries. Ask for the *Old Cromwell Town Historic Precinct* map at the i-SITE. During summer an excellent farmers market kicks off at 8am every Sunday.

Goldfields Jet JETBOATING
(☎03-445 1038, 0800 111 038; www.goldfieldsjet.co.nz; adult/child $90/49) Zip around the Kawarau River on a 40-minute jetboat ride with Goldfields Jet.

Central Otago Motorcycle Hire MOTORBIKE RENTAL
(☎03-445 4487; www.comotorcyclehire.co.nz; 271 Bannockburn Rd; motorcycle hire per day from $275)

WORTH A TRIP

SEARCHING FOR THE PERFECT PINOT NOIR

The Bannockburn Valley near Cromwell is home to NZ's finest pinot noir wines, and accounts for over half of Central Otago's total wine production. Vineyards to visit include **Mt Difficulty Wines** (03-445 3445; www.mtdifficulty.co.nz; Felton Rd; platters $17-50, mains $30-33; cellar door 10.30am-4.30pm, restaurant noon-3pm) and **Carrick Wines** (03-445 3480; www.carrick.co.nz; Cairnmuir Rd; platters $12-25, mains $18-25; cellar door 11am-4pm, restaurant noon-3pm). Both vineyards also have highly regarded restaurants open for lunch; it's worth phoning head to book. Before you head off to Bannockburn, visit the Cromwell i-SITE and check out the handy display showcasing the area's vineyards. Pick up the *Central Otago Wine Map* brochure.

Central Otago vineyard tours can be arranged through **Active Travel** (0800 326 228, 03-445 4927; www.activetravelco.com; 8 Pinot Noir Dr; per person $140). Tours include visiting four different vineyards and a high-country sheep station. Other options include exploring Bannockburn's gold-mining heritage with **Bannockburn Historic Goldfields Tours** (03-445 1559, 027 221 0799; www.bannockburngold.co.nz; per person $15-29).

See www.otagowine.com and www.cowa.org.nz.

The sinuous and hilly roads of Central Otago are perfect for negotiating on two wheels. Hire a bike – including Harley Davidson – from Central Otago Motorcycle Hire. Much smaller Italian scooters ($90 per day) are perfect for zipping around the area's lakes, orchards and vineyards, and only require a car driver's licence. The company can also advise on improbably scenic routes around Queenstown, Glenorchy and Wanaka.

Sleeping

Most of Cromwell's motels are huddled near the town's central shopping mall.

Burn Cottage Retreat COTTAGE $$
(03-445 3050; www.burncottageretreat.co.nz; 168 Burn Cottage Rd; d $185) In a rural setting 3km northwest of Cromwell, Burn Cottage has three luxury self-contained cottages set in walnut trees and flower-studded woodland. Decor is classy and chic including king-size beds, spacious self-contained kitchens and modern bathrooms. Ask about the cosy Rascal Cottage, the most secluded of the three. Bed-and-breakfast accommodation (double $165) is available in the main house.

Carrick Lodge MOTEL $$
(0800 445 495, 03 445 4519; www.carricklodge.co.nz; 10 Barry Ave; d $138-160) One of Cromwell's more stylish motels, with spacious, modern rooms just a short stroll from good restaurants and cafes in the town's mall. Ask the owners about viewing the DVD about when the original Cromwell village was flooded to accommodate the construction of the Clyde Dam and Lake Dunstan.

Cromwell Top 10 Holiday Park HOLIDAY PARK $
(0800 107 275, 03-445 0164; www.cromwellholidaypark.co.nz; 1 Alpha St; sites from $40, units $75-135;) The size of a small European nation, packed with cabins, self-contained units and rooms of various descriptions, all set in tree-lined grounds.

Eating & Drinking

Armando's Kitchen ITALIAN $$
(71 Melmore Tce, Old Cromwell Town; mains $25-32; 9am-4pm Tue-Sun, 6.30-10pm Thu-Sat) Old Cromwell Town is best enjoyed with an espresso or gourmet ice cream – try the Thai coconut and lime – on the heritage veranda of Armando's Kitchen. Excellent cake, gourmet pies, and open sandwiches are other daytime distractions. Italian-influenced dinner options include wild mushroom risotto with pancetta, and slow-braised lamb shank with polenta and silverbeet.

Feast RESTAURANT $$
(The Mall; mains $25-35; 5pm-late Tue-Sat) Ignore the incongruous location in Cromwell's shopping mall, and stop by for tasty gourmet pizzas ($22.50), including woodfired spins on Moroccan lamb and Peking duck. Central Otago lamb and briny South Island blue cod and scallops also make an appearance, all served with local wine.

Grain & Seed Café CAFE $
(meals $10-15; 9am-4pm) Set in a beautiful stone building that was once Jolly's Grain Store, this cute cafe serves up big, delicious, inexpensive meals. Grab an outside table beside the lake.

Cider House Cafe & Bar CAFE $$
(SH8; $10-30; ⏲7.30am-4pm Sun-Thu, 7.30am-late Fri-Sat) Sitting beside the state highway at the entry to town, this sunny little cafe dishes up healthy salads, good pizzas ($22.50) and world-famous-in-Cromwell fresh fruit smoothies ($7). Try a glass of their wild apple cider – tart and very tasty.

Getting There & Away

Atomic Shuttles (☎03-349 0697; www.atomictravel.co.nz), **InterCity** (www.intercity.co.nz), **Naked Bus** (www.nakedbus.com) and **Wanaka Connexions** (☎03-443 9122; www.alpinecoachlines.co.nz) all run to/from Queens-town (one hour) and Alexandra (30 minutes). Some services connect to Christchurch and Invercargill. Catch-a-Bus (p189) runs a convenient service linking Dunedin and Wanaka, stopping at Middlemarch, Ranfurly, Alexandra and Cromwell. Other stops near the Otago Central Rail Trail (including Naseby) can also be requested.

Clyde

POP 850

On the banks of the emerald-green Clutha River, the little village of Clyde (www.clyde.co.nz) looks more like a cute 19th-century gold-rush film set than a real town. Despite a recent influx of retirees, Clyde retains a friendly, small-town feel, and even when holidaymakers arrive in numbers over summer, it's a great place to chill out. It's also one end of the Otago Central Rail Trail.

Sights & Activities

Pick up a copy of *Walk Around Historic Clyde* from the Alexandra i-SITE (p209). The **Alexandra–Clyde 150th Anniversary Walk** (three hours one-way) is a riverside trail that's fairly flat with ample resting spots and shade.

Clyde Historical Museum MUSEUM
(Blyth St; adult/child $3/1; ⏲2-4pm Tue-Sun) Showcases Maori and Victorian exhibits and provides information about the Clyde Dam.

Trail Journeys BICYCLE RENTAL
(☎0800 724 587; www.trailjourneys.co.nz; Clyde Railhead; ⏲tours Sep-Apr) Trail Journeys rents bikes (from $35 per day) and offers cycling tours.

Festivals & Events

Clyde Wine & Food Festival WINE & FOOD
(www.promotedunstan.org.nz; ⏲Easter Sunday) Showcasing the region's produce and wines.

Sleeping

In February and March Clyde gets very busy so advance booking of accommodation is recommended.

Oliver's Lodge B&B $$$
(☎03-449 2600; www.oliverscentralotago.co.nz; 34 Sunderland St; d $195-315; 📶) Showcasing an outstanding collection of old maps, Oliver's Lodge fills a 19th-century merchant's house and stables with luxurious rooms decked out with Oriental rugs, heritage furniture and claw-foot baths. Most rooms open onto a secluded garden courtyard, and breakfast of freshly baked bread, homemade yoghurt and preserves is included.

Hartley Arms Backpackers HOSTEL $
(☎03-449 2700; hartleyarms@xtra.co.nz; 25 Sunderland St; per person $40) In the old stables behind a beautiful 1869 building that was once the Hartley Arms Hotel, these three cosy rooms look out to a peaceful, private, stone-walled garden and share a small kitchen and lounge. Tables and chairs in the shade of the cherry tree are a fine place to stretch limbs weary from 150km of cycling. The cat's called Radler, German for cyclist.

Dunstan House B&B $$
(☎03-449 2295; www.dunstanhouse.co.nz; 29 Sunderland St; d incl breakfast $120-220; ⏲Sep-May; @) This restored Victorian-age, balconied inn has lovely bar and lounge areas. Rooms with ensuite bathrooms, individually decorated in period style, are a little pricier, but most have claw-foot tubs. Less expensive (but still comfortable) rooms are next door in 'Miners Lane'.

Old Postmaster's House B&B $
(☎03-449 2488; www.postofficecafeclyde.co.nz; Blyth St; d $95-125) Has lovely rooms dotted with antique furnishings.

EATING

Bank Café CAFE $
(31 Sunderland St; $10-18; ⏲9am-4.30pm) Owned by a group of passionate local foodies, everything at the Bank Café is made fresh daily. That includes cakes and slices, corn fritters for breakfast and robust takeaway sandwiches that are perfect for lunch on two wheels.

Post Office Café & Bar CAFE $$
(2 Blyth St; mains $15-30; ⏲10am-9pm) Clyde's 1899 post office houses a popular restaurant famous for its garden tables and favourites such as grilled chicken sandwiches and hot-

WORTH A TRIP

TWO WHEELS GOOD: OTAGO CENTRAL RAIL TRAIL

Stretching from Dunedin to Clyde, the Central Otago rail branch linked small, inland goldfield towns with the big city from the early 20th century through to the 1990s. After the 150km stretch from Middlemarch to Clyde was permanently closed, the rails were ripped up and the trail resurfaced. The result is a year-round trail that takes bikers, walkers and horseback riders along a historic route containing old rail bridges, viaducts and tunnels. With excellent trailside facilities (toilets, shelters and information), no steep hills, gob-smacking scenery and profound remoteness, the trail attracts well over 25,000 visitors annually. March to April is the busiest time, when the trail is packed with urban visitors from Auckland, Wellington, Christchurch and Australia.

The trail can be followed in either direction. One option is to travel from Dunedin on the scenic Taieri Gorge Railway (p200), cycle from Pukerangi to Middlemarch (19km by road) and begin the trail the following day. The entire trail takes approximately four to five days to complete by bike (or a week on foot), but you can obviously choose to do as short or long a stretch as suits your plans. There are also easy detours to towns such as Naseby and St Bathans. Many settlements along the route offer accommodation and dining, including lodgings in restored cottages and rural farmhouses.

Mountain bikes can be rented in Dunedin, Middlemarch, Alexandra and Clyde. Any of the area's major i-SITEs can provide detailed information. See www.otagocentralrailtrail.co.nz and www.otagorailtrail.co.nz for track information, recommended timings, accommodation options and tour companies.

pots. There's loads of nooks and crannies conducive to reading fascinating newspapers featuring momentous days in NZ history.

The Packing Shed CAFE $
(68 Boulton Rd; $10-20) An interesting sculpture garden and a funky rural ambience make the Packing Shed a popular detour for Rail Trailers from Clyde to Alexandra.

Shopping

Central Gourmet Galleria FOOD
(www.centralone.co.nz; 27 Sunderland St) Expect a great collection of award-winning local wines, many of which you won't find anywhere else. There's also plenty of Central Otago foodie treats such as jams and chutneys – all easy-to-transport gifts and souvenirs.

Getting There & Away

Although no company has a dedicated stop here, buses travelling between Cromwell and Alexandra pick up and drop off in Clyde on request (it may incur a small surcharge).

Alexandra

POP 4620

Unless you've come here especially for the Easter Bunny Hunt or September's NZ Merino Shearing Championships, the best reason to visit Alexandra is the nearby mountain biking. Some travellers stay for seasonal fruit-picking work.

Sights & Activities

Mountain bikers will love the old gold trails weaving through the hills. Collect maps from the i-SITE (p209). **Altitude Adventures** (☎03-448 8917; www.altitudeadventures.co.nz; 88 Centennial Ave) and **Trail Journeys** (☎0800 724 587; www.trailjourneys.co.nz; Clyde Railhead) both rent bikes, offer backcountry cycling tours and provide transport to trailheads.

Central Stories MUSEUM
(www.centralstories.co.nz; 21 Centennial Ave; admission by donation; ⏲9am-5pm) Visit this excellent regional museum in the Alexandria i-SITE to understand Central Otago's history of gold-mining, winemaking and sheep farming.

Clutha River Adventures KAYAKING
(☎03-449 3155; www.cluthariveradventures.co.nz; from $95) Commandeer inflatable kayaks to explore Lake Roxburgh. A popular self-guided option is from Alexandra to the interesting Doctor's Point gold-mining town.

Clutha River Cruise BOAT TOUR
(☎03-449 3155; www.clutharivercruises.co.nz; adult/child $90/40; ⏲11am & 2pm Boxing Day-Feb, 1pm Oct-Christmas Eve & Mar-Apr) To experience the scenery and history of the region

by boat, join a 2½-hour Clutha River Cruise. Book at the Alexandra i-SITE.

Sleeping

Motels line Centennial Ave on the way into town.

Quail Rock B&B $$

(☎03-448 7224; www.quailrock.co.nz; 5 Fairway Dr; s/d from $100/150; @📶) Perched high above town, this very comfortable B&B offers equal servings of privacy and mountain views. Homemade preserves give breakfast a unique touch, and dinners are also available. And yes, quail are often seen scratching around the rocks in the garden.

Marj's Place HOSTEL $

(☎03-448 7098; www.marjsplace.co.nz; 5 Theyers St; per person $35; @📶) Two houses have myriad higgledy-piggledy shared rooms and a nice communal vibe, helped by the peaceful rose garden out back. There's a compact Finnish sauna onsite, and friendly owner Marj can also arrange seasonal work. Cash only.

Alexandra Holiday Park HOLIDAY PARK $

(☎03-448 8297; www.alexandraholidaypark.com; 44 Manuherikia Rd; sites from $30, units $50-70; @📶) Sitting beside the road to Ranfurly, with plenty of shade and backing onto the swimmer-friendly Manuherikia River, this holiday park is close to where the Rail Trail enters town. Self-contained units (sleeping up to six) start at $95 for two.

Eating

Tin Goose Cafe CAFE $

(www.thetingoosecafe.com; 22 Centennial Ave; $10-20) Home-style baking and superior counter food – try the chicken, cranberry and cream cheese pizza – combine with interesting salads and Alexandra's best coffee. Local mushrooms on ciabatta or the omelette of the day are healthy ways to start the day, especially if you're en route to the Rail Trail in nearby Clyde.

Red Brick Café CAFE $$

(Centrepoint car park off Limerick St; lunch $15-30, dinner $30-35) This funky cafe-wine bar with a sunny courtyard is positioned beside an Alexandra shoppers' carpark, the last place you'd expect to find blue cod, venison and pork belly so well prepared. Most ingredients and wines are locally sourced. The building was originally Alexandra's first bakery, and a hip utilitarian warehouse ambience lingers.

Shaky Bridge Café CAFE $$

(Graveyard Gully Rd; mains $15-30) Over a 110-year-old footbridge near the Rail Trail, Shaky Bridge is a winery-cafe in a heritage mudbrick building with views of the Manuherikia River. Tuck into locally sourced delicacies such as venison, duck or salmon. Coffee and cake come with a side order of vineyard views.

Foursquare SUPERMARKET $

(91 Tarbert St) Self-catering central.

Information

Alexandra i-SITE (☎03-448 9515; www.centralotagonz.com; 22 Centennial Ave; ⏰9am-6pm; @) The Alexandra i-SITE has internet access and a necessary free map of this very spread-out town.

Getting There & Away

See Cromwell for buses that pass along this route. From Alexandra you can head north-west past Cromwell towards Queenstown, or south past Roxburgh towards the east coast.

Alexandra to Palmerston

Northeast of Alexandra an irrigated strip of land tags alongside the highway, with the Dunstan and North Rough Ranges rising impressively on either side. This is the Manuherikia Valley, which tumbles into the Maniototo Plain as State Hwy 85 (SH85).

Chatto Creek Tavern (☎03-447 3710; www.chattocreektavern.co.nz; SH85; meals $12-23) is a cute 1880s stone hotel beside the Rail Trail and the highway. Pop in for a whitebait fritter (in season) or steak sandwich, or rest your weary calf muscles in a dorm bed ($50) or double room ($120). Rates include breakfast.

Made up of half a handful of historic buildings, and home to just 50 souls, tiny **Ophir** lies across the Manuherikia River and lays claim to the country's largest range of temperatures (from 35°C above to 22°C below). Take the gravel exit south off SH85 to rattle across the cute, 1870s wooden-planked Dan O'Connell Bridge, a bumpy but scenic crossing. **Black's Hotel** (☎03-447 3826; steven.chapman@clear.net.nz; per person incl breakfast $60) has cycle-friendly accommodation.

Back on SH85, **Omakau** and **Lauder** are good stops if you're a hungry rail-trailer with a sore bum and a need for a bed. Good-value rooms, excellent food and local company are all on tap at the **Omakau Commercial Hotel** (☎03-447 3715; www.omakauhotel.co.nz; 1 Harvey

St; dm/s/d from $35/45/80). Accommodation in nearby Lauder includes **Pedal Inn** (03-447 3460; benandcatherine@farmside.co.nz; SH85; d $120), which has two modern self-contained units on a working farm, and the cosy **Muddy Creek Cutting** (03-447 3682; www.muddycreekcutting.co.nz/; per person $60), a charmingly restored 1930s mudbrick farmhouse. Dinners with a local, organic spin are also available ($50 per person).

In Omakau township, take a break from the Rail Trail at the **Muddy Creek Cafe** (2 Harvey St; pies & mains $10-15), a friendly spot festooned with old radios. Organic ice cream and deservedly famous chicken and mushroom pies are some of the treats your tired legs have earned. Just up the road in Lauder, trailside **Stationside Cafe** (Lauder; snacks & mains $10-20) has healthy salads, sandwiches, soups and pasta. You'll probably hear Rosemary, the pet sheep, before you see her.

Take the turn-off north, into the foothills of the imposing Dunstan Range and on to diminutive **St Bathans**, 17km from SH85. This once-thriving gold-mining town of 2000 people is now home to only half a dozen permanent residents. Blue Lake is an accidental attraction: a large hollow filled with amazingly blue mineral water that has run off abandoned gold workings. Walk around the alien-looking lake's edge to a lookout (one hour return).

The **Vulcan Hotel** (03-447 3629; www.stbathansnz.co.nz; Main Rd; r per person $50; meals $20-25) is an atmospheric spot to drink in or stay. Considering it has a population of only six people (plus one Labrador and a ghost or two), you'll find the bar here pretty busy on a Friday night as thirsty shearers from around the valley descend en masse. The Vulcan also rents out some empty houses nearby. Jack (the black Labrador) will escort you down to a handful of cute cottages (doubles from $100 to $220 per night) including the old gaol. He's also very keen on his battered old rugby ball. Try not to lose it like we almost did.

Back on SH85, the road swings around to run southeast and passes the historic **Wedderburn Tavern** (03-444 9548; www.wedderburntavern.co.nz; SH85; per person incl breakfast $55). Seven kilometres later is the turn-off for Naseby; otherwise it's straight through to Ranfurly.

NASEBY

Cute as a button, surrounded by forest and dotted with 19th-century stone buildings, Naseby is the kind of small town where life moves slowly. That the town is pleasantly obsessed with the fairly insignificant world of NZ curling indicates there's not much else going on. It's that lazy small-town vibe, along with good mountain-biking and walking trails through the surrounding forest, that make Naseby an interesting place to stay for a couple of days.

Sights & Activities

Naseby Information & Crafts (03-444 9961; Derwent St; 11am-2pm Fri-Mon), in the old post office, has information on local walks and bike trails. For more mountain-biking information and to hire a bike, head to **Kila's Bike Shop** (03-444 9088; kilasbikeshop@xtra.co.nz; Derwent St; per day $35) near the Black Forest Café. **Naseby Forest Headquarters** (03-444 9995; Derwent St) is also good for maps of walks through the Black Forest.

All year round you can shimmy after curling stones at the indoor ice rink in the **Naseby Alpine Park** (03-444 9878; www.curling.co.nz; Channel Rd; curling per hr adult/family $20/50; 10am-5pm). Curling tuition is also available. From June to August there's ice skating at an adjacent outdoor rink, and a seasonal ice **luge** (03-444 9270; www.lugenz.co.nz; Jul-Aug) runs for a thrilling 360m down a nearby hillside. The luge is open to the public, but booking ahead is essential.

Sleeping & Eating

Church Mouse RENTAL HOUSE $$
(03-444 9440, 027 714 1209; www.holidayhouses.co.nz; d $190) For a romantic stay, consider the Church Mouse, a lovingly restored former Catholic church, now revitalised as luxury rental accommodation. Rich wooden floors are partnered with stylish modern furniture, and the main bedroom fills a private mezzanine floor. Mod cons include a brand-new kitchen, and there's a private sunny courtyard for enjoying those southern summer nights.

Naseby Trail Lodge LODGE $$
(03-444 8374, 0508 627 329; www.nasebylodge.co.nz; cnr Derwent & Oughter Sts; d $160) Popular with international luging visitors, the Nasbey Trail Lodge features modern units constructed of environmentally friendly straw-bale walls sheathed in rustic corrugated iron.

Ancient Briton PUB $
(03-444 9990; www.ancientbriton.co.nz; 16 Leven St; s $60, d from $105) A mudbrick ho-

tel dating from 1863, Ancient Briton has a rambling range of basic-to-comfortable accommodation. Have some traditional pub grub (mains from $17 to $27), or prop yourself up at the bar to admire the trophies of the pub's 'Blue Hats' curling team and get to know the locals.

Royal Hotel HOTEL $
(03-444 9990; www.naseby.co.nz; Earne St; dm $30, d $89-115) Another pub with good food and accommodation is the Royal Hotel, right beside what just may be NZ's most rustic garden bar.

Larchview Holiday Park HOLIDAY PARK $
(03-444 9904; www.larchviewholidaypark.co.nz; Swimming Dam Rd; sites from $26, units $45-81; @) Set in 17 acres of woods, Larchview Holiday Park has an alpine feel, a small on-site playground and swimming at a dam nearby. There are also basic timber cabins and cottages.

Black Forest Café CAFE $
(03-444 9820; 5 Derwent St; mains $10-15; 9am-4pm) Fresh baking and good coffee features at the Black Forest Café, gorgeous inside with its stone walls, bright colours and warm polished wood. The wide-ranging menu features bagels, panini and creamy smoothies using local Central Otago fruit.

Getting There & Away

The Ancient Briton pub (p210) has a courtesy van and will pick up from Ranfurly or the Rail Trail. If prebooked, **Catch-a-Bus** (03-449 2024; www.catchabus.co.nz) stops in Naseby on its Dunedin–Cromwell route. If you're driving, take the exit off SH85, just north of Ranfurly. From Naseby, you can wind your way northeast through spectacular scenery to Danseys Pass and through to Duntroon and the Waitaki Valley.

RANFURLY

Ranfurly is trying hard to cash in on its art deco buildings – much of the town was rebuilt in the architecture of the day after a series of fires in the 1930s – and a few attractive buildings and antique shops line its sleepy main drag. The town holds an annual **Art Deco Festival** (www.ranfurlyartdeco.co.nz) on the last weekend of February.

The **Ranfurly i-SITE** (03-444 1005; www.maniototo.co.nz; Charlemont St; 10am-4pm daily Oct-Apr, Mon-Fri May-Sep; @) is in the old train station. Grab a copy of *Rural Art Deco – Ranfurly Walk* for a self-guided tour.

The art deco **Ranf**
444 9140; www.ranfurlyhote
St; s $55-70, d $75-98; @) ha
rooms and a couple of bars,
stantial pub meals (dinner
$27). All you'll need after a long
wheels and a bike seat.

Cheery and warm, with an open fire
art and the Maniototo sports wall of fa
E-Central Café (03-444 8300; 14 Charlemo
St; mains $7-15; breakfast & lunch) is definitely
the best lunch option in town.

To explore the rugged terrain made famous by local landscape artist Grahame Sydney, contact **Maniototo 4WD Safaris** (03-444 9703; www.maniototo4wdsafaris.co.nz; per person half-/full day $80/140).

A daily **Catch-a-Bus** (03-449 2024; www.catchabus.co.nz) shuttle passes through Ranfurly on its way between Wanaka and Dunedin.

WAIPIATA

About 10km southeast of Ranfurly and right on the Rail Trail, tiny Waipiata has the **Waipiata Country Hotel** (03-444 9470; www.waipiatahotel.co.nz; dinner mains $20-25; @). There's a sunny CYO ('Cook Your Own') barbecue area, and the restaurant menu includes goodies such as Pig Root Spare Ribs and Bike Faster Pasta. It's the only pub on the Rail Trail serving Dunedin's Emerson's beer, and comfortable accommodation is available from $70 per person. Ask about the recently refurbished Mudbrick room.

Set on farmland 4km from Waipiata, **Peter's Farm Lodge** (0800 472 458, 027 686 1692; www.petersfarm.co.nz; Tregonning Rd; per person incl breakfast $50) has simple, comfortable rooms in a rustic 19th-century farmhouse. Shared dining tables encourage an end-of-the-day social vibe, and hearty barbecue dinners are $25. Kayaks, fishing rods and gold pans are all available, so it's worth staying a couple of nights. Peter also runs the nearby Tregonnings Cottage, built in 1880, but now with a well-equipped, modern kitchen. He'll also pick you up for nix from the Waipiata stop on the Rail Trail.

RANFURLY TO DUNEDIN

After Ranfurly, SH85 runs 62km to Palmerston, then 55km south to Dunedin or 59km north to Oamaru. Another option is to hop on the southbound SH87 directly to Dunedin, 129km via **Hyde** and Middlemarch. In Hyde, the **Otago Central Hotel** (03-444 4800; www.hydehotel.co.nz; s/d with shared bathroom $80-130, s/d with ensuite $100-190) provides

...nger in the sun-
...spresso before
...n.
...nge as an im-
...vn of **Middle-**
...z) is one end
...lso a start or
...il Trail. Rent
...ry (03-464
...Ave; per day
...nch at the

...iddlemarch Singles**
...held across Easter in odd-numbered years, southern men from the region gather to woo city gals.

On a family-owned farm just a few hundred metres from the Rail Trail, **Trail's End** (03-464 3474; www.trailsend.co.nz; 91 Mason Rd; d incl breakfast $150) combines secluded cabins with views of the Rock and Pillar Mountain Range, and has the muscle-easing diversion of a spa pool.

Opposite the railway station, **Quench Café & Bar** (03-464 3070; 29 Snow Ave; mains $10-30; 8am-late) is versatility plus, with goodies such as the Rail Burger ($15 – recommended if you're beginning the Rail Trail) and ice-cold Speight's on tap (*definitely* recommended if you've just finished the trail).

Alexandra to Dunedin

Heading south from Alexandra, SH8 winds along rugged, rock-strewn hills above Lake Roxburgh, then follows the Clutha River as it passes lush fruit farms and Central Otago's famous orchards. In season, roadside fruit stalls sell just-picked stone fruit, cherries and berries. En route are a number of small towns, many from gold-rush days.

Only 13km south of Alexandra, **Speargrass Inn** (03-449 2192; www.speargrassinn.co.nz; SH8; d $155-170) has three units in attractive gardens behind a charming 1860s building with elegant guest areas. An on-site **restaurant** (SH8; mains $15-30; 9am-4pm Mon & Thu,9am-7pm Fri & Sat, 9am-6pm Sun) offers cosmopolitan tastes including beef parmigiana and mushroom-and-blue-cheese tart. At the very least, stop for coffee and cake, and stock up on tasty homemade preserves and chutneys.

From here, the road passes through Roxburgh, Lawrence and the Manuka Gorge Scenic Reserve, a scenic route through wooded hills and gullies. SH8 joins SH1 in Milton.

ROXBURGH

The orchards surrounding Roxburgh provide excellent roadside stalls and equally plentiful seasonal fruit-picking work. **Roxburgh i-SITE** (03-446 8920; www.centralotagonz.com; 120 Scotland St; 9.30am-4pm) has information on mountain biking and water sports.

Villa Rose Backpackers (03-446 8761; www.villarose.co.nz; 79 Scotland St; dm/unit $30/95) is an old-fashioned villa with spacious dorm rooms and a huge modern kitchen. Adjacent heritage-style, self-contained units are supercomfortable. The manager can help sort out seasonal fruit-picking work, and provide discounted weekly rates.

Stop at Roxburgh's iconic **Jimmy's Pies** (03-444-8596; 143 Scotland St; pies $4-6; 7.30am-5pm Mon-Fri). Renowned across the South Island since 1960, Jimmy's pastry delights are at their best just out of the oven. Try the apricot and apple flavour – you're in orchard country after all. Heading south, you'll find Jimmy's on your right just as you're leaving town.

Clutha District

The mighty Clutha River is NZ's highest-volume river, and is dammed in several places to feed hydroelectric power stations. **Balclutha** is South Otago's largest town but is of little interest to travellers other than as a place to stock up on supplies before setting off into the Catlins. The **Balclutha i-SITE** (03-418 0388; www.cluthacountry.co.nz; 4 Clyde St) has local info and internet access. For more local information, see www.cluthacountry.co.nz.

NORTH OTAGO & WAITAKI

The broad, braided Waitaki River rushes across the northern boundary of Otago, setting the boundary with Canterbury to the north. South of the river, on the coast, lies Oamaru, a town of penguins and glorious heritage architecture. The Waitaki Valley is an alternative route inland, featuring freaky rock formations, Maori rock paintings and ancient fossils. The area is also one of NZ's newest winemaking regions, and a major component of the new Alps2Ocean Cycle Trail, linking Aoraki/Mt Cook National Park to Oamaru. See www.nzcycletrail.com for more information.

Oamaru

POP 12,700

Nothing moves very fast in Oamaru. Tourists saunter, locals linger and penguins waddle. Even oft-celebrated heritage modes of transport – penny farthings and steam trains – reflect an unhurried pace. For travellers, the focus is mostly on penguins and the historic district, but eccentric gems such as the South Island's yummiest cheese factory, cool galleries and a peculiar live-music venue provide other distractions. Another recent layer to Oamaru's unique appeal is the quirky Steampunk movement, boldly celebrating the past and the future with an ethos of 'tomorrow as it used to be'.

A history of refrigerated-meat shipping made Oamaru prosperous enough in the 19th century to build the imposing limestone buildings that grace the town today. In its 1880s heyday, Oamaru was about the same size as Los Angeles was at the same time. Oamaru also has an affinity with the arts that may well be rooted in its claim to Janet Frame, but extends to a lively arty and crafty community today.

Sights

HARBOUR-TYNE HISTORIC PRECINCT

Oamaru has some of NZ's best-preserved historic commercial buildings, particularly around the harbour and Tyne St, an area designated the **Historic Precinct**. They were built from the 19th century, largely using the local limestone (known as Oamaru stone or whitestone) in fashionable classic forms, from Gothic revival to neoclassical Italianate and Venetian palazzo. Pop into the Oamaru Whitestone Civic Trust (p218) for information and the *Victorian Oamaru* pictorial guide. On Thames St, Oamaru's expansive main drag – laid out to accommodate the minimum turning circle of a bullock cart – don't miss the **National Bank** at No 11 and the **Oamaru Opera House** at No 92.

The fascinating area of narrow streets in the historic precinct is now home to bookshops, antique stores, galleries, vintage clothing shops and craft bookbinders. Guided walking tours ($10) leave from the Oamaru i-SITE at 10am daily from November to April.

The **Woolstore** (1 Tyne St) has a cafe and souvenirs, and the **Auto Museum** (1 Tyne St; adult/child $6/free; ⏲10am-4.30pm) is perfect for *Top Gear* fans. On adjoining Harbour St, the **Grainstore Gallery** (☎027-261 3764; ⏲noon-4pm Mon-Fri, 10am-2pm Sat & Sun) features an ever-changing array of quirky artwork. Another thoroughly Victorian-era thrill is steering a penny farthing bicycle from **Oamaru Cycle Works** (☎03-439 5333, 027 439 5331; Wansbeck St; lesson & afternoon tea $25). Ask David the owner about his intrepid penny farthing trek down the entire length

OAMARU IN FRAME

One of NZ's best-known novelists, Janet Frame, is intimately linked with Oamaru. The town, disguised in her novels as 'Waimaru', was Frame's home throughout most of her early years. Her writing is often described as 'dense', with early books also somewhat grim, a reflection of her own troubled life. But they are also unique in the construction of their stories and the nature in which the story is told. Later books remain intense, with wordplays, mythological clues and illusions, but are less gloomy.

It was in 1951 that Frame, a (misdiagnosed) sufferer of schizophrenia at Seacliff Lunatic Asylum, found sudden recognition as a writer, happily causing her doctors to rethink her planned lobotomy. Released, with frontal lobe intact, she moved on to gain international recognition in 1957 with her first novel *Owls Do Cry*, in which 'Waimaru' features strongly. Her subsequent literary accomplishments include *Faces in the Water* (1961), *The Edge of the Alphabet* (1962), *Scented Gardens for the Blind* (1963), *A State of Siege* (1967) and *Intensive Care* (1970). Jane Campion's film version of *An Angel at My Table* (1990), is based on the second volume of Frame's autobiographical trilogy. Pick up a free copy of *Janet Frame's Oamaru* from the Oamaru i-SITE (p218) and follow the 1½-hour self-guided tour.

Frame received numerous NZ and international awards, and was twice short-listed for the Nobel Prize for literature, most recently in 2003. She died the following year.

Janet Frame's **childhood house** (56 Eden St; $6; ⏲2-4pm Nov-Apr) is also open for viewing.

of New Zealand. He also rents out retro 1940s bikes (half/full day $15/20).

Try to visit this historical precinct at the weekend, especially on a Sunday for the excellent **Oamaru Farmers Market** (www.oamarufarmersmarket.co.nz; Tyne St; ⌚9.30am-1pm Sun). Note that some historic precinct shops and attractions are closed on a Monday.

Also check out the Oamaru limestone being carved at **Ian Andersen's gallery** (www.ianandersensculptor.co.nz; 15 Tyne St) and buy some smaller works to take home. Art buffs should seek out the *Oamaru Arts & Crafts* brochure at the i-SITE.

ELSEWHERE IN OAMARU

Blue-Penguin Colony WILDLIFE

(www.penguins.co.nz; adult/child/family $25/10/65; ⌚10am-sunset) In an old limestone quarry near the waterfront, you can see the little tykes from Oamaru's blue-penguin colony surfing in and wading ashore. The penguins arrive just before dark (around 5.30pm in midwinter and 9.30pm midsummer), and it takes them about an hour to all come ashore. You'll see the most penguins (up to 150) in November and December. From March to August there may be only 30 to 50 birds. Nightly viewing times are posted at the i-SITE (p218). Use of camera flashes is prohibited, and you should dress warmly.

To understand the centre's conservation work, take the 30-minute, daytime, behind-the-scenes tour (self-guided adult/child/family $12/5/30 or guided $18/8/50). Forward bookings can be made on www.penguins.co.nz, and packages combining night viewing and the behind-the-scenes tour are also available. Drop some coins in the centre's donation box. Their conservation efforts have helped increase the bird population dramatically.

Do not under any circumstances wander around the rocks beside the sea here at night looking for penguins. It's damaging to their environment as well as stuffing up studies on the effect of humans on the little birds.

FREE **Yellow-Eyed Penguin Colony** WILDLIFE

There are large hides and good trails to the yellow-eyed penguin colony at Bushy Beach, where the penguins come ashore in late afternoon to feed their young. Two hours before dark is the best time to see them.

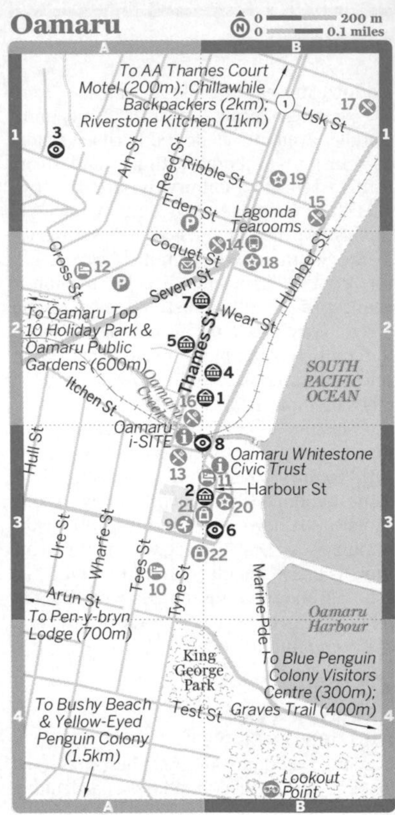

Despite their Maori name, *hoiho* (noisy shouter), they're extremely shy; if they see or hear you they'll head back into the water. Graves Trail, a 2.5km low-tide walk, starts from the end of Waterfront Rd and follows the rugged coastline around to the yellow-eyed colony at Bushy Beach. Watch out for fur seals, and do not use a flash when photographing the penguins.

FREE **Steampunk HQ** GALLERY

(www.steampunkoamaru.co.nz; 1 Itchen St; ⌚10am-4pm) Discover the past – or maybe a quirky version of the future – in this wonderful gallery celebrating Steampunk culture. Ancient machines wheeze and splutter, and the industrial detritus of the last century or so is repurposed and reimagined to funky effect. Don't miss firing up the sparking, space-age locomotive out the front – definitely at its best after dark.

Oamaru

Sights

	Auto Museum	(see 11)
1	Forrester Gallery	B2
2	Grainstore Gallery	B3
3	Janet Frame's House	A1
4	National Bank	B2
5	North Otago Museum	A2
6	NZ Malt Whisky Company	B3
7	Oamaru Opera House	B2
8	Steam Train	B3
	Steampunk HQ	(see 8)

Activities, Courses & Tours

9	Oamaru Cycle Works	A3

Sleeping

10	Anne Mieke Guest House	A3
11	Criterion Hotel	B3
12	Red Kettle YHA	A2

Eating

13	Annie's Victorian Tearooms	A3
14	Countdown Supermarket	B2
	Harbour St Bakery	(see 11)
	Loan & Merc Tavern & Eating House	(see 6)
15	Midori	B1
16	Steam	A2
17	Whitestone Cheese Factory & Café	B1

Drinking

	Birdlands Wine Company	(see 11)
	Criterion Hotel	(see 11)
	Fat Sallys	(see 5)

Entertainment

18	Globe	B2
19	Movie World 3	B1
20	Penguin Club	B3

Shopping

21	Ian Andersen's Gallery	B3
22	Oamaru Farmers Market	A3
	Woolstore	(see 11)

FREE **Forrester Gallery** GALLERY
(www.forrestergallery.com; 9 Thames St; 10.30am-4.30pm) Housed in a beautiful, columned 1880s bank building, the Forrester Gallery has an excellent collection of regional and NZ art. This gallery is a good place to see works by Colin McCahon, renowned for his darkly melancholic style. Check the website for regular special exhibitions.

FREE **North Otago Museum** MUSEUM
(www.northotagomuseum.co.nz; 60 Thames St; 10.30am-4.30pm Mon-Fri, 1-4.30pm Sat & Sun) In the grand 19th-century library, the North Otago Museum has exhibits on Maori and Pakeha history, writer Janet Frame, architecture and geology.

Steam Train TRAIN
(www.oamaru-steam.org.nz; adult/child/family one-way $5/2/12, return $8/3/20; 11am-4pm Sun & Public Holidays) On Sundays ride the old Steam Train from the historic district to the waterfront area. The two steam trains date from 1877 and 1924, although in winter they're occasionally replaced by a diesel.

NZ Malt Whisky Company DISTILLERY
(03-434 8842; www.nzmaltwhisky.co.nz; 14 Harbour St; gallery free, tastings $10-15; 11am-5pm) The NZ Malt Whisky Company offers whisky tastings amid the heritage bones of a former Victorian warehouse. Don't miss taking the labyrinthine wooden stairs to the art gallery on the upper floors.

FREE **Oamaru Public Gardens**
(main entry on Severn St) The Oamaru public gardens were first opened in 1876 and are a lovely place to chill out on a hot day, with endless lawns, waterways, bridges and a children's playground.

Activities

Vertical Ventures MOUNTAIN BIKING, CLIMBING
(021 894 427, 03-434 5010; www.verticalventures.co.nz) Contact Rob to rent mountain bikes ($45 per day), or join guided mountain-biking trips along forest tracks and coastal roads (from $100 per person). To get vertical, join an abseiling or climbing group (from $130). Locations include the Elephant Rocks in the Waitaki Valley.

Festivals & Events

Oamaru Wine & Food Festival FOOD & WINE
(www.oamaruwineandfoodfest.co.nz; 3rd Sun in Feb) Showcasing North Otago's food and wine scene.

Victorian Heritage Celebrations CULTURAL
(www.historicoamaru.co.nz; ⏲late November) Five days of locals wearing Victorian garb, with penny-farthing races, singing, dancing and street theatre.

Tours

MP3 players ($15) for self-guided tours are available at the i-SITE (p218). Ask about guided walking tours of Oamaru's historic precinct, often with a ghostly spin.

Penguins Crossing WILDLIFE
(☎03-477 9083; www.travelheadfirst.com; adult/child/family $50/25/125) Door-to-door, 2½-hour tour taking in the blue and yellow-eyed colonies. Price includes admission to the blue penguin colony. Pick up times vary from 4pm to 7pm throughout the year.

Sleeping

Oamaru's motel mile kicks off at the northern end of town as SH1 morphs into Thames St. There's also good accommodation a short drive from Oamaru at Old Bones Backpackers (p220) and the Olive Grove Lodge and Holiday Park (p220).

Pen-y-bryn Lodge LODGE $$$
(☎03-434 7939; www.penybryn.co.nz; 41 Towey St; d incl breakfast/breakfast & dinner $625/875; @) Well-travelled foodie owners have thoroughly revitalised this beautiful 125-year-old residence. Rates include a full breakfast, predinner drinks in the antiques-studded drawing room, and a four-course, gourmet dinner in the fabulous dining room. Retire afterwards to the billiard room and show off on the full-sized table. Dinner is also available to outside guests by prior arrangement (three/four courses $85/135).

Chillawhile Backpackers HOSTEL $
(☎03-437 0168; www.chillawhile.co.nz; 1 Frome St; dm $29-31, s $48, d/tw 58-66; @📶) Unleash your creative spirit at this funky and colourful hostel in a restored two-storey Victorian residence. Guests are encouraged to draw and paint, or create sweet soul music on the hostel's guitars, pianos, didgeridoo and African drums. With all that creative energy, there's definitely a laidback social vibe, and Chillawhile is one of NZ's best and most unique hostels.

Criterion Hotel HOTEL $$
(☎03-434 6247; www.criterion.net.nz; 3 Tyne St; d with bathroom $165, s/tw/d without bathroom $85/100/135, all incl breakfast) Period rooms at this 1877 hotel are smallish, but the guest lounge is large, and both are lovingly restored with glowing wooden floors and Turkish rugs. Rates also include home baking and preserves in the cosy dining room. Downstairs there's the distraction of a great corner pub with more than a few good beers on tap.

Anne Mieke Guest House B&B $
(☎03-434 8051; www.theoamarubnb.com; 47 Tees St; s/d incl $60/90) The decor is a tad chintzy, and the ambience hushed like your Nana's house, but visitors are guaranteed harbour views at this good-value B&B. Look forward to spotless shared bathrooms and a spacious guest lounge.

Red Kettle YHA HOSTEL $
(☎03-434 5008; www.yha.co.nz; cnr Reed & Cross Sts; dm/d $28/62; @📶) This red-roofed cottage has colourfully painted inner walls, a well-equipped kitchen and a cosy lounge. A good old-school vinyl collection will keep you and fellow guests entertained. It's on a quiet side street, a short walk from the town centre.

AAA Thames Court Motel MOTEL $$
(☎0800 223 644, 03-434 6963; www.aaathamescourt.co.nz; 252 Thames St; d $115-140; @📶) Good option for families with comfortable, recently renovated units and a play area for kids. All bookings include free wi-fi, and the cafes and pubs of Oamaru are a pleasant 500m stroll away.

Oamaru Top 10 Holiday Park HOLIDAY PARK $
(☎03-434 7666, 0800 280 202; www.oamarutop10.co.nz; Chelmer St; sites from $40, units $65-140; @📶) Grassy and well maintained, with trees out the back and the public gardens next door. Cabins are basic, but units with kitchen (with varying levels of self-contained comfort) are much nicer.

Eating

TOP CHOICE **Riverstone Kitchen** RESTAURANT $$
(☎03-431 3505; www.riverstonekitchen.co.nz; 1431 SH1; brunch & lunch mains $15-20, dinner mains $29-32; ⏲9am-5pm Thu-Mon, 6pm-late Thu-Sun; 🖉) This award-winning haven 12km north of Oamaru on SH1 blends leather couches and polished concrete for a sophisticated ambience. Much of Riverstone's produce is from their own onsite gardens, with standout options including free-range pork with fennel and apple slaw, or delicious panko-crumbed red cod with chunky hand-cut

chips. Beers and wines showcase smaller vineyards and craft breweries. Booking for dinner is recommended.

Loan & Merc Tavern & Eating House RESTAURANT **$$**
(www.loanandmerc.co.nz; 14 Harbour St; mains $20-30, dinner carvery $32.50) Attention travelling carnivores. Here's your opportunity to tuck into superbly roasted meats including lamb, beef and pork, all served with overflowing platters of innovatively prepared vegetables. Ask if the honey-roasted fennel bulbs are in season. À la carte offerings include rabbit, venison and pickled walnut pies, and during the day, the high-ceilinged heritage warehouse showcases ploughman's lunches with smoked and cured meats.

Annie's Victorian Tearooms CAFE **$**
(cnr Itchen & Thames St; afternoon tea $10; ⏲10am-7pm Thu-Mon) Step into a gracious past courtesy of the delightful Annie Baxter. Waitstaff are dressed in Victorian period costume, the heritage ambience is thoroughly authentic and the afternoon tea spread includes delicate sandwiches and freshly baked cakes. Sipping on Earl Grey tea from bone china cups, you won't mind off switching off your flash 21st-century smartphone at all.

Harbour St Bakery BAKERY **$**
(Harbour St; ⏲Tue-Sun) In the historic precinct the Harbour St Bakery has the South Island's best sourdough bread – just perfect with a slab of local Whitestone cheese. Another tasty option is to buy a freshly baked gourmet pie. Grab an outdoor seat and watch Oamaru's heritage vibe scroll past like an old-time movie.

Midori JAPANESE **$$**
(cnr Humber & Ribble Sts; sushi $8-11, mains $12-18; ⏲11am-2.30pm & 5-8.30pm Mon-Wed, 11.30am-9pm Thu-Sat) Housed in a heritage whitestone building, this Japanese restaurant makes the most of the South Island's good seafood. Sashimi and sushi are super-fresh, and other carefully prepared dishes include salmon on rice and teriyaki blue cod. Here's your tasty opportunity to (kind of) replicate the diet of a little blue penguin.

Steam CAFE **$**
(7 Thames St; mains $10-18) Steam specialises in coffees and fruit juices, and is a good spot to stock up on freshly ground java for your own travels. Settle in for breakfast, or partake of a freshly baked Mainland-sized muffin.

Whitestone Cheese Factory & Café CAFE **$**
(www.whitestonecheese.co.nz; 3 Torridge St) The home of tasty, award-winning organic cheeses. Try the creamy Mature Windsor Blue or the ultrarich Mt Domet Double Cream. Sample the $5 cheese tasting plate or the $18 charcuterie platter. The cheese rolls are an Otago delicacy, and there are also local fruit juices and Central Otago wines. Unsurprisingly, the cheesecake is also very good.

Countdown Supermarket SUPERMARKET **$**
(cnr Thames & Coquet Sts) Centrally located.

Drinking

Criterion Hotel PUB
(3 Tyne St) This restored property is the ultimate corner pub. The owner maintains an ever-changing selection of draught beers – look for brews from Christchurch's Harrington Breweries and Dunedin's Green Man – and there's also excellent pub food. Don't blame us if you progress to the single-malt heaven also on offer. Weekend evenings sometimes see impromptu gigs from local musos.

Birdlands Wine Company WINE BAR
(3 Harbour St; 4pm-late Thu-Sat, 1pm-late Sun) Oamaru's hippest spot is this cool wine bar in the historic precinct. Local wines and Kiwi craft beers combine with antipasto platters and Whitestone cheese boards, and there's chilled live music or DJs most Saturday nights.

Fat Sallys PUB
(☎03-434 8368; 84 Thames St; ⏲Tue-Sun) Popular with locals, especially early on when they're often tucking into a substantial pub meal. Come along on a Wednesday night for the rollicking pub quiz.

Entertainment

Check out the Criterion Hotel (p217) and Birdlands Wine Company (p217) for occasional live music.

Penguin Club LIVE MUSIC
(☎03-434 1402; www.thepenguinclub.co.nz; Emulsion Lane off Harbour St; admission varies) Tucked down a sleepy alley off a 19th-century street, the Penguin's bizarre location matches its acts: everything from touring Kiwi bands to punky/grungy/rocky/country locals. Fridays are open-stage jam night. It's nominally Members Only, so ask at the Oamaru i-SITE about scoring a guest pass. See the website for listings.

Movie World 3 CINEMA
(☎03-434 1070; www.movieworld3.co.nz; 239 Thames St; adult/child $13.50/8.50) Cheaper on Tuesdays.

Globe CLUB
(12 Coquet St; ⊙Fri & Sat) Oamaru's sole nightclub.

Information

Oamaru i-SITE (☎03-434 1656; www.visitoamaru.co.nz; 1 Thames St; ⊙9am-5pm Mon-Fri, 10am-4pm Sat-Sun; @) Mountains of information including details on local walking trips and wildlife. There's internet, bike hire and an interesting 10-minute DVD on the history of the town. Daily penguin-viewing times are also posted outside.

Oamaru Whitestone Civic Trust (☎03-434 5385; www.historicoamaru.co.nz; 2 Harbour St; ⊙10am-4pm) Vintage B&W photos of Oamaru's heritage, maps, information and walking tours of the historic precinct.

Post Office (cnr Coquet & Severn Sts)

Getting There & Around

Bookings can be made through the i-SITE (p218) and at the **Lagonda Tearooms** (191 Thames St; ⊙9am-4.30pm). Buses and shuttles depart from here.

The following companies have shuttles to Dunedin (two hours) and Christchurch (3½ hours).

Atomic Shuttles (☎03-349 0697; www.atomictravel.co.nz)

Coastline Tours (☎03-434 7744, 027 256 5651; www.coastline-tours.co.nz) Runs to/from Dunedin and will detour to Dunedin airport

InterCity (www.intercity.co.nz)

Knightrider (www.knightrider.co.nz) Handy for morning flights from Christchurch airport.

Naked Bus
(☎0900 625 33; www.nakedbus.com)

Southern Link (☎0508 458 835; www.southernlink.co.nz)

Waitaki Valley

The little-travelled Waitaki Valley includes some unique sights and scenery between the turn-off at SH1 and Omarama. The valley is also an outdoors paradise, and is a good place to catch trout and salmon, or waterski on the strikingly blue hydrolakes. This is a possible route to Wanaka and Queenstown if you're heading south, or to Twizel and Mt Cook if you're heading north.

After following SH83 almost to Duntroon, detour left at the turn-off to Danseys Pass. Nearby on the left, under an impressive limestone overhang, are the Maraewhenua **Maori rock paintings**. The charcoal-and-ochre paintings date back several centuries, tracing everything from pre-European hunting to sailing ships.

Follow the road another 4km then turn left towards Ngapara. Two kilometres further on are **Elephant Rocks**. Sculpted by wind, rain and rivers, the huge limestone boulders of this bizarre landscape were utilised as Aslan's Camp in the NZ-filmed *Narnia* blockbuster (2005). If you're feeling adventurous, continue over Danseys Pass to Naseby from 2km back at the intersection.

Back on SH83 at Duntroon is the **Vanished World Centre** (www.vanishedworld.co.nz; 7 Campbell St; adult/family $5/10; ⊙10am-4pm Oct-Jun, 11am-3pm Sat-Sun only Jul-Sep), with interesting displays of 25-million-year-old fossils, including NZ's shark-toothed dolphins and giant penguins. Pick up a copy of the *Vanished World Fossil Trail* map outlining 20 different locations around North Otago. Just west of Duntroon is the **Takiroa Maori Rock Art Site**, with more drawings dating back many centuries.

Tiny **Kurow** is at the junction of the Waitaki and Hakataramea Rivers. For good coffee, stop at the **Te Kohurau Restaurant & Café** (⊙8am-6pm Thu-Tue). Pop into the **Kurow Heritage & Information Centre** (☎03-436 0950; museum@kurow.co.nz; SH83), which has an interesting museum, including a mini-shrine to local boy Richie McCaw, captain of the mighty All Blacks when they won the Rugby World Cup in 2011.

Instead of continuing west from Kurow on SH83, take the 21km scenic detour over the Aviemore Dam, around the northern lake shore past walking tracks and scenic campsites ($10), then over the huge Benmore Dam earthworks. Rejoin SH83 just west of Otematata.

OMARAMA

POP 360

At the head of the Waitaki Valley, Omarama is surrounded by mountain ranges and fabulous landscapes. Busy times in town include the Omarama rodeo (28 December) and the Omarama sheepdog trials (March).

Sights & Activities

Clay Cliffs CLIFFS
(admission $5) The bizarre moonscape of the Clay Cliffs is the result of two million years of erosion on layers of silt and gravel that

WAITAKI WINE ON THE WAY UP

The wines of nearby Central Otago already have a robust global reputation, but a few winemaking pioneers in North Otago's Waitaki Valley are also making international wine experts drink up and take notice. Pop into the **Vintner's Drop** (☎03 436 0545, 021 431 559; www.ostlerwine.co.nz; 45 Bledisloe St; ⏲noon-2pm Thu-Sun Dec-Apr, 11am-4pm Thu & noon-2pm Sun Jul-Oct) – housed in Kurow's old post office – to taste a wide range of wines from the emerging vineyards of the Waitaki, including varietals from Ostler Wines.

Just 4km east of Kurow on SH83, the **Kurow Winery** (☎03 3 436 0443; www.kurow winery.co.nz; Duntroon Rd; ⏲cellar door 11am-5pm, reduced hours in winter) offers well-balanced Riesling, and smoky and spicy pinot noir. Drop in for a wine-tasting session and a winery platter ($38), including smoked Aoraki salmon, Whitestone cheese from nearby Oamaru, and local venison salami.

Pinot gris and pinot noir are the stars at **Sublime Wine** (www.sublimewine.co.nz; 511 Grants Rd, RD7K), a compact, family-owned vineyard around 2km further east on SH83 past the Kurow Winery. The well-travelled owners also operate the funky **Sublime Bed & Breakfast** (☎03-436 0089, 021 943 969; www.sublimewine.co.nz; d $150; wi-fi). The rambling old homestead is surrounded by vineyards and mountain valleys, and a twin and double room are decorated with an eclectic combo of old advertising signs and retro furniture. Special Taste of Waitaki three-course dinners ($50 per person including wine) showcasing local produce are available.

were exposed along the active Osler fault line. The cliffs are on private land; the turn-off is 3.5km north of Omarama, then it's another 10km on an unsealed road. Pay $5 for admission at Omarama Hot Tubs.

Wrinkly Rams ANIMAL SHOW
(☎03-438 9751; www.thewrinklyrams.co.nz; SH8; adult/child/family $25/12.50/60) Wrinkly Rams does 30-minute stage shows of merino sheep being shorn using both modern and traditional methods, along with a sheepdog show. A barbecue lunch is included. Phone ahead to tag along with a tour group, or book your own one-off show. Attached to Wrinkly Rams is one of the town's better restaurants (p220).

Omarama Hot Tubs
(☎03-438 9703; www.hottubsomarama.co.nz; 25 Omamara Ave; ⏲10am-10pm) If your legs are weary after mountain biking or hiking, or you just want to cosy up with your significant other, pop into the Omarama Hot Tubs. The concept, combining private hot tubs (per person $30 to $40), and private 'wellness pods' ($125 for two people) including intimate, personal saunas, is Japanese, but with the surrounding mountain ranges and a pristine night sky, you could only be on the South Island of New Zealand. Therapeutic massages (30/60 minutes $40/80) are another relaxing option. The chemical-free mountain water is changed daily, and used water is recycled for irrigation.

Omarama Hot Tubs also doubles as the local information office, and can assist with accommodation and transport information. See www.discoveromarama.co.nz for more information.

GLIDING

The area's westerlies and warm summer thermals allow for world-class gliding over the hills and spectacular Southern Alps, and a national gliding meet is held here in December or January. Two companies will get you aloft from around $325:

Glide Omarama
(☎03-438 9555; www.glideomarama.com)

Southern Soaring
(☎0800 762 746; www.soaring.co.nz)

Sleeping & Eating

Buscot Station FARMSTAY $
(☎027 222 1754, 03-438 9646; SH8; dm/s/d $23/43/55; @) A slightly chintzy but very comfortable farmhouse on a huge sheep farm with expansive views. Large doubles in the main house and a large modern dormitory out back are all comfortable. Tony the owner shares his kitchen and lounge, as well as his theories on farming and politics. You'll find the turn-off to Buscot Station 10km north of Omarama.

Omarama Top 10 Holiday Park HOLIDAY PARK $
(☎03-438 9875; www.omaramatop10.co.nz; SH8; sites from $32, units $54-125; @☎) Streamside and duck-ponded, this is a peaceful green space to camp in. Cabins are compact, and larger ensuite and self-contained motel units cost $110 for two.

Ladybird Hill Vineyard Restaurant RESTAURANT $$
(www.ladybirdhill.co.nz; lunch $10-29, dinner $26-32; ⏱10.30am-late Thu-Sun) Drop into this slice of Tuscany for a leisurely lunch of venison open sandwich or wild rabbit pie, or come back at night for pan-fried salmon or prime rib-eye steak with roasted beetroot. Wines include the restaurant's own tipples, and vintages from the nearby Waitaki Valley. Other attractions include a kids' playground and walking tracks through the hillside vineyard.

Wrinkly Rams RESTAURANT $$
(☎03-438 9751; www.thewrinklyrams.co.nz; SH8; breakfast $10-15, lunch & dinner $15-30) Restaurants attached to tourist attractions can be dodgy, but the dinners here (pan-fried cod, tender lamb shanks) are quite delicious. Big glass windows and outside tables give a nice view of the mountains while you eat. Wines from the nearby Waitaki Valley also feature.

ℹ Getting There & Away

From Omarama head north up SH8 past beautiful Lake Ohau to Twizel and Mt Cook, or southwest through the striking Lindis Pass towards Cromwell and Queenstown. Stop before the Lindis Pass to add your own roadside cairn.

Omarama is on the route from Christchurch (five hours) to Lake Tekapo and Mt Cook. Both **Atomic Shuttles** (☎03-349 0697; www.atomictravel.co.nz) and **InterCity** (www.intercity.co.nz) swing by.

Oamaru to Dunedin

It's a 114km blast along SH1 from Oamaru to Dunedin, but the narrow, ocean-hugging road travelling south from Oamaru provides a break from the main highway. Take Wharfe St out of town (following the signs for Kakanui) for gorgeous coastal views.

About 5km south of Oamaru on this coast road, **Old Bones Backpackers** (☎03-434 8115; www.oldbones.co.nz; Beach Rd; per person $45, campervans per person $20; @☎) has spacious rooms off a sunny, central space. Close enough to the sea to hear the surf at night, this is a place to just relax in front of the huge windows looking over farmland to the sea, or get stuck into your favourite book. It's under new ownership, but is still one of NZ's best hostels.

Rejoining SH1 again at Waianakarua, backtrack 300 metres north to the **Olive Grove Lodge and Holiday Park** (☎03-439 5830; www.olivebranch.co.nz; SH1, Waianakarua; sites from $24, dm/s $27/45, d/tw $60-70). Surrounded by farmland and encircled by the Waianakarua River, this is a popular camping ground during summer. The rooms are brightly painted with interesting artworks, and the sunny communal lounge is a treat. Kids will love the adventure playground and highland cattle; parents will love the spa, eco lifestyle, organic vegies and peaceful vibe. En suite rooms (doubles $70) are good options for families.

Further south on SH1, 30km south of Oamaru, stop to check out the **Moeraki Boulders** (*Te Kaihinaki*), a collection of large spherical boulders on a stunning stretch of beach, scattered about like a giant kid's discarded marbles. Try to time your visit for low tide.

Moeraki township is a charming fishing village. It's a nice 1½-hour walk along the beach between the village and the boulders. Head in the other direction towards the Kaiks wildlife trail and a cute old wooden lighthouse – a great spot to see yellow-eyed penguins and fur seals. Moeraki has nurtured the creation of several national treasures, from Frances Hodgkins' paintings to Keri Hulme's *The Bone People*...and Fleur Sullivan's cooking.

Fleur's Place (☎03-439 4480; www.fleursplace.com; Old Jetty; mains $25-38; ⏱10.30am-late Wed-Sat) has a rumble-tumble look about it, but this timber hut serves up some of the South Island's best food. The speciality is seafood, fresh off Moeraki's fishing boats. Head for the upstairs deck and tuck into fresh chowder, tender mutton bird and other briny-fresh ocean bounty. Bookings are strongly recommended, but they'll probably squeeze you in between the busy lunch and dinner times. Fleur is also the energy behind Oamaru's Loan & Merc (p217).

Moeraki Motel (☎03-439 4862; www.moerakibeachmotels.co.nz; cnr Beach & Haven Sts; d $100) has self-contained units with balconies, while the **Moeraki Village Holiday Park** (☎03-439 4759; www.moerakivillageholidaypark.co.nz; 114 Haven St; sites from $29, units $55-130; @☎) has cabins and motel units.

Queenstown & Wanaka

Includes »

Best Places to Eat

- » Bella Cucina (p236)
- » Fishbone Bar & Grill (p236)
- » Amisfield Winery & Bistro (p239)
- » Vudu Cafe & Larder (p236)
- » Federal Diner (p255)

Best Places to Stay

- » The Dairy (p233)
- » Glenorchy Lake House (p246)
- » Wanaka Bakpaka (p253)
- » Riversong (p253)
- » Warbrick Stone Cottage (p233)

Why Go?

With a cinematic background of mountains and lakes you actually have seen in the movies, and a 'what can we think of next?' array of adventure activities, it's little wonder Queenstown tops the itineraries of many travellers.

Slow down (slightly) in Wanaka – Queenstown's junior cousin – which also has good restaurants, bars, and outdoor adventures on tap. Explore nearby Mt Aspiring National Park to reinforce the fact that you're only a short drive from true New Zealand wilderness.

Slow down even more in Glenorchy, an improbably scenic reminder of what Queenstown and Wanaka were like before the adventure groupies moved in. Negotiate the Greenstone and Routeburn Tracks for extended outdoor thrills, or kayak the upper reaches of Lake Wakatipu.

Across in historic Arrowtown, consider the town's gold-mining past over a chilled craft beer or dinner in a cosy bistro. The following day there'll be plenty more opportunities to dive into Queenstown's cavalcade of action.

When to Go

The fine and settled summer weather from January to March is the perfect backdrop to Queenstown's active menu of adventure sports and lake and alpine exploration. From June to August, the ski slopes surrounding Queenstown and Wanaka are flush with an international crew of ski and snowboard fans. For the best in local festivals, make a date for June's exciting Queenstown Winter Festival, or experience the region's food and wine scene at March's Gibbston Valley Festival and Wanaka Fest in October.

Getting There & Around

Air New Zealand (03-441 1900; www.airnewzealand.co.nz; 8 Church St) links Queenstown to Auckland, Wellington and Christchurch, and Sydney and Melbourne. Virgin Australia has flights between Queenstown and Sydney and Brisbane. Jetstar links Queenstown with Auckland, Christchurch and Wellington, and Sydney, Melbourne and the Gold Coast. From Wanaka, Air New Zealand flies to Christchurch. Bus and shuttle companies criss-cross Otago from Dunedin to Queenstown and Wanaka. Several divert south to Te Anau and Invercargill, and others migrate north to Christchurch or travel through the Haast Pass and up the West Coast. The major operators include InterCity, Atomic Shuttles, Naked Bus, Tracknet, Alpine Coachlines and Wanaka Connexions.

QUEENSTOWN REGION

POP 11,000

Surrounded by the soaring indigo heights of the Remarkables, crowned by Coronet Peak, and framed by the meandering coves of Lake Wakatipu, it's little wonder that Queenstown is a show-off. The town wears its 'Global Adventure Capital' badge proudly, and most visitors take the time to do crazy things they've never done before. But a new Queenstown is also emerging, with a cosmopolitan restaurant and arts scene and excellent vineyards. Go ahead and jump off a bridge or out of a plane, but also slow down and experience Queenstown without the adrenaline. And once you've eased up, look forward to more of the same in historic Arrowtown or beautiful Glenorchy.

Queenstown

No one's ever visited Queenstown and said, 'I'm bored'. Looking like a small town, but displaying the energy of a small city, Queenstown offers a mountain of outdoor activities.

Maximise bragging rights with your souvenir T-shirt in the town's atmospheric restaurants, laid-back cafes and bustling bars. Be sure to also find a lakeside bench at sunrise or dusk and immerse yourself in one of NZ's most beautiful views.

Queenstown is well used to visitors with international accents, so expect great tourist facilities, but also great big crowds, especially in summer and winter. Autumn (March to May) and spring (October to November) are slightly quieter, but Queenstown is a true year-round destination. The town's restau-

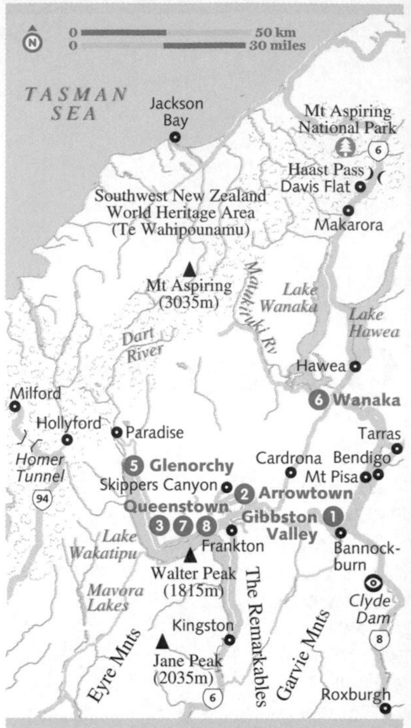

Queenstown & Wanaka Highlights

1. Sampling superb wines amid the dramatic scenery of the **Gibbston Valley** (p239)
2. Relaxing and dining in **Arrowtown** (p241) after the last of the day-trippers have left
3. Doing things you've only dreamed about in **Queenstown** (p222), the adrenaline-rush capital of NZ
4. Walking the peaceful **Routeburn Track** (p247)
5. Exploring by horseback, kayak and jetboat the upper reaches of Lake Wakatipu from sleepy and stunning **Glenorchy** (p245)
6. Watching a flick at **Cinema Paradiso** (p256) in Wanaka, with pizza during intermission
7. **Bar-hopping** (p238) and **dining** (p236) in cosmopolitan Queenstown
8. Experiencing Queenstown's **mountain biking** (p229) mecca on two knobbly wheels

ESSENTIAL QUEENSTOWN & WANAKA

» **Eat** A leisurely lunch at a vineyard restaurant

» **Drink** One of Wanaka Beerworks' (p249)' surprising seasonal brews

» **Read** *Walking the Routeburn Track* by Philip Holden for a wander through the history, flora and fauna of this tramp

» **Listen to** The silence as you kayak blissfully around Glenorchy and Kinloch

» **Watch** Art-house movies at Arrowtown's quirky Dorothy Browns (p245) boutique cinema

» **Online** www.queenstownnz.co.nz; www.lakewanaka.co.nz; www.lonelyplanet.com/new-zealand/queenstown

» **Area code** ☎03

rants and bars are regularly packed with a mainly young crowd that really know how to enjoy themselves on holiday. If you're a more private soul, drop in to see what all the fuss is about, but then get out and about by exploring the sublime wilderness further up the lake at Glenorchy.

History

The region was deserted when the first Pakeha (white person) arrived in the mid-1850s, although there is evidence of previous Maori settlement. Sheep farmers came first, but after two shearers discovered gold on the banks of the Shotover River in 1862, a deluge of prospectors followed. Within a year Queenstown was a mining town with streets, permanent buildings and a population of several thousand. It was declared 'fit for a queen' by the NZ government, hence Queenstown was born. Lake Wakatipu was the principal means of transport, and at the height of the boom there were four paddle steamers and 30 other craft plying the waters.

By 1900 the gold had petered out and the population was a mere 190. It wasn't until the 1950s that Queenstown became a popular holiday destination.

Sights

Skyline Gondola CABLE CAR
(Map p226; www.skyline.co.nz; Brecon St; adult/child/family return $25/14/71) Hop on the Skyline Gondola for fantastic views of Queenstown, the lake and the mountains. At the top are a cafe, a restaurant with regular Maori cultural shows (p240), and souvenir shops. Walking trails include the loop track (30 minutes return), or you can try the Luge or new mountain-bike trails. The energetic can forgo the gondola and hike to the top; take the upper, left-hand gravel track from the trailhead on Lomond Cres for an hour's uphill hike.

Kiwi Birdlife Park WILDLIFE
(Map p230; www.kiwibird.co.nz; Brecon St; adult/child $38/19; ⌚9am-5pm, shows 11am & 3pm) Here's your best bet to spy a kiwi. There are also 10,000 native plants and scores of birds, including the rare black stilt, kea, morepork and parakeets. Stroll around the sanctuary, watch the conservation show and tiptoe quietly into the darkened kiwi houses.

The Kingston Flyer TRAIN EXCURSION
(☎03-248 8888, 0800 435 937; www.kingstonflyer.co.nz; Kingston; adult/child/family 1 way $35/17.50/87.50, return $45/22.50/112.50; ⌚departs Kingston 10am & 1.30pm) Based in Kingston, a lakeside village 40 minutes south of Queenstown, this restored 130 year-old steam train runs on a preserved 14km stretch of track linking Kingston and Fairlight. Shuttles ($20 return) are available from Queenstown if you don't have transport.

Williams Cottage HISTORIC BUILDING
(Map p230; cnr Marine Pde & Earl St; ⌚10am-5.30pm) Williams Cottage is Queenstown's oldest home. An annexe of Arrowtown's Lake District Museum and Gallery, it was built in 1864 and retains plenty of character, including 1930s wallpaper. The cottage and its 1920s garden are now home to the very cool Vesta store showcasing local designers and artists. Much of the work is exclusive to Vesta.

Church of St Peter CHURCH
(Map p230; www.stpeters.co.nz; cnr Church & Camp Sts; ⌚services 10am Wed, 10.30am Sun) This pretty wood-beamed building has a beautiful organ and colourful stained glass. Take a look at the cedar lectern, which was

MAORI NZ: QUEENSTOWN & WANAKA

Kiwi Haka (p240) perform nightly atop the Queenstown gondola. Two Queenstown galleries worth checking out for contemporary Maori art and design are Kapa (p240) and toi o tahuna (p240).

Queenstown Region

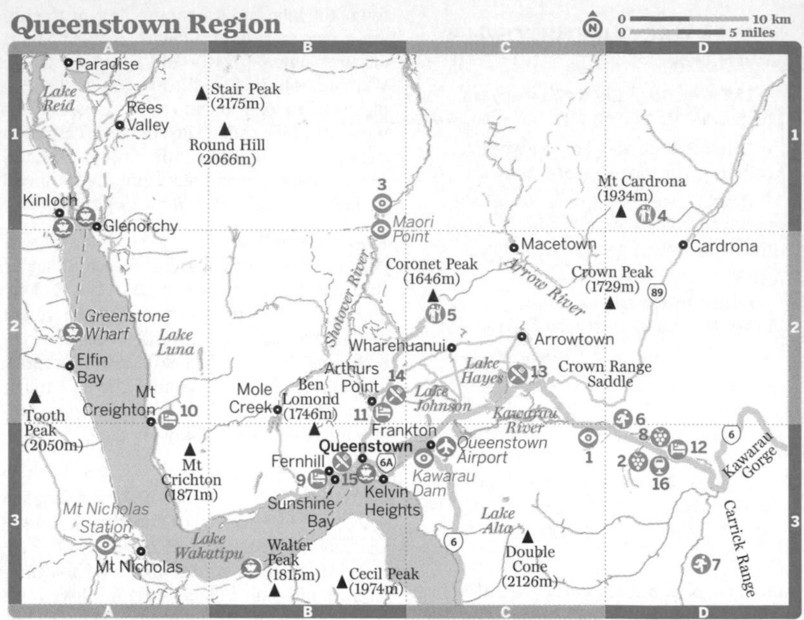

Queenstown Region

Sights

1 Chard Farm C3
2 Gibbston Valley Wines D3
3 Skippers Canyon B1

Activities, Courses & Tours

4 Cardrona D1
5 Coronet Peak C2
6 Kawarau Bridge D2
Kawarau Bungy Centre (see 6)
7 Nevis Highwire D3
Onsen Hot Pools (see 14)
8 Peregrine D3

Sleeping

9 Evergreen Lodge B3
10 Little Paradise Lodge A2
11 Shotover Top 10 Holiday Park B2
12 Warbrick Stone Cottage D3

Eating

13 Amisfield Winery & Bistro C2
14 Gantley's B2
15 VKnow B3
Winehouse & Kitchen (see 6)

Drinking

16 Gibbston Tavern D3

carved by Ah Tong, a Chinese immigrant, in the 1870s. On Saturday mornings in summer, the church grounds host the Queenstown Farmers Market.

Underwater Observatory WILDLIFE

(Map p230; Queenstown Bay Jetty; adult/child/family $5/3/10; 9am-5pm) Underwater Observatory has six giant windows showcasing life under the lake. Brown trout abound, and look out for freshwater eels and scaup (diving ducks), which cruise right past the windows.

Activities

Purchase discounted combination tickets from **Queenstown Combos** (03-442 7318, 0800 423 836; www.combos.co.nz). Some activity operators have offices on Shotover St, or you can book at the i-SITE or your accommodation.

Bungy Jumping

Queenstown is famous for bungy jumping. For all the following bungy jumping and bungy variations, contact AJ Hackett Bungy at the Station (p241) or book through your accommodation or the i-SITE. Most bungy trips also include transport to the jump location.

Kawarau Bridge BUNGY
(Map p224; per person $180) The historic 1880 Kawarau Bridge, 23km from Queenstown, became the world's first commercial bungy site in 1988 and allows you to leap 43m.

FREE **Kawarau Bungy Centre** BUNGY
(Map p224; SH6; 8am-5.45pm) Looks through the Secrets of Bungy Tour, explaining the history of bungy; you can try the more gentle Bungy Trampoline (adult/child $20/15). It's loads of fun for children, even two-year-olds.

Ledge Bungy BUNGY
(Map p226; Brecon St; per person $180) From atop the Skyline Gondola, the 47m-high Ledge Bungy also operates after dark.

Nevis Highwire BUNGY
(Map p224; per person $260) Jump from a 134m-high pod above the Nevis River.

Bungy Variations

Shotover Canyon Swing BUNGY
(0800 279 464, 03-442 6990; www.canyonswing.co.nz; per person $199, additional swings $39) Be released loads of different ways – backwards, in a chair, upside down. From there it's a 60m free fall and a wild swing across the canyon at 150km/h.

Nevis Arc BUNGY
(0800 286 4958; www.nevisarc.co.nz) Fly in tandem ($320) or go it alone ($180) on the planet's highest swing.

Ledge Sky Swing BUNGY
(Map p226; 0800 286 4958; www.bungy.co.nz; per person $150) A shorter swing than at the Nevis Arc, but equally stunning views of Queenstown from atop the Skyline Gondola.

Jetboating

The Shotover and Kawarau are Queenstown's most popular rivers to hurtle along. The lengthier and more scenic Dart River is less travelled.

Shotover Jet JETBOATING
(0800 746 868; www.shotoverjet.co.nz; adult/child $119/69) Half-hour trips through the rocky Shotover Canyons, with lots of thrilling 360-degree spins.

Kawarau Jet JETBOATING
(Map p230; 03-442 6142, 0800 529 272; www.kjet.co.nz; Queenstown Bay Jetty; adult/child $110/65) Does one-hour trips on the Kawarau and Lower Shotover Rivers.

Skippers Canyon Jet JETBOATING
(03-442 9434, 0800 226 996; www.skipperscanyon.co.nz; adult/child $129/79) Incorporates a 30-minute blast in the narrow gorges of **Skippers Canyon** (Map p224) in three-hour trips that also cover the area's gold-mining history.

White-Water Rafting

The choppy Shotover and calmer Kawarau Rivers are both great for rafting. Trips take four to five hours with two to three hours on the

QUEENSTOWN IN...

Two Days

Start your day with breakfast at **Vudu Cafe & Larder** before heading to Shotover St to book your adrenaline-charged activities for the next day. Spend the rest of the day visiting **Williams Cottage** and the **Kiwi Birdlife Park**, before boarding the exciting **Shotover Jet** or taking a lake cruise on the **TSS Earnslaw**. Wind up with a walk through **Queenstown Gardens** to capture dramatic views of the **Remarkables** at dusk. Have a sunset drink at **Pub on Wharf** or the **Atlas Beer Cafe** before dinner at **Fishbone Bar & Grill** or **Wai Waterfront Restaurant & Wine Bar**. The evening's still young, so head to **Minibar** or **Bardeaux**. Devote the next morning to bungy jumping, skydiving or white-water rafting, and take to two wheels at the **Queenstown Bike Park** in the afternoon. If you're a wine buff, book a cycle tour through the **Gibbston Valley** with **Cycle de Vine**. Enjoy dinner at **Winnies**, and stay on for the live music or DJs.

Four Days

Follow the two-day itinerary, then head to **Arrowtown** to wander the enigmatic **Chinese settlement**, browse the local shops and sample the beers at the **Arrow Brewing Company**. The following day drive along the shores of Lake Wakatipu to tiny **Glenorchy.** Have lunch at the **Glenorchy Café** and then strap on your hiking boots and head into **Mt Aspiring National Park** to do some wonderful short tramps in the vicinity of the **Routeburn Track.** If you'd rather exercise your arms, go kayaking across the lake at **Kinloch**.

Queenstown

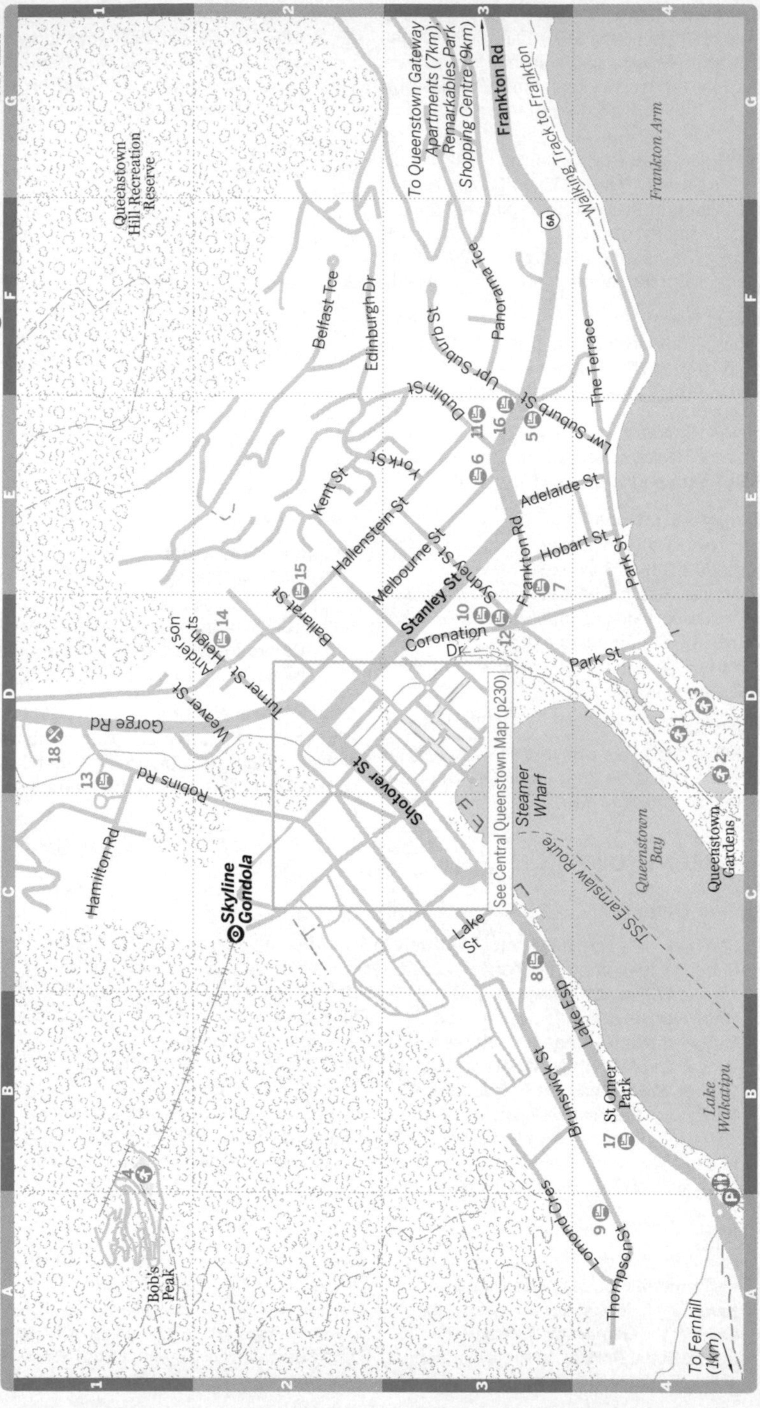

0 500 m
0 0.25 miles
Queenstown Hill Recreation Reserve
Bob's Peak
4
18
13
Hamilton Rd
Robins Rd
Gorge Rd
Weaver St
Anderson Heights
14
Skyline Gondola
Turner St
Ballarat St
15
Kent St
Belfast Tce
Edinburgh Dr
Hallenstein St
York St
Shotover St
Melbourne St
Stanley St
Sydney St
Coronation Dr
10
12
Dublin St
Upr Suburb St
6
11
16
Panorama Tce
To Queenstown Gateway Apartments (7km); Remarkables Park Shopping Centre (9km)
Frankton Rd
6A
Walking Track to Frankton
5
Lwr Suburb St
Adelaide St
Hobart St
Frankton Rd
7
The Terrace
Park St
Park St
Lake St
See Central Queenstown Map (p230)
Steamer Wharf
8
Lake Esp
Brunswick St
Lomond Cres
9
Thompson St
17
St Omer Park
TSS Earnslaw Route
Queenstown Bay
Queenstown Gardens
1
2
3
Frankton Arm
Lake Wakatipu
To Fernhill (1km)

Queenstown

river. There's generally a minimum age of 13 years and a minimum weight of around 40kg. An exciting alternative are heli-rafting trips.

Queenstown Rafting RAFTING
(☎03-442 9792, 0800 723 8464; www.rafting.co.nz; rafting/heli-rafting $195/279) One of Queenstown's most established rafting companies.

Extreme Green Rafting RAFTING
(☎03-442 8517; www.nzraft.com; rafting/heli-rafting $195/279) Trips on both the Kawarau and Shotover Rivers.

Challenge Rafting RAFTING
(☎03-442 7318, 0800 423 836; www.raft.co.nz; rafting/heli-rafting $195/279) On the Shotover and Kawarau Rivers.

QUEENSTOWN & WANAKA ON A RAINY DAY

Book in for a Japanese-style spa experience at Onsen Hot Pools (p228), or catch a bus across to Arrowtown for a movie at the quirky cinema Dorothy Browns (p245). If you're holed up in Wanaka, Cinema Paradiso (p256) or Ruby's (p256) are equally cool. Other all-weather attractions in Wanaka include Puzzling World (p251) and the excellent Wanaka Transport & Toy Museum (p250) or Warbirds & Wheels (p249). If you're visiting from April to October, go ice-skating at the Queenstown Ice Arena (p230).

Family Adventures RAFTING
(☎03-442 8836, 0800 4723 8464; www.familyadventures.co.nz; adult/child $179/120) Gentler (Grade I to II) trips on the Shotover suitable for children three years and older. Operates in summer only.

River Surfing & White-Water Sledging

Serious Fun RIVER SLEDGING
(☎03-442 5262, 0800 737 468; www.riversurfing.co.nz; per person $175) The only company to raft the infamous Chinese Dogleg section of the Kawarau River.

Frogz Have More Fun RIVER SLEDGING
(☎0800 437 649, 03-441 2318; www.frogz.co.nz; per person $175) Steer buoyant sleds on the rapids and whirlpools of the Kawarau River.

Canyoning

Canyoning.co.nz CANYONING
(☎03-441 3003; www.canyoning.co.nz; per person $185) Half-day trips in the nearby 12-Mile Delta Canyons. Canyoning in the remote Routeburn Valley ($210) is also available.

Flying, Gliding & Skydiving

Tandem Paragliding PARAGLIDING
(Map p226; ☎0800 759 688, 03-441 8581; www.nzgforce.com; per person $199) Tandem paragliding from the top of the gondola or from Coronet Peak (9am departures are $20 cheaper).

Skytrek Hang Gliding HANG GLIDING
(☎0800 759 873; www.skytrek.co.nz; flights from $210) Soar on tandem flights from Coronet Peak or the Remarkables.

REMEMBER, YOU'RE ON HOLIDAY...

So much of the Queenstown experience is about active adventure and adrenaline-fuelled shenanigans. Here's our pick of the best experiences to slow down, recharge and remind your body there's more to the travelling life than scaring yourself silly.

» **Onsen Hot Pools** (Map p224; ☎03-442 5707; www.onsen.co.nz; 160 Arthurs Point Rd; adult/child $46/10; ⊙11am-10pm) has private Japanese-style hot tubs with mountain views. Book ahead and one will be warmed up for you.

» To reboot your system after a few days of bungying, biking and jetboating, ease into in-room massage and spa treatments with the **Mobile Massage Co** (☎027 442 6161, 0800 426 161; www.queenstownmassage.co.nz; 1hr from $125; ⊙9am-9pm).

» Slow down even more by checking into **Hush Spa** (Map p230; ☎03-4009 0901; www.hushspa.co.nz; 1st fl, 32 Rees St; 30/60min massage from $70/125; ⊙9am-9pm Tue-Fri, to 7pm Sat) for a massage, aroma stone therapy or a deep bath soak.

» For truly world-class spa treatments, make the short trek to Millbrook near Arrowtown, where the Spa at Millbrook (p242) has been voted one of the world's top 10 spas.

» Queenstown's newest spa escape is **Eforea: Spa at Hilton** (☎03-450 9416; www.queenstownhilton.com; Peninsula Rd, Hilton Queenstown; treatments from $120), enjoying a lakeside location at Kawarau Village, a short water-taxi ride from Steamer Wharf.

Flight Park Tandems PARAGLIDING
(☎0800 467 325; www.tandemparagliding.com; 1140m/1620m $185/205) Offering spectacular takeoffs from Coronet Peak. Rates apply to winter months.

Queenstown Paraflights PARAGLIDING
(Map p230; ☎0800 225 520; www.paraflights.co.nz; adult & child solo $139, adult/child tandem $109/$79) Glide 200m above the lake as you're pulled behind a boat.

Elevation Paragliding School PARAGLIDING
(☎0800 359 444; www.elevation.co.nz; instruction from $240) Learn the paragliding ropes and graduate to four solo flights.

NZONE SKYDIVING
(☎03-442 5867, 0800 376 796; www.nzone.biz; jumps from $269) Jump out of a perfectly good airplane – with a tandem skydiving expert.

Tramping & Climbing

Pick up the *Wakatipu Walks* brochure ($2) from DOC for local tramping tracks ranging from easy one-hour strolls to tough eight-hour slogs.

Bob's Peak WALKING
Walk up Bob's Peak to the gondola terminus. The walk is not particularly scenic, but the views at the top are excellent.

Queenstown Hill WALKING
Another short climb is up 900m Queenstown Hill (two to three hours return). Access is from Belfast Tce.

Ben Lomond WALKING
Climb 1746m Ben Lomond (six to eight hours return), accessed from Lomond Cres. It's a difficult tramp requiring a high level of fitness and shouldn't be underestimated.

Encounter Guided Day Walks TRAMPING
(☎03-442 8200; www.ultimatehikes.co.nz; Routeburn Track adult/child $145/85; Milford Track adult/child $165/95; Mt Cook adult/child $105/65; ⊙Oct-Apr) Day walks on the Routeburn Track, the Milford Track and near Mt Cook, as well as multiday tramps.

Guided Nature Walks WALKING
(☎03-442 7126; www.nzwalks.com; adult/child from $105/65) Excellent walks in the Queenstown area, including a Walk and Wine option and even snow-shoeing in winter.

Climbing Queenstown CLIMBING
(☎03-450 2119; www.climbingqueenstown.com; rock climbing from $139, abseiling adult/child $139/99, Via Ferrata adult/child $139/89 and mountaineering from $499.) Rock climbing, abseiling, Via Ferrata (climbing fixed metal rungs, rails, pegs and cables) and mountaineering. All activities are run by qualified guides.

Horse Treks

Moonlight Stables HORSE RIDING
(☎03-442 1229; www.moonlightcountry.co.nz; adult/child $120/95) Ride through a stunning landscape on a 324-hectare working farm. Horseriding is also on offer around **Cardrona** (☎03-443 8151; www.backcountrysadddles.

co.nz; Crown Range Rd; adult/child from $80/60) and Glenorchy (p246).

Fishing

The rivers and lakes around Queenstown are home to brown and rainbow trout. All companies practise catch-and-release.

Stu Dever Fishing Charters FISHING
(☎03-442 6371; www.fishing-queenstown.co.nz; per hour from $60) Salmon and trout fishing from the 34ft launch *Chinook*. Owner Stu can arrange for your catch to be cooked at a local restaurant.

Other Activities

You can also golf, minigolf, quad bike, sail, dive and much more.

Central Otago Wine Experience WINE TASTING
(Map p230; ☎03-409 2226; www.winetastes.com; 14 Beach St; tasting cards $20; ⏰10am-10pm) A $20 card provides tastes of around eight to 10 different wines from a menu of 80. Cheese and antipasto platters ($28 to $34) accompany the tasty tastings, and all wine can be shipped home.

Ziptrek Ecotours ZIPLINE
(Map p226; ☎0800 947 8735; www.ziptrek.com; Brecon St; adult/child from $129/79) Incorporating a series of zip-lines (flying foxes), this harness-clad thrill-ride takes you from treetop to treetop high above Queenstown. Ingenious design and ecofriendly values are a bonus on this adrenaline-fuelled activity. Choose from the two-hour, four-line 'Moa' tour or the gnarlier three-hour, six-line 'Kea' option (adult/child $179/129).

Luge LUGE
(Map p226; ☎03-441 0101; www.skyline.co.nz; Brecon St; 1/2/3/5 rides incl gondola ride adult $33/38/43/48, child $23/28/33/38; ⏰daylight hours) Hop on a three-wheeled cart to ride the Luge at the top of the gondola. Nail the 'scenic' run once, and then you're allowed on the advanced track with its banked corners and tunnel.

MOUNTAIN-BIKING MECCA

With the opening of the Queenstown Bike Park the region is now firmly established as an international focus for the sport. See also www.wakatiputrails.co.nz for details on the ongoing development of new mountain-bike trails around the area. Visit in late March for the annual Queenstown Bike Festival (www.queenstownbikefestival.co.nz).

The Queenstown Trail – more than 90km in total – links five scenic smaller trails showcasing Queenstown, Arrowtown, the Gibbston Valley, Lake Wakatipu and Lake Hayes. Overall the trail is technically easy and suitable for cyclists of all levels.

Pop into Outside Sports or Vertigo for more trail information. If you're in town for a while, consider joining the **Queenstown Mountain Bike Club** (www.queenstownmtb.co.nz).

Queenstown Bike Park (Map p226; ☎03-441 0101; www.skyline.co.nz; Brecon St; ⏰half-day pass adult/child/family $45/25/115, day pass adult/child/family $60/30/150) Nine different trails – from easy to extreme – traverse Bob's Peak high above the lake. Once you've descended on two wheels, simply jump on the gondola and do it all over again. The best trail for novice riders is the 6km-long Hammy's Track, which is studded with lake views and picnic spots all the way down.

Vertigo (Map p230; ☎03-442 8378, 0800 837 8446; www.vertigobikes.co.nz; 4 Brecon St; rental from $79 per day) Options include downhill rides into Skippers Canyon ($169) and a Remarkables helibike option ($399). Skills training (from $139) and guided sessions ($159) on the Queenstown Bike Park are also available. If you're serious about getting into mountain biking QT-style, Vertigo is an essential first stop.

Fat Tyre Adventures (☎0800 328 897; www.fat-tyre.co.nz; from $199) Tours cater to different abilities with day tours, multiday tours, helibiking and singletrack riding. Bike hire and trail snacks are included.

Outside Sports (Map p230; www.outsidesports.co.nz; 36-38 Shotover St) One-stop shop for bike rentals and trail information.

Queenstown Bike Hire (Map p230; cnr Marine Pde & Church St) Best for tandems and lakefront rides.

Central Queenstown

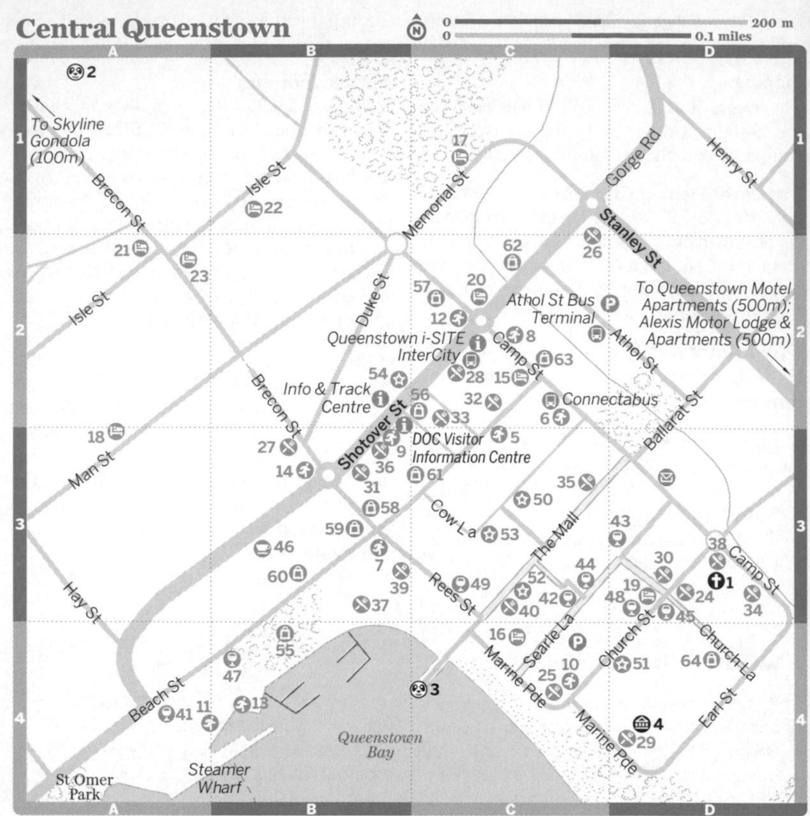

Frisbee Golf FRISBEE
(Map p226; www.queenstowndiscgolf.co.nz) On a marked course in Queenstown Gardens. Targets are tree-mounted chain baskets. BYO frisbee.

Queenstown Ice Arena ICE SKATING
(Map p226; ☎03-441 8000; www.queenstowniceArena.co.nz; 29 Park St; adult/child incl skate hire $20/15; ⊙10am-6pm, to 9.30pm Fri Apr-Oct) Come for a skate or a game of ice hockey. Closed in summer.

☞ Tours

Scenic Flights

Aerostunts SCENIC FLIGHT
(☎0800 788 687; www.aerostunts.co.nz; 15/25 minutes $310/400) To see the sights upside down, take a G-force-defying aerobatic flight.

Over the Top Helicopters SCENIC FLIGHT
(☎03-442 2233, 0800 123 359; www.flynz.co.nz; from $265) Around Queenstown and beyond.

Sunrise Balloons BALLOONING
(☎03-442 0781, 0800 468 247; www.ballooningnz.com; adult/child $445/295) One-hour rides including a champagne breakfast.

4WD Tours

Nomad Safaris 4WD TOUR
(☎03-442 6699, 0800 688 222; www.nomadsafaris.co.nz; adult/child from $130/65) Trips take in stunning scenery and hard-to-get-to backcountry vistas around Skippers Canyon and Macetown. The operators will even let you drive ($260), or you can quad-bike it ($245).

Off Road Adventures 4WD TOUR
(☎03-442 7858, 0800 633 7623; www.offroad.co.nz; 4WD adult/child from $99/49) Exciting off-road 4WD, quad-bike (from $189) and dirt-bike ($249) tours.

Skippers Canyon Heritage Tours 4WD TOUR
(☎03-442 5949; www.queenstown-heritage.co.nz; adult/child $160/80) Skippers Canyon is

Central Queenstown

Sights

1 Church of St Peter ... D3
2 Kiwi Birdlife Park ... A1
3 Underwater Observatory ... C4
4 Williams Cottage ... D4

Activities, Courses & Tours

5 Central Otago Wine Experience ... C3
6 Double-Decker Bus Tour ... C2
7 Hush Spa ... B3
Kawarau Jet ... (see 3)
8 Kiwi Discovery ... C2
9 Outside Sports ... B3
10 Queenstown Bike Hire ... C4
Queenstown Paraflights ... (see 3)
11 Real Journeys ... A4
12 The Station ... C2
13 TSS Earnslaw ... B4
14 Vertigo ... B3

Sleeping

15 Adventure Queenstown Hostel & Chalet ... C2
16 Eichardt's Private Hotel ... C4
17 Last Resort ... C1
18 Lomond Lodge ... A3
19 Nomads ... D3
20 Queenstown Accommodation Centre ... C2
21 Queenstown Lakeview Holiday Park ... A2
22 Southern Laughter ... B1
23 The Dairy ... A2

Eating

24 @Thai ... D3
25 Aggy's Shack ... C4
26 Alpine Supermarket ... C2
27 Bella Cucina ... B3
28 Bob's Weigh ... C2
29 Botswana Butchery ... D4
30 Devil Burger ... D3
Fergbaker ... (see 31)
31 Fergburger ... B3
32 Fishbone Bar & Grill ... C2
33 Habebes ... C2
34 Halo ... D3
35 Kappa Sushi Cafe ... C3
36 Lick & Slurp Soup ... B3
37 Patagonia ... B3
38 Queenstown Farmers Market ... D3
39 Vudu Cafe & Larder ... B3
Wai Waterfront Restaurant & Wine Bar ... (see 11)
40 Winnies ... C3

Drinking

41 Atlas Beer Cafe ... A4
Ballarat Trading Company ... (see 52)
42 Bardeaux ... C3
43 Barmuda ... D3
44 Minibar ... C3
45 Monty's ... D3
46 Motogrill ... B3
47 Pub on Wharf ... B4
48 Searle Lane & Social ... D3
49 Surreal ... C3

Entertainment

50 Debajo ... C3
51 Dux de Lux ... D4
52 Reading Cinemas ... C3
Subculture ... (see 45)
53 Tardis Bar ... C3
54 The World Bar ... B2

Shopping

55 Arts & Crafts Market ... B4
56 Fetch ... C2
57 Green Toad ... C2
58 Kapa ... B3
59 Kathmandu ... B3
Outside Sports ... (see 9)
60 Rockies ... B3
61 Small Planet Outlet Store ... C3
62 Small Planet Sports Co ... C2
63 Snowrental ... C2
64 toi o tahuna ... D4

reached by a narrow, winding road which was built by gold panners in the 1800s. This scenic but hair-raising 4WD route runs from Arthurs Point towards Coronet Peak and then above the Shotover River, passing along the way some gold-rush sights. Specialist wine and photography tours are also available.

Lake Cruises

TSS Earnslaw BOAT TOUR

(Map p230; ☎0800 656 503; www.realjourneys.co.nz; Steamer Wharf, Beach St) The stately, steam-powered *TSS Earnslaw* celebrated a centenary of continuous service in 2012. Once the lake's major means of transport, it originally carried more than 800 passengers. Climb aboard for the standard

1½-hour Lake Wakatipu tour (adult/child $50/22) or take a 3½-hour excursion to the high-country Walter Peak Farm (adult/child $75/22) for sheep-shearing demonstrations and sheep-dog performances.

Milford Sound

Day trips via Te Anau to Milford Sound take 12 to 13 hours and cost around $225/115 per adult/child, including a two-hour cruise on the sound. Bus–cruise–flight options are also available, as is pick-up from the Routeburn Track finish line. To save on travel time and cost, consider visiting Milford from Te Anau.

Real Journeys GUIDED TOURS
(Map p230; ☎03-249 7416, 0800 656 501; www.realjourneys.co.nz; Beach St, Steamer Wharf) Lake trips and tours.

BBQ Bus TOUR
(☎03-442 1045, 0800 421 045; www.milford.net.nz; adult/child $182/100) Smaller groups (up to 22 people) and a barbecue lunch.

Winery Tours

Most tours include a visit to the wineries around Banockburn (p206).

Appellation Central Wine Tours WINE TASTING
(☎03-442 0246; www.appellationcentral.co.nz; $165-215) Tours include an all-day gourmet excursion that also samples local cheeses.

Cycle de Vine WINE TASTING
(☎0800 328 897; www.queenstown-trails.co.nz; adult/child $155/95; ⏰Sep-Jun) Cruise on a retro bicycle around the Gibbston Valley. Tours include two different wineries and a picnic lunch beside the meandering Kawarau River.

Queenstown Wine Trail WINE TASTING
(☎03-441 3990, 0800 827 8464; www.queenstownwinetrail.co.nz; adult $129, shorter tour with lunch $148) Choose from a five-hour tour with tastings at four wineries or a shorter tour with lunch included.

Other Tours

Double-Decker Bus Tour BUS TOUR
(Map p230; www.doubledecker.co.nz; adult/child $48/25) Visits historic Arrowtown, taking in Gibbston Valley Wines and Lake Hayes. The three-hour tours depart from in front of O'Connell's Shopping Centre at 9.30am.

Segway on Q GUIDED TOUR
(☎03-442 8687, 0800 734 386; www.segwayonq.com) Explore the town and Queenstown Gardens on a two-hour spin (adult/child/family $109/99/375), or cruise for an hour around Queenstown Bay on Lake Wakatipu (adult/child/family $75/65/250).

Art Adventures GUIDED TOUR
(☎0800 582 878; www.artadventures.co.nz; studio & gallery tours half/full day $180/350, tuition from $300) Art Adventures provide studio and gallery tours – including lunch and wine-tasting at local vineyards – or the opportunity to work with professional tutors on your own masterpiece.

Festivals & Events

Gibbston Harvest Festival FOOD & WINE
(www.gibbstonharvestfestival.com; ⏰mid-Mar) Food and wine buffs should time their visit to coincide with this annual festival.

Queenstown Winter Festival SPORTS
(www.winterfestival.co.nz; ⏰late Jun/early Jul) Wacky ski and snowboard activities, live mu-

GETTING ACTIVE ON THE SLOPES

The ski season generally lasts from around June to September. Time your visit for the loads-of-fun Queenstown Winter Festival (p232).

Around Queenstown, the Remarkables and Coronet Peak ski fields are the key snow-sport centres. Across the Crown Range near Wanaka, Treble Cone and Cardrona host the downhill action, and you can try cross-country skiing at **Snow Farm New Zealand** (☎03-443 7542; www.snowfarmnz.com). **Snowpark NZ** (☎03-443 9991; www snowparknz.com) is a winter wonderland of freestyle terrain with half-pipes and rails. For serious skiers, check out **Heli Ski Queenstown** (☎03-442 7733; www.flynz.co.nz; from $895), **Harris Mountains Heli-Ski** (☎03-442 6722; www.heliski.co.nz; from $795) or **Southern Lakes Heliski** (☎03-442 6222; www.southernlakesheliski.co.nz; from $6729).

Tune into 99.2FM from 6.45am to 9am to hear snow reports. Online, visit www.snowreports.co.nz. For equipment hire, including apparel, toboggans and snowboards, see Green Toad (p240) in Queenstown and Outside Sports (p240) in Queenstown and Wanaka.

sic, a Mardi Gras party, fireworks and plenty of frigid frivolity.

Queenstown Bike Festival SPORTS
(www.queenstownbikefestival.co.nz) Ten full days of two-wheeled action and fun; held in late March.

Sleeping

Queenstown has endless places to stay, but many visitors seeking accommodation. Midrange travellers won't find much choice. Consider a top-end place or go for one of the excellent budget options and spend up on activities. Places book out and prices rocket during the peak summer (December to February) and ski (June to September) seasons; book well in advance at these times. Rooms with guaranteed lake views often have a surcharge.

The **Queenstown Accommodation Centre** (Map p230; ☎03-442 7518; www.qac.co.nz; 1st fl, 19 Camp St) has a range of holiday homes and apartments on its website, with prices ranging from around $200 to $500 per week. There is often a minimum-stay period.

Ask at the DOC office for directions to the **12-Mile Delta campsite**, 11km out of town towards Glenorchy, and **Skippers campsite**, near Coronet Peak.

The Dairy B&B $$$
(Map p230; ☎03-442 5164, 0800 333 393; www.thedairy.co.nz; 10 Isle St; s/d incl breakfast from $435/465, Jun-Aug 3-night packages d $900-990; P@) Once a corner store, the Dairy is now a luxury B&B with 13 rooms packed with classy touches like designer bed linen, silk cushions and luxurious mohair rugs. Rates also include freshly baked afternoon tea. From June to August three-night packages are good value for skiers.

Warbrick Stone Cottage COTTAGE $$
(☎03-442 7520, 021 558 321; www.gibbston.co.nz; 2403 Gibbston Hwy; d $150) Relax in this Gibbston Valley (p239) heritage cottage restored by an award-winning architect. A modern kitchen and bathroom partner wooden floors and walls made of local schist (river stone), and there's an outdoor table perfect for lazy breakfasts or a twilight tipple from one of the local vineyards. The cottage is around 30km from Queenstown, en route to Cromwell and Central Otago.

Chalet Queenstown B&B B&B $$$
(Map p226; ☎0800 222 457, 03-442 7117; www.chaletqueenstown.co.nz; 1 Dublin St; d $195-225; P) This chic and friendly B&B is one of the best boutique accommodation options in Queenstown. Perfectly appointed rooms sparkle with flat-screen TVs, interesting original artworks and quality bed linen. Book well ahead to secure one of the rooms with a lake view – easily one of the best vistas in town.

QUEENSTOWN ON A BUDGET

Play Frisbee golf (p230) in the Queenstown Gardens, or hire a **bike** or **kayak** at the lakefront. For more thrilling two-wheeled action, consider a half-day pass at the Queenstown Bike Park (p229), or getting active on the many bike trials around the town. Foodies should head to the Mediterranean Market (p238) for lakeside picnic supplies, or graze the tasty – and often free – samples at the Queenstown Farmers Market (p238). Market fans should also check out the Saturday morning arts and crafts market (p240).

Eichardt's Private Hotel BOUTIQUE HOTEL $$$
(Map p230; ☎03-441 0450; www.eichardtshotel.co.nz; cnr Marine Pde & Searle Lane; d $1639-1892; P) Originally opened in the 1860s, this re-opened and restored boutique hotel enjoys an absolute lakefront location. Each of the five giant suites has a fireplace, lake views and a blend of antique and modern decor. King-sized beds, heated floors and lake sized bath tubs provide the ideal welcome after a day cruising the vineyards of Central Otago. Four newer lakeside apartments (double $1190 to $1449) are equally luxurious.

Evergreen Lodge B&B $$$
(Map p224; ☎03-442 6636; www.evergreenlodge.co.nz; 28 Evergreen Pl; d $895; P@) Handcrafted wooden furniture from a local Queenstown artisan is showcased at this modern lodge. Add in a supremely private location with unfettered views of the Remarkables, complimentary beer and wine, and a sauna and gym, and you've got a very relaxing escape from Queenstown's global hoi polloi.

Central Ridge Boutique Hotel BOUTIQUE HOTEL $$$
(Map p226; ☎03-442 8832; www.centralridge.co.nz; 4 Sydney St; d incl breakfast $270-455; P) Visitors rave about the breakfasts, but there's more to be effusive about, such as pre-dinner canapés with Central Otago wines, underfloor

QUEENSTOWN FOR CHILDREN

While Queenstown is brimming with activities, some of them have age restrictions that may exclude the youngest in your group. Nevertheless, you shouldn't have any trouble keeping the youngsters busy.

For a high that will make sugar rushes seem passé, take wilder kids on the Shotover Jet (p225). For older kids, consider a tamer variation on the classic bungy jump with the Ledge Sky Swing (p225) or go tandem with them on Queenstown Paraflights (p228). At Kawarau Bungy Centre, (p225) kids can watch people plunging off the bridge, and also challenge gravity themselves on the bungy trampoline.

The Skyline Gondola (p223) offers a slow-moving activity from dizzying heights. At the top of the hill lies the wonderfully curvy Luge (p229), suitable for ages three and up. An alternative way of getting down the hill is with Ziptrek Ecotours (p229), suitable for zipline daredevils six years and older. Supervised kids from five to 14 can also zig and zag at the Queenstown Bike Park (p229).

Several places in town hire out tandem bicycles and child-sized mountain bikes. Queenstown Bike Hire (p229) also rents foot scooters and baby buggies, plus toboggans in winter. Rockies (p240) hires out snowsuits for children.

The conservation shows at Kiwi Birdlife Park (p223) are especially geared to a younger crowd. **Queenstown Gardens** (Map p226) has a good beachside playground near the entrance on Marine Pde. Also in the park, Queenstown Ice Arena (p230) is great for a rainy day, and there's Frisbee Golf (p230).

Consider also lake cruises on the TSS *Earnslaw* (p231) and 4WD tours of narrow, snaking Skippers Canyon (p230). Train buffs will love the Kingston Flyer (p223), and family rafting trips are run by Family Adventures (p227).

For more ideas and information – including details of local babysitters – see the i-SITE (p240) or visit online at www.kidzgo.co.nz.

heating, and spacious, modern bathrooms. With only 14 rooms here, you're guaranteed a winning way with personal service.

Adventure Queenstown Hostel & Chalet HOSTEL $
(Map p230; ☎03-409 0862; www.aqhostel.co.nz; 36 Camp St; dm $29-35, d/tw/tr $120/110/135; @ wi-fi) Run by experienced travellers, the Adventure Queenstown Hostel & Chalet has spotless dorms, modern kitchens and bathrooms, and double, twin and triple rooms. Free this and free that includes international calling to 30 countries, bicycles and frisbees. It's got a more subdued ambience than other hostels, but the best of Queenstown's nightlife is nearby.

Amity Lodge MOTEL $$
(Map p226; ☎0800 556 000; www.amitylodge.co.nz; 7 Melbourne St; d from $165; P wi-fi) In a quiet street around five minutes' (uphill) walk from central Queenstown, Amity Lodge combines older but recently renovated units, and more comfortable and modern two-bedroom units. The friendly owners offer a wealth of local information, and in an expensive destination, Amity Lodge is good value.

Historic Stonehouse APARTMENT $$$
(Map p226; ☎03-442 9812; www.historicstonehouse.co.nz; 47 Hallenstein St; d $225-395; P) One of Queenstown's loveliest old private residences – built in 1874 – now houses three very comfortable self-contained apartments. Formerly the mayor's digs, the apartments are surrounded by established gardens and trimmed with antique furniture and a heritage vibe. They're not at all stuffy though, and mod cons include modern kitchens and bathrooms and an outdoor spa pool.

Bumbles HOSTEL $
(Map p226; ☎03-442 6298, 0800 286 2537; www.bumblesbackpackers.co.nz; cnr Lake Esplanade & Brunswick St; sites/dm/tw/d $20/29/62/62; P @ wi-fi) This popular hostel is colourfully decorated. Its prime lakeside location near the heart of town ensures excellent views and easy access to the best of Queenstown. It's an easygoing spot, with a quieter and more laidback vibe compared to other larger hostels around town. There's also limited space for tents and campervans.

Last Resort HOSTEL $
(Map p230; ☎03-442 4320; www.tlrqtn.com; 6 Memorial St; dm $30; @ wi-fi) Super-central, this

friendly smaller hostel is reached by a tiny brick-and-timber bridge traversing a bubbling brook in the backyard. It's just a short stroll from where most transport will drop you off, and you can expect an excited canine welcome from Cocco, an Alaskan Malamute.

Coronation Lodge MOTEL $$
(Map p226; ☎0800 420 777, 03-442 0860; www.coronationlodge.co.nz; 10 Coronation Dr; d $150-220; @☎) Right beside the Queenstown Gardens, this lodge has plush bed linen, wooden floors and cosy Turkish rugs. In a town that's somewhat lacking in good midrange accommodation, Coronation Lodge is recommended. Larger rooms have kitchenettes, and some of Queenstown's best restaurants and bars are a short stroll downhill.

Little Paradise Lodge LODGE $$
(Map p224; ☎03-442 6196; www.littleparadise.co.nz; Glenorchy-Queenstown Rd; s $45, d $120-160; ≋) Wonderfully eclectic, this slice of arty paradise is the singular vision of its Swiss owner. Each rustic room features wooden floors, quirky artwork and handmade furniture. Outside the fun continues with a back-to-nature swimming hole and well-crafted walkways along a nearby hillside. Outside visitors are welcome to enjoy afternoon tea and stroll around the gardens for $6.

Queenstown Gateway Apartments MOTEL $$
(☎0800 656 665, 03-442 3599; www.gateway.net.nz; 1066 Frankton Rd; d from $160; P☎) This modern motel complex near the airport is handy if you're flying in and picking up transport to explore other parts of the South Island. It's also a good base if you're planning on visiting Central Otago, Wanaka and Arrowtown on day trips.

Nomads HOSTEL $
(Map p230; ☎03-441 3922; www.nomadshostels.com; 5 Church St; dm $29-34, tw/d $130-150; @☎) With a prime location near Queenstown's nightlife, Nomad's has top-notch facilities including its own mini-cinema, ensuite rooms aplenty, massive kitchens and an onsite travel agency. The only potential downside is its size – Nomads is massive – so it's not the place to stay if you're looking for a quieter, more laidback ambience.

Southern Laughter HOSTEL $
(Map p230; ☎03-441 8828; www.southernlaughter.co.nz; 4 Isle St; dm $26-28, tw $58, d $60-75; @☎) This funky hostel has various kitchens scattered throughout the sprawling complex. Check out the retro B&W pics of old Queenstown before strolling into town to see new Queenstown. Free vegie soup and a spa pool are added benefits.

Hippo Lodge HOSTEL $
(Map p226; ☎03-442 5785; www.hippolodge.co.nz; 4 Anderson Heights; dm $28, s/d from $41/68; @☎) Well-maintained, relaxed hostel with good views and a correspondingly high number of stairs. Pitch a tent for $19 per person.

Butterfli Lodge HOSTEL $
(Map p226; ☎03-442 6367; www.butterfli.co.nz; 62 Thompson St; dm/d/tr $26/62/78; @) This smaller hostel sits in a quiet hillside suburb. Commandeer the barbecue on the deck and take in beaut views as you turn your steaks and sausages.

Lomond Lodge LODGE $$
(Map p230; ☎03-442 8235; www.lomondlodge.com; 33 Man St; d $138-169; P@☎) A recent make-over has modernised Lomond Lodge's cosy decor. Share your on-the-road stories with fellow travellers in the communal kitchen and around the garden barbecue. Larger family apartments ($270 for up to four people) are also available.

Alexis Motor Lodge & Apartments MOTEL $$
(Map p226; ☎03-409 0052; www.alexisqueenstown.co.nz; 69 Frankton Rd; d $170; @☎) This modern hillside motel with self-contained units is an easy 10-minute walk from town along the lakefront. Ask for an end unit with snap-happy views of one of the best mountain and lake views on the planet.

Queenstown Motel Apartments MOTEL $$
(Map p226; ☎0800 661 668, 03-442 6095; www.qma.co.nz; 62 Frankton Rd; d $35-195; P) This well-run spot has newer units with spa bathrooms, trendy decor and private mini gardens, and older 1970s-style units that represent good value for budget travellers. There's a handy onsite laundry, and the lake and mountain views are uniformly great – even from the cheaper, budget accommodation.

Black Sheep Lodge HOSTEL $
(Map p226; ☎03-442 7289; www.blacksheepbackpackers.co.nz; 13 Frankton Rd; dm/d from $25/70; @☎) This place keeps younger social types happy with a spa, a pool table and a truckload of DVDs. Rooms are recently decorated, and it's a friendly affair that maximises plenty of R&R before your next Queenstown outdoor adventure. Newer rooms are

excellent value, and there are plenty of private nooks and crannies for escaping with your favourite book.

YHA Queenstown Lakefront HOSTEL $
(Map p226; ☎03-442 8413; www.yha.co.nz; 88-90 Lake Esplanade; dm/d from $36/87; @📶) This friendly alpine lodge has staff well versed in Queenstown's myriad activities. Rooms are basic but clean; some rooms and the dining area have lake and mountain views. Queenstown's nightlife is a 10- to 15-minute lakeside stroll away.

Creeksyde Top 10 Holiday Park HIOLIDAY PARK $
(Map p226; ☎0800 786 222, 03-442 9447; www.camp.co.nz; 54 Robins Rd; sites $47, d $62-164; 📶) In a garden setting, this pretty spot has accommodation ranging from basic tent sites to self-contained motel units. An ecofriendly green tinge is added with a disciplined approach to recycling and a commitment to increase planting of native trees.

Shotover Top 10 Holiday Park HOLIDAY PARK $
(Map p224; ☎03-442 9306; www.shotoverholidaypark.co.nz; 70 Arthurs Point Rd; sites from $35, units $65-155; @📶) High above the Shotover River, this family-friendly park is 10 minutes' drive from the hustle and bustle of Queenstown. Fall out of your campervan straight onto the famous Shotover Jet.

Queenstown Lakeview Holiday Park HOLIDAY PARK $
(Map p230; ☎0800 482 735, 03-442 7252; www.holidaypark.net.nz; Brecon St; sites $40, units $140-200; @📶) A short stroll from the gondola, this park has a big open field to camp in and great facilities. A few larger trees would soften the slightly spartan ambience for campers, but there are also flasher motel units and lodges.

Eating

Queenstown's town centre is peppered with busy eateries. Many target the tourist dollar, but dig a little deeper and you'll discover local favourites covering a surprising range of international cuisines. At the more popular places, it's wise to make a reservation for evening dining.

TOP CHOICE **Fishbone Bar & Grill** SEAFOOD $$
(Map p230; ☎03-442 6768; www.fishbonequeenstown.co.nz; 7 Beach St; mains $26-32) Queenstown's more than a few miles inland, but that doesn't stop Fishbone from sourcing the best of NZ seafood. Everything from scallops to snapper is treated with a light and inventive touch. Try the zingy prawn tacos on handmade tortillas or the robust South Indian-style seafood curry. A recent makeover has reinforced Fishbone's coolly cosmopolitan ambience.

Vudu Cafe & Larder CAFE $
(Map p230; 16 Rees St; mains $10-18) Excellent home-style baking – try the pork and fennel sausage rolls or the delicate mini-pavlovas – feature at this cosmopolitan cafe. Top-notch breakfast and lunch options include buttermilk pancakes and a cheesy quesadilla. Check out the huge photo inside of a much less populated Queenstown, or head through to the rear garden for lake and mountain views.

Bella Cucina ITALIAN $$
(Map p230; ☎03-442 6762; www.bellacucina.co.nz; 6 Brecon St; pizza & pasta $29, mains $29-34; ⏰5pm-late) Fresh pasta and risotto are highlights at Bella Cucina, while the rustic woodfired pizzas are perfect for sharing. Beautifully simple food done just right and a perfectly concise winelist, all served in one of Queenstown's cosiest and most romantic dining rooms.

VKnow RESTAURANT $$
(Map p224; ☎03-442 5444; www.vknow.co.nz; 155 Fernhill Rd; mains $26-36) This bistro/wine bar is located in the suburb of Fernhill, but it's definitely worth the short taxi or bus ride (Bus 9 to the Aspen on Queenstown stop). Gourmet pizzas ($19 to $27) feature smoked salmon, Indian and vegetarian spins, and the main menu showcases local venison, blue cod and Canterbury lamb. Look forward to a casual ambience that's like dining at a friend's place.

Wai Waterfront Restaurant & Wine Bar MODERN NZ $$$
(Map p230; ☎03-442 5969; www.wai.net.nz; Steamer Wharf, Beach St; mains $40-55, 7-course degustation menu without wine $138, with wine $215; ⏰11am-10pm) Small and intimate, Wai (meaning 'water' in Maori) is white-linen classy with lake and mountain views. It's known for lamb and seafood, and the Oyster Bar does the world's favourite bivalve five different ways. The seven-course degustation menu is a splurge-worthy opportunity for a great culinary adventure. Think about it seriously. It's actually about how much you'll spend on another round of outdoor adventure activities, and will last a lot longer.

Botswana Butchery MODERN NZ **$$$**
(Map p230; ☎03-442 6994; Marine Pde; mains $35-45; ⏰noon-late) Botswana Butchery's meals are a divine combination of seasonal vegetables augmenting prime cuts of beef, lamb, poultry and seafood. The winelist is almost as long as a telephone directory. Come along for the $15 Express Lunch menu for a more affordable slice of the Botswana Butchery experience.

@Thai THAI **$$**
(Map p230; www.atthai.co.nz; 3rd fl, 8 Church St; mains $16-24) Head up the semi-hidden set of stairs for pad Thai worth writing home about, and the *hor-mok* seafood red curry will blow your mind. Definitely kick off your meal with the coconut prawns ($12) and an icy Singha beer. Takeaways are also available.

Winnies PIZZA **$$**
(Map p230; www.winnies.co.nz; 1st fl, 7 The Mall; pizza $16-27) Part-bar and part restaurant, Winnies alway seems busy. Guess why? Pizzas with a Thai, Mexican or Moroccan accent, massive burgers, pasta and steaks, and occasional live music and DJs keep energy levels high. If you need more convincing, happy hour kicks in at 9pm.

Gantley's MODERN NZ **$$$**
(Map p224; ☎03-442 8999; www.gantleys.co.nz; Arthurs Point Rd; mains $35-42; ⏰6.30pm-late) This atmospheric dining experience is showcased in a historic 1863 stone-and-timber house. The contemporary NZ cuisine and highly regarded wine list are worth the journey. Reservations are essential. A courtesy bus is availabe to ferry diners from town. A six-course degustation menu is $90 per person.

Motogrill CAFE
(Map p230; 62 Shotover St; snacks & mains $10-15; 📶) Squeeze in beside off-duty adventure guides and other discerning locals for eggy breakfasts, chunky toasted sandwiches and great coffee from hip and savvy baristas. The coffee has actually been judged Central Otago's finest by NZ's *Cuisine* magazine.

Kappa Sushi Cafe JAPANESE **$$**
(Map p230; Level 1, 36a The Mall; sushi $7-13, lunch $9-5, dinner mains $13-29; ⏰noon-2.30pm Mon-Sun, 5.30pm-late Mon-Sat) Queenstown's best Japanese eatery is also its most casual. Fresh tuna and salmon feature in good-value bento boxes for lunch. Later at night linger longer with excellent tempura and Japanese beer and sake. In summer watch the passing parade in the Mall from the upstairs deck.

Halo CAFE **$$**
(Map p230; Camp St; breakfast & lunch $10-20, dinner $24; ⏰7am-9pm) A stylish and sunny place that effortlessly blurs the line between breakfast, lunch and dinner. The breakfast burrito will definitely set you up for a day's adventuring. Come back at night for a Moroccan lamb burger and a glass of local wine. There's plenty of outdoor seating.

Bob's Weigh CAFE **$**
(Map p230; 6 Shotover St; snacks & mains $7-17) Bob's Weigh is the perfect start to any day promising extreme sports and active adventure. Join a steady stream of locals grabbing their first caffeine fix of the day, and boost your own energy levels with muesli or bagels. Lunch options include regular pasta and soup specials.

Patagonia CAFE **$**
(Map p230; www.patagoniachocolates.co.nz; 50 Beach St; coffee & chocolate $6-8; 📶) Delicious hot chocolate, homemade choccies and Queenstown's best ice cream. What more do you want? How about a lakefront location and free wi-fi? Patagonia is open until 10pm, so it's your best bet for a late-night coffee. The warm *churros* (Spanish doughnuts) will probably have you coming back for a second (or third) night.

Lick & Slurp Soup ICE-CREAM
(Map p230; 40 Shotover St; ice cream from $4.50, soups from $7; ⏰10am-10pm) Winter? Summer? Soup? Ice-cream? Head to this versatile spot for gourmet treats like toffee apple or macadamia-nut ice cream, or hearty cool-weather concoctions including mushroom and thyme soup.

Fergburger BURGERS **$**
(Map p230; www.fergburger.com; 42 Shotover St; burgers $10-17; ⏰8.30am-5am) Queenstown's iconic Fergburger has now become a tourist attraction in itself, forcing a few locals to look elswhere for their regular gourmet burger fix. Ferg's was the innovative original in town, though, and international travellers of all ages still crowd in for their burger fix. Queue nicely, please.

Devil Burger BURGERS **$**
(Map p230; www.devilburger.com; 5-11 Church St; burgers and wraps $10-18) Look out Ferg – you've got competition in the Queenstown burger wars. This diabolical new kid on the block also does tasty wraps. Try the hangover-busting Walk of Shame wrap, stuffed with bacon, egg, hash browns and grilled mushrooms.

Fergbaker BAKERY $

(Map p230; 42 Shotover St; pies $5-7; ⌚7.30am-5am) Hearty pies including lamb and kumara (sweet potato), and assorted baked goodies including ciabatta sandwiches and banoffee pie tart. A perfect early morning treat after an extended bar hop.

Habebes MIDDLE EASTERN $

(Map p230; btwn Beach & Shotover Sts; meals $7-12; ✎) Middle Eastern–inspired salads and wraps are the go at Habebes. Soups and yummy pies – try the chicken, kumara and mushroom one – are tasty diversions if you're in town for a winter-sports sojourn.

Aggy's Shack FISH & CHIPS $

(Map p230; Church St; $10-20; ⌚11am-10pm) Pull up a chair at this simple lakeside gazebo for fish and chips, including juicy blue cod and the opportunity to try a few local flavours like smoked eel and *titi* (muttonbird).

Queenstown Farmers Market FARMERS MARKET $

(Map p230; cnr Church & Camp Sts; ⌚9am-12.30pm Sat Dec-Mar) Gourmet goodies and ethical foodie choices from all around Central Otago.

Mediterranean Market SELF CATERING $

(cnr Gorge & Robins Rds) Fill up a basket for a lakeside picnic from this fantastic deli and bakery.

New World Wakatipu SUPERMARKET $

(Remarkables Park Shopping Centre) Near the airport and convenient if you've just picked up a campervan.

Freshchoice SUPERMARKET $

(Map p226; 64 Gorge Rd) Queenstown's biggest supermarket.

Alpine Supermarket SUPERMARKET $

(Map p230; cnr Stanley & Shotover Sts) Queenstown's most central supermarket.

Drinking

Drinking is almost a competitive sport in Queenstown, and there's a good range of options for after-dark carousing. Bars shut at 4am.

Atlas Beer Cafe CRAFT BEER

(Map p230; Steamer Wharf, Beach St; ⌚10am-2am) Perched at the end of Steamer Wharf, this pint-sized bar specialises in beers from Dunedin's Emerson's Brewery and regular guest beers from further afield. A concise but tasty food menu includes good-value sandwiches and wraps for lunch (around $10), and shared plates and tapas ($10 to $15) for dinner. If you're a craft beer fan, also head to Dux de Lux (p240).

Searle Lane & Social BAR

(Map p230; www.searlelane.co.nz; 11 Church St) Pool tables, pizza and lunch specials, and shared rotisserie chickens make this a top spot for getting to know any new arrivals at your hostel. Free-flowing beer and well-mixed cocktails definitely enhance the Social part. DJs kick in around 11pm from Wednesday to Saturday.

Ballarat Trading Company PUB

(Map p230; www.ballarat.co.nz; 7-9 The Mall) Stuffed bears, rampant wall-mounted ducks and a recreated colonial general store – there's really no competition for the title of Queenstown's most eclectic decor. Beyond the grab bag of infuences, Ballarat's gastro pub combo is quite a traditional spot, with gleaming beer taps, occasional lapses into 1980s music, and robust meals, including confit duck leg, lamb pie, burgers and steaks.

Pub on Wharf PUB

(Map p230; www.pubonwharf.co.nz; Steamer Wharf) Ubercool interior design meets handsome woodwork and lighting fit for a hipster hideaway. Stuffed animal heads reinforce that you're still in NZ, and Mac's beers on tap, scrummy nibbles and a decent wine list make this a great place to settle in for the evening. Check the website for live-music listings.

Bardeaux WINE BAR

(Map p230; Eureka Arcade, 11 The Mall; ⌚6pm-late) This small, low-key wine bar is all class. Under a low ceiling await plush leather armchairs and a fireplace made from Central Otago's iconic schist rock. Come along for one of Queenstown's best wine selections, many also from Central Otago.

Surreal COCKTAIL BAR

(Map p230; www.surrealbar.co.nz; 7 Rees St) With funky music, low lighting and red-velvet booths, this unpretentious and private spot is good for a quiet drink and nibbling on tasty shared platters. Later in the evening DJ-inspired goings-on kick off and the dance floor comes to life. Happy hour is from 10pm.

Monty's PUB

(Map p230; www.montysbar.co.nz; Church St) On warm summer days the patio at Monty's is prime real estate. Most nights the band cranks up and gets the crowd tapping their feet as they down a few.

EXPLORING THE GIBBSTON VALLEY

Gung-ho visitors to Queenstown might be happiest dangling off a giant rubber band, but as they're plunging towards the Kawarau River, they'll be missing out on some of Central Otago's most interesting winemaking areas just up the road in the stunning Gibbston Valley.

On a spectacular river terrace near the Kawarau Bridge, AJ Hackett's original bungy partner Henry van Asch set up the **Winehouse & Kitchen** (Map p224; ☎03-442 7310; www.winehouse.co.nz; mains $15-30; ⏰10am-5pm). A restored wooden villa includes a garden cafe, and in early 2012, the Winehouse's annual Summer Playgound Series music festival was also launched from January to April. Check the website for listings.

Almost opposite, a winding and scenic road leads to beautiful **Chard Farm** (Map p224; ☎03-442 6110; www.chardfarm.co.nz; ⏰11am-5pm), and a further 700m along is **Gibbston Valley Wines** (Map p224; www.gvwines.co.nz), the area's largest wine producer. Try its pinot noir and take a tour of the impressive wine cave. There are also a 'cheesery' and a restaurant.

A further 4km along SH6, **Peregrine** (Map p224; ☎03-442 4000; www.peregrinewines.co.nz; ⏰10am-5pm) produces excellent sauvignon blanc, pinot noir and pinot gris, and hosts occasional outdoor concerts during summer, sometimes featuring international names.

Further west near the shores of Lake Hayes, the **Amisfield Winery & Bistro** (Map p224; ☎03-442 0556; www.amisfield.co.nz; small plates $16.50; ⏰11.30am-8pm Tue-Sun) is regularly lauded by NZ's authoritative *Cuisine* magazine. The highly regarded eatery serves tapas-sized plates perfect for sharing with a few friends on the sunny deck, and Amisfield's pinot noir has been awarded internationally. Also available is the 'Trust the Chef' menu (per person $55), where Amisfield's canny chefs magic up tasty diversions based on whatever is in season. Bookings recommended.

Ask at the Queenstown i-SITE (p240) for maps and information about touring the Gibbston Valley. Recent developments in the area include mountain biking and walking trails along the spidery Kawarau River. You could also join a guided wine tour. A fun option is by retro bicycle with Cycle de Vine (p232). Visit www.gibbstonvalley.co.nz for more info about this compact wine-growing area with its own unique microclimate.

For accommodation, the cosy Warbrick Stone Cottage (p233) is a convenient option en route from Queenstown to Cromwell. Campervan travellers can park up at the compact well-equipped campsite at the **Gibbston Tavern** (☎03-409 0508; www.gibbstontavern.co.nz; 8 Coal Pit Rd; sites $30). Expect a warm welcome from the locals at the adjacent pub. Ask to try the tavern's own Moonshine Wines, as you won't find them anywhere else.

Barmuda BAR

(Map p230; Searle Lane; ⏰3pm-late) A huge open fire makes Barmuda's atmospheric courtyard the place to be in cooler weather. In summer, live jazz on Friday and Saturday nights is sometimes on the cards.

Minibar CRAFT BEER

(Map p230; Eureka Arcade, 11 The Mall; ⏰4pm-late) Beer, beer and more beer. More than 100 local and international beers are poured in this compact space. A cool name for a cool bar, oozing with style.

☆ Entertainment

Pick up the *Source* (www.thesourceonline.com), a free weekly flyer with a gig guide and events listings. Live music and clubbing are a nightly affair and most Queenstown venues stay open until the wee hours.

Nightclubs

Subculture CLUB

(Map p230; www.subculture.net.nz; downstairs 12-14 Church St) Drum 'n' bass, hip-hop, dub and reggae noises that get the crowds moving.

Debajo CLUB

(Map p230; Cow Lane) The perennial end-of-night boogie spot – house and big-beat gets the dance floor heaving till closing time.

Tardis Bar BAR

(Map p230; www.tardisbar.com; 20 Cow Lane, Skyline Arcade) A good dance bar. Regular DJs play hip-hop, dancehall and dub. Like Dr Who's phone booth, it's surprisingly roomy inside.

Cinema

Reading Cinemas CINEMA

(Map p230; ☎03-442 9990; www.readingcinemas.co.nz; 11 The Mall; adult/child $16.20/10.50) Discounts on Tuesdays.

Live Music

The World Bar BAR

(Map p230; www.theworldbar.co.nz; 27 Shotover St; ⏲4pm to late) Still retaining its raucous backpacker roots, the World Bar is also one of Queenstown's best music clubs with regular DJs and live gigs. Check the website for what's on, or drop by for teapot cocktails and legendary Fat Badgers pizzas.

Dux de Lux PUB

(Map p230; 14 Church St) Lots of live bands and DJs with everything from reggae to drum 'n' bass. Look forward to occasional summer visits from NZ's biggest touring acts. The 'Dux' also brew their own beers.

Haka

Kiwi Haka TRADITIONAL DANCE

(Map p226; ☎03-441 0101; www.skyline.co.nz; Brecon St; adult/child/family incl gondola $59/32/166; ⏲from 5.15pm) For traditional Maori dancing and singing, come watch this group at the top of the gondola. There are four 30-minute shows nightly, but bookings are essential.

Shopping

Queenstown is a good place to shop for souvenirs and gifts. Many shops also specialise in outdoor and adventure gear. Begin your shopping along the Mall, Shotover St and Beach St. Explore Church Lane linking Church St to Earl St for art galleries.

Fetch CLOTHING

(Map p230; www.fetchnz.com; 34 Shotover St) Grab an iconic Kiwi T-shirt - our favourite is 'New Zealand – Damn Better than Old Zealand' or create your own design as a wearable souvenir of the time you bungyed, mountain-biked and ziplined to adventure-sports Nirvana.

Kapa ARTS & CRAFTS

(Map p230; www.kapa.co.nz; 29 Rees St) Quirky and eclectic NZ design infused with a healthy dose of contemporary Maori culture.

Rockies CLOTHING

(Map p230; www.rockies.co.nz; 49 Beach St) Rent or buy kids' clothes from Rockies to keep them cosy on the slopes.

Kathmandu OUTDOOR EQUIPMENT

(Map p230; wwww.kathmandu.co.nz; 88 Beach St) A well-known and good-value chain with regular sales making things even cheaper. Join Kathmandu's 'Summit Club' for extra discounts on its rugged backpacks, active footwear and stylish travel and adventure clothing.

Green Toad OUTDOOR EQUIPMENT

(Map p230; ☎03-442 5311; www.greentoad.co.nz; 48 Camp St) Equipment hire including apparel, snowboards and toboggans.

Snowrental OUTDOOR EQUIPMENT

(Map p230; www.snowrental.co.nz; 39 Camp St) Ski-equipment hire company.

Outside Sports OUTDOOR EQUIPMENT

(Map p230; www.outsidesports.co.nz; 36 Shotover St) Ski-equipment hire, mountain-bike hire and outdoor gear for sale

Small Planet Sports Co OUTDOOR EQUIPMENT

(Map p230; www.smallplanetsports.co.nz; 17 Shotover St) New and used outdoor equipment. It's also got a cheaper **outlet store** (Map p230; www.smallplanetsports.co.nz; 23 Beach St).

toi o tahuna ARTS & CRAFTS

(Map p230; www.toi.co.nz; 11 Church Lane) Exclusively NZ art, with around half the work from contemporary Maori artists. Around toi o tahuna, you can also explore other galleries in chic Church Lane. Ask for the *Fine Arts Galleries Walking Trail* map at the i-SITE.

Arts & Crafts Market ARTS & CRAFTS

(Map p230; www.marketplace.net.nz; ⏲9am 4.30pm Nov-Apr, 10am-3.30pm May-Oct) On Saturdays, visit this creative market at Earnslaw Park on the lakefront beside Steamer Wharf. Here's your chance to get a few truly local gifts or souvenirs.

Information

Emergency

Ambulance, fire service and police (☎111)

Post

Post Office (13 Camp St)

Tourist Information

Queenstown i-SITE (☎03-442 4100, 0800 668 888; www.queenstownnz.co.nz; Clocktower Centre, cnr Shotover & Camp Sts; ⏲8am-6.30pm) Booking service, accommodation and information on Queenstown, Arrowtown and Glenorchy.

DOC Visitor Centre (Department of Conservation; ☎03-442 7935; www.doc.govt.nz; 38 Shotover St; ⏲8.30am-5.30pm) Backcountry Hut Passes and weather and track updates; on the mezzanine floor above Outside Sports. Head here to pick up confirmed bookings for the Milford, Kepler and Routeburn Tracks.

Info & Track Centre (☎03-442 9708; www.infotrack.co.nz; 37 Shotover St; ⏲7am-9pm) Information on transport to trailheads.

Travel Agencies

Kiwi Discovery (Map p230; ☎03-442 7340, 0800 505 504; www.kiwidiscovery.com; 37 Camp St) Ski packages and tramping and trailhead transport.

Real Journeys (☎03-249 7416, 0800 656 501; www.realjourneys.co.nz; Beach St, Steamer Wharf) Lake trips and tours.

The Station (Map p230; ☎03-442 5252; www.thestation.co.nz; cnr Camp & Shotover Sts) Houses AJ Hackett Bungy and Shotover Jet.

 Getting There & Away

Air

Air New Zealand (p222) links Queenstown to Auckland, Wellington and Christchurch, and Sydney and Melbourne. Virgin Australia has flights between Queenstown and Sydney and Brisbane.

Jetstar (☎0800 800 995; www.jetstar.com) links Queenstown with Auckland, Christchurch and Wellington, and Sydney, Melbourne and the Gold Coast.

Bus

Most buses and shuttles leave from the **Athol St bus terminal** or the Station (p241). Check when you book. Approximate times from Queenstown are the following: Christchurch (seven hours), Dunedin (4½ hours), Invercargill (three hours), Te Anau (two hours), Milford Sound (six hours), Wanaka (30 minutes), Cromwell (one hour), Haast (four hours), Greymouth (nine hours), West Coast glaciers (six hours).

InterCity (www.intercity.co.nz) Book at the i-SITE. Travels to Christchurch, Te Anau, Milford Sound, Dunedin and Invercargill, plus a daily West Coast service to the glaciers and Haast.

Naked Bus (www.nakedbus.com) To the West Coast, Te Anau, Christchurch, Dunedin, Cromwell, Wanaka and Invercargill.

Atomic Shuttles (www.atomictravel.co.nz) To Wanaka, Christchurch, Dunedin and Greymouth.

Catch-a-Bus (☎03-479 9960; www.catchabus.co.nz) To Dunedin and Central Otago – also links to the Taeri Gorge Railway.

Bottom Bus (☎03-477 9083; www.bottombus.co.nz) Does a loop service around the south of the South Island.

Wanaka Connexions (☎03-443 9120; www.alpinecoachlines.co.nz) Links Queenstown with Wanaka and the Rail Trail towns of Central Otago.

Trampers' & Skiers' Transport

Bus services between Queenstown and Milford Sound via Te Anau can also be used for track transport.

For the ski slopes, catch a shuttle ($15 return) to Coronet Peak or the Remarkables from the Queenstown Snow Centre at the Station (p241). The Info & Track Centre (p240) and Kiwi Discovery (p241) both provide transport to trailheads.

See **Alpine Coachlines** (☎03-443 9120; www.alpinecoachlines.co.nz) and Kiwi Discovery (p241) for details of transport to Cardrona and Treble Cone.

Trackhopper (☎021-187 7732; www.trackhopper.co.nz; from $230 plus fuel costs) Offers a handy car-relocation service from either end of the Routeburn Track, so you don't have to backtrack over parts of the country you've already seen. Similar services are available for the Greenstone & Caples Track and the Rees-Dart Track.

 Getting Around

To/From the Airport

Queenstown Airport (ZQN; ☎03-450 9031; www.queenstownairport.co.nz; Frankton) is 8km east of town. **Super Shuttle** (☎0800 748 885; www.supershuttle.co.nz) picks up and drops off in Queenstown (around $20). **Connectabus** (☎03-441 4471; www.connectabus.com; cnr Beach & Camp Sts) runs to to the airport ($6) every 15 minutes from 6.50am to 10.20pm. **Alpine Taxis** (☎0800 442 6666) or **Queenstown Taxis** (☎03-442 7788) charge around $30.

Public Transport

Connnectabus (☎03-441 4471; www.connectabus.com) has various colour-coded routes. Catch the blue route for accommodation in Fernhill and the red routes for accommodation in Frankton. A day pass (adult/child $17/12) allows travel on the entire network. Pick up a route map and timetable from the i-SITE. Buses leave from the corner of Beach and Camp Sts.

Arrowtown

POP 2400

Beloved by day-trippers from Queenstown, exceedingly quaint Arrowtown sprang up in the 1860s following the discovery of gold in the Arrow River. Today the town retains more than 60 of its original wooden and stone buildings, and has pretty, tree-lined avenues, excellent galleries and an expanding array of fashionable shopping opportunities.

The only gold being flaunted these days is on credit cards, and surrounded by a bonanza of daytime tourists, you might grow wary of the quaint historical ambience. Instead take advantage of improved public transport to stay in the town, and use it as a base for exploring Queenstown and the wider region. That way you can enjoy Arrowtown's history, charm and excellent restaurants when the tour buses have decamped back to Queenstown.

Sights & Activities

Try your luck **gold panning** on the Arrow River. Rent pans from the visitor information centre ($3) and head to the northern edge of town. This is also a good spot for **walking**. Pick up *Arrowtown Area Walks* (free) from the visitor information centre. You'll find routes and history on walks to **Macetown** (14km, seven hours) and on **Tobins Track** (one hour).

Chinese Settlement HISTORIC SITE
(admission by gold coin donation; ⌚24hr) Arrowtown has NZ's best example of a gold-era Chinese settlement. Interpretive signs explain the lives of Chinese 'diggers' during and after the gold rush, while restored huts and shops make the story more tangible. Subjected to significant racism, the Chinese often had little choice but to rework old tailings rather than seek new claims. The Chinese settlement is off Buckingham St.

Lake District Museum & Gallery MUSEUM
(www.museumqueenstown.com; 49 Buckingham St; adult/child $8/2; ⌚8.30am-5pm) Exhibits on the gold-rush era and the early days of Chinese settlement around Arrowtown. Younger travellers will enjoy the Museum Fun Pack ($5), which includes activity sheets, museum treasure hunts, stickers and a few flecks of gold.

Millbrook Golf Course GOLF
(☎03-441 7010; www.millbrook.co.nz; Malaghans Rd; green fees $180, club hire $60) Flasher golfers should head to Millbrook Golf Course.

Arrowtown Bike Hire BICYCLE RENTAL
(☎03-442 1466; www.arrowtownbikehire.co.nz; Ramshaw Lane; half/full day rental $35/49) Get active on two wheels on the many new mountain-biking trails around Arrowtown, or join a Mountain Bike Mania tour ($199, October to April) combining 4WD and mountain-biking action and exploring the former gold-rush village of Macetown. Multiday rentals are also available. Rent bikes on Ramshaw Lane or visit Poplar Lodge (p242) for bookings and track information.

Tours

Southern Explorer 4WD TOUR
(☎03-441 1144; www.southernexplorer.co.nz; 4 Merioneth St; day tours per person $65-140) 4WD day tours exploring the improbably scenic landscapes and old mining history around Arrowtown, Skippers Canyon and Glenorchy. Options include overnight camping in Skippers Canyon or Macetown. Based at Poplar Lodge (p242).

Sleeping

There's accommodation from budget to top end, but during summer rooms fill up fast.

The Arrow BOUTIQUE HOTEL **$$$**
(☎03-409 8600; www.thearrow.co.nz; 63 Manse Rd; d from $415) Five understated but luxurious suites feature at this modern property set in stunning landscapes on the outskirts of Arrowtown. Accommodation is chic and contemporary with huge picture windows showcasing the countryside. Breakfast is included, and there's an original stone cottage that's the perfect socialising hub for guests. The bright lights of Arrowtown are a picturesque five-minute walk away.

Millbrook RESORT **$$$**
(☎03-441 7000, 0800 800 604; www.millbrook.co.nz; Malaghans Rd; d from $499; P@) Just outside Arrowtown, this enormous resort is a town unto itself. Cosy private villas have recently been refurbished and there's a top-class golf course right at your front door. At the end of the day, take your pick from four restaurants, or relax at the **Spa at Millbrook** (☎03-441 7017; www.millbrook.co.nz; Malaghans Rd; treatments from $230), recently voted one of the world's top 10 hotel spas.

Arrowtown Lodge B&B **$$**
(☎03-442 1101; www.arrowtownlodge.co.nz; 7 Anglesea St; d incl breakfast $160; @) From the outside, the guest rooms look like heritage cottages, but inside they're cosy and modern. The family owners are friendly, the breakfast is hearty and some of the units include compact private gardens,

Poplar Lodge HOSTEL **$**
(☎03-442 1466; www.poplarlodge.co.nz; 4 Merioneth St; dm/s/d $29/62/70;) Budget accommodation options are limited in A-town, but this is your best bet. A converted house, Poplar Lodge has a cosy feel and is off the bus-bound tourist trail. A couple of self-contained units ($99 to $120) are also available. It's also home base for Arrowtown Bike Hire (p242) and Southern Explorer (p242).

Shades MOTEL **$$**
(☎03-442 1613; www.shadesofarrowtown.co.nz; cnr Buckingham & Merioneth Sts; d $100-155;) A garden setting gives these bungalow-style cottages a relaxed air. Sleeping up to eight, the two-storey family unit (from $175) is

Arrowtown

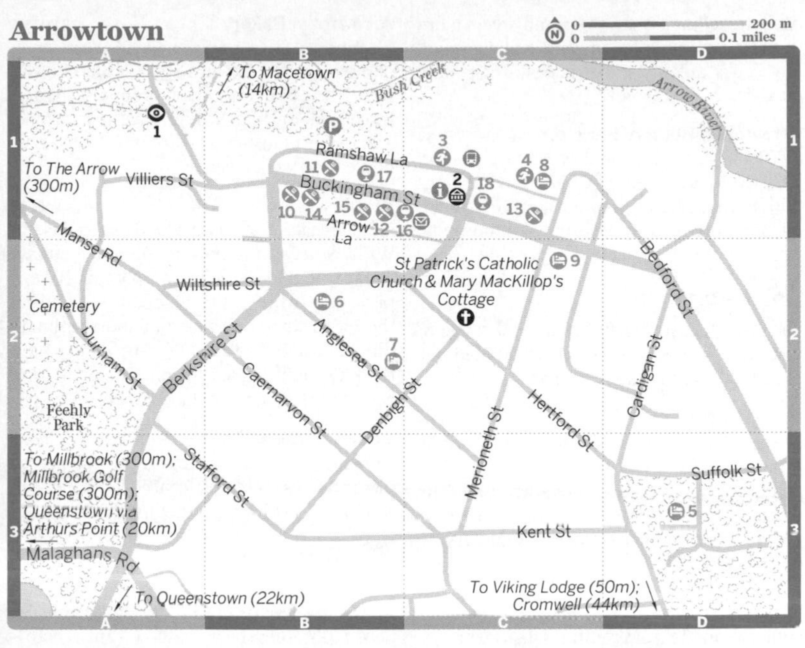

Arrowtown

Sights

1 Chinese Settlement A1
2 Lake District Museum & Gallery C1

Activities, Courses & Tours

3 Arrowtown Bike Hire C1
4 Southern Explorer C1

Sleeping

5 Arrowtown Holiday Park D3
6 Arrowtown Lodge B2
7 Old Villa Homestay B&B B2
8 Poplar Lodge C1
9 Shades C2

Eating

10 Arrowtown Bakery B1
11 Bonjour Cafe B1
12 Cook's Store & Deli B1
Pesto .... (see 14)
13 Provisions C1
14 Saffron B1
15 Stables B1

Drinking

16 Arrow Brewing Company C1
Blue Door .... (see 14)
17 New Orleans Hotel B1
18 The Tap C1

Entertainment

Dorothy Browns .... (see 14)

good value if you're travelling with the whole clan. Savvy budget travellers should book the more compact studio units ($100).

Old Villa Homestay B&B B&B **$$**
(☎03-442 1682; www.arrowtownoldvilla.co.nz; 13 Anglesea St; s/d $120/160) Freshly baked bread and homemade preserves welcome visitors to this heritage-style villa with a garden just made for summer barbecues. Two en-suite double rooms come trimmed with fresh sprigs of lavender. One of the rooms has an additional single bed if you've got an extra travelling companion.

Viking Lodge MOTEL **$$**
(☎03-442 1765; www.vikinglodge.co.nz; 21 Inverness Cres; d $95-150; @🛜≋) These older A-frame units have a comfortable and family-friendly stamp. If the kids still have energy after a

day's travelling, wear them out even more in the swimming pool or on the playground. Barbecues aplenty make it easy to to dine alfresco.

Arrowtown Holiday Park HOLIDAY PARK **$$**
(☎03-442 1876; www.arrowtownholidaypark.co.nz; 11 Suffolk St; sites $36, d $65-140; @📶) Mountain views come as standard, even if you're paying more for the flash new studio units. Amenities blocks are equally pristine.

Eating

For its size, Arrowtown has a good range of restaurants. Booking is recommended for evening dining during summer.

Provisions CAFE **$**
(www.provisions.co.nz; 65 Buckingham St; snacks & meals $8-15) One of Arrowtown's oldest cottages is now a cute cafe surrounded by fragrant gardens. Pop in for breakfast or a coffee, and don't leave town without trying one of their deservedly famous sticky buns. Foodie goodies to stock up the campervan with include still-warm bread, and jams and chutneys made from Central Otago fruit.

Saffron INTERNATIONAL **$$$**
(☎03-442 0131; www.saffronrestaurant.co.nz; 18 Buckingham St; lunch $20-30, dinner mains $38-40; ⊙noon-late) Saffron has grown-up food, including lamb rump or Hereford beef with interesting variations on local vegetables. The trio of curries featuring pork, duck and king prawns effortlessly traverses Asia, and you can also purchase the *Saffron* cookbook, showcasing the restaurant's most iconic recipes. The ambience is more formal and sophisticated than the buzz of adjacent Pesto.

Pesto ITALIAN **$$**
(☎03-442 0885; 18 Buckingham St; mains $18-33; ⊙5pm-late) This candlelit restaurant serves Italian food with a contemporary spin. It's Saffron's slightly rowdier, younger, family-friendly sibling, and the culinary expectations are kept high with good pasta and gourmet pizzas ($20 to $34).

Bonjour Cafe FRENCH **$$**
(☎03-409 8946; www.bonjour-arrowtown.com; Ramshaw Lane; mains $18-30; ⊙8.30am-3pm Sun & Sat, 5.30-9pm Thu-Sat) Come for breakfast and tuck into one of the 18 different crepe options – you'll definitely struggle to choose. Come back for dinner to treat yourself to cheese fondue or the Kiwi-French combo of herb-crusted rack of lamb.

Arrowtown Bakery BAKERY **$**
(Buckingham St; gourmet pies $5.50) We can recommend the bacon and egg or satay chicken pies. Don't blame us if you order a second. A tasty back-up plan would have to be coffee and a slice of just maybe Central Otago's best boysenberry cheesecake.

Stables CAFE **$$**
(28 Buckingham St; lunch $10-18, dinner $14-30) With courtyard tables adjoining a grassy square, Stables is a good spot to share a pizza and wine. Later at night, step inside the 1860s stone building for a more intimate dining experience. If you're travelling with the kids, they can let off some steam tearing around the adjacent village green.

Cook's Store & Deli DELI **$**
(www.cooksdeli.co.nz; 44 Buckingham St) Pick up picnic fixings including local cheeses and artisan breads at this retro-themed deli and cafe.

Drinking

Arrow Brewing Company CRAFT BEER
(www.arrowbrewing.co.nz; 48-50 Buckingham St) Seven different beers and a sunny courtyard make the Arrow Brewing Company an essential stop. We're especially keen on the honey-infused Gentle Annie lager and the hoppy Arrow Pilz pilsner. Occasional seasonal beers create havoc for the indecisive drinker, and good-value meals and bar snacks include quite possibly the South Island's best lamb burger.

Blue Door BAR
(18 Buckingham St; ⊙3pm-late) Hidden away behind a tricky-to-find blue door. Low ceilings, diffuse light and abundant candles create an intimate quaffing location. Blue Door has a formidable wine list and enough rustic ambience to keep you entertained for the evening.

New Orleans Hotel PUB
(27 Buckingham St) With looks transplanted more from the Wild West than the Deep South, this heritage pub is a good escape from Arrowtown's array of expensive designer shops. The hearty meals are a step back in time, too, and occasional live music infiltrates the town's hushed ambience most weekends.

The Tap PUB
(51 Buckingham St) The Tap dates back to the gold rush. Inside, there are wines, a pool table, pub grub and liquid gold on tap. Sit outside in the sunny garden bar and slow down to Arrowtown's languid pace.

☆ Entertainment

Dorothy Browns CINEMA

(☎03-442 1964; www.dorothybrowns.com; Ballarat Arcade, Buckingham St; adult/child/student $18.50/8/12.50) This is what a cinema should be. Ultra-comfortable seating with the option to cuddle with your neighbour. Fine wine and cheese boards are available to accompany the mostly art-house films on offer. Every screening has an intermission – the perfect opportunity to tuck into a tub of gourmet ice cream.

Information

Arrowtown Visitor Information Centre (☎03-442 1824; www.arrowtown.com; 49 Buckingham St; ⌚8.30am-5pm; @📶) Shares premises with the Lake District Museum & Gallery.

Getting There & Away

From Queenstown, **Connectabus** (☎03-441 4471; www.connectabus.com) runs regular services (7.45am to 11pm) on its No 10 route from Frankton to Arrowtown. You'll need to catch a No 11 bus from Queenstown to the corner of Frankton and Kawarau Rd, and change to a No 10 bus there. The cheapest way is a one-day pass (adult/child $17/12).

The **Double-Decker Bus Tour** (☎03-441 4421; www.doubledeckerbus.co.nz; $48) does a three-hour round-trip tour to Arrowtown (departs Queenstown at 9.30am). **Arrowtown Scenic Bus** (☎03-442 1900; www.arrowtownbus.co.nz) runs a daily four-hour round trip from Queenstown at 10am ($69).

Around Arrowtown

Fourteen kilometres north of Arrowtown lies Macetown, a ghost town reached via a rugged, flood-prone road (the original miners' wagon track), which crosses the Arrow River more than 25 times. Don't even think about taking the rental car here – instead four-hour trips are made from Queenstown and Arrowtown by 4WD vehicle, with gold panning included. Operators include **Nomad Safaris** (☎03-442 6699, 0800 688 222; www.nomadsafaris.co.nz; adult/child from $165/80) and Southern Explorer (p242), and you can also join a mountain-bike trip there with Arrowtown Bike Hire (p242).

Glenorchy

POP 220

Set in achingly beautiful surroundings, postage-stamp-sized Glenorchy is the perfect low-key antidote to Queenstown. An expanding range of adventure operators will get you active on the lake and in nearby mountain valleys by kayak, horse or jetboat, but if you prefer to strike out on two legs, tiny Kinloch, just across the lake, is the starting point for some of the South Island's finest tramps. Glenorchy lies at the head of Lake Wakatipu, a scenic 40-minute (68km) drive northwest from Queenstown.

Activities

Almost all organised activities offer shuttles to and from Queenstown for a small surcharge. Other activities on offer include farm tours – complete with the opportunity to shear sheep – trout fishing, guided photography tours and cookery classes. See www.glenorchyinfocentre.co.nz or ask at the Queenstown i-SITE (p240).

Tramping & Scenic Driving

The DOC brochure *Head of Lake Wakatipu* ($2) details an easy waterside walk around the outskirts of town, and other tramps from two hours to two days, taking in the Routeburn Valley, Lake Sylvan, Dart River and Lake Rere. For track snacks or meals, stock up on groceries in Queenstown. If you're planning on doing short day walks around the region, note that track transport can be at a premium during summer, as it is the Great Walks season. Try to book transport in advance if possible. Those with sturdy wheels can explore the superb valleys north of Glenorchy. **Paradise** lies 15km northwest of town, just before the start of the Dart Track. Keep your expectations low: Paradise is just a paddock, but the gravel road there runs through beautiful farmland fringed by majestic mountains. You can also explore the Rees Valley or take the road to Routeburn, which goes via the Dart River Bridge. Near the start of the Routeburn Track is the Routeburn Nature Walk (one hour) and the Lake Sylvan tramp (one hour 40 minutes).

Glenorchy Base TRAMPING

(☎03-409 0960; www.glenorchybase.co.nz; adult/child from $60) Specialises in guided walks (two hours to one day) in the Glenorchy area. Highlights include birdwatching around Lake Sylvan and a Routeburn Track day walk.

Rural Discovery Tours 4WD

(☎03-442 2299; www.rdtours.co.nz; adult/child $185/92) Half-day tours of a high-country sheep station in a remote valley between Mts Earnslaw and Alfred.

LOCAL KNOWLEDGE

THE REES VALLEY
JANE CAMPION

As many times a year as I can, I travel to a holiday hut up the Rees Valley, at the top end of Lake Wakatipu. I love the lake, the majesty of the surrounding mountains, the good weather in the basin, the walks, the rivers, the end-of-the-world feeling and the laconic people who live nearby. Everyone who has visited me up here is infected by the ready magic of the landscape and the sensation of worldly troubles dissolving. Lake Sylvan is one of many good bush walks in the area – a fairly short walk for this scale of landscape, but the intimacy of being inside the bush immediately gives you a sense of delight. Recently the lake has been high and is phenomenal to swim in.

Jane Campion,
film director, writer & producer.

Jetboating & Kayaking

Dart River Safaris JET BOATING
(☎03-442 9992, 0800 327 8538; www.dartriver.co.nz; adult/child $219/119) Journeys into the heart of the spectacular Dart River wilderness, followed by a short nature walk and a 4WD trip. The round trip from Glenorchy takes three hours. You can also combine a jetboat ride with a river descent in an inflatable three-seater 'funyak' (adult/child $289/189).

Kayak Kinloch KAYAKING
(☎03-442 4900; www.kayakkinloch.co.nz; adult $40-80, child $35-50) Excellent guided trips exploring the lake. Trips depart from Queenstown, Glenorchy or Kinloch.

Other Activities

Dart Stables HORSE RIDING
(☎0800 474 3464, 03-442 5688; www.dartstables.com) Offer a two-hour ride ($129), a full-day trot ($279) and a 1½-hour Ride of the Rings trip ($169) for Hobbitty types. If you're really keen, consider the overnight two-day trek with a sleepover in Paradise ($695). All trips can be joined in Queenstown.

Paradise Skydive SKYDIVING
(☎03-442 8333, 0800 475 934; www.skydiveparadise.co.nz; Glenorchy Airport; $325-399) Tandem skydiving above some the planet's most spectacular scenery.

High Country Horses HORSE RIDING
(☎0508 595 959, 03-442 9915; www.high-country-horses.co.nz) Runs two-hour rides ($125) and full-day rides ($295). Trips can be joined in Queenstown.

Sleeping & Eating

At the base of the Kinloch Lodge there's a DOC campsite ($6), which has basic lakeside facilities.

Glenorchy Lake House B&B $$$
(☎03-442 7084; www.glenorchylakehouse.co.nz; Mull St; d incl breakfst $325-400) This luxury lakefront B&B features Egyptian cotton sheets, flat-screen TVs and luxury toiletries. Good luck tearing yourself away to get active out and about in the Wakatipu area. Once you return, recharge in the spa or with a massage. An award-winning chef is in residence (dinner per person $85), and transfers to the Routeburn and Greenstone Tracks are available.

Kinloch Lodge LODGE
(☎03-442 4900; www.kinlochlodge.co.nz; Kinloch Rd; dm $33, d $82-132) Across Lake Wakatipu from Glenorchy, this is a great place to unwind or prepare for a tramp. Rooms in the bunkhouse are comfy and colourful, and there's a hot tub. The 19th-century Heritage Rooms are small but plusher, and come with breakfast and dinner (double $278 to $298). A bar and a good restaurant are on-site. Kinloch is a 26km drive from Glenorchy, or you can organise a five-minute boat ride across the lake. Kinloch Lodge can also arrange track transfers to various trailheads.

Glenorchy Holiday Park HOLIDAY PARK $
(☎03-441 0303; www.glenorchyaccommodation.co.nz; 2 Oban St; sites $28, dm $20, units $32-80; @) Set up camp in a field surrounded by basic cabins and handy barbecues. Out front is a small shop and information centre.

Glenorchy Lodge PUB $$
(☎03-442 9968; www.wakatipu.com; Mull St; d $30-150) Tidy yet tiny rooms live upstairs from this centrally located pub. Some rooms have loft-style ceilings and some have en suites – all have great views.

Glenorchy Hotel HOSTEL $
(☎03-442 9902; www.glenorchy-nz.co.nz; Mull St; dm $30-35) Basic dorms and an adequate base for returning trampers.

Glenorchy Café CAFE $$
(Mull St; breakfast & lunch mains $15-20, pizza $25; ⏲8am-5pm May-Oct, dinner Nov-Apr) Pizza and

breakfast stacks are perennial favourites with locals.

Information

The best place for local information, weather and track information is the **Glenorchy visitor information centre** (☎03-409 2049; www.glenorchy-nz.co.nz; Oban St) in the Glenorchy Hotel. It's website is also an excellent resource. Fishing rods and mountain bikes can be hired. Ask about trail maps for walking or mountain biking in the nearby **Whakaari Conservation Area.**

There is a petrol station in Glenorchy, but fill up with cheaper fuel before you leave Queenstown. There's an ATM at the Glenorchy Hotel.

Getting There & Away

With sweeping vistas and gem-coloured waters, the sealed Glenorchy to Queenstown Rd is wonderfully scenic. Its constant hills are a killer for cyclists. Pick up the *Queenstown to Glenorchy Road* leaflet from the Queenstown i-SITE (p240) for points of interest along the way. The Info & Track Centre (p240) provides transport to Glenorchy from Queenstown. It also services the trailheads of the Routeburn and Greenstone Tracks.

Lake Wakatipu Region

The mountainous region at the northern head of Lake Wakatipu showcases gorgeous, remote scenery, best viewed while tramping along the famous Routeburn and lesser-known Greenstone, Caples and Rees-Dart Tracks. For shorter tracks, see the DOC brochure *Wakatipu Walks* ($5). Glenorchy is a convenient base for all these tramps.

Ultimate Hikes (☎03-450 1940; www.ultimatehikes.co.nz) has a three-day guided tramp on the Routeburn ($1125/1270 low/high season); a six-day Grand Traverse ($1560/1765), combining walks on the Routeburn and Greenstone Tracks; and a one-day Routeburn Encounter ($169), available November to mid-April.

TRACK INFORMATION

For details on accommodation, transport to and from all trailheads, and DOC centres, see coverage of Queenstown and Te Anau. DOC staff advise on maps and sell Backcountry Hut Passes and Great Walks passes. Before setting out, it's essential that you contact them for up-to-date track conditions. Be sure to register your intentions with DOC. For more details on all these tracks, see Lonely Planet's *Tramping in New Zealand.*

ROUTEBURN TRACK

Passing through a huge variety of landscapes with fantastic views, the 32km-long, two- to four-day Routeburn Track is one of the most popular rainforest/subalpine tracks in NZ. Increased pressure on the track has necessitated the introduction of a booking system. Reservations are required throughout the main season (October to April). Book huts or campsites online at www.doc.govt.nz or at a DOC office prior to the trip. Hut fees are $54 per person and camping fees are $18.

For the Routeburn Track, trampers must call in to the DOC visitor centres in either Queenstown (p240) or Te Anau (p266) to collect actual tickets, either the day before or on the day of departure.

Outside the main season, passes are still required; huts cost $15/free per adult/child per night. Camping is $5/free in the off season. The Routeburn track remains open in winter. However, to traverse the alpine section after the snow falls is not recommended for hikers, as winter mountaineering skills required. There are 32 avalanche paths across the section between Routeburn Falls hut and Howden hut, and avalanche risk remains until spring. Always check conditions with DOC.

There are car parks at the Divide and Glenorchy ends of the Routeburn, but they're unattended, so don't leave any valuables in your car. If you do have a car, a relocation service is offered by Trackhopper (p241) in Queenstown from either end of the track.

The track can be started from either end. Many people travelling from Queenstown try to reach the Divide in time to catch the bus to Milford and connect with a cruise on the sound. En route, you'll take in breathtaking views from Harris Saddle and the top of nearby Conical Hill, from where you can see waves breaking at Martins Bay. From Key Summit, there are panoramic views of the Hollyford Valley and the Eglinton and Greenstone River Valleys.

Estimated walking times:

ROUTE	TIME
Routeburn Shelter to Flats Hut	1½-2½hr
Flats Hut to Falls Hut	1-1½hr
Falls Hut to Mackenzie Hut	4½-6hr
Mackenzie Hut to Howden Hut	3-4hr
Howden Hut to the Divide	1-1½hr

Routeburn, Greenstone & Caples Tracks

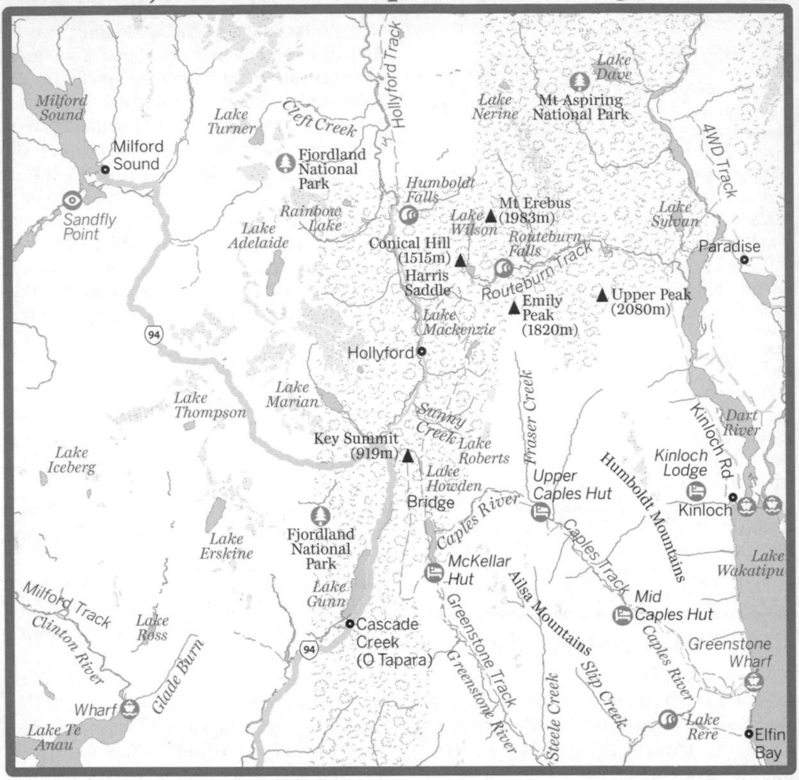

GREENSTONE & CAPLES TRACKS

Following meandering rivers through lush, peaceful valleys, these two tracks form a loop that many trampers stretch out into a moderate four- or five-day tramp. Basic huts en route are **Mid Caples**, **Upper Caples**, **McKellar** and Greenstone. All are $15/5 per adult/child (11 to 17 years) per night, and Backcountry Hut Passes must be pre-purchased.

You can camp for free 50m away from the main track, but not on the private land and around the McKellar Saddle. Check the Environment Care Code on the DOC website. Both tracks meet up with the Routeburn Track; you can either follow its tail end to the Divide or (if you've prebooked) pursue it back to Glenorchy.

From McKellar Hut you can tramp two or three hours to Howden Hut on the Routeburn Track (you'll need to book this hut from October to April), which is an hour from the Divide.

Access to the Greenstone and Caples Tracks is from **Greenstone Wharf**; nearby you'll find unattended parking. Bus transport by Info & Track (p240) runs betwen the Greenstone Car Park and Glenorchy and Queenstown. Another option is the car relocation service offered by Trackhopper (p241).

Estimated walking times:

ROUTE	TIME
Greenstone Wharf to Mid Caples Hut	3hr
Mid Caples Hut to Upper Caples Hut	2-3hr
Upper Caples Hut to McKellar Hut	5-8hr
McKellar Hut to Greenstone Hut	5-7hr
Greenstone Hut to Greenstone Wharf	4-6hr

REES-DART TRACK

This is a difficult, demanding four- to five-day circular route from the head of Lake

Wakatipu, taking you through valleys and over an alpine pass, with the possibility of a side trip to the Dart Glacier if you're suitably equipped and experienced. Access by vehicle is possible as far as Muddy Creek on the Rees side, from where it's six hours to Shelter Rock Hut.

Park your car at Muddy Creek or arrange transport with Queenstown's Info & Track Centre (p240). Another option is the car relocation service offered by Trackhopper (p241). Most people go up the Rees track first and come back down the Dart. The three basic DOC huts (Shelter Rock, Daleys Flat and the Dart) cost $15 per person and Backcountry Hut Passes must be purchased in advance.

Estimated walking times:

ROUTE	TIME
Muddy Creek to Shelter Rock Hut	6hr
Shelter Rock Hut to Dart Hut	5-7hr
Dart Hut to Daleys Flat Hut	6-8hr
Daleys Flat Hut to Paradise	6-8hr

WANAKA REGION

With overgrown valleys, unspoiled rivers and tumbling glaciers, the Wanaka region is crowned with the colossal Mt Aspiring (Tititea; 3035m), the highest peak outside the Mt Cook region. Enter this area from the north via Haast Pass, and you encounter Lakes Wanaka and Hawea, wedged between awesome hills and cliffs. From the south via Cardrona, stunning valley views and mountain vistas are on tap. The Wanaka region, and especially the activity-filled town of Wanaka itself, is seeing more and more travellers, but it's still quieter than Queenstown. It's also very easy to escape the town's growing tourist buzz by exploring Mt Aspiring National Park or the forested wilderness around Makarora.

Wanaka

POP 5000

Beautiful scenery, tramping and skiing opportunities and a huge roster of adrenaline-inducing activities have transformed the lakeside town of Wanaka into a year-round tourist destination. Travellers come here as an alternative to Queenstown, and while some locals worry their home is starting to resemble its hyped-up Central Otago sibling across the Crown Range, Wanaka's lakefront area retains a laid-back, small-town feel. It's definitely not a sleepy hamlet anymore, though, and new restaurants and bars are adding a veneer of sophistication. Note that Wanaka wakes up in a big way for New Year's Eve.

Wanaka is located at the southern end of Lake Wanaka, just over 100km northeast of Queenstown via Cromwell. It's the gateway to Mt Aspiring National Park and to the Treble Cone, Cardrona, Harris Mountains and Pisa Range Ski Areas.

Sights

With its emphasis on the stunning outdoors, Wanaka isn't brimming with conventional sights, but you can keep surprisingly busy on a rainy day.

Warbirds & Wheels MUSEUM
(www.warbirdsandwheels.com; Wanaka Airport, 11 Lloyd Dunn Av; adult/child/family $20/5/45; ⌚9am-5pm) Dedicated to NZ combat pilots, the aircraft they flew, and the sacrifices they made, this excellent museum features Hawker Hurricanes, a de Havilland Vampire and vintage Soviet fighter planes. Classic cars make up the 'wheels' part. Grab a bite to eat and fire up the jukebox in the retro diner.

Wanaka Beerworks BREWERY
(www.wanakabeerworks.co.nz; SH6; tours & tasting $10; ⌚9am-4pm) This small brewery's three main beers, a Vienna lager, a German-style black beer and a hops-laden Bohemian pilsner are complemented by up to 12 different seasonal brews each year. Dave the owner is a real-deal Belgian brewing supremo, and is usually available for tastings and brewery tours.

Wanaka Transport & Toy Museum MUSEUM
(www.wanakatransportandtoymuseum.com; SH6; adult/child/family $12/5/30; ⌚8.30am-5pm) Around 30,000 items include a Cadillac Coupe de Ville, a mysteriously acquired MiG jet fighter, and toys you're guaranteed to remember from rainy childhood afternoons.

Puzzling World AMUSEMENT PARK
(www.puzzlingworld.com; 188 Main Hwy 84; adult/child $15/10; ⌚8.30am-5.30pm) A 3-D Great Maze and lots of 'now-you-see-it, now-you-don't' visual tomfoolery to keep kids of all ages bemused, bothered and bewildered. It's en route to Cromwell, 2km from town.

Wanaka

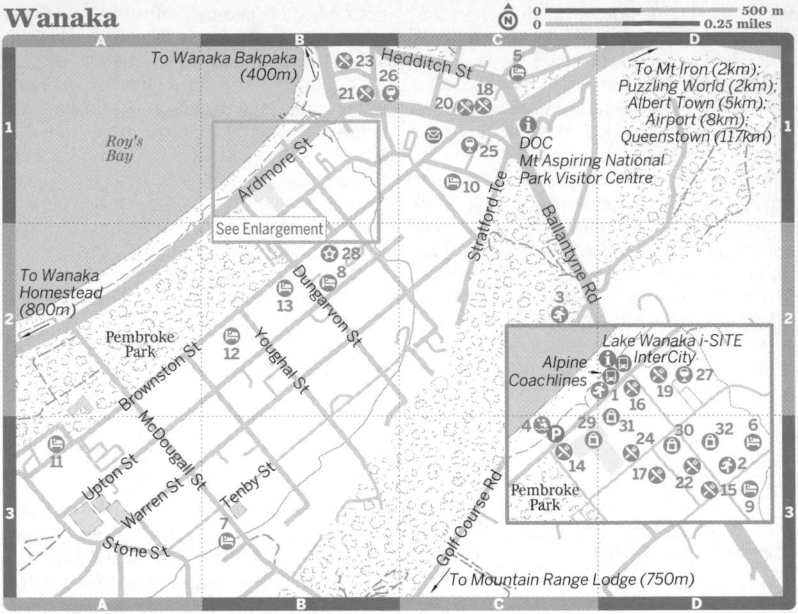

Wanaka

Activities, Courses & Tours

1	Lakeland Adventures	D2
2	Thunderbikes	D3
3	Wanaka Golf Club	C2
4	Wanaka Kayaks	C3

Sleeping

5	Archway Motels	C1
6	Brook Vale	D3
7	Harpers	B3
8	Holly's	B2
9	Matterhorn South	D3
10	Mountain View Backpackers	C1
11	Wanaka Lakeview Holiday Park	A3
12	Wanaka View Motel	B2
13	YHA Wanaka Purple Cow	B2

Eating

14	Bistro on Ardmore	C3
	Botswana Butchery	(see 25)
	Café Gusto	(see 23)
15	Federal Diner	D3
16	Kai Whakapai	D2
17	New World Supermarket	D3
18	Red Star	C1
19	Relishes	D2
20	Sasanoki	C1
21	Soulfood Store & Cafe	B1
22	Spice Room	D3
23	The Landing	B1
24	Yohei	D3

Drinking

25	Barluga	C1
26	Opium	B1
27	Uno	D2
	Wanaka Ale House	(see 14)

Entertainment

28	Cinema Paradiso	B2

Shopping

29	Chop Shop	C3
30	Gallery Thirty Three	D3
31	MT Outdoors	D3
32	Picture Lounge	D3

Activities

Wide valleys, alpine meadows, more than 100 glaciers and sheer mountains make **Mt Aspiring National Park** an outdoor enthusiast's paradise. Protected as a national park in 1964, and later included in the Southwest New Zealand (Te Wahipounamu) World Heritage Area, the park now blankets more than 3500 sq km along the Southern Alps, from the Haast River in the north to its border with Fiordland National Park in the south.

Tramping

While the southern end of Mt Aspiring National Park is well trafficked by visitors and includes popular tramps such as the Routeburn Track, there are great short walks and more demanding multiday tramps in the Matukituki Valley, close to Wanaka; see the DOC brochure *Matukituki Valley Tracks* ($2). The dramatic **Rob Roy Valley Track** (two to three hours return) takes in glaciers, waterfalls and a swing bridge. It's a moderate walk, but some parts are quite steep. The road to the carpark also crosses many streams. The **West Matukituki Valley** track goes on to Aspiring Hut (four to five hours return), a scenic walk over mostly grassy flats. For overnight or multiday tramps, continue up the valley to **Liverpool Hut** for great views of Mt Aspiring.

Many of these tramps are subject to snow and avalanches and can be treacherous. Register your intentions, and it is also extremely important you consult DOC in Wanaka before heading off. Also purchase hut tickets. Tracks are reached from Raspberry Creek at the end of Mt Aspiring Rd, 54km from Wanaka.

For walks closer to town, pick up the DOC brochure *Wanaka Outdoor Pursuits* ($3.50). This includes the easy lakeside stroll to **Eely Point** (20 minutes) and on to **Beacon Point** (30 minutes), as well as the **Waterfall Creek Walk** (1½ hours return) east along the lakeshore.

The fairly gentle climb to the top of **Mt Iron** (549m, 1½ hours return) reveals panoramic views. After a view, fit folks can undertake the taxing, winding 11km tramp up **Roy's Peak** (1578m, five to six hours return), starting 6km from Wanaka on Mt Aspiring Rd. The high track crosses private land and is closed from October to mid-November for lambing. From Roy's Peak continue along the **Skyline Route** (five to six hours) to Cardrona Rd, 10km south of Wanaka. Don't do this in winter; low cloud eliminates views and makes it treacherous.

To the north of Wanaka, the **Minaret Burn Track** (six to seven hours) in the Mt Alta Conservation Area is suitable for walking and mountain biking. You can pick up a map ($1) at DOC.

Many outfits offer guided walking tours around Wanaka, some into Mt Aspiring National Park.

Alpinism & Ski Wanaka TRAMPING
(☎03-442 6593; www.alpinismski.co.nz; from $200) Day walks and overnight tramps.

Eco Wanaka Adventures TRAMPING
(☎0800 926 326; www.ecowanaka.co.nz; half-/full day from $105/170) Day, half-day and multiday trips.

Wild Walks TRAMPING
(☎03-443 9422; www.wildwalks.co.nz; 3 days from $960) Multiday tramps.

Jetboating & Rafting

Pioneer Rafting RAFTING
(☎03-443 1246; www.ecoraft.co.nz; half-day adult/child $145/85, full day $195/105) Ecorafting on the high-volume Clutha, with Grade II to III rapids, gold panning and birdwatching.

Lakeland Adventures JETBOATING
(☎03-443 7495; www.lakelandadventures.co.nz; i-SITE; adult/child $109/55) One-hour jetboat trips across the lake and including the winding Clutha River.

Wanaka River Journeys JETBOATING
(☎0800 544 555; www.wanakariverjourneys.co.nz; adult/child $240/145) Combination bush walk (50 minutes) and jetboat ride in the stunning Matukituki Valley.

Canyoning & Kayaking

Deep Canyon CANYONING
(☎03-443 7922; www.deepcanyon.co.nz; from $240; ⏲mid-Nov–Apr) Loads of climbing, swimming and waterfall-absciling through confined, wild gorges.

Alpine Kayak Guides KAYAKING
(☎03-443 9023; www.alpinekayaks.co.nz; half-/full day $149/195; ⏲Nov-May) Paddles down the Hawea, Clutha and Matukituki Rivers. Kids can join a more leisurely half-day Grandview trip (two adult and two kids $450).

Wanaka Kayaks KAYAKING
(☎0800 926 925; www.wanakakayaks.co.nz; from per hour $12; ⏲summer only) Rents kayaks and offers guided lake tours (from $75 per person).

Lakeland Adventures KAYAKING
(☎03-443 7495; www.lakelandadventures.co.nz) Hire kayaks on the waterfront for $15 per hour.

Skydiving & Paragliding

Skydive Lake Wanaka SKY DIVING
(☎03-443 7207; www.skydivewanaka.com; from $329) Jumps from 12,000ft and a scary 15,000ft; the latter lets you fall for 60 seconds.

Wanaka Paragliding PARAGLIDING
(☎0800 359 754; www.wanakaparagliding.co.nz; $189) Count on around 20 minutes soaring on the Central Otago thermals.

Rock Climbing & Mountaineering

Mt Aspiring National Park is a favourite playground of mountaineering and alpine climbing companies. The following all offer beginners' courses and multiday guided ascents of Mts Aspiring, Tasman and Tutoko.

Aspiring Guides MOUNTAINEERING
(☎03-443 9422; www.aspiringguides.com; 3 days from $960) Over 20 years of alpine experience.

Adventure Consultants MOUNTAINEERING
(☎03-443 8711; www.adventureconsultants.com; 5 days from $4100) Also offers two- and three-day excursions on Brewster Glacier and Gillespies Pass in Mt Aspiring National Park ($880 to $990).

Hospital Flat CLIMBING
Excellent rock climbing can be found at Hospital Flat – 25km from Wanaka towards Mt Aspiring National Park.

Wanaka Rock Climbing ROCK CLIMBING
(☎03-443 6411; www.wanakarock.co.nz; from $140) Introductory rock-climbing course (half/full day $140/210), a half-day abseiling intro ($140), and bouldering and multipitch climbs for the experienced.

Basecamp Wanaka ROCK CLIMBING
(www.basecampwanaka.co.nz; 50 Cardrona Valley Rd; adult/child $20/17; ⊙noon-8pm Mon-Fri, from 10am Sat & Sun) Before you hit the mountains, learn the ropes on climbing walls. Climbing gear can also be hired.

Mountain Biking

Many tracks and trails in the region are open to cyclists. Pick up the DOC brochure *Wanaka Outdoor Pursuits* ($3.50), describing mountain-bike rides ranging from 2km to 24km, including the Deans Bank Loop Track (11.5km).

The *Bike Wanaka Cycling Map* ($2) is available at local cycle shops and features forested tracks for more adventurous riders. To hire a bike and get local track information go to **Thunderbikes** (cnr Helwick & Bronwston St).

Freeride NZ MOUNTAIN BIKING
(☎0800 743 369, 021 712 996; www.freeridenz.com; per person from $185) Guided full-day trips including helibiking options, and a three-day ($1370) Central Otago adventure. Self-guided tours and rental is $95.

Fishing

Lakes Wanaka and Hawea (16km away) have excellent trout fishing, and the surrounding rivers are also popular angling spots.

Hatch FISHING
(☎03-443 8446; www.hatchfishing.co.nz; 2 adults half-/full day $490/750) Adventure fishing trips incorporating hiking and including an overnighter (one/two persons $1690/1890) with gourmet food, wine and beer.

Riversong FISHING
(☎03-443 8567, 021 113 6396; www.wanakaflyfishingguides.co.nz; half-/full day $400/600) For $75 per hour, tuition in the dark art of fly-fishing.

Other Activities

Wanaka Golf Club GOLF
(☎03-443 7888; www.wanakagolf.co.nz; Ballantyne Rd; green fees $60, club hire from $20) A spectacular 18-hole course.

 Tours

Book at the i-SITE.

Aerial Sightseeing

Classic Flights SCENIC FLIGHTS
(☎03-443 4043, 0508 435 9464; www.classicflights.co.nz; from $235) Runs sightseeing flights in a vintage Tigermoth. 'Biggles' goggles provided, but BYO flowing silk scarf.

The Silver Demon SCENIC FLIGHT
(☎0508 435 9464; www.silverdemon.co.nz; $185-285) G-force-defying, upside-down, loop-the-loop aerobatic madness.

Wanaka Flightseeing SCENIC FLIGHTS
(☎03-443 8787; www.flightseeing.co.nz; adult/child from $200/120) Spectacular flyovers of Mt Aspiring, Milford Sound and Mt Cook.

Helicopter Rides

The following offer 20-minute flights around Wanaka for about $195, and 60-minute tours of Mt Aspiring and the glaciers for about $495.

Alpine Helicopters SCENIC FLIGHTS
(☎03-443 4000; www.alpineheli.co.nz) Also offer views-a-plenty alpine picnics.

Aspiring Helicopters SCENIC FLIGHTS
(☎03-443 7152; www.aspiringhelicopters.co.nz) Also includes flights to Milford Sound.

Wanaka Helicopters SCENIC FLIGHTS
(☎03-443 1085; www.heliflights.co.nz) Snow landings from $199 per person.

Other Tours

Lakeland Adventures BOAT TOUR
(☎03-443 7495; www.lakelandadventures.co.nz; Wanaka i-SITE) Has 2½-hour trips to Stevensons Island (adult/child $85/55 and a 3½-hour trip with a guided bushwalk on Mou Waho (adult/child $145/55). Kayaks ($15 per hour) and aqua bikes ($15 per 20 minutes) are also available.

Lake Wanaka Cruises BOAT CRUISE
(☎03-443 1230; www.wanakacruises.co.nz; from $70) Lake cruising aboard a catamaran with overnight options.

Ridgeline WINE TASTING
(☎0800 234 000; www.ridgelinenz.com; per person from $165) Tours incorporating wine, spas and 4WD excursions.

Festivals & Events

Warbirds over Wanaka AIRSHOW
(☎0800 496 920, 03-443 8619; www.warbirdsoverwanaka.com; Wanaka Airport; 3-day adult/child from $170/25, 1st day only from $50/10, each of last 2 days from $75/10) Every second Easter (even-numbered years) Wanaka hosts this incredibly popular international airshow attracting 100,000 people. With a backdrop of sun-kissed summertime mountains, it's hard to imagine a more spectacular location to watch heritage and iconic aircraft strut their stuff.

Rippon Festival MUSIC
(www.ripponfestival.co.nz) Music fans should diarise this popular festival held every second year in early February at the lakeside Rippon Vineyard. Big-name Kiwi acts headline with a variety of styles represented – dance, reggae, rock and electronica to name a few. If the music doesn't relax you (highly unlikely), the wine certainly will.

Wanaka Fest ARTS & CULTURAL
(www.wanakafest.co.nz; ⊙mid-Oct) This four-day event has the feel of a small-town fair. Street parades, live music and wacky competitions get the locals saying g'day to the warmth of spring. Look forward to also sampling fine Central Otago produce.

Sleeping

Like Queenstown, Wanaka is bursting with hostels and luxury accommodation, but good midrange options are harder to find. Across summer, and especially around New Year, prices and demand increase considerably. During winter, the town is hit with an influx of international snowboarders.

TOP CHOICE **Riversong** B&B $$
(☎03-443 8567; www.riversongwanaka.co.nz; 5 Wicklow Tce; d $160-180) On the banks of the Clutha River in nearby Albert Town, Riversong has two rooms in a lovely heritage B&B. The well-travelled owners may well have the best nonfiction library in NZ, and if you can tear yourself away from the books, there's excellent trout fishing just metres away. Dinner including wine is $55 per person.

Wanaka Bakpaka HOSTEL $
(☎03-443 7837; www.wanakabakpaka.co.nz; 117 Lakeside Rd; dm $27, s $53, d & tw $64-80; @☜) An energetic husband-and-wife team run this friendly hostel high above the lake with just about the best views in town. Amenities are top-shelf and the onto-it staff consistently offer a red carpet welcome to weary travellers. The rooms are good value and the outlook from the spacious lounge will inspire you to (finally) get your blog up to date.

Wanaka Homestead LODGE $$$
(☎03-443 5022; www.wanakahomestead.co.nz; 1 Homestead Close; d $265, cottages $410-525; @☜) Wooden interiors, oriental rugs and local artwork punctuate this boutique lodge, which has won awards for its ecofriendly approach to sustainability. Despite the focus on green good deeds, it's still luxurious, with underfloor heating and an under-the-stars hot tub. Choose from rooms in the main lodge or in self-contained cottages. Say g'day to Douglas, the friendly canine host, for us.

Mountain Range Lodge LODGE $$$
(☎03-443 7400; www.mountainrange.co.nz; Heritage Park, Cardrona Valley Rd; d incl breakfast $320-335; @☜) Seven rooms named after nearby mountain ranges showcase comfy duvets, fluffy robes and views that'll distract you from the nearby skiing and tramping options. Cool touches like a complimentary glass of Central Otago wine and an on-site hot tub complete an already pretty picture. There's a minimum stay of two nights.

Archway Motels MOTEL $$
(☎0800 427 249, 03-443 7698; www.archwaymotels.co.nz; 64 Hedditch St; $105-150; 📶) This older motel with clean and spacious units and chalets is a short uphill walk from the lakefront. Friendly and helpful owners, new flat screen TVs, and cedar hot tubs with mountain views make Archway great value in a sometimes expensive town. Check online for good offpeak discounts.

Altamont Lodge LODGE $
(☎03-443 8864; www.altamontlodge.co.nz; 121 Mt Aspiring Rd; s/d $49/69; @📶) At the quieter end of town, natural wood gives this place a ski-lodge ambience. Tennis courts, a spa pool and a lounge with a big fire provide plenty of off-piste action. There's also a spacious and well-equipped kitchen. Altamont Lodge is often booked by groups, so it's worthwhile booking ahead. Bathroom facilities are shared.

Aspiring Campervan & Holiday Park HOLIDAY PARK $
(☎03-443 6603, 0800 229 8439; www.campervanpark.co.nz; Studholme Rd; sites fom $37, units $65-160; @📶) Grassy sites for tents and campervans, lots of trees and pretty views add up to a relaxing spot. Superior facilities include a barbecue area with gas heaters, and free wi-fi, spa pool and sauna. Older-style motel units have all been totally renovated, and the newest budget cabins are warm and cosy with wooden floors.

Brook Vale MOTEL $$
(☎0800 438 333, 03-443 8333; www.brookvale.co.nz; 35 Brownston St; d $145-185; 📶🏊) Self-contained studio and family units with a few classy touches; patios open onto a grassy lawn complete with a gently flowing creek. You'll also find a barbecue, a spa and a swimming pool for those sunny Central Otago days.

Wanaka View Motel MOTEL $$
(☎03-443 7480; www.wanakaviewmotel.co.nz; 122 Brownston St; d $110-150) Formerly called Fern Lodge, the relaunched and refurbished Wanaka View Motel has comfortable doubles through to flasher chalet rooms with Sky TV, spa baths and ritzy gas kitchens. The common themes throughout are excellent value for money and mountain views.

YHA Wanaka Purple Cow HOSTEL $
(☎03-443 1880; www.yha.co.nz; 94 Brownston St; dm $28-35, d $86-130) Warmed by a wood stove, the lounge at this ever-popular hostel holds commanding lake and mountain views; that's if you can tear yourself away from the regular movie nights. There are four- and six-bed dorms and a small array of nice doubles with en suites.

Harpers B&B $$
(☎03-443 8894; www.harpers.co.nz; 95 McDougall St; d incl breakfast $140-160; 📶) The garden (with pond and waterfall no less…) is a labour of love at this friendly B&B in a quiet location down a long driveway. Legendary breakfasts are served on a sunny deck with expansive views. You'd be wise to factor a leisurely second cup of breakfast coffee into your day's plans.

Matterhorn South HOSTEL $
(☎03-443 1119; www.matterhornsouth.co.nz; 56 Brownston St; ⏲dm $26-30, s $68, d $68-95, tr $115, q $125; @📶) Right at the edge of central Wanaka, this friendly spot has clean, good-value dorms and studios, and a sunny TV and games room. It has a shared country-style kitchen and a private garden to relax in after a day's outdoor adventuring.

Mountain View Backpackers HOSTEL $
(☎03-443 9010, 0800 112 201; www.wanakabackpackers.co.nz; 7 Russell St; dm $26-28, d $68; @📶) Run by a friendly family, this colourfully renovated and characterful house features an expansive lawn and warm, comfortable rooms. Fire up the alfresco barbecue after a busy day's exploring.

Holly's HOSTEL $
(☎03-443 8187; www.hollys-backpacker.co.nz; 71 Upton St; dm $27-29, d/tw $66; @📶) A family-run, low-key hostel that's a good antidote to busier places around town. Showing a bit of wear and tear, but a friendly spot. Bikes are for hire, and it's a good-value place to stay if you're looking to hit Wanaka for an extended snowboarding sojourn.

Wanaka Lakeview Holiday Park HOLIDAY PARK $
(☎03-443 7883; www.wanakalakeview.co.nz; 212 Brownston St; sites $34, units $55-100) Grassy sites set amid established pine trees with a kids' playground and lots of space to set up camp. Rooms range from basic cabins to en-suite flats.

Eating

Wanaka has a surprising range of places to eat, drink and generally celebrate the fact that you're on holiday. The best coffee in town is at Chop Shop (p256) in Pembroke Mall.

Federal Diner CAFE
(www.federaldiner.co.nz; 47 Helwick St; snacks & mains $10-20; ⏲7.30am-4pm, open later for tapas in summer) Seek out this cosmopolitan cafe tucked away off Wanaka's main shopping street. The all-day menu delivers robust spins on breakfast, excellent coffee and chunky gourmet sandwiches. Try the 'Roaster Coaster' with slow-roasted pork shoulder and apple sauce on ciabatta. Beers and wines are proudly local, and there's occasional live music with a blues or folk flavour on Friday nights.

Spice Room INDIAN $$
(www.spiceroom.co.nz; 43 Helwick St; mains $20-25;) The combo of an authentic curry, crispy garlic naan and cold beer is a great way to recharge after a day's snowboarding or tramping. Beyond the spot-on renditions of all your subcontinental favourites, the Spice Room springs a few surprises with starters including a zingy scallops masala salad. Time for one more chilled Kingfisher, maybe?

Kai Whakapai CAFE $$
(cnr Helwick & Ardmore Sts; meals $10-30;) An absolute Wanaka institution, Kai (the Maori word for food) is definitely the place to be on a sunny day. Massive sandwiches and pizzas, great coffee and occasionally slow service are all a part of the experience. Locally brewed Wanaka Beerworks beers are on tap – often including the brewery's regular seasonal concoctions – and there are Central Otago wines as well.

Relishes CAFÉ $$
(99 Ardmore St; breakfast & lunch $12-20, dinner $27-34) A cafe by day with good breakfast and lunch options, this place whips out the white tablecloths at night and becomes a classy restaurant with a good wine list. Try the free-range pork belly or Aoraki salmon, and toast the lakefront setting with a glass of Central Otago's finest.

Botswana Butchery MODERN NZ $$$
(☎03-443 6745; Post Office Lane; mains $30-45; ⏲5pm-late) In a sophisticated dining room, locally inspired dishes like Central Otago hare and Cardrona Merino lamb shoulder go head to head with Botswana Butchery's signature aged beef steaks. Definitely food for grown-ups, as is the serious Central Otago-skewed wine list. After dinner, pop next door for a night cap at Barluga.

Soulfood Store & Cafe ORGANIC $
(74 Ardmore St; mains $8-16;) Park yourself in a rustic wooden booth and stay healthy with organic soups, pizza, pasta and muffins. Not everything's strictly vegetarian, and breakfast with free-range eggs breaks the spell in a tasty way. The attached organic food store, which has freshly baked bread, is a good spot for a pre-picnic stock-up. Juices and smoothies are both tasty and virtuous.

The Landing MODERN NZ $$$
(www.missyskitchen.com; Level 1, 80 Ardmore St; mains $25-37; ⏲from 4pm) A dramatic upstairs dining room with equally spectacular lake views serves up local beef, lamb and salmon in innovative and award-winning ways. Try the Asian-style pork belly with black-pepper caramel and mashed aubergine and coriander with a Central Otago pinot gris.

Yohei SUSHI
(Spencer House Mall, 23 Dunmore St; snacks $8-12;) Tucked away in a shopping arcade, this funky Japanese-inspired eatery does interesting local spins on sushi (how about venison or lamb?), and superlative juices and smoothies. Very cool music, a good range of vego options and free wi-fi with any $4 purchase.

Bistro on Ardmore CAFE
(155 Ardmore St; meals $12-20;) This cosmopolitan lakefront cafe has everything from muffins the size of Mt Aspiring to equally robust steak sandwiches and lamb burgers. The food is hearty and honest, the welcome genuine, and it's all washed down with good coffee, free wi-fi and a concise but considered array of local wines and beers.

Café Gusto CAFE $
(1 Lakeside Rd; mains $15-20) Gusto provides robust meals like a breakfast burrito with jalapeno peppers, or smoked salmon and scrambled eggs. Both will set you up for the most active of days, and after you've kayaked/mountain biked/rafted/hiked, come back in the afternoon for excellent cakes and good coffee.

Sasanoki JAPANESE $
(26 Ardmore St; mains $10-15) Good value, sushi, sashimi, and noodle and rice dishes. Push the boat out with a bento box ($28) and a few Japanese beers if you're feeling flush.

Red Star BURGERS
(26 Ardmore St; burgers $10-15;) Red Star spoils diners with a menu featuring inventive

ingredients and 21 different burgers. Everybody is catered for – even vegetarians, who get a show-stopping three options.

New World Supermarket SELF-CATERING $
(Dunmore St) Excellent deli, wine and beer selection.

Drinking

Barluga BAR
(Post Office Lane; ⏲4pm-late) In the funky Post Office Lane area, Barluga's leather armchairs and coolly retro wallpaper at first make you think of a refined gentlemen's club. Wicked cocktails and killer back-to-back beats soon smash that illusion.

Wanaka Ale House PUB
(155 Ardmore St) Celebrating a lakefront location, this place also owns the coveted corner office. The rustic ambience morphs into a Southern Man reverie of exposed beams and mountain views, and an ample supply of Monteith's beer flows like water.

Uno BAR
(99 Ardmore St; ⏲5pm-late) This slick and contemporary wine bar is the perfect place to watch the sun go down. It's a pretty good spot to head back to after dinner as well.

Opium CLUB
(Level 1, 68 Ardmore St; ⏲5pm-late) Asian-themed bar with DJs and occasional live music. It's popular in winter with the snowboarder crowd, but in summer the lakefront bars are busier.

Entertainment

Cinema Paradiso CINEMA
(☎03-443 1505; www.paradiso.net.nz; 72-76 Brownston St; adult/child $16/10; @) Wanaka's original Cinema Paradiso in Ardmore St was a true NZ icon, and it reopened at these more modern and spacious premises in March 2012. Look forward to an entertaining slice of the old Paradiso magic with comfy couches and extra cushions on the floor to stretch out on. At intermission the smell of freshly baked cookies wafts through the theatre, and you can also order light meals to be ready for you at the break. Try the homemade ice cream and don't forget to arrive early to get a good couch. The best of Hollywood and arthouse flicks run across three screens.

Ruby's CINEMA
(www.rubyscinema.co.nz; 50 Cardrona Valley Rd; adult/child $18.50/12.50) Channelling a lush New York or Shanghai vibe, this hip arthouse cinema meets chic cocktail bar is a real surprise in outdoorsy Wanaka. Luxuriate in the huge cinema seats, or chill out in the red velvet lounge with craft beers, classic cocktails and sophisticated bar snacks ($6 to $14). You'll find Ruby's concealed within the Basecamp Wanaka building on the outskirts of town.

Shopping

Picture Lounge PHOTOGRAPHY
(48 Helwick St) Showcase gallery and shop for stunning large-format shots by local and NZ photographers. Central Otago's rugged scenery has never looked so good.

Chop Shop CLOTHING
(www.chop.co.nz; Pembroke Mall) The best coffee in town, funky alfresco seating and a natty range of locally designed beanies and cool T-shirts for the discerning snowboarder

Gallery Thirty Three ARTS & CRAFTS
(www.gallery33.co.nz; 33 Helwick St) Has pottery, glass and jewellery from local artists.

MT Outdoors OUTDOOR EQUIPMENT
(www.mtoutdoors.co.nz; Dunmore St) Camping and tramping gear.

Outside Sports OUTDOOR EQUIPMENT
(www.outsidesports.co.nz; 17-23 Dunmore St) Both winter and summer outdoor equipment for sale or rent.

Information

DOC Mt Aspiring National Park Visitor Centre (☎03-443 7660; www.doc.govt.nz; Ardmore St; ⏲8am-5pm Nov-Apr, 8.30-5pm Mon-Fri, 9.30am-4pm Sat May-Oct) In an A-framed building on the edge of town. Enquire about tramps. There's a small museum (admission free) on Wanaka geology, flora and fauna.

Lake Wanaka i-SITE (☎03-443 1233; www.lakewanaka.co.nz; 100 Ardmore St; ⏲8.30am-5.30pm, to 7pm in summer) In the log cabin on the lakefront.

Wanaka Medical Centre (☎03-443 7811; www.wanakamedical.co.nz; 23 Cardrona Valley Rd; ⏲9am-5pm Mon-Fri, clinics at 9am & 5pm Sat & Sun) Patches up adventure-sports mishaps.

Getting There & Away

Air

Air New Zealand (☎0800 737 000; www.airnewzealand.co.nz) has daily flights between Wanaka and Christchurch (from $99).

Bus

InterCity (www.intercity.co.nz) The bus stop is outside the lakefront i-SITE. Wanaka receives daily buses from Queenstown (two hours), which motor on to Franz Josef (six hours) via Haast Pass (three hours). For Christchurch (6½ hours) you'll need to change at Tarras.

Atomic Shuttles (www.atomictravel.co.nz) Services to Christchurch (seven hours), Dunedin (4½ hours) and the West Coast.

Catch-a-Bus (☎03-479 9960; www.catchabus.co.nz) Links Wanaka with Dunedin and the Rail Trail towns of Central Otago.

Naked Bus (www.nakedbus.com) Services to Queenstown, Christchurch, Cromwell and the West Coast.

connectabus (☎0800 405 066; www.connectabus.com; one-way/return $35/65) Handy twice-daily service linking Wanaka with the Queenstown airport and Queenstown. Free pickup from most accommodation.

Wanaka Connexions (☎03-443-9120; www.alpinecoachlines.co.nz) Links Wanaka with Queenstown and the Rail Trail towns of Central Otago.

Getting Around

Alpine Coachlines (☎03-443 7966; www.alpinecoachlines.co.nz; Dunmore St) meets and greets flights at Wanaka Airport ($15), and in summer has twice-daily shuttles for trampers ($35) to Mt Aspiring National Park and Raspberry Creek. See it also for winter transport to Treble Cone. **Wanaka Taxis** (☎0800 272 2700) also looks after airport transfers, while **Adventure Rentals** (☎03-443 6050; www.adventurerentals.co.nz; 20 Ardmore St) hires cars and 4WDs, and **Yello** (☎0800 443 5555; www.yello.co.nz) provide charter transport, airport transfers and regional sightseeing.

Makarora

POP 40

At Makarora you've left the West Coast and entered Otago, but the township still has a West Coast frontier feel. Visit the **DOC Visitor Information Centre** (DOC; ☎03-443 8365; www.doc.govt.nz; SH6; ⏰8am-5pm Dec-Mar, Mon-Fri only Nov & Apr) for conditions and routes before undertaking any regional tramps. The **Makarora Tourist Centre** (☎03-443 8372, 0800 800 443; www.makarora.co.nz; ⏰8am-8pm) can help with accommodation and booking tours and activities.

Activities

Tramping

Short tramps in this secluded area include the **Bridal Track** (1½ hours one-way, 3.5km), from the top of Haast Pass to Davis Flat, and the **Blue Pools Walk** (30 minutes return), where you can see huge rainbow trout.

Longer tramps go through magnificent countryside but shouldn't be undertaken lightly. Changeable alpine and river conditions mean you must be well prepared; consult with DOC before heading off. DOC's brochure *Tramping in the Makarora Region* ($1) is a worthwhile investment.

Gillespie Pass TRAMPING

The three-day Gillespie Pass loop tramp goes via the Young, Siberia and Wilkin Valleys. This is a high pass with avalanche danger in winter and spring. With a jetboat ride down the Wilkin to complete it, this rates alongside the Milford Track as one of NZ's must-do tramps.

Wilkin Valley Track TRAMPING

The Wilkin Valley Track heads off from Kerin Forks Hut – at the top of the Wilkin River – and on to Top Forks Hut and the picturesque Lakes Diana, Lucidus and Castalia (one hour, 1½ hours and three to four hours respectively from Top Forks Hut). Jetboats go to Kerin Forks, and a service goes across the Young River mouth when the Makarora floods. Another option is to use the High River Route from the Blue Pools (7km and two hours). Enquire at Wilkin River Jets or DOC.

Other Activities

Siberia Experience ADVENTURE TOUR

(☎03-443 8666, 0800 345 666; www.siberiaexperience.co.nz; adult/child $355/285) The Siberia Experience is a thrill-seeking extravaganza combining a half-hour scenic small-plane flight, a three-hour bush walk through a remote mountain valley and a half-hour jetboat trip down the Wilkin and Makarora Rivers in Mt Aspiring National Park. To avoid getting lost, keep your eye on the markers as you descend from Siberia Valley. It's possible to join in Wanaka.

Wilkin River Jets JET BOATING

(☎0800 538 945, 03-443 8351; www.wilkinriverjets.co.nz; Kerin Forks transfer $85) A superb 50km, one-hour jetboating trip (adult/child $98/57) into Mt Aspiring National Park, following the Makarora and Wilkin Rivers. It's cheaper than Queenstown options, and also offers trips including helicopter rides or tramping.

Southern Alps Air SCENIC FLIGHTS

(☎03-443 4385, 0800 345 666; www.southernalpsair.co.nz) Trip to Mt Cook and the glaciers (adult/child $410/215) or landings at Milford Sound ($395/245).

Sleeping & Eating

The nearest DOC camping grounds (adult/child $6/3) are on SH6 at Cameron Flat, 10km north of Makarora, and at Boundary Creek Reserve, 18km south of Makarora on the shores of Lake Wanaka.

Makarora Homestead Wilderness Accommodation B&B $$
(☎03-443 1532; www.makarora.com; Rapid 53 Rata Rd; d $130-150) Country-style studio units and cottages have compact kitchenettes, or you can stay on a B&B basis in the sprawling main homestead. Look forward to a quiet rural location with the occasional company of deer, lambs and native birds. Cottages have wide verandas and tranquil country views.

Makarora Tourist Centre HOLIDAY PARK
(☎03-443 8372; www.makarora.co.nz; SH6; sites from $24, dm $30, units $70-120; @) In scrubby bush are self-contained chalets, basic cabins, and backpacker doubles and dorms. They've all got a snug, alpine feel, and you'll also find a cafe, an outdoor pool, a grocery store and a petrol station. Campervan travellers are also welcome, and later at night the cafe assumes the role of Makarora's pub.

Getting There & Away

InterCity (www.intercity.co.nz) and **Atomic Shuttles** (www.atomictravel.co.nz) both travel through Makarora en route to Haast and the West Coast.

Hawea

POP 1600

The small town of Hawea, 15km north of Wanaka, has spectacular lake and mountain views. From Lake Hawea look out at the indomitable Corner Peak on the western shore and out to the distant Barrier Range. Separated from Lake Wanaka by a narrow isthmus called the Neck, Lake Hawea is 35km long and 410m deep, and home to trout and landlocked salmon. The lake was raised 20m in 1958 to facilitate the power stations downriver.

Lake Hawea Motor Inn (☎03-443 1224, www.lakehawea.co.nz; 1 Capell Ave; dm $30, d $150-180) has smart recently refurbished rooms with unbeatable views across the lake. Downstairs is the cosy Stag's Head bar and restaurant with equally stellar vistas.

On the lakeshore is the spacious and relatively peaceful **Lake Hawea Holiday Park** (☎03-443 1767; www.haweaholidaypark.co.nz; SH6; sites from $30, units $50-120; @), a favourite of fishing and boating enthusiasts.

Cardrona

The sealed **Crown Range Road** from Wanaka to Queenstown via Cardrona is shorter than the route via Cromwell, but it's a narrow, twisting-and-turning mountain road that needs to be tackled with care, especially in poor weather. In winter it is often snow covered, necessitating chaining up the wheels, and is often subject to closure because of snow. You've been warned.

With views of lush valleys, foothills and countless snowy peaks, this is one of the South Island's most scenic drives. The road passes through tall, swaying tussock grass in the **Pisa Conservation Area**, which has a number of short walking trails. There are plenty of rest stops to drink in the view. Particularly good ones are at the Queenstown end of the road, as you switchback down towards Arrowtown.

The unpretentious-looking **Cardrona Hotel** (☎03-443 8153; www.cardronahotel.co.nz; Crown Range Rd; d $135-185) first opened its doors in 1863. Today you'll find lovingly restored, peaceful rooms with snug, country-style furnishings and patios opening onto a garden. You'll also find a deservedly popular pub with a good **restaurant** (mains $15-20) and a great garden bar.

The hotel is located near the turn-off for Snow Farm New Zealand (p232). In winter this is home to fantastic cross-country skiing. Lessons and ski hire are available ($90 for both). Also nearby is Snowpark NZ (p232), the country's only specialist freestyle and snowboard area.

Also situated nearby is Backcountry Saddle Expeditions (p228), with horse treks through the Cardrona Valley on Appaloosa horses.

Alternatively, the altogether less placid **Cardrona Adventure Park** (www.adventurepark.co.nz; monster trucks from $140, quad-bikes from $75, go-karts from $60; ⏰10am-5pm) is a rambunctious and noisy collection of monster trucks (including a self-drive option), quad-bikes, and off-road go-karts.

Fiordland & Southland

Includes »

Best Outdoors

» Milford Sound (p269)
» Doubtful Sound (p272)
» Nugget Point (p283)
» Ulva Island (p286)

Best Places to Stay

» Misty Mountain Eco-Retreat (p271)
» Milford Sound Lodge (p269)
» Hilltop (p282)
» Pounawea Motor Camp (p284)

Why Go?

Welcome to scenery that travellers dream of and cameras fail to capture.

To the west is Fiordland National Park, with jagged misty peaks, glistening lakes and a remote and pristine stillness. Enter this beautiful isolation via the world-famous Milford Track, one of the various trails that meander through dense forest and past spectacular mountains and glacier-sculpted canyons. Fiordland is also home to Milford and Doubtful Sounds, with verdant cliffs soaring almost vertically from deep, indigo waters. Both fiords are relatively easy to access by road, boat or kayak.

In Southland's east, a sharp left turn off the beaten track, the peaceful Catlins showcase bird-rich native forests and rugged, windswept coasts. Abundant southern Pacific waters host penguins, seals, sea lions, dolphins and the occasional whale.

Keep heading south for the rugged isolation of Stewart Island, and the opportunity to spy New Zealand's beloved kiwi in the wild.

When to Go

Visit from February to March for the best opportunity of settled weather amid Fiordland's notoriously fickle climate. Linger until May for the opportunity to sample local beers and NZ's favourite bivalve and at the annual Bluff Oyster and Food Festival. The Milford, Kepler and Routeburn Tracks are three of NZ's iconic tramping routes, and classified as Great Walks by NZ's Department of Conservation. During the Great Walks season from late October to late April you'll need to book your time exploring these three popular tracks in advance.

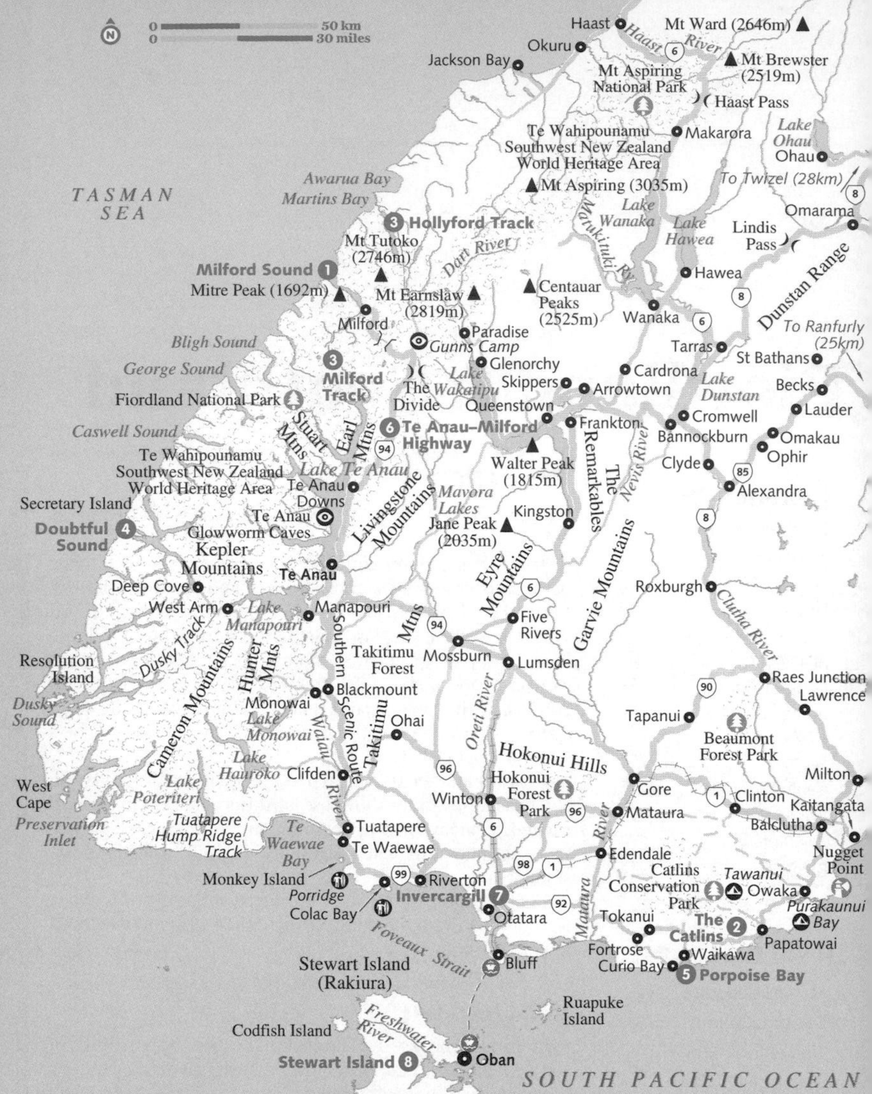

Fiordland & Southland Highlights

1. Sea kayaking, dwarfed by the steep cliffs of **Milford Sound** (p269)
2. Exploring side roads, forest waterfalls and lonely southern beaches in the peaceful, windswept **Catlins** (p279)
3. Walking through forest and mountains on the **Milford** and **Hollyford Tracks** (p267)
4. Overnighting on the vast, remote **Doubtful Sound** (p272)
5. Sharing a beach with dolphins, whales, sea lions and penguins at **Porpoise Bay** (p281) in the Catlins
6. Diverting from **Te Anau–Milford Hwy** (p266) to explore forest walks and still mountain lakes
7. Saying g'day to the tuatara, New Zealand's living dinosaurs, at Invercargill's **Southland Museum & Art Gallery** (p275)
8. Chancing on a snuffling, shuffling band of kiwi on a twilight kiwi-spotting expedition on **Stewart Island** (p284)

 Getting There & Around

Air New Zealand (p278) connects Invercargill with Christchurch, while Stewart Island Flights (p278) connects Invercargill with Oban.

Major bus operators shuttle to Te Anau and Invercargill from Queenstown or Dunedin, and some ply the Southern Scenic Route and take in Milford Sound. These include Tracknet, InterCity, Topline Tours, Atomic Shuttles, Bottom Bus and Naked Bus.

FIORDLAND

Fiordland is NZ's rawest wilderness area, a jagged, mountainous, forested zone sliced by numerous deeply recessed sounds (which are technically fiords) reaching inland like crooked fingers from the Tasman Sea. Part of the Te Wahipounamu Southwest New Zealand World Heritage Area, it remains formidable and remote.

Of the region's wonderful bushwalks, Milford Track may be king, but Kepler and Hollyford are worthy knights, and the Routeburn, Greenstone and Caples Tracks all link Fiordland with the Queenstown region.

ESSENTIAL FIORDLAND & SOUTHLAND

» **Eat** Bluff oysters in Bluff or Tuatapere sausages in Tuatapere

» **Drink** The fine beers crafted by the Invercargill Brewery

» **Read** *The Gorse Blooms Pale* by Dan Davin, a collection of Southland short stories

» **Listen to** The sound of silence while kayaking in Doubtful Sound

» **Watch** *South* (2009), a TV series (available on DVD) hosted by quirky local media identity Marcus Lush

» **Go green** Take ecologically focused tours by boat on Doubtful Sound or by foot in the Catlins

» **Online** www.fiordland.org.nz, www.southlandnz.com

» **Area Code** ☎03

Te Anau

POP 3000

Peaceful, lakeside Te Anau township is a good base for trekkers and visitors to Milford Sound, and an ideal place to recharge or get active in the surrounding landscapes.

To the east are the pastoral areas of central Southland, while west across Lake Te Anau lie the rugged forested mountains of Fiordland. The lake, NZ's second largest, was gouged out by a huge glacier and has several arms that penetrate into the mountainous forested western shore. Its deepest point is 417m, about twice the depth of Loch Ness.

Sights

Te Anau Glowworm Caves CAVE

Once present only in Maori legends, these impressive caves were rediscovered in 1948. Accessible only by boat, the 200m-long system of caves is a magical place with sculpted rocks, waterfalls small and large, whirlpools and a glittering glowworm grotto in its inner reaches. **Real Journeys** (☎0800 656 501; www.realjourneys.co.nz) runs 2¼-hour guided tours ($70/22 per adult/child), reaching the heart of the caves by a walkway and a short underground boat ride.

DOC Te Anau Wildlife Centre WILDLIFE CENTRE

(☎03-249 0200; Te Anau-Manapouri Rd; admission by donation; ⏲dawn-dusk) Native bird species – including the rare flightless takahe, NZ pigeons, tui, kaka and weka.

Fiordland Astronomy ASTRONOMY

(☎0508 267 667; www.astronomyfiordland.co.nz; adult/child $45/35) See the Southern Cross and Milky Way in Fiordland's pristine skies; weather permitting.

Stardome ASTRONOMY

(☎0508 267 667; www.astronomyfiordland.co.nz; Events Centre, Luxmore Dr; adult/child $30/20) Book at the i-SITE for this interactive digital planetarium.

Activities

Tramping

Register your intentions at the Department of Conservation Visitor Centre (p266).

KEPLER TRACK

This 60km circular Great Walk starts less than an hour's walk from Te Anau and heads west into the Kepler Mountains, taking in the lake, rivers, gorges, glacier-carved valleys and beech forest. The walk can be done in four days, or three if you exit at Rainbow Reach. On the first day you reach the tree line, giving panoramic views. The alpine stretch between Luxmore and Iris Burn

Te Anau

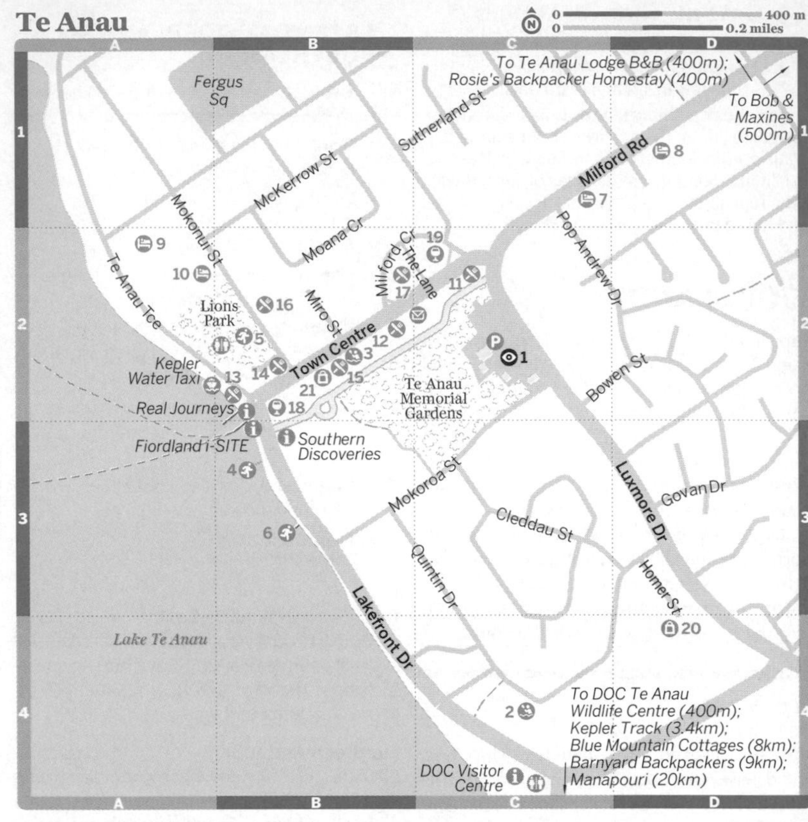

Te Anau

Sights

1 Stardome C2

Activities, Courses & Tours

2 Fiordland Wilderness Experiences C4
3 Rosco's Milford Kayaks B2
4 Southern Lakes Helicopters B3
5 Te Anau Bike Hire B2
6 Wings & Water Te Anau B3

Sleeping

7 Cosy Kiwi C1
8 Keiko's B&B D1
9 Te Anau Top 10 Holiday Park A2
10 Te Anau YHA A2

Eating

11 Fat Duck C2
Fresh Choice Supermarket .... (see 17)
12 Kebabs 2 Go B2
13 Mainly Seafood B2
14 Miles Better Pies B2
15 Olive Tree Café & Restaurant B2
16 Redcliff Bar & Restaurant B2
17 Sandfly Café B2

Drinking

18 Moose B2
19 Ranch Bar & Grill C2

Entertainment

Fiordland Cinema .... (see 17)

Shopping

20 Bev's Tramping Gear D4
21 Te Anau Outside Sports B2

Kepler Track

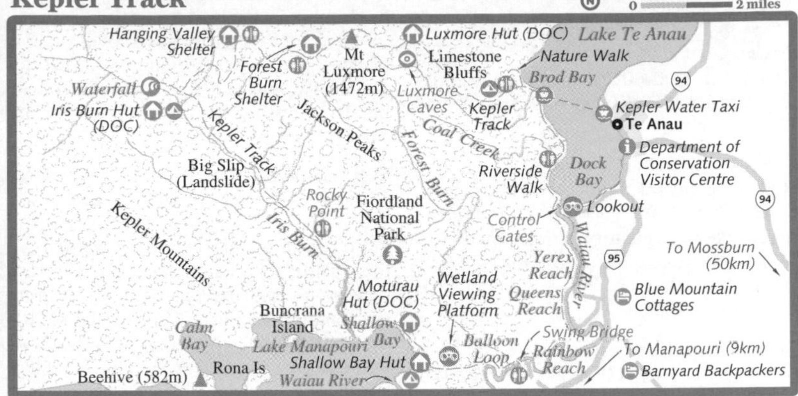

Huts goes along a high ridge, well above the bush, and offers fantastic views when it's clear; in poor weather it can be treacherous. It's recommended that the track be done in the Luxmore–Iris Burn–Moturau direction.

The weather impacts greatly on this walk, and you should expect rain and be prepared for wading. Good rain gear is essential. The alpine sections require a good level of fitness and may be closed in winter. Other sections are considered moderate, with climbs and descents of up to 1000m and unbridged stream crossings.

During the main walking season (October to April), advance bookings must be made by all trampers online at www.doc.govt.nz or at any DOC visitor centre. Pick up tickets at Te Anau's DOC visitor centre before departure.

Accommodation here is in three well-maintained huts. A **camping pass** (per night adult/child $18/free) allows camping at two designated campsites. Outside the main season, a **Backcountry Hut Pass** (per night adult/child $15/free) must be prepurchased, but no heating or cooking is on offer. Off-season camping is free.

Estimated walking times:

DAY	ROUTE	TIME
1	Te Anau DOC visitor centre to control gates	45min
1	Control gates to Brod Bay	1½hr
1	Brod Bay to Luxmore Hut	3½-4½hr
2	Luxmore Hut to Iris Burn Hut	5-6hr
3	Iris Burn Hut to Moturau Hut	5-6hr
4	Moturau Hut to Rainbow Reach	1½-2hr
4	Rainbow Reach to control gates	2½-3½hr

Tracknet (☎0800 483 262; www.tracknet.net) and **Topline Tours** (☎03-249 8059; www.toplinetours.co.nz) provide trailhead transport.

SHORT WALKS

Set out along the Kepler Track on free day walks. **Kepler Water Taxi** (☎03-249 8364; stevsaunders@xtra.co.nz; one-way/return $25/50) will scoot you over to Brod Bay from where you can walk to Mt Luxmore (seven to eight hours) or along the southern lakeshore back to Te Anau (two to three hours). Regular shuttles leave Te Anau lakefront at 8.30am and 9.30am during summer.

During summer, **Trips'n'Tramps** (☎03-249 7081, 0800 305 807; www.tripsandtramps.com; ⊙Oct-Apr) offers small-group, guided hikes on sections of the Routeburn and Kepler and Hollyford Tracks. Some departures incorporate kayaking on Milford Sound. **Real Journeys** (☎800 656 501; www.realjourneys.co.nz) runs guided day hikes (adult/child $195/127, November to mid-April) along an 11km stretch of the Milford Track.

Grab a copy of *Fiordland National Park Day Walks* ($1 from the Fiordland i-SITE or free at www.doc.govt.nz).

Kayaking & Jetboating

Fiordland Wilderness Experiences KAYAKING
(☎0800 200 434; www.fiordlandseakayak.co.nz; from $145) One-day and multiday kayaking explorations of Lake Te Anau and Lake Manapouri.

Rosco's Milford Kayaks KAYAKING
(☎0800 476 726; www.roscosmilfordkayaks.com; 72 Town Centre; ⊙9am-5pm) A good local operator. Has a booking and information kiosk

on the main drag that focuses mainly on adventure activities such as kayaking.

Luxmore Jet JETBOATING
(☎03-249 6951, 0800 253 826; www.luxmorejet.com; adult/child $99/49) On the Upper Waiau River.

Other Activities

High Ride Adventures QUAD BIKES, HORSE RIDING
(☎03-249 7570, 0508 444 474; www.highride.co.nz) Offers backcountry trips on quad bikes ($155) and horseback rides ($80 to $95) along the Upukerora River. Combo deals ($235) are available.

Te Anau Bike Hire BICYCLE RENTAL
(7 Mokonui St; mountain bikes per hr/day from $12/30; ⏲from 10am Sep-Apr) Mountain bikes, kids' bikes and tandems.

Tours

Southern Lakes Helicopters SCENIC FLIGHTS
(☎03-249 7167; www.southernlakeshelicopters.co.nz; Lakefront Dr) Flights over Te Anau for 25 minutes ($195), longer trips over Doubtful, Dusky and Milford Sounds (from $540), and a chopper/walk/boat option on the Kepler Track ($185).

Wings & Water Te Anau SCENIC FLIGHTS
(☎03-249 7405; www.wingsandwater.co.nz; Lakefront Dr) Ten-minute local flights (adult/child $95/55), and longer flights over the Kepler Track and Doubtful and Milford Sounds (from $225).

Sleeping

Accommodation can get booked out in the peak season (late December to February). Book early if possible.

Ask at DOC for directions to **Queens Reach campsite**, 6km south of town towards Manapouri. Basic facilities only (no toilets).

Te Anau Lodge B&B B&B $$$
(☎03-249 7477; www.teanaulodge.com; 52 Howden St; d $240-350; @🛜) The former 1930s-built Sisters of Mercy Convent, relocated to a grand location just north of town, is a positively decadent accommodation option. Sip your drink in a chesterfield in front of the fire, retire to your spa before collapsing on a king-size bed, then awaken to a fresh, delicious breakfast in the old chapel.

Blue Mountain Cottages LODGE $$$
(☎03-249 9030; www.bluemountaincottages.co.nz; Hwy 95; cabins $260) These family-friendly self-contained cabins surrounded by farmland 8km south of town sleep up to four. Fresh baked goods and organic produce and vegies are often available for guests. The owners' son Jayden is usually keen to show visitors around the 8-hectare rural property.

Bob & Maxines HOSTEL $
(☎03-249 7429; bob.anderson@woosh.co.nz; 20 Paton Pl, off Oraka St; dm/d $31/82; @) Only 2.5km out of town, off the Te Anau–Milford Hwy, this relaxed and modern hostel gets rave reviews for the big mountain vistas from the communal lounge. Warm up beside the woodburner, cook up a storm in the spacious well-equipped kitchen, or just chill out. Bikes are available to get you back into town.

Keiko's B&B B&B $$
(☎03-249 9248; www.keikos.co.nz; 228 Milford Rd; d $165-195; ⏲closed Jun-Aug; 🛜) The private, self-contained cottages here are lovely, and the entirety is surrounded by Japanese-style gardens. A Japanese breakfast in the morning and a bamboo-bordered hot tub in the evening are other essential extras.

Cosy Kiwi MOTEL $$
(☎0800 249 700, 03-249 7475; www.cosykiwi.com; 186 Milford Rd; d $150-210; @🛜) This smart motel with modern, well-appointed rooms is just a short stroll from bustling downtown Te Anau. Breakfast is included, and host Eleanor usually offers a couple of cooked options.

Barnyard Backpackers HOSTEL $
(☎03-249 8006; www.barnyardbackpackers.com; 80 Mt York Rd, off SH95; dm $29-33, d $76; @) On a deer farm 9km south of town, this rustic communal building and its collection of log cabins sit on a view-laden hillside. Cabins are comfortable, with en-suite bathrooms, and the main lodge is great for playing pool or sitting around the central fireplace.

Rosie's Backpacker Homestay HOSTEL $
(☎03-249 8431; backpack@paradise.net.nz; 23 Tom Plato Dr; dm/d $31/74; ⏲closed Jun-Jul; @🛜) You're immediately made to feel part of the family in this small and intimate homestay. It's a short walk north of the town centre.

Te Anau Top 10 Holiday Park HOLIDAY PARK $
(☎03-249 7462, 0800 249 746; www.teanautop10.co.nz; 128 Te Anau Tce; sites $38, units $72-160; @🛜) Near the town and lake with private camping sites, a playground, a sauna, bike hire, a barbecue area and modern kitchen facilities. Cabins and units run from basic to fancy.

Te Anau Lakeview Holiday Park HOLIDAY PARK $
(☎03-249 7457, 0800 483 262; www.teanauholidaypark.co.nz; 77 Te Anau-Manapouri Rd; sites from $20, dm $35, s $40, units $84-270) This sprawling lakeside complex combines the Te Anau Lakeview campsite with West Arm singles accommodation (pretty basic and institutional, but more private than dorms), and Steamers backpackers (characterless rooms but sharing modern communal areas). The new Marakura Apartments are chic and modern.

Te Anau YHA HOSTEL $
(☎03-249 7847; www.yha.co.nz; 29 Mokonui St; dm $33-42, s $70, d $90-120; @📶) This centrally located and modern hostel has great facilities and comfortable, colourful rooms. Lounge in the hammock, barbecue in the grassy backyard, or get cosy by the wood fire.

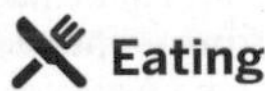

Eating

Fat Duck RESTAURANT $$
(☎03-249 8480; 124 Town Centre; breakfast $10-17, lunch & dinner mains $22-38; ⊙8.30am-late; 📶) Dishes are tasty and hearty in proportions, with imaginative variations on crispy duck, pork belly and salmon. There's a bar as long as Doubtful Sound if you just want a drink before kicking on somewhere else. Sometimes closed Monday and Tuesday outside the peak season.

Redcliff Bar & Restaurant RESTAURANT $$$
(☎03-249 7431; 12 Mokonui St; mains $29-42; ⊙5pm-late) Housed in a replica old settler's cottage, Redcliff showcases locally sourced produce in a convivial atmosphere. Try the wild Fiordland venison or tender herby hare. Bookings aren't taken, so kick off with a drink in the rustic front bar. There's occasional live music and a permanent friendly vibe with excellent service.

Sandfly Café CAFE $
(9 The Lane; breakfast & lunch $7-17) This is a lovely, chilled-out place to relax. Enjoy excellent coffee and cruisy music, all-day breakfasts, and yummy baking including excellent wraps, muffins and hearty bacon-and-egg pies.

Olive Tree Café & Restaurant CAFE $$
(52 Town Centre; snacks & burgers $10-15, mains $23-34) Olive Tree is warm and funky inside, with excellent outdoor areas to sip coffee in the sun or enjoy a tasty Mediterranean-tinged meal. Build up your pre-Milford Track energy reserves with eggs Benedict or hearty pizzas with organic toppings.

Miles Better Pies PIES $
(cnr Town Centre & Mokonui St; pies $4-6) The selection includes gourmet venison, Thai curry or apricot pies. There are a few pavement tables, but sitting beside the lake is nicer; the pies also make a good snack for the road.

Mainly Seafood FISH & CHIPS $
(Te Anau Tce; snacks & burgers $6-15; ⊙noon-9pm) A lakefront location, mountain views and perfectly executed fish and chips and gourmet burgers. Make this humble food truck your Te Anau snack stop of choice.

Kebabs 2 Go KEBABS $
(Town Centre; kebabs & burgers $10-16) Celebrate your return to civilisation after the Kepler or Milford Tracks with the gulity pleasure of a chilli lamb kebab and a sweet slice of baklava.

Fresh Choice Supermarket SUPERMARKET
(1 The Lane) Good wine and beer selection.

Drinking & Entertainment

Ranch Bar & Grill PUB
(Town Centre) Look forward to happy hour from 8pm to 9pm and good-value Sunday-night roast dinners ($15). It's the locals' choice for the best pub meals in town.

Moose PUB
(84 Lakefront Dr) The cavernous lakefront Moose has big-screen sports and a sunny patio. It also does meals ($20 to $35) and bar snacks.

Fiordland Cinema CINEMA
(☎03-249 8812; www.fiordlandcinema.co.nz; 7 The Lane; 📶) In between back-to-back showings of the excellent *Ata Whenua* (adult/child $10/5), essentially a 32-minute advertisement for stunning Fiordland scenery, Fiordland Cinema also screens Hollywood and art-house titles. The cinema's Black Dog Bar has occasional live gigs.

Shopping

Bev's Tramping Gear OUTDOOR EQUIPMENT
(☎03-249 7389; www.bevs-hire.co.nz; 16 Homer St; ⊙9am-noon & 5.30-7pm Nov-Apr, closed Sun morning) Topographical maps for sale and tramping and camping equipment for hire. From May to October, open by prior arrangement.

Te Anau Outside Sports OUTDOOR EQUIPMENT
(www.outsidesports.co.nz; 38 Town Centre) Tramping and camping equipment for sale or hire.

Information

Department of Conservation Visitor Centre (DOC; ☎03-249 0200; www.doc.govt.nz; cnr Lakefront Dr & Te Anau-Manapouri Rd; ⊙8.30am-4.30pm) Includes the Great Walks counter for bookings and confirmed tickets for the Milford, Routeburn and Kepler Tracks. Computer terminals with NZ-wide DOC information are also available.

Fiordland i-SITE (☎03-249 8900; www.fiordland.org.nz; 85 Lakefront Dr; ⊙8.30am-5.30pm) Activities, accommodation and bus bookings.

Fiordland Medical Centre (☎03-249 7007; Luxmore Dr; ⊙8am-5.30pm Mon-Fri, 9am-noon Sat)

Post office (102 Town Centre) Located in bookshop.

Real Journeys (☎0800 656 501; www.realjourneys.co.nz; Lakefront Dr; ⊙9am-5pm) Fiordland-focused tours and activities.

Southern Discoveries (☎0800 264 536; www.southerndiscoveries.co.nz; Lakefront Dr; ⊙8am-6pm Mon-Fri & 9.30am-6pm Sat-Sun) For information and booking activities. Outside opening hours there's a handy 24-hour information touch screen.

Getting There & Away

InterCity (www.intercity.co.nz) has daily bus services between Te Anau and Queenstown (2½ hours), Invercargill (2½ hours) and Dunedin (4¾ hours). Buses depart outside Kiwi Country on Miro St.

Bottom Bus (☎03-477 9083; www.travelheadfirst.com) is a hop-on, hop-off bus service linking Te Anau to Queenstown, Invercargill and Milford Sound (1½ hours). **Naked Bus** (www.nakedbus.com) links Te Anau with Queenstown, Invercargill and Milford Sound.

From November to April, **Topline Tours** (☎03-249 8059; www.toplinetours.co.nz) run a Te Anau–Queenstown shuttle.

For trampers:

Tracknet (☎0800 483 262; www.tracknet.net) has daily shuttles to the Kepler, Hollyford and Milford Tracks, and to the western end of the Routeburn, Greenstone and Caples Tracks at the Divide. The Kepler Water Taxi (p263) runs regularly across the lake to Brod Bay on the Kepler Track in summer. **Wings & Water** (☎03-249 7405; www.wingsandwater.co.nz) provides transport to Supper Cove ($330 per person, minimum two passengers) for Dusky Sound trampers.

Te Anau–Milford Hwy

If you don't have the opportunity to hike into Fiordland's wilderness, the 119km road from Te Anau to Milford (SH94) is the most easily accessible taste of its vastness and beauty.

Head out from Te Anau early (8am) or later in the morning (11am) to avoid the tour buses heading for midday sound cruises. See the Milford Sound section for important information about chains and avalanches (in winter) and petrol (always).

The trip takes two to 2½ hours if you drive straight through, but take time to stop and experience the majestic landscape. Pull off the road and explore the many viewpoints and nature walks en route. Pick up the *Fiordland National Park Day Walks* brochure ($1 from the DOC or Fiordland i-SITE in Te Anau or free at www.doc.govt.nz).

The first part of the road meanders through rolling farmland atop the lateral moraine of the glacier that once gouged out Lake Te Anau. The road passes **Te Anau Downs** (there's accommodation here at Fiordland National Park Lodge) after 29km and heads towards the entrance of Fiordland National Park, passing patches of beech (red, silver and mountain), alluvial flats and meadows.

Just past the **McKay Creek** campsite (at 51km) are great views over Eglinton Valley with sheer mountains either side and Pyramid Peak (2295m) and Ngatimamoe Peak (2164m) ahead. The boardwalk at Mirror Lakes (at 58km) takes you through beech forest and wetlands, and on a calm day the lakes reflect the mountains across the valley. **Knob's Creek** (at 63km) also has accommodation.

At the 77km mark is the area referred to as O Tapara, or more commonly as **Cascade Creek**. O Tapara is the original name of nearby Lake Gunn, and was a stopover historically for Maori parties heading to Anita Bay in search of *pounamu* (greenstone). A walking track (45 minutes return) passes through tall red beech forest ringing with bird calls. Side trails lead to quiet lakeside beaches.

At 84km the vegetation changes as you pass across the **Divide**, the lowest east–west pass in the Southern Alps. There's a large roadside shelter here for walkers either finishing or starting the Routeburn, Greenstone or Caples Tracks; it's also used as a terminal for trampers' bus services. A walk from the shelter, initially through beech forest along the start of the Routeburn, then climbing up alpine tussockland to **Key Summit** (two hours return), offers spectacular views of the three valleys that radiate from this point.

From the Divide, the road falls into the beech forest of the **Hollyford Valley** (stop at Pop's View for a great outlook) and there's a worthwhile detour to Gunns Camp (p269) 8km along an unsealed road. About 9km further, at the end of that road, is a walk to the high **Humboldt Falls** (30 minutes return) and the start of the Hollyford Track.

Back on the main road to Milford, the road climbs to the **Homer Tunnel**, 101km from Te Anau and framed by a spectacular, high-walled, ice-carved amphitheatre. The tunnel is one-way outside avalanche season, with the world's most alpine set of traffic lights to direct traffic. Kea (alpine parrots) hang around the eastern end of the tunnel looking for food from tourists. Don't feed them as it's bad for their health. Dark, magnificently rough-hewn and dripping with water, the 1207m-long tunnel emerges at the other end at the head of the spectacular **Cleddau Valley**.

About 10km before Milford, the **Chasm Walk** (20 minutes return and even accessible by wheelchair, though you might appreciate assistance on the steeper parts) is well worth a stop. The forest-cloaked Cleddau River plunges through eroded boulders in a narrow chasm, creating deep falls and a natural rock bridge. From here, watch for glimpses of **Mt Tutoko** (2746m), Fiordland's highest peak, above the beech forest just before Milford.

TE WAHIPOUNAMU SOUTHWEST NEW ZEALAND WORLD HERITAGE AREA

In the southwest corner of New Zealand, the combination of four huge national parks make up Te Wahipounamu Southwest New Zealand World Heritage Area. Te Wahipounamu (the Place of Greenstone) covers 2.6 million hectares and is recognised internationally for its cultural significance to the Ngai Tahu, as well as for the area's unique fauna and wildlife. Te Wahipounamu incorporates the following national parks:

» Fiordland National Park

» Aoraki/Mt Cook National Park

» Westland Tai Poutini National Park

» Mt Aspiring National Park

HOLLYFORD TRACK

This dramatic track starts in the midst of lowland forest, crossing mountain streams and passing pretty waterfalls as it follows the broad Hollyford River valley all the way to the sea. The Tasman coast makes a satisfying end point, with dolphins, seals and penguins often greeting hikers on their arrival. However, it does mean backtracking another four days back to your start point unless you take one of the sneaky shortcut options.

The 56km track is graded as a moderate hike, but involves some creek crossings and suffers frequent flash floods that can leave trekkers waiting it out en route for several days until the trail becomes passable. The trickiest part of the route is the ominously named Demon Trail (10km) alongside Lake McKerrow. It's imperative that you check with DOC in Te Anau for the latest track and weather conditions and have detailed maps.

Tracknet (☎0800 483 262; www.tracknet.net) has shuttles between the Hollyford Rd turn-off and Te Anau ($52, one hour) and Queenstown ($90, 3¾ hours).

Options for reducing the length of the there-and-back journey include hitching a jetboat ride south with **Hollyford Track Guided Walks** (☎03-442 3000, 0800 832 226; www.hollyfordtrack.com; $110) for the length of Lake McKerrow; book in advance. A more luxurious, three-day guided walk ($1795) includes fancy accommodation, jetboat trips in both directions along Lake McKerrow and a flight back to Milford Sound from the coastal finish line at Martins Bay.

You can also arrange a flight between Martins Bay and civilisation with **Air Fiordland** (☎03-249 6720; www.airfiordland.com) for up to four people (Te Anau/Milford Sound $620/1240). The price is per flight, so you can share the cost. Hollyford Track Guided Walks sometimes has empty seats when it flies from Milford Sound to pick up its walkers at Martins Bay, and can drop you at Martins Bay by plane ($145) or helicopter ($195).

These services run only on specific dates from October to April, and independent walkers must pre-book with Hollyford Track Guided Walks.

MILFORD TRACK

The 53.5km Milford Track is one of the world's finest walks. The number of walkers is limited in the Great Walks season (late October to late April), and you must follow a one-way, four-day set itinerary. Accommodation is only in huts (camping isn't allowed).

Even in summer, expect *lots* of rain, in the wake of which water will cascade everywhere and small streams will become raging torrents within minutes.

In the off-season, there's limited trail transport, the huts aren't staffed, and some

Milford Track

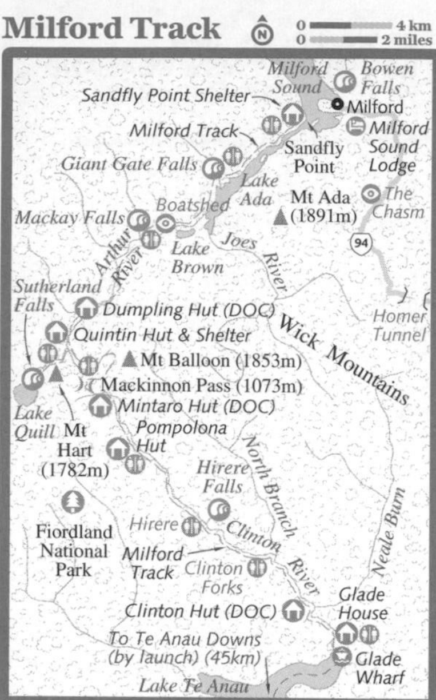

bridges are removed. During winter, snow and avalanches make it unsafe. It's vital to check avalanche risk with DOC.

BOOKINGS

You can walk the track independently or with a guided tour. For independent bookings, contact DOC in Te Anau or book online at www.doc.govt.nz. Pick up track tickets at DOC in Te Anau before departure.

The track must be booked during the Great Walks season (late October to late April). Book as far ahead as possible. Bookings open up 12 months before the start of the following season.

Ultimate Hikes (☎03-450 1940, 0800 659 255; www.ultimatehikes.co.nz; adult/child Dec-Mar from $1995/1790, Apr & Nov $1830/1640) has five-day guided walks staying at private lodges. A one-day 11km sampler is also available (adult/child $195/123).

WALKING THE TRACK

The trail starts at Glade House, at the northern end of Lake Te Anau, accessed by boat from Te Anau Downs or Te Anau. The track follows the flat bottom of the Clinton River Valley up to its head at Lake Mintaro, passing through rainforest and crystal-clear streams. From Mintaro you cross the dramatic **Mackinnon Pass**, which on a clear day gives spectacular views back to yesterday's Clinton Valley and forward to tomorrow's Arthur Valley. (If the pass appears clear when you arrive at Mintaro Hut, make the effort to climb it, as it may not be clear the next day.) From the pass a long, wooden staircase leads you down to Arthur River, following alongside the rapids. The trail then continues down to Quintin and Dumpling Huts and through the valley rainforest to Milford Sound. You can leave your pack at the Quintin public shelter while you make the return walk to the graceful, 630m-high **Sutherland Falls**, NZ's tallest falls.

Estimated walking times:

DAY	ROUTE	TIME
1	Glade Wharf to Glade House	20min
1	Glade House to Clinton Hut	1-1½hr
2	Clinton Hut to Mintaro Hut	6hr
3	Mintaro Hut to Dumpling Hut	6-7hr
3	Side trip to Sutherland Falls	1½hr return
4	Dumpling Hut to Sandfly Point	5½-6hr

TRANSPORT TO GLADE WHARF

During the Great Walks season, **Tracknet** (☎0800 483 262; www.tracknet.net) drives up from Te Anau to Te Anau Downs ($22). Tracknet also offers the option of transport from Queenstown to Te Anau Downs ($65). **Real Journeys** (☎0800 656 501; www.realjourneys.co.nz; adult/child $190/123.50; ⊙Nov–mid-Apr) will then run you by boat from Te Anau Downs to Glade Wharf near the start of the track. Both of these trips can be booked at DOC in Te Anau at the same time as you book your walk. Outside the Great Walks season, talk to Tracknet about transport the whole way to Glade Wharf.

TRANSPORT FROM SANDFLY POINT

There are ferries leaving Sandfly Point at 2pm and 3.15pm for the Milford Sound cruise wharf (adult/child $34/19.50). From there you can bus back to Te Anau with Tracknet ($47, 2½ hours). These can both be booked via DOC at Te Anau.

PACKAGES

Cruise Te Anau (☎03-249 7593; www.cruiseteanau.co.nz) does a bus-boat combination trip for around $180.

Sleeping

Along SH94 are basic DOC campsites ($6 per person), the majority of them situated between 45km and 81km from Te Anau. You'll find them in *Conservation Campsites – South Island* (free from DOC in Te Anau) or at www.doc.govt.nz.

Milford Sound Lodge LODGE $$
(☎03-249 8071; www.milfordlodge.com; just off SH94; sites per person from $18, dm $30-33, d $85) Alongside the Cleddau River, this simple but comfortable lodge has an unhurried, ends-of-the-earth air. There's no TV, and travellers and trampers relax in the large lounges to discuss their experiences. There's a tiny shop/cafe/bar and a free shuttle to Milford Sound, just 1.5km away. Very comfortable chalets ($255) enjoy an absolute riverside location. Booking ahead is strongly recommended.

Gunns Camp CABINS $
(gunnscamp@ruralinzone.net; Hollyford Rd; sites/dm/cabins $12/20/55) Gunns Camp, also known as Hollyford Camp, is on Hollyford Rd about halfway between SH94 (8km) and the start of the Hollyford Track (9km). The old Public Works cabins are very basic (linen hire is $5 per bed), and heating is via a coal or wood-fired stove (fuel provided). A generator supplies limited electricity, turning off at 10pm, and there are hot showers and a spacious new kitchen block. There's also a small shop and an eccentric museum (adult/child $1/30c; guests free) with pioneering memorabilia. Cash and credit cards only – no Eftpos.

Knob's Flat MOTEL $$
(☎03-249 9122; www.knobsflat.co.nz; sites per person $10, studio/motel units $120/150) In the grassy Eglinton Valley, 63km from Te Anau, Knob's Flat has comfortable units catering to walkers and anglers. TV, email and stress have no place here, and mountain bikes can be hired. Recent developments include a campsite (unpowered sites only) and a spacious amenities block.

Fiordland National Park Lodge LODGE $$
(☎0800 500 805, 03-249 7811; www.teanau-milfordsound.co.nz; SH94; dm $28, d hotel $65-75, d motel $130; @📶) At Te Anau Downs (29km from Te Anau) at the head of the lake where boats depart for the Milford Track, Fiordland National Park Lodge has accommodation ranging from dorms and backpacker doubles to self-contained motel units. It's popular with Milford Track walkers, but other travellers are also welcome.

Milford Sound

POP 170

The first sight of Milford Sound is stunning. Sheer rocky cliffs rise out of still, dark waters, and forests clinging to the slopes sometimes relinquish their hold, causing a 'tree avalanche' into the waters. The spectacular, photogenic 1692m-high Mitre Peak rises dead ahead.

A cruise on Milford Sound is Fiordland's most accessible experience, complete with seals, dolphins and an average annual rainfall of 7m – more than enough to fuel cascading waterfalls and add a shimmering moody mist to the scene.

Milford Sound receives about half a million visitors each year, many of them crammed into the peak months (January and February). Some 14,000 arrive by foot, via the Milford Track, which ends at the sound. Many more drive from Te Anau, but most arrive via the multitude of bus tours. But don't worry. Out on the water all this humanity seems tiny compared to nature's vastness.

Sights & Activities

Unique environmental circumstances have allowed the sound to become home to some rarely glimpsed marine life. Heavy rainfall sluicing straight off the rocky slopes washes significant organic matter into the ocean, creating a 5m-deep permanent tannin-stained freshwater layer above the warmer sea water. This dark layer filters out much of the sunlight and, coupled with the sound's calm, protected waters, replicates deep-ocean conditions. The result is that deep-water species thrive not far below the surface. A similar situation exists at Doubtful Sound. One of the best perspectives you can get of Milford Sound is from a kayak at water level, dwarfed by the cliffs.

Rosco's Milford Kayaks KAYAKING
(☎03-249 8500, 0800 476 726; www.roscosmilfordkayaks.com; trips $130-175) Recommended excursions include the 'Morning Glory', a challenging early-morning kayak (around five hours in the boat) the full length of the fiord to Anita Bay, and the 'Stirling Sunriser', which includes kayaking under the 151m-high Stirling Falls. Another option includes a 20-minute paddle around Deepwater Basin to Sandfly Point and a 3½-hour walk on the Milford Track ($89). Rosco's has a booking office in Te Anau's main drag.

Fiordland Wilderness Experiences KAYAKING
(☎0800 200 434, 03-249-7700; www.seakayakfiordland.co.nz; per person $145; ⏲Sep-Apr) Guided six-hour paddles on Milford Sound.

Milford Discovery Centre AQUARIUM
(adult/child $36/18; ⏲9am-3.45pm) Incorporates interactive displays on the natural history, geology and environment of Milford Sound, and the Deep Underwater Observatory, a five-storey mostly submerged building suspended from pontoons. Four storeys underwater are deep-water corals, tube anemones and bottom-dwelling sea perch. The Discovery Centre can be visited on boat trips with Milford Sound Cruises and Mitre Peak Cruises.

Tawaki Adventures DIVING
(☎0800 829 254; www.southernaqua.co.nz) Trips include a three-hour boat cruise and two guided dives of a total of 30 minutes ($159); it's an extra $99 for gear hire. If you don't dive you can join the boat trip anyway ($99 plus $45 to hire snorkelling gear).

Tours

Each Milford Sound cruise company claims to be quieter, smaller, bigger, cheaper or in some way preferable to the rest. What really makes a difference is the timing of the cruise. Most bus tours aim for 1pm sailings so if you avoid that time of day there'll be less people on the boat (and on the road). With some companies you get a better price on cruises outside rush hour too.

If you're particularly keen on wildlife, ask whether there'll be a nature guide on board. It's wise to book ahead regardless. You generally need to arrive 20 minutes before departure. Most companies offer coach transfers from Te Anau for an additional cost. Day trips from Queenstown make for a very long 13-hour day.

All the cruises visit the mouth of the sound, only 15km from the wharf, poking their prow into the choppy waves of the Tasman Sea. The shorter cruises visit less of the en route 'highlights', which include Bowen Falls, Mitre Peak, Anita Bay and Stirling Falls. You'll have a good chance of seeing dolphins, seals and penguins. All cruises leave from the huge **cruise terminal** (⏲8am-5.15pm Oct-Apr, 9am-4.15pm May-Sep), a 10-minute walk from the cafe and car park.

Real Journeys BOAT TOUR
(☎03-249 7416, 0800 656 501; www.realjourneys.co.nz; adult/child from $68/22) Lots of cruises from this big company including 1¾-hour scenic cruises (adult $68 to $90, child $22). The company also does 2½-hour nature cruises (adult $75 to $95, child $22) with a nature guide for commentary and Q&A. Real Journeys does overnight cruises on two of its boats. You can kayak and take nature tours in tender crafts en route. The cost includes all meals but transport from Te Anau is additional. All depart from the Milford terminal around 4.30pm and return around 9.30am the following day. Cheaper prices apply in May and September. The *Milford Wanderer*, modelled on an old trading scow, accommodates 36 passengers in two- and four-bunk cabins (with shared bathrooms) and costs $325/162.50 per adult/child. The *Milford Mariner* sleeps 60 in more upmarket, en-suite, twin-share cabins ($495/247.50 per adult/child).

Jucy Cruize BOAT TOUR
(☎0800 500 121; www.jucycruize.co.nz; adult/child from $65/15) A smaller, less-crowded experience with 1½-hour trips on a comfortable boat with lots of deck space.

Mitre Peak Cruises BOAT TOUR
(☎0800 744 633, 03-249 8110; www.mitrepeak.com; adult/child from $68/16.50) Cruises in smallish boats with a maximum capacity of 75. The 4.30pm cruise is good because many larger boats are heading back at this time.

Milford Sound Cruises BOAT TOUR
(☎03-441 1137, 0800 264 536; www.southerndiscoveries.co.nz; adult/child from $73/15) A range of trips exploring Milford Sound, all lasting around two hours. The 2¼-hour wildlife cruise (adult $73 to $90, child $15) is more intimate, and operates on a smaller boat.

Eating & Drinking

Blue Duck Café & Bar CAFE $$
(snacks $5-15, buffet lunch $17-21; ⏲cafe 8.30am-4pm, bar 4pm-late; @) Serving sandwiches and a lunch buffet, and at night the attached bar sees a mix of travellers and trampers tucking in to the $25 beer and pizza deal. You'll find the Blue Duck on the edge of the main carpark at Milford Sound.

Getting There & Away

Bus

InterCity (www.intercity.co.nz) runs daily bus services from Queenstown (4½ hours) and Te Anau (1½ hours) to Milford Sound. **Naked Bus** (www.nakedbus.com) also runs from Te Anau to the sound. Many bus trips include a boat cruise on the sound; most are around $150 from Te Anau (or around $200 from Queenstown).

Trampers' buses from **Tracknet** (☎0800 483 262; www.tracknet.net) also operate from Te Anau and Queenstown and will pick up at the Milford Sound Lodge. All these buses pass the Divide and the start/end of the Routeburn, Greenstone and Caples Tracks.

Car

Fill up with petrol in Te Anau before setting off. Chains must be carried on avalanche-risk days from May to November (there will be signs on the road), and can be hired from most service stations in Te Anau.

Manapouri

POP 210

Manapouri is largely used as a jumping-off point for cruises to the sublime Doubtful Sound, and as a base for walking expeditions.

In 1969, Manapouri was the site of NZ's first major environmental campaign. The original plan for the West Arm power station, built to provide cheap electricity for the aluminium smelter near Invercargill, included raising the level of the lake by 30m. A petition gathered a staggering 265,000 signatures (17% of voting-age New Zealanders at the time) and the issue contributed to the downfall of the government at the following election. The action was successful: the power station was built but the lake's level remains unchanged. It was a success that spawned increasing national environmental action through the 1970s and '80s. West Arm power station is NZ's largest producer of electricity: a tunnel dug through the mountain from Lake Manapouri to Doubtful Sound drops a hefty 180m from lake to sound, driving the power station's turbines.

Activities

Day Walks TRAMPING

With some form of water transport (kayak, dinghy or water taxi), you can cross the Waiau River for some easy low-altitude day walks, detailed in the DOC brochure *Fiordland National Park Day Walks* (www.doc.govt.nz). A walk along the **Circle Track** (three hours return) can be extended to **Hope Arm** (five to six hours return), crossing the uninvitingly named Stinking Creek. Although Te Anau is the usual access point for the Kepler Track, the trail touches the northern end of Lake Manapouri and part of it can be done as a day walk from Manapouri; access is via the swing bridge at Rainbow Reach, 10km north of town. From Pearl Harbour there's also a walk that doesn't require crossing the river: to **Frasers Beach** (1½ hours return), from where you can gaze across the beautiful lake.

Dusky Track TRAMPING

Manapouri is also a staging point for the remote 84km Dusky Track, a walk that takes eight days if you tramp between Lakes Manapouri and Hauroko, with an extra two-day detour possible from Loch Maree Hut to Supper Cove on Dusky Sound. With regular tree falls, deep mud, river crossings, delaying floods and 21 three-wire bridges, this is an extremely challenging wilderness walk, suitable only for well-equipped, very experienced trampers. Contact DOC, and read Lonely Planet's *Tramping in New Zealand,* for more details. For transport options from either Te Anau or Tuatapere to the Dusky Track, contact **Lake Hauroko Tours** (☎03-226 6681; www.duskytrack.co.nz).

Adventure Kayak & Cruise KAYAKING

(☎0800 324 966; www.fiordlandadventure.co.nz) Rents kayaks from $50 per person per day for paddles on Lake Manapouri from October to April; will rent only to groups of two paddlers or more, and provide VHF radios free of charge for safety. Also offers kayaking trips on Doubtful Sound (from $239 per person).

Adventure Manapouri BOATING

(☎03-249 8070; www.adventuremanapouri.co.nz) Rowboat hire ($20 per day), water taxis and fishing trips.

Manapouri Stores BOATING

Rowboats for rent ($30 per day) and a handy map showing nearby walking trails.

Sleeping

Misty Mountain Eco-Retreat RENTAL HOUSE $$

(☎03-249 6661; www.waitahanui-hideaway.co.nz; 313 Hillside-Manapouri Rd; d $150) Surrounded by native trees and birdsong, this cosy cottage combines timber from seawashed logs retrieved from Doubtful Sound with a modern kitchen and bathroom. Decor is stylish with wooden floors and Oriental rugs, and there's a sunny deck with mountain views.

Freestone Backpackers HOSTEL $

(☎03-249 6893; www.freestone.co.nz; 270 Hillside-Manapouri Rd; dm $22-33, d $66-150) These clean, comfortable and rustic cabins nestle on a hillside about 3km east of town. Each cabin has a small kitchen, potbelly stove and verandah. Bathrooms are communal. Dorms and bedrooms in a shared house are also available. More comfortable options include accommodation ($75) with a kitchen and private bathroom, and a deluxe bed and breakfast ($150) with a spa.

Manapouri Lakeview Chalets & Motor Park HOLIDAY PARK $
(☎03-249 6624; www.manapourimotels.co.nz; SH95; sites from $33, units $58-130; @📶) This camping ground features eclectic cabins, ranging from mock Swiss Alpine to mock shanty town. There's a fabulous fleet of old Morris Minors in various states of repair and a vintage pinball-machine collection to relive your youth.

Possum Lodge HOLIDAY PARK $
(☎03-249 6623; www.possumlodge.co.nz; 13 Murrell Ave; sites $34, dm $23, units $55-105; ⏲Oct-Easter; @📶) A charming, shady little campsite near the lakeside, this property has old-school, relatively basic cabins and modern motel-style units. Best bring some sandfly repellent.

Eating & Drinking

Lakeside Café & Bar PUB
(68 Cathedral Dr; pizza $18-20, mains $18-34; @📶) Serves substantial meals with a generous side order of lake views from the sunny garden bar. The public bar attached is a large, cheery affair, with crazy silver helicopters providing the wacky ventilation.

Getting There & Away

On request, **Topline Tours** (☎03-249 8059; www.toplinetours.co.nz; $20) can divert to Manapouri on their from Queenstown to Te Anau.

Doubtful Sound

Massive, magnificent Doubtful Sound is a wilderness area of rugged peaks, dense forest and thundering post-rain waterfalls. It's one of NZ's largest sounds: three times the length and 10 times the area of Milford Sound. Doubtful is also much, *much* less trafficked. If you have the time and the money, it's an essential experience. Fur seals, dolphins, Fiordland crested penguins and seals are also regular visitors.

Until relatively recently, only the most intrepid tramper or sailor ever explored Doubtful Sound. Even Captain Cook only observed it from off the coast in 1770, because he was 'doubtful' whether the winds in the sound would be sufficient to blow the ship back out to sea. The sound became more accessible when the road over Wilmot Pass opened in 1959 to facilitate construction of the West Arm power station.

Tours

Doubtful Sound is only accessible by tour. You'll cross Lake Manapouri by boat from Manapouri to the West Arm power station, drive by bus the winding 22km through dense rainforest to Deep Cove (permanent population: one), then head out on Doubtful Sound on another boat. Many tours include the power station. The easiest place to base yourself is Manapouri, although many tours pick up in Te Anau and Queenstown.

Real Journeys BOAT TOUR
(☎0800 656 501; www.realjourneys.co.nz) Has a Wilderness Cruise day trip (adult/child $235/65), beginning with a 45-minute boat ride across Lake Manapouri to West Arm power station, followed by a bus ride over Wilmot Pass to the sound, which you explore on a three-hour cruise. Pick up options from Te Anau or Queenstown are also available. To venture underground and admire a power station, take a separate Lake Manapouri cruise (adult/child $70/22, October to April). From September to May, Real Journeys also runs a Doubtful Sound overnight cruise. The *Fiordland Navigator* sleeps 70 and has twin-share, en-suite cabins (per adult/child from $675/337.50) and quad-share bunkrooms ($375/187.50). Transport to and from Te Anau or Queenstown is available. Prices include meals and kayaking or tender-craft trips.

Adventure Kayak & Cruise KAYAKING
(☎0800 324 966; www.fiordlandadventure.co.nz; ⏲late Sep-May) Kayaking day trips ($239) and overnight kayaking and camping trips ($269).

Fiordland Wilderness Experiences KAYAKING
(☎0800 200 434; www.seakayakfiordland.co.nz; per person $399-2250; ⏲Oct-Apr) Two- to five-day kayaking and camping trips around Doubtful Sound, and five-day kayaking trips in remote Dusky Sound. Accommodation is on the expedition vessel *Breaksea Girl* and includes all meals and helicopter transfers.

Deep Cove Charters CRUISE
(☎0800 249 682; www.doubtful-sound.com; bunk beds per person $500, private cabin $1200) Intimate overnight cruises with a maximum of

12 passengers. Includes meals, and you can fish for your own dinner.

Fiordland Cruises CRUISE
(☎0800 483 262; www.fiordlandcruises.co.nz; from $550) Overnight cruise including wildlife viewing and fishing. Maximum 12 passengers. Includes meals and transfers to/from Te Anau.

Fiordland Expeditions CRUISE
(☎0508 888 656; www.fiordlandexpeditions.co.nz; from $495) Overnight cruise. Ten-passenger maximum. Kayaking, diving, fishing, and dinner is whatever is caught from the boat.

Fiordland Explorer Charters CRUISE
(☎0800 434 673; www.doubtfulsoundcruise.com; day cruise adult/child $220/80) Day cruise with maximum of 20 people. Includes power-station tour and three hours on the sound.

Sleeping

Simple accommodation is available on the sound, but most travellers join an overnight cruise or kayak/camping trip to stay on the sound.

Deep Cove Hostel HOSTEL $
(☎03-218 7655; www.deepcovehostel.co.nz; per person $26-41; @) Bunks, cooking facilities and dinghies, all situated right on Doubtful Sound with a number of bush walks radiating from it. It's predominantly used by school groups, but casual guests are welcome. Booking ahead is essential.

SOUTHERN SCENIC ROUTE

The quiet, unhurried Southern Scenic Route begins in Queenstown and heads south via Te Anau to Tuatapere, Riverton and Invercargill. From Invercargill it continues north through the Catlins to Dunedin. See www.southernscenicroute.co.nz or pick up the free *Southern Scenic Route* map. Public transport is limited, but **Bottom Bus** (☎03-477 9083; www.travelheadfirst.com) offers regular shuttles.

From Manapouri the road follows the Waiau River south between the forested Takitimu and Hunter Mountains. Near Clifden is the elegant **Clifden Suspension Bridge**, built in 1899 and one of the longest bridges in the South Island. **Clifden (Waiau) Caves** are signposted on Otautau Rd, 2km from the Clifden Rd corner. These caves offer a scramble through crawl spaces and up ladders. Bring a friend, a spare torch and lots of caution. Visit Tuatapere visitor information centre for conditions and a map beforehand.

Just south of the suspension bridge is a turn-off to a walking track through **Dean Forest**, a reserve of ancient totara trees, 23km off the main road. From Clifden you can drive 30km of mostly unsealed road to Lake Hauroko, the deepest lake in NZ and surrounded by dark, brooding, steeply forested slopes. The area has many ancient *urupa* (burial sites) so be respectful and keep to trails. The Dusky Track also ends (or begins) here. **Lake Hauroko Tours** (☎03-226 6681; www.duskytrack.co.nz; tours incl lunch $120; ⏲Nov-Apr) has day-trip return tours from Tuatapere.

Tuatapere

POP 740

Formerly a timber-milling town, sleepy Tuatapere is now largely a farming centre. Those early woodcutters were very efficient, so only a remnant of a once large tract of native podocarp (conifer) forest remains.

Tuatapere visitor information centre (☎03-226 6739, 0800 486 774; www.humpridgetrack.co.nz; 31 Orawia Rd; ⏲9.30am-5pm, limited hours in winter) assists with visits to the Clifden Caves, Hump Ridge hut passes and transport. Adjacent is the **Bushman's Museum** (admission by donation), featuring an interesting photographic record of the area's timber-milling past

For more information on Tuatapere and the Western Southland area, see www.westernsouthland.co.nz. Don't leave without trying some of the excellent local sausages.

Activities

Tuatapere Hump Ridge Track TRAMPING
(☎03-226 6739; www.humpridgetrack.co.nz) The excellent 53km Tuatapere Hump Ridge Track climbs to craggy subalpine heights with views north to Fiordland and south to Stewart Island, and then descends through lush native forests of rimu and beech to the rugged coast. There's bird life aplenty, and the chance to see Hector's dolphins on the lonely windswept coast back to the start point. En route the path crosses a number of towering historic wooden viaducts, including NZ's highest. Beginning and ending at Bluecliffs Beach on Te Waewae Bay, 20km from Tuatapere, the track takes three fairly long days to complete.

Estimated walking times:

ROUTE	TIME
Bluecliffs Beach Car Park to Okaka Lodge	7-9hr
Okaka Lodge to Port Craig Village	7-9hr
Port Craig Village to Bluecliffs Beach Car Park	5-6hr

It's essential to book for this track, which is administered privately rather than by DOC. No-frills summer bookings cost from $130 for two nights, and there are also guided, jetboating and helihiking options.

Humpridge Jet JETBOATING
(☎0800 270 556; www.wildernessjet.co.nz; from $210) Options include a jetboat/helicopter combo or overnighting at the remote Waitutu Lodge.

W-Jet JETBOATING
(☎0800 376 174; www.wjet.co.nz; from $225) Includes a guided nature walk and barbecue.

Sleeping & Eating

Last Light Lodge HOLIDAY PARK $
(☎03-226 6667; www.lastlightlodge.com; 2 Clifden Hwy; sites from $15, dm $30, units $56-66) A funky spot in Tuatapere with loads of simple overnight options including camping, dorms and cabins. The attached Last Light Cafe does robust breakfasts and yummy snacks amid coolly retro furniture. Most of the food is organic, and lots of ingredients are sourced from their own gardens.

Shooters Backpackers & Tuatapere Motel HOLIDAY PARK $
(☎03-226 6250; www.tuataperaccommodation.co.nz; 73 Main St; sites from $30, dm $28, units $60-110; @ wi-fi) Communal spaces include a spacious kitchen with a wood stove, a big deck and barbecue, plus a spa and sauna. Camping is on a grassy lawn; more private are double rooms and self-contained units. Jetboating, diving and fishing trips can also be arranged.

Yesteryears Café CAFE $
(3a Orawia Rd; light meals $10-15) Rip into Aunt Daisy's sugar buns and a quintessentially Kiwi milkshake, and buy homemade jams for on-the-road breakfasts. There's an interesting jumble of quirky household items from local Tuatapere families.

Tuatapere to Riverton

On SH99, around 10km south of Tuatapere, stop at the spectacular lookout at **McCracken's Rest**. Cast your eye down the arcing sweep of **Te Waewae Bay** – where Hector's dolphins and southern right whales are sometimes seen – to the snowy peaks of Fiordland.

Colac Bay is a popular holiday place and a good surfing spot. Southerlies provide the best swells here, but it's pretty consistent year-round and never crowded. **Dustez Bak Paka's & Camping Ground** (☎03-234 8399; www.dustezbakpakas.co.nz; 15 Colac Bay Rd; sites from $29, dm $29, units $55-59) has basic rooms and campsites in a grassy field. Guests can borrow surfboards. Get dinner next door at the Colac Bay Tavern. Down at the beach, the Pavilion is known around Southland for its fish, organic lamb and garden-fresh herbs. It's also a top spot for a coffee and cake break.

Riverton

POP 1850

Quiet little Riverton, only 38km short of Invercargill, is worth a lunch stop and, if near-Antarctic swimming takes your fancy, the **Riverton Rocks** area and **Taramea Bay**

LOCAL KNOWLEDGE

COLAC BAY *KERI HULME*

Where two different strands of my ancestry found themselves: an American whaler captain, rumoured to be part-Tahitian, and a Kai Tahu/Kati Mamoe woman had a son who was my great-grandfather. There's not a lot in Colac Bay except beach and surf and the local *marae*. Oh, and there's Surfer Dude riding his wave at a slant angle. Classic baches and rock-fishing…a bit of fossicking along the low-tide line, and perhaps a trip to Cozy Nook? But the quintessential attraction of Colac Bay is the sound of those seas, that surf homing in: I have spent days, listening, wandering, listening, pondering, going to sleep with sea-song in my ears. It's a really choice place to blob out for a day or three or more. Be warned that the winds can be exceedingly strong, and bear Antarctic coldness with them – but there is also frequent calm and sun…

Keri Hulme, author & poet

(don't venture past the point) are good for a dip. A few **funky galleries** are definitely worth a browse.

Riverton visitor information centre (☎03-234 8260; www.riverton-aparima.co.nz; 127 Palmerston St; ⏲10am-4pm Oct-Apr, 11am-3pm Nov-Mar) has information about exploring the region's interesting geological heritage and can advise on accommodation.

Inside the centre, **Te Hikoi Southern Journey** (☎03-234 8260; www.tehikoi.co.nz; adult/child $5/free; ⏲10am-4pm summer, 11am-3pm winter) tells the story of the area's early Maori and Pakeha history.

Beach House (126 Rocks Hwy; mains $20-34; @) is a stylish, comfortable cafe that is famous for its seafood, especially its creamy chowder. On a sunny day with a warm breeze wafting off Foveaux Strait, the outside tables are a must. The other 90% of the time, retire inside to admire the sea view warm behind the windows. To find the cafe, follow signs along the coast to the lookout.

The chic little **Mrs Clark's Café** (108 Palmerston St; meals $12-123), with lots of reused timbers, chilled-out music and South Island beers and wines, occupies an insanely turquoise building that has been various forms of eatery since 1891. We doubt if its espressos and big breakfasts were quite so delicious back then.

The **South Coast Environment Centre** (www.sces.org.nz; 154 Palmerston St) has a good range of organic fruit, vegies and meats, is the local WWOOF (World Wide Opportunities on Organic Farms) agent, and organises the Riverton farmers market (Friday afternoons).

CENTRAL SOUTHLAND

Central Southland is the gateway to Stewart Island, and also a good jumping-off point for the Catlins and Fiordland.

Invercargill

POP 50,328

Flat and suburban, with endlessly treeless streets, Invercargill won't enthrall you if you came here via the Catlins or Fiordland. Nevertheless, most travellers in Southland will find themselves here at some point – perhaps stocking up on supplies and equipment before setting off to the Catlins or Stewart Island. Discover the town's arty bits, some good restaurants and a great little microbrewery.

Sights & Activities

Southland Museum & Art Gallery GALLERY
(www.southlandmuseum.com; Queens Park, 108 Gala St; admission by donation; ⏲9am-5pm) The art gallery hosts visiting exhibitions from contemporary Maori and local artists and occasional international shows. If you're headed for Stewart Island, visit the museum's 'Beyond the Roaring Forties' exhibition.

The museum's rock stars are undoubtedly the tuatara, NZ's unique lizardlike reptiles, unchanged for 220 million years. If the slow-moving 100-years-old-and-counting patriarch Henry is any example, they're not planning to do much for the next 220 million years either.

You'll find Henry and his reptilian mates in the tuatara enclosure. Feeding time is 4pm on Fridays, and outside opening hours, there are viewing windows at the rear of the pyramid.

Burt Munro MOTORBIKES, FILM LOCATION
If you're a fan of motorcyclist Burt Munro's speedy achievements, captured in *The World's Fastest Indian* (2005), you can see his famous motorbike at **E Hayes & Sons** (www.ehayes.co.nz; 168 Dee St). Other retro two-wheelers are on display and film merchandise is for sale. **Oreti Beach** (site of Burt's race against the troop of insolent young tearaways) is 10km to the southwest and a nice spot for a swim. The **Burt Munro Challenge** (www.burtmunrochallenge.com) is a popular motorbike event held each November. There's also a good display of Munrobilia at the Southland Museum.

Invercargill Brewery BREWERY
(☎03-214 5070; www.invercargillbrewery.co.nz; 8 Wood St; ⏲11am-5.30pm Mon-Thu, to 6.30pm Fri, to 4pm Sat) Tastings are free of charge, and if you're a real beer buff, the staff may be able to show you around the brewery. Phone ahead to check. Our favourites are the crisp Biman Pilsner and the hoppy Stanley Green Pale Ale. Regular seasonal brews include the Smokin' Bishop, a German-style *rauchbier* made with smoked malt.

Anderson Park Art Gallery GALLERY
(McIvor Rd; admission by donation; ⏲gallery 10.30am-5pm, gardens 8am-dusk) This excellent gallery in a 1925 Georgian-style manor contains works from many NZ artists. The landscaped gardens are studded with trees and trails, and include a children's playground and *wharepuni* (sleeping house). The gallery is 7km north of the city centre; follow North Rd then turn right into McIvor Rd.

Queens Park PARK

Wander around the half-wild, half-tamed Queens Park, with its trees, duck ponds, children's playground and Alice's castle.

Sleeping

Many places will store luggage for guests heading to Stewart Island. Motels cluster along Hwy 1 East (Tay St) and Hwy 6 North (North Rd).

TOP CHOICE **Bushy Point Fernbirds** HOMESTAY $$

(☎03-213 1302; www.fernbirds.co.nz; 197 Grant Rd; s/d incl breakfast $115/135) Two friendly corgis are among the hosts at this eco-aware homestay set on the edge of 4.5 hectares of private forest reserve and wetlands. Fernbirds is very popular with birding types, so booking ahead is essential. It's five minutes' drive from central Invercargill, and rates include a guided walk in the forest reserve.

Sparky's Backpackers HOSTEL $

(☎03-217 2905; www.sparkysbackpackers.co.nz; 271 Tay St; dm/d incl breakfast $25/60) Free breakfast, Sparky's chocolate cake and a genuine Southland welcome all feature at this quirky cross between a homestay and a hostel. The friendly owners were busy installing a new bathroom and an outdoor spa pool when we dropped by.

Victoria Railway Hotel HISTORIC HOTEL $$

(☎03-218 1281, 0800 777 557; www.hotelinvercargill.com; cnr Leven & Esk Sts; d $145-195) For a spot of 19th-century luxury, the plush rooms and swanky guests' areas in this grand old refurbished hotel fit the bill. The guests' dining room is elegant and the opulent house bar is crammed with South Island wines and local beers.

Living Space HOTEL $$

(☎03-211 3800; www.livingspace.net; 15 Tay St; d $75-129; @ wi-fi) Colourful, modern decor, ergonomically savvy design and relaxed service are showcased at this transformed 1907 warehouse. The studios are not huge, but feature self-contained kitchenettes and compact bathrooms.

Southern Comfort Backpackers HOSTEL $

(☎03-218 3838; 30 Thomson St; dm/s/d $28/65/66) Mellow, comfortable house with a TV-free lounge (hooray!), colourful rooms and a modern, well-equipped kitchen. Doubles are spacious and the lovely gardens are crammed with fresh herbs for cooking. Cash only.

388 Tay MOTEL $$

(☎0508 388 829, 03-217 3881; www.388taymotel.co.nz; 388 Tay St; d $120-160; wi-fi) Modern and spacious units and a friendly welcome are standard at this well-run spot that's a standout along Invercargill's Tay St motel alley.

Tuatara Lodge HOSTEL $

(☎03-214 0954; www.tuataralodge.co.nz; 30-32 Dee St; dm $29, d $69-80; @ wi-fi) Rooms here are fairly basic, but they're clean and comfortable and it's the most central of Invercargill's budget accommodation. Staff are friendly and downstairs is a groovy traveller-focused cafe-bar. Transport to/from Bluff for Stewart Island stops just outside.

Invercargill Top 10 Holiday Park HOLIDAY PARK $

(☎0800 486 873, 03-215 9032; www.invercargilltop10.co.nz; 77 McIvor Rd; sites from $19, units $78-150; @) This quiet leafy place 6.5km north of town has private sites and good communal facilities. Modern, comfortable studios and self-contained cabins have en suites.

Eating

Duo RESTAURANT $$

(☎03-218 8322; 16 Kelvin St; lunch $16-22, dinner $32; ⊙11.30am-2pm & 5.30pm-late) The elegant Duo has good-value lunch specials and a more expensive evening menu. Standouts include smoked salmon, herb-and-feta-crusted pork steaks and oven-baked blue cod. The wine list travels mainly to nearby Central Otago for some hard-to-find boutique tipples. Booking for dinner is recommended.

The Batch CAFE $$

(173 Spey St; snacks & mains $8-15) Lots of shared tables, a relaxed beachy ambience and top-notch coffee and smoothies add up to the cafe being regularly voted Southland's best. Delicious counter food includes bagels and brownies, and a smallish wine and beer list partners healthy lunch options. Open later on Friday nights, until 7.30pm.

Seriously Good Chocolate Company CAFE $

(147 Spey St; ⊙Mon-Fri) This sunny spot a short walk from central Invercargill specialises in individual artisan chocolates (around $1.50 each). Order a coffee and then abandon yourself to the difficult task of choosing flavours. The chilli and peanut cluster variations were both good enough for us to return a second day. Like it says on the tin… seriously good.

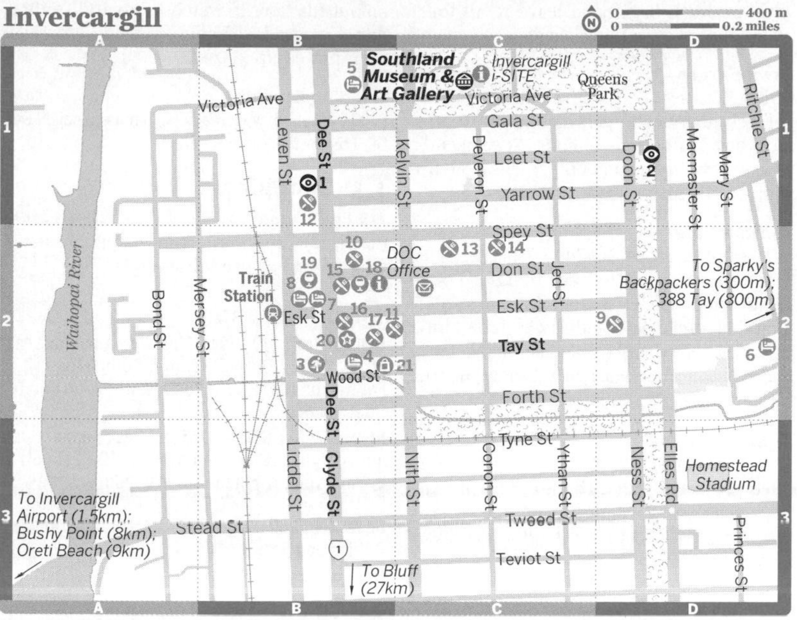

Invercargill

Top Sights
- Southland Museum & Art Gallery C1

Sights
- 1 E Hayes & Sons B1
- 2 Water Tower D1

Activities, Courses & Tours
- 3 Invercargill Brewery B2

Sleeping
- 4 Living Space B2
- 5 Southern Comfort Backpackers B1
- 6 Sparky's Backpackers D2
- 7 Tuatara Lodge B2
- 8 Victoria Railway Hotel B2

Eating
- 9 Countdown D2
- 10 Devil Burger B2
- 11 Duo B2
- 12 Louie's Café B1
- 13 Seriously Good Chocolate Company C2
- 14 The Batch C2
- 15 Three Bean Café B2
- Tuatara Café .... (see 7)
- 16 Turkish Kebabs B2
- 17 Zookeepers Cafe B2

Drinking
- 18 Kiln B2
- 19 Speight's Ale House B2

Entertainment
- 20 Reading Cinemas B2
- Tillermans Music Lounge .... (see 10)

Shopping
- 21 H&J's Outdoor World B2

Zookeepers Cafe CAFE $$
(50 Tay St; meals $15-30) The Zookeepers is easily spotted by the giant corrugated-iron elephant on the roof. Staff are laid-back and friendly, and the meals are good value and tasty. Tuck into a warm balsamic beef salad or sip an Invercargill Brewery beer. Try the Wasp lager, a southern honey-infused spin on a traditional Pilsner.

Three Bean Café CAFE $
(73 Dee St; meals $12-16) Some of Invercargill's best coffee and casual eats are at this cosmopolitan main-drag cafe. Kick your day off

with a salmon bagel, and leave room for a baked slice of something sweet.

Devil Burger BURGERS $
(16 Don St; burgers $10-16, wraps $12-16; ⊙from 11am; ✎) Tasty gourmet burgers and healthy wraps, including lots of vegie options. At weekends, expect crowds of hungry burger fans from upstairs at Tillermans Music Lounge.

Tuatara Café CAFE $
(30-32 Dee St; meals $10-20; ⊙7am-late; @☎) The cafe attached to the Tuatara Lodge backpackers hostel is cool in a traveller-focused, dreadlocks-and-Kiwi dub kinda way. Scrambled eggs on toast make for a hearty good-value start to the day and the burgers are tasty and interesting.

Turkish Kebabs TURKISH $
(29 Esk St; from $13.50; ✎) Tasty hummusy felafels and kebabs, all with the option of dine-in or takeaway. For indecisive diners, there's also Japanese and Indian food a few doors either side.

Countdown SUPERMARKET
(cnr Doon & Tay Sts) This is Invercargill's biggest supermarket.

Drinking & Entertainment

Louie's Café CAFE
(142 Dee St; ⊙Wed-Sat) This cosy cafe-bar specialises in tapas-style snacks ($12), and there's also a concise blackboard menu (mains $20 to $30). Relax near the fireside, tuck yourself away in various nooks and crannies, or spread out on a comfy padded sofa and enjoy the chilled-out music. There are occasional live gigs.

Tillermans Music Lounge LIVE MUSIC
(16 Don St; ⊙9pm-late) Tillerman's is an alternative live-music/DJ venue, with live music ranging from local thrash bands to visiting rock or reggae talents. DJs spin mostly dub and house. Decrepit black couches and a battered old dance floor prove its credentials.

Kiln PUB
(7 Don St) Stylish bar with hanging lampshades, underlit bar and Great Aunt Edith's wallpaper. Easily the most civilised drinking option in town and surprisingly good food too. Try the parmesan-crusted blue cod with a Summer Ale.

Speight's Ale House PUB
(38 Dee St) Big-screen TVs for live sport, and Speight's brews south from Dunedin. Grab an outside table to watch Invercargill's after-dark cavalcade of annoying boy racers in their hotted-up Mazdas.

Reading Cinemas CINEMA
(☎03-211 1555; www.readingcinemas.co.nz; 29 Dee St) Discounts on Tuesdays.

Shopping

H&J's Outdoor World OUTDOOR EQUIPMENT
(32 Tay St) Everything from maps and boots to sleeping bags and dried food.

Information

DOC office (☎03-211 2400; www.doc.govt.nz; 7th fl, 33 Don St; ⊙8.30am-4.30pm Mon-Fri) For info on tracks around Stewart Island and Southland.

Invercargill i-SITE (☎03-211 0895; www.invercargillnz.com; Queens Park, 108 Gala St; ⊙8am-5pm; @) In the same building as the Southland Museum & Art Gallery. Bikes can be rented, and it's good for information on the Catlins and Stewart Island.

Post office (51 Don St)

Getting There & Away

Air

Air New Zealand (☎0800 737 000; www.airnewzealand.co.nz) flights link Invercargill to Christchurch (from $89, one hour) several times a day. **Stewart Island Flights** (☎03-218 9129; www.stewartislandflights.com) link Stewart Island and Invercargill (adult/child one-way $115/75, return $195/115, 20 minutes) three times a day. Ask about discounted standby fares.

Bus

Buses leave from the Invercargill i-SITE, where you can also book your tickets. Travel time to Dunedin is four hours, Te Anau three hours, Queenstown four hours, and Christchurch 10 hours. The Catlins Coaster (p281) and Bottom Bus (p273) also pass through Invercargill.

InterCity (www.intercity.co.nz) To Te Anau, Dunedin and Christchurch.

Atomic Shuttles (www.atomictravel.co.nz) To Dunedin and Christchurch.

Knightrider (www.knightrider.co.nz) Overnight to Dunedin and Christchurch; good to catch morning flights from either city.

Naked Bus (www.nakedbus.com) To Te Anau, Queenstown and Dunedin.

Tracknet (www.tracknet.net) To Te Anau and Queenstown.

Getting Around

Invercargill Airport (☎03-218 6920; www.invercargillairport.co.nz; 106 Airport Ave) is 3km west of central Invercargill. The door-to-door **Airport Shuttle** (☎03-214 3434) costs $12 from the city centre to the airport; more for residential pick-up. By taxi it's around $20; try **Blue Star Taxis** (☎03-218 6079) or **City Cabs** (☎03-214 4444).

Bluff

POP 2100

Bluff is Invercargill's port, 27km south of the city. The main reasons to come here are to catch the ferry to Stewart Island, pose for photos beside the **Stirling Point signpost**, or buy famous Bluff oysters. Also at Stirling Point is a huge chain-link sculpture by NZ artist Russell Beck. It symbolises the Maori legend where the South Island is the canoe of Maui and Stewart Island is the boat's anchor. At Stirling Point, the chain disappears into the ocean, and a companion sculpture on Stewart Island represents the other end of the anchor chain.

While Bluff isn't the South Island's southernmost point (that claim belongs to Slope Point in the Catlins), and even though Stewart Island and other dots of rock lie even further south, the phrase 'from Cape Reinga to Bluff' is oft-quoted to signify the entire length of NZ. NZ's main highway, SH1, terminates south of Bluff at Stirling Point, so it really does feel like the end of the country.

Kids will enjoy the small **Bluff Maritime Museum** (☎03-212 7534; 241 Foreshore Rd; adult/child $2/free; ⏰10am-4.30pm Mon-Fri, 1-5pm Sat & Sun) and clambering over a century-old oyster boat, while steam nerds will love the big old 600hp steam engine. There are interesting displays on Bluff's history complete the exhibition.

The **Bluff Oyster & Food Festival** (www.bluffoysterfest.co.nz) celebrates Bluff's most famous exports, and is held annually, usually in May. The oysters are in season from late March to late August. To buy fresh Bluff oysters, visit **Fowlers Oysters** (Ocean Beach Rd; ⏰9am-5pm Mar-Aug) on the way into town on the left.

Near the Four Square supermarket, **Stella's** (64 Gore St; ⏰6.30am-2pm) is your best bet for a coffee before braving the ferry crossing to Stewart Island. The seafood chowder and pies are pretty good too.

For more information, see www.bluff.co.nz.

Invercargill to Dunedin

Following SH1 is the most direct route between Invercargill and Dunedin. The pastoral scenery is pretty, but not as spectacular as the SH92 route via the Catlins. If you've got time, opt for the latter.

THE CATLINS

If you veer off SH1 and head for the coastal route between Invercargill and Dunedin (via SH92), you wind through the enchanting Catlins, a region that combines lush farmland, native forests and rugged bays. With bushwalks, wildlife-spotting opportunities and lonely beaches to explore, the Catlins is well worth a couple of days.

On a clear summer's day, surrounded by forest greens and ocean blues, there's nothing more beautiful than the Catlins coast. In the face of a sleety Antarctic southerly, it's a very different environment. Good luck.

The Catlins

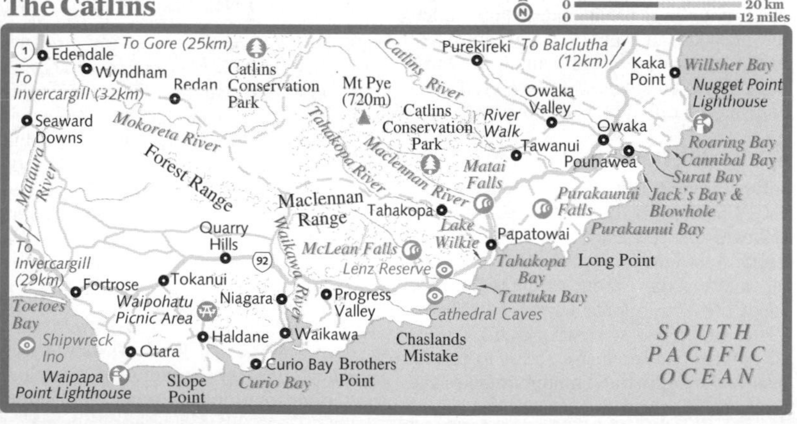

WORTH A TRIP

GORE

Around 66km northeast of Invercargill, Gore is the proud 'home of country music' in New Zealand, with the annual **Gold Guitar Week** (www.goldguitars.co.nz) in late May and early June ensuring all the town's accommodation is booked out for at least 10 days per year. For the other 355 days, good reasons to stop include a surprisingly cool art gallery, vintage biplanes and whisky tasting at the Hokonui Moonshine Museum. See www.gorenz.com for more local information.

The interesting **Hokonui Moonshine Museum** (www.hokonuiwhiskey.com; admission $5; ⌚9am-4.30pm Mon-Fri, 10am-3.30pm Sat & Sun) and the **Gore Historical Museum** (admission by donation; ⌚9am-4.30pm Mon-Fri, 10am-3.30pm Sat & Sun) share the same building and celebrate Gore's proud history of fishing, farming and illegal distilleries. Admission to the Moonshine Museum includes a wee dram of the local liquid gold.

The outstanding **Eastern Southland Gallery** (☎03-208 9907; 14 Hokonui Dr; admission by donation; ⌚10am-4.30pm Mon-Fri, 1-4pm Sat & Sun), in Gore's century-old former public library, houses a hefty collection of NZ art including a large Ralph Hotere collection. The amazing John Money Collection combines indigenous folk art from West Africa and Australia with works by iconic New Zealand artist Rita Angus.

Croydon Aircraft Company (☎03-208 9755; www.croydonaircraft.com; SH94), 16km down the road to Queenstown, restores vintage aircraft and, for wannabe WWI flying aces, offers flights in a two-seater 1930s Tiger Moth biplane ($55/160 for 10/30 minutes) or other wee aircraft. There's also good eating at the **Moth** (www.themoth.co.nz; 1558a Waimea Hwy; lunch & pizza $11-24, 2-/3-course dinner $42/52; ⌚10am-4pm Mon-Tue, 10am-late Wed-Sun) restaurant.

This route has many twists, turns and narrow sections, and while it's similar in distance, it's slower going than the inland route along SH1.

Flora & Fauna

The Catlins is a wonderful place for independent wildlife-watching. Fur seals and sea lions laze along the coast, while elephant seals breed at Nugget Point. In spring, keep your eyes peeled for southern right whales. Dolphins are also frequent visitors.

Unlike much of Southland, tall kahikatea, totara and rimu forests still exist in the Catlins. Prolific bird life includes the wonderfully noisy tui, and you'll also see kereru (NZ pigeons). Other sea, estuary and forest birds include the endangered yellow-eyed penguin and the rare mohua (yellowhead).

Activities

Catlins Adventures ADVENTURE TOUR
(☎03-415 8339, 027 416 8822; www.catlinsadventures.co.nz; per person 1/2 days $175/295) Energetic, switched-on operators offering one- and two-day Catlins scenic tours, river walking ($75), rainforest kayaking ($75) and yellow-eyed penguin viewing ($89). Catlins Adventures have exclusive access to certain areas of the Catlins, and mountain bikes and kayaks are also available for hire.

Catlins Wildlife Trackers WILDLIFE
(☎0800 228 5467, 03-415 8613; www.catlins-ecotours.co.nz) Papatowai-based Catlins Wildlife Trackers offer eco-centric guided walks and tours (three nights/two days $800), including all food, accommodation and transport. These conservation gurus have been running tours since 1990 and also manage Top Track, a 26km self-guided walk through beaches and a private forest; it costs $25 if you walk it in a 10-hour day, or $45 if you do it in two, including overnighting in a converted trolley bus. Guided trips focusing on wildlife are also available.

Catlins Surf School SURFING
(☎03-246 8552; www.catlins-surf.co.nz) Located in Porpoise Bay near Curio Bay, the Catlins Surf School runs 90-minute surfing lessons for $50. The occasional group of dolphin spectators is free of charge. If you're already confident on the waves, hire a board and wetsuit (very necessary) for three hours ($40). Owner Nick also offers tuition in stand-up paddleboarding (2½ hours, $75).

Catlins Marine Encounters BOAT TOUR
(☎03-929 6580, 027 212 1327; www.catlinsmarineencounters.co.nz) This Waikawa-based company offers a variety of ways to explore the Catlins' marine environment including

sea-mammal watching ($80), birdwatching and scenic harbour cruises ($45), and diving and fishing charters.

Catlins Horse Riding HORSE RIDING
(☎03-415 8368, 027 269 2904; www.catlinshorseriding.co.nz; 41 Newhaven Rd, Owaka; 1/2/3hr rides $40/70/90) the idiosyncratic coastline and landscapes on four legs with Catlins Horse Riding. Full-day rides including lunch are $180.

Tours

Bottom Bus TOUR
(☎03-477 9083; www.bottombus.co.nz; from $175) Does a regular loop from Queenstown to Dunedin, south through the Catlins to Invercargill, along the Southern Scenic Route to Te Anau, then back to Queenstown. It stops at all main points of interest, and you can hop off and catch the next bus coming through. There are lots of pass options. The Southlander pass ($375) lets you start anywhere on the loop and includes a Milford Sound cruise.

Catlins Coaster TOUR
(☎03 477 9083; www.catlinscoaster.co.nz; from $210) Run by Bottom Bus and offering day tours and trips through the Catlins from Dunedin and Invercargill. Check the website for details. Departures are more limited in winter.

Information

Contact the main **Catlins information centre** (☎03-415 8371; www.cluthacountry.co.nz; 20 Ryley St; ⏰9.30am-1pm & 1.30-4.30pm Mon-Fri, 10am-4pm Sat & Sun) in Owaka or the smaller **Waikawa visitors centre** (☎03-205 8006; waikawamuseum@hyper.net.nz; Main Rd; ⏰10am-5pm; @). The I-SITEs in Invercargill and Balclutha also have lots of Catlins information. Online, see www.catlins.org.nz and www.catlins-nz.com.

The Catlins has no banks and limited options for eating out or grocery shopping (except in Owaka). There's an ATM at the 4 Square supermarket in Owaka, and petrol stations (hours can be irregular) in Fortrose, Papatowai and Owaka. Stock up and fill up before you arrive.

Invercargill to Papatowai

Heading east and south from Invercargill, SH92 enters the Catlins region at Fortrose, from where the **Shipwreck Ino** is visible across the sandy harbour at low tide. Take the turn-off here towards Waipapa Point and use the coastal route via Haldane, Waikawa and Niagara (where you rejoin SH92). It's a slower, but more beautiful route, with lots to check out along the way. The **Waipapa Point lighthouse** dates from 1884, three years after a terrible maritime disaster when SS *Tararua* sank and 131 people drowned.

Turn off at Haldane and drive 5km to **Slope Point**, the South Island's southernmost point. A 20-minute walk across farmland leads to a stubby beacon and stubbier signpost atop a windswept spur with views up and down the coast. The track is closed in September and October for lambing.

Further east at **Curio Bay**, fossilised Jurassic-age trees are visible for four hours either side of low tide. The lookout is the place to be an hour or so before sunset, when you'll see yellow-eyed penguins waddling ashore. Just before Curio Bay, neighbouring **Porpoise Bay** has excellent accommodation and a beach that's safe for swimming. Blue penguins nest in the dunes and in summer Hector's dolphins come here to rear their young. Whales are occasional visitors, and fur seals and sea lions are often lounging on the rocks. It's also a good place to learn to surf.

A 4km drive past the McLean Falls Holiday Park, the walk to **McLean Falls** (40 minutes return) passes through tree ferns and rimu. Don't stop at the first falls – the real thing is a bit further on.

Cutting back into cliffs right on the beach, the huge, arched **Cathedral Caves** (www.cathedralcaves.co.nz; adult/child $5/1) are accessible only for two hours either side of low tide (tide timetables are posted on the website, at the highway turn-off and at visitor information centres). If you're happy to wade, you can walk in one entrance and out the other. From SH92 it's 2km to the car park, then a peaceful 15-minute forest walk down to the beach and a further 25 minutes to the caves.

Around 10km further east, an easy forest walk leads down to the dark peaty waters of Lake Wilkie (30 minutes return). A turn-off soon leads to secluded **Tahakopa Bay**. Just before the descent into Papatowai, stop at the **Florence Hill Lookout** with spectacular views of the sweeping arc of **Tautuku Bay**.

Papatowai provides a base for forays into the nearby forests. There's a handful of accommodation options and a general store selling petrol. There's also good picnicking at the mouth of the Tahakopa River.

Lost Gypsy Gallery (☎03-415 8908; SH92; ⏰11am-5pm Thu-Tue; 📶) occupies a roadside house-bus at Papatowai. Based on found objects, specialising in self-wound automata and things that go whirrr, this place is guaranteed to make you laugh. A fascinating gallery (admission $5, young children not allowed, sorry...) showcases some of artist Blair Sommerville's larger one-off pieces. We especially like the TV that runs on bicycle power. Blair's always up for a good chat, and there's also a funky coffee caravan and wi-fi.

Sleeping

SLOPE POINT

Slope Point Backpackers HOSTEL $
(☎03-246 8420; www.slopepoint.co.nz; 164 Slope Point Rd; sites per person from $12, dm $22-27, d $47, unit $87; wi-fi) Surrounded by trees, this rural property has modern dorms and rooms, along with a great-value self-contained unit. There's plenty of grass to pitch a tent or park a campervan, and the owners' children are always keen to show off the working farm. Board games, puzzles and loads of magazines take the place of TV.

Nadir Outpost GUESTHOUSE $
(☎03-246 8544; www.catlins-slopepoint.com; 174 Slope Point Rd; d $90) Nadir offers double rooms inside the owners' house, and a cosy, standalone cabin with kitchen facilities. There's a shop selling basic supplies and a forested area to pitch a tent ($12 per person) or park a van ($29 for two people). Meals are also available (breakfast $7 to $14, dinner $25).

CURIO BAY

Curio Bay Boutique Studios APARTMENT $$
(☎03-246 8797; www.curiobay.co.nz; 501 Curio Bay Rd; d $220) With big windows and an even bigger deck, these two plush beachside units are open to awesome sea views. Recline on the giant, rustic, timber-framed bed to feel like a king or queen. A splurgeworthy and romantic retreat if you're celebrating someone or something special.

Lazy Dolphin Lodge HOSTEL $
(☎03-246 8579; www.lazydolphinlodge.co.nz; 529 Curio Bay Rd; dm/d/tw $33/72/72; @ wi-fi) New owners have given this long-established place a renewed energy, and the views from the big lounge and deck towards the Porpoise Bay breakers are still among the South Island's finest. Other traveller-friendly benefits include private beach access and occasional sightings of seals and dolphins.

Curio Bay Holiday Park HOLIDAY PARK $
(☎03-246 8897; valwhyte@hotmail.com; 601 Curio Bay Rd; sites from $15) Very private campsites lost in a sea of tall flax make this a beautiful spot to camp. The camping ground nestles up to the small outcrop between Curio and Porpoise Bays, within easy walking distance to both. Guided nature walks are available.

Catlins Beach House RENTAL HOUSE $
(☎03-246 8340; www.catlinsbeachhouse.co.nz; 499 Curio Bay Rd; dm $25, d $70-95) This extremely comfortable house has a cosy woodburner for heating, a good kitchen, and a deck that opens onto a grassy lawn sloping down to the beach. Blue penguins nest hereabouts and can be heard waddling past making cute penguin sounds at night.

Catlins Surf Cottages RENTAL HOUSE $$
(☎03-246 8552; www.catlins-surf.co.nz; houses $110-190) A range of self-contained cottages and houses around Curio Bay can be rented from Catlins Surf. One-night rentals are fine, and it's a good option for travelling families or groups of three or four.

WAIKAWA

Penguin Paradise Holiday Lodge HOSTEL $
(☎03-246 8552; www.catlins-surf.co.nz; 612 Niagara-Waikawa Rd; dm/d/tw $25/56/56) Laid-back backpackers in a heritage cottage in Waikawa village near the estuary. Special combo deals ($70) of one night's accommodation and a 1½-hour surf lesson are also available.

Waikava Harbourview RENTAL HOUSE $$
(☎03-246 8866; www.southcatlins.co.nz; 14 Larne St; d $130-170) Waikava Harbourview is a four-bedroom house that's a good option for families or a group; up to 10 people can be accommodated. Opened in 2009, the newer one- and two-bedroom Harakeke and Toi Tois units are also good value.

MCLEAN FALLS

McLean Falls Holiday Park HOLIDAY PARK $
(☎03-415 8338; www.catlinscamping.com; SH92; sites per person $20, units $75-195; @ wi-fi) Just off the main road, McLean Falls Holiday Park has a number of Kiwiana-style cabins, newer chalets, and sites for vans and tents. The amenities blocks are spacious and very well maintained. The attached **Whistling Frog Café & Bar** (meals $10-30; ⏲8.30am-9pm) does breakfast, lunch and dinner with a surprisingly cosmopolitan spin, and there's a good selection of South Island beer and wine.

PAPATOWAI

TOP CHOICE **Hilltop** LODGE $
(☎03-415 8028; www.hilltopcatlins.co.nz; 77 Tahakopa Valley Rd; dm $34, d $85-100) High on a hill

1.5km out of town, with native forest at the back door and surrounded by a sheep farm, this lovely old renovated pair of houses has spectacular views of the surrounding hills and the ocean. The en-suite double makes for a luxurious mini-splurge.

Catlins Wildlife Trackers COTTAGES $$
(0800 228 5467; www.catlins-ecotours.co.nz; d $145-170) This tour company offers a variety of accommodation around Papatowai, including the modern Pipipi eco-cottage, and four very comfortable, ecofriendly cottages (www.catlinsmohuapark.co.nz) on the edge of a native forest reserve.

Eating

You'll find roadside takeaways in Waikawa and Papatowai. The Papatoawi general store has a limited range of groceries.

TOP CHOICE **Niagara Falls Café** CAFE $$
(www.niagarafallscafe.co.nz; Main Rd; meals $13-24; 8am-10pm;) Sharing a restored schoolhouse with a local art gallery, this is a friendly spot for a meal. Tuck into delicious, good-value cooking including steaks, blue cod and rack of lamb, or linger over coffee and home-cooked cakes and muffins. The beer and wine list is impressive, and the mighty falls themselves are nearby. Vegetarian and gluten-free options abound.

Papatowai to Balcutha

From Papatowai, follow the highway north to **Matai Falls** (a 30-minute return walk) on the Maclennan River, then head southeast on the signposted road to the tiered **Purakaunui Falls** (20 minutes return). Both falls are reached via cool, dark forest walks through totara and tree fern.

Continue along the gravel road from Purakaunui Falls to the 55m-deep **Jack's Blowhole**. In the middle of a sheep paddock 200m from the sea but connected by a subterranean cavern, this huge cauldron was named after Chief Tuhawaiki, nicknamed Bloody Jack for his cussin'. It's a fairly brisk 30-minute walk each way.

Owaka is the Catlins' main town (population a hefty 395), with a good information centre, a 4 Square grocery store – including an ATM – and a petrol station. An excellent **museum** (adult/child $5/free; 9.30am-1pm & 1.30-4.30pm Mon-Fri, 10am-4pm Sat & Sun), attached to the information centre, has displays on local history. An attached theatrette shows interesting videos on the Catlins' deserved reputation as a shipwreck coast. Once you've stocked up or stopped for a meal, venture off to more remote, more attractive parts of the Catlins.

Pounawea, 4km east, is a beautiful little riverside town with some lovely places to stay. Across the inlet, **Surat Bay** is even quieter and also has accommodation. Sea lions are often seen on the beach between here and **Cannibal Bay**, a 30-minute beach walk away.

Heading north from Owaka, detour off SH92 to **Nugget Point**, stopping for the short walk out to the lighthouse at the end – the last 900m or so, with drops to the ocean on either side, is breathtaking, and the view of wave-thrashed vertical rock formations from the end is great, too. A spacious DOC viewing platform huddles around the lighthouse. Fur seals, sea lions and elephant seals occasionally bask together on the rocks down to your left, a rare and noisy coexistence. Yellow-eyed and blue penguins, shags and sooty shearwaters all breed here. Ten minutes' walk down from a car park is **Roaring Bay**, where a well-placed hide allows you to see yellow-eyed penguins coming ashore (best two hours before sunset). The best viewing is from a newly constructed hide. You should not use a flash when photographing the penguins. If you don't have your own transport, nightly **twilight tours** (0800 525 278; www.catlins.co.nz; per person $30) are run by the Nugget View and Kaka Point Motels.

From Nugget Point the road loops back through the little township of **Kaka Point**, which has a sandy, quiet beach and accommodation and is a nice spot for a meal. The road continues north from here to Balclutha.

Sleeping

OWAKA & PURAKAUNUI

DOC Camping Grounds CAMPSITE $
(www.doc.govt.nz; campsites $6) There are DOC camping grounds at Purakaunui Bay and inland at Tawanui.

POUNAWEA

Pounaewa Grove Motel MOTEL $$
(03-415 8339; www.pounaweagrove.co.nz; 5 Ocean Grove; d $120;) Well managed by a friendly Kiwi–South African couple, these chic and stylish units are literally metres from the ocean. Flat-screen TVs, free wi-fi and modern bathrooms are thoroughly 21st century, but the enduring grandeur and energy of the Catlins coastline is on tap just outside. The motel is also the home base for the excellent Catlins Adventures (p280).

Pounawea Motor Camp HOLIDAY PARK $
(☎03-415 8483; www.catlins-nz.com/pounawea-motor-camp; Park Lane; sites from $28, units $45-80) Sitting right on the estuary and surrounded by native bush ringing with birdsong, this is a gem of a place to park your tent. Others think so too, and in the frenzied post-Christmas season you'll be sharing this beautiful spot with many Kiwi and international holidaymakers.

SURAT BAY

Newhaven Holiday Park HOLIDAY PARK $
(☎03-415 8834; www.newhavenholiday.com; Newhaven Rd; sites from $30, units $66-120; @☜) A few minutes' walk from the beach is this little camping area with modern cabins and facilities and three self-contained flats. Rent kayaks and bikes from Surat Bay Lodge, next door.

Surat Bay Lodge HOSTEL $
(☎03-415 8099; www.suratbay.co.nz; Surat Bay Rd; dm/d $29/68; @) Right beside the start of the track down to the beach, and next-door neighbours with the sea lions, this superbly located hostel has cosy, brightly decorated rooms and a friendly vibe. Rent a kayak ($12 to $40) or bike ($30 per day) and get exploring.

NUGGET & KAKA POINTS

Nugget Lodge LODGE $$
(☎03-412 8783; www.nuggetlodge.co.nz; Nugget Rd; d $165; ☜) Perched above the sea on the road south to the lighthouse, this pair of self-contained units has spectacular views up and down the coast. It's worth including their huge breakfast ($12.50 per person) with freshly baked bread and homemade muesli. If you're lucky you might spy a couple of resident sea lions lolling on the beach below you.

Nugget View & Kaka Point Motels MOTEL $$
(☎0800 525 278; www.catlins.co.nz; 11 Rata St; d $95-200; ☜) A veritable mini-village of motel options ranging from excellent-value older units through to more modern accommodation with private spa baths and verandahs. The friendly owners also operate one- and two-day tours of the Catlins, and twilight tours ($30 per person) to view Nugget Point and the penguin colony at Roaring Bay.

Kaka Point Camping Ground HOLIDAY PARK $
(☎03-412 8801; www.kakapointcamping.co.nz; 39 Tarata St; sites from $13.50, cabins per person $24; ☜) Cabins are basic but functional, and there is a lovely grassy, hedged area to pitch tents. There are bushwalks into the surrounding forest, and it's a short, though steep, stroll downhill to the beach and town.

Fernlea Backpackers HOSTEL $
(☎03-418 0117, 03-412 8834; Moana St; dm/d $25/55) Perched atop a hill, and a leafy, zigzag path above the street below, this tiny, basic bungalow is ultra-snug, with lovely sea views and basic facilities. Sometimes closed from May to September so phone ahead.

Eating

OWAKA

Catlins Cafe CAFE $$
(www.catlinscafe.co.nz; 3 Main Rd; mains $12-25; ☜) This super-cosy highway culinary diversion comes with loads of retro Kiwiana touches including comfy old sofas and rustic wooden furniture. The food's equally hearty and familiar from muesli and eggs Benedict for breakfast, through to top-notch burgers for lunch, and steak and blue cod for dinner. South Island wines and beers partner a serious approach to coffee.

Lumberjack Bar & Café CAFE $$
(3 Saunders St; mains $15-30; ⊙Tue-Sun) Park yourself at one of the Lumberjack's trademark rustic wooden tables and tuck into huge Catlins-sized meals including good burgers, steaks and seafood.

4 Square SUPERMARKET
(3 Ovenden St) Stock up for self-catering.

KAKA POINT

Point Café & Bar PUB $$
(58 Esplanade; bar menu $5-15, mains $27-30) Prop yourself at the driftwood bar for a cool beer, or grab a window seat for a sea view. Takeaways are also available at the attached store – grab a burger ($5) for the road.

Stewart Island

Travellers who undertake the short jaunt to Stewart Island will be rewarded with a warm welcome from both the local kiwi and the local Kiwis. New Zealand's 'third' island is a good place to spy the country's shy, feathered icon in the wild, and the close-knit community of Stewart Islanders (population 420) are relaxed hosts. If you're staying on the island for just a few days, don't be too surprised if most people quickly know who you are and where you came from – especially if you mix and mingle over a beer at NZ's southernmost pub, in the main settlement of Oban.

Once you've said g'day to the locals, there's plenty of active adventure on offer including kayaking and setting off on a rewarding tramp in Stewart Island's Rakiura National Park. With a worthwhile injection of effort, relative newcomers to tramping can easily complete one of NZ's Great Walks, and be surprised and entertained with an uninterrupted aria from native birds. And if a multiday tramp still sounds too intense, spying a kiwi in the wild can also be achieved with the straightforward combination of a short boat ride and an even shorter bush and beach walk.

History

Stewart Island's Maori name is Rakiura (Glowing Skies), and catch a glimpse of a spectacular blood-red sunset or the aurora australis and you'll quickly know why. According to myth, NZ was hauled up from the ocean by Maui, who said, 'Let us go out of sight of land, far out in the open sea, and when we have quite lost sight of land, then let the anchor be dropped.' The North Island was the fish that Maui caught, the South Island his canoe and Rakiura was the anchor – Te Punga o te Waka o Maui.

There is evidence that parts of Rakiura were occupied by moa hunters as early as the 13th century. The titi (muttonbird or sooty shearwater) on adjacent islands were an important seasonal food source for the southern Maori.

The first European visitor was Captain Cook, who sailed around the eastern, southern and western coasts in 1770 but couldn't figure out if it was an island or a peninsula. Deciding it was attached to the South Island, he called it South Cape. In 1809 the sealing vessel *Pegasus* circumnavigated Rakiura and named it after its first officer, William Stewart.

In June 1864 Stewart and the adjacent islets were bought from local Maori for £6000. Early industries were sealing, timber-milling, fish-curing and shipbuilding, with a short-lived gold rush towards the end of the 19th century. Today the island's economy is dependent on tourism and fishing, including crayfish (lobster), paua (abalone), salmon, mussels and cod.

Stewart Island (Rakiura)

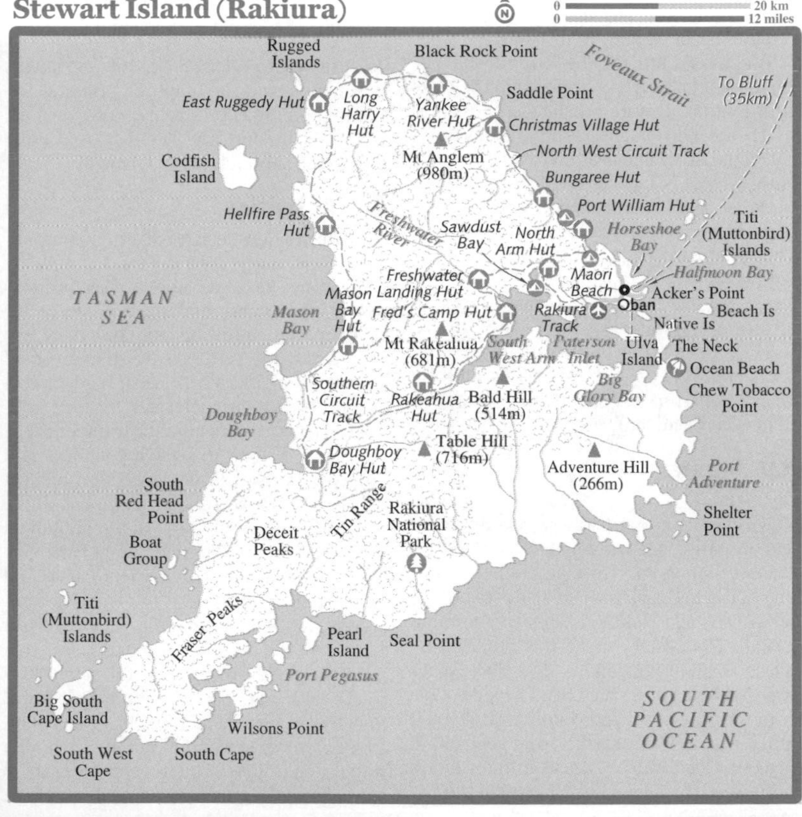

THE IMPORTANCE OF BEING PREPARED

Stewart Island's changeable weather can bring four seasons in one day. Frequent downpours create a misty, mysterious air and lots of mud, making boots and waterproof clothing mandatory. Make sure you're prepared for a variety of seasons. Nevertheless, the temperature is milder than you'd expect, with winter averaging around 10°C and summer 16.5°C.

Flora & Fauna

Nature has cranked the birdsong up to 11 here; you can't miss the tui, parakeets, kaka, bellbirds, fernbirds, robins and dotterels that constantly flap overhead and serenade you from gardens. You can also see kiwi and Fiordland crested, yellow-eyed and blue penguins. Ask locals about the evening parade of penguins on a small beach near the wharf. Don't feed any of the birds, as you run the risk of passing on diseases.

Two species of deer, the red and the Virginia (whitetail), were introduced in the early 20th century, as were brush-tailed possums, which are now numerous in the northern half of the island and destructive to the native bush. Stewart Island also has NZ fur seals.

Unlike NZ's North and South Islands, there is no beech forest on Stewart Island. The predominant lowland vegetation is hardwood but there are also lots of tree ferns, ground ferns and several types of orchid. Along the coast there's muttonbird scrub, grass tree, tree daisies, supplejack and leatherwood. Around the shores are clusters of bull kelp, fine red weeds, delicate green thallus and bladder ferns.

Sights

Ulva Island ISLAND

This island is a tiny paradise covering only 250 hectares. An early naturalist, Charles Traill, was honorary postmaster here. He'd hoist a flag to signal that mail had arrived and hopefuls would paddle in from surrounding islands. His postal service was replaced by one at Oban in 1921, and in 1922 Ulva Island was declared a bird sanctuary. The air is alive with the song of tui and bellbirds, and you'll also see kaka, weka, kakariki and kereru (NZ pigeon). Good walking tracks in the island's northwest are detailed in *Ulva: Self-Guided Tour* ($2), available from the DOC visitor centre. Popular routes include **Flagstaff Point Lookout** (20 minutes return) and **Boulder Beach** (1½ hours return). Many paths intersect amid beautiful stands of rimu, miro, totara and rata. During summer, water taxis go from Golden Bay wharf to Ulva Island. To get the most out of the island, consider going with a guide from Ruggedy Range Wilderness Experience or Ulva's Guided Walks.

Rakiura Museum MUSEUM

(Ayr St; adult/child $2/50c; ⏲10am-1.30pm Mon-Sat, noon-2pm Sun) Models of various ferries from over the years, Maori artifacts, and exhibitions on whaling and early European settlement.

Presbyterian Church Hall CHURCH

(Kamahi Rd) The wooden Presbyterian Church Hall was relocated to Oban from a whaling base in Paterson Inlet in 1937.

Stone House HISTORIC BUILDING

At Harrold Bay, 2.5km southwest of Oban, is a stone house built by Lewis Acker around 1835, one of NZ's oldest stone buildings.

Rakiura Environmental Centre WILDLIFE

Learn about the Halfmoon Bay Habitat Rehabilitation Project restoring native bird life around Halfmoon Bay. The display is adjacent to the supermarket in Oban.

Activities

NZ's third-largest island features unspoilt wilderness and is a haven for a symphony of birdsong. Rakiura National Park protects 85% of the island, making it a mecca for trampers and birdwatchers, and there are countless sandy, isolated coves that are good for swimming if you're brave or mad enough to venture into the cool water.

Even if you're not a gung-ho tramper, Stewart Island is great to stretch your legs and immerse yourself in wilderness on a short tramp. For more serious trampers, there are excellent, multiday, DOC-maintained trails. The DOC Rakiura National Park Visitor Centre sells Backcountry Hut Passes and has detailed pamphlets on local tramps. Store gear here in small/large lockers for $10/20 for the duration of the hire.

In the north, there's a good network of tracks with huts occupied on a first-come, first-served basis. Each hut has foam mattresses, wood stoves for heating, running water and toilets. You'll need to carry a stove, food, sleeping bags, utensils and first-aid equipment. A tent can be useful over the busy summer holidays and Easter period. The southern part of the island is undeveloped and remote, and you shouldn't tramp on your own or go off the established tracks.

Day Walks TRAMPING

There are a number of short tramps, ranging from half an hour to seven hours; the majority are easily accessed from Halfmoon Bay. Pick up Day Walks ($2) from DOC Rakiura National Park Visitor Centre. The walk to **Observation Rock** (30 minutes return) has good views over Paterson Inlet. Continue past the old stone house at Harrold Bay to **Acker's Point Lighthouse** (three hours return), for good views of Foveaux Strait and the chance to see blue penguins and a colony of titi.

Rakiura Track TRAMPING

(www.doc.govt.nz) The 30km, three-day Rakiura Track is a well-defined, easy circuit starting and ending at Oban with copious bird life, beaches and lush bush en route. It requires a moderate level of fitness and is suitable for tramping year-round. The entire circuit is 37km in total (including the road sections) and showcases spectacular scenery. The circuit follows the open coast, climbs over a 250m-high forested ridge and traverses the sheltered shores of Paterson Inlet/Whaka a Te Wera. It passes sites of historical interest and introduces many of the common sea and forest birds of the island.

The Rakiura Track is one of NZ's Great Walks and bookings are required all year round to stay in the huts and at campsites. These must be made in advance, either online at www.doc.govt.nz or at the DOC Rakiura National Park Visitor Centre. There is a limit of two consecutive nights in any one hut.

Once an online booking has been received a confirmation letter may be printed from email. This is your ticket – read all the information contained within and bring a copy with you. All trampers are required to register their intentions at the visitor centre prior to departure for the Rakiura Track.

North West Circuit Track TRAMPING

(www.doc.govt.nz) Following the northern coast is the North West Circuit Track, a 125km trail taking 10 to 12 days. The 56km four-day **Southern Circuit Track** branches off the North West Circuit Track. Both tracks are suitable only for fit, well-equipped and experienced trampers. Mud is widespread and often deep and thick on the tracks, regardless of the season. Track times are an indication only, and extra time should be allowed in adverse conditions.

The North West Circuit Pass provides for a night in each of the backcountry huts. A Backcountry Hut Pass can be purchased for use in the huts; however, both the Port William and North Arm huts still need to be booked via the DOC website. The cost for these two huts is additional.

Bravo Adventure Cruises BIRDWATCHING

(☎03-219 1144; www.kiwispotting.co.nz) To see a kiwi in the wild, Bravo Adventure Cruises runs twilight tours ($140). In order to protect the kiwi, numbers are limited so make sure you book *well* ahead. Kiwi-spotting is also available with Ruggedy Range Wilderness Experience (p287).

Ruggedy Range Wilderness Experience TOURS, BIRDWATCHING

(☎0508 484 337, 03-219 1066; www.ruggedyrange.com; cnr Main Rd & Dundee St) Excellent guide Furhana Ahmad takes small groups on guided walks with an ecofriendly, conservation angle. A very popular excursion is the half-day trip to Ulva Island ($110); one- and two-night expeditions to see kiwi in the wild ($470 to $860) are also available. Ruggedy Range also specialises in the viewing of pelagic seabirds. Guided sea kayaking starts at $95, and you can also buy tramping and camping gear.

Rakiura Kayaks KAYAKING

(☎027 868 0318; www.rakiura.co.nz) Paterson Inlet consists of 100 sq km of sheltered, kayak-friendly waterways, with 20 islands, DOC huts and two navigable rivers. A popular trip is a paddle to Freshwater Landing (7km upriver from the inlet) followed by a three- to four-hour walk to Mason Bay to see kiwi in the wild. Rakiura Kayaks rents kayaks (half/full day $50/65) and also run guided paddles around the inlet ($65 to $105).

Ulva's Guided Walks WALKING TOUR

(☎03-219 1216; www.ulva.co.nz) Excellent three- to five-hour tours costing from $120 to $150 (transport included). Options include Ulva Island and Port William, a historic Maori and sealing site. Book at the Fernery (p290). If you're a mad-keen twitcher, see the website for the Birding Bonanza trip ($400) taking in everything avian.

Rakiura Charters FISHING

(☎03-219 1487, 0800 725 487; www.rakiuracharters.co.nz; adult/child from $100/70) Sightseeing and fishing outings on the *Rakiura Suzy*. Most popular is the half-day fishing cruise including a stop at the historic Whalers' Base. Multiday diving, fishing and hunting charters, and overnight trips are also available.

Stewart Island Experience GUIDED TOURS
(☎0800 000 511; www.stewartislandexperience.co.nz) Runs 2½-hour Paterson Inlet cruises (adult/child $85/22) via Ulva Island; 1½-hour minibus tours of Oban and the surrounding bays ($45/22); and 45-minute semisubmersible cruises ($85/42.50).

Stewart Island Spa DAY SPA
(☎03-219 1422; www.stewartislandspa.co.nz; Main Rd; treatments from $95; ⏰Dec-Mar) In a refurbished hilltop cottage, with options including crystal healing, a rainforest bath and a sauna and massage. Premium organic beauty products are used for all treatments. See Britt at the Kiwi-French Crepery for more information and bookings.

Sleeping

Finding accommodation can be difficult, especially in the low season when many places shut down. Booking ahead is recommended.

Self-contained rental houses offer good value, especially for families and groups. Note that many accommodation options have a two-night minimum stay or charge a surcharge for one night.

See www.stewartisland.co.nz for options.

Jo & Andy's B&B B&B $
(☎03-219 1230; jariksem@clear.net.nz; cnr Morris St & Main Rd; s $45-60, d & tw $90; @📶) An excellent option for budget travellers, this cosy blue home squeezes in twin, double and single rooms. A big breakfast of muesli, fruit and homemade bread prepares you for the most active of days. Jo and Andy are both great company, and there's hundreds of books if the weather packs up.

Observation Rock Lodge LODGE $$$
(☎03-219 1444, 027 444 1802; www.observationrocklodge.co.nz; 7 Leonard St; d from $195) Tucked away in native bush with views south to Golden Bay, this luxury lodge is run by the lovely Annett Eiselt from Perfect Dinner (p289). A sauna, hot tub and plenty of hidden sanctuaries around the bird-studded property add up to a relaxing island escape.

Greenvale B&B B&B $$$
(☎03-219 1357; www.greenvalestewartisland.co.nz; Elgin Tce; s/d $300/385; 📶) Just 50m from the sea, this modern home has stunning views over the strait. Both rooms have quality cotton bed linen and contemporary furnishings. It's a five-minute walk to Halfmoon Bay, and a two-second transition to the sunny deck.

Stewart Island Lodge LODGE $$$
(☎03-219 1085; www.stewartislandlodge.co.nz; Nichol Rd; d incl breakfast $390) This upmarket retreat with six rooms features king-size beds, a shared deck and a garden teeming with bird life. On a hill at the edge of town, the lodge commands magnificent views. Look forward to complimentary drinks and nibbles at 5pm every night.

Bunkers Backpackers HOSTEL $
(☎03-219 1160; www.bunkersbackpackers.co.nz; 13 Argyle St; dm/s/d $28/48/76; @📶) A renovated wooden villa houses Stewart Island's newest hostel. Shared areas are modern and sunny, and the rooms are spacious and spotless.

Pilgrim Cottage RENTAL HOUSE $$
(☎03-219 1144; www.kiwispotting.co.nz; 8 Horseshoe Bay Rd; d $140) This quaint, weatherboard cottage in a leafy oasis near town has wooden furnishings, a potbelly stove and a well-equipped kitchen. Expect lots of bird life.

Port of Call B&B B&B $$$
(☎03-219 1394; www.portofcall.co.nz; Leask Bay Rd; s/d incl breakfast $345/385) Take in ocean views, get cosy before an open fire, or explore an isolated beach. Port of Call is 1.5km southwest of Oban on the way to Acker's Point. It has a two-night minimum stay, and guided walks and water taxi trips can also be arranged.

Bay Motel MOTEL $$$
(☎03-219 1119; www.baymotel.co.nz; 9 Dundee St; d $165-185) Modern, comfortable units with lots of light and views over the harbour. Some units have big spa tubs, all rooms have full kitchens and two are wheelchair-accessible. When you've exhausted the island's bustling after-dark scene, Sky TV's on hand for on-tap entertainment.

Te Tahi Bed & Breakfast B&B $$$
(☎03-219 1487, 0800 725 487; www.rakiuracharters.co.nz; 14 Kaka Ridge Rd; d $200) A sunny conservatory immersed in verdant bush, ocean views and colourfully decorated bedrooms are the standouts at this friendly B&B just five minutes' walk from the bustling hub of Oban and Halfmoon Bay.

Kaka Retreat MOTEL $$$
(☎03-219 1252; www.kakaretreat.net; 7 & 9 Miro Cres; d from $260; @📶) These self-contained

SPOTTING A KIWI: A BRUSH WITH THE GODS

Considered the king of the forest by Maori, the kiwi has been around for 70 million years and is related to the now-extinct moa. Brown feathers camouflage the kiwi against its bush surroundings and a nocturnal lifestyle means spying a kiwi in the wild is a challenge. They're a smart wee bird – they even build their burrows a few months before moving in so newly grown vegetation can further increase their privacy.

Stewart Island is one of the few places on earth where you can spot a kiwi in the wild. As big as a barnyard chicken and numbering around 15,000 to 18,000 birds, the tokoeka (Stewart Island brown kiwi) is larger in size and population than other subspecies. They are also the only kiwi active during daylight hours. About two hours after sunrise and an hour before sunset, tokoeka forage for food in grassed areas, particularly on Mason Bay. Watch for white kiwi poo and telltale holes made by their long hunting beaks. When you spot one, keep silent, and stay still and well away. The birds' poor eyesight and single-mindedness in searching for food will often lead them to bump right into you.

The Stewart Island kiwi *(Apteryx australis lawryi)* is a distinct subspecies, with a larger beak and longer legs than its northern cousins. Kiwi are common over much of Stewart Island, particularly foraging around beaches for sandhoppers under washed-up kelp. Unusually, Stewart Island's kiwi are active during the day as well as at night – the birds are forced to forage for longer to attain breeding condition. Many trampers on the North West Circuit Track spot them. Because of Stewart Island's often-fickle weather, tours are sometimes cancelled, and you may need to spend a few nights on the island to finally see a kiwi.

studio units have luxury interiors and cosy verandah. With crisply modern decor and flash bathrooms, the superior units are among the island's best. An older-style family unit is good value for up to six people.

Stewart Island Backpackers HOSTEL **$**
(☎03-219 1114; www.stewartsislandbackpackers.com; cnr Dundee & Ayr Sts; dm/s/d $30/50/70) Friendly new management are breathing new life into this hostel. Recently renovated rooms are brightly painted, and many open onto a courtyard. There are only three beds per dorm, and table tennis and a shared barbecue keep things nicely social. There's an additional surcharge of $5 if you stay only one night, and tenting is $18 per person.

The Bach RENTAL HOUSE **$$$**
(☎03-219 1394; www.portofcall.co.nz; Leask Bay Rd; d $260) A modern self-contained studio unit, 1.5km southwest of Oban on the way to Acker's Point. It has a two-night minimum stay, and guided walks and water taxi trips can also be arranged.

Eating & Drinking

South Sea Hotel PUB **$$**
(26 Elgin Tce; mains $20-30; ⏲7am-9pm; 📶) This cafe-style spot does superb fish and robust seafood chowder. The attached pub is the town's main drinking hole, enlivened by occasional weekend bands and a loads-of-fun pub quiz that kicks off at 6.30pm on Sunday nights. Say hi to Vicky, quiz-mistress extraordinaire for us.

Perfect Dinner INTERNATIONAL **$$**
(☎027 444 1802, 03-219 1444; perfectdinner@observationrocklodge.co.nz; 3-course menu per person $89; ⏲Oct-May) Relocated from Germany, Annett Eiselt specialises in 'movable feasts'. She's available to provide three-course menus or gourmet platters ($69) wherever you desire on the island; at your accommodation, on a beach or somewhere else with equally terrific views. Produce is always seasonal, and ideally organic and sourced locally.

Kiwi-French Crepery CREPERIE **$$**
(Main Rd; crepes $13-28; ⏲9am-9pm) Savoury and sweet crepes are made to order in this cosy cafe, and the coffee is the best on the island. Try the chicken, pesto and camembert, or apple and cinnamon flavours. There's also regular soup specials, and owner Britt also sells gemstone jewellery and designs made from paua shells.

Church Hill Cafe, Bar & Restaurant RESTAURANT **$$$**
(☎03-219 1323; www.churchhillrestaurant.com; 36 Kamahi Rd; 2/3 courses $65/75; ⏲6pm-late) During summer this heritage villa's sunny deck provides hilltop views, and in cooler months you can get cosy inside beside the open fire. Regular highlights include manuka (tea

tree) smoked Stewart Island salmon, and old-fashioned dessert treats like apple and rhubarb crumble. It's essential to book for dinner, and by 5pm at the latest.

Kai Kart FISH & CHIPS $
(☎03-219 1225; Ayr St; meals $5-20; ⏲11.30am-2.30pm & 5-9pm Nov-Apr, reduced hours in winter) This caravan of cuisine serves up delicious blue cod, and the mussels with spicy satay sauce aren't far behind in the flavour stakes.

Ship to Shore SUPERMARKET $
(Elgin Tce; ⏲7.30am-7.30pm) Groceries and beer and wine, and sandwiches and baked goodies ($4 to $6) are also available.

Fishermen's Co-op SELF-CATERING $$
Fresh fish and crayfish from the main wharf.

Shopping

Glowing Sky CLOTHING
(www.glowingsky.co.nz; Elgin Tce; ⏲11am-3pm) Hand-printed T-shirts with Maori designs and NZ-made merino clothing.

Fernery ARTS & CRAFTS
(www.theferneryznz.com; Main Rd; ⏲10.30am-5pm Dec-Apr, to 2pm Oct-Nov) Crafts, paintings and island-themed books.

Information

There are no banks on Stewart Island. Credit cards are accepted for most activities but it's wise to bring enough cash for your stay. There's internet access, including wi-fi, at the South Sea Hotel, and most accommodation.

The Invercargill i-SITE has a wide range of information. Online, see www.stewartisland.co.nz.

DOC Rakiura National Park Visitor Centre (☎03-219 0002; www.doc.govt.nz; Main Rd; ⏲8am-5pm daily Jan-Mar, 8.30am-4.30pm Mon-Fri & 10am-2pm Sat-Sun Apr-late Oct, 8am-5pm Mon-Fri late Oct-Dec) Visit the free exhibition here to understand Stewart Island's flora and fauna. Backcountry Hut Passes and detailed maps of local tracks are also available. Please ensure if you are heading into the bush that you complete an intentions form to inform them of your whereabouts. Purchase books and cards with conservation themes, tramping supplies, and possum and merino clothing.

Post office (Elgin Tce) At Stewart Island Flights.

Ruggedy Range Birds & Forest Booking Office (☎0508 484 337, 03-219 1066; www.ruggedyrange.com; cnr Main Rd & Dundee St; ⏲7.30am-8pm Mon-Sun Sep-May, 8.30am-5.30pm Mon-Fri & 9.30am-2pm Sat & Sun Jun-Aug) Dedicated booking and information office for Ruggedy Range Wilderness Experience with birdwatching, tramping and water taxis on offer. Note that Ruggedy Range is not represented by other information centres on the island.

Stewart Island Experience (☎03-219 1456; www.stewartislandexperience.co.nz; 12 Elgin Tce; ⏲8.30am-6pm) In the big red building; books accommodation and activities. Also handles sightseeing tours and rents scooters, cars, fishing rods, dive gear and golf clubs.

Stewart Island Health Centre (☎03-219 1098; Argyle St; ⏲10am-12.30pm) 24-hour on-call service.

Getting There & Away

Air

Rakiura Helicopters (☎03-219 1155; www.rakiurahelicopters.co.nz; 151 Main Rd) This is the only helicopter company based on Stewart Island. It's available for transfers from Bluff ($250 per person), scenic flights ($50 to $785 per person) and charter flights for hunters and trampers.

Stewart Island Flights (☎03-218 9129; www.stewartislandflights.co.nz; Elgin Tce; adult/child one-way $115/75, return $195/115) Flies between the island and Invercargill three times daily. Phone ahead for good standby discounts.

Boat

Stewart Island Experience (☎03-212 7660, 0800 000 511; www.stewartislandexperience.co.nz; Main Wharf) The passenger-only ferry runs between Bluff and Oban (adult/child $69/34.50) around three times daily. Book a few days ahead in summer. The crossing takes one hour and can be a rough ride. The company also runs a shuttle between Bluff and Invercargill (adult/child $25/11) with pick-up and drop-off in Invercargill at the i-SITE, Tuatara Backpackers and Invercargill Airport. Cars and campervans can be stored in a secure car park at Bluff for an additional cost.

A shuttle also runs between Bluff and Queenstown (adult/child $69/34.50), and Bluff and Te Anau (adult/child $69/34.50) with pick-up and drop-off at the Real Journeys offices.

Getting Around

Water taxis offer pick-ups and drop-offs to remote parts of the island – a handy service for trampers. The taxis also service Ulva Island (return $25).

Stewart Island Water Taxi & Eco Guiding (☎03-219 1394)

Aihe Eco Charters & Water Taxi (☎03-219 1066; www.aihe.co.nz)

Sea View Water Taxi (☎03-219 1014; www.seaviewwatertaxi.co.nz)

Rakiura Helicopters can also provide remote access.

Rent a scooter (per half/full day $60/70) or a car (per half/full day $70/115) from Stewart Island Experience.

Understand the South Island

population per sq km

NORTH ISLAND | SOUTH ISLAND | AUSTRALIA

≈ 3 people

The South Island Today

Shaky Isle

There's no denying it. New Zealand, and especially the South Island, has had it tough during the past few years. The country may be geographically isolated, but it's definitely not been immune to the vagaries of the global economy. In September 2010, just as New Zealand was edging out of its worst recession in 30 years, a magnitude 7.1 earthquake struck near Christchurch, the South Island's social and economic hub. The damage was extensive but miraculously no life was lost, partly because it occurred in the early hours of the morning when people were in their beds. By way of comparison, Haiti's slightly smaller earthquake earlier that year killed more than 316,000 people.

While the earthquake clean up was continuing on the East Coast, tragedy struck on the West Coast of the South Island when an explosion occurred at the Pike River coalmine near Greymouth, sealing 29 men inside. All hope of rescue ended on 24 November when a second large explosion ripped through the mine.

Then in the early afternoon of 22 February 2011, a magnitude 6.3 earthquake struck Christchurch. This time the city wasn't so lucky and 185 people lost their lives. Canterbury has barely had a break since then, experiencing literally hundreds of aftershocks: a 6.4 earthquake killed an elderly man in June; a 5.8 rattled Christmas shoppers on 23 December; and a 5.5 got the new year off to a shaky start on 2 January 2012.

Following the first anniversary of the February 2011 earthquake, Christchurch's seismic nightmare has slowed, and there's evidence the progression of tremors is moving further eastwards into the Pacific Ocean. Despite the renewed calm, the challenges and opportunities facing the South Island's biggest city remain significant, as it copes with

» Population: 1.04 million

» Area: 151,215 sq km (smaller than Victoria, bigger than Tasmania)

» Total number of snakes: 0

» Distance between North and South Islands: 23km

» In the eight months following the February 2011 earthquake, 6000 Christchurch residents emigrated to Australia; a 62% increase in the corresponding period for the previous year.

You'll need

» A travel-insurance policy covering high-risk activities.

» Insect repellent to keep the sandflies at bay.

» The ability to feign enthusiasm over rugby.

» A bottomless appetite for Kiwi food and wine.

Faux Pas

» Don't refer to the fuzzy green fruit as kiwis, they're kiwifruit. A kiwi is a bird or a nationality.

» Don't insist that Phar Lap, the pavlova, and Crowded House are Australian icons.

» Jokes about sheep just aren't funny.

Top Films

The Lord of the Rings trilogy (2001–03) Dir: Peter Jackson

In My Father's Den (2004) Dir: Brad McGann

Out of the Blue (2006) Dir: Robert Sarkies

The Hobbit: An Unexpected Journey (2012) Dir: Peter Jackson

Where they live
(% of New Zealanders)

if the South Island were 100 people

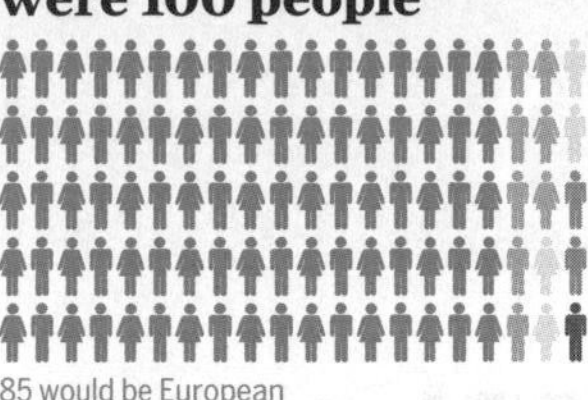

85 would be European
8 would be Maori
4 would be Asian
2 would be Pacific Islanders
1 would be other

reconstruction and renewal from history's third most expensive natural disaster, in terms of insurance claims.

Pause, Engage

In the midst of all this doom and gloom, South Islanders have soldiered on stoically, with the people of Christchurch proving remarkably resilient in the face of what's been occurring for more than 18 months.

Throughout September and October 2011, the influx of tourists for the Rugby World Cup provided a welcome distraction. Kiwis love sharing their spectacular country with visitors, and in turn seeing it anew through foreign eyes. They never tire of being reminded of the rugged beauty of their beaches, mountains, fiords, glaciers and native forests.

Although Christchurch missed out on hosting any games – its recently renovated stadium was damaged irreparably – the city's rattled residents couldn't help but be cheered by the feel-good success of the tournament and the national team's victory. By April 2012, a new rugby stadium in Christchurch had opened, and All Blacks superstars such as Richie McCaw and Dan Carter were again steering the city's beloved Crusaders Super 15 team to hometown victories.

In the face of all that's occurred, you might be surprised by the extent to which the average South Islander will genuinely want you to have a good time during your stay. It's in these interactions with everyday, easygoing Kiwis that lasting memories are made, especially in Christchurch where your visit to a city undergoing an exciting rebirth will be overwhelmingly welcomed.

Top Books

The Bone People (1988) Keri Hulme
The Carpathians (1988) Janet Frame
Denniston Rose (2003) & **Heart of Coal** (2004) Jenny Patrick
The Hut Builder (2011) Laurence Fearnley

Top Beers

Hopwired IPA 8 Wired Brewing Company
Stonecutter Scotch Ale Renaissance Brewing Company
Smokin' Bishop Rauch Bier Invercargill Brewery
Sauvin Pilsner The Twisted Hop

Top Anthems

Tally Ho (1981) The Clean
Death & the Maiden (1982) The Verlaines
Pink Frost (1984) The Chills
North by North (1987) The Bats
Not Given Lightly (1990) Chris Knox

History

James Belich

One of New Zealand's foremost modern historians, James Belich has written a number of books on NZ history and hosted the TV documentary series *The New Zealand Wars*.

New Zealand's history is not long, but it is fast. In less than a thousand years these islands have produced two new peoples: the Polynesian Maori and European New Zealanders. The latter are often known by their Maori name, 'Pakeha' (though not all like the term). NZ shares some of its history with the rest of Polynesia, and with other European settler societies, but has unique features as well. It is the similarities that make the differences so interesting, and vice versa.

Making Maori

Despite persistent myths, there is no doubt that the first settlers of NZ were the Polynesian forebears of today's Maori. Beyond that, there are a lot of question marks. Exactly where in east Polynesia did they come from – the Cook Islands, Tahiti, the Marquesas? When did they arrive? Did the first settlers come in one group or several? Some evidence, such as the diverse DNA of the Polynesian rats that accompanied the first settlers, suggests multiple founding voyages. On the other hand, only rats and dogs brought by the founders have survived, not the more valuable pigs and chickens. The survival of these cherished animals would have had high priority, and their failure to be successfully introduced suggests fewer voyages.

> *'Kaore e mau te rongo – ake, ake!'* (Peace never shall be made – never, never!) War chief Rewi Maniapoto in response to government troops at the battle of Orakau, 1864

NZ seems small compared with Australia, but it is bigger than Britain, and very much bigger than other Polynesian islands. Its regions vary wildly in environment and climate. Prime sites for first settlement were warm coastal gardens for the food plants brought from Polynesia (kumara or sweet potato, gourd, yam and taro); sources of workable stone

TIMELINE

AD 1000–1200

Possible date of the arrival of Maori in NZ. Solid archaeological evidence points to about AD 1200, but much earlier dates have been suggested for the first human impact on the environment.

1642

First European contact: Abel Tasman arrives on an expedition from the Dutch East Indies (Indonesia) to find the 'Great South Land'. His party leaves without landing, after a sea skirmish with Maori.

1769

European contact recommences with visits by James Cook and Jean de Surville. Despite some violence, both manage to communicate with Maori. This time NZ's link with the outside world proves permanent.

for knives and adzes; and areas with abundant big game. NZ has no native land mammals apart from a few species of bat, but 'big game' is no exaggeration: the islands were home to a dozen species of moa (a large flightless bird), the largest of which weighed up to 240kg, about twice the size of an ostrich. There were also other species of flightless birds and large sea mammals such as fur seals, all unaccustomed to being hunted. For people from small Pacific islands, this was like hitting the jackpot. The first settlers spread far and fast, from the top of the North Island to the bottom of the South Island within the first 100 years. High-protein diets are likely to have boosted population growth.

By about 1400, however, with big-game supply dwindling, Maori economics turned from big game to small game – forest birds and rats – and from hunting to gardening and fishing. A good living could still be made, but it required detailed local knowledge, steady effort and complex communal organisation, hence the rise of the Maori tribes. Competition for resources increased, conflict did likewise, and this led to the building of increasingly sophisticated fortifications, known as *pa*. Vestiges of *pa* earthworks can still be seen around the country (on the hilltops of Auckland, for example).

The Maori had no metals and no written language (and no alcoholic drinks or drugs). But their culture and spiritual life was rich and distinctive. Below Ranginui (sky father) and Papatuanuku (earth mother) were various gods of land, forest and sea, joined by deified ancestors over time. The mischievous demigod Maui was particularly important. In legend, he vanquished the sun and fished up the North Island before meeting his death between the thighs of the goddess Hine-nui-te-po in an attempt to conquer the human mortality embodied in her.Maori traditional performance art, the group singing and dancing known as *kapa haka,* has real power, even for modern audiences. Visual art, notably

For a thorough overview of NZ history from Gondwanaland to today, visit history-nz.org.

Rumours of late survivals of the giant moa bird abound, but none have been authenticated. So if you see a moa in your travels, photograph it – you have just made the greatest zoological discovery of the last 100 years.

THE MORIORI & THEIR MYTH

One of NZ's most persistent legends is that Maori found mainland NZ already occupied by a more peaceful and racially distinct Melanesian people, known as the Moriori, whom they exterminated. This myth has been regularly debunked by scholars since the 1920s, but somehow hangs on.

To complicate matters, there were real 'Moriori', and Maori did treat them badly. The real Moriori were the people of the Chatham Islands, a windswept group about 900km east of the mainland. They were, however, fully Polynesian, and descended from Maori – 'Moriori' was their version of the same word. Mainland Maori arrived in the Chathams in 1835, as a spin-off of the Musket Wars, killing some Moriori and enslaving the rest. But they did not exterminate them. The mainland Moriori remain a myth.

» Statue of James Cook

1772

Marion du Fresne's French expedition arrives; it stays for some weeks at the Bay of Islands. Relations with Maori start well, but a breach of Maori *tapu* (sacred law) leads to violence.

1790s

Whaling ships and sealing gangs arrive in the country. Relations are established with Maori, with Europeans depending on the contact for essentials such as food, water and protection.

1818–36

Intertribal Maori 'Musket Wars' take place: tribes acquire muskets and win bloody victories against tribes without them. The war tapers off in 1836, probably due to the equal distribution of weapons.

woodcarving, is something special – 'like nothing but itself', in the words of 18th-century explorer-scientist Joseph Banks.

Enter Europe

NZ became an official British colony in 1840, but the first authenticated contact between Maori and the outside world took place almost two centuries earlier in 1642, in Golden Bay at the top of the South Island. Two Dutch ships sailed from Indonesia, to search for southern land and anything valuable it might contain. The commander, Abel Tasman, was instructed to pretend to any natives he might meet 'that you are by no means eager for precious metals, so as to leave them ignorant of the value of the same'.

Similarities in language between Maori and Tahitian indicate close contact in historical times. Maori is about as similar to Tahitian as Spanish is to French, despite the 4294km separating these island groups.

When Tasman's ships anchored in the bay, local Maori came out in their canoes to make the traditional challenge: friends or foes? Misunderstanding this, the Dutch challenged back, by blowing trumpets. When a boat was lowered to take a party between the two ships, it was attacked. Four crewmen were killed. Tasman sailed away and did not come back; nor did any other European for 127 years. But the Dutch did leave a name: 'Nieuw Zeeland' or 'New Sealand'.

Contact between Maori and Europeans was renewed in 1769, when English and French explorers arrived, under James Cook and Jean de Surville. Relations were more sympathetic, and exploration continued, motivated by science, profit and great power rivalry. Cook made two more visits between 1773 and 1777, and there were further French expeditions.

Unofficial visits, by whaling ships in the north and sealing gangs in the south, began in the 1790s. The first mission station was founded in 1814, in the Bay of Islands, and was followed by dozens of others: Anglican, Methodist and Catholic. Trade in flax and timber generated small European–Maori settlements by the 1820s. Surprisingly, the most numerous category of European visitor was probably American. New England whaling ships favoured the Bay of Islands for rest and recreation; 271 called there between 1833 and 1839 alone. To whalers, 'rest and recreation' meant sex and drink. Their favourite haunt, the little town of Kororareka (now Russell) was known to the missionaries as 'the hellhole of the Pacific'. New England visitors today might well have distant relatives among the local Maori.

The Ministry for Culture & Heritage's history website (www.nzhistory.net.nz) is an excellent source of info on NZ history.

One or two dozen bloody clashes dot the history of Maori–European contact before 1840 but, given the number of visits, interracial conflict was modest. Europeans needed Maori protection, food and labour, and Maori came to need European articles, especially muskets. Whaling stations and mission stations were linked to local Maori groups by intermarriage, which helped keep the peace. Most warfare was between

1837

Possums are introduced to New Zealand from Australia. Brilliant.

1840

Starting at Waitangi in the Bay of Islands on 6 February, around 500 chiefs countrywide sign the Treaty of Waitangi to 'settle' sovereignty once and for all. NZ becomes a nominal British colony.

1844

Young Ngapuhi chief Hone Heke challenges British sovereignty, first by cutting down the British flag at Kororareka (now Russell), then by sacking the town itself. The ensuing Northland war continues until 1846.

1858

The Waikato chief Te Wherowhero is installed as the first Maori King.

CAPTAIN JAMES COOK *TONY HORWITZ*

If aliens ever visit earth, they may wonder what to make of the countless obelisks, faded plaques and graffiti-covered statues of a stiff, wigged figure gazing out to sea from Alaska to Australia, from NZ to North Yorkshire, from Siberia to the South Pacific. James Cook (1728–79) explored more of the earth's surface than anyone in history, and it's impossible to travel the Pacific without encountering the captain's image and his controversial legacy in the lands he opened to the West.

For a man who travelled so widely, and rose to such fame, Cook came from an extremely pinched and provincial background. The son of a day labourer in rural Yorkshire, he was born in a mud cottage, had little schooling, and seemed destined for farm work – and for his family's grave plot in a village churchyard. Instead, Cook went to sea as a teenager, worked his way up from coal-ship servant to naval officer, and attracted notice for his exceptional charts of Canada. But Cook remained a little-known second lieutenant until, in 1768, the Royal Navy chose him to command a daring voyage to the South Seas.

In a converted coal ship called *Endeavour,* Cook sailed to Tahiti, and then became the first European to land at NZ and the east coast of Australia. Though the ship almost sank after striking the Great Barrier Reef, and 40% of the crew died from disease and accidents, the *Endeavour* limped home in 1771. On a return voyage (1772–75), Cook became the first navigator to pierce the Antarctic Circle and circle the globe near its southernmost latitude, demolishing the myth that a vast, populous and fertile continent surrounded the South Pole. Cook criss-crossed the Pacific from Easter Island to Melanesia, charting dozens of islands between. Though Maori killed and cooked 10 sailors, the captain remained sympathetic to islanders. 'Notwithstanding they are cannibals,' he wrote, 'they are naturally of a good disposition.'

On Cook's final voyage (1776–79), in search of a northwest passage between the Atlantic and Pacific, he became the first European to visit Hawaii, and coasted America from Oregon to Alaska. Forced back by Arctic pack ice, Cook returned to Hawaii, where he was killed during a skirmish with islanders who had initially greeted him as a Polynesian god. In a single decade of discovery, Cook had filled in the map of the Pacific and, as one French navigator put it, 'left his successors with little to do but admire his exploits'.

But Cook's travels also spurred colonisation of the Pacific, and within a few decades of his death, missionaries, whalers, traders and settlers began transforming (and often devastating) island cultures. As a result, many indigenous people now revile Cook as an imperialist villain who introduced disease, dispossession and other ills to the Pacific (hence the frequent vandalising of Cook monuments). However, as islanders revive traditional crafts and practices, from tattooing to *tapa* (traditional barkcloth), they have turned to the art and writing of Cook and his men as a resource for cultural renewal. For good and ill, a Yorkshire farm boy remains the single most significant figure in the shaping of the modern Pacific.

Tony Horwitz is a Pulitzer-winning reporter and nonfiction author. In researching Blue Latitudes (or Into the Blue), Tony travelled the Pacific – 'boldly going where Captain Cook has gone before'.

1860–69

First and Second Taranaki wars, starting with the controversial swindling of Maori land by the government at Waitara, and continuing with outrage over the confiscation of more land as a result.

1861

Gold discovered in Otago by Gabriel Read, an Australian prospector. As a result, the population of Otago climbs from less than 13,000 to over 30,000 in six months.

1863–64

Waikato Land War. Up to 5000 Maori resist an invasion mounted by 20,000 imperial, colonial and 'friendly' Maori troops. Despite surprising successes, Maori are defeated and much land is confiscated.

1868–72

East Coast war. Te Kooti, having led an escape from his prison on the Chatham Islands, leads a holy guerrilla war in the Urewera region. He finally retreats to establish the Ringatu Church.

Maori and Maori: the terrible intertribal 'Musket Wars' of 1818–36. Because Northland had the majority of early contact with Europe, its Ngapuhi tribe acquired muskets first. Under their great general Hongi Hika, Ngapuhi then raided south, winning bloody victories against tribes without muskets. Once they acquired muskets, these tribes saw off Ngapuhi, but also raided further south in their turn. The domino effect continued to the far south of the South Island in 1836. The missionaries claimed that the Musket Wars then tapered off through their influence, but the restoration of the balance of power through the equal distribution of muskets was probably more important.

Abel Tasman named NZ Statenland, assuming it was connected to Staten Island near Argentina. It was subsequently named after the province of Zeeland in Tasman's Holland.

Europe brought such things as pigs (at last) and potatoes, which benefited Maori, while muskets and diseases had the opposite effect. The negative effects have been exaggerated, however. Europeans expected peoples like the Maori to simply fade away at contact, and some early estimates of Maori population were overly high – up to one million. Current estimates are between 85,000 and 110,000 for 1769. The Musket Wars killed perhaps 20,000, and new diseases did considerable damage too (although NZ had the natural quarantine of distance: infected Europeans usually recovered or died during the long voyage, and smallpox, for example, which devastated native Americans, did not make it here). By 1840, the Maori had been reduced to about 70,000, a decline of at least 20%. Maori bent under the weight of European contact, but they certainly did not break.

Making Pakeha

By 1840, Maori tribes described local Europeans as 'their Pakeha', and valued the profit and prestige they brought. Maori wanted more of both, and concluded that accepting nominal British authority was the way to get them. At the same time, the British government was overcoming its reluctance to undertake potentially expensive intervention in NZ. It too was influenced by profit and prestige, but also by humanitarian considerations. It believed, wrongly but sincerely, that Maori could not handle the increasing scale of unofficial European contact. In 1840, the two peoples struck a deal, symbolised by the treaty first signed at Waitangi on 6 February that year. The Treaty of Waitangi now has a standing not dissimilar to that of the Constitution in the US, but is even more contested. The original problem was a discrepancy between British and Maori understandings of it. The English version promised Maori full equality as British subjects in return for complete rights of government. The Maori version also promised that Maori would retain their chieftainship, which implied local rights of government. The problem was not great at first, because the Maori version applied outside the small European settlements. But as those settlements grew, conflict brewed.

'God's own country, but the devil's own mess.' Prime Minister Richard (King Dick) Seddon, speaking on the source of NZ's self-proclaimed nickname 'Godzone'.

1886–87

Tuwharetoa tribe gifts the mountains of Ruapehu, Ngauruhoe and Tongariro to the government to establish the world's fourth national park.

» Mt Ngauruhoe, Tongariro National Park

1893

NZ becomes the first country in the world to grant the vote to women, following a campaign led by Kate Sheppard, who petitioned the government for years.

In 1840, there were only about 2000 Europeans in NZ, with the shanty town of Kororareka (now Russell) as the capital and biggest settlement. By 1850, six new settlements had been formed with 22,000 settlers between them. About half of these had arrived under the auspices of the New Zealand Company and its associates. The company was the brainchild of Edward Gibbon Wakefield, who also influenced the settlement of South Australia. Wakefield hoped to short-circuit the barbarous frontier phase of settlement with 'instant civilisation', but his success was limited. From the 1850s, his settlers, who included a high proportion of upper-middle-class gentlefolk, were swamped by succeeding waves of immigrants that continued to wash in until the 1880s. These people were part of the great British and Irish diaspora that also populated Australia and much of North America, but the NZ mix was distinctive. Lowland Scots settlers were more prominent in NZ than elsewhere, for example, with the possible exception of parts of Canada. NZ's Irish, even the Catholics, tended to come from the north of Ireland. NZ's English tended to come from the counties close to London. Small groups of Germans, Scandinavians and Chinese made their way in, though the last faced increasing racial prejudice from the 1880s, when the Pakeha population reached half a million.

Much of the mass immigration from the 1850s to the 1870s was assisted by the provincial and central governments, which also mounted large-scale public works schemes, especially in the 1870s under Julius Vogel. In 1876, Vogel abolished the provinces on the grounds that they were hampering his development efforts. The last imperial governor with substantial power was the talented but Machiavellian George Grey, who ended his second governorship in 1868. Thereafter, the governors (governors-general from 1917) were largely just nominal heads of state; the head of government, the premier or prime minister, had more power. The central government, originally weaker than the provincial governments, the imperial governor and the Maori tribes, eventually exceeded the power of all three.

The Maori tribes did not go down without a fight, however. Indeed, their resistance was one of the most formidable ever mounted against European expansion, comparable to that of the Sioux and Seminole in the US. The first clash took place in 1843 in the Wairau Valley, now a wine-growing district. A posse of settlers set out to enforce the myth of British control, but encountered the reality of Maori control. Twenty-two settlers were killed, including Wakefield's brother, Arthur, along with about six Maori. In 1845, more serious fighting broke out in the Bay of Islands, when Hone Heke sacked a British settlement. Heke and his ally Kawiti baffled three British punitive expeditions, using a modern variant of the traditional *pa* fortification. Vestiges of these innovative earthworks

Maurice Shadbolt's *Season of the Jew* (1987) is a semifictionalised story of bloody campaigns led by warrior Te Kooti against the British in Poverty Bay in the 1860s. Te Kooti and his followers compared themselves to the Israelites who were cast out of Egypt.

To find out more about the New Zealand Wars, visit www.newzealandwars.co.nz.

'I believe we were all glad to leave New Zealand. It is not a pleasant place. Amongst the natives there is absent that charming simplicity...and the greater part of the English are the very refuse of society.' Charles Darwin, referring to Kororareka (Russell), in 1860.

1901

NZ politely declines the invitation to join the new Commonwealth of Australia.

1908

NZ physicist Ernest Rutherford is awarded the Nobel Prize in chemistry for 'splitting the atom', investigating the disintegration of elements and the chemistry of radioactive substances.

1914–18

NZ's contribution to WWI is staggering for a country of just over one million people: about 100,000 NZ men serve overseas. Some 60,000 become casualties, mostly on the Western Front in France.

1931

Napier earthquake kills 131 people.

can still be seen at Ruapekapeka (south of Kawakawa). Governor Grey claimed victory in the north, but few were convinced at the time. Grey had more success in the south, where he arrested the formidable Ngati Toa chief Te Rauparaha, who until then wielded great influence on both sides of Cook Strait. Pakeha were able to swamp the few Maori living in the South Island, but the fighting of the 1840s confirmed that the North Island at that time comprised a European fringe around an independent Maori heartland.

The Six o'clock Swill referred to the frantic after-work drinking at pubs when men tried to drink as much as possible from 5.05pm until strict closing time at 6pm.

In the 1850s, settler population and aspirations grew, and fighting broke out again in 1860. The wars burned on sporadically until 1872 over much of the North Island. In the early years, a Maori nationalist organisation, the King Movement, was the backbone of resistance. In later years, some remarkable prophet-generals, notably Titokowaru and Te Kooti, took over. Most wars were small-scale, but the Waikato war of 1863–64 was not. This conflict, fought at the same time as the American Civil War, involved armoured steamships, ultramodern heavy artillery, telegraph and 10 proud British regular regiments. Despite the odds, the Maori won several battles, such as that at Gate Pa, near Tauranga, in 1864. But in the end they were ground down by European numbers and resources. Maori political, though not cultural, independence ebbed away in the last decades of the 19th century. It finally expired when police invaded its last sanctuary, the Urewera Mountains, in 1916.

Wellington-born Nancy Wake (codenamed 'The White Mouse') led a guerrilla attack against the Nazis with a 7000-strong army. She had the multiple honours of being the Gestapo's most-wanted person and being the most decorated Allied servicewoman of WWII.

Welfare & Warfare

From the 1850s to the 1880s, despite conflict with Maori, the Pakeha economy boomed on the back of wool exports, gold rushes and massive overseas borrowing for development. The crash came in the 1880s, when NZ experienced its Long Depression. In 1890, the Liberals came to power, and stayed there until 1912, helped by a recovering economy. The Liberals were NZ's first organised political party, and the first of several governments to give NZ a reputation as 'the world's social laboratory'. NZ became the first country in the world to give women the vote in 1893, and introduced old-age pensions in 1898. The Liberals also introduced a long-lasting system of industrial arbitration, but this was not enough to prevent bitter industrial unrest in 1912–13. This happened under the conservative 'Reform' government, which had replaced the Liberals in 1912. Reform remained in power until 1928, and later transformed itself into the National Party. Renewed depression struck in 1929, and the NZ experience of it was as grim as any. The derelict little farmhouses still seen in rural areas often date from this era.

1935–49

First Labour government in power, under Michael Savage. This government creates NZ's pioneering version of the welfare state, and also takes some independent initiatives in foreign policy.

1936

NZ aviatrix Jean Batten becomes the first aviator to fly solo from Britain to NZ.

1939–45

NZ troops back Britain and the Allied war effort during WWII; from 1942 a hundred thousand or so Americans arrive to protect NZ from the Japanese.

1948

Maurice Scheslinger invents the Buzzy Bee, NZ's most famous children's toy.

In 1935, a second reforming government took office: the First Labour government, led by Michael Joseph Savage, easily NZ's favourite Australian. For a time, the Labour government was considered the most socialist government outside Soviet Russia. But, when the chips were down in Europe in 1939, Labour had little hesitation in backing Britain.

NZ had also backed Britain in the Boer War (1899–1902) and WWI (1914–18), with dramatic losses in WWI in particular. You can count the cost in almost any little NZ town. A central square or park will contain a memorial lined with names – more for WWI than WWII. Even in WWII, however, NZ did its share of fighting: a hundred thousand or so New Zealanders fought in Europe and the Middle East. NZ, a peaceful-seeming country, has spent much of its history at war. In the 19th century it fought at home; in the 20th, overseas.

LAND WARS *ERROL HUNT*

Five separate major conflicts made up what are now collectively known as the New Zealand Wars (also referred to as the Land Wars or Maori Wars). Starting in Northland and moving throughout the North Island, the wars had many complex causes, but *whenua* (land) was the one common factor. In all five wars, Maori fought both for and against the government, on whose side stood the Imperial British Army, Australians and NZ's own Armed Constabulary. Land confiscations imposed on the Maori as punishment for involvement in these wars are still the source of conflict today, with the government struggling to finance compensation for what are now acknowledged to have been illegal seizures.

Northland war (1844–46) 'Hone Heke's War' began with the famous chopping of the flagpole at Kororareka (now Russell) and 'ended' at Ruapekapeka (south of Kawakawa). In many ways, this was almost a civil war between rival Ngapuhi factions, with the government taking one side against the other.

First Taranaki war (1860–61) Starting in Waitara, the first Taranaki war inflamed the passions of Maori across the North Island.

Waikato war (1863–64) The largest of the five wars. Predominantly involving Kingitanga, the Waikato war was caused in part by what the government saw as a challenge to sovereignty. However, it was land, again, that was the real reason for friction. Following defeats such as Rangiriri, the Waikato people were pushed entirely from their own lands, south into what became known as the King Country.

Second Taranaki war (1865–69) Caused by Maori resistance to land confiscations stemming from the first Taranaki war, this was perhaps the war in which the Maori came closest to victory, under the brilliant, one-eyed prophet-general Titokowaru. However, once he lost the respect of his warriors (probably through an indiscretion with the wife of one of his warriors), the war too was lost.

East Coast war (1868–72) Te Kooti's holy guerrilla war.

1953

New Zealander Edmund Hillary, with Tenzing Norgay, 'knocks the bastard off'; the pair become the first men to reach the summit of Mt Everest.

1973

Fledgling Kiwi prog-rockers Split Enz enter a TV talent quest... finishing second to last.

1974

Pacific Island migrants who have outstayed visas ('overstayers') are subjected to Dawn Raids by immigration police under Robert Muldoon and the National government. These raids continue until the early 1980s.

1981

Springbok rugby tour divides the nation. Many New Zealanders show a strong anti-apartheid stance by protesting the games. Others feel sport and politics shouldn't mix, and support the tour going ahead.

Better Britons?

British visitors have long found NZ hauntingly familiar. This is not simply a matter of the British and Irish origin of most Pakeha. It also stems from the tightening of NZ links with Britain from 1882, when refrigerated cargoes of food were first shipped to London. By the 1930s, giant ships carried frozen meat, cheese and butter, as well as wool, on regular voyages taking about five weeks one way. The NZ economy adapted to the feeding of London, and cultural links were also enhanced. NZ children studied British history and literature, not their own. NZ's leading scientists and writers, such as Ernest Rutherford and Katherine Mansfield, gravitated to Britain. This tight relationship has been described as 'recolonial', but it is a mistake to see NZ as an exploited colony. Average living standards in NZ were normally better than in Britain, as were the welfare and lower-level education systems. New Zealanders had access to British markets and culture, and they contributed their share to the latter as equals. The list of 'British' writers, academics, scientists, military leaders, publishers and the like who were actually New Zealanders is long. Indeed, New Zealanders, especially in war and sport, sometimes saw themselves as a superior version of the British – the Better Britons of the south. The NZ–London relationship was rather like that of the American Midwest and New York.

The Waitangi Treaty Grounds, where the Treaty of Waitangi was first signed in 1840, is now a tourist attraction for Kiwis and non-Kiwis alike. Each year on 6 February, Waitangi hosts treaty commemorations and protests

TREATY OF WAITANGI

'Recolonial' NZ prided itself, with some justice, on its affluence, equality and social harmony. But it was also conformist, even puritanical. Until the 1950s, it was technically illegal for farmers to allow their cattle to mate in fields fronting public roads, for moral reasons. The 1953 American movie, *The Wild One,* was banned until 1977. Sunday newspapers were illegal until 1969, and full Sunday trading was not allowed until 1989. Licensed restaurants hardly existed in 1960, nor did supermarkets or TV. Notoriously, from 1917 to 1967, pubs were obliged to shut at 6pm. Yet the puritanical society of Better Britons was never the whole story. Opposition to Sunday trading stemmed, not so much from belief in the sanctity of the Sabbath, but from the belief that workers should have weekends too. Six o'clock closing was a standing joke in rural areas, notably the marvellously idiosyncratic region of the South Island's West Coast. There was always something of a Kiwi counterculture, even before imported countercultures took root from the 1960s.

There were also developments in cultural nationalism, beginning in the 1930s but really flowering from the 1970s. Writers, artists and film-makers were by no means the only people who 'came out' in that era.

1985

Rainbow Warrior is sunk in Auckland Harbour by French government agents to prevent the Greenpeace protest ship from making its intended voyage to Moruroa, where the French are conducting nuclear tests.

JENNY & TONY ENDERBY / LONELY PLANET IMAGES ©

» Memorial to the sunken ship, *Rainbow Warrior*

1992

Government begins reparations for the Land Wars, and confirms Maori fishing rights in the 'Sealord deal'. Major settlements follow, including, in 1995, reparations for the Waikato land confiscations.

Coming In, Coming Out

The 'recolonial' system was shaken several times after 1935, but managed to survive until 1973, when Mother England ran off and joined the Franco-German commune now known as the EU. NZ was beginning to develop alternative markets to Britain, and alternative exports to wool, meat and dairy products. Wide-bodied jet aircraft were allowing the world and NZ to visit each other on an increasing scale. NZ had only 36,000 tourists in 1960, compared with more than two million a year now. Women were beginning to penetrate first the upper reaches of the workforce and then the political sphere. Gay people came out of the closet, despite vigorous efforts by moral conservatives to push them back in. University-educated youths were becoming more numerous and more assertive.

Scottish influence can still be felt in NZ, particularly in the south of the South Island. NZ has more Scottish pipe bands per capita than Scotland itself.

From 1945, Maori experienced both a population explosion and massive urbanisation. In 1936, Maori were 17% urban and 83% rural. Fifty years later, these proportions had reversed. The immigration gates, which until 1960 were pretty much labelled 'whites only', widened, first to allow in Pacific Islanders for their labour, and then to allow in (East) Asians for their money. These transitions would have generated major socioeconomic change whatever happened in politics. But most New Zealanders associate the country's recent 'Big Shift' with the politics of 1984.

In 1984, NZ's third great reforming government was elected – the Fourth Labour government, led nominally by David Lange and in fact by Roger Douglas, the Minister of Finance. This government adopted an antinuclear foreign policy, delighting the left, and a more-market economic policy, delighting the right. NZ's numerous economic controls were dismantled with breakneck speed. Middle NZ was uneasy about the antinuclear policy, which threatened NZ's ANZUS alliance with Australia and the US. But in 1985, French spies sank the antinuclear protest ship *Rainbow Warrior* in Auckland Harbour, killing one crewman. The lukewarm American condemnation of the French act brought middle NZ in behind the antinuclear policy, which became associated with national independence. Other New Zealanders were uneasy about the more-market economic policy, but failed to come up with a convincing alternative. Revelling in their new freedom, NZ investors engaged in a frenzy of speculation, and suffered even more than the rest of the world from the economic crash of 1987.

NZ's staunch antinuclear stance earned it the nickname 'The Mouse that Roared'.

The early 21st century is an interesting time for NZ. Food, wine, film and literature are flowering as never before, and the new ethnic mix is creating something very special in popular music. There are continuities, however – the pub, the sportsground, the quarter-acre section, the bush, the beach and the bach – and they too are part of the reason people like to come here. Realising that NZ has a great culture, and an intriguing history, as well as a great natural environment, will double the bang for your buck.

1995

Peter Blake and Russel Coutts win the Americas Cup for NZ, sailing *Black Magic;* red socks become a matter of national pride.

2004

Maori TV begins broadcasting – for the first time, a channel committed to NZ content and the revitalisation of Maori language and culture hits the small screen.

2010

A cave-in at Pike River coalmine on the South Island's West Coast kills 29 miners.

2011

A severe earthquake strikes Christchurch, killing 185 people and badly damaging the central business district. NZ hosts (and wins) the Rugby World Cup.

Environment

Vaughan Yarwood

Vaughan Yarwood is a historian and travel writer who is widely published in New Zealand and internationally. His most recent book is *The History Makers: Adventures in New Zealand Biography*.

The Land

New Zealand is a young country – its present shape is less than 10,000 years old. Having broken away from the supercontinent of Gondwanaland (which included Africa, Australia, Antarctica and South America) in a stately geological dance some 85 million years ago, it endured continual uplift and erosion, buckling and tearing, and the slow fall and rise of the sea as ice ages came and went. Straddling the boundary of two great colliding slabs of the earth's crust – the Pacific plate and the Indian/Australian plate – to this day NZ remains the plaything of nature's strongest forces.

The result is one of the most varied and spectacular series of landscapes in the world, ranging from snow-dusted mountains and drowned glacial valleys to rainforests, dunelands and an otherworldly volcanic plateau. It is a diversity of landforms you would expect to find across an entire continent rather than a small archipelago in the South Pacific.

Evidence of NZ's tumultuous past is everywhere. The South Island's mountainous spine – the 650km-long ranges of the Southern Alps – is a product of the clash of the two plates; the result of a process of rapid lifting that, if anything, is accelerating. Despite NZ's highest peak, Aoraki/Mt Cook, losing 10m from its summit overnight in a 1991 landslide, the Alps are on an express elevator that, without erosion and landslides, would see them 10 times their present height within a few million years.

On the North Island, the most impressive changes have been wrought by volcanoes. Auckland is built on an isthmus peppered by scoria cones, on many of which you can still see the earthworks of *pa* (fortified villages) built by early Maori. The city's biggest and most recent volcano, 600-year-old Rangitoto Island, is just a short ferry ride from the downtown wharves. Some 300km further south, the classically shaped cone of snowcapped Mt Taranaki/Egmont overlooks tranquil dairy pastures.

But the real volcanic heartland runs through the centre of the North Island, from the restless bulk of Mt Ruapehu in Tongariro National Park northeast through the Rotorua lake district out to NZ's most active volcano, White Island, in the Bay of Plenty. Called the Taupo Volcanic Zone, this great 250km-long rift valley – part of a volcano chain known as the 'Pacific Ring of Fire' – has been the seat of massive eruptions that have left their mark on the country physically and culturally.

Most spectacular were the eruptions that created Lake Taupo. Considered the world's most productive volcano in terms of the amount of material ejected, Taupo last erupted 1800 years ago in a display that was the most violent anywhere on the planet within the past 5000 years.

You can experience the aftermath of volcanic destruction on a smaller scale at Te Wairoa (the Buried Village), near Rotorua on the shores of Lake Tarawera. Here, partly excavated and open to the public, lie the remains of a 19th-century Maori village overwhelmed when nearby Mt Tarawera erupted without warning. The famous Pink and White Terraces (one of several claimants to the popular title 'eighth wonder of the world') were destroyed overnight by the same upheaval.

But when nature sweeps the board clean with one hand she often rebuilds with the other: Waimangu Valley, born of all that geothermal violence, is the place to go to experience the hot earth up close and personal amid geysers, silica pans, bubbling mud pools, and the world's biggest hot spring. Or you can wander around Rotorua's Whakarewarewa Thermal Village, where descendants of Maori displaced by the eruption live in the middle of steaming vents and prepare food for visitors in boiling pools.

A second by-product of movement along the tectonic plate boundary is seismic activity – earthquakes. Not for nothing has NZ been called 'the Shaky Isles'. Most quakes only rattle the glassware, but one was indirectly responsible for creating an internationally celebrated tourist attraction...

In 1931 an earthquake measuring 7.9 on the Richter scale levelled the Hawke's Bay city of Napier, causing huge damage and loss of life. Napier was rebuilt almost entirely in the then-fashionable art-deco architectural style, and walking its streets today you can relive its brash exuberance in what has become a mecca for lovers of art deco.

However, the North Island doesn't have a monopoly on earthquakes. In September 2010 Christchurch was rocked by a magnitude 7.1 earthquake. Less than six months later, in February 2011, a magnitude 6.3 quake destroyed much of the city's historic heart and claimed 185 lives, making it the country's second-deadliest natural disaster. NZ's second city continues to be jostled by aftershocks as it begins to build anew.

The South Island can also see some evidence of volcanism – if the remains of the old volcanoes of Banks Peninsula weren't there to repel the sea, the vast Canterbury Plains, built from alpine sediment washed down the rivers from the Alps, would have eroded away long ago.

But in the south it is the Southern Alps themselves that dominate, dictating settlement patterns, throwing down engineering challenges and offering outstanding recreational opportunities. The island's mountainous backbone also helps shape the weather, as it stands in the path of the prevailing westerly winds which roll in, moisture-laden, from the Tasman Sea. As a result bush-clad lower slopes of the western Southern Alps are among the wettest places on earth, with an annual precipitation of some 15,000mm. Having lost its moisture, the wind then blows dry across the eastern plains towards the Pacific coast.

The North Island has a more even rainfall and is spared the temperature extremes of the South – which can plunge when a wind blows in from Antarctica. The important thing to remember, especially if you are tramping at high altitude, is that NZ has a maritime climate. This means weather can change with lightning speed, catching out the unprepared.

NZ is one of the most spectacular places in the world to see geysers. Rotorua's short-lived Waimangu geyser, formed after the Mt Tarawera eruption, was once the world's largest, often gushing to a dizzying height of 400m.

GEYSERS

Wildlife

NZ may be relatively young, geologically speaking, but its plants and animals go back a long way. The tuatara, for instance, an ancient reptile unique to these islands, is a Gondwanaland survivor closely related to the dinosaurs, while many of the distinctive flightless birds (ratites) have distant African and South American cousins.

Due to its long isolation, the country is a veritable warehouse of unique and varied plants, most of which are found nowhere else. And with separation of the landmass occurring before mammals appeared on the scene, birds and insects have evolved in spectacular ways to fill the gaps.

ENVIRONMENTAL ISSUES IN AOTEAROA NEW ZEALAND

NANDOR TANCZOS

Aotearoa New Zealand likes to sell itself as clean and green. We have the NZ Forest Accord to protect native forests. National parks and reserves now cover a third of the country. Marine reserves continue to pop up around the coast. Our antinuclear legislation seems unassailable. A closer look, however, reveals a dirtier picture.

New Zealand is one of the highest per-capita emitters of greenhouse gases. We are one of the most inefficient users of energy in the developed world. Public transport is negligible in most places. Add the ongoing battle in many communities to stop the pumping of sewage and toxic waste into waterways, a conflict often spearheaded by *tangata whenua* (Maori), and the 'clean and green' label looks a bit tarnished.

One of our challenges is that our biggest polluting sector is also our biggest export earner. Pastoral farming causes half of our greenhouse-gas emissions. Clearing forests to grow cows and sheep has left many hillsides scoured by erosion. Grazing animals damage stream edges and lake margins and farm run-off has left many waterways unsafe for swimming or drinking. The worse culprit is dairy farming, and while regional councils and farming groups are fencing and planting stream banks to protect water quality, their efforts are outstripped by the sheer growth in dairying. Meanwhile governments are reluctant to take on the powerful farming lobby.

Our other major challenge is around mining and drilling. The state-owned company Solid Energy plans to expand coalmining on the West Coast and convert lignite (the dirtiest form of coal) into fertiliser and diesel. The government is also encouraging overseas companies to prospect for off-shore oil in what would be some of the deepest and most difficult waters for drilling in the world. Once again local *iwi* (tribes) such as Te Whanau a Apanui are in the front lines alongside environmental groups like Greenpeace, fighting to prevent the marine ecosystems of the East Coast being put at risk.

Despite these things, New Zealand has some good things going on. A high proportion of our energy is from renewable sources. Farm animals, except for pigs and chickens, are mostly grass fed and free range. We are getting better with waste minimisation and resource recovery. Like most countries, though, we need to make a stronger effort to develop not just sustainable, but regenerative economic systems.

Our biggest saving grace is our small population. As a result, Aotearoa is a place well worth visiting. This is a beautiful land with enormous geographical and ecological diversity. Our forests are unique and magnificent, and the bird species that evolved in response to an almost total lack of mammalian life are spectacular, although now reduced in numbers from introduced predators such as rats, stoats and hedgehogs.

Visitors who want to help protect our ecological integrity can make the biggest impact by asking questions of their hosts: every time you ask where the recycling centre is; every time you question wasteful energy use, car use and water use; every time you ask for organic or free-range food at a cafe or restaurant; you affect the person you talk to.

Aotearoa New Zealand has the potential to be a world leader in ecological wisdom. We have a strong tradition to draw from – the careful relationship of reciprocity that Maori developed with the natural world over the course of many, many generations. We live at the edge of the Pacific, on the Rim of Fire, a remnant of the ancient forests of Gondwanaland. We welcome conscious travellers.

Nandor Tanczos is a social ecologist based in Ngaruawahia. He was a Member of Parliament for the Green Party from 1999 to 2008.

The now extinct flightless moa, the largest of which grew to 3.5m tall and weighed over 200kg, browsed open grasslands much as cattle do today (skeletons can be seen at Auckland Museum), while the smaller kiwi still ekes out a nocturnal living rummaging among forest leaf litter for insects and worms much as small mammals do elsewhere. One of the country's most ferocious-looking insects, the mouse-sized giant weta, meanwhile, has taken on a scavenging role elsewhere filled by rodents.

As one of the last places on earth to be colonised by humans, NZ was for millennia a safe laboratory for such risky evolutionary strategies, but with the arrival first of Maori and soon after of Europeans, things went downhill fast.

Many endemic creatures, including moa and the huia, an exquisite songbird, were driven to extinction, and the vast forests were cleared for their timber and to make way for agriculture. Destruction of habitat and the introduction of exotic animals and plants have taken a terrible environmental toll and New Zealanders are now fighting a rearguard battle to save what remains.

Birds & Animals

The first Polynesian settlers found little in the way of land mammals – just two species of bat – but forests, plains and coasts alive with birds. Largely lacking the bright plumage found elsewhere, NZ's birds – like its endemic plants – have an understated beauty that does not shout for attention.

Among the most musical is the bellbird, common in both native and exotic forests everywhere except Northland, though like many birds it is more likely to be heard than seen. Its call is a series of liquid bell notes, most often sounded at dawn or dusk.

The tui, another nectar eater and the country's most beautiful songbird, is a great mimic, with an inventive repertoire that includes clicks, grunts and chuckles. Notable for the white throat feathers that stand out against its dark plumage, the tui often feeds on flax flowers in suburban gardens but is most at home in densely tangled forest ('bush' to New Zealanders).

B Heather and H Robertson's *Field Guide to the Birds of New Zealand* is a comprehensive guide for birdwatchers and a model of helpfulness for anyone even casually interested in the country's remarkable bird life.

Fantails are commonly encountered on forest trails, swooping and jinking to catch insects stirred up by passing hikers, while pukeko, elegant swamp-hens with blue plumage and bright-red beaks, are readily seen along wetland margins and even on the sides of roads nearby – be warned, they have little road sense.

If you spend any time in the South Island high country, you are likely to come up against the fearless and inquisitive kea – an uncharacteristically drab green parrot with bright-red underwings. Kea are common in the car parks of the Fox and Franz Josef Glaciers, where they hang out for food scraps or tear rubber from car windscreens.

Then there is the takahe, a rare flightless bird thought extinct until a small colony was discovered in 1948, and the equally flightless kiwi, NZ's national emblem and the nickname for New Zealanders themselves.

The kiwi has a round body covered in coarse feathers, strong legs and a long, distinctive bill with nostrils at the tip for sniffing out food. It is not easy to find them in the wild, but they can be seen in simulated environments at excellent nocturnal houses. One of the best is the Otorohanga Kiwi House, which also has other birds, including native falcons, moreporks (owls) and weka.

To get a feel for what the bush used to be like, take a trip to Tiritiri Matangi island. This regenerating island is an open sanctuary and one of the country's most successful exercises in community-assisted conservation.

BIRDWATCHING

The flightless kiwi is the species most sought after by birdwatchers. Sightings of the Stewart Island subspecies are common at all times of the year. Elsewhere, wild sightings of this increasingly rare nocturnal species are difficult, apart from in enclosures. Other birds that twitchers like to sight are the royal albatross, white heron, Fiordland crested penguin, yellow-eyed penguin, Australasian gannet and wrybill.

On the Coromandel Peninsula, the Firth of Thames (particularly Miranda) is a haven for migrating birds, while the Wharekawa Wildlife

KIWI SPOTTING

A threatened species, the kiwi is also nocturnal and difficult to see in the wild, although you can do this in Okarito on the West Coast and on Stewart Island. They can, however, be observed in many artificially dark 'kiwi houses':

» West Coast Wildlife Centre (p123), Franz Josef
» Orana Wildlife Park (p139), Christchurch
» Willowbank Wildlife Reserve (p140), Christchurch
» Kiwi Birdlife Park (p223), Queenstown

Refuge at Opoutere Beach is a breeding ground of the endangered NZ dotterel. There's also a very accessible Australasian gannet colony at Muriwai, west of Auckland, and one in Hawke's Bay. There are popular trips to observe pelagic birds out of Kaikoura, and royal albatross viewing on the Otago Peninsula.

Two good guides are the revised *Field Guide to the Birds of New Zealand,* by Barrie Heather and Hugh Robertson, and *Birds of New Zealand: Locality Guide* by Stuart Chambers.

MARINE MAMMAL-WATCHING

Kaikoura, on the northeast coast of the South Island, is NZ's nexus of marine mammal-watching. The main attraction here is whale-watching, but this is dependent on weather conditions, so don't expect to just be able to rock up and head straight out on a boat for a dream encounter. The sperm whale, the largest toothed whale, is pretty much a year-round resident, and depending on the season you may also see migrating humpback whales, pilot whales, blue whales and southern right whales. Other mammals – including fur seals and dusky dolphins – are seen year-round.

Nature Guide to the New Zealand Forest, by J Dawson and R Lucas, is a beautifully photographed foray into the world of NZ's forests. Far from being drab and colourless, these lush treasure houses are home to ancient species dating from the time of the dinosaurs. This guidebook will have you reaching for your boots.

Kaikoura is also an outstanding place to swim with dolphins. Pods of up to 500 playful dusky dolphins can be seen on any given day. Dolphin swimming is common elsewhere in NZ, with the animals gathering off the North Island near Whakatane, Paihia, Tauranga, and in the Hauraki Gulf, and off Akaroa on the South Island's Banks Peninsula. Seal swimming is possible in Kaikoura and in the Abel Tasman National Park.

Swimming with sharks is also possible, though with a protective cage as a chaperone; you can do it in Gisborne.

Trees

No visitor to NZ (particularly Australians!) will go for long without hearing about the damage done to the bush by that bad-mannered Australian import, the brush-tailed possum. The long list of mammal pests introduced to NZ accidentally or for a variety of misguided reasons includes deer, rabbits, stoats, pigs and goats. But the most destructive by far is the possum, 70 million of which now chew through millions of tonnes of foliage a year despite the best efforts of the Department of Conservation (DOC) to control them.

Among favoured possum food are NZ's most colourful trees: the kowhai, a small-leaved tree growing to 11m, that in spring has drooping clusters of bright-yellow flowers (NZ's national flower); the pohutukawa, a beautiful coastal tree of the northern North Island which bursts into vivid red flower in December, earning the nickname 'Christmas tree'; and a similar crimson-flowered tree, the rata. Rata species are found on both islands; the northern rata starts life as a climber on a host tree (that it eventually chokes).

The few remaining pockets of mature centuries-old kauri are stately emblems of former days. Their vast hammered trunks and towering, epiphyte-festooned limbs, which dwarf every other tree in the forest, are reminders of why they were sought after in colonial days for spars and building timber. The best place to see the remaining giants is Northland's Waipoua Kauri Forest, home to three-quarters of the country's surviving kauri.

National Parks

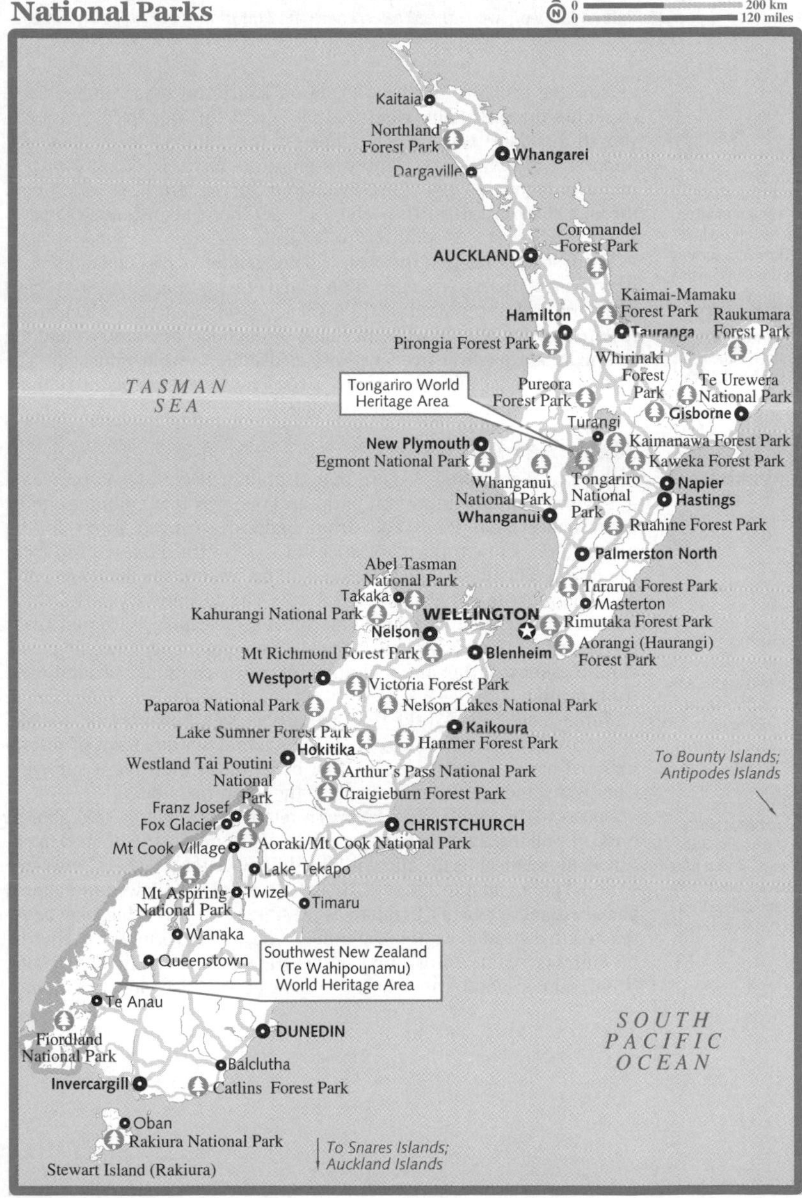

TOWERING KAURI

When Chaucer was born this was a sturdy young tree. When Shakespeare was born it was 300 years old. It predates most of the great cathedrals of Europe. Its trunk is sky-rocket straight and sky-rocket bulky, limbless for half its height. Ferns sprout from its crevices. Its crown is an asymmetric mess, like an inverted root system. I lean against it, give it a slap. It's like slapping a building. This is a tree out of Tolkien. It's a kauri.

Joe Bennett (A Land of Two Halves) referring to the McKinney kauri in Northland.

Now the pressure has been taken off kauri and other timber trees, including the distinctive rimu (red pine) and the long-lived totara (favoured for Maori war canoes), by one of the country's most successful imports – *Pinus radiata*. Pine was found to thrive in NZ, growing to maturity in just 35 years, and plantation forests are now widespread through the central North Island – the southern hemisphere's biggest, Kaingaroa Forest, lies southeast of Rotorua.

The icon in this book marks places that demonstrate a commitment to sustainability. Travellers seeking other sustainable tourism operators should look for operators accredited with Qualmark Green (www.qualmark.co.nz) or listed at Organic Explorer (www.organicexplorer.co.nz).

You won't get far into the bush without coming across one of its most prominent features – tree ferns. NZ is a land of ferns (more than 80 species) and most easily recognised are the mamaku (black tree fern) – which grows to 20m and can be seen in damp gullies throughout the country – and the 10m-high ponga (silver tree fern) with its distinctive white underside. The silver fern is equally at home as part of corporate logos and on the clothing of many of the country's top sportspeople.

National Parks

A third of the country – more than 5 million hectares – is protected in environmentally important parks and reserves that embrace almost every conceivable landscape: from mangrove-fringed inlets in the north to the snow-topped volcanoes of the Central Plateau, and from the forested fastness of the Ureweras in the east to the Southern Alps' majestic mountains, glaciers and fiords. The 14 national parks, three marine parks and more than 30 marine reserves, along with numerous forest parks, offer huge scope for wilderness experiences, ranging from climbing, snow skiing and mountain biking to tramping, kayaking and trout fishing.

The Department of Conservation website (www.doc.govt.nz) has useful information on the country's national parks, tracks and walkways. It also lists backcountry huts and campsites.

Three places are World Heritage areas: NZ's Subantarctic Islands, Tongariro National Park and Te Wahipounamu, an amalgam of several national parks in southwest NZ that boast the world's finest surviving Gondwanaland plants and animals in their natural habitats.

Access to the country's wild places is relatively straightforward, though huts on walking tracks require passes and may need to be booked in advance. In practical terms, there is little difference for travellers between a national park and a forest park, though dogs are not allowed in national parks without a permit. Camping is possible in all parks, but may be restricted to dedicated camping grounds – check first. Permits are required for hunting (game birds), and licences are needed for inland fishing (trout, salmon); both can be bought online at www.fishandgame.org.nz.

Maori Culture

John Huria

John Huria (Ngai Tahu, Muaupoko) has an editorial, research and writing background with a focus on Maori writing and culture. He was senior editor for Maori publishing company Huia (NZ) and now runs an editorial and publishing services company, Ahi Text Solutions Ltd (www.ahitextsolutions.co.nz).

'Maori' once just meant 'common' or 'everyday', but now it means...let's just begin by saying that there is a lot of 'then' and a lot of 'now' in the Maori world. Sometimes the cultural present follows on from the past quite seamlessly; sometimes things have changed hugely; sometimes we just want to look to the future.

Maori today are a diverse people. Some are engaged with traditional cultural networks and pursuits; others are occupied with adapting tradition and placing it into a dialogue with globalising culture. The Maori concept of *whanaungatanga* – family relationships – is important to the culture. And families spread out from the *whanau* (extended family) to the *hapu* (subtribe) and *iwi* (tribe) and even, in a sense, beyond the human world and into the natural and spiritual worlds.

Maori are New Zealand's *tangata whenua* (people of the land), and the Maori relationship with the land has developed over hundreds of years of occupation. Once a predominantly rural people, many Maori now live in urban centres, away from their traditional home base. But it's still common practice in formal settings to introduce oneself by referring to home: an ancestral mountain, river, sea or lake, or an ancestor. There's no place like home, but it's good to be away as well.

The best way to learn about the relationship between the land and the *tangata whenua* is to get out there and start talking with Maori.

If you're looking for a Maori experience in NZ you'll find it – in performance, in conversation, in an art gallery, on a tour...

Maori Then

Some three millennia ago people began moving eastward into the Pacific, sailing against the prevailing winds and currents (hard to go out, easier to return safely). Some stopped at Tonga and Samoa, and others settled the small central East Polynesian tropical islands.

The Maori colonisation of Aotearoa began from an original homeland known to Maori as Hawaiki. Skilled navigators and sailors travelled across the Pacific, using many navigational tools – currents, winds, stars, birds and wave patterns – to guide their large, double-hulled ocean-going craft to a new land. The first of many was the great navigator Kupe, who arrived, the story goes, chasing an octopus named Muturangi. But the distinction of giving NZ its well-known Maori name – Aotearoa – goes to his wife, Kuramarotini, who cried out, '*He ao, he ao tea, he ao tea roa!*' (A cloud, a white cloud, a long white cloud!).

Kupe and his crew journeyed around the land, and many places around Cook Strait (between the North and South Islands), and the Hokianga in Northland still bear the names that they gave them and the marks of his passage. Kupe returned to Hawaiki, leaving from (and naming) Northland's Hokianga. He gave other seafarers valuable navigational information. And then the great *waka* (ocean-going craft) began to arrive.

The *waka* that the first setters arrived on, and their landing places, are immortalised in tribal histories. Well-known *waka* include *Takitimu, Kurahaupo, Te Arawa, Mataatua, Tainui, Aotea* and *Tokomaru*. There are many others. Maori trace their genealogies back to those who arrived on the *waka* (and further back as well).

Arriving for the first time in NZ, two crew members of *Tainui* saw the red flowers of the pohutukawa tree, and they cast away their prized red feather ornaments, thinking that there were plenty to be had on shore.

What would it have been like making the transition from small tropical islands to a much larger, cooler land mass? Goodbye breadfruit, coconuts, paper mulberry; hello moa, fernroot, flax – and immense space (relatively speaking). NZ has over 15,000km of coastline. Rarotonga, by way of contrast, has a little over 30km. There was land, lots of it, and a flora and fauna that had developed more or less separately from the rest of the world for 80 million years. There was an untouched, massive fishery. There were great seaside mammalian convenience stores – seals and sea lions – as well as a fabulous array of birds.

The early settlers went on the move, pulled by love, by trade opportunities and greater resources; pushed by disputes and threats to security. When they settled, Maori established *mana whenua* (regional authority), whether by military campaigns, or by the peaceful methods of intermarriage and diplomacy. Looking over tribal history it's possible to see the many alliances, absorptions and extinctions that went on.

Histories were carried by the voice, in stories, songs and chants. Great stress was placed on accurate learning – after all, in an oral culture where people are the libraries, the past is always a generation or two away from oblivion.

Maori lived in *kainga,* small villages, which often had associated gardens. Housing was quite cosy by modern standards – often it was hard

HOW THE WORLD BEGAN

In the Maori story of creation, first there was the void, then the night, then Rangi-nui (sky father) and Papa-tu-a-nuku (earth mother) came into being, embracing with their children nurtured between them. But nurturing became something else. Their children were stifled in the darkness of their embrace. Unable to stretch out to their full dimensions and struggling to see clearly in the darkness, their children tried to separate them. Tawhiri-matea, the god of winds, raged against them; Tu-mata-uenga, the god of war, assaulted them. Each god child in turn tried to separate them, but still Rangi and Papa pressed against each other. And then Tane-mahuta, god of the great forests and of humanity, placed his feet against his father and his back against his mother and slowly, inexorably, began to move them apart. Then came the world of light, of demigods and humanity.

In this world of light Maui, the demigod ancestor, was cast out to sea at birth and was found floating in his mother's topknot. He was a shape-shifter, becoming a pigeon or a dog or an eel if it suited his purposes. He stole fire from the gods. Using his grandmother's jawbone, he bashed the sun so that it could only limp slowly across the sky, so that people would have enough time during the day to get things done (if only he would do it again!). Using the South Island as a canoe, he used the jawbone as a hook to fish up Te Ika a Maui (the fish of Maui) – the North Island. And, finally, he met his end trying to defeat death itself. The goddess of death, Hine Nui Te Po, had obsidian teeth in her vagina (obsidian is a volcanic glass that takes a razor edge when chipped). Maui attempted to reverse birth (and hence defeat death) by crawling into her birth canal to reach her heart as she slept. A small bird – a fantail – laughed at the absurd sight. Hine Nui Te Po awoke, and crushed Maui between her thighs. Death one, humanity nil.

to stand upright while inside. From time to time people would leave their home base and go to harvest seasonal foods. When peaceful life was interrupted by conflict, the people would withdraw to *pa,* fortified dwelling places.

And then Europeans began to arrive.

Maori Today

Today's culture is marked by new developments in the arts, business, sport and politics. Many historical grievances still stand, but some *iwi* (Ngai Tahu and Tainui, for example) have settled historical grievances and are major forces in the NZ economy. Maori have also addressed the decline in Maori language use by establishing *kohanga reo, kura kaupapa Maori* and *wananga* (Maori-medium preschools, schools and universities). There is now a generation of people who speak Maori as a first language. There is a network of Maori radio stations, and Maori TV is attracting a committed viewership. A recently revived Maori event is becoming more and more prominent – Matariki, or Maori New Year. The constellation Matariki is also known as Pleiades. It begins to rise above the horizon in late May or early June and its appearance traditionally signals a time for learning, planning and preparing as well as singing, dancing and celebrating. Watch out for talks and lectures, concerts, dinners, and even formal balls.

You can check out a map that shows *iwi* distribution and a good list of *iwi* (tribe) websites on Wikipedia (www.wikipedia.org).

Religion

Christian churches and denominations are important in the Maori world: televangelists, mainstream churches for regular and occasional worship, and two major Maori churches (Ringatu and Ratana) – we've got it all.

But in the (non–Judaeo Christian) beginning there were the *atua Maori,* the Maori gods, and for many Maori the gods are a vital and relevant force still. It is common to greet the earth mother and sky father when speaking formally at a *marae*. The gods are represented in art and carving, sung of in *waiata* (songs), invoked through *karakia* (prayer and incantation) when a meeting house is opened, when a *waka* is launched, even (more simply) when a meal is served. They are spoken of on the *marae* and in wider Maori contexts. The traditional Maori creation story is well known and widely celebrated.

The Arts

There are many collections of Maori *taonga* (treasures) around the country. Some of the largest and most comprehensive are at Wellington's Te Papa Museum and the Auckland Museum. Canterbury Museum in Christchurch also has a good collection, and Hokitika Museum has an exhibition showing the story of *pounamu* (nephrite jade, or greenstone).

You can stay up to date with what is happening in the Maori arts by reading *Mana* magazine (available from most newsagents), listening to *iwi* stations (www.irirangi.net) or weekly podcasts from Radio New Zealand (www.radionz.co.nz). Maori TV also has regular features on the Maori arts – check out www.maoritelevision.com.

Maori TV went to air in 2004, an emotional time for many Maori who could at last see their culture, their concerns and their language in a mass medium. Over 90% of content is NZ-made, and programs are in both Maori and English: they're subtitled and accessible to everyone. If you want to really get a feel for the rhythm and meter of spoken Maori from the comfort of your own chair, switch to Te Reo, a Maori-language-only channel.

TA MOKO

Ta moko is the Maori art of tattoo, traditionally worn by men on their faces, thighs and buttocks, and by women on their chins and lips. *Moko* were permanent grooves tapped into the skin using pigment (made from burnt caterpillar or kauri gum soot), and bone chisels: fine, sharp combs for broad work, and straight blades for detailed work. Museums in the major centres – Auckland, Wellington and Christchurch – all display traditional implements for *ta moko*.

The modern tattooist's gun is common now, but bone chisels are coming back into use for Maori who want to reconnect with tradition. Since the general renaissance in Maori culture in the 1960s, many artists have taken up *ta moko* and now many Maori wear *moko* with quiet pride and humility.

See Ngahuia Te Awekotuku's *Mau Moko: The World of Maori Tattoo* (2007) for the big picture, with powerful, beautiful images and an incisive commentary.

Can visitors get involved, or even get some work done? The term *kirituhi* (skin inscriptions) has arisen to describe Maori motif-inspired modern tattoos that non-Maori can wear.

CARVING

Traditional Maori carving, with its intricate detailing and curved lines, can transport the viewer. It's quite amazing to consider that it was done with stone tools, themselves painstakingly made, until the advent of iron (nails suddenly became very popular).

Some major traditional forms are *waka* (canoes), *pataka* (storage buildings), and *wharenui* (meeting houses). You can see sublime examples of traditional carving at Te Papa in Wellington, and at the following:

» **Maori & Colonial Museum** (p158) A *waka taua* (war canoe) dating back to 1867; Okains Bay, Banks Peninsula.

» **Otago Museum** (p189) Nice old *waka* and *whare runanga* (meeting house) carvings; Dunedin.

» **Canterbury Museum** (p137) A magnificent *poutokomanawa* or male ancestor figure, Christchurch.

The apex of carving today is the *whare whakairo* (carved meeting house). A commissioning group relates its history and ancestral stories to a carver, who then draws (sometimes quite loosely) on traditional motifs to interpret or embody the stories and ancestors in wood or composite fibreboard.

Rongomaraeroa Marae, by artist Cliff Whiting, at Te Papa in Wellington is a colourful example of a contemporary re-imagining of a traditional art form. The biggest change in carving (as with most traditional arts) has been in the use of new mediums and tools. Rangi Kipa uses a synthetic polymer called Corian to make his *hei tiki* (figure motif worn around the neck), the same stuff that is used to make kitchen benchtops. You can check out his gallery at www.rangikipa.com.

For information on Maori arts today, check out Toi Maori www.maoriart.org.nz.

WEAVING

Weaving was an essential art that provided clothing, nets and cordage, footwear for rough country travel, mats to cover earthen floors, and *kete* (bags). Many woven items are beautiful as well as practical. Some were major works – *korowai* (cloaks) could take years to finish. Woven predominantly with flax and bird feathers, they are worn now on ceremonial occasions, a stunning sight.

Working with natural materials for the greater good of the people involved getting things right by maintaining the supply of raw material and ensuring that it worked as it was meant to. Protocols were necessary, and women were dedicated to weaving under the aegis of the gods.

VISITING MARAE

As you travel around NZ, you will see many *marae* complexes. Often *marae* are owned by a descent group. They are also owned by urban Maori groups, schools, universities and church groups, and they should only be visited by arrangement with the owners. Some *marae* that may be visited include Huria Marae in Tauranga; Koriniti Marae on the Whanganui River Rd; Te Manuka Tutahi Marae in Wakatane; and Te Papa in Wellington.

Marae complexes include a *wharenui* (meeting house), which often embodies an ancestor. Its ridge is the backbone, the rafters are ribs, and it shelters the descendants. There is a clear space in front of the *wharenui* (ie the *marae atea*). Sometimes there are other buildings: a *wharekai* (dining hall); a toilet and shower block; perhaps even classrooms, play equipment and the like.

Hui (gatherings) are held at *marae*. Issues are discussed, classes conducted, milestones celebrated and the dead farewelled. *Te reo Maori* (the Maori language) is prominent, sometimes exclusively so.

Visitors sleep in the meeting house if a *hui* goes on for longer than a day. Mattresses are placed on the floor, someone may bring a guitar, and stories and jokes always go down well as the evening stretches out...

The Powhiri

If you visit a *marae* as part of an organised group, you'll be welcomed in a *powhiri* (formal welcome). The more common ones are outlined here.

There may be a *wero* (challenge). Using *taiaha* (quarter-staff) moves, a warrior will approach the visitors and place a baton on the ground for a visitor to pick up.

There is a *karanga* (ceremonial call). A woman from the host group calls to the visitors and a woman from the visitors responds. Their long, high, falling calls begin to overlap and interweave and the visiting group walks on to the *marae atea*.

It is then time for *whaikorero* (speechmaking). The hosts welcome the visitors, the visitors respond. Speeches are capped off by a *waiata* (song), and the visitors' speaker places *koha* (gift, usually an envelope of cash) on the *marae*. The hosts then invite the visitors to *hariru* (shake hands) and *hongi* (press foreheads together). Visitors and hosts are now united and will share light refreshments or a meal.

The Hongi

Press forehead and nose together firmly, shake hands, and perhaps offer a greeting such as *'Kia ora'* or *'Tena koe'*. Some prefer one press (for two or three seconds, or longer), others prefer two shorter (press, release, press). Men and women sometimes kiss on one cheek. Some people mistakenly think the *hongi* is a pressing of noses only (awkward to aim!) or the rubbing of noses (even more awkward).

Tapu

Tapu (spiritual restrictions) and *mana* (power and prestige) are taken seriously in the Maori world. Sit on chairs or seating provided (never on tables), and walk around people, not over them. The *powhiri* is *tapu*, and mixing food and *tapu* is right up there on the offence-o-meter. Do eat and drink when invited to do so by your hosts. You needn't worry about starvation: an important Maori value is *manaakitanga* (kindness).

Depending on the area, the *powhiri* has gender roles: women *karanga* (call), men *whaikorero* (orate); women lead the way on to the *marae*, men sit on the *paepae* (the speakers' bench at the front). In a modern context, the debate around these roles continues.

Today, tradition is greatly respected, but not all traditions are necessarily followed.

Flax was (and still is) the preferred medium for weaving. To get a strong fibre from flax leaves, weavers scraped away the leaves' flesh with a mussel shell, then pounded until it was soft, dyed it, then dried it. But contemporary weavers are using everything in their work: raffia, copper wire, rubber – even polar fleece and garden hoses!

Kupe's passage is marked around NZ: he left his sails (Nga Ra o Kupe) near Cape Palliser as triangular landforms; he named the two islands in Wellington Harbour Matiu and Makoro after his daughters; his blood stains the red rocks of Wellington's south coast.

The best place to experience weaving is to contact one of the many weavers running workshops. By learning the art, you'll appreciate the examples of weaving in museums even more. And if you want your own? Woven *kete* and backpacks have become fashion accessories and are on sale in most cities. Weaving is also found in dealer art galleries around the country.

HAKA

Experiencing *haka* can get the adrenaline flowing, as it did for one Pakeha observer in 1929 who thought of dark Satanic mills: 'They looked like fiends from hell wound up by machinery'. *Haka* can be awe-inspiring; they can also be uplifting. The *haka* is not only a war dance – it is used to welcome visitors, honour achievement, express identity or to put forth very strong opinions.

Haka involve chanted words, vigorous body movements, and *pukana* (when performers distort their faces, eyes bulging with the whites showing, perhaps with tongue extended).

The well-known *haka* 'Ka Mate', performed by the All Blacks before rugby test matches, is credited to the cunning fighting chief Te Rauparaha. It celebrates his escape from death. Chased by enemies, he hid himself in a food pit. After they had left, a friendly chief named Te Whareangi (the 'hairy man' referred to in the *haka*), let him out; he climbed out into the sunshine and performed 'Ka Mate'.

In the South Island you can experience *haka* at various cultural performances including at Ko Tane (p140) at Willowbank in Christchurch; Maori Tours (p74) in Kaikoura, Myths & Legends Eco-tours (p58) in Picton, and Kiwi Haka (p240) in Queenstown.

But the best displays of *haka* are at the national Te Matatini National Kapa Haka Festival when NZ's top groups compete. It is held every two years, with the next festival in February 2013 to take place in Rotorua.

Maori legends are all around you as you tour NZ: Maui's *waka* became today's Southern Alps; a *taniwha* (aupernatural creature) formed Lake Waikaremoana in its death throes; and a rejected Mt Taranaki walked into exile from the central North Island mountain group, carving the Whanganui River.

CONTEMPORARY VISUAL ART

A distinctive feature of Maori visual art is the tension between traditional Maori ideas and modern artistic mediums and trends. Shane Cotton produced a series of works that conversed with 19th-century painted meeting houses, which themselves departed from Maori carved houses. Kelcy Taratoa uses toys, superheroes and pop urban imagery alongside weaving and carving design.

Of course not all Maori artists use Maori motifs. Ralph Hotere is a major NZ artist who 'happens to be Maori' (his words), and his careerlong exploration of black speaks more to modernism than the traditional *marae* context.

Contemporary Maori art is by no means only about painting. Many other artists use installations as the preferred medium – look out for work by Jacqueline Fraser and Peter Robinson.

There are some great permanent exhibitions of Maori visual arts in the major centres. Both the Auckland and Christchurch Art Galleries hold strong collections, as does Wellington's Te Papa.

CONTEMPORARY THEATRE

The 1970s saw the emergence of many Maori playwrights and plays, and theatre is a strong area of the Maori arts today. Maori theatre drew heavily on the traditions of the *marae*. Instead of dimming the lights and immediately beginning the performance, many Maori theatre groups began with a stylised *powhiri,* had space for audience members to respond to the play, and ended with a *karakia* or a farewell.

Taki Rua is an independent producer of Maori work for both children and adults and has been in existence for over 25 years. As well as staging its shows in the major centres, it tours most of its work – check out its website (www.takirua.co.nz) for the current offerings. Maori drama is also often showcased at the professional theatres in the main centres as well as the biennial New Zealand International Festival. Hone Kouka and Briar Grace-Smith (both have published playscripts available) have toured their works around NZ and to festivals in the UK.

See Hirini Moko Mead's *Tikanga Maori,* Pat and Hiwi Tauroa's *Visiting a Marae,* and Anne Salmond's *Hui* for detailed information on Maori customs.

CONTEMPORARY DANCE

Contemporary Maori dance often takes its inspiration from *kapa haka* and traditional Maori imagery. The exploration of pre-European life also provides inspiration. For example, a Maori choreographer, Moss Patterson, used *kokowai* (a body-adorning paste made from reddish clay and shark oil) as the basis of his most recent piece of the same name.

NZ's leading specifically Maori dance company is the Atamira Dance Collective (www.atamiradance.co.nz), which has been producing critically acclaimed, beautiful and challenging work since 2000. If that sounds too earnest, another choreographer to watch out for is Mika Torotoro, who happily blends *kapa haka* (cultural dance), drag, opera, ballet and disco into his work. You can check out clips of his work at www.mika.co.nz.

Music plays an important role in traditional and contemporary Maori culture.

MAORI FILM-MAKING

Although there had already been successful Maori documentaries (*Patu!* and the *Tangata Whenua* series are brilliant, and available from some urban video stores), it wasn't until 1987 that NZ had its first fiction feature-length movie by a Maori director with Barry Barclay's *Ngati*. Mereta Mita was the first Maori woman to direct a fiction feature, with *Mauri* (1988). Both Mita and Barclay had highly political aims and ways of working, which involved a lengthy pre-production phase, during which they would consult with and seek direction from their *kaumatua* (elders). Films with significant Maori participation or control include the harrowing *Once Were Warriors* and the uplifting *Whale Rider*. Oscar-shortlisted Taika Waititi, of Te Whanau-a-Apanui descent, wrote and directed *Eagle vs Shark*.

The New Zealand Film Archive (www.filmarchive.org.nz) is a great place to experience Maori film, with most showings being either free or relatively inexpensive. It has offices in Auckland and Wellington.

The first NZ hip-hop song to become a hit was Dalvanius Prime's 'Poi E', which was sung entirely in Maori by the Patea Maori Club. It was the highest-selling single of 1984 in NZ, outselling all international artists.

MAORI WRITING

There are many novels and collections of short stories by Maori writers, and personal taste will govern your choices. How about approaching Maori writing regionally? Read Patricia Grace *(Potiki, Cousins, Dogside Story, Tu)* around Wellington, and maybe Witi Ihimaera *(Pounamu, Pounamu, The Matriarch, Bulibasha, The Whale Rider)* on the North Island's East Coast. Keri Hulme *(The Bone People, Stonefish)* and the South Island go together like a mass of whitebait bound in a frying pan by a single egg (ie very well). Read Alan Duff *(Once Were Warriors)* anywhere, but only if you want to be saddened, even shocked.

Definitely take James George *(Hummingbird, Ocean Roads)* with you to Auckland's West Coast beaches and Northland's Ninety Mile Beach. Paula Morris *(Queen of Beauty, Hibiscus Coast, Trendy but Casual)* and Kelly Ana Morey *(Bloom, Grace Is Gone)* – hmm, Auckland and beyond? If poetry appeals you can't go past the giant of Maori poetry in English, the late, lamented Hone Tuwhare *(Deep River Talk: Collected Poems)*. Famously sounding like he's at church and in the pub at the same time, you *can* take him anywhere.

The Kiwi Psyche

What Makes Kiwis Tick?

New Zealand is like that little guy at school when they're picking rugby teams – quietly waiting to be noticed, desperately wanting to be liked. Then, when he does get the nod, his sheer determination to prove himself propels him to score a completely unexpected try. When his teammates come to congratulate him he stares at the ground and mumbles, 'It was nothing, ay'.

While NZ is a proud little nation, Kiwis traditionally don't have time for show-offs. Jingoistic flag-waving is generally frowned upon. People who make an impression on the international stage are respected and admired, but flashy tall poppies have traditionally had their heads lopped off. This is perhaps a legacy of NZ's early egalitarian ideals – the ones that sought to avoid the worst injustices of the 'mother country' (Britain) by breaking up large land holdings and enthusiastically adopting a 'cradle to grave' welfare state. 'Just because someone's got a bigger car than me, or bigger guns, doesn't make them better' is the general Kiwi attitude.

People born in other countries make up 23% of NZ residents. Of these, the main regions of origin are the UK and Ireland (29%), the Pacific Islands (15%), Northeast Asia (15%) and Australia (7%).

NZ has rarely let its size get in the way of making a point on the international stage. A founding member of the League of Nations (the precursor to the UN), it ruffled feathers between the world wars by failing to blindly follow Britain's position. It was in the 1980s, however, that things got really interesting.

A Turbulent Decade

Modern Kiwi culture pivots on that decade. Firstly, the unquestioned primacy of rugby union as a source of social cohesion (which rivalled the country's commitment to the two world wars as a foundation of nation-building) was stripped away when tens of thousands of New Zealanders took to the streets to protest a tour by the South African rugby side in 1981. The protestors held that the politics of apartheid not only had a place in sport, they trumped it. The country was starkly divided; there were riots in paradise. The scar is still strong enough that most New Zealanders over the age of 40 will recognise the simple phrase 'The Tour' as referring to those events.

NZ is defined as a state in the Australian constitution. At the time of Australia's federation into one country it was hoped that NZ would join. On this side of the Tasman that idea proved as unpopular then as it does now.

The tour protests both harnessed and nourished a political and cultural renaissance among Maori that had already been rolling for a decade. Three years later, that renaissance found its mark when a reforming Labour government gave statutory teeth to the Waitangi Tribunal, an agency that has since guided a process of land return, compensation for past wrongs and interpretation of the Treaty of Waitangi – the 1840 pact between Maori and the Crown – as a living document.

At the same time antinuclear protests that had been rumbling for years gained momentum, with mass blockades of visiting US naval ships. In 1984 Prime Minister David Lange barred nuclear-powered or armed ships from entering NZ waters. The mouse had roared. As a result the US

'SO, WHAT DO YOU THINK OF NEW ZEALAND?' *RUSSELL BROWN*

That, by tradition, is the question that visitors are asked within an hour of disembarking in NZ. Sometimes they might be granted an entire day's research before being asked to pronounce, but asked they are. The question – composed equally of great pride and creeping doubt – is symbolic of the national consciousness.

When George Bernard Shaw visited for four weeks in 1934, he was deluged with what-do-you-think-of questions from newspaper reporters the length of the country. Although he never saw fit to write a word about NZ, his answers to those newspaper questions were collected and reprinted as *What I Saw in New Zealand: the Newspaper Utterances of George Bernard Shaw in New Zealand*. Yes, people really were that keen for vindication.

Other visitors were more willing to pronounce in print, including the British Liberal MP, David Goldblatt, who wrote an intriguing and prescient little book called *Democracy At Ease: a New Zealand Profile*. Goldblatt found New Zealanders a blithe people: kind, prosperous and fond of machines.

For the bon vivant Goldblatt, the attitude towards food and drink was all too telling. He found only 'the plain fare and even plainer fetch and carry of the normal feeding machine of this country' and shops catering 'in the same pedestrian fashion for a people never fastidious – the same again is the order of the day'.

Thus, a people with access to some of the best fresh ingredients on earth tended to boil everything to death. A nation strewn almost its entire length with excellent microclimates for viticulture produced only fortified plonk. Material comfort was valued, but was a plain thing indeed.

It took New Zealanders a quarter of a century more to shuck 'the same dull sandwiches', and embrace a national awareness – and, as Goldblatt correctly anticipated, it took 'hazards and misfortunes' to spur the 'divine discontent' for change.

But when it did happen, it really happened.

Russell Brown is a journalist and manager of the popular Public Address blog site (www.publicaddress.net).

threw NZ out of ANZUS, the country's main strategic military alliance, which also included Australia, declaring NZ 'a friend but not an ally'.

However, it was an event in the following year that completely changed the way NZ related to the world, when French government agents launched an attack in Auckland Harbour, sinking Greenpeace's antinuclear flagship *Rainbow Warrior* and killing one of its crew. Being bombed by a country that NZ had fought two world wars with – and the muted or nonexistent condemnation by other allies – left an indelible mark. It strengthened NZ's resolve to follow its own conscience in foreign policy, and in 1987 the New Zealand Nuclear Free Zone, Disarmament, and Arms Control Act became law.

'...a sordid act of international state-backed terrorism...' – Prime Minister David Lange, describing the bombing of the *Rainbow Warrior* (1986)

From the Boer to Vietnam Wars, NZ had blithely trotted off at the behest of the UK or US. Not anymore, as is demonstrated by its lack of involvement in the invasion of Iraq. That's not to say that the country shirks its international obligations: NZ troops continue to be deployed in peacekeeping capacities throughout the world and are currently active in Afghanistan.

If that wasn't enough upheaval for one decade, 1986 saw another bitter battle split the community – this time over the decriminalisation of homosexuality. The debate was particularly rancorous, but the law that previously incarcerated consenting gay adults was repealed, paving the way for the generally accepting society that NZ is today. In 1999 Georgina Beyer, an openly transsexual former prostitute, would win a once-safe rural seat off a conservative incumbent – an unthinkable achievement in most of the world, let alone in the NZ of 13 years earlier.

Yet while the 1980s saw the country jump to the left on social issues, simultaneously economic reforms were carried out that were an extreme step to the right (to paraphrase one-time Hamiltonian Richard O'Brien's song 'The Time Warp'). The bloated public sector was slashed, any state assets that weren't bolted to the floor were sold off, regulation was removed from many sectors, trade barriers dismantled and the power of the unions greatly diminished.

If there is broad agreement that the economy had to be restructured, the reforms carried a heavy price. The old social guarantees are not as sure. New Zealanders work long hours for lower wages than their Australian cousins would ever tolerate. Compared with other Organisation for Economic Co-operation and Development (OECD) nations, NZ family incomes are low, child poverty rates are high and the gap between rich and poor is widening.

Ironically, the person responsible for the nuclear age was a New Zealander. In 1917 Ernest Rutherford was the first to split the nucleus of an atom. His face appears on the $100 note.

Yet there is a dynamism about NZ that was rare in the 'golden weather' years before the reforms. NZ farmers take on the world without the massive subsidies of yore, and Wellington's inner city – once virtually closed after dark by oppressive licensing laws – now thrives with great bars and restaurants.

As with the economic reforms, the 'Treaty process' of redress and reconciliation with Maori makes some New Zealanders uneasy, more in their uncertainty about its extent than that it has happened at all. The Maori population sat somewhere between 85,000 and 110,000 at the time of first European contact 200 years ago. Disease and warfare subsequently decimated the population, but a high birth rate now sees about 15% of New Zealanders (565,000 people) identify as Maori, and that proportion is likely to grow.

The implication of the Treaty is one of partnership between Maori and the British Crown, together forging a bicultural nation. After decades of attempted cultural assimilation it's now accepted in most quarters that the indigenous culture has a special and separate status within the country's ethnic mix. For example, Maori is an official language and there is a separate electoral roll granting Maori guaranteed parliamentary seats.

Yet room has had to be found for the many New Zealanders of neither British nor Maori heritage. In each new wave of immigration there has been a tendency to demonise before gradually accepting and celebrating what the new cultures have to offer. This happened with the Chinese in the mid-19th century, Croatians at the beginning of the 20th, Pacific Islanders in the 1970s and, most recently, the Chinese again in the 1990s. That said, NZ society is more integrated and accepting than most. People of all races are represented in all levels of society and race isn't an obstacle to achievement.

IT'S A WOMAN'S WORLD

New Zealand is justifiably proud of being the first country in the world to give women the vote (in 1893). Kate Sheppard, the hero of the women's suffrage movement, even features on the country's $10 bill. Despite that early achievement, the real role for women in public life was modest for many years. That can hardly be said now. Since 1997 the country has had two female prime ministers and for a time in 2000 every key constitutional position was held by a woman, including the prime minister, attorney general, chief justice, governor general and head of state – although New Zealanders can't take credit for choosing Betty Windsor for that last role. At the same time a Maori queen headed the Kingitanga (King Movement; see p301) and a woman led NZ's biggest listed corporation. Things have slipped a little since and only two of those roles are held by women – and, yes, one of those is filled by Queen Elizabeth II.

A SPORTING CHANCE

The arena where Kiwis have most sated their desperation for recognition on the world stage is sport. In 2011, NZ was ranked the third most successful sporting nation per capita in the world (behind only Jamaica and Norway). NZ's teams are the current world champions in Rugby Union and Rugby League, holding both the men's and women's world cup in each code.

For most of the 20th century, NZ's All Blacks dominated international rugby union, with one squad even dubbed 'The Invincibles'. Taking over this pastime of the British upper class did wonders for national identity and the game is now interwoven with NZ's history and culture. The 2011 Rugby World Cup victory did much to raise spirits after a year of tragedy and economic gloom.

For all rugby's influence on the culture, don't go to a game expecting to be caught up in an orgy of noise and cheering. Rugby crowds at Auckland's Eden Park are as restrained as their teams are cavalier, but they get noisier as you head south. In contrast, a home game for the NZ Warriors rugby league team at Auckland's Mt Smart Stadium is a thrilling spectacle, especially when the Polynesian drummers kick in.

Despite the everyman appeal of rugby union in NZ (unlike in the UK), rugby league retains the status of the working-class sport and support is strongest from Auckland's Maori, Polynesian and other immigrant communities. Still, taking the Rubgy League World Cup off the Australians – NZ's constant arch-rivals – brought a smile to the faces of even the staunchest supporters of the rival rugby code.

Netball is the leading sport for women and the one in which the national team, the Silver Ferns, perpetually vies for world supremacy with the Australians – one or other of the countries has taken the world championship at every contest (except for a three-way tie in 1979).

In 2010 the All Whites, NZ's national soccer (football) squad, competed in the FIFA World Cup for the second time ever, emerging with the totally unanticipated distinction of being the only unbeaten team in the competition. They didn't win any games either, but most Kiwis were overjoyed to have seen their first ever World Cup goals and three draws.

Other sports in which NZ punches above its weight include sailing, rowing, canoeing, equestrian, cycling and triathlon. The most Olympic medals NZ has won have been in athletics, particularly in track and field events. Cricket is the established summer team sport, although not one in which the Kiwis are currently setting the world alight.

If you truly want to discover the good, the bad and the ugly of the national psyche, the sporting field isn't a bad place to start.

For the younger generation, for whom the 1980s are prehistory, political apathy is the norm. Perhaps it's because a decade of progressive government has given them little to kick against – unlike those politicised by the anti–Iraq War movements elsewhere. Ironically, as NZ has finally achieved its own interesting, independent cultural sensibility, the country's youth seem more obsessed with US culture than ever. This is particularly true within the hip-hop scene, where a farcical identification with American gangsta culture has developed into a worrying youth gang problem.

For many, Sir Edmund Hillary, the first person to climb Mt Everest, was the consummate New Zealander: humble, practical and concerned for social justice. A public outpouring of grief followed his death in 2008.

A Long Way From Britain

Most Kiwis (except perhaps the farmers) would probably wish it rained a little less and they got paid a little more, but it sometimes takes a few years travelling on their 'Big OE' (Overseas Experience – a traditional rite of passage) before they realise how good they've got it. In a 2011 study of the quality of life in the world's major cities, Auckland was rated third and Wellington 13th.

Despite all the change, key elements of the NZ identity are an unbroken thread, and fortune is still a matter of economics rather than class. If you are well served in a restaurant or shop, it will be out of politeness or pride in the job, rather than servility.

In country areas and on bushwalks don't be surprised if you're given a cheery greeting from passers-by, especially in the South Island. In a legacy of the British past, politeness is generally regarded as one of the highest virtues. A 'please' and 'thank you' will get you a long way. The three great exceptions to this rule are: a) on the road, where genteel Dr Jekylls become raging Mr Hydes, especially if you have the misfortune of needing to change lanes in Auckland; b) if you don't speak English very well; and c) if you are Australian.

The latter two traits are the product of insularity and a smallness of world view that tends to disappear among Kiwis who have travelled (and luckily many do). The NZ/Australian rivalry is taken much more seriously on this side of the Tasman Sea. Although it's very unlikely that Kiwis will be rude outright, visiting Aussies must get pretty sick of the constant ribbing, much of it surprisingly ill-humoured. It's a sad truth that while most Australians would cheer on a NZ sports team if they were playing anyone other than their own, the opposite is true in NZ.

In 2009 and 2010 NZ topped the Global Peace Index, earning the distinction of being rated the world's most peaceful country. In 2011 it dropped to second place behind Iceland – something to do with all those *haka* performed during the Rugby World Cup, perhaps?

Number-Eight Wire

You might on your travels hear the phrase 'number-eight wire' and wonder what on earth it means. It's a catchphrase New Zealanders still repeat to themselves to encapsulate a national myth: that NZ's isolation and its pioneer stock created a culture in which ingenuity allowed problems to be solved and tools to be built from scratch. A NZ farmer, it was said, could solve pretty much any problem with a piece of number-eight wire (the gauge used for fencing on farms).

It's actually largely true – NZ farms are full of NZ inventions. One reason big offshore film and TV producers bring their projects here – apart from the low wages and huge variety of locations – is that they like the can-do attitude and ability to work to a goal of NZ technical crews. Many more New Zealanders have worked as managers, roadies or chefs for famous recording artists (everyone from Led Zeppelin and U2 to Madonna) than have enjoyed the spotlight themselves. Which just goes to show that New Zealanders operate best at the intersection of practicality and creativity, with an endearing (and sometimes infuriating) humility to boot.

No matter where you are in NZ, you're never more than 128km from the sea.

Arts & Music

It took a hundred years for post-colonial New Zealand to develop its own distinctive artistic identity. In the first half of the 20th century it was writers and visual artists who led the charge. By the 1970s, NZ pub rockers had conquered Australia, while in the 1980s, indie-music obsessives the world over hooked into Dunedin's weird and wonderful alternative scene. However, it took the success of the film industry in the 1990s to catapult the nation's creativity into the global consciousness.

Literature

A nationalist movement first arose in NZ literature in the 1930s, striving for an independent identity and challenging the notion of NZ simply being an annexe of the 'mother country'.

Katherine Mansfield's work began a NZ tradition in short fiction, and for years the standard was carried by novelist Janet Frame, whose dramatic life was depicted in Jane Campion's film of her autobiography, *An Angel at My Table*. Frame's novel *The Carpathians* (1989) won the Commonwealth Writers' Prize. A new era of international recognition began in 1985 when Keri Hulme's haunting *The Bone People* won the Booker Prize (the world is still waiting for the follow-up, *Bait*).

It wasn't until 2007 that another Kiwi looked likely to snag the Booker. Lloyd Jones' *Mister Pip* was pipped at the post, but the nomination rocketed his book up literature charts the world over; a film version is due in 2012.

Less recognised internationally, Maurice 'gee-I've-won-a-lot-of-awards' Gee has gained the nation's annual top fiction gong six times, most recently with *Blindsight* (2005) and *Live Bodies* (1998). His much-loved children's novel *Under the Mountain* (1979) was made into a seminal NZ TV series in 1981 and then a major motion picture in 2009. In 2004 the adaptation of another of his novels, *In My Father's Den* (1972), won major awards at international film festivals and is one of the country's highest grossing films. His latest novel is *Access Road* (2009).

Maurice is an auspicious name for NZ writers, with the late Maurice Shadbolt achieving much acclaim for his many novels, particularly those set during the NZ Wars. Try *Season of the Jew* (1987) or *The House of Strife* (1993).

MAORI VOICES IN PRINT

Some of the most interesting and enjoyable NZ fiction voices belong to Maori writers, with Booker-winner Keri Hulme leading the way. Witi Ihimaera's novels give a wonderful insight into small-town Maori life on the East Coast – especially *Bulibasha* (1994) and *The Whale Rider* (1987), which was made into an acclaimed film – while *Nights in the Gardens of Spain* (1996) casts a similar light on Auckland's gay scene. Patricia Grace's work is similarly filled with exquisitely told stories of rural *marae*-centred life: try *Mutuwhenua* (1978), *Potiki* (1986), *Dogside Story* (2001) or *Tu* (2004).

MIDDLE-EARTH TOURISM

If you are one of those travellers inspired to come down under by the scenery of the *LOTR* movies, you won't be disappointed. Jackson's decision to film in NZ wasn't mere patriotism. Nowhere else on earth will you find such wildly varied, unspoiled landscapes – not to mention poorly paid actors.

You will doubtless recognise some places from the films. For example, Hobbiton (near Matamata), Mt Doom (instantly recognisable as towering Ngauruhoe) or the Misty Mountains (the South Island's Southern Alps). The visitor information centres in Twizel or Queenstown should be able to direct you to local *LOTR* sites of interest. If you're serious about finding the exact spots where scenes were filmed, buy a copy of Ian Brodie's nerdtastic *The Lord of the Rings: Location Guidebook*, which includes instructions, and even GPS coordinates, for finding all the important places.

Keep an eye out for new tours visiting locations from *The Hobbit*, Jackson's new Middle Earth opus due to be released late 2012.

Cinema & TV

If you first got interested in NZ by watching it on the silver screen, you're in good company. Sir Peter Jackson's NZ-made *Lord of the Rings* (*LOTR*) trilogy was the best thing to happen to NZ tourism since Captain Cook.

Other than 2003's winner *Return of the King*, *The Piano* is the only NZ movie to be nominated for a Best Picture Oscar. Jane Campion was the first Kiwi nominated as Best Director and Peter Jackson the first to win it.

Yet NZ cinema is hardly ever easygoing. In his BBC-funded documentary, *Cinema of Unease,* NZ actor Sam Neill described the country's film industry as 'uniquely strange and dark', producing bleak, haunted work. One need only watch Lee Tamahore's harrowing *Once Were Warriors* (1994) to see what he means.

The *Listener*'s film critic, Philip Matthews, makes a slightly more upbeat observation: 'Between (Niki Caro's) *Whale Rider,* (Christine Jeffs') *Rain* and *Lord of the Rings,* you can extract the qualities that our best films possess. Beyond slick technical accomplishment, all share a kind of land-mysticism, an innately supernatural sensibility'.

You could add to this list Jane Campion's *The Piano* (1993), Brad McGann's *In My Father's Den* (2004) and Jackson's *Heavenly Creatures* (1994) – all of which use magically lush scenery to couch disturbing violence. It's a land-mysticism constantly bordering on the creepy.

Even when Kiwis do humour it's as resolutely black as their rugby jerseys; check out Jackson's early splatter-fests and Taika Waititi's *Boy* (2010). Exporting NZ comedy hasn't been easy, yet the HBO-produced TV musical parody *Flight of the Conchords* – featuring a mumbling, bumbling Kiwi folk-singing duo trying to get a break in New York – has found surprising international success.

The TV show *Popstars* originated in New Zealand, though the resulting group, True Bliss, was short-lived. The series concept was then picked up in Australia, the UK, and the US, inspiring the *Idol* series.

It's the Polynesian giggle-factor that seems likeliest to break down the bleak house of NZ cinema, with feel-good-through-and-through *Sione's Wedding* (2006) netting the second-biggest local takings of any NZ film.

New Zealanders have gone from never seeing themselves in international cinema to having whole cloned armies of Temuera Morrisons invading the universe in *Star Wars*. Familiar faces such as Cliff Curtis and Karl Urban seem to constantly pop up playing Mexican or Russian gangsters in action movies. Many of them got their start in long-running soap opera *Shortland St* (7pm weekdays, TV2).

While the tourist industry waits for Jackson's *The Hobbit* (due late 2012), the NZ film industry has quietly continued producing well-crafted, affecting movies, such as *The Topp Twins: Untouchable Girls* (people's choice documentary winner at the Toronto and Melbourne film festivals, 2009).

Music

NZ music began with the *waiata* (singing) developed by Maori following their arrival in the country. The main musical instruments were wind instruments made of bone or wood, the most well known of which is the *nguru* (also known as the 'nose flute'), while percussion was provided by chest- and thigh-slapping. These days, the liveliest place to see Maori music being performed is at *kapa haka* competitions in which groups compete with their own routines of traditional song and dance. In a similar vein is the Pasifika Festival in Auckland, which has areas to represent each of the Pacific Islands. It is a great place to see both traditional and modern forms of Polynesian music, whether that means modern hip-hop beats or throbbing Cook Island drums, or island-style guitar, ukulele and slide guitar.

Gareth Shute

Gareth Shute wrote this music section. He is the author of four books, including *Hip Hop Music in Aotearoa* and *NZ Rock 1987–2007.* He is also a musician and has toured the UK, Europe and Australia as a member of The Ruby Suns and The Brunettes. He now plays in indie soul group The Cosbys.

Early European immigrants brought their own styles of music and gave birth to local variants during the early 1900s. In the 1950s Douglas Lilburn became one of the first internationally recognised NZ classical composers. More recently the country has produced a number of world-renowned musicians in this field, including opera singer Dame Kiri Te Kanawa, million-selling pop diva Hayley Westenra, composer John Psathas (who created music for the 2004 Olympic Games) and composer/percussionist Gareth Farr (who also performs in drag under the name Lilith). Each of the main universities in NZ has its own music school and these often have free concerts, which visitors can attend. Many of Christchurch's traditional venues were damaged in the earthquakes, and concerts in the city are often now held at the Events Village in Hagley Park.

NZ also has a strong rock-music scene, its most acclaimed exports being the revered indie label Flying Nun and the music of the Finn Brothers. In 1981 Flying Nun was started by Christchurch record store owner Roger Shepherd (who sold it in the '90s, but bought back partial ownership in 2009). Many of the early groups came from Dunedin, where local musicians took the DIY attitude of punk but used it to produce a lo-fi indie-pop that received rave reviews from the likes of *NME* in the UK and *Rolling Stone* magazine in the US. Billboard even claimed in 1989: 'There doesn't seem to be anything on Flying Nun Records that is less than excellent.'

For indie rock fans, a great source of local information is www.cheeseontoast. co.nz, which lists gigs and has interviews/photographs of bands (both local and international). Local hip hop, pop, and rock is also discussed at www.thecorner.co.nz. One of the longest running local music websites is www.muzic.net.nz.

Many of the musicians from the Flying Nun scene still perform live to this day, including David Kilgour (from The Clean), Martin Phillipps (from The Chills), and Shayne Carter (from the Straitjacket Fits, now fronting Dimmer and The Adults). These days, the spirit of the scene is kept alive at Chick's Hotel (p199) in Port Chalmers (near Dunedin). The indie scene in NZ is being kept fresh by newer labels such as Lil Chief Records and Arch Hill Recordings. For more adventurous listeners, Bruce Russell continues to play in influential underground group The Dead C, and releases music through his Corpus Hermeticum label.

Since the millennium, the NZ music scene has developed a new vitality after the government convinced commercial radio stations to adopt a voluntary quota of 20% local music. This enabled commercially oriented musicians to develop solid careers. Rock groups such as Shihad, The Feelers and Op-shop have thrived in this environment, as have a set of soulful female solo artists (who all happen to have Maori heritage): Bic Runga, Anika Moa, and Brooke Fraser (daughter of All Black Bernie Fraser).

However, the genres of music that have been adopted most enthusiastically by Maori and Polynesian New Zealanders have been reggae (in the 1970s) and hip-hop (in the 1980s), which has led to distinct local forms. In Wellington, a thriving jazz scene took on a reggae influence to create a host of groups that blend dub, roots, and funky jazz – most notably Fat Freddy's Drop. The national public holiday, Waitangi Day, on 6 February, also happens to fall on the birthday of Bob Marley and annual reggae concerts are held on this day in Auckland and Wellington.

The local hip-hop scene has its heart in the suburbs of South Auckland, which have a high concentration of Maori and Pacific Island residents. This area is home to one of NZ's foremost hip-hop labels, Dawn Raid, which takes its name from the infamous early-morning house raids of the 1970s that police performed on Pacific Islanders suspected of outstaying their visas.

Dawn Raid's most successful artist is Savage, who sold a million copies of his single 'Swing' after it was featured in the movie *Knocked Up*. Within NZ, the most well-known hip-hop acts are Scribe, Che Fu, and Smashproof (whose song 'Brother' held number one on the NZ singles charts longer than any other local act).

Early in the new millennium, NZ also produced two internationally acclaimed garage rock acts: the Datsuns and the D4.

Dance music had its strongest following in Christchurch in the 1990s, spawning dub/electronica outfit Salmonella Dub and its offshoot act, Tiki Taane. Drum 'n' bass remains popular locally and has spawned internationally renowned acts such as Concord Dawn and Shapeshifter. Unfortunately the music scene in Christchurch was crippled by the earthquakes in late 2010 and early 2011. In the interim, a number of temporary spaces have opened up as gig venues; a full list of events can be found at www.christchurchmusic.org.nz. Further south, many local bands tour through Queenstown during the ski season, with the main venue being Dux de Lux (p240). Christchurch venues to look out for include Dux Live (p153) and Darkroom (p153).

An up-to-date list of gigs in the main centres is listed at www.grooveguide.co.nz. Tickets for most events can be bought at: www.ticketek.co.nz, www.ticketmaster.co.nz, or, for smaller gigs, www.undertheradar.co.nz.

THE BROTHERS FINN

There are certain tunes that all Kiwis can sing along to, given a beer and the opportunity. A surprising proportion of these were written by Tim and Neil Finn, and many of their songs have gone on to be international hits.

Tim Finn first came to prominence in the 1970s group Split Enz. When the original guitarist quit, Neil flew over to join the band in the UK despite being only 15 at the time. Split Enz amassed a solid following in Australia, New Zealand and Canada before disbanding in 1985.

Neil then formed Crowded House with two Australian musicians (Paul Hester and Nick Seymour) and one of their early singles, 'Don't Dream It's Over', hit number two on the US charts. Tim later did a brief spell in the band, during which the brothers wrote 'Weather With You' – a song that reached number seven on the UK charts, pushing their album *Woodface* to gold sales. The original line-up of Crowded House played their final show in 1996 in front of 100,000 people on the steps of the Sydney Opera House (though Finn and Seymour reformed the group in 2007 and continue to tour and record occasionally). Tim and Neil have both released a number of solo albums, as well as releasing material together as the Finn Brothers.

More recently, Neil has also remained busy, organising a set of shows/releases under the name Seven Worlds Collide, which is a collaboration with well-known overseas musicians, including Jeff Tweedy (Wilco), Johnny Marr (The Smiths) and members of Radiohead. His latest band is the Pajama Club, a collaboration with wife Sharon and Auckland musicians Sean Donnelly and Alana Skyring.

Neil's son Liam also has a burgeoning solo career, which has seen him tour the US with Eddie Vedder and The Black Keys, as well as appearing on the David Letterman show. Both Tim and Neil were born in the small town of Te Awamutu and the local museum has a collection that documents their work.

In summer, many of the beachfront towns throughout the country are visited by touring bands (winery shows are also popular).

A number of South Island festivals take place throughout the summer months, including Rhythm and Alps at Mt Hutt near Christchurch, and the funky Rippon Open Air Festival in a lakeside vineyard near Wanaka

Visual Arts

The NZ 'can do' attitude extends to the visual arts. If you're visiting a local's home don't be surprised to find one of the owner's paintings on the wall or one of their mate's sculptures in the back garden, pieced together out of bits of shell, driftwood and a length of the magical 'number-eight wire'.

This is symptomatic of a flourishing local art and crafts scene cultivated by lively tertiary courses churning out traditional carvers and weavers, jewellery makers, multimedia boffins, and moulders of metal and glass. The larger cities have excellent dealer galleries representing interesting local artists working across all media.

Not all the best galleries are in Auckland or Wellington. The energetic Govett-Brewster Art Gallery – home to the legacy of sculptor and film-maker Len Lye – is worth a visit to the North Island's New Plymouth in itself, and Gore's Eastern Southland Gallery (p280) has an important and growing collection.

A wide range of cultural events is listed on www.eventfinder.co.nz. This is a good place to find out about concerts, classical music recitals and *kapa haka* performances. For more specific information on the NZ classical music scene, see www.sounz.org.nz.

Traditional Maori art has a distinctive visual style with well-developed motifs that have been embraced by NZ artists of every race. In the painting medium, these include the cool modernism of the work of Gordon Walters and the more controversial pop-art approach of Dick Frizzell's *Tiki* series. Likewise, Pacific Island themes are common, particularly in Auckland. An example is the work of Niuean-born Auckland-raised John Pule.

It should not be surprising that in a nation so defined by its natural environment, landscape painting constituted the first post-European body of art. John Gully and Petrus van der Velden were among those to arrive and paint memorable (if sometimes overdramatised) depictions of the land.

A little later, Charles Frederick Goldie painted a series of compelling, realist portraits of Maori, who were feared to be a dying race. Debate over the political propriety of Goldie's work raged for years, but its value is widely accepted now: not least because Maori themselves generally acknowledge and value them as ancestral representations.

From the 1930s NZ art took a more modern direction and produced some of the country's most celebrated artists including Rita Angus, Toss Woollaston and Colin McCahon. McCahon is widely regarded to have been the country's most important artist. His paintings might seem inscrutable, even forbidding, but even where McCahon lurched into Catholic mysticism or quoted screeds from the Bible, his spirituality was rooted in geography. His bleak, brooding landscapes evoke the sheer power of NZ's terrain.

Survival Guide

Accommodation

Across the South Island you can bed down in historic guesthouses, facility-laden hotels, uniform motel units, beautifully situated campsites, and hostels that range in character from clean-living to tirelessly party-prone.

Accommodation listings are in order of authorial preference, based on our assessment of atmosphere, cleanliness, facilities, location and bang for your buck.

If you're travelling during peak tourist seasons, book your bed well in advance. Accommodation is most in demand (and at its priciest) during the summer holidays from Christmas to late January, at Easter and during winter in snowy resort towns like Queenstown.

Note that booking ahead for accommodation in Christchurch is strongly recommended, as hostels, motels and hotels are often busy with consultants and tradespeople working on the city's rebuild.

Visitor information centres in places such as Queenstown and Wanaka provide reams of local accommodation information, often in the form of folders detailing facilities and up-to-date prices; many can also make bookings on your behalf.

For online listings, visit **Automobile Association** (AA; www.aa.co.nz) and **Jasons** (www.jasons.com).

B&Bs

Bed and breakfast (B&B) accommodation is a growth industry across NZ's South Island, popping up in the middle of cities, in rural hamlets and on stretches of isolated coastline, with rooms on offer in everything from suburban bungalows to stately manors owned by one family for generations.

Breakfast may be 'continental' (cereal, toast and tea or coffee), 'hearty continental' (add yoghurt, fruit, home-baked bread or muffins), or a stomach-loading cooked meal including eggs, bacon and sausages. Some B&B hosts may also cook dinner for guests and advertise dinner, bed and breakfast (DB&B) packages.

B&B tariffs are typically in the $120 to $180 bracket (per double), though some places charge upwards of $300 per double. Some hosts continue to be cheeky-as-a-kea, charging hefty prices for what is, in essence, a bedroom in their home.

Online resources:

Bed & Breakfast Book (www.bnb.co.nz)

Bed and Breakfast Directory (www.bed-and-breakfast.co.nz)

Camping & Holiday Parks

Campers and campervan drivers alike converge upon NZ's hugely popular 'holiday parks', slumbering peacefully in powered and unpowered sites, cheap bunk rooms (dorm rooms), cabins and self-contained units that are often called motels or tourist flats. Well-equipped communal kitchens, dining areas and games and TV rooms often feature. In cities, holiday parks are usually a fair way from the action, but in smaller towns they can be impressively central or near lakes, beaches, rivers and forests.

The nightly cost of holiday-park camping is usually between $15 and $20 per adult, with children charged half-price; powered sites are a couple of dollars more. Cabin/unit accommodation normally ranges from $60 to $120 per double. Unless noted otherwise, the prices we've listed for campsites, campervan sites, huts and

BOOK YOUR STAY ONLINE

For more accommodation reviews by Lonely Planet authors, check out http://hotels.lonelyplanet.com. You'll find independent reviews, as well as recommendations on the best places to stay. Best of all, you can book online.

SLEEPING PRICE RANGES

The following price ranges refer to a double with en suite.

- **$ Budget** Less than $100
- **$$ Midrange** $100–180
- **$$$ Top end** More than $180

Prices generally increase by 20% to 25% in Christ church and Queenstown. Here you can still find budget accommodation at up to $100 per double, but midrange stretches from $100 to $200, with top-end rooms more than $200.

cabins are for two people. The 'big three' holiday park operators around NZ – Top 10, Kiwi Parks and Family Parks – all offer discount cards for loyal slumberers.

DOC CAMPSITES & FREEDOM CAMPING

A fantastic option for those in campervans are the 250-plus vehicle-accessible 'Conservation Campsites' run by the **Department of Conservation** (DOC; www.doc.govt.nz), with fees ranging from free (basic toilets and fresh water) to $19 per adult (flush toilets and showers). DOC publishes free brochures with detailed descriptions and instructions to find every campsite (even GPS coordinates). Pick up copies from DOC offices before you hit the road, or visit the website.

DOC also looks after hundreds of 'Backcountry Huts', which can only be reached on foot. See the website for details.

Never just assume it's OK to camp somewhere. Always ask a local first. Check at the local i-SITE or DOC office, or with commercial camping grounds. If you are freedom camping treat the area with respect (p349). Instant fines can be charged for camping in prohibited areas, or irresponsible disposal of waste.

For more freedom camping info see, www.camping.org.nz.

Farmstays

Farmstays open the door on the agricultural side of South Island life, with visitors encouraged to get some dirt beneath their fingernails at orchards, and dairy, sheep and cattle farms. Costs can vary widely, with B&Bs generally ranging from $80 to $120. Some farms have separate cottages where you can fix your own food, while others offer low-cost, shared, backpacker-style accommodation.

Farm Helpers in NZ (FHINZ; www.fhinz.co.nz) produces a booklet ($25) that lists around 350 NZ farms providing lodging in exchange for four to six hours' work per day. **Rural Holidays NZ** (www.ruralholidays.co.nz) lists farmstays and homestays throughout the country on its website.

Hostels

The South Island is packed to the rafters with backpacker hostels, both independent and part of large chains, ranging from small, homestay-style affairs with a handful of beds to refurbished hotels and towering modern structures in the big cities. Hostel bed prices listed throughout this book are nonmember rates, usually between $25 and $35 per night.

If you're a Kiwi travelling in your own country, be warned that some hostels only admit overseas travellers, typically inner-city places. If you encounter such discrimination, either try another hostel or insist that you're a genuine traveller and not a bedless neighbour.

Online, www.hostelworld.com is useful for pre-trip planning.

HOSTEL ORGANISATIONS

Budget Backpacker Hostels (BBH; www.bbh.co.nz)

PRACTICALITIES

- **News** Leaf through Christchurch's *The Press* newspaper, or Dunedin's *Otago Daily Times*. Online check out www.stuff.co.nz and www.odt.co.nz.
- **TV** Watch one of the national government-owned TV stations (TV One, TV2, TVNZ 6, TVNZ 7, Maori TV and the 100% Maori language Te Reo) or the subscriber-only Sky TV (www.skytv.co.nz).
- **Radio** Tune in to Radio National for current affairs and Concert FM for classical and jazz (see www.radionz.co.nz for frequencies). Kiwi FM (www.kiwifm.co.nz) showcases lots of NZ music; Radio Hauraki (www.hauraki.co.nz) cranks out classic rock (the national appetite for Fleetwood Mac is insatiable...).
- **DVDs** Kiwi DVDs are encoded for Region 4, which includes Mexico, South America, Central America, Australia, the Pacific and the Caribbean.
- **Electrical** To plug yourself into the electricity supply (230V AC, 50Hz), use a three-pin adaptor (the same as in Australia; different from British three-pin adaptors).
- **Weights & measures** NZ uses the metric system.

WWOOFING

If you don't mind getting your hands dirty, an economical way of travelling around NZ involves doing some voluntary work as a member of **Willing Workers on Organic Farms** (WWOOF; ☎03-544 9890; www.wwoof.co.nz). Membership of this popular, well-established international organisation scores you access to hundreds of organic and permaculture farms, market gardens and other environmentally sound cottage industries across the country. Down on the farm, in exchange for a hard day's work, owners provide food, accommodation and some hands-on organic farming experience. Contact farm owners a week or two beforehand to arrange your stay, as you would for a hotel or hostel – don't turn up unannounced!

A one-year online membership costs $40; an online membership and a farm-listing book, which is mailed to you, costs $50. You should be part of a Working Holiday Scheme when you visit NZ, as the immigration department considers WWOOFers to be working.

NZ's biggest hostel group, with around 300 hostels on its books, including homestays and farmstays. Membership costs $45 and entitles you to stay at member hostels at rates listed in the annual (free) *BBH Backpacker Accommodation* booklet. Nonmembers pay an extra $3 per night, though not all hostel owners charge the difference. Pick up a membership card from any member hostel, or have one mailed to you overseas for $50 (see the website for details).

YHA New Zealand (Youth Hostels Association; www.yha.co.nz) More than 25 hostels in prime South Island locations. The YHA is part of the **Hostelling International** (HI; www.hihostels.com) network, so if you're already an HI member in your own country, membership entitles you to use NZ hostels. If you don't already have a membership card from home, you can buy one at major NZ YHA hostels for $42 for 12 months, or book online and have your card mailed to you overseas for the same price. Hostels also take non-YHA members for an extra $3 per night. NZ YHA hostels also supply bed linen, so you don't need to bring a sleeping bag.

VIP Backpackers (www.vipbackpackers.com) International organisation affiliated with around 20 NZ hostels (not BBH or YHA), mainly in the cities and tourist hot-spots. For around $63 (including postage) you'll receive a 12-month membership entitling you to a $1 discount off nightly accommodation. You can join online, at VIP hostels or at larger agencies dealing in backpacker travel.

Nomads Backpackers (www.nomadsworld.com) One South Island franchise in Queenstown. Membership costs AUD$37 for 12 months and like VIP offers NZ$1 off the cost of nightly accommodation. Join at participating hostels, backpacker travel agencies or online.

Base Backpackers (www.stayatbase.com) Nationwide chain with two South Island locations in Queenstown and Wanaka. Expect clean dorms, girls-only areas and party opportunities aplenty. Offers a 10-night 'Base Jumping' accommodation card for $239, bookable online.

Pubs, Hotels & Motels

Pubs The least expensive form of South Island hotel accommodation is the humble pub. As is often the case elsewhere, some of the South Island's old pubs are full of character (and characters), while others are grotty, ramshackle places that are best avoided, especially by women travelling solo. Also check whether there's a band cranking out the tunes the night you plan to be in town, as you could be in for a sleepless night. In the cheapest pubs, singles/doubles might cost as little as $30/60 (with a shared bathroom down the hall), though $50/80 is more common.

Hotels At the top end of the hotel scale are five-star international chains, resort complexes and architecturally splendorous boutique hotels, all of which charge a hefty premium for their mod cons, snappy service and/or historic opulence. We quote 'rack rates' (official advertised rates) for such places throughout this book, but discounts and special deals often mean you won't have to pay these prices.

Motels NZ's towns have a glut of nondescript, low-rise motels and 'motor lodges', charging between $80 and $180 for double rooms. These tend to be squat structures congregating just outside CBDs, or skulking by highways on the edge of towns. Most are modernish (though decor is often mired in the '90s) and have similar facilities, namely tea- and coffee-making equipment, fridge, and TV – prices vary with standard.

Rental Accommodation

The basic Kiwi holiday home is called a 'bach' (short for 'bachelor', as they were often used by single men as hunting and fishing hideouts); in Otago and Southland they're known as 'cribs'. These are simple self-contained cottages that can be rented in rural and coastal areas, often in isolated locations. Prices are typically $80 to $130 per night, which isn't bad for a whole house or self-contained bungalow.

For more upmarket holiday houses, the current trend is to throw rusticity to the wind and erect luxurious cottages on beautiful nature-surrounded plots. Expect to pay anything from $130 to $400 per double.

Online resources:

» www.holidayhomes.co.nz
» www.bookabach.co.nz
» www.holidayhouses.co.nz
» www.nzapartments.co.nz

Business Hours

Note that most attractions close on Christmas Day and Good Friday.

Shops & businesses 9am to 5.30pm Monday to Friday, and 9am to 12.30pm or 5pm Saturday. Late-night shopping (until 9pm) in larger cities on Thursday and/or Friday nights. Sunday trading in most big towns and cities.

Supermarkets 8am to 7pm, often 9pm or later in cities.

Banks 9.30am to 4.30pm Monday to Friday; some city branches also open Saturday mornings.

Post offices 8.30am to 5pm Monday to Friday; larger branches also 9.30am to 1pm Saturday. Postal desks in newsagencies open later.

Restaurants Food until 9pm, often until 11pm on Fridays and Saturdays.

Cafes 7am to 4pm or 5pm.

Pubs Noon until late; food from noon to 2pm and from 6pm to 8pm.

Children

Accommodation Many motels and holiday parks have playgrounds, games and DVDs, and occasionally fenced swimming pools and trampolines. Cots and highchairs aren't always available at budget and midrange accommodation, but top-end hotels supply them and often provide child-minding services.

B&Bs aren't usually amenable to families – many promote themselves as kid-free. Hostels focusing on the backpacker demographic don't welcome kids either, but there are plenty of other hostels (including YHA hostels) that do.

Babysitting For specialised childcare, try www.rockmybaby.co.nz, or look under 'babysitters' and 'child care centres' in the *Yellow Pages* directory.

Car seats Some smaller car-hire companies don't provide baby seats – double-check that your company can supply the right-sized seat for your child, and that the seat will be properly fitted.

Some companies may legally require you to fit the seat yourself.

Change rooms & breastfeeding Cities and most major towns have public rooms where parents can go to nurse a baby or change a nappy (diaper); check with the local visitor info centre or council, or ask a local.

Concessions Kids' and family rates are often available for accommodation,

Climate

Nelson

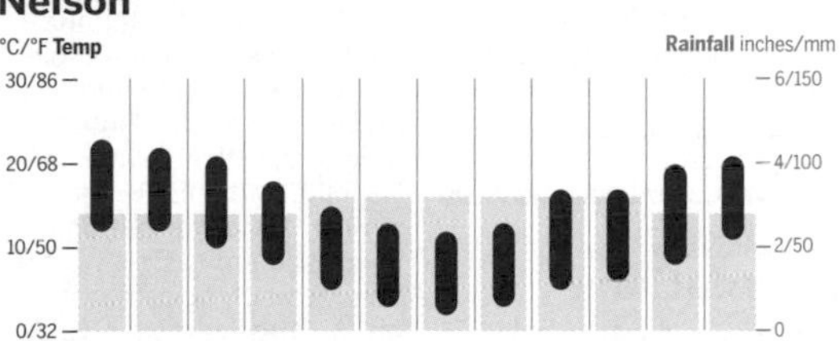

Christchurch

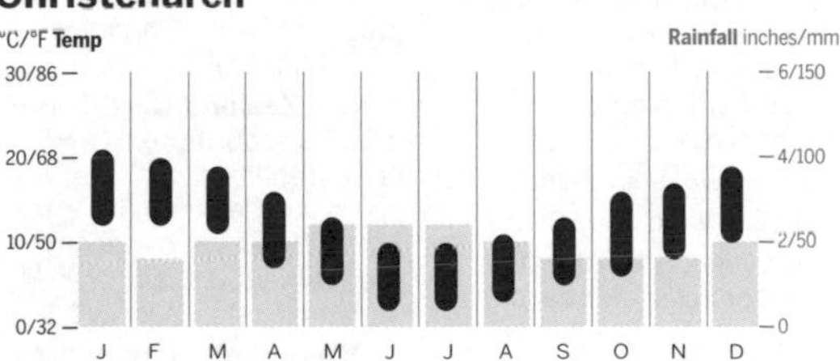

Queenstown

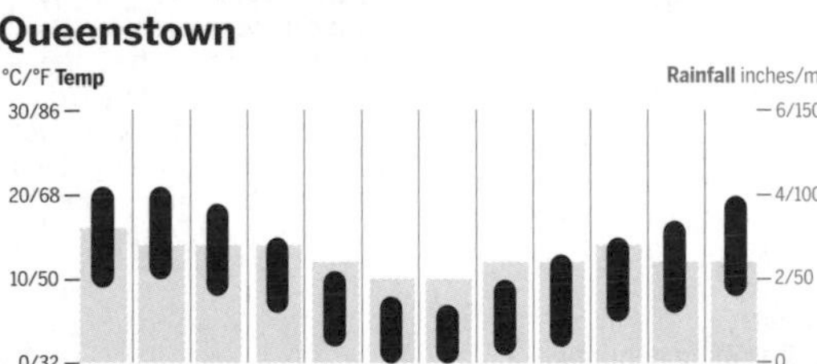

tours, entry fees, and air, bus and train transport, with discounts of as much as 50% off the adult rate. The definition of 'child' can vary from under 12 to under 18 years; toddlers (under four years old) usually get free admission and transport.

Eating out There are plenty of family-friendly restaurants in NZ with highchairs and kids' menus. Pubs often serve kids' meals and most cafes and restaurants (with the exception of upmarket eateries) can handle the idea of child-sized portions.

Health NZ's medical services and facilities are world-class, with goods like formula and disposable nappies widely available.

For helpful general tips, see Lonely Planet's *Travel with Children*. Handy online resources for kid-centric activities and travel info:

» www.kidzgo.co.nz

» www.kidspot.co.nz

» www.kidsnewzealand.com

» www.kidsfriendlynz.com

Customs Regulations

For the low-down on what you can and can't bring into NZ, see the **New Zealand Customs Service** (www.customs.govt.nz) website.

Per-person duty-free allowances:

» 1125mL of spirits or liqueur

» 4.5L of wine or beer

» 200 cigarettes (or 50 cigars or 250g of tobacco)

» dutiable goods up to the value of $700.

It's a good idea to declare any unusual medicines. Biosecurity is another customs buzzword – authorities are serious about keeping out any diseases that may harm NZ's agricultural industry.

Tramping gear such as boots and tents will be checked and may need to be cleaned before being allowed in. You must declare any plant or animal products (including anything made of wood), and food of any kind.

You'll also come under greater scrutiny if you've arrived via Africa, Southeast Asia or South America. Weapons and firearms are either prohibited or require a permit and safety testing.

Discount Cards

» **International Student Identity Card** The internationally recognised ISIC is produced by the **International Student Travel Confederation** (ISTC; www.istc.org), and issued to full-time students aged 12 and over. It provides discounts on accommodation, transport and admission to attractions. The ISTC also produces the International Youth Travel Card, available to folks between 12 and 26 who are not full-time students, with equivalent benefits to the ISIC. Also similar is the International Teacher Identity Card, available to teaching professionals. All three cards (NZ$25 each) are available online at www.isiccard.co.nz, or from student travel companies like STA Travel.

» **New Zealand Card** This is a $35 discount **pass** (www.newzealandcard.com) that'll score you between 5% and 50% off a range of accommodation, tours, sights and activities.

» **Other cards** Senior and disabled travellers who live overseas will find that discount cards issued by their respective countries are not always 'officially' recognised in NZ, but that many places still acknowledge such cards.

Electricity

Embassies & Consulates

Most principal diplomatic representations to NZ are in Wellington, with a few in Auckland.

Remember that while in NZ you are bound by NZ laws. Your embassy will not be sympathetic if you end up in jail after committing a crime locally, even if such actions are legal in your own country.

In genuine emergencies you may get some assistance, but only if other channels have been exhausted. For example, if you need to get home urgently, a free ticket is unlikely as the embassy would expect you to have insurance. If you have all your money and documents stolen, it might assist with getting a new passport, but a loan for onward travel is out of the question.

Embassies, consulates and high commissions include the following:

Australia (☎04-473 6411; www.australia.org.nz; 72-76

Hobson St, Thorndon, Wellington)

Canada (☎04-473 9577; www.newzealand.gc.ca; L11, 125 The Terrace, Wellington)

China (☎04-472 1382; www.chinaembassy.org.nz; 2-6 Glenmore St, Kelburn, Wellington)

Fiji (☎04-473 5401; www.fiji.org.nz; 31 Pipitea St, Thorndon, Wellington)

France (☎04-384 2555; www.ambafrance-nz.org; 34-42 Manners St, Wellington)

Germany (☎04-473 6063; www.wellington.diplo.de; 90-92 Hobson St, Thorndon, Wellington)

Israel (☎04-439 9500; info@wellington.mfa.gov.il; L13, Bayley's Building, 36 Brandon St, Wellington)

Ireland (☎09-977 2252; www.ireland.co.nz; L7, Citigroup Bldg, 23 Customs St E, Auckland)

Japan (☎04-473 1540; www.nz.emb-japan.go.jp; L18, The Majestic Centre, 100 Willis St, Wellington)

Netherlands (☎04-471 6390; www.netherlandsembassy.co.nz; L10, PSIS House, cnr Featherston & Ballance Sts, Wellington)

UK (☎04-924 2888; www.britain.org.nz; 44 Hill St, Thorndon, Wellington)

USA (☎04-462 6000; http://wellington.usembassy.gov; 29 Fitzherbert Tce, Thorndon, Wellington)

EATING PRICE RANGES

The following price ranges refer to a main course.

» **$ Budget** Less than $15

» **$$ Midrange** $15 to $32

» **$$$ Top end** More than $35

Food & Drink

The NZ foodie scene once slavishly reflected Anglo-Saxon stodge, but nowadays the country's restaurants and cafes are adept at throwing together traditional staples (lamb, beef, venison, green-lipped mussels) with Asian, European and pan-Pacific flair.

Eateries themselves range from fry-'em-up fish-and-chip shops and pub bistros to cafes drowned in faux-European, grungy or retro stylings; to restaurant-bars with full à-la-carte service; to fine-dining establishments with linen so crisp you'll be afraid to prop your elbows on it. Listings are in order of authorial preference, based on our assessment of ambience, service, value and, of course, deliciousness. For online listings:

» www.dineout.co.nz

» www.menus.co.nz

On the liquid front, NZ wine is world class (especially sauvignon blanc and pinot noir), and you'll be hard-pressed to find a NZ town of any size without decent espresso. NZ microbrewed beers have also become mainstream.

Practicalities

Smoking Banned in all restaurants, pubs and bars.

Tipping Not mandatory, but feel free if you've had a happy culinary experience (about 10% of the bill).

Opening hours Restaurants to 9pm, often 11pm Friday and Saturday. Cafes 7am to 4pm or 5pm. Pub food noon to 2pm, and 6pm to 8pm.

Vegetarians & Vegans

Most large urban centres have at least one dedicated vegetarian cafe or restaurant. See the **New Zealand Vegetarian Society** (www.vegsoc.org.nz) restaurant guide for listings. Also look for the vegetarian icon in Eating listings in this book, as it indicates a good vegetarian selection.

Beyond this, almost all restaurants and cafes offer vegetarian menu choices (although sometimes only one or two). Many eateries also provide gluten-free and vegan options. Always check that stocks and sauces are vegetarian too.

TO MARKET, TO MARKET

There are more than 20 farmers markets held around the South Island. Most happen on weekends and are happy local affairs where visitors will meet local producers and find fresh regional produce. Mobile coffee is usually present, and tastings are offered by enterprising and innovative stall holders.

Always take a bag to carry purchases, as many of the sustainably minded markets ban the use of plastic bags. And arrive as early as possible – the best produce sells out quickly.

Check out www.farmersmarkets.org.nz for dates and times of farmers markets throughout the South Island.

Gay & Lesbian Travellers

The gay and lesbian tourism industry in NZ isn't as high-profile as it is in neighbouring Australia, but homosexual communities are prominent across both islands, with myriad support organisations. NZ has relatively progressive laws protecting the rights of gays and lesbians; the legal minimum age for sex between consenting persons is 16. Generally speaking, Kiwis are fairly relaxed and accepting about homosexuality, but that's not to say that homophobia doesn't exist.

Resources

There are loads of websites dedicated to gay and lesbian travellers. **Gay Tourism New Zealand** (www.gaytourismnewzealand.com) is a good starting point, with links to various sites.
Other worthwhile queer websites include the following:

- » www.gaynz.com
- » www.gaynz.net.nz
- » www.lesbian.net.nz
- » www.gaystay.co.nz

Check out the nationwide magazine *express* (www.gayexpress.co.nz) every second Wednesday for the latest happenings, reviews and listings on the NZ gay scene.

Festivals & Events

Gay Ski Week (www.gayskiweeknz.com) Annual Queenstown snow-fest in August/September.

Health

New Zealand is one of the healthiest countries in the world in which to travel. Diseases such as malaria and typhoid are unheard of, and the absence of poisonous snakes or other dangerous animals makes this a very safe region to get off the beaten track and out into the beautiful countryside.

Before You Go

MEDICATIONS

Bring medications in their original, clearly labelled containers. A signed and dated letter from your physician describing your medical conditions and medications, including generic names, is also a good idea. If carrying syringes or needles, be sure to have a physician's letter documenting their medical necessity.

VACCINATIONS

NZ has no vaccination requirements for any traveller, but the World Health Organization recommends that all travellers should be covered for diphtheria, tetanus, measles, mumps, rubella, chickenpox and polio, as well as hepatitis B, regardless of their destination. Ask your doctor for an International Certificate of Vaccination (or 'the yellow booklet'), which will list all the vaccinations you've received.

INSURANCE

If your current health insurance doesn't cover you for medical expenses incurred overseas, you should think about getting extra insurance – check out www.lonelyplanet.com for more information. Find out in advance if your insurance plan will make payments directly to providers or reimburse you at a later date for overseas health expenditures. (In many countries doctors expect payment in cash.)

In New Zealand

AVAILABILITY & COST OF HEALTH CARE

Health insurance is essential for all travellers. While health care in NZ is of a high standard and not overly expensive by international standards, considerable costs can be built up and repatriation can be extremely expensive.

NZ does not have a government-funded system of public hospitals. All travellers are, however, covered for medical care resulting from accidents that occur while in NZ (eg motor-vehicle accidents, adventure-activity accidents) by the Accident Compensation Corporation (ACC). Costs incurred due to treatment of a medical illness that occurs while in NZ will only be covered by travel insurance. For more details, see www.moh.govt.nz and www.acc.co.nz.

The 24-hour, free-call **Healthline** (☎0800 611 116; www.healthline.govt.nz) offers health advice throughout NZ.

PHARMACEUTICAL SUPPLIES

Over-the-counter medications are widely available in NZ through private chemists. These include painkillers, antihistamines for allergies, and skin-care products.

Some medications that are available over the counter in other countries are only available by a prescription obtained from a general practitioner. These include the oral contraceptive pill, most medications for asthma and all antibiotics. If you take medication on a regular basis, bring an adequate supply and ensure you have details of the generic name, as brand names differ between countries. The majority of medications in use outside the region are available.

INFECTIOUS DISEASES

The giardia parasite is widespread in the waterways of NZ. Drinking untreated water from streams and lakes is not recommended. Using water filters and boiling or treating water with iodine are effective ways of preventing the disease. Symptoms consist of intermittent bad-smelling diarrhoea, abdominal bloating and wind. Effective treatment is available (tinidazole or metronidazole).

ENVIRONMENTAL HAZARDS

Hypothermia This is a significant risk, especially during the winter months or year-round in the mountains of the North Island and all of the South Island. Mountain ranges and/or strong winds produce a high chill factor, which can result in hypothermia, even in moderately cool temperatures. Early signs include the inability to perform fine movements (such as doing up buttons), shivering and a bad case of the 'umbles' (fumbles, mumbles, grumbles, stumbles). The key element of treatment are changing the environment to one where heat loss is minimised: changing out of wet clothing, adding dry clothes with wind- and waterproof layers, adding insulation and providing fuel (water and carbohydrates) to allow shivering to build the internal temperature. In severe hypothermia, shivering actually stops; this is a medical emergency requiring rapid evacuation in addition to the above measures.

Surf Beaches & Drowning NZ has exceptional surf beaches. The power of the surf can fluctuate as a result of the varying slope of the seabed at many beaches. Check with local surf lifesaving organisations before entering the surf and be aware of your own limitations and expertise.

Insurance

A watertight travel-insurance policy covering theft, loss and medical problems is essential. Some policies specifically exclude designated 'dangerous activities' such as scuba diving, parasailing, bungy jumping, white-water rafting, motorcycling, skiing and even tramping. If you plan on doing any of these things (a distinct possibility in NZ), make sure the policy you choose covers you fully.

You may prefer a policy that pays doctors or hospitals directly rather than you having to pay on the spot and claim later. If you have to claim later, make sure you keep all documentation. Some policies ask you to call back (reverse charges) to a centre in your home country where an immediate assessment of your problem is made. Check that the policy covers ambulances and emergency medical evacuations by air.

It's worth mentioning that under NZ law, you cannot sue for personal injury (other than exemplary damages). Instead, the country's **Accident Compensation Corporation** (ACC; www.acc.co.nz) administers an accident compensation scheme that provides accident insurance for NZ residents and visitors to the country, regardless of fault. This scheme, however, does not cancel out the necessity for your own comprehensive travel-insurance policy, as it doesn't cover you for such things as loss of income or treatment in your home country or ongoing illness.

Worldwide cover for travellers from over 44 countries is available online at www.lonelyplanet.com/bookings/insurance.do.

Internet Access

Getting online in NZ is easy in all but the most remote locales.

Internet Cafes

Internet cafes in the bigger urban centres or tourist areas are usually brimming with high-speed terminals. Facilities are a lot more haphazard in small, out-of-the-way towns, where a so-called internet cafe could turn out to be a single terminal in the corner of a DVD store.

Most hostels make an effort to hook you up, with internet access sometimes free for guests. Many public libraries have free internet access too, but there can be a limited number of terminals.

Internet access at cafes ranges anywhere from $4 to $6 per hour. There's often a minimum period of access, usually 10 or 15 minutes.

Wireless Access & Internet Service Providers

Increasingly, you'll be able to find wi-fi access around the country, from hotel rooms to pub beer gardens to hostel dining rooms. Usually you have to be a guest or customer to access the internet at these locations – you'll be issued with a code, a wink and a secret handshake to enable you to get online. Sometimes it's free; sometimes there's a charge.

The country's main telecommunications company is **Telecom New Zealand** (www.telecom.co.nz), which has wireless hot spots around the country. If you have a wi-fi-enabled device, you can purchase a Telecom wireless prepaid card from participating hot spots. Alternatively, you can purchase a prepaid number from the login page and any wireless hotspot using your credit card. See the website for hot spot listings.

If you've brought your palmtop or notebook computer, you might consider buying a prepay USB modem (aka a 'dongle') with a local SIM card: both Telecom and **Vodafone** (www.vodarent.co.nz) sell these from around $100. If you want to get connected via a local internet service provider (ISP), there are plenty of options, though some companies limit their dial-up areas to major cities or particular regions. ISPs include the following:

Clearnet (☎0508 888 800; www.clearnet.co.nz)

Earthlight (☎03-479 0303; www.earthlight.co.nz)

Freenet (☎0800 645 000; www.freenet.co.nz)

Slingshot (☎0800 892 000; www.slingshot.co.nz)

Maps

The **Automobile Association** (AA; ☎0800 500 444; www.aa.co.nz/travel) produces excellent city, town, regional, island and highway maps, available from its local offices. The AA also produces a detailed *New Zealand Road Atlas*. Other reliable countrywide atlases, available from visitor information centres and bookshops, are published by Hema, KiwiMaps and Wises.

Land Information New Zealand (LINZ; www.linz.govt.nz) publishes several exhaustive map series, including street, country and holiday maps, national park and forest park maps, and topographical trampers' maps. Scan the larger bookshops, or try the nearest DOC office or visitor information centre for topo maps.

Online, log onto **AA SmartMap** (www.aamaps.co.nz) or **Yellow Maps** (www.maps.yellowpages.co.nz) to pinpoint exact addresses in NZ cities and towns.

Money

ATMs & Eftpos

Branches of the country's major banks, including the Bank of New Zealand, ANZ, Westpac and ASB, have 24-hour ATMs that accept cards from other banks and provide access to overseas accounts. You won't find ATMs everywhere, but they're widespread across both islands.

Many NZ businesses use electronic funds transfer at point of sale (Eftpos), a convenient service that allows you to use your bank card (credit or debit) to pay directly for services or purchases, and often withdraw cash as well. Eftpos is available practically everywhere, even in places where it's a long way between banks. Just like an ATM, you need to know your personal identification number (PIN) to use it.

Bank Accounts

We've heard mixed reports on how easy it is for nonresidents to open a bank account in NZ. Some sources say it's as simple as flashing a few pieces of ID, providing a temporary postal address (or your permanent address) and then waiting a few days while your request is processed. Other sources say that many banks won't allow visitors to open an account with them unless they're planning to stay in NZ for at least six months, or unless the application is accompanied by some proof of employment. Bank websites are also rather vague on the services offered to short-term visitors. If you think you'll need to open an account, do your homework before you arrive in the country and be prepared to shop around to get the best deal.

Credit & Debit Cards

Perhaps the safest place to keep your NZ travelling money is inside a plastic card! The most flexible option is to carry both a credit and a debit card.

CREDIT CARDS

Credit cards (Visa, Master Card etc) are widely accepted for everything from a hostel bed to a bungy jump. Credit cards are pretty much essential if you want to hire a car. They can also be used for over-the-counter cash advances at banks and from ATMs, depending on the card, but be aware that such transactions incur charges. Charge cards such as Diners Club and Amex are not as widely accepted.

DEBIT CARDS

Apart from losing them, the obvious danger with credit cards is maxing out your limit and going home to a steaming pile of debt. A safer option is a debit card, with which you can draw money directly from your home bank account using ATMs, banks or Eftpos machines. Any card connected to the international banking network (Cirrus, Maestro, Visa Plus and Eurocard) should work, provided you know your PIN. Fees for using your card at a foreign bank or ATM vary depending on your home bank; ask before you leave. Companies such as Travelex offer debit cards (Travelex calls them Cash Passport cards) with set withdrawal fees and a balance you can top-up from your personal bank account while on the road – nice one!

Currency

NZ's currency is the NZ dollar, comprising 100 cents. There are 10c, 20c, 50c, $1 and $2 coins, and $5, $10, $20, $50 and $100 notes. Prices are often still marked in single cents and then rounded to the nearest 10c when you hand over your money.

Moneychangers

Changing foreign currency or travellers cheques is usually no problem at banks throughout NZ or at licensed moneychangers such as Travelex in the major cities. Moneychangers can be found in all major tourist areas, cities and airports.

Taxes & Refunds

The Goods and Services Tax (GST) is a flat 15% tax on all domestic goods and services. Prices in this book include GST. There's no GST refund available when you leave NZ.

Tipping

Tipping is completely optional in NZ – the total at the bottom of a restaurant bill is all you need to pay (note that sometimes there's an additional service charge). That said, it's totally acceptable to reward good service – between 5% and 10% of the bill is fine.

Travellers Cheques

Amex, Travelex and other international brands of travellers cheques are a bit old-fashioned these days, but they're easily exchanged at banks and moneychangers. Present your passport for identification when cashing them; shop around for the best rates/lowest fees.

Post

The services offered by **New Zealand Post** (☎0800 501 501; www.nzpost.co.nz) are reliable and reasonably inexpensive. Within NZ, standard postage is 60c for regular letters and postcards, and $1.20 for larger letters.

International destinations are divided into two zones: Australia and the South Pacific, and the rest of the world. The standard rate for postcards is $1.90 worldwide, and for regular letters $1.90 to Australia and the South Pacific and $2.40 elsewhere. Express rates are also available. Check out the incredibly precise calculator on the website for more details, including info on parcels.

Public Holidays

NZ's main public holidays:

New Year 1 and 2 January

Waitangi Day 6 February

Easter Good Friday and Easter Monday; March/April

Anzac Day 25 April

Queen's Birthday First Monday in June

Labour Day Fourth Monday in October

Christmas Day 25 December

Boxing Day 26 December

In addition, each NZ province has its own anniversary-day holiday. The dates of these provincial holidays vary – when these dates fall on Friday to Sunday, they're usually observed the following Monday; if they fall on Tuesday to Thursday, they're held on the preceding Monday.

South Island's anniversary holidays:

Southland 17 January

Nelson 1 February

Otago 23 March

South Canterbury 25 September

Marlborough 1 November

Westland 1 December

Canterbury 16 December

School Holidays

The Christmas holiday season, from mid-December to late January, is part of the summer school vacation. It's the time you'll most likely to find transport and accommodation booked out, and long, grumpy queues at tourist attractions. There are three shorter school-holiday periods during the year: from mid- to late April, early to mid-July, and mid-September to early October. For exact dates see the **Ministry of Education** (www.minedu.govt.nz) website.

Safe Travel

Although it's no more dangerous than other developed countries, violent crime does happen in NZ, so it's worth taking sensible precautions on the streets at night or if staying in remote areas. Gang culture permeates some parts of the country; give any black-jacketed, insignia-wearing groups a wide berth.

Theft from cars is a problem around NZ – travellers are viewed as easy marks. Avoid leaving valuables in vehicles, no matter where they're parked; you're tempting fate at tourist parking areas and trailhead car parks.

Don't underestimate the dangers posed by NZ's unpredictable, ever-changing climate, especially in high-altitude areas. Hypothermia is a real risk.

NZ has been spared the proliferation of venomous creatures found in neighbouring Australia (spiders, snakes, jellyfish...). Sharks patrol NZ waters, but rarely nibble on humans. Much greater ocean hazards are rips and undertows, which can quickly drag swimmers out to sea: heed local warnings.

Kiwi roads are often made hazardous by speeding locals, wide-cornering campervans and traffic-ignorant sheep. Set yourself a reasonable itinerary and keep your eyes on the road. Cyclists take care: motorists can't always overtake easily on skinny roads.

In the annoyances category, NZ's sandflies are a royal pain. Lather yourself with insect repellent in coastal areas.

Shopping

NZ isn't one of those countries where it's necessary to buy a T-shirt to help you remember your visit, but there are some unique locally crafted items you might consider.

Clothing

Queenstown and Dunedin boast fashion-conscious boutiques ablaze with the sartorial flair of NZ designers. In Christchurch, the fashion scene is in the suburb of Addington, the city's new Re:START shopping precinct. Check out www.fashionz.co.nz for up-to-date information. Keep an eye out for labels such as Zambesi, Kate Sylvester, Karen Walker, Trelise Cooper, NOM D and Little Brother.

From the backs of NZ sheep come sheepskin products such as footwear (including the much-loved ugg boot) and beautiful woollen jumpers (jerseys or sweaters) made from hand-spun, hand-dyed wool. Other knitted knick-knacks include hats, gloves and scarves.

Long woollen Swanndri jackets, shirts and pullovers are so ridiculously practical, they're almost the national garment in country areas. Most common are the red-and-black or blue-and-black plaid ones; pick up 'Swannies' in outdoor-gear shops.

Maori Art

Maori *whakairo rakau* (woodcarving) features intricate forms like leaping dolphins, as well as highly detailed traditional carvings. You'll pay a premium for high-quality work; avoid the poor examples in some Queenstown souvenir shops.

Maori artisans have always made bone carvings in the shape of humans and animals, but nowadays they cater to the tourist industry. Bone fish-hook pendants, carved in traditional Maori and modernised styles, are most common, worn on a leather string around the neck.

Paua

Abalone shell, called paua in NZ, is carved into some beautiful ornaments and jewellery and is often used as an inlay in Maori carvings. Be aware that it's illegal to take natural paua shells out of the country – only processed ornaments can be taken with you.

Pounamu

Maoris consider *pounamu* (greenstone, or jade or nephrite) to be a culturally invaluable raw material. It's found predominantly on the west coast of the South Island – Maoris called the island Te Wahi Pounamu (The Place of Greenstone) or Te Wai Pounamu (The Water of Greenstone).

One of the most popular Maori *pounamu* motifs is the *hei tiki*, the name of which literally means 'hanging human form'. They are tiny, stylised Maori figures worn on a leather string or chain around the neck. They've got great *mana* (power), but they also serve as fertility symbols.

The best place to buy *pounamu* is Hokitika, which is strewn with jade workshops and gift shops. Rotorua also has its fair share of *pounamu* crafts.

Traditionally, *pounamu* is bought as a gift for another person, not for yourself. Ask a few questions to ensure you're buying from a local operator who crafts local stone, not an offshore company selling imported (usually Chinese or European) jade.

Telephone

Telecom New Zealand (www.telecom.co.nz) The country's key domestic player, with a stake in the local mobile (cell) market.

Vodafone (www.vodafone.co.nz) Alternative mobile network option.

International Calls

Payphones allow international calls, but the cost and international dialling code for calls will vary depending on which provider you're using. International calls from NZ are relatively inexpensive and subject to specials that reduce the rates even more, so it's worth shopping around – consult the Yellow Pages for providers.

To make international calls from NZ, you need to dial the international access code (☎00), the country code and the area code (without the initial 0). So for a London number, you'd dial ☎00-44-20, then the number.

If dialling NZ from overseas, the country code is ☎64, followed by the appropriate area code minus the initial zero.

Local Calls

Local calls from private phones are free! Local calls from payphones cost $1 for the first 15 minutes, and 20c per minute thereafter, though coin-operated payphones are scarce – you'll need a phonecard. Calls to mobile phones attract higher rates.

Long Distance Calls & Area Codes

NZ uses regional two-digit area codes for long-distance calls, which can be made from any payphone. If you're making a local call (ie to someone else in the same town), you don't need to dial the area code. But if you're dialling within a region (even if it's to a nearby town with the same area code), you do have to dial the area code.

Information & Toll-Free Calls

Numbers starting with ☎0900 are usually recorded information services, charging upwards of $1 per minute (more from mobiles); these numbers cannot be dialled from payphones.

Toll-free numbers in NZ have the prefix ☎0800 or ☎0508 and can be called free of charge from anywhere in the country, though they may not be accessible from certain areas or from mobile phones. Telephone numbers beginning with ☎0508, ☎0800 or ☎0900 cannot be dialled from outside NZ.

Mobile Phones

Local mobile phone numbers are preceded by the prefix ☎021, ☎022, ☎025 or ☎027. Mobile phone coverage is good in cities and towns but can be patchy away from urban centres on the South Island.

If you want to bring your own phone and use a prepaid service with a local SIM card, **Vodafone** (www.vodafone.co.nz) is a practical option. Any Vodafone shop (found in most major towns) will set you up with a SIM card and phone number (about $40); top-ups can be purchased at newsagencies, post offices and petrol stations practically anywhere.

Alternatively, if you don't bring your own phone from home, you can rent one from **Vodafone Rental** (www.vodarent.co.nz) priced from $5 per day (for which you'll also need a local SIM card), with pick-up and drop-off outlets at NZ's major airports. We've also had some positive feedback on **Phone Hire New Zealand** (www.phonehirenz.com), which hires out mobile phones, SIM cards, modems and GPS systems.

Phonecards

NZ has a wide range of phonecards available, which can be bought at hostels, newsagencies and post offices for a fixed dollar value (usually $5, $10, $20 and $50). These can be used with any public or private phone by dialling a toll-free access number and then the PIN number on the card. Shop around – rates vary from company to company.

Time

NZ is 12 hours ahead of GMT/UTC and two hours ahead of Australian Eastern Standard Time. The Chathams are 45 minutes ahead of NZ's main islands.

In summer, NZ observes daylight-saving time, where clocks are wound forward by one hour on the last Sunday in September; clocks are wound back on the first Sunday of the following April.

Tourist Information

Local Tourist Offices

Almost every South Island city or town seems to have a visitor information centre. The bigger centres stand united within the outstanding **i-SITE** (www.newzealand.com/travel/i-sites) network, affiliated with Tourism New Zealand (the official national tourism body). i-SITEs have trained staff, information on local activities and attractions, and free brochures and maps. Staff can also book activities, transport and accommodation.

Bear in mind that many information centres only promote accommodation and tour operators who are paying members of the local tourist association, and that sometimes staff aren't supposed to recommend one activity or accommodation provider over another.

There's also a network of **Department Of Conservation** (DOC; www.doc.govt.nz) visitor centres to help you plan activities and make bookings. Visitor centres – in national parks, regional centres and major cities – usually also have displays on local lore, flora, fauna and biodiversity.

Tourist Offices Abroad

Tourism New Zealand (www.newzealand.com) has representatives in various countries around the world. A good place for pretrip research is the official website (emblazoned with the hugely successful 100% Pure New Zealand branding), which has information in several languages, including German and Japanese. Overseas offices:

Australia (☎0415-123 362; L12, 61 York St, Sydney)

UK & Europe (☎020-7930 1662; L7, New Zealand House, 80 Haymarket, London, UK)

USA & Canada (☎310-395 7480; Suite 300, 501 Santa Monica Blvd, Santa Monica, USA)

Travellers with Disabilities

Kiwi accommodation generally caters fairly well for travellers with disabilities, with a significant number of hostels, hotels, motels and B&Bs equipped with wheelchair-accessible rooms. Many tourist attractions similarly provide wheelchair access, with wheelchairs often available.

Tour operators with accessible vehicles operate from most major centres. Key cities are also serviced by 'kneeling' buses (buses that hydraulically stoop down to kerb level to allow easy access); taxi companies offer wheelchair-accessible vans. Large car-hire firms (Avis, Hertz etc) provide cars with hand controls at no extra charge (advance notice required). Mobility parking permits are available from branches of **CCS Disability Action** (☎0800 227 200, 04-384 5677; www.ccsdisabilityaction.org.nz) in the main centres.

For good general information, see NZ's disability information website **Weka** (www.weka.net.nz), which has categories including Transport and Travel.

Want to tackle a wilderness pathway? Pick up a copy of *Accessible Walks* by Anna and Andrew Jameson ($26), with first-hand descriptions of 100-plus South Island walks. It's available online at www.accessiblewalks.co.nz. If cold-weather activity is more your thing, see the **Adaptive Snow Sports NZ** (www.disabledsnowsports.org.nz) website.

Visas

Visa application forms are available from NZ diplomatic missions overseas, travel agents and **Immigration New Zealand** (☎0508 558 855, 09-914 4100; www.immigration.govt.nz). Immigration New Zealand has over a dozen offices overseas; consult the website.

Visitor's Visa

Citizens of Australia don't need a visa to visit NZ and can stay indefinitely (provided they have no criminal convictions). UK citizens don't need a visa either and can stay in the country for up to six months.

Citizens of another 56 countries that have visa-waiver agreements with NZ don't need a visa for stays of up to three months, provided they have an onward ticket and sufficient funds to support their stay: see the website for details. Nations in this group include Canada, France, Germany, Ireland, Japan, the Netherlands and the USA.

Citizens of other countries must obtain a visa before entering NZ. Visas come with three months' standard validity and cost $110 if processed in Australia or certain South Pacific countries (eg Samoa, Fiji), or around $140 if processed elsewhere in the world.

A visitor's visa can be extended for stays of up to nine months within one 18-month period, or to a maximum of 12 months in the country. Applications are assessed on a case-by-case basis; visitors will need to meet criteria such as proof of ongoing financial self-support. Apply for extensions at any Immigration New Zealand office – see the website for locations.

Work Visa & Working Holiday Scheme

WORK VISA

It's illegal for foreign nationals to work in NZ on a visitor's visa, except for Australians who can legally gain work without a visa or permit. If you're visiting NZ to find work, or you already have an employment offer, you'll need to apply for a work visa, which translates into a work permit once you arrive and is valid for up to three years. You can apply for a work permit after you're in NZ, but its validity will be backdated to when you entered the country. The fee for a work visa ranges from NZ$200 to NZ$310, depending on where and how it's processed (paper or online) and the type of application.

WORKING HOLIDAY SCHEME

Eligible travellers who are only interested in short-term employment to supplement their travels can take part in one of NZ's working-holiday schemes (WHS). Under these schemes citizens aged 18 to 30 years from 36 countries – including Canada, France, Germany, Ireland, Japan, Malaysia, the Netherlands, Scandinavian countries, the UK and the USA – can apply for a visa. For most nationalities the visa is valid for 12 months. It's only issued to those seeking a genuine working holiday, not permanent work, so you're not supposed to work for one employer for more than three months.

Most WHS-eligible nationals must apply for this visa from within their own country; residents of some countries can apply online. Applicants must have an onward ticket, a passport valid for at least three months from the date they will leave NZ and evidence of at least NZ$4200 in accessible funds. The application fee is NZ$140 regardless of where you apply, and isn't refunded if your application is declined.

The rules vary for different nationalities, so make sure you read up on the specifics of your country's agreement with NZ at www.immigration.govt.nz/migrant/stream/work/workingholiday.

Women Travellers

NZ is generally a very safe place for women travellers, although the usual sensible precautions apply: avoid walking alone late at night and never hitchhike alone. If you're out on the town, always keep enough money aside for a taxi back to your accommodation. Lone women should also be wary of staying in basic pub accommodation unless it looks safe and well managed. Sexual harassment is not a widely reported problem in NZ, but of course it does happen.

See www.womentravel.co.nz for more information.

Work

If you arrive in NZ on a visitor's visa, you're not allowed to work for pay. If you're caught breaching this (or any other) visa condition, you could be booted back to where you came from.

If you have been approved for a WHS visa, look into the possibilities for temporary employment. There's plenty of casual work around, mainly in agriculture (fruit picking, farming, wineries), hospitality or ski resorts. Office-based work can be found in IT, banking, finance and telemarketing. Register with a local office-work agency to get started.

Seasonal fruit picking, pruning and harvesting is prime short-term work for visitors. More than 300 sq km of apples, kiwifruit and other fruit and veg are harvested from December to May. Rates are around $10 to $15 an hour for physically taxing toil – turnover of workers is high. You're usually paid by how much you pick (per bin, bucket or kilogram). Prime South Island picking locations include Nelson (Tapawera), Marlborough (around Blenheim) and Central Otago (Alexandra and Roxburgh).

VOLUNTOURISM

NZ presents a swathe of active, outdoorsy volunteer opportunities for travellers to get some dirt under their fingernails and participate in conservation programs. Programs can include anything from tree-planting and weed removal to track construction, habitat conservation and fencing. Ask about local opportunities at any regional i-SITE visitor information centre, or check out www.conservationvolunteers.org.nz and www.doc.govt.nz/getting-involved, both of which allow you to browse for opportunities by region.

Winter work at ski resorts and their service towns includes bartending, waiting, cleaning, ski-tow operation and, if you're properly qualified, ski or snowboard instructing.

Resources

Backpacker publications, hostel managers and other travellers are the best sources of info on local work possibilities. **Base Backpackers** (www.stayatbase.com/work) runs an employment service via its website, while the Notice Boards page on **Budget Backpacker Hostels** (BBH; www.bbh.co.nz) lists job vacancies in BBH hostels and a few other possibilities.

Kiwi Careers (www.kiwicareers.govt.nz) lists professional opportunities in various fields (agriculture, creative, health, teaching, volunteer work and recruitment), while **Seek** (www.seek.co.nz) is one of the biggest NZ job-search networks, with thousands of jobs listed.

Check ski-resort websites for work opportunities in the snow, and in the fruit-picking/horticultural realm, try the following websites:

» www.seasonalwork.co.nz

» www.seasonaljobs.co.nz

» www.picknz.co.nz

» www.pickingjobs.com

Income Tax

Death and taxes – no escape! For most travellers, Kiwi dollars earned in NZ will be subject to income tax, deducted from payments by employers – a process called Pay As You Earn (PAYE). Standard NZ income tax rates are 12.5% for annual salaries up to $14,000, then 19.5% up to $48,000, 32% up to $70,000, then 35% for higher incomes. A NZ Accident Compensation Corporation (ACC) scheme levy (2%) will also be deducted from your pay packet. Note that these rates tend to change slightly year to year.

If you visit NZ and work for a short time (eg on a working holiday scheme), you may qualify for a tax refund when you leave. Complete a *Refund Application – People Leaving New Zealand IR50* form and submit it with your tax return, along with proof of departure (eg air-ticket copies) to the **Inland Revenue Department** (www.ird.govt.nz). For more info, see the IRD website, or contact the **Inland Revenue Non-Resident Centre** (☎03-951 2020; nonres@ird.govt.nz; Private Bag 1932).

IRD Number

Travellers undertaking paid work in NZ must obtain an IRD number. Download the *IRD Number Application – Individual IR595* form from the **Inland Revenue Department** (www.ird.govt.nz) website. IRD numbers normally take eight to 10 working days to be issued.

Transport

GETTING THERE & AWAY

Flights, tours and rail tickets can be booked online at lonelyplanet.com/bookings.

Entering the Country

Disembarkation in New Zealand is generally a straightforward affair, with only the usual customs declarations to endure and the uncool scramble at the luggage carousel.

Recent global instability has resulted in increased security in NZ airports, in both domestic and international terminals, and you may find customs procedures more time-consuming. One procedure has the Orwellian title Advance Passenger Screening, a system whereby documents that used to be checked after you touched down in NZ (passport, visa etc) are now checked before you board your flight – make sure all your documentation is in order so that your check-in is stress-free.

Passport

There are no restrictions when it comes to foreign citizens entering NZ. If you have a current passport and visa (or don't require one), you should be fine.

Air

There's a number of competing airlines servicing NZ and a wide variety of fares to choose from if you're flying in from Asia, Europe or North America, though ultimately you'll still pay a lot for a flight unless you jet in from Australia.

NZ's inordinate popularity and abundance of year-round activities mean that almost any time of year airports can be swarming with inbound tourists – if you want to fly at a particularly popular time of year (eg over the Christmas period), book well in advance.

High season for flights into NZ is summer (December to February), with slightly less of a premium on fares during the shoulder months (October/November and March/April). The low season generally tallies with the winter months (June to August), though this is still a busy time for airlines ferrying ski bunnies and powder hounds to Queenstown.

Airports & Airlines

Three South Island airports handle international flights:

Christchurch Airport (CHC; ☎03-358 5029; www.christchurchairport.co.nz; Memorial Ave)

Dunedin Airport (DUD; ☎03-486 2879; www.dnairport.co.nz; Miller Rd)

Queenstown Airport (ZQN; ☎03-450 9031; www.queenstownairport.co.nz; Sir Henry Wigley Dr)

AIRLINES FLYING TO & FROM NEW ZEALAND

Winging-in from Australia, Virgin Australia, Qantas and Air New Zealand are the key players. Air New Zealand also flies in from North

DEPARTURE TAX

An international departure tax of NZ$25 applies when leaving NZ at Queenstown Airport and payable by anyone aged 12 and over (NZ$10 for children aged two to 11, free for those under two years of age). The tax is not included in the price of airline tickets, but must be paid separately at the airport before you board your flight (via credit card or cash). Departing Auckland, Christchurch and Dunedin, a NZ$12.50 Passenger Service Charge (PSC) applies, which is included in your ticket price. If you're leaving NZ from Christchurch or Dunedin airports, the departure tax is included in the cost of your airline tickets.

CLIMATE CHANGE & TRAVEL

Every form of transport that relies on carbon-based fuel generates CO_2, the main cause of human-induced climate change. Modern travel is dependent on aeroplanes, which might use less fuel per kilometre per person than most cars but travel much greater distances. The altitude at which aircraft emit gases (including CO_2) and particles also contributes to their climate change impact. Many websites offer 'carbon calculators' that allow people to estimate the carbon emissions generated by their journey and, for those who wish to do so, to offset the impact of the greenhouse gases emitted with contributions to portfolios of climate-friendly initiatives throughout the world. Lonely Planet offsets the carbon footprint of all staff and author travel.

America, but you can also head south with Air Canada and American Airlines.

From Europe, the options are a little broader, with British Airways, Lufthansa and Virgin Atlantic entering the fray, and several others stopping in NZ on broader round-the-world routes.

NZ's own overseas carrier is Air New Zealand, which flies to runways across Europe, North America, eastern Asia and the Pacific. Airlines that connect NZ with international destinations include the following (note that 0800 and 0508 phone numbers mentioned here are for dialling from within NZ only):

Aerolineas Argentinas (AR; ☎09-379 3675; www.aerolineas.com.ar)

Aircalin (SB; ☎09-977 2238; www.aircalin.com)

Air Canada (AC; ☎09-969 7470; www.aircanada.com)

Air China (CA; ☎09-379 7696; www.airchina.com.cn)

Air New Zealand (NZ; ☎09-357 3000, 0800 737 000; www.airnewzealand.co.nz)

Air Pacific (FJ; ☎09-379 2404, 0800 800 178; www.airpacific.com)

Air Tahiti Nui (YN; ☎09-308 3360; www.airtahitinui.com.au)

Air Vanuatu (NF; ☎09-373 3435; www.airvanuatu.com)

American Airlines (AA; ☎09-912 8814, 0800 445 442; www.aa.com)

British Airways (BA; ☎09-966 9777; www.britishairways.com)

Cathay Pacific (CX; ☎09-379 0861, 0800 800 454; www.cathaypacific.com)

China Airlines (CI; ☎09-308 3364; www.china-airlines.com)

China Southern (CZ; ☎09-302 0666; www.flychinasouthern.com)

Emirates (EK; ☎09-968 2208, 0508 364 728; www.emirates.com)

Etihad Airways (EY; ☎09-977 2207; www.etihadairways.com)

Japan Airlines (JL; ☎0800 525 747; www.jal.com)

Jetstar (JQ; ☎0800 800 995; www.jetstar.com)

Korean Air (KE; ☎09-914 2000; www.koreanair.com)

LAN (LA; ☎09-308 3352; www.lan.com)

Lufthansa (LH; ☎09-303 1529; www.lufthansa.com)

Malaysia Airlines (MH; ☎09-379 3743, 0800 777 747; www.malaysiaairlines.com)

Qantas (QF; ☎09-357 8900, 0800 808 767; www.qantas.com.au)

Singapore Airlines (SQ; ☎09-379 3209, 0800 808 909; www.singaporeair.com)

South African Airways (SA; ☎09-977 2237; www.flysaa.com)

Thai Airways International (TG; ☎09-377 3886; www.thaiairways.com)

Virgin Atlantic (VS; ☎09-308 3377; www.virginatlantic.com)

Virgin Australia (DJ; ☎0800 670 000; www.virginaustralia.com)

Virgin Samoa (☎0800 670 000; www.virginaustralia.com)

Tickets

Automated online ticket sales work well if you're doing a simple one-way or return trip on specified dates, but are no substitute for a travel agent with the low-down on special deals, strategies for avoiding layovers and other useful advice.

ROUND-THE-WORLD (RTW) TICKETS

If you're flying to New Zealand from the other side of the world, RTW tickets can be bargains. They're generally put together by the big airline alliances, and give you a limited period (usually a year) in which to circumnavigate the globe. You can go anywhere the participating airlines go, as long as you stay within the prescribed kilometre extents or number of stops and don't backtrack when flying between continents.

Ticket providers include the following:

Oneworld (www.oneworld.com)

Skyteam (www.skyteam.com)

Star Alliance (www.staralliance.com)

CIRCLE PACIFIC TICKETS

A Circle Pacific ticket is similar to a RTW ticket but covers a more limited region, using a combination of airlines to connect Australia, NZ, North America and Asia, with stopover options in the Pacific islands.

As with RTW tickets, there are restrictions on how many stopovers you can take.

ONLINE TICKET SALES

For online ticket bookings, including RTW fares, start with the following websites:

AirTreks (www.airtreks.com) A US company with some tasty round-the-world fares.

Cheap Flights (www.cheapflights.com) Global sites (US, Australia/NZ, Spain, Germany, UK/Ireland, France, Canada and Italy) with specials, destination information and flight searches.

Cheapest Flights (www.cheapestflights.co.uk) Cheap worldwide flights from the UK; get in early for the bargains.

Co-operative Travel (www.co-operativetravel.co.uk) International site for affordable holiday packages.

Expedia (www.expedia.com) Microsoft's travel site; good for USA-related flights.

Flight Centre International (www.flightcentre.com) Respected operator handling direct flights, with sites for NZ, Australia, the UK, the USA, Canada and South Africa.

Roundtheworldflights.com (www.roundtheworldflights.com) Build your own adventure from the UK with up to six stops, including Asia, Australia, NZ and the USA. Good rates in the NZ winter.

STA Travel (www.statravel.com) The full package: flights (including RTW), tours, accommodation and insurance.

Travel Online (www.travelonline.co.nz) Good place to check worldwide flights from NZ.

Travel.com.au (www.travel.com.au) Solid Australian site; look up fares and flights to/from the country.

Travelocity (www.travelocity.com) Global site that allows you to search fares from/to practically anywhere.

Sea

It's possible (though by no means easy or safe) to make your way between NZ and Australia, and some smaller Pacific islands, by hitching rides or crewing on yachts. Try asking around at harbours, marinas, and yacht and sailing clubs.

Popular yachting harbours in NZ include the Bay of Islands and Whangarei (both in Northland), Auckland and Wellington. March and April are the best months to look for boats heading to Australia. From Fiji, October to November is a peak departure season to beat the cyclones that soon follow in that neck of the woods.

There are no passenger liners operating to/from NZ, and finding a berth on a cargo ship (much less enjoying the experience) is no easy task.

GETTING AROUND

Air

Those who have limited time to get between NZ's attractions can make the most of a widespread network of intra- and inter-island flights.

Airlines in New Zealand

The country's major domestic carrier, Air New Zealand, has an aerial network covering most of the country. Australia-based Jetstar also flies between main urban areas. Between them, these two airlines service the main routes and carry the vast majority of domestic passengers in NZ.

Beyond this, several small-scale regional operators provide services, including between the North Island and South Island, to Stewart Island, and around the glaciers and mountains of the South Island.

Operators include the following:

Air Fiordland (☎0800 107 505, 03-249 6720; www.airfiordland.com) Services around Milford Sound, Te Anau and Queenstown.

Air New Zealand (NZ; ☎09-357 3000, 0800 737 000; www.airnewzealand.co.nz) Offers flights between 30-plus domestic destinations.

Air West Coast (☎03-738 0524, 0800 247 937; www.airwestcoast.co.nz) Operates charter and scenic flights ex-Greymouth, winging over the West Coast glaciers and Aoraki/Mt Cook, and stopping in Milford Sound, Queenstown and Christchurch.

Air2there.com (☎04-904 5130, 0800 777 000; www.air2there.com) Connects destinations across Cook Strait, including Paraparaumu, Wellington, Nelson and Blenheim.

Golden Bay Air (☎03-525 8725, 0800 588 885; www.goldenbayair.co.nz) Flies regularly between Wellington and Takaka in Golden Bay. Also connects to Karamea for Heaphy Track trampers.

Jetstar (JQ; ☎0800 800 995; www.jetstar.com) Joins the dots between key tourism centres: Auckland, Wellington, Christchurch, Dunedin and Queenstown (and flies Queenstown to Sydney).

Soundsair (☎0800 505 005, 03-520 3080; www.soundsair.co.nz) Numerous flights each day between Picton and Wellington, with connections to Blenheim and Nelson.

Stewart Island Flights (☎03-218 9129; www.stewartislandflights.com) Flies between Invercargill and Stewart Island.

Air Passes

With discounting being the norm these days, and a number of budget airlines now serving the trans-Tasman route as well as the Pacific islands, the value of air passes isn't as red-hot as in the past.

From Los Angeles return, **Air New Zealand** (NZ; ☎09-357 3000, 0800 737 000; www.airnewzealand.co.nz) offers the Explore New Zealand Airpass, which includes a stop in either Wellington, Queenstown or Christchurch plus three other domestic NZ destinations. Prices at the time of research started at around US$1150.

Star Alliance (www.staralliance.com) offers the coupon-based South Pacific Airpass, valid for selected journeys within NZ, and between NZ, Australia and several Pacific islands, including Fiji, New Caledonia, Tonga, the Cook Islands and Samoa.

Passes are available to nonresidents of these countries, must be issued outside NZ in conjunction with Star Alliance international tickets, and are valid for three months. A typical Sydney–Christchurch–Wellington–Auckland–Nadi pass cost NZ$1050 at the time of research.

Bicycle

Touring cyclists proliferate in NZ, particularly over summer. NZ is clean, green and relatively uncrowded, and has lots of cheap accommodation (including camping) and abundant fresh water.

The roads are generally in good nick, and the climate is generally not too hot or cold. Road traffic is the biggest danger: trucks overtaking too close to cyclists are a particular threat. Bikes and cycling gear (to rent or buy) are readily available in the main centres, as are bicycle repair shops.

By law all cyclists must wear an approved safety helmet (or risk a fine); it's also vital to have good reflective safety clothing. Cyclists who use public transport will find that major bus lines and trains only take bicycles on a 'space available' basis and charge up to $10.

Some of the smaller shuttle bus companies, on the other hand, make sure they have storage space for bikes, which they carry for a surcharge.

If importing your own bike or transporting it by plane within NZ, check with the relevant airline for costs and the degree of dismantling and packing required.

See www.nzta.govt.nz/traffic/ways/bike for more bike safety and legal tips.

Hire

The rates offered by most outfits for renting road or mountain bikes range from $10 to $20 per hour and $30 to $50 per day.

Longer-term rentals are often available by negotiation.

Boat

NZ may be an island nation but there's virtually no long-distance water transport around the country. Obvious South Island exceptions include the inter-island ferries between Auckland and various islands in the Hauraki Gulf, the inter-island ferries that chug across Cook Strait between Wellington and Picton, and the passenger ferry that negotiates Foveaux Strait between Bluff and the town of Oban on Stewart Island.

Bus

Bus travel in NZ is relatively easy and well organised, with services transporting you to the far reaches of both islands (including the start/end of various walking tracks), but it can be expensive, tedious and time-consuming.

NZ's dominant bus company is **InterCity** (☎09-583 5780; www.intercity.co.nz), which also has an extra-comfort travel and sightseeing arm called **Newmans Coach Lines** (☎09-583 5780; www.newmanscoach.co.nz). InterCity can drive you to just about anywhere on the South Island. **Naked Bus** (☎0900 625 33; www.nakedbus.com) is the main competition, a budget operator with fares as low as $1 (!).

Seat Classes

There are no allocated economy or luxury classes on NZ buses; smoking is a no-no.

Reservations

Over summer, school holidays and public holidays, book well in advance on popular routes. At other

NGA HAERENGA, NEW ZEALAND CYCLE TRAIL

The **Nga Haerenga, New Zealand Cycle Trail** (www.nzcycletrail.com) is a major nationwide project that has been in motion since 2009, expanding and improving NZ's extant network of bike trails. Funded to the tune of around $46 million, the project currently has 18 'Great Rides' under construction across both islands, most of which are already open to cyclists in some capacity. See the website for info and updates.

times a day or two ahead is usually fine.

The best prices are generally available online, booked a few weeks in advance.

Bus Passes

If you're covering a lot of ground, both **InterCity** (☎09-583 5780, 0800 222 146; www.intercity.co.nz) and **Naked Bus** (☎0900 625 33; www.nakedbus.com) offer bus passes that can be cheaper than paying as you go, but they do of course lock you into using their respective networks.

InterCity also offers a 15% discount for YHA, BBH and VIP backpacker members. All the following passes are valid for 12 months.

Backpacker Buses also offers fixed-itinerary bus-pass options for dorm dwellers.

NATIONWIDE PASSES

Flexipass A hop-on, hop-off InterCity pass, allowing travel to pretty much anywhere in NZ, in any direction. The pass is purchased in blocks of travel time: minimum 15 hours ($117), maximum 60 hours ($449). The average cost of each block becomes cheaper the more hours you buy. You can top up the pass if you need more time.

Flexitrips An InterCity bus-pass system whereby you purchase a specific number of bus trips (eg Christchurch to Dunedin would count as one trip) in blocks of five, with or without the north–south ferry trip included. Five/15/30 trips including the ferry cost $210/383/550 (subtract $54 if you don't need the ferry).

Naked Passport A Naked Bus **pass** (www.nakedpassport.com) that allows you to buy trips in blocks of five, which you can add to any time, and book each trip as needed. Five/15/30 trips cost $157/330/497. An unlimited pass costs $597 – great value if you're travelling NZ for many moons.

SOUTH ISLAND PASSES

On the South Island, InterCity offers 11 hop-on, hop-off, fixed-itinerary passes, ranging from $43 trips between Christchurch and Kaikoura, to $583 loops around the whole island.

See www.travelpass.co.nz for details.

Shuttle Buses

Other than InterCity and Naked Bus, South Island regional shuttle-bus operators include the following:

Abel Tasman Coachlines (☎03-548 0285; www.abeltasmantravel.co.nz) Traverses the tarmac between Nelson, Motueka, Golden Bay, and Kahurangi and Abel Tasman National Parks.

Alpine Scenic Tours (☎07-378 7412; www.alpinescenictours.co.nz) Has services around Taupo and into Tongariro National Park, plus the ski fields around Mt Ruapehu and Mt Tongariro.

Atomic Shuttles (☎03-349 0697; www.atomictravel.co.nz) Has services throughout the South Island, including to Christchurch, Dunedin, Invercargill, Picton, Nelson, Greymouth/Hokitika, Te Anau and Queenstown/Wanaka

Cook Connection (☎0800 266 526; www.cookconnect.co.nz) Triangulates between Mt Cook, Twizel and Lake Tekapo.

East West Coaches (☎03-789 6251, 0800 142 622; eastwestcoaches@xtra.co.nz) Offers a service between Christchurch and Westport via Reefton.

Hanmer Connection (☎0800 242 663; www.atsnz.com) Twice-daily services between Hanmer Springs and Christchurch.

Knightrider (☎03-342 8055, 0800 317 057; www.knightrider.co.nz) Runs a nocturnal service from Christchurch to Dunedin return. David Hasselhoff nowhere to be seen...

Southern Link Travel (☎0508 458 835; www.southernlinkkbus.co.nz) Roams across most of the South Island, taking in Christchurch, Nelson, Picton, Greymouth, Queenstown and Dunedin, among others.

Topline Tours (☎03-249 8059; www.toplinetours.co.nz) Connects Te Anau and Queenstown.

Tracknet (☎03-249 7777, 0800 483 262; www.tracknet.net) Daily track transport (Milford, Routeburn, Hollyford, Kepler etc) between Queenstown, Te Anau, Milford Sound, Invercargill, Fiordland and the West Coast.

West Coast Shuttle (☎03-768 0028; www.westcoastshuttle.co.nz) Daily bus from Greymouth to Christchurch and back.

Backpacker Buses

If you feel like clocking up some kilometres with like-minded fellow travellers, the following operators run fixed-itinerary bus tours, nationwide or on the North or South Island.

Accommodation and hop-on/hop-off flexibility are often included.

Adventure Tours New Zealand (☎09-526 2149; www.adventuretours.com.au)

Flying Kiwi (☎03-547 0171, 0800 693 296; www.flyingkiwi.com)

Kiwi Experience (☎09-336 4286; www.kiwiexperience.com)

Haka Tours (☎03-980 4252; www.hakatours.com)

Magic Travellers Network (☎09-358 5600; www.magicbus.co.nz)

Stray Travel (☎09-526 2140; www.straytravel.com)

Car & Motorcycle

The best way to explore NZ in depth is to have your own wheels. It's easy to hire cars and campervans at good rates; alternatively, consider buying your own vehicle.

Automobile Association (AA)

NZ's **Automobile Association** (AA; ☎0800 500 444; www.aa.co.nz/travel) provides emergency breakdown services, maps and accommodation guides (from holiday parks to motels and B&Bs).

Members of overseas automobile associations should bring their membership cards – many of these bodies have reciprocal agreements with the AA.

Driving Licences

International visitors to NZ can use their home country's driving licence – if your licence isn't in English, it's a good idea to carry a certified translation with you.

Alternatively, use an International Driving Permit (IDP), which will usually be issued on the spot (valid for 12 months) by your home country's automobile association.

Fuel

Fuel (petrol, aka gasoline) is available from service stations across NZ. LPG (gas) is not always stocked by rural suppliers; if you're on gas, it's safer to have dual-fuel capability.

Aside from remote locations like Milford Sound and Mt Cook, petrol prices don't vary much from place to place (very democratic): per-litre costs at the time of research were around $2.10.

Hire

CAMPERVAN

Check your rear-view mirror on any far-flung NZ road and you'll probably see a shiny white campervan (aka mobile home, motor home, RV) packed with liberated travellers, mountain bikes and portable barbecues cruising along behind you.

Most towns of any size have a campground or holiday park with powered sites for around $35 per night. There are also 250-plus vehicle-accessible **Department of Conservation** (DOC; www.doc.govt.nz) campsites around NZ, ranging in price from free to $19 per adult: check the website.

You can hire campervans from dozens of companies, prices varying with season, vehicle size and length of rental.

A small van for two people typically has a minikitchen and foldout dining table, the latter transforming into a double bed when dinner is done and dusted.

Larger 'superior' two-berth vans include shower and toilet. Four- to six-berth campervans are the size of trucks (and similarly sluggish) and, besides the extra space, usually contain a toilet and shower.

During summer, rates offered by the main rental firms for two-/four-/six-berth vans start at around $160/260/300 per day, dropping to as low as $45/60/90 in winter for month-long rentals.

Major operators include the following:

Apollo (☎09-889 2976, 0800 113 131; www.apollocamper.co.nz)

Britz (☎09-255 3910, 0800 831 900; www.britz.co.nz)

Kea (☎09-448 8800, 0800 520 052; www.keacampers.com)

Maui (☎09-255 3910, 0800 651 080; www.maui.co.nz)

Pacific Horizon (☎09-257 4331; www.pacifichorizon.co.nz)

United Campervans (☎09-275 9919; www.unitedcampervans.co.nz)

BACKPACKER VAN RENTALS

Budget players in the campervan industry offer slick deals and funky, well-kitted-out vehicles for backpackers.

Rates are competitive (from $35 per day May to September; from $80 per day December to February). Operators include the following:

Backpacker Campervans (☎0800 422 267; www.backpackercampervans.co.nz) Reliable operator, affiliated with Britz and Maui.

Backpacker Sleeper Vans (☎03-359 4731, 0800 325 939; www.sleepervans.co.nz) The name says it all.

Escape Rentals (☎0800 216 171; www.escaperentals.co.nz) Loud, original paintwork, plus DVDs, TVs and outdoor barbecues for hire.

Hippie Camper (☎0800 113 131; www.hippiecamper.co.nz) Think Combi vans for the new millennium.

Jucy (☎0800 399 736; www.jucy.co.nz)

Spaceships (☎09-526 2130, 0800 772 237; www.spaceshipsrentals.co.nz) The customised 'Swiss Army

FREEDOM CAMPING

NZ is so photogenic, it's tempting to just pull off the road at a gorgeous viewpoint and camp the night. But never just assume it's OK to camp somewhere: always ask a local or check with the local i-SITE, DOC office or commercial campground. If you are freedom camping, treat the area with respect – if your van doesn't have toilet facilities, find a public loo. Legislation allows for $200 instant fines for camping in prohibited areas, or improper disposal of waste (in cases where dumping waste could damage the environment, fees are up to $10,000). See www.camping.org.nz for more freedom camping tips, and www.tourism.govt.nz for info on where to find dump stations.

ROAD DISTANCES (KM)

	Aoraki/Mt Cook	Arthur's Pass	Blenheim	Christchurch	Dunedin	Franz Josef Glacier	Greymouth	Hanmer Springs	Hokitika	Invercargill	Kaikoura	Milford Sound	Nelson	Oamaru	Picton	Queenstown	Te Anau	Timaru	Wanaka
Arthur's Pass	410																		
Blenheim	635	420																	
Christchurch	330	150	310																
Dunedin	325	455	665	360															
Franz Josef Glacier	485	230	500	390	560														
Greymouth	510	95	330	250	550	180													
Hanmer Springs	460	265	260	140	490	395	215												
Hokitika	510	100	370	250	550	135	40	255											
Invercargill	440	660	870	570	210	530	710	700	665										
Kaikoura	505	290	130	185	535	540	330	135	390	745									
Milford Sound	540	840	1060	760	410	630	805	890	770	275	930								
Nelson	745	370	115	425	775	470	290	310	335	990	245	1100							
Oamaru	210	340	550	250	115	510	430	375	435	325	420	525	660						
Picton	660	450	30	340	690	530	355	290	400	900	160	1090	120	580					
Queenstown	260	565	785	480	285	355	530	610	490	190	660	290	820	290	815				
Te Anau	420	725	945	640	295	515	690	770	650	160	815	120	980	410	975	170			
Timaru	210	260	465	165	200	490	350	295	360	410	340	605	580	85	495	330	490		
Wanaka	210	510	730	430	280	285	465	555	420	245	600	345	755	230	760	70	230	275	
Westport	610	195	260	340	650	280	100	220	145	810	330	905	230	535	290	630	790	455	565

Knife of campervans', with extras including DVD and CD players, roof racks and solar showers.

Wicked Campers (☎09-634 2994, 0800 246 870; www.wicked-campers.co.nz) Spray-painted vans bedecked with everything/everyone from Mr Spock to Sly Stone.

CAR

Competition between car-rental companies in NZ is torrid, particularly in the big cities and Picton.

Remember that if you want to travel far, you need unlimited kilometres. Some (but not all) companies require drivers to be at least 21 years old – ask around.

Most car-hire firms suggest (or insist) that you don't take their vehicles between islands on the Cook Strait ferries. Instead, you leave your car at either Wellington or Picton terminal and pick up another car once you've crossed the strait.

This saves you paying to transport a vehicle on the ferries, and is a pain-free exercise.

INTERNATIONAL RENTAL COMPANIES

The big multinational companies have offices in most major cities, towns and airports.

Firms sometimes offer one-way rentals (eg collect a car in Auckland, leave it in Wellington), but there are often restrictions and fees. On the other hand, an operator in Christchurch may need to get a vehicle back to Auckland and will offer an amazing one-way deal (sometimes free!).

The major companies offer a choice of either unlimited kilometres, or 100km (or so) per day free, plus so many cents per subsequent kilometre.

Daily rates in main cities typically start at around $40 per day for a compact, late-model, Japanese car, and around $75 for medium-sized cars (including GST, unlimited kilometres and insurance).

Avis (☎09-526-2847, 0800 655 111; www.avis.co.nz)

Budget (☎09-529 7784, 0800 283 438; www.budget.co.nz)

Europcar (☎03-357 0920, 0800 800 115; www.europcar.co.nz)

Hertz (☎03-520 3044, 0800 654 321; www.hertz.co.nz)

Thrifty (☎03-359 2720, 0800 737 070; www.thrifty.co.nz)

LOCAL RENTAL COMPANIES

Local rental firms dapple the *Yellow Pages*. These are almost always cheaper than the big boys – sometimes half the price – but the cheap rates may come with serious restrictions: vehicles are often older, and with less formality sometimes comes a less protective legal structure for renters.

Rentals from local firms start at around $30 per day for the smallest option. It's obviously cheaper if you rent for a week or more, and there are often low-season and weekend discounts.

Affordable and independent operators with national networks include the following:

a2b Car Rentals (☎0800 666 703; www.a2b-carrentals.co.nz)

Ace Rental Cars (☎09-303 3112, 0800 502 277; www.acerentalcars.co.nz)

Apex Rentals (☎03-379 6897, 0800 939 597; www.apexrentals.co.nz)

Ezy Rentals (☎09-374 4360, 0800 399 736; www.ezy.co.nz)

Go Rentals (☎09-525 7321, 0800 467 368; www.gorentals.co.nz)

Omega Rental Cars (☎09-377 5573, 0800 525 210; www.omegarentalcars.com)

Pegasus Rental Cars (☎03-548 2852, 0800 803 580; www.rentalcars.co.nz)

MOTORCYCLE

Born to be wild? NZ has great terrain for motorcycle touring, despite the fickle weather in some regions.

Most of the South Island's motorcycle-hire shops are in Christchurch, where you can hire anything from a little 50cc moped (aka nifty-fifty) to a throbbing 750cc touring motorcycle and beyond.

Recommended operators (who also run guided tours) with rates from $80 to $345 per day:

New Zealand Motorcycle Rentals & Tours (☎09-486 2472; www.nzbike.com)

Te Waipounamu Motorcycle Tours (☎03-377 3211; www.motorcycle-hire.co.nz)

Insurance

Rather than risk paying out wads of cash if you have an accident, you can take out your own comprehensive insurance policy, or (the usual option) pay an additional fee per day to the rental company to reduce your excess.

This brings the amount you must pay in the event of an accident down from around $1500 or $2000 to around $200 or $300.

Smaller operators offering cheap rates often have a compulsory insurance excess, taken as a credit-card bond, of around $900.

Most insurance agreements won't cover the cost of damage to glass (including the windscreen) or tyres, and insurance coverage is often invalidated on beaches and certain rough (4WD) unsealed roads – read the fine print.

Purchase

Buying a car then selling it at the end of your travels can be one of the cheapest and best ways to see NZ. Christchurch is the easiest place to buy a car on the South Island: scour the hostel notice boards. **Turners Auctions** (☎03-343 9850, 09-525 1920; www.turners.co.nz) is NZ's biggest car-auction operator, with 10 locations.

LEGALITIES

Make sure your prospective vehicle has a Warrant of Fitness (WoF) and registration valid for a reasonable period: see the **Land Transport New Zealand** (www.landtransport.govt.nz) website for details.

Buyers should also take out third-party insurance, covering the cost of repairs to another vehicle in an accident that is your fault: try the **Automobile Association** (AA; ☎0800 500 444; www.aa.co.nz/travel).

NZ's no-fault Accident Compensation Corporation scheme covers personal injury, but make sure you have travel insurance too.

Various car-inspection companies inspect cars for around $150; find them at car auctions, or they will come to you.

Try **Vehicle Inspection New Zealand** (VINZ; ☎09-573 3230, 0800 468 469; www.vinz.co.nz) or the AA.

Before you buy it's wise to confirm ownership of the vehicle, and find out if there's anything dodgy about the car (eg stolen, or outstanding debts).

The AA's **LemonCheck** (☎09-414 6665, 0800 536 662; www.lemoncheck.co.nz) offers this service.

BUY-BACK DEALS

You can avoid the hassle of buying/selling a vehicle privately by entering into a buy-back arrangement with a dealer. Predictably, dealers often find sneaky ways of knocking down the return-sale price, which may be 50% less than what you paid.

Hiring or buying and selling a vehicle yourself (if you have the time) is usually a better bet.

Road Hazards

Kiwi traffic is usually pretty light, but it's easy to get stuck behind a slow-moving truck or campervan – pack plenty of patience. There are also lots of slow wiggly roads, one-way bridges and plenty of gravel roads, all of which require a more cautious driving approach.

And watch out for sheep!

Road Rules

Kiwis drive on the left-hand side of the road; cars are right-hand drive. Give way to the right at intersections.

At single-lane bridges (of which there are a surprisingly

large number), a smaller red arrow pointing in your direction of travel means that *you* give way.

Speed limits on the open road are generally 100km/h; in built-up areas the limit is usually 50km/h. Speed cameras and radars are used extensively.

All vehicle occupants must wear a seatbelt or risk a fine. Small children must be belted into approved safety seats.

Always carry your licence when driving. Drink-driving is a serious offence and remains a significant problem in NZ, despite widespread campaigns and severe penalties.

The legal blood alcohol limit is 0.08% for drivers over 20, and 0% (zero!) for those under 20.

Hitching & Ride-Sharing

NZ is no longer immune from the perils of solo hitching (especially for women). Those who decide to hitch are taking a small but potentially serious risk. That said, it's not unusual to see hitchhikers along country roads.

Alternatively, check hostel notice boards for ride-share opportunities, or have a look at www.carpoolnz.org or www.nationalcarshare.co.nz.

Local Transport

Bus, Train & Tram

NZ's larger cities have extensive bus services but, with a few honourable exceptions, they are mainly daytime, weekday operations; weekend services can be infrequent or nonexistent.

Christchurch has a free city shuttle service and the historic tramway (closed post-earthquake at the time of research).

The bigger South Island cities have late-night buses on boozy Friday and Saturday nights.

Taxi

The main cities have plenty of taxis and even small towns may have a local service.

Train

NZ train travel is about the journey, not about getting anywhere in a hurry.

KiwiRail Scenic Journeys (☎04-495 0775, 0800 872 467; www.tranzscenic.co.nz) operates operates two routes in the South Island:

Coastal Pacific Between Christchurch and Picton.

TranzAlpine Over the Southern Alps between Christchurch and Greymouth.

Reservations can be made through KiwiRail Scenic Journeys directly, or at most train stations, travel agents and visitor information centres. Discounts on the *Coastal Pacific* and *TranzAlpine* apply for children and seniors (30% off) and backpacker cardholders (20% off).

Train Passes

Tranz Scenic's **KiwiRail Scenic Journeys** (www.tranzscenic.co.nz) allows unlimited travel on all of its rail services, including passage on the Wellington–Picton Interislander ferry. A two-week pass costs $528/402 per adult/child. There's also a seven-day *TranzAlpine* and *Coastal Pacific* pass for $307/215.

Language

WANT MORE?

For in-depth language information and handy phrases, check out Lonely Planet's *South Pacific Phrasebook*. You'll find it at **shop.lonelyplanet.com**, or you can buy Lonely Planet's iPhone phrasebooks at the Apple App Store.

New Zealand has three official languages: English, Maori and NZ sign language. Although English is what you'll usually hear, Maori has been making a comeback. You can use English to speak to anyone in New Zealand, but there are some occasions when knowing a small amount of Maori is useful, such as when visiting a *marae*, where often only Maori is spoken. Some knowledge of Maori will also help you interpret the many Maori place names you'll come across.

KIWI ENGLISH

Like the people of other English-speaking countries in the world, New Zealanders have their own, unique way of speaking the language. The flattening of vowels is the most distinctive feature of Kiwi pronunciation. For example, in Kiwi English, 'fish and chips' sounds more like 'fush and chups'. On the North Island sentences often have 'eh!' attached to the end. In the far south a rolled 'r' is common, which is a holdover from that region's Scottish heritage – it's especially noticeable in Southland.

MAORI

The Maori have a vividly chronicled history, recorded in songs and chants that dramatically recall the migration to New Zealand from Polynesia as well as other important events. Early missionaries were the first to record the language in a written form using only 15 letters of the English alphabet.

Maori is closely related to other Polynesian languages such as Hawaiian, Tahitian and Cook Islands Maori. In fact, New Zealand Maori and Hawaiian are quite similar, even though more than 7000km separates Honolulu and Auckland.

The Maori language was never dead – it was always used in Maori ceremonies – but over time familiarity with it was definitely on the decline. Fortunately, recent years have seen a revival of interest in it, and this forms an integral part of the renaissance of *Maoritanga* (Maori culture). Many Maori people who had heard the language spoken on the *marae* for years but had not used it in their day-to-day lives, are now studying it and speaking it fluently. Maori is taught in schools throughout New Zealand, some TV programs and news reports are broadcast in it, and many English place names are being renamed in Maori. Even government departments have been given Maori names: for example, the Inland Revenue Department is also known as Te Tari Taake (the last word is actually *take*, which means 'levy', but the department has chosen to stress the long 'a' by spelling it 'aa').

In many places, Maori have come together to provide instruction in their language and culture to young children; the idea is for them to grow up speaking both Maori and English, and to develop a familiarity with Maori tradition. It's a matter of some pride to have fluency in the language. On some *marae* only Maori can be spoken.

Pronunciation

Maori is a fluid, poetic language and surprisingly easy to pronounce once you remember to split each word (some can be amazingly long) into separate syllables. Each syllable ends in a vowel. There are no 'silent' letters.

Most consonants in Maori – *h, k, m, n, p, t* and *w* – are pronounced much the same as in English. The Maori *r* is a flapped sound (not rolled) with the tongue near the front of the mouth. It's closer to the English 'l' in pronunciation.

The *ng* is pronounced as in the English words 'singing' or 'running', and can be used at the beginning of words as well as at the end. To practise, just say 'ing' over and over, then isolate the 'ng' part of it.

The letters *wh,* when occuring together, are generally pronounced as a soft English 'f'. This pronunciation is used in many place names in New Zealand, such as Whakatane, Whangaroa and Whakapapa (all pronounced as if they begin with a soft 'f'). There is some local variation: in the region around the Whanganui River, for example, *wh* is pronounced as in the English word 'when'.

The correct pronunciation of the vowels is very important. The examples below are a rough guideline – it helps to listen carefully to someone who speaks the language well. Each vowel has both a long and a short sound, with long vowels often denoted by a line over the letter or a double vowel. We have not indicated long and short vowel forms in this book.

Vowels

a	as in 'large', with no 'r' sound
e	as in 'get'
i	as in 'marine'
o	as in 'pork'
u	as the 'oo' in 'moon'

Vowel Combinations

ae, ai	as the 'y' in 'sky'
ao, au	as the 'ow' in 'how'
ea	as in 'bear'
ei	as in 'vein'
eo	as 'eh-oh'
eu	as 'eh-oo'
ia	as in the name 'Ian'
ie	as the 'ye' in 'yet'
io	as the 'ye o' in 'ye old'
iu	as the 'ue' in 'cue'
oa	as in 'roar'
oe	as in 'toe'
oi	as in 'toil'
ou	as the 'ow' in 'how'
ua	as the 'ewe' in 'fewer'

Greetings & Small Talk

Maori greetings are becoming increasingly popular – don't be surprised if you're greeted with *Kia ora*.

Welcome!	*Haere mai!*
Hello./Good luck./ Good health.	*Kia ora.*
Hello. (to one person)	*Tena koe.*
Hello. (to two people)	*Tena korua.*
Hello. (to three or more people)	*Tena koutou.*
Goodbye. (to person staying)	*E noho ra.*
Goodbye. (to person leaving)	*Haere ra.*
How are you? (to one person)	*Kei te pehea koe?*
How are you? (to two people)	*Kei te pehea korua?*
How are you? (to three or more people)	*Kei te pehea koutou?*
Very well, thanks./ That's fine.	*Kei te pai.*

Maori Geographical Terms

The following words form part of many Maori place names in New Zealand, and help you understand the meaning of these place names. For example: Waikaremoana is the Sea *(moana)* of Rippling *(kare)* Waters *(wai)*, and Rotorua means the Second *(rua)* Lake *(roto)*.

a – of
ana – cave
ara – way, path or road
awa – river or valley
heke – descend
hiku – end; tail
hine – girl; daughter
ika – fish
iti – small
kahurangi – treasured possession; special greenstone
kai – food
kainga – village
kaka – parrot
kare – rippling
kati – shut or close
koura – crayfish
makariri – cold
manga – stream or tributary
manu – bird

maunga – mountain
moana – sea or lake
moko – tattoo
motu – island
mutu – finished; ended; over
nga – the (plural)
noa – ordinary; not *tapu*
nui – big or great
nuku – distance
o – of, place of...
one – beach, sand or mud
pa – fortified village
papa – large blue-grey mudstone
pipi – common edible bivalve
pohatu – stone
poto – short
pouri – sad; dark; gloomy
puke – hill
puna – spring; hole; fountain
rangi – sky; heavens
raro – north
rei – cherished possession
roa – long
roto – lake
rua – hole in the ground; two
runga – above
tahuna – beach; sandbank
tane – man
tangata – people
tapu – sacred, forbidden or taboo
tata – close to; dash against; twin islands
tawaha – entrance or opening
tawahi – the other side (of a river or lake)
te – the (singular)
tonga – south
ure – male genitals
uru – west
waha – broken
wahine – woman
wai – water
waingaro – lost; waters that disappear in certain seasons
waka – canoe
wera – burnt or warm; floating
wero – challenge
whaka... – to act as ...
whanau – family
whanga – harbour, bay or inlet
whare – house
whenua – land or country
whiti – east

Here are some more place names composed of words in the list:

Aramoana – Sea *(moana)* Path *(ara)*
Awaroa – Long *(roa)* River *(awa)*
Kaitangata – Eat *(kai)* People *(tangata)*
Maunganui – Great *(nui)* Mountain *(maunga)*
Opouri – Place of *(o)* Sadness *(pouri)*
Te Araroa – The *(te)* Long *(roa)* Path *(ara)*
Te Puke – The *(te)* Hill *(puke)*
Urewera – Burnt *(wera)* Penis *(ure)*
Waimakariri – Cold *(makariri)* Water *(wai)*
Wainui – Great *(nui)* Waters *(wai)*
Whakatane – To Act *(whaka)* as a Man *(tane)*
Whangarei – Cherished *(rei)* Harbour *(whanga)*

GLOSSARY

Following is a list of abbreviations, 'Kiwi English', Maori, and slang terms used in this book and which you may hear in New Zealand.

All Blacks – NZ's revered national rugby union team
ANZAC – Australia and New Zealand Army Corps
Aoraki – *Maori* name for Mt Cook, meaning 'Cloud Piercer'
Aotearoa – *Maori* name for NZ, most often translated as 'Land of the Long White Cloud'

aroha – love

B&B – 'bed and breakfast' accommodation
bach – holiday home (pronounced 'batch'); see also crib
black-water rafting – rafting or tubing underground in a cave
boozer – public bar
bro – literally 'brother'; usually meaning mate
BYO – 'bring your own' (usually applies to alcohol at a restaurant or cafe)

choice/chur – fantastic; great
crib – the name for a bach in Otago and Southland

DB&B – 'dinner, bed and breakfast' accommodation
DOC – Department of Conservation (or Te Papa Atawhai); government department that administers national parks, tracks and huts

eh? – roughly translates as 'don't you agree?'

farmstay – accommodation on a Kiwi farm

football – rugby, either union or league; occasionally soccer

Great Walks – a set of nine popular tramping tracks within NZ

greenstone – jade; *pounamu*

gumboots – rubber boots or Wellingtons; originated from diggers on the gum-fields

Hawaiki –an original homeland of the *Maori*

haka – any dance, but usually a war dance

hangi – oven whereby food is steamed in baskets over embers in a hole; a *Maori* feast

hapu – subtribe or smaller tribal grouping

hei tiki – carved, stylised human figure worn around the neck; also called a *tiki*

homestay – accommodation in a family house

hongi – *Maori* greeting; the pressing of foreheads and noses, and sharing of life breath

hui – gathering; meeting

i-SITE – information centre

iwi – large tribal grouping with common lineage back to the original migration from Hawaiki; people; tribe

jandals – a contraction of Japanese sandals; flip-flops; thongs; usually rubber footwear

jersey – jumper, usually woollen; the shirt worn by rugby players

kauri – native pine

kia ora – hello

Kiwi – A New Zealander; an adjective to mean anything relating to NZ

kiwi – flightless, nocturnal brown bird with a long beak

Kiwiana – things uniquely connected to NZ life and culture, especially from bygone years

kiwifruit – small, succulent fruit with fuzzy brown skin and juicy green flesh; aka Chinese gooseberry or zespri

kumara – Polynesian sweet potato, a *Maori* staple food

Kupe – early Polynesian navigator from *Hawaiki*, credited with the discovery of the islands that are now NZ

mana – spiritual quality of a person or object; authority or prestige

Maori – indigenous people of NZ

Maoritanga – things *Maori*, ie *Maori* culture

marae – the sacred ground in front of the *Maori* meeting house; more commonly used to refer to the entire complex of buildings

Maui – a figure in *Maori* (Polynesian) mythology

mauri – life force/principle

moa – large, extinct flightless bird

moko – tattoo; usually refers to facial tattoos

munted –damaged or destroyed

nga – the (plural); see also *te*

ngai/ngati – literally, 'the people of' or 'the descendants of'; tribe (pronounced 'kai' on the South Island)

NZ – the universal term for New Zealand; pronounced 'en zed'

pa – fortified *Maori* village, usually on a hilltop

Pacific Rim – modern NZ cuisine; local produce cooked with imported styles

Pakeha – *Maori* for a white or European person

Pasifika – Pacific Island culture

paua – abalone; iridescent paua shell is often used in jewellery

pavlova – meringue cake topped with cream and kiwifruit

PI – Pacific Islander

poi – ball of woven flax

pounamu – *Maori* name for *greenstone*

powhiri – traditional *Maori* welcome onto a marae

rip – dangerously strong current running away from the shore at a beach

Roaring Forties – the ocean between 40° and 50° south, known for very strong winds

silver fern – the symbol worn by the *All Blacks* and other national sportsfolk on their jerseys; the national netball team is called the Silver Ferns

sweet, sweet as – all-purpose term like choice; fantastic, great

tapu – a strong force in *Maori* life, with numerous meanings; in its simplest form it means sacred, forbidden, taboo

te – the (singular); see also *nga*

te reo – literally 'the language'; the *Maori* language

tiki – short for *hei tiki*

tiki tour – scenic tour

tramp – bushwalk; trek; hike

tuatara – prehistoric reptile dating back to the age of dinosaurs

tui – native parson bird

wahine – woman

wai – water

wairua – spirit

Waitangi – short way of referring to the Treaty of Waitangi

waka – canoe

Warriors – NZ's popular rugby league club, affiliated with Australia's NRL

Wellywood – Wellington, because of its thriving film industry

zorbing – rolling down a hill inside an inflatable plastic ball

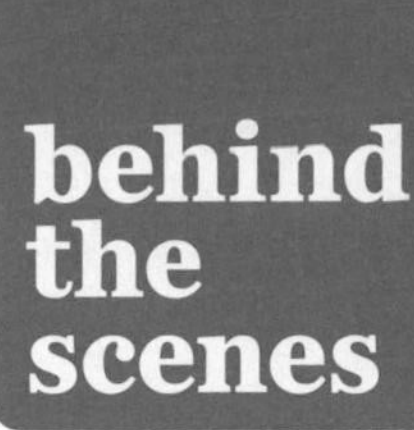

SEND US YOUR FEEDBACK

We love to hear from travellers – your comments keep us on our toes and help make our books better. Our well-travelled team reads every word on what you loved or loathed about this book. Although we cannot reply individually to postal submissions, we always guarantee that your feedback goes straight to the appropriate authors, in time for the next edition. Each person who sends us information is thanked in the next edition – the most useful submissions are rewarded with a selection of digital PDF chapters.

Visit **lonelyplanet.com/contact** to submit your updates and suggestions or to ask for help. Our award-winning website also features inspirational travel stories, news and discussions.

Note: We may edit, reproduce and incorporate your comments in Lonely Planet products such as guidebooks, websites and digital products, so let us know if you don't want your comments reproduced or your name acknowledged. For a copy of our privacy policy visit lonelyplanet.com/privacy.

OUR READERS

Many thanks to the travellers who used the last edition and wrote to us with helpful hints, useful advice and interesting anecdotes:

Penny Cruickshank, John England, Eli Faen, Peter Geddes, Emily Hui, Karel Kovanda, Dirk Latijnouwers & Loeki Bouwmans, Marc Leyton-Smith, Diana Parr, Vivien Priestley, Pascal Reichmuth, Koos Reitsma, Nicola Simpson, Judi Strickland, James Sumner, Kristy White

AUTHOR THANKS

Brett Aktinson

Thanks to all the i-SITE and DOC staff I tapped for vital information. In Christchurch, special thanks to Kelly Wilkes, Monique Devereux, Roger Sutton, and Jeff and Naomi Peters. Cheers to Richard Emerson in Dunedin, and to Scott Kennedy in Queenstown. At Lonely Planet, it's always great to work with Errol Hunt and the NZ author crew, ably assisted this time around by Jani Patokallio. Final thanks to Carol back at Casa Loma in Auckland.

Sarah Bennett & Lee Slater

Thanks to everyone who helped us on the road, including RTO and i-SITE staff , tourism operators and travellers. Many thanks DOC, especially Penny McIntosh, Katrina Henderson and Diana Parr. Big ups to everyone in-house at Lonely Planet, and to Team NZ, including Errol, Peter, Brett, Charles, Sarah Ewing, and by proxy Arnott Potter at CPP. To all who provided a park for our camper, a fridge for the flagon, and even turkey for thanksgiving: *arohanui, e hoa ma*, especially the Bennetts, Parsons, Pauls, Betzy Iannuzzi and John Kelly.

Peter Dragicevich

Special thanks to Shenita Prasad, Tania Wong, Joanne Cole, Matt Swaine and Donna Jarden for their company on the road, and to Tony Dragicevich and Debbie Debono for the writing retreat.

Charles Rawlings-Way

Thanks to the many generous, knowledgeable and quietly self-assured Kiwis I met on the road. Thanks to Errol Hunt for the gig, and the everimpressive LP production staff (including the Lords of SPP). Humongous gratitude to my tireless, witty and professional co-authors: Sarah, Brett, Peter and Lee. Thanks also to Warren for Wellington, and to Meg, Ione and Remy for holding the fort while I was away.

ACKNOWLEDGMENTS

Climate map data adapted from Peel MC, Finlayson BL & McMahon TA (2007) 'Updated World Map of the Köppen-Geiger Climate Classification', *Hydrology and Earth System Sciences*, 11, 163344.

Cover photograph: Moeraki Boulders, Otago, Massimo Ripani/4Corners. Many of the images in this guide are available for licensing from Lonely Planet Images: www.lonelyplanetimages.com.

THIS BOOK

This 3rd edition of Lonely Planet's *New Zealand's South Island* guidebook was coordinated by Brett Atkinson, and researched and written by Brett, Sarah Bennett, Peter Dragicevich, Charles Rawlings-Way and Lee Slater. It includes content from the 16th edition of the *New Zealand* guide, coordinated by Charles Rawlings-Way. This guidebook was commissioned in Lonely Planet's Melbourne office, and produced by the following:

Commissioning Editor Errol Hunt

Coordinating Editor Amanda Williamson

Coordinating Cartographer Laura Matthewman

Coordinating Layout Designer Jacqui Saunders

Managing Editors Barbara Delissen, Martine Power

Managing Cartographers Shahara Ahmed, Corey Hutchison

Managing Layout Designer Jane Hart

Assisting Layout Designer Wibowo Rusli

Cover Research Naomi Parker

Internal Image Research Rebecca Skinner

Language Content Branislava Vladisavljevic

Thanks to

Anita Banh, Imogen Bannister, David Carroll, David Connolly, Daniel Corbett, Laura Crawford, Ryan Evans, Larissa Frost, Chris Girdler, Paul Iacono, Alison Lyall, Ross Macaw, Erin McManus, Anna Metcalfe, Jane Nethercote, Susan Paterson, Trent Paton, Anthony Phelan, Kirsten Rawlings, Jessica Rose, Dianne Schallmeiner, Amanda Sierp, Gina Tsarouhas, Diana Von Holdt, Gerard Walker

index

000 Map pages
000 Photo pages

000 Map pages
000 Photo pages

D

E

000 Map pages
000 Photo pages

S

T

000 Map pages
000 Photo pages

how to use this book

These symbols will help you find the listings you want:

- Sights
- Beaches
- Activities
- Courses
- Tours
- Festivals & Events
- Sleeping
- Eating
- Drinking
- Entertainment
- Shopping
- Information/ Transport

These symbols give you the vital information for each listing:

- Telephone Numbers
- Opening Hours
- Parking
- Nonsmoking
- Air-Conditioning
- Internet Access
- Wi-Fi Access
- Swimming Pool
- Vegetarian Selection
- English-Language Menu
- Family-Friendly
- Pet-Friendly
- Bus
- Ferry
- Metro
- Subway
- Tram
- Train

Reviews are organised by author preference.

Look out for these icons:

TOP CHOICE Our author's recommendation

FREE No payment required

A green or sustainable option

Our authors have nominated these places as demonstrating a strong commitment to sustainability – for example by supporting local communities and producers, operating in an environmentally friendly way, or supporting conservation projects.

Map Legend

Sights
- Beach
- Buddhist
- Castle
- Christian
- Hindu
- Islamic
- Jewish
- Monument
- Museum/Gallery
- Ruin
- Winery/Vineyard
- Zoo
- Other Sight

Activities, Courses & Tours
- Diving/Snorkelling
- Canoeing/Kayaking
- Skiing
- Surfing
- Swimming/Pool
- Walking
- Windsurfing
- Other Activity/ Course/Tour

Sleeping
- Sleeping
- Camping

Eating
- Eating

Drinking
- Drinking
- Cafe

Entertainment
- Entertainment

Shopping
- Shopping

Information
- Post Office
- Tourist Information

Transport
- Airport
- Border Crossing
- Bus
- Cable Car/ Funicular
- Cycling
- Ferry
- Metro
- Monorail
- Parking
- S-Bahn
- Taxi
- Train/Railway
- Tram
- Tube Station
- U-Bahn
- Other Transport

Routes
- Tollway
- Freeway
- Primary
- Secondary
- Tertiary
- Lane
- Unsealed Road
- Plaza/Mall
- Steps
- Tunnel
- Pedestrian Overpass
- Walking Tour
- Walking Tour Detour
- Path

Boundaries
- International
- State/Province
- Disputed
- Regional/Suburb
- Marine Park
- Cliff
- Wall

Population
- Capital (National)
- Capital (State/Province)
- City/Large Town
- Town/Village

Geographic
- Hut/Shelter
- Lighthouse
- Lookout
- Mountain/Volcano
- Oasis
- Park
- Pass
- Picnic Area
- Waterfall

Hydrography
- River/Creek
- Intermittent River
- Swamp/Mangrove
- Reef
- Canal
- Water
- Dry/Salt/ Intermittent Lake
- Glacier

Areas
- Beach/Desert
- Cemetery (Christian)
- Cemetery (Other)
- Park/Forest
- Sportsground
- Sight (Building)
- Top Sight (Building)

Contributing Authors

Professor James Belich wrote the History chapter (p294). James is one of NZ's pre-eminent historians and the award-winning author of *The New Zealand Wars, Making Peoples* and *Paradise Reforged*. He has also worked in TV – *New Zealand Wars* was screened in NZ in 1998.

Tony Horwitz wrote the Captain James Cook boxed text (p297) in the History chapter. Tony is a Pulitzer-winning reporter and nonfiction author. His fascination with James Cook, and with travel, took him around NZ, Australia and the Pacific while researching *Blue Latitudes* (alternatively titled *Into the Blue*), part biography of Cook and part travelogue.

John Huria (Ngai Tahu, Muaupoko) wrote the Maori Culture chapter (p311). John has an editorial, research and writing background with a focus on Maori writing and culture. He was senior editor for Maori publishing company Huia and now runs an editorial and publishing services company, Ahi Text Solutions Ltd (www.ahitextsolutions.co.nz).

Josh Kronfeld wrote the Surfing in New Zealand boxed text (p46) in the Extreme New Zealand chapter. Josh is an ex–All Black flanker, whose passion for surfing NZ's beaches is legendary and who found travelling for rugby a way to surf other great breaks around the world.

Gareth Shute wrote the Music section (p326) in the Arts & Music chapter. Gareth is the author of four books, including *Hip Hop Music in Aotearoa* and *NZ Rock 1987–2007*. He is also a musician and has toured the UK, Europe and Australia as a member of The Ruby Suns and The Brunettes. He now plays in indie soul group The Cosbys.

Nandor Tanczos wrote the Environmental Issues in Aotearoa New Zealand boxed text (p306) in the Environment chapter. NZ's first Rastafarian Member of Parliament (NZ Greens Party), and the first to enter parliament in dreadlocks and a hemp suit, he was also the Green Party's spokesperson on constitutional issues and the environment from 1999 to 2008.

Vaughan Yarwood wrote the Environment chapter (p304). Vaughan is an Auckland-based writer whose most recent book is *The History Makers: Adventures in New Zealand Biography*. Earlier work includes *The Best of New Zealand, a Collection of Essays on NZ Life and Culture by Prominent Kiwis*, which he edited, and the regional history *Between Coasts: from Kaipara to Kawau*. He has written widely for NZ and international publications and is the former associate editor of *New Zealand Geographic*, for which he continues to write.

Thanks to Dr David Millar for his help with the Health content, Grace Hoet for her contribution to the Maori Culture chapter, and all the NZ regional tourism organisations for their help with pre-research briefings.

OUR STORY

A beat-up old car, a few dollars in the pocket and a sense of adventure. In 1972 that's all Tony and Maureen Wheeler needed for the trip of a lifetime – across Europe and Asia overland to Australia. It took several months, and at the end – broke but inspired – they sat at their kitchen table writing and stapling together their first travel guide, *Across Asia on the Cheap*. Within a week they'd sold 1500 copies. Lonely Planet was born.

Today, Lonely Planet has offices in Melbourne, London and Oakland, with more than 600 staff and writers. We share Tony's belief that 'a great guidebook should do three things: inform, educate and amuse'.

OUR WRITERS

Brett Atkinson

Coordinating author, Plan your Trip, Christchurch & Canterbury, Dunedin & Otago, Queenstown & Wanaka, Fiordland & Southland, South Island Today On his third research trip to the 'mainland', Brett explored Maori rock art, stayed in a historic cottage in the Gibbston Valley, and negotiated a penny-farthing bicycle around Oamaru. Two weeks researching earthquake-damaged Christchurch left him even more impressed with the resilience and determination of the people of Canterbury. Brett has covered ten countries for Lonely Planet, and more than 40 countries as a freelance travel and food writer. See also www.brett-atkinson.net.

Sarah Bennett & Lee Slater

Marlborough & Nelson, The West Coast Raised at the top of the South, Sarah migrated to Wellington at 16 and has lived there ever since, except for various travels and a stint in London working at Lonely Planet's UK office. During research, she strives to find fault, particularly in relation to baked goods and beer selection. Sarah is joined in this endless quest by her husband and co-writer, Lee. English by birth and now a naturalised New Zealander, Lee's first career as an engineer has seen him travel extensively around Europe, the Middle East, North Africa and the Caucasus. Sarah and Lee are co-authors of *Let's Go Camping* and *The New Zealand Tramper's Handbook*. They are also freelance feature writers for newspapers and magazines, including the *Dominion Post* and *Wilderness*.

Peter Dragicevich

The Kiwi Psyche, Arts & Music After nearly a decade working for off-shore publishing companies, Peter's life has come full circle, returning to West Auckland where he was raised. As managing editor of Auckland-based *Express* newspaper he spent much of the '90s writing about the local arts, club and bar scenes. Peter has worked on several of Lonely Planet's guides to New Zealand and, after dozens of Lonely Planet assignments, it remains his favourite gig.

Charles Rawlings-Way

Survival Guide English by birth, Australian by chance, All Blacks fan by choice: Charles' early understanding of Aotearoa was less than comprehensive (sheep, mountains, sheep on mountains...). He realised there was more to it when a wandering uncle returned with a faux-jade *tiki* in 1981. Mt Taranaki's snowy summit, Raglan's point breaks and Whanganui's raffish charm have enthralled. He's once again smitten with NZ's phantasmal landscapes, disarming locals and determination to sculpt its own political and indigenous destiny.

OVER PAGE MORE WRITERS

Published by Lonely Planet Publications Pty Ltd
ABN 36 005 607 983
3rd edition – September 2012
ISBN 978 1 74220 212 9

10 9 8 7 6 5 4 3 2 1
Printed in China